WITHDRAWN

90

Also by Ted Steinberg

American Green: The Obsessive Quest for the Perfect Lawn

Down to Earth: Nature's Role in American History

Acts of God: The Unnatural History of Natural Disaster in America

Slide Mountain, or the Folly of Owning Nature

Nature Incorporated: Industrialization and the Waters of New England

GOTHAM UNBOUND

The Ecological History of Greater New York

Ted Steinberg

Simon & Schuster

New York London Toronto Sydney New Delhi

Simon & Schuster
1230 Avenue of the Americas
New York, NY 10020

First Simon & Schuster hardcover edition June 2014

SIMON & SCHUSTER and colophon are registered trademarks of Simon & Schuster, Inc.

For information about special discounts for bulk purchases, please contact Simon & Schuster Special Sales at 1-866-506-1949 or business@simonandschuster.com.

The Simon & Schuster Speakers Bureau can bring authors to your live event. For more information or to book an event, contact the Simon & Schuster Speakers Bureau at 1-866-248-3049 or visit our website at www.simonspeakers.com.

Interior design by Nancy Singer
Jacket design by Michael Accordino
Jacket photographs: One World Trade Center © Andrew Burton/Getty Images;
The Museum of the City of New York/Art Resource;
E. L. King in Tuttlingen © The Museum of the City of New York/Art Resource
Maps by Jeffrey Ward
Illustrations by Kris Tobiassen
Historical GIS Maps by Jesse Tarbert

Manufactured in the United States of America

10 9 8 7 6 5 4 3 2 1

Library of Congress Cataloging-in-Publication Data

Steinberg, Theodore.
Gotham unbound : an ecological history of greater New York,
from Henry Hudson to Hurricane Sandy / Ted Steinberg.
pages   cm
1. Natural history—New York (State)—New York.   I. Title.
QH105.N7S77   2014
508.747—dc23   2013036197

ISBN 978-1-4767-4124-6
ISBN 978-1-4767-4130-7 (ebook)

For the folks at 603 East Ninety-Fourth (1940–1973)

Excepting Rippy

CONTENTS

Introduction   xv

PART 1
UNDER WATER, 1609–1789

1 Entrepôt   3
2 George Washington Stepped Here   22

PART 2
THE GREAT TRANSFORMATION, 1790–1920

3 The Reticulation   41
4 Adventures in Drainage   66
5 The Revenge of Thomas Dongan   89
6 The Open Loop   109
7 The Exploding Metropolis   126
8 Two-Dimensional Gotham   152

PART 3
NIGHT COMES TO THE MARSHES, 1900–1980

9 The Road to Hermitville   183
10 The Landscapers of Queens   208
11 The Wilds of Staten Island   226

12 The Massifs of Fresh Kills   238

13 The Great Hackensack Disappearing Act   259

PART 4
THE GREEN COLOSSUS, 1960–2012

14 The Age of Limits   283

15 The Big Apple Biome   304

16 The Future of New York   326

Appendixes   353

A Note on Sources   367

Historical Geographic Information

    Systems Sources   379

Art Credits   383

Acknowledgments   385

Notes   389

Index   495

New York City was the beneficiary but the
victim of its geography.

—*Raymond Moley*, 1970

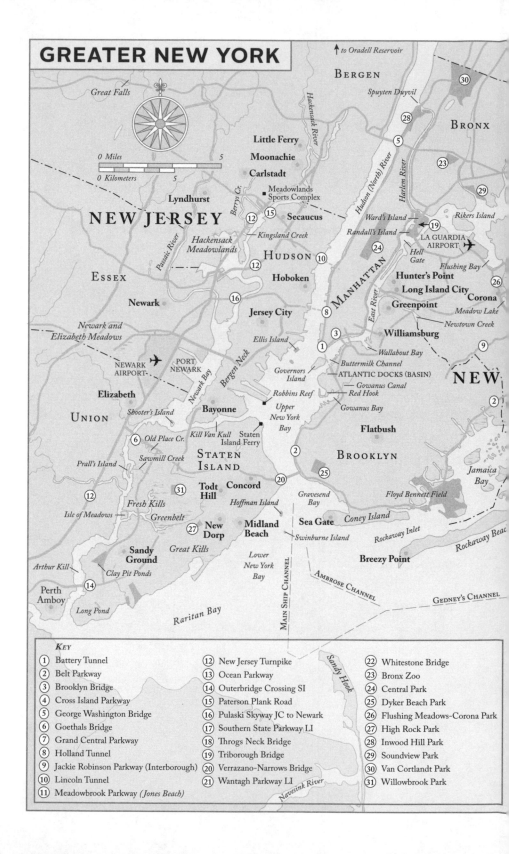

GREATER NEW YORK

↑ to Oradell Reservoir

BERGEN

BRONX

Great Falls

Spuyten Duyvil

30

28

5

23

29

Little Ferry

Moonachie

Carlstadt

Meadowlands
Sports Complex

Hudson (North) River

Harlem River

Rikers Island

Ward's Island

Randall's Island

19

LA GUARDIA
AIRPORT

Lyndhurst

NEW JERSEY

12 15 Secaucus

Hackensack
Meadowlands

Kingsland Creek

HUDSON 10

24

Hell
Gate

Flushing Bay

26

MANHATTAN

Hunter's Point

Long Island City Corona

Essex

12

Hoboken

Passaic River

Berrys Cr.

Newark

16

Jersey City 8

Greenpoint

Meadow Lake

Newtown Creek

Ellis Island

3

Williamsburg

9

Newark and
Elizabeth Meadows

1

Wallabout Bay

NEW

NEWARK
AIRPORT

PORT
NEWARK

Governors
Island

Buttermilk Channel

ATLANTIC DOCKS (BASIN)

Gowanus Canal

Red Hook

Elizabeth

Newark Bay

Bergen Neck

Robbins Reef

Gowanus Bay

2

UNION

Shooter's Island

Bayonne

Upper
New York
Bay

Flatbush

6 Old Place Cr.

Kill Van Kull Staten
Island Ferry

BROOKLYN

Prall's Island

Sawmill Creek

STATEN
ISLAND

2

25

Jamaica
Bay

12

31 Todt
Hill

Concord

Gravesend
Bay

Floyd Bennett Field

Isle of Meadows

Fresh Kills

Hoffman Island

20

Greenbelt

27 New
Dorp

Midland
Beach

Sea Gate Coney Island

Sandy
Ground

Great Kills

Swinburne Island

Rockaway Inlet

Rockaway Beac

Arthur Kill

Clay Pit Ponds

Lower
New York
Bay

Breezy Point

Perth
Amboy

14

AMBROSE CHANNEL

GEDNEY'S CHANNEL

Long Pond

MAIN SHIP CHANNEL

Raritan Bay

Sandy Hook

KEY

①	Battery Tunnel	⑫	New Jersey Turnpike	㉒	Whitestone Bridge
②	Belt Parkway	⑬	Ocean Parkway	㉓	Bronx Zoo
③	Brooklyn Bridge	⑭	Outerbridge Crossing SI	㉔	Central Park
④	Cross Island Parkway	⑮	Paterson Plank Road	㉕	Dyker Beach Park
⑤	George Washington Bridge	⑯	Pulaski Skyway JC to Newark	㉖	Flushing Meadows-Corona Park
⑥	Goethals Bridge	⑰	Southern State Parkway LI	㉗	High Rock Park
⑦	Grand Central Parkway	⑱	Throgs Neck Bridge	㉘	Inwood Hill Park
⑧	Holland Tunnel	⑲	Triborough Bridge	㉙	Soundview Park
⑨	Jackie Robinson Parkway (Interborough)	⑳	Verrazano-Narrows Bridge	㉚	Van Cortlandt Park
⑩	Lincoln Tunnel	㉑	Wantagh Parkway LI	㉛	Willowbrook Park
⑪	Meadowbrook Parkway (Jones Beach)				

Navesink River

0 Miles 5

0 Kilometers 5

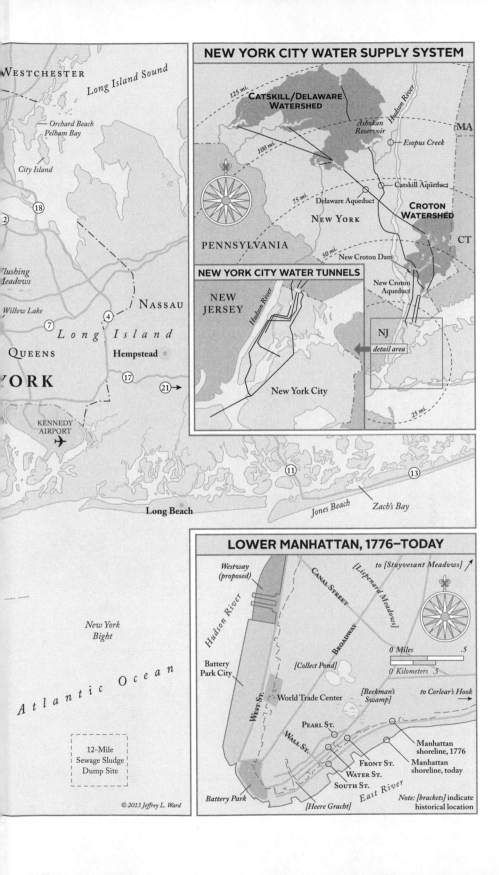

NEW YORK CITY WATER SUPPLY SYSTEM

WESTCHESTER

Long Island Sound

125 mi.

CATSKILL/DELAWARE WATERSHED

Ashokan Reservoir

Hudson River

MA

Orchard Beach
Pelham Bay

Esopus Creek

City Island

100 mi.

Catskill Aqueduct

18

75 mi.

Delaware Aqueduct

CROTON WATERSHED

2

Flushing Meadows

NEW YORK

CT

PENNSYLVANIA

50 mi.

New Croton Dam

New Croton Aqueduct

Willow Lake

NEW YORK CITY WATER TUNNELS

7

NASSAU

NEW
JERSEY

NJ

QUEENS

Hempstead

detail area

YORK

17

Hudson River

4

21

25 mi.

New York City

KENNEDY
AIRPORT

11

13

Long Beach

Jones Beach

Zach's Bay

New York Bight

LOWER MANHATTAN, 1776–TODAY

Westway (proposed)

CANAL STREET

to [Stuyvesant Meadows]

[Lispenard Meadows]

Hudson River

BROADWAY

Battery Park City

[Collect Pond]

0 Miles   .5

Atlantic Ocean

0 Kilometers .5

WEST ST.

World Trade Center

[Beekman's Swamp]

to Corlear's Hook

PEARL ST.

Manhattan shoreline, 1776

WALL ST.

FRONT ST.

Manhattan shoreline, today

WATER ST.

12-Mile
Sewage Sludge
Dump Site

Battery Park

SOUTH ST.

East River

[Heere Gracht]

Note: [brackets] indicate historical location

© 2013 Jeffrey L. Ward

GOTHAM UNBOUND

For an unparalleled nature adventure, head for the Island of Many Hills. This place lives up to its name with 573 prominences of one kind or another. But the topography is in some ways the least of the adventure. With fifty-five different ecological communities packed into just twenty-odd square miles, the island is a veritable Garden of Eden. From marine eelgrass meadow to shrub swamp, low salt marsh to brackish intertidal mudflats, blueberry bog thicket to oak-tulip forest, this spot is a living embodiment of the phrase "wealth of nature." There are more than twenty ponds and over sixty miles of streams and perhaps as many as three hundred springs gurgling away. There are oysters galore. There are black bears, wolves, mountain lions, whales, and porpoises. There are red-winged blackbirds, American redstarts, red-bellied woodpeckers, clapper rails, and great horned owls. There are, in the sedge department alone, densetuft, oval-leaf, hop, broadleaf, parasol, threeway, Muhlenberg's, Schweinitz's, Pennsylvania, and hairy umbrella-sedge. This is Mannahatta: a place we are all four hundred years too late to visit.[1]

As it turned out, this landmass on the Atlantic Coast of North America did not become a nature preserve. It emerged instead as an urban giant: the Borough of Manhattan—the heart of one of the most drastically transformed natural environments in the world. New York is the most populous city in the United States and has been for the last two centuries. In 1609, less than 1 percent of the Manhattan landscape showed evidence of human influence. By the early twenty-first century, 97 percent of the land had been converted to buildings, sidewalks, parking lots, streets, recreational areas, and other artifacts of civilization. The dominant species by this time was, of course, neither the oyster nor the mountain lion but *Homo sapiens sapiens.* Today a stunning 69,464 people per square mile live in Manhattan. And as goes Manhattan, so goes the rest of the New York metropolitan area.[2]

This book is about the struggle between New York and the natural world. At its core, the story is about how, over centuries, people have come to understand, define, and ultimately transform New York's land, water, and its plant and animal life. The metropolitan area assumed its current shape by way of a set of contingent decisions. Which is precisely why we want to study its history: to understand how ecological change has made New York what it is today, while acknowledging that, present concerns aside, the past has a logic all its own. The struggle at the center of this story has been overwhelmingly one-sided; a man-bites-dog story, if you will. To cite just one measure, between 1900 and 2010, development had whittled down Staten Island's monumental 5,099 acres of marsh—wildlands more than a third the size of all Manhattan, filled with night herons, belted kingfishers, dragonflies, and snails—to a fractional existence the size of a mere city park (865 acres).[3] Part of the story, too, is that sometimes the dog bit back.

To examine New York is to confront what has always been—in one form or another—a high-density place. The key to appreciating this point is to first understand that New York exists in the estuary of the Hudson River, where freshwater meets the Atlantic Ocean. Estuaries are very special environments and, from an ecological perspective, highly productive ones. They are located at the point where freshwater and salt water join together, and play a role not only as habitat for birds and other wildlife but also in the health of oceans, by filtering water and acting as nursery grounds for fish. They tend to be crammed with life. Estuaries trap nutrients from the adjoining watershed and thus are capable of supplying food to enormous populations of species, from oysters to grasses to waterfowl. Not for nothing is the New York area one of the great stopping points for birds migrating along the Atlantic Flyway, the avian world's version of an interstate.[4]

The ecological history of New York, then, can be summed up very simply: an estuary with a high natural density was replaced by one with an astonishingly high unnatural (for lack of a better word) density. Human beings overshadow the area, but that has hardly led to the end of nature, as it were. In fact, just the reverse. Though the diversity of the plant and animal world is less encyclopedic than what it was back when Henry Hudson made his famed voyage in 1609, some species—gulls, Phragmites (common reed), various kinds of plankton—have thrived on the disruption caused by squeezing more than 6 percent of the entire population of the nation into one small space. Those who see the swarms of people at Times Square and think New York is an exceptionally dense environment don't know the half of it.[5]

There has been a sense that New York's success as a city was somehow foreordained, that the place was geographically destined for greatness. It is an old idea. Isaac Newton Phelps Stokes, the author of an epic early-twentieth-century study of Manhattan and its topography, wrote that commerce was "naturally attracted" to the "splendid harbor." More recently, Harvard economist Edward Glaeser has offered a more sophisticated analysis. Acknowledging that Gotham's rise was a multi-dimensional process, he nevertheless pinpointed the ramifying economic impact of the city's status as a port, which itself was based on geographic advantages such as proximity to the ocean and a location along the wide and navigable Hudson River. "In this case," he writes, "geography really was destiny, and the significance of trade and immigration to the early republic ensured that New York would dominate." A recent popular history echoes that conclusion: "Geography would prove to be destiny—more, perhaps, than in the history of any other city on earth."[6]

There is little doubting the importance of geography. But it is wrong to view it as static. For New York has undergone profound geographic transformations, especially in the last two centuries. The harbor is hardly one that George Washington (who was inaugurated here), much less Henry Hudson, would recognize. Between the early nineteenth century and 1980, an area of marshland four times the size of the island of Manhattan was destroyed. Nearly three Manhattan Islands' worth of open water, moreover, was filled, explaining why Upper New York Bay is now only three-quarters the size it was in 1845. Altogether, an area of tidal marsh and underwater land in the Hudson estuary amounting to almost half the size of the five boroughs has been lost to urban development. It is not too much to call New York one giant reclamation project.[7]

Hence, my argument is not that geography is destiny but, in a sense, the reverse. A dense city evolved in the Hudson estuary largely because of the trust in constant population and economic growth—New York's destiny as articulated by those who have run it.

When the growth fetish began is a little hard to say, but it was almost certainly manifest by the middle of the nineteenth century. By that point, the idea that progress rested on what one historian has called "a condition of never-ending growth" had taken root more broadly in the nation. Eventually this fascination with expansion would come to inform the thinking of New York's boosters as they vied to shake off the restraining grip of the natural world and reshape relations with land and sea. And this faith in the virtues of the onward march of progress continues to weigh heavily on the minds of those who rule the city. "Growth," professor of urban planning Tom Angotti put it recently, "is always presumed to be good, even in a Manhattan that is already densely packed with buildings and has little breathing room." That said, I am not unsympathetic to the importance of economic advancement. What inspires me instead is the necessity to accurately depict the consequences of growth for the region's ecological fabric.[8]

Historians of New York have tended to see natural forces as a backdrop to what they consider the more important matters of politics and economics. Even the most comprehensive historical works seem to view the natural environment as little more than a preface to the tale of New York's rise from trading post to metropolis to megalopolis. And yet, crusades to control nature are as central to New York's history as battles are to the Civil War. Driving the Grand Central Parkway near La Guardia Airport, you might never know that you are passing by Meadow Lake, a man-made body of water that was once a prodigious salt marsh carved up by rivers and sporting panicled expanses of green cordgrass. That was before a war was waged to fend off the sea and make way for the appropriately named lake—New York City's largest. The reinvention of a marsh as a lake gives us an inkling of the task this book takes up. We must examine how the landscape changed, who was responsible for those changes, and what environmental and social impacts grew out of them. The population density of the New York metropolitan area, after all, rests on a set of ecological imperatives such as the need for water and a place to discharge all the waste produced when millions of people live side by side. What happens in Vegas may stay there, but the same does not hold true for New York.[9]

Gotham Unbound forgoes the tidy political watersheds that have defined the study of this great city and emphasizes a new set of turning points. Not simply the shift from Dutch to English rule, but the market in underwater land is what concerns me in Part 1. This was a development that not only betrayed the colonists' approach to the natural world but also set the stage for the far more massive efforts to reshape the region and profit off the land that came later.

Part 2 places considerable emphasis on the 1811 grid plan, which was indeed a major change that built on the earlier underwater history of Manhattan Island while laying the groundwork for the high-density living that would come to define the region. Altogether, the grid, the development of an off-island water supply, and other trends associated with the quest for limitless growth combined to cause the most radical alteration of the waters of New York Harbor in recorded history.

What the transformation of the harbor was to the nineteenth century, the makeover of wetlands was to the hundred years that followed. Once marshlands dominated the waterfront from Long Island on the east to the Hackensack Meadowlands on the west—little more than wind blowing across these sweeping expanses of grass. Probing the fate of the marshlands in the shadow of one of the densest urban agglomerations in the world is the subject of Part 3.

Then the fourth and final part explores the period since 1960 as the environmental movement began to blossom. It focuses on the limits to growth in a metropolis long defined by rampant development and ends with Hurricane Sandy. In sum, *Gotham Unbound* tells the story of New York over the last four centuries from the ground up, a vantage point that reveals a world of change and dislocation that is otherwise difficult to discern.

I freely admit that it is a little hard to define exactly where this book takes place. My main concern is with New York Harbor, broadly construed, and the land surrounding it. Starting with Manhattan and using the coordinates found on a compass, this means that I will examine the expanse stretching from as far east as Jones Beach on Long Island, as far west as the Meadowlands, and as far south as the edge of the New York Bight—the shallow water extending seaward from where the coasts of New York and New Jersey meet to the edge of the continental shelf. To sum up in a word or two this far-reaching tidal network of marshes, rivers, and bays—the habitats mainly dealt with below—is a tall order. I simply call it Greater New York.[10]

Rather than offer a comprehensive portrait of all that has happened across this vast terra *in*firma, I aim instead to simply make New York a less familiar proposition—to show that there is much still to know and understand about a place that many think they know so well. Put somewhat differently, without the changes described in this study, Fresh Kills today would be a wetland and not a mountain chain. Without them, people might be fishing the pond in lower Manhattan or donning waders to walk along the aptly named Water Street. Flushing Meadows would be a meadow instead of the city's largest lake, Coney Island a real island, and the Meadowlands a place people think of for its snapping turtles and the whistling call of osprey, not for its football or harness racing.

It might be tempting to write off New York Harbor's ecological history as a simple tale of decline and fall. But that would be inaccurate. There is no question that, by the 1920s, the harbor had reached a nadir in terms of the oxygen saturation necessary to sustain marine life and that, later on, Staten Island's Fresh Kills was buried under several colossal mountains of garbage. But the waters have since recovered to a great extent, and Fresh Kills, now no longer a landfill, is being turned into a city park. By the 1970s, herons and egrets had returned to the gritty Arthur Kill separating Staten Island and New Jersey, one of the most industrialized areas of the entire harbor. Today seal-watching cruises depart from Rockaway, Queens.[11]

So I am not contending that the Big Apple has the biggest ecological problems in the world.[12] My focus instead is on relationships: on the link between new ways of understanding land, especially underwater land, and the changing geography of the city; on the transcendence of the local water supply and the decline in marine life; on the rise of a vision of New York as an infinite proposition and the quest to encroach on the sea; on the relationship between the overproduction of waste and the making of urban mountains; and of course on the link between the present shape of the metropolitan area and the past. An ecological history of New York can help us see that it is wrong to take the city for granted but right to question how the landscape we see driving along the Belt Parkway or strolling along the Hudson River came to be.

These connections are important to recognize because it seems fair to say, as at least one writer has, that today comparatively few New Yorkers realize that they are living in the estuary of the Hudson River.[13] This lack of knowledge is perhaps understandable in a place known to many as a concrete jungle. Why *would* contemporary New Yorkers think of themselves as residents in an environment where river and ocean meet when so much of that environment—its smooth cordgrass, fiddler crabs, marsh hens—has been overshadowed by monumental building exploits? And yet there is nothing natural or inevitable about the lapse. Understanding the forces that have made New York what it is will not only place the city in a new light. It will illuminate how this estrangement from the natural world came about. An ecological history has the potential to reconnect people not just with the past but also with the natural environment as it exists today.

It can also change how we think about the future. By midcentury, the projection is that seven out of every ten people on earth will live in a city. Urbanization is remaking landscapes across the globe and playing out with particular force in estuaries, where the bulk of the largest cities in the world are located. Moreover, New York, like other sister cities located in tidal environments, must face up to the realities of climate change. It is more than a little ironic that the celebration of New York's ecological virtues—as a dense city with less per capita energy use than rural areas—has occurred concurrently with grim forecasts about its vulnerability to extreme weather. Hurricane Sandy in 2012 made it clear that the threat is real. Historians are not in the business of prediction, but exploring ecological history, which studies humankind's struggle with natural constraints, is a uniquely good way to begin a discussion about the future of the world's first megacity.[14]

In the depths of the fiscal crisis back in the 1970s, the critic Gilbert Millstein wrote that New York was "still the scale on which all other cities must be measured, precisely because of the destruction it has wreaked on itself, precisely because of the insane, unbalanced behavior of those who run it, tear it down and build it and decide what shall happen to it." And it remains such a yardstick today. For all the oceans of ink spilled on New York, we have yet to fully understand the environmental transformation that underwrote what is one of the most creative acts of vandalism ever perpetrated on a natural landscape.[15]

PART 1
UNDER WATER

1609–1789

1 ENTREPÔT

When we say that Henry Hudson explored New York, what we really mean is that he explored *lost* New York. The bulk of the landscape that Hudson saw on his 1609 visit has vanished—erased by storms, wave action, rising sea level, and the transformation of the land and waterscape. The changes have been so vast and thoroughgoing that it is not even possible to pinpoint with certainty where Hudson ventured on his travels.

Much of what we know about Hudson's expedition to New York comes from the journal of an officer on the vessel, one Robert Juet of London. On September 2, 1609, the *Half Moon* arrived, as best we can tell, at a point to the east of Sandy Hook, a barrier spit jutting north along the coast of New Jersey and guarding Lower New York Bay's southerly entrance. Here the crew found what Juet described as "drowned Land, which made it to rise like Ilands." It was an apt description in light of geological history. New York Harbor is sometimes described in the scientific literature as a "drowned estuary," a shallow arm of the sea fed by the Hudson River that was literally swamped by the rise in water level that came with the melting of the glaciers. When the last ice sheet began its retreat about twelve thousand years ago, a ridge of rock and sediment was left behind spanning Staten Island and Long Island. Meltwater from the retiring glacier eventually perforated the ridge to produce a

narrow channel, eventually named for the Florentine explorer Giovanni
da Verrazano, who weighed anchor there in 1524. As the so-called Wisconsin glacier withdrew, its waters ran off to fill glacial lakes Hackensack
and Flushing, giant old bodies of water that became marshes as the rise
in sea level slowed down about five thousand years ago.[1]

Riding at anchor off Sandy Hook, Juet spied what he took to be
"three great Rivers." One of them was the Verrazano Narrows. A second,
bona fide river off to the west was the Raritan. At an earlier time, the
Raritan had hosted the primordial Hudson River as it flowed along a
much different path toward the sea than it does today. The third so-called
river, and the closest one at hand to the ship, was actually Rockaway
Inlet. It was located at the western end of a peninsula formed as wind
and wave action channeled sediment west along Long Island's coast, a
process known as littoral drift. We know the identity of Juet's "rivers"
thanks to the work of Douglas Hunter, a writer and seasoned sailor who
in the twenty-first century set out to trace Hudson's path. Hunter relied
on soundings recorded by Juet during the 1609 voyage. These are measurements of the ocean's depth using a weighted and measured line. The
soundings guided a ship in the days when mariners were as yet unable to
establish longitude and when even latitude readings taken with a cross
staff were subject to error. Hunter used the soundings in conjunction
with old nautical charts to re-create the explorer's itinerary. What he discovered was that Henry Hudson probably began his visit to the region in
Brooklyn, not too far from present-day Flatbush Avenue.[2]

Entering Rockaway Inlet, the *Half Moon* encountered Jamaica Bay.
Juet recorded seeing "many Salmons, and Mullets, and Rayes, very great,"
though the mention of salmon has raised some eyebrows and caused a
biologist to conclude instead that the men had found weakfish or sea
trout. The next day, if Hunter is correct in his sleuthing, the *Half Moon*
ventured farther into the bay, where the crew discovered an island that
later would be called Beeren Eylant, Dutch for "Bear Island." According
to Juet's account, some of the crew then "went on Land with our Net to
Fish, and caught ten great Mullets, of a foot and a halfe long a peece,
and a Ray as great as foure men could hale into the ship." What the

men thought of Jamaica Bay itself we do not know. But the bay back in Hudson's time looked much different than it does today now that its tidal wetlands—extending across more than twenty-five square miles as late as 1907—have been filled to construct, among other things, John F. Kennedy International Airport. Even Beeren Eylant (later called Barren Island) is gone, absorbed into Long Island. By 1970, the marshlands were just a shadow of their former existence, reduced by at least 75 percent.[3]

The salt marshes of Jamaica Bay, teeming with plant and animal life, had themselves only arrived on the scene a few thousand years before Hudson himself—yesterday in geological time. They were the product of a more stabilized set of sea level conditions. One archaeologist has called such marshlands "one of the most productive landforms in the world, rivaling intensive agricultural lands in food productivity."[4]

It is not surprising that Hudson stumbled upon native people living in such a bounteous environment. Because the bulldozing of the landscape has swept away much of the archaeological record, the Canarsie Indians, part of a broader Algonquian-speaking people named the Lenape, are difficult for us to fathom. Huge, heaping mounds of shells found on Long Island suggest that, like the other Indians of this region, they were a coastal people, though when Juet encountered the Canarsie, he found them in possession of a "great store of Maiz, or Indian Wheate, whereof they make good Bread." Juet's journal entry notwithstanding, maize, beans, and squash probably did not play as important a role for them as it did for other Native American groups in the Northeast. The rock-strewn and sandy soil would have discouraged agriculture, as did a diverse array of habitats (open ocean, salt and freshwater marshes, mudflats, meadows, and forest) that placed prolific food sources near at hand. The Lenape likely viewed horticulture as peripheral to their diet, though this did not mean that they lacked a rootedness and attachment to place, as even Hudson's crew was starting to learn.[5]

In their peregrinations about New York Harbor, the crew of the *Half Moon* came well equipped for estuarine travel. The ship itself was a form of *vlieboat*—the Vlie being the medieval name for the estuary of the river IJssel. More precisely, the boat was what the Dutch called a *jaght*, a word that means "hunter" and the root of the English word *yacht*. The *Half Moon* also stowed a smaller ship's boat, which Hudson decided should be sent out on September 6 to "sound the other River, being foure leagues from us." That "River" was evidently the Verrazano Narrows. Hudson chose John Colman, an Englishman and veteran of an earlier Hudson voyage, to lead the expedition and instructed him to take four crewmembers along. They departed west along the south shore of Long Island past Coney Island, which was still an actual island back then. They then steered through the Narrows and ultimately emerged in Upper New York Bay. Soon after, they crossed into "a narrow River to the Westward, between two Ilands." In other words, they proceeded down the Kill Van Kull, a tidal strait separating Staten Island from Bergen Neck in New Jersey. The men saw lands that were "pleasant with Grasse and Flowers, and goodly Trees as ever they had seene." They pressed on until they came upon "an open Sea" known to us today as Newark Bay. Beyond the bay stretched the Hackensack and Newark Meadows, the former named for a Lenape group, the latter for the Connecticut Puritans' New Ark of the Covenant.[6]

These tidal wetlands once extended over forty-two square miles; the Indians called them the Great Marsh, or Mankachkewachky. At the time Colman and the others arrived, an Atlantic white cedar swamp blanketed about a third of the land.* It would be almost impossible to exaggerate the multitude of life-forms that inhabited this place: spoonbills waded in shallow waters; coots plucked away at wild rice that flanked the edges of streams; shad, carp, perch, suckers, sunfish, and pike swarmed through the rivers; lobsters crawled across sandy bottoms feeding on crabs and mussels; the loud gobbling call of wild turkey reverberated through the woods; mountain lions, bears, deer, wolves, and foxes roved the uplands while bald eagles, falcons, and hawks soared overhead.[7]

It was a stunning landscape, and the last one John Colman ever saw.

---

* The so-called Little Ice Age, a five-hundred-year period of unstable climatic conditions, beginning in 1300, may have encouraged the northward spread of this southern bog species.

Later, a group of Indians attacked the crew and Colman wound up "with an Arrow shot into his throat."[8]

The men eventually escaped and brought Colman's body back to be buried at a point named in his memory. But exactly where the grave was dug, nobody can say. The *Half Moon* prepared to leave Rockaway Inlet and on September 10 cruised toward the Verrazano Narrows, passing Coney Island, a place arguably named, assuming various Dutch and English corruptions of language, for the departed Colman.[9]

On the following day, after coming through the Narrows, the crew dropped anchor and "saw that it was a very good Harbour for all windes." The *Half Moon* had arrived in Upper New York Bay. Like Jamaica Bay, it was a lot roomier back then. Off on the west side, the men might have seen mudflats that eventually came to be called the Jersey Flats. Hoboken would have been little more than an island at high tide, having yet to be reclaimed as part of the mainland. Nor had Gowanus Bay been filled in with the remains of a bluff, a change Walt Whitman would later lament. Lower Manhattan looked more like a peninsula than the bulbous landmass it is today.[10]

The *Half Moon* had voyaged into a world not simply of mudflats, wetlands, bays, and deep-water habitats, but a place with an unrivaled biota. In Henry Hudson's day, oysters and grasses, not people, crowded the estuary that would come to bear his name. Hundreds of square miles of oyster beds dominated the harbor, making it one of the world's greatest collections of filter feeders (a species that feeds by straining out waterborne suspended matter such as plankton). The bivalve's inescapable presence would eventually be etched right into the landscape from Oyster Island in Upper New York Bay to Oyster Bay in Long Island Sound to Pearl Street in lower Manhattan, named after the pile of oyster shells the Indians left behind.[11]

The grasses of New York were even more prolific. The crew on board the *Half Moon* would have discovered tall, bright green expanses of salt marsh cordgrass, giving off a sulfurous odor that mingled with the briny smell of the sea. This perennial grass species has few competitors in the intertidal zone because it evolved to deal effectively with the high fluctuations in salinity found in this environment. Behind it, on higher, drier terrain, the men found shorter stands of salt meadow hay with its purple flowers and its stems bent into cowlicks by the wind. And beyond that, yet more sod as far as the eye could see: spike grass, switchgrass, rushes. Grass was everywhere, even underwater where eelgrass flourished, creating a habitat for everything from sea horses to sea turtles. Henry Hudson had chanced upon an extraordinarily rich and productive natural environment.[12]

From the days of Henry Hudson to those of George Washington, some 150 years later, coastal New York likely remained a largely intact set of ecosystems with some localized depletions. There was only one exception to this generalization: lower Manhattan, or *Manna-hatta*, to use Juet's name for the area. The spot of earth that would evolve into the linchpin of the global economy underwent intensive change from a place organized mainly around harvesting marine life to one that quickly assumed a new status as an entrepôt. A place notable for its natural wealth went on to distinguish itself as a place in the business of producing riches of a different sort. The change happened under the leadership of the Dutch, a people who embraced some quintessentially modern economic ideas.[13]

Not for nothing is the word *landscape* of Dutch origin. In the late sixteenth century, the United Provinces rose to become the world capital of landscape change. This happened at the same time that the Dutch overtook Spain to reign over the global capitalist economy. The Dutch had their work cut out for them. Nearly half the land area of the Netherlands would be swamped if not for the system of dikes built to defend the country from river and sea. So as the Dutch etched out their political identity, they got down in the muck and took control over their ecological destiny as well. For two thousand years, the Dutch had battled the marshes, and the marshes had won. But beginning in the fifteen hundreds, as the Dutch Golden Age began, the mud workers broke out their pumps and set about reclaiming two hundred thousand acres of land. The high point came in the period between 1600 and 1625, just as the city of New Amsterdam across the Atlantic was getting off the ground. "Don't fight the sea with brute force but with soft persuasion," intoned Andries Vierlingh, the hydraulic engineer and dike master to William the Silent. The Dutch had persuaded a whole new landscape into existence, and now they headed west to try their hand abroad.[14]

In the wake of Hudson's voyage, the English sea captain Samuel Argall paid a visit to Manhattan. Hudson's discovery briefly seemed in jeopardy, but then the Dutch, under the auspices of the West India Company, took over. Chartered in 1621, after the Twelve Years' Truce with Spain ended, the West India Company was charged with containing the spread of Catholicism while vying with the Spanish for commercial dominance. The company would soon dispatch ships to North America and, though the evidentiary record is not entirely clear, it seems as if a ship named the *Eendracht* arrived there with a small number of colonists in 1624. In an effort to lay claim to as much territory as possible, the vessel dispatched settlers along the South River (Delaware River), the Fresh River (Connecticut River), and the North River (Hudson). On the lower Hudson, the colonists disembarked at a place they called Nooten Eylandt, or nut island, because of its oak, hickory, and chestnut trees. Today it is known as Governors Island.[15]

The following year, the company appointed Willem Verhulst as the colony's director. He was instructed to round up the colonists into one main settlement, presumably to serve as a military and commercial hub for the company's far-flung trading network. Many people, including the company's officers, its chief farmers, and skippers, participated in the decision. The company directors back at headquarters in the Netherlands voiced the opinion that the best place for a fort was "where the river is narrow, where it cannot be fired upon from higher ground, where large ships cannot come too close, where there is a distant view unobstructed by trees or hills, where it is possible to have water in the moat, and where there is no sand, but clay or other firm earth." They suggested three possibilities: High Island on the South River, a spot not far from where Trenton, New Jersey, is today; the west side of the North River (or Jersey City, roughly speaking); or "the hook of the Manattes." Verhulst was also warned in making the choice to see that "the place chosen is well provided with water and with timber for fuel and building, and that the rivers thereabout are full of fish." Evidently Verhulst was not a particularly likable fellow. Before he could proceed too far with the consolidation plan, he was replaced by Peter Minuit. Minuit is of course legendary for having (as reported in a 1626 letter from Pieter Schaghen) "purchased the Island Manhattes from the Indians for the value of 60 guilders." The directors, perhaps not surprisingly, given their lack of firsthand knowledge of this part of the world, got their third choice.[16]

The gaps in the historical record make it impossible to say definitively why Nooten Eylandt was abandoned for another larger island first mapped by the Dutch trader Adriaen Block as "Manhates." We can, however, draw inferences. By the spring of 1626, the Dutch colonists at Fort Orange (Albany, New York) became embroiled in a battle with the Mohawks that left Daniel van Crieckenbeeck, the commander of the fort, dead. The news of the disastrous attack made its way down the Hudson and prompted Minuit to send a letter, dated May 11, 1626, to one Pieter Barentsz, instructing him to proceed to Fort Orange to take control in Van Crieckenbeeck's absence. It seems plausible that Minuit, fearing an all-out battle with the Indians, felt compelled to gather the settlers dispersed at Fort Orange and to the south on tiny High Island (Hooghe Eylandt) in the Delaware River into one central location. He likely was inclined toward an island because of its military advantages and even better if there was room to spread out. However it happened, the decision would put Manhattan on the map.[17]

Having selected a location, the Dutch, under orders from Amsterdam not to stoop to force or fraud, proceeded to make one of the most famous transactions in world history. Some have tried to establish whether the sixty-guilder sum employed to purchase Manhattan (eventually reckoned, in the nineteenth century, it is believed, as twenty-four dollars) represented a fair valuation. Others have come to dismiss the issue of computing the island's worth as beside the point because the Indians had no choice. "Had the Indians not sold Manhattan to the Dutch," writes one historian, "the inevitable rise in the English population in the area later in the seventeenth century, driven by the advantages of New York as a harbor, would have put steadily mounting pressure on the Indians to sell."[18]

The real issue here is less the inevitability of New York City based on its natural attributes or the morality of the exchange. It is instead the two very different systems for organizing relations with the land that came into conflict as the European settlement developed. As best as anyone can tell, the idea of selling land would never have occurred to the Indians. A Dutch visitor to New Netherland named Adriaen van der Donck (of whom more in a moment) put his finger on one of the key features of the Indian land regime: their belief in collective stewardship. To the Indians, "wind, stream, bush, field, sea, beach, and riverside are open and free to everyone of every nation with which the Indians are not embroiled in open conflict." An archaeologist who has studied land transactions between the Lenape and the colonists found that the Indians practiced a form of land tenure founded on temporary usufructuary rights rather than permanent title. This is an understanding of ownership based on the idea of mutual rights to harvest the bounty of the land. The colonists, meanwhile, had a different idea. They had come to embrace the notion of private property, a concept that turned the land into a commodity.[19]

It is important not to present too stark a picture of the differences between the Indians and the colonists on the matter of land ownership. Both groups held the land in trust: the Lenape in the name of the Great Spirit, *Kishelemukunk*; the colonists in the name of God. Both also recorded the transactions: the Lenape with wampum, the colonists with deeds. And both, despite the innovation of private property, shared in the experience of communal rights to the land—an agrarian custom known in Europe as the commons. Further, in light of the Manhattan-for-twenty-four-dollars debate, it is instructive to note that the Indians seem to have initially accepted relatively low prices for their land, perhaps hoping to establish a reciprocal relationship that would obligate the colonists to provide them with short-term protection. This strategy, it has been argued, helped the Lenape to fend off complete subjugation for almost a century and a half.[20]

With respect to the land, the date 1638 has retreated into the shadows of history, and yet it is arguably as important if not more so than what happened in 1626. The former date marks the year when the institution of real property surfaced in Manhattan. The new director general, Willem Kieft, a merchant, arrived to issue the first land patent, or *grond-brieven*, to Andries Hudde for one hundred morgens of land in Harlem.* The idea of land patents was not something Kieft dreamed up on his own. Private ownership of land was a custom with which settlers coming from the urbanized world of the Netherlands would have been intimately familiar. That it took over a decade after settlement for land patents to be issued suggests what an utterly fragile affair the entire New Amsterdam enterprise was during its early years. With the granting of the first patents, the Dutch colonists received the legal right to sell, lease, and bequeath the land. They also found themselves charged with improving the lots on penalty of forfeiture. It would be some years before John Locke published a work that spelled out a formal theory of property, but, in essence, the Dutch had taken a page straight out of the Englishman's book.[21]

As the colonists set about making history in this new land, their thoughts—not surprisingly, given their country of origin—turned to water. We have seen how the West India Company sent its settlers out to the major waterways of the region. Minuit had originally been summoned to New Netherland not to replace Verhulst but to survey rivers and size up the prospects for settlement. Unused to clearing forests and likely intimidated by the lush old-growth oaks, chestnuts, and hemlocks that carpeted perhaps three-quarters of Manhattan, the Dutch flocked to the more familiar marshy terrain. They settled the wetlands of southern Manhattan, a place that the Mohawk called *Gänóno*, or "place of

---

* A morgen was about two acres, or the amount of land that could be plowed in one morning.

reeds." In 1636 they colonized the tidal inlet and saltwater marsh at Gowanus. Ten years later, they founded Breucklen, named after a Dutch town famous for its brooks. In 1645 Vlissingen, after a town in the Netherlands, was incorporated on what would come to be the Flushing Meadows. In 1654 they peopled the marshland near Jamaica Bay with its prized salt meadow hay, ideal for forage, establishing Middlewout, later called Vlachte Bos, or Flatbush. In 1658 they voyaged to a marsh on the eastern part of Manhattan Island's northernmost reaches and named it Nieuw Haarlem. In 1671 they set off to establish Nieu Dorp (New Town) near the Great Kills, a wetland on Staten Island. It was as if the Dutch sought to comfort themselves in this new world with scenes reminiscent of their Fatherland.[22]

Nevertheless, the southern part of Manhattan facing New York Bay remained at the center of Dutch ambitions. To this place, a newly minted lawyer named Adriaen van der Donck journeyed in May 1641.

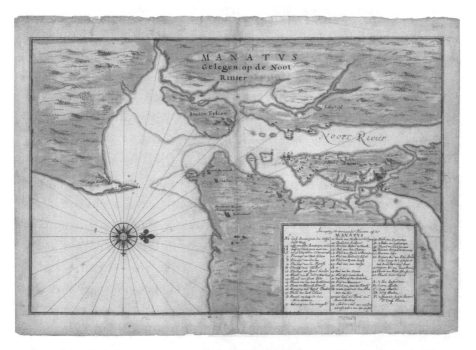

Thought to have been drawn about 1670, this map is a copy of a 1639 map showing the settlements around what became New York Harbor.

He set sail across the ocean aboard a ship named *Den Eyckenboom* (the Oak Tree), en route to govern the vast landholdings along the Hudson River of the diamond merchant Kiliaen van Rensselaer. When Van der Donck arrived, New Amsterdam was about to undergo a renaissance of sorts. Until this point, the city had been best known for its barroom brawls and prostitutes, a lawless trading post in a colony run by an imperious private company. But in 1639 the Dutch States General approved a new set of provisions that forced the West India Company to relinquish its monopoly on trade. The move opened the floodgates of the free market, making Amsterdam's private merchants eager in anticipation. As a result, a burgeoning merchant elite began to consider New Amsterdam home, and the city took a more assertive approach toward the land.[23]

Sometime before 1643, the Dutch settlers of Manhattan undertook their first drainage project. A wetland they called Blommaert's Vly occupied the southern tip of the island. A little brook meandered through it. Using the brook to get a head start on the project, the colonists dug two canals to drain the boggy land, acting in the spirit of an old proverb that went, "*dien water deert, die water keert*" meaning "if water hurts you, you may turn it away." The settlers called the larger, main canal (approximating the course of today's Broad Street) the Heere Gracht. A smaller canal built as a spur was christened the Prinzen Gracht. Both were named after conduits in Amsterdam and translate as the Gentleman's (Herengracht) and Prince's (Prinsengracht) canals. Built in the early seventeenth century, the Amsterdam canals formed part of a complex development project that sought to marry sea power to the urban landscape. More specifically, the canals reclaimed land for purposes of housing developments designed to appeal to those who had struck it rich during the Dutch Golden Age. Their considerably less elegant counterparts in the New World served less ambitious but nonetheless important ends. The New Amsterdam watercourses transformed a marsh in lower Manhattan into land suitable for a sheep pasture. Equally important, the canals furthered transportation around the small city by allowing small vessels, at high tide at least, to enter into the town from the harbor. As one historian has written, the waterways "brought the waterfront deep into the settlement."[24]

Van der Donck ignored the New Amsterdam canals in a book he wrote in 1656 describing New Netherland. But he did pay special attention to the topography of this new land. What struck him were New Amsterdam's wetlands, "some so big that one cannot see across them." Van der Donck was especially impressed by the "double formation" of New York's coastline. There he looked out at "islands or barrier beaches, beyond which lie spacious marshes, waterways, and creeks, many of them navigable and affording convenient passage from one place to another." Then there were the major rivers. The North River "carries most of the trade and commerce" and was already well populated by the time that Van der Donck wrote. In the river, he came across "sturgeon, rockfish, black bass, and sheepshead." He also mentioned whales, which on one occasion apparently managed to travel far upstream from the ocean by taking advantage of the wedge of salt water that runs up the Hudson. One wayward animal beached forty-three miles from the sea and was turned into so much "train oil" (a word that comes from Dutch for *tear* and referenced the extraction of the oil in droplets). On the eastern side of New Amsterdam, there was the East River. Some settlers correctly perceived that this was not a river at all but a "bay" (in reality, a tidal strait) that connected two parts of the ocean. "River or bay, as one pleases, it is one of the best, commodious, and commendable attributes a country could be desired to have," Van der Donck observed. The East River brimmed with "bays, harbors, creeks, inlets, rivers, and other places, in such number on both the island and the inland that we should be unable to find its match in the Netherlands."[25]

Tremendous diversity of species and large wildlife populations characterized the world Van der Donck encountered. The landscape was as densely packed as it is today, but with plants and animals, not towers and people. Van der Donck wrote of beaver, a keystone species, which meant that it shaped the environment and the possibilities for other organisms to a degree out of proportion to its own numbers. The large beaver population thrived in all the freshwater swamps and bogs spread throughout the island. Van der Donck also happened upon a place rich in fish such as shad and sturgeon, which migrate up rivers to spawn, and a great range of avian life including eagles, falcons, hawks, sandhill cranes, herons, bitterns, pileated woodpeckers, red-winged blackbirds, and passenger pigeons, the last nesting "together in enormous numbers of countless thousands." He marveled at the waterfowl, the whistling swans, Canada geese, pintails, widgeons, loons, cormorants, and shovelers. He glimpsed seals, tuna, and dolphins, and uncovered estuaries overrun with mussels, clams, and oysters—a world of incredible abundance that offered a stark contrast with the depleted coastal ecosystems of Europe where people had relentlessly fished the inshore for over six hundred years.[26]

It was, above all, the "potential utility of nature," as one historian has written, that most excited Dutch visitors like Van der Donck, especially the navigational prospects of the harbor. The North and East Rivers, after all, flowed into yet another bay. Not just any bay, but a place "preeminently known as The Bay." Its fame rested on several factors. Multiple waterways, apart from the North and East Rivers, emptied into New York Bay, including the Raritan River, the Kill Van Kull, and the Navesink River. "A further reason for its fame is that this bay can easily provide berthing protected from all dangerous winds to more than a thousand cargo ships." A wide entrance welcomed visiting ships; on a single tide vessels could sail several miles straight to New Amsterdam. To the Lenape, the estuary was a gift of simple abundance. To the Dutch, who judged any land in relation to its rivers and bays, New Amsterdam was God's gift to maritime commerce, an activity at which the Dutch had come to excel by the middle of the sixteenth century.[27]

Naturally enough, trends in the Netherlands shaped the Dutch approach to New York Harbor. In the half century following 1570, Dutch trade evolved away from inland waterways toward the expansion of harbors to accommodate international trade. By the second third of the seventeenth century, New York Harbor too was in the throes of a dramatic reorientation as it gravitated toward a new existence as an entrepôt and away from its long history as a place valued chiefly for its marine life. This is not to say that the Dutch turned their backs on the ecological bounty they found in New Amsterdam's marine environment. As early as 1658, the productivity of the oyster reefs surrounding Manhattan had degraded enough to precipitate what may have been New York's first conservation ordinance barring "all persons from continuing to dig or dredge any Oyster shells on the East River or on the North River." But there is no doubt that, by the 1650s, New Amsterdam had become an increasingly important point in a sweeping transatlantic trading network. The growth of the slave-based Caribbean sugar plantations set the stage for New Amsterdam's emergence as a "convenient entrepôt for the slave trade in North America and a source of vital supplies for the plantation economies developing to the south." It would be hard to overstate the importance—much less the stunning environmental implications—of the reconceptualization of New Amsterdam from coastal cornucopia to port.[28]

Across the ocean, the burgeoning Atlantic economy helped to underwrite rapid urban growth in Holland and Zeeland during the Dutch Golden Age and inspired some to envision great possibilities for New Amsterdam. Visitors such as Van der Donck argued that the old Netherlands and the new one were cut from the same ecological mold, implying that they would chart similar economic destinies. The two places bore, he offered, a striking likeness in "opportunity for trade, seaports, watercourses, fisheries, weather, and wind." In large part, Van der Donck surmised, the similarities stemmed from natural predisposition. But he also hazarded, "There is scope for man-made improvements in many places."[29]

These improvements began under the leadership of Petrus (Peter) Stuyvesant, governor of New Netherland from 1647 through 1664. In the 1630s, the West India Company had stationed Stuyvesant in Curaçao, where he oversaw the mushrooming Dutch commodities trade. He later rose to acting governor of the Lesser Antilles and in 1645—after losing a leg to a Spanish cannonball—director-general of New Netherland. Stuyvesant arrived in New Amsterdam in May 1647. Two months later, he made clear his intention to orient the city around the commercial potential of its waterfront. He authorized an excise tax to pay for "a Pier for the convenience of the Merchants and Citizens" and a bulkhead to ward off erosion along the East River. He would later go on to reclaim vacant riverine lots "from the water and morass" in order to build a new residence. Stuyvesant seemed bent on reshaping the New Amsterdam landscape after its Dutch namesake.[30]

In the 1650s, as the city evolved from a company town into an independent municipality, New Amsterdam's economic center of gravity shifted more toward the waterfront. By turns erratic and tyrannical, Stuyvesant, who once threatened to make anyone who appealed his dictates "a foot shorter, and send the pieces to Holland," ran into opposition from Van der Donck, who favored a more decentralized form of government. Although Stuyvesant responded to the criticism by banishing Van der Donck from the colony, the increasingly embattled West India Company forced Stuyvesant to form a municipal government in 1652. Emboldened perhaps by its new legal status, the city began widening the Heere Gracht and lining it with wooden sheathing to keep the sides from caving in, a project designed to internalize the waterfront within the city and make it even more accessible to navigation by small boats. The authorities also approved a new municipal pier at the southern tip of Manhattan and remodeled the City Tavern, a gathering spot built to emulate Amsterdam's Stadts Herbergh. The building became the Stadhuis, or city hall, and a more solid monument to government—literally—as workers excavated earth from a nearby hill to fill in the space between the structure and the water. In a sign of the waterfront's new significance for economic life, the city hall's main entrance was relocated to the East River side of the building.[31]

The rise of New Amsterdam's waterfront in the 1650s, it turned out, was inauspiciously timed to coincide with a new era of increasing pressure on Dutch commercial hegemony. The year 1652 marked the start of the First Anglo-Dutch War and the beginning of a quarter century of attacks on the maritime supremacy of the United Provinces, a trend that eventually resulted in England's conquest of New Netherland and the transformation of New Amsterdam into New York.[32]

While British mercantilism by the early 1660s had thrown the Dutch on the defensive economically (by requiring that only English ships be employed in the Atlantic trade to England), James, Duke of

York, the brother of the newly restored king, Charles II, salivated over the prospect of replacing the Netherlands at the helm of Europe's trading empire. The English had already been busy colonizing the vicinity around New Amsterdam. Earlier in 1656, Stuyvesant had made peace with the Indians of western Long Island and, while Dutch settlement increased shortly thereafter, ultimately it was the English who benefited. By the 1660s, the English had established thirteen settlements on that island, compared to only five for the Dutch; the Indians had been driven from what is today Kings and Queens Counties. Then, in 1664, Charles II gave his brother what is certainly one of the largest gifts in history: a huge expanse from the Connecticut River to Delaware Bay, throwing in parts of Maine, Martha's Vineyard, Nantucket, and Long Island for good measure. With the gift, New Amsterdam's geopolitical importance became paramount. The present, in other words, opened the way for New York to evolve into the seat of British control over the entire stretch of coast spanning from Maine to Cape Fear, North Carolina. It also bolstered New York's prospects as an entrepôt for supplying the West Indies with slaves and food.[33]

Shortly thereafter, British warships under the command of Colonel Richard Nicolls swept into New York Harbor to claim James's present. Stuyvesant was vastly outmatched and, under pressure from city fathers, capitulated without a fight.[34]

Even so, Dutch influence over the landscape persisted. The rivers emptying into the Hudson on the western side of what was now New York continued to be called *kills* as opposed to the English equivalent, *brooks*. *Bays* remained *reaches*. Dutch place names survived, and so too did the canals in southern Manhattan.[35]

Not until the 1670s did the Heere Gracht finally succumb. Why the English filled in the canal remains something of a mystery. What we do know is that the conduit had become fouled over time. In 1657 a New Amsterdam ordinance prohibited people from throwing "rubbish, filth, ashes, oyster-shells, dead animal or anything like it" into it. No one seems to have paid the law much attention. So another ordinance was soon passed increasing the fine for violating the rule. In the 1660s, the government set about collecting a tax from those with property adjoining the canal to pay for sheeting to repair its walls. Two years later, the money left over was used to finance a lock to keep the canal full and at the ready in the event of fire. Even after the lock went in, the canal was described as "very foul and muddy."[36]

It is conceivable that the watercourse may have deteriorated even further by the 1670s. In 1675, with the British now firmly in control of New York (after repossessing it from the Dutch, who briefly reoccupied the city in 1673), a committee was appointed to oversee "the cleansing the great Graft or Ditch." Not long thereafter, the Common Council, the governing body of the city of New York, ordered that people "Liueing within the Streete Called Heregraft: Shall forth with & without: delay fill up the graft Ditch." As one historian writing in the early twentieth century put it, "Thus, probably with no malice aforethought, the newly created English common council abolished this reminder of the Dutch 'Vaterland.'" Filling in land under water eventually burgeoned into a fixation for the English colonists.[37]

Rather than building canals and internalizing the waterfront as the Dutch had, the British focused on extending the existing littoral outward. Major Edmund Andros played an important role in this regard. Appointed governor of New York in 1674, Andros proved eager to enhance New York's mission as a purveyor of food and supplies to the plantations of the West Indies, and thus did all he could to aid the city's merchants in monopolizing this trade. He also personally oversaw the building of a proper and truly permanent pier, called the Great Dock. Although there had been two earlier efforts to build rudimentary piers beginning in 1647 and 1659, this was a far more ambitious public works project anticipated to involve eighteen thousand cartloads of stone. According to one report, Andros had plans in the autumn of 1676 to visit John Winthrop, the governor of Connecticut, but chose to delay the trip after "having undertaken a great worke of making [a] new wharfe." When completed in November, the imposing stone and timber breakwater formed a near perfect semicircle beginning at Whitehall Street and ending at city hall. A neat little passage at the apex allowed vessels to pass into the now protected harbor.[38]

By 1684, Andros's great work, the port of New York, had grown to support a resident fleet of roughly eighty vessels; trade with the West Indies plantations in wheat, lumber, and meat thrived.[39] To this point in New York's history, the English were simply building on the philosophy of the Dutch, a people enamored of trade whose legacy would survive on the island long after they lost control of it. Even so, the waterfront of southern Manhattan had undergone an important change. A place prized mainly for its ecological abundance had become a point on a trading network. This small but significant toehold on an island off the coast of North America would mature into the nexus for one of the most thoroughly transformed environments on the face of the earth.

2 GEORGE WASHINGTON STEPPED HERE

Even more than half a century after the Europeans first settled the island, Manhattan was probably more known for its wolves than its waterfront. But in 1686, less than a year after an order giving "license to the inhabitants of the island of Manhatans, to hunt and destroy wolves," that was about to change.

Colonial agriculture, with its private property, fences, and domesticated animals such as pigs and cattle, caused sweeping ecological change: novel weeds, pests, and the complete silencing of the wolves who had once preyed on the colonists' sheep. As important as these shifts were, there was one way in which the English approach to Manhattan triggered an even more dramatic transformation. Unlike their Native American counterparts, the colonists were bent on changing the very geography of the island.[1]

With the Lenape Indians being driven out by military assault and smallpox, the English began reconfiguring the waterfront, soon to be New York's most important natural resource. In pursuit of this goal, they did something previously unknown to the island. They made underwater land into a form of property that could be bought and sold like any other commodity.

It is not that the Indians never contemplated changing the land.

As Van der Donck observed, the Lenape burned the woods and marsh-lands every fall to facilitate their hunting exploits. But they had never envisioned a facelift on the scale that the colonists had in mind. What happened in 1686 marked the start of a new chapter in Manhattan Is-land's geography, a process of physical expansion that over the years has added an area equivalent to more than seventeen hundred football fields to the landmass.[2]

The transformation of southern Manhattan began with a document called the Dongan Charter. It was named for Governor Thomas Don-gan, a fifty-two-year-old Irishman born in County Kildare, who signed it on April 27, 1686. The charter accomplished several things. First, it upheld the sanctity of private property. Second, it reinforced the power of the merchant elite by confirming the city's monopoly power over the export trade in flour. That trade had grown considerably in importance as settlers fanned out across the Hudson River valley and took up ag-riculture. But, from an environmental perspective, the single most im-portant aspect of the Dongan Charter was its grant of all vacant land on "Manhattans Island aforesaid Extending and reaching to the Low water marke." A later section conferred the right to "take in fill and make up and laye out" land along the coast. In 1686 the shore along the East River extended to Pearl Street, three blocks inland from where it is today. Along the Hudson River, the waterfront ended at roughly Green-wich Street, four blocks from where it now stands. The Dongan Charter, in other words, helped to remake the New York landscape.[3]

Granting the land around southern Manhattan down to the low-water mark was meant to enrich commercial prospects. There was prece-dent for the idea of such grants. The Massachusetts colonial government had an ordinance on the books since the 1640s permitting landowners to colonize the intertidal area. But it would be wrong to conclude that there was anything particularly natural about the idea of ownership over the shore.[4]

If they were not making land anymore, as the old saying goes, some-one forgot to tell New York. As late as the mid–sixteen hundreds, a nar-row reddish sand beach or strand, as the Dutch called it, hugged the coast of southern Manhattan along the East River. With the Dongan Charter in hand, however, the city began doling out "water-lot" grants, underwriting a new coastline in the process. Evidently the water near to shore was too shallow to allow larger vessels to tie up. Building out the shorefront would solve this problem and also provide room for warehouses. Unlike in England or the Netherlands, where pumps and dikes drained existing land, New Yorkers created new ground by building retaining structures and depositing material behind them. The English colonists called it "wharfing out."[5]

The goal was to extend the shore into deep enough water to allow vessels to tie up and discharge their goods. Wooden cribs made of timber fashioned into a kind of underwater log cabin created the foundation for the new wharves. Slaves probably did most of the labor. Although early water-lot grants specified that only "Dock Mudd" be used to make the new land (the word *dock* originally referred to the water in the slip, not a discrete physical structure), over time the quality of the fill declined. It was not unheard of for the owners of water lots to jump-start the process by hauling in abandoned ships and sinking them down to the ocean floor with sand and granite. Ship ballast was a much-favored form of fill; modern-day archeologists have unearthed everything from Caribbean coral to English flint. It is not too much to say that the whole world had a role in building New York.[6]

The process of making land out of water was also helped along by the fact that from the very start it was a challenge to handle all the waste produced by New York. It was customary, for example, to dump tubs of excrement into the street or directly into the East River (the designated repository after a 1700 Common Council ordinance). In 1745 the slips along the river had filled so high with "filth & nastiness" that they were said to have "a most offensive abominable smell in them." By the end of the eighteenth century, people were tossing in "dead horses, dogs, cats, hogs." When the slips brimmed with everything from unwanted ballast to scraps of leather to butcher offal and bones, the entire intervening area was filled in, and the wharfing out began again.[7]

The sale of underwater land seemed to go hand in hand with the merchant elite's increasing control of the waterfront. Of the ninety-four water lots sold between 1686 and 1722, nearly three-fifths of the grantees described themselves as merchants, gentlemen, or esquire (a term denoting English gentry or the holder of a public office). Eight alone went to merchants Stephanus van Cortlandt (1643–1700) and his brother Jacobus (1658–1739). Their father, Oloff Stevensen van Cortlandt (1600–1684), who served as a soldier with the Dutch West India Company, rose to become one of the richest men in the entire colony. Men from more middling social positions, especially those involved in trades associated with shipping (coopers, shipwrights, boatmen*), rounded out the list of grantees. But there seems no escaping the conclusion that the initial burst in water-lot sales delivered a great deal of what was fast becoming the most valuable land in the city into the hands of the ruling merchant class, including the Philipse, Forster, Kip, French, Schuyler, and Beekman families.[8]

One grant at a time, development worked its way north along the East River waterfront, helping the port to flourish. As late as 1678, the city's fleet, according to Governor Edmund Andros, consisted of some "smale shipps and a Ketch." By the mid-1690s, the fleet had grown to a total of more than 160 ships, sloops, and riverboats. In 1694 the Common Council demolished the defensive barricade initially built in the 1650s to guard against the English and, by the end of the decade, Wall Street had lost its wall. At the time, the densely settled area of the city took up just a small fraction of the island, though the demolition of the palisade cleared the way for northward expansion. In 1700 New York even began to rival Boston, exceeding it in terms of tonnage and the clearance of vessels.[9]

By the turn of the century, only a couple hundred feet of foreshore, the land between the high- and low-water marks, from Whitehall north to Beekman's Swamp (a tad south of today's Brooklyn Bridge) remained to be developed into wharves. But an economic downturn made the

---

* Coopers made and repaired wooden containers that held the goods, which were, in turn, carried on boats built by shipwrights and piloted by boatmen.

issue of further water-lot expansion moot. Boston carriers, with cheaper rates, trounced the New York merchant marine, exports plummeted, and specie all but disappeared. Worse, in 1702 tensions escalated between England and France, and the latter's new ally, Spain, over who would control North America. Queen Anne's War was the result. The conflict precipitated a Spanish embargo of New York's British West Indies trade, crushing commercial prospects still further. Only with the Peace of Utrecht in 1713, which brought the war to a close, did the economy turn around. Vessels clearing the port and tonnage both rose significantly between 1714 and 1721, as New York merchants forged a booming West Indian trade. Merchants shipped flour, corn, and other products from farms in the hinterland to Caribbean plantations for sugar that wound up on British tables. As prosperity returned, so did the desire to impinge farther on the East River.[10]

In a rendering of the city circa 1716, the artist William Burgis showed the waterfront extending a full block beyond where the colonists found the shore of the East River on arrival. Now some among the mercantile elite tried to expand the island's landmass still farther by making private entreaties to the colonial authorities to grant more underwater land. Appalled by the special pleading, New York City's Common Council intervened, asking Governor William Burnet for a grant "beyond the present low water mark round the whole Island Manhattans." To make sure the governor credited its position, the Common Council appointed a committee to consult with the governor's council and "make a hansome Entertainmt" for it. Perhaps the entertainment left something to be desired: New York's request went nowhere.[11]

By the 1720s, land expansion had reached the limits of the Dongan grant. A howling coastal storm, and the costly damage that resulted, added pressure on the city to renew its request. On July 29, 1723, a nor'easter hammered New York and its roughly seven thousand inhabitants. The storm broke up "Wharffs from one end of the City to the other, drove all the Vessels ashore, except three, and broke three Sloops to pieces: the Tide higher than ever was known here." The wharves surrounding the Great Dock "are almost Intirely Ruined and washed Away." The significant expense of rebuilding the Great Dock strained the municipal budget, and, with revenue now a priority, inspired another trip to the authorities, this time to see Governor John Montgomerie about a new grant.[12]

What the city had in mind was a stretch of underwater land encompassing "four hundred feet beyond low-water mark" beginning at Bestevars Killitie, a turbulent stream that the Lenape called "Mannette" or "Devil's Water" and which ran along the foot of sand dunes draining today's Washington Square Park and Greenwich Village. From Bestevars Killitie, the proposed grant extended south around the tip of Manhattan and then up the east side of the island as far as Corlaers (later Corlear's) Hook. The surveyor general of the province, Cadwallader Colden, had determined earlier that such a grant would amount to 82.5 acres of land along the Hudson and 127 acres along the East River. Apart from more than two hundred acres around the southern part of the island, the new charter granted the city "all the waste, vacant, unpatented and unappropriated lands" and even control of the foreshore on "Nassaw Island" (Brooklyn) from "Wallabout to red Hook." One need only point out the extensive land reserves of European cities (and the democratic effects of this open space) to realize the possibilities of the new charter. But New York's government at this time was firmly under the rule of the merchant elite, and they had no intention of allowing the new underwater land to lie idle. There is little doubt that the city's most powerful traders— including Frederick Philipse, John Cruger, and John Roosevelt, all of whom sat on the Common Council—favored the granting of what came to be known as the Montgomerie Charter.[13]

The Montgomerie Charter forsook such natural boundaries as the "shore" and the "low-water mark" for an arbitrary mathematical one more in concert with the intention to reshape New York's geography toward commercial ends. In a further sign of the triumph of economic rationality, the city in the early 1730s began charging a yearly rent on the water lots, thereby ending the policy of conveying them in fee-simple absolute. As a result, as one authority on municipal landownership put

it, "their history branches off from that of the upland." No longer would
those who purchased the lots have unconditional control of the property. The new legal status betrayed the recognition not simply of the
economic potential of the water lots, but a willingness to conceptualize
them as a distinct species of real estate different from ordinary land away
from the coast.[14]

It is probably not a coincidence that following the signing of the
Montgomerie Charter, there appeared the first map to depict New York
Harbor as a whole. Published by William Bradford in 1735, *A New Map
of the Harbour of New-York by a Late Survey* gave an overview of the stretch
from Jamaica Bay west to Newark Bay and south to Sandy Hook, replete
with soundings showing the depth of water in the main ship channels
leading to York Island. (That was the name sometimes used for Manhattan.) On the map, the harbor seems to overwhelm the city, which appears
as a small urban outpost in an intricate marine complex. Next to the city
is a tiny mark designating the waterfront on the East River as a proper
anchorage. John Peter Zenger, who apprenticed at Bradford's Pearl Street
shop and is famous for his arrest on charges of seditious libel, published
an edition of the Montgomerie Charter bundled with a copy of the new
harbor map. The two documents taken together reflect the growing consciousness of the surrounding waters. New York Harbor was born.[15]

By the 1750s, New York's economy was pulsating away like never before.
Borne along by the money to be made by war and industrial revolution
in Europe, trade flourished as merchants rushed to capitalize on the out-
fitting of His Majesty's troops, plundered ships on the high seas, and
supplied the sugar-producing West Indies. A mighty wave of economic
good fortune washed over the waterfront. The wharves and the narrow streets raying back from them swarmed with people as oystermen
pushed their barrows and merchants shouted to be heard over the whis-
tle of the wind and the cry of heavy tackle. Sailmakers and provisioners,
meantime, did a booming business as vessels heaved into the slips that
fingered their way along the shore and opened out onto a harbor of bil-
lowing canvas and flapping flags.[16]

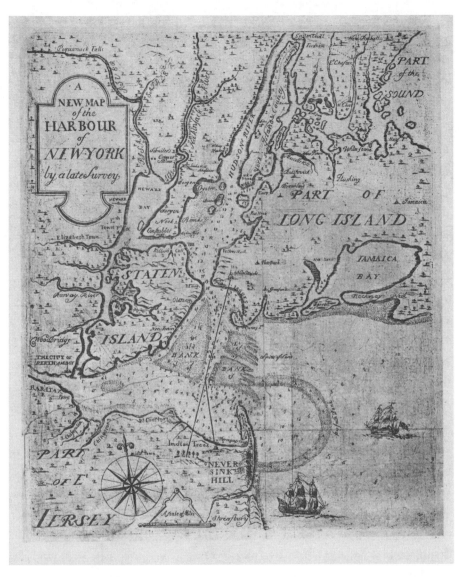

This map depicts the depth soundings taken for the harbor, with Roman numerals delineating anchorages.

Expectations puffed up like wind-inflated sails as boosters went to work selling New York as ideally located for business. A periodical called the *Independent Reflector*, for example, contemplated "the natural Advantages of New-York." It described the colony's central location on the Atlantic Coast, "happily situated for supporting a Trade with all the

Plantations from *Georgia* to *Halifax*." It pointed out that "[n]ot one of the Provinces has a River so far navigable into the Country as ours; whence it is that the Indian Trade from those vast Territories on the North, determines its Course to *Albany*, and thence down *Hudson's* River to *New-York*, as naturally as a Stream gliding in its proper Channel." It sang the virtues of New York Harbor as follows: "Our Harbour, or rather Road, is as safe as others generally are, most of them being subject to important Objections, and often indebted for their Security to very expensive Improvements of Art. The mooring Ground is good, free from Bars, and not incommoded by Rocks, the Water of an equal and convenient Depth, and the Shore bold to the very Edges; and but for floating Cakes of Ice in the Winter, our Shipping would be entirely exempted from Danger." To this day, those inclined to see geography as the root cause of New York's rise to power echo these very same sentiments. But tellingly, at the same time that the case was being made for New York's "natural advantages," the city embarked on its first concerted assault on the sea. Which is to say that New Yorkers stood poised to take geography into their own hands.[17]

The mid–eighteenth century represents a turning point in New York's relationship with its surrounding waters. This was the moment when New Yorkers decided, in earnest, to turn water into land through intensive action. The driving force behind the change was the booming economy, itself driven by shifts in global politics and economics: that is, King George's War followed by the Seven Years' War in conjunction with the British industrial revolution. Although this bid to control nature was a bit chaotic, the results in the end were clear. First, there was a visible change in the shape of southern Manhattan as the city disbursed a swath of water lots and New York ventured farther into the sea. Second, the merchant elite over time consolidated its control over the resulting value created. Here, in microcosm, was a process that would recur.

This second development is in need of some explanation. It is important to understand who bought the water lots, because it is easy to assume that they normally went "to the rich and powerful," making the elite's hold on the waterfront seem like a timeless phenomenon.[18] In fact, the near total dominion over the shore by the merchant class was a contingent development and in no way foreordained. Above all, it had an identifiable starting point in the period after the American Revolution. Put differently, waterfront development started out as a more pluralistic exercise.

The numbers tell the story. In the two decades following 1740, the city matured from a remote outpost into a prospering metropolis. By 1760, New York, with a population of about eighteen thousand, had surpassed Boston to become the second most populous American city after Philadelphia. Nevertheless, the city doled out just five water lots in the 1740s. But the following decade, the number of grants jumped to fifty-seven. Significantly, while nearly half of the grants went to the upper class (merchants, gentlemen, and esquires), 44 percent of the water lots went to entrepreneurial artisans such as shipwrights, bakers, and sailmakers. In other words, at midcentury the water-lot market was by no means the exclusive province of the most privileged.[19]

One of the reasons that the market in water lots was open to people outside the elite was the greater concern at the time for popular rights. The *Independent Reflector*, for example, made a point of condemning a legal right held dear by mercantile interests with land along the waterfront: a right of first refusal respecting adjoining underwater land. This "preemptive" right grew out of a broader sense that landowners were entitled to the "quiet enjoyment" of their estates. But by the mid–eighteenth century, the idea that a waterfront owner ought to have first dibs on the purchase of adjacent underwater land struck those with affection for the free market as wrongheaded. Why should "the Contiguity of their Lands," asked the magazine, entitle these owners to special privilege when "Sale at public Vendue" would bring the city more money, especially in light of the fact that "the Water Lots are now of greater Value than formerly." With these kinds of thoughts circulating, it is plausible that the Common Council—despite being dominated by the affluent in the forty years prior to the Revolution—felt inclined to indulge those somewhat lower down the social scale.[20]

The liberal strain could even interfere with the business of well-to-do families. Consider the case of William Walton, whose father owned a shipyard on Water Street and capitalized on the West Indian trade. When his father died in 1747, William and his brother took over the family business, though his sibling passed on shortly thereafter, leaving William to go it alone. William profited handsomely as a merchant and went on in 1752 to erect one of the most famous houses in all of New York, an elaborate Georgian-style mansion meant to convey the sense of refinement that by midcentury had become fashionable among Manhattan's upper class. He built the mansion on the edge of what was later described as "literally a *swamp*, being a wet, boggy waste, covered with trees and bushes, where wild birds built their nests." Two years later, Walton decided to enrich his estate through some urban renewal along the eastern shore of lower Manhattan at Rotten Row—a dank, filthy area where once a barrel filled with body parts was found bobbing along. Dirty as it was, Rotten Row served as an ice-free refuge for the market boats and larger vessels called coasters that helped provision the city. These small-scale operators found the fees for dockage at private wharves onerous. Hence, alarm spread in 1754 when Walton sought a grant of two hundred feet beyond the low-water mark.[21]

More than simply a safe, ice-free harbor was at stake. For some, there inhered in the wharves at Rotten Row a kind of customary "use-right." A writer in the *New-York Gazette* argued that the city had a tradition at Rotten Row of making water-lot grants that preserved the right to the slips in common. In 1717 Walton's father had been granted permission to wharf out twenty-five feet into the East River, but it came with a reservation permitting "any of the merchants and inhabitants of the said city as for all strangers trading to and from the Same" to load and unload vessels. Such language caused our correspondent to object to the plans of the younger Walton and to argue for "a free and common Wharf" as well as for a public say in rights to underwater land more generally. The right to Rotten Row "is a Right in common to all Mankind; they are in the Nature of Trustees for every Inhabitant in this City." It is important to understand that the colonial charters granted the city "exclusive dominion" over the foreshore and other vacant land and made no provision for so-called use-rights. But the idea of common rights to hunt, pasture animals, cut wood, and engage in other subsistence pursuits had a rich tradition in both England and parts of America, and there is reason to suspect that the agitation over Rotten Row had some effect, because Walton did not receive the water lot.[22]

That was then. In the decade that followed, the social elite mobilized to protect their interests and increasingly came to dominate the market in water-lot grants. In 1768, merchants organized "for promoting and encouraging commerce." So began the New York Chamber of Commerce. By this point, William Walton had died, childless, but his heirs, including his nephew and namesake William Walton Jr., were among the founding members of the new commercial group, which evolved into the most important lobby for mercantile interests in New York City. The following year, William Jr., who had married the daughter of Lieutenant Governor James De Lancey, himself a key representative of the mercantile interest, received (along with others) the water-lot grant sought earlier by his uncle. While the grant continued to make a provision for public access, it limited a right of entry to the two slips at either end of Rotten Row. This was typical of the new grants.[23]

Moreover, this limitation of common right of access to the shore paralleled the merchant elite's mounting command of the waterfront. In contrast with the 1750s, when artisans and merchants shared equally in the water-lot grants, in the following decade merchants received more than two and a half times the number of grants that tradesmen did. Things equalized again in the 1770s—not surprising in light of the democratic upsurge. Then in the postrevolutionary era, the merchant class further strengthened its grip on the waterfront. The broader trend was clear. Breaking the century into three parts—before the Montgomerie Charter, from the charter to the Revolution, and the postrevolutionary period—we find that the elite saw its share of the water-lot grants rise, respectively, from 60 percent to 70 percent to 85 percent. Increasingly, over the course of the eighteenth century, some of the choicest real estate on the island was filed away on the account books of the rich.[24]

By the end of the century, the geography of the lower part of the island had experienced a far-reaching transformation. On the eve of the

American Revolution, a realization seemed to dawn on the conquerors of the East River; a recognition of the boundary-breaking impulse that had come to shape the city's relations with the natural world. Instead of simply describing the location of the water lot with respect to its ward, the grants affirmed, for the first time, that the spot in question would be "made Land & Gained out of the East River." By the stroke of a pen, guided by imagination under the influence of economic gain, land was conjured where once there had been only water. When it came to land and sea, New York City launched its infamous crusade in creative destruction early in its history. Karl Marx had it wrong. It was not "[a]ll that is solid melts into air," but something close to the reverse.[25]

New York was still a little city in a wilderness when George Washington arrived in 1776 to protect the fledgling nation from the British onslaught. Less than a fifth of the island had come under colonial occupation. An infinitesimal 3 percent of its total land area could be characterized as built up.[26] Hemming in what scant urban development existed was a belt of marshy land punctuated by a pond running from today's Lower East Side across town to TriBeCa. New York was no more than a small island on an island.

Nevertheless, York Island had changed significantly since the days of Henry Hudson. Most obviously, it had grown. At the southern end of Manhattan, fifty-six football fields' worth of made land (seventy-four acres) had replaced open water or marsh. Broad Street now curved atop solid ground before moving on to meet the East River, sketching a path once penetrated by shallow salt water; along the river itself, what had been a quiet, sandy beach and bay water beyond had materialized into new city blocks. Change was even taking place in the swampy northern reaches of New York, where solid ground was also being wrested from the marshland extending across the island—on the west side by Greenwich Street and on the east side by city lots. A 1775 map noted that the remaining marsh on the southeastern flank was "constantly filling up in order to Build on." The seventy-four new acres of terra firma were a notable addition that was almost equivalent in size to the entire densely settled portion of the city in 1695.[27]

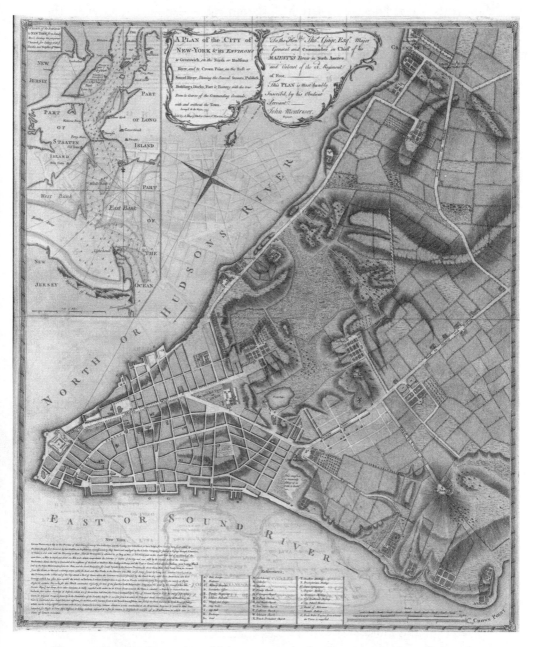

The marshland in the center of this 1775 map is shown cut by drainage ditches. A central ditch follows the path of present-day Canal Street, extending northwest to the Hudson River from a starting point slightly above and to the right of the map's center.

These were all major changes, but war brought still more alterations in its wake. For one, it left Manhattan more denuded than ever. The woods had been under very heavy pressure as early as Thomas Dongan's day. In 1683 the Common Council observed that "moste of the firewood braught to this Citty is Cutt in Other Parts of the Province," presumably Long Island and New Jersey. Firewood prices began to increase in the 1730s, as the logging out of the forest nearest the city proper sent axmen farther afield. The impact of the Little Ice Age—a period of erratic conditions involving cold, harsh winters alternating with mild ones that lasted, roughly speaking, from about 1300 to 1850—may have added to the pressure on the Manhattan woods. The winter of 1760–61 drove the price of a cord of wood up to forty or even fifty shillings. Four years later, the temperature in New York dropped so low that the Hudson River froze almost completely solid all the way to the Jersey shore. In February 1765, slave trader John Watts wrote that "for this six weeks we have been in Greenland." During the American Revolution, British troops competed with Loyalists for firewood, putting a significant dent in the forests on the upper part of the island. Literally miles of defensive fortifications had already robbed the land of much of its timber.[28]

Then came the brutal winter of 1779–80. It was so cold that a giant ice sheet drew up to surround Manhattan. People and even loaded sleighs made the five-mile trip from Staten Island to Manhattan across the frozen waters of Upper New York Bay. The pressure on the woodlands must have been intense. Another devastatingly cold winter followed the year after. While scrutinizing the British occupation from a vantage point in New Jersey, Washington found that "the Island is totally stripped of Trees, & wood of every kind; but low bushes (apparently as high as a Mans waste) appear in places which were covered with Wood in the year 1776." Nearly three-quarters of the island in 1782 consisted of what two ecologists have dubbed "degraded forest and shrub." The island's vast old-growth forest veered toward extinction.[29]

Deforestation increased erosion and storm-water runoff, overwhelming what few culverts existed. By the late eighteenth century, New York had major drainage trouble. Cellars and streets flooded, and the making of new land along the waterfront only aggravated the situation. In 1795, while approving plans for yet another street to be gained out of the East River (South Street), the Common Council observed that the prior water-lot grants "hath long been conceived injurious if not ruinous to the internal and low parts of this City through want of the necessary Descent for carrying off the Water out of the Streets into the River."[30]

It was this damp New York, a city that trailed the Philadelphia metropolitan area in population, to which George Washington traveled en route to the presidency. "About ten o'clock," confided Washington in his diary entry of April 16, 1789, "I bade adieu to Mount Vernon, to private life, and to domestic felicity; and with a mind oppressed with more anxious and painful sensations than I have words to express, set out for New York." Accompanied by escorts, Washington trekked north by coach to Alexandria, Georgetown, Baltimore, Havre de Grace, Wilmington, Chester, and Philadelphia. He then crossed the Delaware—again—and we imagine his mind must have turned to the earlier crossing of that river on a stormy Christmas night thirteen years before. This time, however, instead of Hessian soldiers, he found crowds of people braving the rain and shouting huzzahs as he came ashore. Washington then set out on horseback for Trenton and eventually rode on to New Brunswick, Woodbridge, and ultimately Elizabeth Town, New Jersey.[31]

From there he stepped aboard an elegantly appointed barge, manned by thirteen oarsmen, who piloted the president-elect across the southern end of Newark Bay and down the Kill Van Kull before dropping into New York Bay. All kinds of vessels turned out to greet the great general, and, after doing so, they dropped back into the wake to form a procession. At one point, a sloop pulled up, and people began singing an ode to the Founding Father set to "God Save the King." According to one firsthand account, it was at this point that "a number of porpoises came playing amongst us." Rounding the southern part of York Island, Washington arrived at Murray's Wharf at the end of Wall Street, its railings bedecked with crimson. It was Thursday, April 23, 1789. Despite the bustle that accompanied the great man's arrival, the city was still a sparsely settled place. Measured by inhabitants per square mile, the island of Manhattan as a whole was barely as dense as Ketchikan, Alaska, is today.[32]

When Washington set foot in New York, with its thirty thousand souls, he entered a place that had experienced a century of significant environmental change. Indeed, the very spot where he disembarked would have been under water and the president-elect in need of a spare pair of breeches had he arrived for the swearing-in at an earlier time.

In the broadest sense, the environmental alterations resulted from Manhattan Island's integration into the North Atlantic capitalist economy. That economy rested, among other things, on an approach to the natural environment unknown in North America before the arrival of the Europeans: namely, an understanding of land as a tool for accumulating wealth.[33] For their part, the colonists of York Island also believed that if they ran out of land they could just make more. New York, in other words, was by Washington's day founded on the idea that land was not a fixed resource. This was a radical notion with important implications not entirely apparent yet in the seventeen hundreds, as the city took its first steps to encroach on the sea. Still, the seed of limitless growth had been sown, and its impact on the region would become all too clear in the decades ahead as New York entered the era of high-density urbanism.

PART 2
THE GREAT TRANSFORMATION

1790–1920

3 THE RETICULATION

When you plan a city around a medieval torture device, you have to be prepared to take some lumps.

Proposed in 1811, the New York street plan, or the "implacable gridiron," as the architectural historian Vincent Scully once put it, was roundly condemned for over a century. Clement Clark Moore, of "'Twas the Night Before Christmas" fame, mourned the "levelling propensities" of the authorities. "The great principle which appears to govern these plans is, to reduce the surface of the earth as nearly as possible to a dead level." As for the men responsible for this act of desecration, they "would have cut down the seven hills of Rome, on which are erected her triumphant monuments of beauty and magnificence, and have thrown them into the Tyber or the Pomptine marshes." The orthogonal plan offended the sensibilities of Walt Whitman, Frederick Law Olmsted, and Henry James. The historian Isaac Newton Phelps Stokes, writing early in the twentieth century, decried it as "entirely deficient in sentiment and charm." The plan marked "the end of the little old city and the beginning of the great modern metropolis," by which he meant a sprawling urban agglomeration where "scarcely anything remains to remind us of the primitive beauty and the fascinating diversity of natural charms which we know Manhattan once possessed."[1]

Knocking New York's grid plan makes great sport but poor history. For the important question is not whether the grid was good or bad but why it surfaced when and in the form that it did. The 1811 grid was, above all, a vision of the landscape, and to understand its full meaning requires us to explore the changes to the land that went on in the years preceding it. Only then can we begin to appreciate how the project shaped Manhattan, not exactly destroying "most of the natural beauty and interest of the island," as Stokes held, but transforming its topography in fundamental ways: leveling rugged terrain, which ranged as high as 154 feet above sea level; burying rippling streams, glistening ponds, and green marsh; and creating one gargantuan drainage dilemma.[2]

Two main developments in lower Manhattan helped usher in the grid: the conquest of the waterlogged frontier north of the city proper, and the expansion of the coast to the limit of the Montgomerie grant. The city tried to grow in every way it could. But it found that there were limitations to island life. New York was trapped by water. A pond and broad, sodden marshlands unfolded north of southern Manhattan's dense settlement, while the Hudson and East Rivers surrounded it on the other three compass points. The gridiron materialized as a consequence of urban expansion encountering the local island geography. Whatever the limitations of the grid, there is no question that it literally laid the groundwork for New York's rise as the nation's dominant city. Ruthless or not, it underwrote a form of high-density life that would eventually transform New York Harbor.[3]

Until the nineteenth century, water still ruled the landscape north of the thickly settled part of the city. The lay of the land was as follows. A swampy thicket tangled with oaks, maples, alders, and blackberries sprawled out to the immediate north. It came to be known as Beekman's Swamp, after the merchant William Beekman (1623–1707). Surrounding the swamp on the north and east and extending down to the East River was salt marsh, oozing tidal land enveloped in a broad sea of green grass. A brief stream wended its way through, named Old Wreck Brook. On the opposite side of the island, on the Hudson shore, unfolded a marsh packed thickly with winnowing snipe probing through the black mud in search of worms.[4]

In between these two wetlands sat a pond that may have once been five acres in extent. It had a depth close to fifty feet in places and was positioned straight in the way of New York's quest for urbanity. A hundred-foot hill called Bayard's Mount loomed to the northeast, close to today's Canal and Centre Streets. The Lenape reportedly took oysters from beds in southern Manhattan and returned to the shores of the pond to prepare and preserve them, scattering the empty shells. So many shells piled up that when the Dutch arrived they called the area Kalch Hoek, or Shell Point. In the eighteenth century, the pond, through some corruption of language, thus came to be named the Collect.[5]

The Collect was once connected to a smaller pond. Springs fed both, though they also may have been subject to the tides. If true, the East and Hudson Rivers must have flowed into this low-lying, boggy expanse. Manhattan—a place we now think of with its towers and pavement as solid as a rock—was literally cut in two by water.[6]

Positioned beyond the defensive palisade built in the 1650s (now Wall Street), this watery world turned into a depository for New York's unwanted. In the 1640s, African slaves granted conditional freedom migrated onto land around the northern part of the Collect and the meadow to the west, serving as a kind of human shield against Indian attacks. An African burial ground was established near the Collect's southern shore. By the 1680s, a Jewish cemetery materialized southeast of the pond. At times, the swampy environs took on the role of a lover's lane. ("I came with her from the bush to the Fresh Water," reads testimony from a 1656 legal case, "and I had such a kiss from her, that I could scarcely compose myself.") One day a man named Hendrik Jansen Smitt "hanged himself and destroyed his life on the branch of a tree at the *Kalck-hoeck*." In the 1670s, the Common Council, concerned about the "inconvenyencyes" posed by slaughterhouses, banished them beyond the defensive palisade to the Cripple Bush, the original Dutch name for Beekman's Swamp (*kreupelbosch* is Dutch for "thicket"). Otherwise the lowland rarely entered the historical record. The place stumbled along as a rural outpost and venue for outcasts, estranged lovers, butchers, and suicidal souls.[7]

As for the waters of the Collect, or, as it was sometimes called, the Fresh Water Pond, they served as a drinking source in a city notorious for its poor supply. Proximity to the ocean had its costs. Salt water intruded on the lower end of the island, making the subsurface water brackish and nearly undrinkable. Not only was the water of poor quality, but also there was too little to go around. Not for nothing did Governor Stuyvesant capitulate to the English in 1664. Holed up in Fort Amsterdam and lacking adequate guns and ammunition, Stuyvesant would later recount that the garrison was also "without either well or cistern." With the Collect positioned a good distance from the densely developed southern tip of the island, New Yorkers relied on cisterns and what few uncontaminated underground sources remained. These included a spring found not too far from the shores of the Hudson, near present-day Thames Street. Masters dispatched slaves to the pump to haul the water back home in kegs, sometimes tying the barrels to their backs. But for those living to the north, beyond the city proper, the Collect was unquestionably the best source around.[8]

So it was a fateful moment when development near the pond picked up in the 1730s. Progress reared its head at precisely the point when the Montgomerie Charter propelled the makeover of New York's waterfront. The most significant reclamation project took place in the meadows west of the Collect, a snarl of vegetation where cows sometimes wandered off. What later in the century came to be the Lispenard Meadows, after Leonard Lispenard, a merchant who amassed a sizable estate through marriage and purchase, remained a place "covered with Breaks and Bushes and small trees" and filled with pools of water. Some nine thousand years of history lay buried here, born of so-called marine transgression: that is, when a rise in sea level began transporting ocean sediment to the meadows. In 1730 a man named Anthony Rutgers, Lispenard's father-in-law, tried to reverse this several-thousand-year-old process by asking King George II of Great Britain for title to the lowland. He claimed the swamp was "filled constantly with standing water for which there is no natural vent." Three years later, George II granted his wish: seventy acres "of a Certain Swamp & fresh pond called the freshwater." The swamp had languished "undrayned" and posed a nuisance to those who had to endure its "Noysom vapours."[9]

Rutgers came from a family of brewers, a trade with a keen appreciation for fresh water. His grandfather, Rutger Jacobsen van Schoenderwoerdt, immigrated to New Netherland in 1636 and had opened a brew house in Albany almost a generation earlier. Anthony Rutgers's father, Harman, grew tired of the Indian attacks on his barley and decided to relocate to New York City, where he purchased a brewery near Whitehall Street. In 1710 Anthony Rutgers moved north of Wall Street and

The Lispenard Meadows with the Collect shown at the lower right-hand corner in 1782.

went on to serve as an alderman from 1727 to 1734, an especially active period in New York's underwater history.[10]

It was probably no coincidence that Rutgers received his grant after an outbreak of yellow fever in 1732. He lost no time in having "the Brush on a great part thereof to be Cut down" and made apparent his intention to "Clear the whole and drain the same, which when perfected, it is believed will greatly Contribute to the health of this City." In an appeal to the Common Council (on which he served at the time), Rutgers asked for permission to construct a drainage apparatus through the wetland leading into the Hudson River. The drain worked—too well. Tanners who had set up shop on the southern shores of the Collect found the water "greatly drawn away," so much so that the Common Council ordered Rutgers in 1734 to fill in the trench and "prevent the same from Draining the said Pond."[11]

It is possible that Rutgers caused even more far-reaching ecological change. A few months before the Common Council curtailed his reclamation project, the city banned the use of all fishing nets in Fresh Water Pond (the Collect). It seems fair to say that the colonists had put some significant pressure on the pond habitat. And the drainage scheme may have aggravated the problem, prompting the government to act. Unsurprisingly, the smaller the volume of water in a pond, the fewer fish it can support. A shallower pond can also lead to more temperature fluctuations and easier predation by birds, and this too translates into fewer fish.[12]

Be that as it may, by the middle of the eighteenth century, the Collect enjoyed a resurgence, as runoff from the hills surrounding the pond channeled enough additional water into it to create two persistent subbasins: Collect and Little Collect. It is possible that a rough patch of weather connected with the Little Ice Age—a period known not just for its harsh winters but also for its torrential spring rains—played a role in the waterscape's revival. If history had ended at this point, lower Manhattan might still be sporting its own little version of Walden Pond.[13]

• • •

The Collect's expansionary prospects were short lived. In 1744 the city encouraged yet more tanners to set up shop by banning tan vats south of the ponds. A "Noisom Smell" that the Common Council believed emanated from "Sundry Tan pitts" prompted the decision. Tanners and butchers worked side by side to transform what had once been a fresh-water pond into something significantly less fresh. Slaughterhouses on the east side of the Collect sent hides to tanneries for processing, with the detritus dumped into the pond or flushed into the Old Wreck Brook before debouching into the East River. By the 1760s, the deep water for which the pond was known accumulated at the Collect's northern main basin. The lower subbasin took on an ephemeral cast, the contaminated pond rising and falling with changes in the groundwater level. With its low-lying, waterlogged land, its industrial disposition, and its fluctuating water levels, the area was the perfect breeding ground for mosquitoes and a vector for yellow-fever epidemics. The outbreaks prefigured the Collect's ultimate demise.[14]

After the American Revolution (with plans afoot to move the capital of the United States to the swampy ground along the Potomac River), New York began the task of dealing with the last vestiges of the soggy ground north of the hurly-burly of the city proper. The Common Council ordered a survey of the "antient Bounds" of the Collect and the following year purchased rights to the marsh west of the pond from the heirs of Anthony Rutgers, who had died in 1746. Then John Jay, first chief justice of the US Supreme Court, pitched in, offering to donate land in the service of "a Canal from the fresh Water Pond to the North River." But before that could happen, an epidemic of yellow fever in 1795 took the lives of more than seven hundred people. The pressure to rid the marshes of water intensified.[15]

The Little Collect succumbed to the forces of development before the century was out. By 1797, the heavily settled part of the city had grown ten times in size since the late seventeenth century; as the population surged north it collided with the slaughterhouses, tanneries, and other factories on the urban frontier. People living around the Little Collect at the foot of Potbaker's Hill complained about "pernicious matter running from a Glue Manufactory." A stream once wound its way from this pond into the larger basin of the Collect, but "a number of Dead animals" had, by 1797, choked it off. The Common Council ordered "all the low & sunken Lots" filled, and the Little Collect eventually disappeared before the relentless roll of the New York City street system.[16]

Water quality in the Fresh Water Pond, now more commonly referred to as the Collect for "all the leakings, scrapings, scourings" that accumulated in it, continued to decline. That was a problem. By the late eighteenth century, population growth had compromised the city's wells, and the only pure alternative was what came from the Collect. "The water is very bad to drink, except at one pump, in Queen-street, which is called the tea-water pump," reported a British textile manufacturer in 1794.[17]

In 1798 New York had reached a turning point in its environmental history. For as long as human beings had inhabited the island, they had depended on ponds, springs, and streams to supply drinking water. As late as the American Revolution, Manhattan still contained an impressive array of water resources. According to one calculation, these included twenty-one ponds, with the Collect being the most substantial, plus approximately sixty-seven miles of streams. The Saw Kill, totaling over eight miles in length, drained what eventually became Central Park. A stream called Minetta Water coursed nearly three miles through the future Greenwich Village. The Great Fresh Kill twisted through Times Square long before balls dropped from the sky on New Year's Eve. The approximately four-mile-long Pension's Creek descended through Morningside Heights to the Harlem Plains. Putting aside the nine salt-water ponds, the remaining ponds and watercourses had for more than three thousand years catered to the island's inhabitants. But in 1798, with New York in the middle of another attack of yellow fever that would claim more than two thousand lives and the already embattled Collect described as "a shocking hole," a Westchester County physician named Joseph Browne stepped forward to suggest that the city tap a source from off the island. Calling the Collect a "large stagnating filthy pond," he nominated "The River Bronx, Whose principal source is from a small lake, about four miles to the Northward of the White Plains" as a solution to the burgeoning need for clean water. More than four decades would elapse before New York contrived an off-island water supply. But Browne's ambitious proposal marked a conceptual shift that would spur New York's rise as a high-density enterprise.[18]

Thinking that the city would eventually be turning to sources outside the island for its water, Browne, now a street commissioner, floated the idea of filling in Manhattan's largest freshwater pond. Concern about the soggy ground around the Collect and the Lispenard Meadows to the west had intensified in the wake of the yellow-fever epidemics. Proposals to build drainage canals proliferated, and in the context of evaluating one of these reclamation efforts, Browne pointed out that the Collect had already filled with fifteen feet of mud. "There is no doubt," Browne wrote about the Collect, "the health of the City, in [a] few Years will require it to be filled up with pure earth, it probably ought to be done immediately while there are high Ground enough to be got in its neighborhood." The following year, plans to follow through on the proposal for a canal from the Collect to the North River went forward. In 1803 the Common Council committee evaluating the plan, which happened to include Browne, approved the first plans to level and fill lower Manhattan.[19]

Much of the earth for eradicating the pond came from Bayard's Mount, which was rechristened Bunker Hill to honor the first major battle of the American Revolution. Issachar Cozzens Jr., of the Lyceum of Natural History of New York, formed in 1817 to promote the study of plants and animals (and later renamed the New York Academy of Sciences), recalled climbing the hill and looking "with delight, to the south, over that beautiful sheet of water." But wiping out the Collect and the surrounding lowlands turned out to be such a vast enterprise that the supply of fill ran short. "The earth is daily becoming more & more scarce," explained the city's comptroller in 1806, "being taken away to various directions for filling places, by no means so important" as for drying out the pond.[20]

By 1807, the Collect was well on its way to wherever old ponds go to die. As if to prove the point, the legislation that would eventually result in the grid plan did not even bother with the pond and the adjoining

Lispenard Meadows. Development seemed to have this quarter well in hand. Instead, those charged with formulating the destiny of the island were instructed to focus on the land to the north. Entombing the Collect marked the final chapter of the old water order, which had served Manhattan since the first human beings arrived. With the prospect raised of bringing in water from fountainheads located outside of the city, the natural features of the island diminished in importance. A new dialogue with the land was set to begin.

If trends taking place inland on the island influenced the emerging grid plan, then so too did changes along the waterfront. The grid was not simply a design for the land, but a manifesto for growth at the expense of the surrounding rivers. How else to make sense of the idea for Twelfth Avenue, a route laid out on the 1811 matrix that, for much of its course, ran right through the Hudson River?[21]

In the period leading up to the grid, New York superseded Philadelphia as the nation's leading port. All US ports benefited from American neutrality during the wars raging in Europe in the 1790s and early 1800s. But the payoff for New York was especially hefty in terms of both imports and exports. Exports alone climbed tenfold between 1792 and 1807. In 1810 New York's population swelled past that of Philadelphia, considered America's largest city at the time.[22]

While geography is not destiny, it might be more accurate for those inclined toward deterministic explanations to argue that geology was the key factor. New York Harbor was the product of events that began during the so-called Pleistocene epoch, the period from roughly two million years ago to ten thousand years before the present. Toward the end of this era, a huge terminal moraine—essentially a giant barricade—extended from what is today Staten Island to Long Island. Behind the moraine, glacial action carved a valley that gave rise to an early version of the Hudson River. As the climate changed when the Pleistocene came to an end, the proto-Hudson (or possibly a large lake) poked a hole in the moraine, and seawater rushed in, giving birth to New York Harbor. The melting of the glaciers, which drove this process, caused the sea level to rise dramatically and provided the city with deep ocean water relatively near to shore. And as an added bonus, the fact that the tides flowed through a narrow opening (the Verrazano Narrows) helped to keep the entrance to Upper New York Bay relatively free of sediment and conducive to navigation. New York's geologic good fortune, however, took on real importance only in the late eighteenth century, as the size and weight of ships began to increase.[23]

The port of New York has the additional virtue of being flanked by two long stretches of land that protect it from wind and surging seas: Rockaway Peninsula and Sandy Hook, the latter a barrier spit that the Dutch called Sant Hoek. These landmasses shelter the mariner heading west into Lower New York Bay. A captain can then tack north and pass through the narrows, a tidal strait between Staten Island and Brooklyn that opens into the security of the upper bay. All that separates the port from the open ocean is a mere seventeen miles. Philadelphia, by contrast, is a hundred miles from Chesapeake Bay. New York Harbor also has a convenient back door: Long Island Sound, which gives the mariner the option to approach the city from the north, sail down the East River, and arrive to take refuge in Upper New York Bay.[24]

But that is not all. The part played by New York Harbor's tidal range is too rarely appreciated, especially among those inclined to give geography the determining role. New York was unlike many European ports, where particularly high tides compelled extravagant docking arrangements. London, where the tide varied by more than twenty feet in the late nineteenth century, is a case in point. The elaborate stone piers built there are a testament to how tidewater influenced the tide of history. The docks of New York, in contrast, were among the simplest in the world, the result of a more advantageous four-and-a-half-foot tidal range. New York's entire waterfront plan was really no plan at all, just the city expanding along the East River—like a balloon slowly inflating with air— when the slips filled with too much garbage and mud.[25]

The strategy continued into the postrevolutionary period. Between 1784 and 1803, the city conveyed water grants at a very low rate of just over one a year. Then, in 1804, with the Jeffersonians having taken over the Common Council, a veritable underwater land rush began. Forty-six water lots were disposed of in that one year. If the Jeffersonian conviction that freedom rested on economic opportunity was behind the surge, the result nevertheless called equality into question. Merchants were the big winners, as becomes clear if we examine trends before and after the Revolution. In 1772, another robust year for water-lot sales, merchants, gentlemen, and tradesmen each received roughly the same number of grants. In 1804, however, the upper class had come to dominate. Further, nearly 80 percent of the grants made in 1804 went to the merchant and governing elite (gentlemen and esquires), reinforcing the world of entrenched wealth along the coast.[26]

In the annals of New York water-lot grants, 1804 stands out for one other reason: this was the year that commerce discovered the Hudson River (still often called the North River). Previously, development favored the East River because it was narrower than the Hudson and close to the nascent town of Brooklyn, the population of which rose from 1,603 in 1790 to 4,402 in 1810. Close to 60 percent of the grants in 1804 (twenty-seven in all) involved underwater land along the Hudson. Nearly as many grants were made along that river in this one single year as had been made in all the years from 1734 to 1803. It is little wonder that for the first time in two hundred years, the city chose to celebrate the anniversary of Henry Hudson's voyage. The first centenary had passed unrecognized. But in 1809, with the river now forging its way into consciousness, the New-York Historical Society celebrated Hudson "and the *river* which has been since called by his name."[27]

The year 1804 is distinctive in one last respect: the grants forgo the natural geography of the shore for the rational geography of the grid. In understanding this change, it is important to first take note of the cramped conditions that were propelling the city farther into the East and Hudson Rivers. Since the 1790s, the city had been suffering from the claustrophobia imposed by the old Montgomerie grant. The waterfront was bulging with wharves and warehouses. In 1796 one traveler visited the shores of the East River and found it "crowded with confused heaps of wooden store houses, built upon wharfs projecting one beyond another in every direction." Silt, waste, and detritus streamed into the slips and had to be cleared with a "Dock Drudge," a rudimentary dredger, purchased by the city in 1791. Burling Slip reeked "from the constant accumulation of dead animals, offals and other perishable substances, which lie putrifying on the mud and stagnant water." Old Slip suffered on as "a Receptacle of Filth." Public slip space also remained in short supply, the result of the relentless privatization of the waterfront in the wake of the Montgomerie Charter. Market boats and coasters (crucial links in the food chain between countryside and city) hustled for what few public landings remained. There seemed to be no escaping the conclusion that the slips had to be enlarged to create more space to unload.[28]

The only way for that to happen was for the city to commission more streets flaring out farther into the water. In 1795 and 1796 the Common Council did just that, authorizing a new street in the East River called South Street and a new one in the Hudson called West Street. But building new thoroughfares to the desired widths would involve expanding into underwater land outside the Montgomerie grant. The city subsequently prevailed on the state of New York to allow it to do so. One of the acts giving the city this right noted that "the curving and other irregularities of the shores of the said rivers in their original state" had made it difficult to improve the waterfront with a straight and nicely aligned street.[29]

Granted ownership of the underwater land, the city proceeded to impose a grid pattern on the waterfront. Grants made prior to 1795 typically described a water lot as extending a certain distance from the low-water mark. But the 1804 grants signaled a departure from this custom. These water-lot grants instead designated the boundaries of the underwater property in relation to a grid network. By laying out the streets in such a fashion it became possible to figure out exactly which ground lot corresponded to which water lot. And that offered speculators a sense of predictability in their purchases, since one could easily target an as yet ungranted water lot simply by buying up the corresponding land. With the help of a grid plan, in other words, water lots made the final leap into the world of real estate.[30]

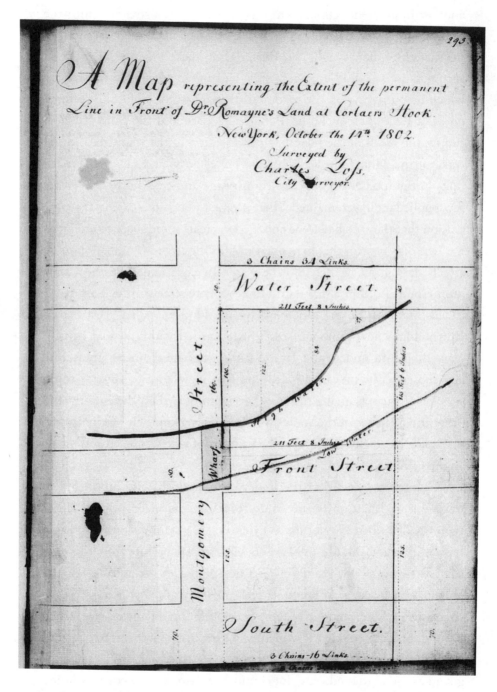

By the nineteenth century, most water-lot grants were accompanied by maps showing a grid pattern imposed over the original high- and low-water marks.

The explosion of water lot grants in 1804 underscored the city's central dilemma: the quest for growth on an island not particularly conducive to it. Bulging at the seams, New York was fighting water on all fronts: to the north at the Collect and Lispenard Meadows and around the island's southern perimeter. This was the context for one of the most important public works projects in Gotham's history: the much maligned gridiron plan in which the same spirit of rationality imposed on the waterfront was applied writ large.

Though once described as "a complete hypocritical, lying nincompoop," John Randel Jr. did more than any other single human being to make New York into the dense conurbation that it is today.[31]

Born in 1787 in Albany, New York, Randel was the son of an Irish brass founder who fought in the Revolution and was captured by the British and then sent to starve at a stinking prison in Halifax, Nova Scotia. Somehow Randel Sr. survived and lived to communicate some of that tenacity to his son, who was nothing if not determined. Randel Jr. is shown in one portrait with dark hair, twisting sideburns, and a look of self-possession. He had a great mind for math, a passion for detail, and a yearning to join the ranks of the booming field of surveying, which looked like a path to success in a young nation whose first three presidents all shared a background in the profession. A highly combustible man, especially later in his life, Randel deployed his measuring rods and compass across upstate New York before being recruited to rationalize Manhattan Island. In carrying out his assignment, he left an indelible mark on the New York landscape.[32]

Beginning in 1808, Randel rose out of bed each morning and trailed north to his office in the suburbs: Greenwich Village, that is, a place with strong rural roots that as late as 1811 was still struggling to foreclose on the "practice of gunning & fowling." Greenwich is an anglicization of the Dutch name for the area: Greenwijck, meaning "pine district." In Randel's day, the place may still have looked in part like a miniature version of the New Jersey Pine Barrens. Sand hills, known by the Dutch as Zantberg, replete with pitch pine and scrub oak traversed the region

from today's Charlton and Varick Streets northeast to a little west of
Astor Place. As Randel later recollected, he "generally crossed *a ditch* cut
through Lispenard's salt meadow" and caught a glimpse on his way to
work of the Collect "at that time filled up by a *collection* of spare earth and
rubbish." On he trudged, turning onto the street that housed his office
"a short distance beyond Manetta water," the trout stream north of the
sand hills that the Indians called Mannette, or "Devil Water," presumably because of its turbulence, and that the Dutch renamed Bestevars
Killitie. Then Randel unpacked his tools and went to work surveying the
land north of a line that stretched across the island (bisecting, roughly
speaking, today's Washington Square). In the process, he helped lay the
foundation for the throngs of people that inhabit Manhattan today.[33]

The idea of laying a rectangular grid over the land was nothing new.
Philadelphia, Albany, and Washington, DC, had already embraced the
idea, as had London, Lima, Peru, and other cities across the world. In
1796 the city of New York, eager to sell off its more rugged common
lands in the center of the island to generate cash, hired a surveyor named
Casimir Goerck to aid in the enterprise. Goerck was a Pole who joined
the American side in the Revolutionary War as an artillery officer. He
was no doubt aware of the Continental Congress's effort, not long after
the war, to divide the new nation's unmapped western lands into rectangular boxes to facilitate their sale and aid in paying off the debts incurred
in the fight for freedom. Goerck tried the same approach in New York.
He imposed a grid design on the land between today's Twenty-Third
and Ninetieth Streets. The map Goerck produced involved just a small
fraction of the land area of Manhattan Island and, in any case, it was
not a full-fledged plan for New York but a survey designed for the
single-minded purpose of disposing of the city's estate.[34]

A year later, the city hired Goerck again, this time to make "a Survey
& Map of this City with all the Streets & Water Lots." The idea was
to have Goerck draw an official map of New York from the Battery to
Sandy Hill Road, "at the two Mile Stone." The city also retained the services of one Joseph Mangin. He had earlier broached the idea of building an elaborate internal dock at the Collect, justifying the endeavor on

the grounds that New York was "designed as the future center and me-tropolis of [the] commercial world." They set to work, but when Goerck died in the yellow-fever outbreak of 1798, Mangin soldiered on alone.[35]

Anticipating generations of developers down to the present, Mangin had a flair for the narcissistic. Though the city had asked for a map of New York as it stood, Mangin arrogantly explained that his map "is not the plan of the city such as it is, but such as it is to be." He went so far as to name one street on the map in his own honor.[36]

In 1803 Mangin finished sketching the map titled *A Plan and Regulation of the City of New York*. The title is suggestive. The word *regulation* took on its modern meaning—to bring under the control of rules or laws—in the seventeenth century, but it also came to mean the idea of making something even. It was the latter sense of the word that Mangin embraced, producing a map that very nearly turned the southern part of the island into one neat little square. Within the square and north of the city proper, he imposed a grid plan. There was only one problem. Not only were some of the streets under water, they were set on "land" that the corporation of the city of New York did not even have title to. The city was thus bound to reject the map, which it did, pointing to its "many inaccuracies." Mangin may have been an odd character, but he did at least raise the idea that New York's future on the island should be a self-consciously planned one.[37]

In 1807 New York was a small city with big plans. The idea of a grid arrangement had been raised, and so had the notion of planning the city's future, instead of stumbling on with the laissez-faire approach. If only New York's leadership could think of a way to follow through instead of being held hostage to the vicissitudes of local politics. The solution was to ask for the intervention of the New York State Legisla-ture, and thereby solve the problem of one Common Council overrul-ing the urban planning decisions of another. The government even had some people in mind who it believed would be "fit and proper persons to be appointed Commissioners of Streets and Roads," namely Simeon De Witt, Gouverneur Morris, and John Rutherfurd.[38]

The state complied. It appointed the three men and gave them four years to come up with a set of maps surveying the city and its "hills, vallies, inlets and streams." The maps would be keyed to a set of "suitable and durable monuments" to be laid out across the land, a task that would occupy John Randel for years. But more than land was at stake. No street plan could be complete without taking into account the waterfront, New York's crowning glory and its very reason for being. So, taking a page out of John Montgomerie's book, the legislature provided the city with title to underwater land along the Hudson "running four hundred feet into the said river from Bestaver's killetje or river [Manetta], to the distance of four miles to the north." It was also granted "land" extending four hundred feet and running two miles "from the north side of Corlear's hook." This single legislative act went well beyond a street plan. It led to the most thoroughgoing reinvention of land and water in the history of the island.[39]

Who were these men appointed to remodel New York? All three were Federalists and thus believers in the discipline of government, as well as college graduates and members of families with large landholdings. Of the group, Gouverneur Morris, age fifty-five, was the most prominent, and author of the most powerful line in the US Constitution: "We the people of the United States." Perhaps it was his stature, or even his skill in thinking clearly about language, that compelled his inclusion on a committee established to bring precision to the landscape. What's more, his views on the natural world are worthy of note. Morris worried that encounters with untamed nature—what he once called "[t]hose awful forests"—could lead to errors of judgment. What better way to ensure the triumph of good sense than to domesticate the wilds of Manhattan?[40]

Simeon De Witt seemed a logical enough appointment. De Witt was born on Christmas Day 1756 about a hundred miles north of New York City in the little town of Wawarsing. The son of a physician, De Witt traveled in well-to-do circles. He learned surveying from his uncle James Clinton, who went on to become a brigadier general in the Continental army and who recommended his nephew to George Washington, who hired him on as a geographer. After the war, the state of New York appointed De Witt its surveyor general. The western part of New

York was described as "still a forest," and it was De Witt's job to ready it "for the residence of civilization." How he went about this project is of some interest. To this point, land surveys typically employed the old metes-and-bounds approach, in which compass directions and distances described a parcel in relation to various natural boundaries—beginning at the such and such river and extending so far to a hemlock tree and so forth. But after the war, Thomas Jefferson was off recommending that western lands be divided into squares, and De Witt took the Founding Father's faith in the grid to heart as he forsook natural features in his quest to divvy up land. He even applied this reticulating logic in places where progress had already swept through, formulating a grid plan for the city of Albany, New York.[41]

John Rutherfurd rounded out the group. Of the three men, he was the only native son, born in Manhattan in 1760 to a family of means. Rutherfurd would go on to become fabulously wealthy. But apart from his wealth and the power that it brought (and perhaps the fact that he was married to Gouverneur Morris's niece), there is little else that explains his inclusion on the commission.[42]

The title given the law empowering the street commissioners was "An Act relative to Improvements, touching the laying out of Streets and Roads in the City of New-York, and for other Purposes." That is a mouthful, but significant in light of the word *improvements*. The word *improve* arrived in the English language as a way of denoting investment with respect to the land, "often the enclosing of common or waste land." By the eighteenth century, the word had a two-hundred-year-old history signifying "profitable operations" with respect to property. As employed in the 1807 act, the term—though it had by then come to mean to make things better—referenced this earlier history.[43]

Gouverneur Morris and Simeon De Witt were big believers in the philosophy of improvement. In 1810, while still working on the formulation of the grid plan, both men assumed posts overseeing one of the greatest improvements in American history: the Erie Canal. Three years later, De Witt gloried in the inventiveness of the American people and wrote of the "boundless field of improvement before us."[44]

But it would be a mistake to somehow imagine that De Witt, who viewed improvement as an unqualified human good, was only interested in bulldozing the natural world. "No approaches can be made to the perfection of Art," he once wrote, "without the habit of attentively observing the attributes and operations of nature." In De Witt's day and circle, the ideas of *art* and *nature* opposed each other. *Art* meant skillful human invention. It meant the Erie Canal or factories driven by waterpower or the wharves of lower Manhattan. *Nature* was another story altogether. To De Witt, it was a force to be reckoned with. He viewed the natural world in Romantic terms, reveling in the beauty of fruits and foliage, rivers and streams, and even the "sublimity of the spectacle" of hurricanes and storms. De Witt's Romantic vision of nature, however at odds with his faith in improvement, meant that he was not inclined to simply run roughshod over the land—the impression sometimes given, from the perspective of hindsight, of the grid's impact on the island.[45]

In any event, he left to his protégé John Randel the messy details of putting improvement into action in the rural hinterland of Manhattan. Beginning in 1808, Randel set about taking measurements for an epic blueprint of New York, and later spent six years inscribing the template onto the land by erecting monuments and sinking iron bolts into rock—more than sixteen hundred markers in all. The landscape Randel found was no virgin wilderness. It is true that Randel did describe making his way north on the Bowery in an area of Manhattan that would have been "impassible without the aid of an axe." But those axes fell on old "hawthorn hedge-fences," a boundary planting in a world that had already paid a visit to the realm of private property. To imagine Randel and his men bushwhacking their way north through a wilderness, while it must certainly have happened at times, is to discount Randel's own observation that they worked "in the suburbs of the city," a world with a system of primitive roads and country residences. Randel even uncovered paths blazed through overgrown parts of Manhattan, including one through the dense grasses of the sweeping Stuyvesant Meadows located in the vicinity of today's Tompkins Square Park.[46]

In the course of his duties, Randel ran into some problems, at one point finding himself detained by some disgruntled New Yorkers. He described "numerous suits instituted against me as agent of the Commissioners, for trespass and damage committed by my workmen, in passing over grounds, cutting off branches of trees." The trouble escalated to the point where the state legislature stepped in. It responded with a law that put the onus on the claimant to bring a bill of particulars before the Common Council within thirty days. No action at law could be brought before the administrative process took its course. If the Common Council made "reasonable compensation" for the problem (damaged trees, for example), "the same shall be a bar to any action to be brought therefor." The law resembled the mill acts popular in New England at this time. These were state laws that allowed mill owners along nonnavigable rivers to erect dams, flood land, and compensate the owners of inundated land according to a specified procedure, and tended to favor the new property of the mill over the old wealth in the land. The New York law was similar in favoring urban development over landed property. It arrogated authority to the Common Council and made its decision the exclusive remedy for damages occasioned by the survey, at least for thirty days. At that point, a landowner could sue, but the new law made that a risky choice since a damage award for less than that of the Common Council's meant a verdict for the city. In other words, an older notion of absolute property rights was swept away in the name of the developmental ethos so central to life in the early republic.[47]

On March 22, 1811, the official commissioner's plan for the city was published. Like much about New York it was big, nearly nine feet in length. It was Randel who drew the three maps that made up the plan, and their physical size betrayed an even larger ambition: to bring more than eleven thousand acres of land under the thumb of urban life. On the maps are found twelve streets running north and south intersected by 155 cross streets, ascending all the way up to Harlem, where the uneven terrain stopped the grid plan dead in its tracks. Altogether, it was an enterprising plan for a city that barely had a population of a hundred thousand people, about a tenth the size of London.[48]

In hindsight, the plan may well be a testament to "ruthless utili-

tarianism" or "real estate logic." But that is not how the commissioners justified their endeavor. In explaining themselves, they noted that
the very first question they faced was whether to "confine themselves to
rectilinear and rectangular streets, or whether they should adopt some
of those supposed improvements, by circles, ovals, and stars." They ultimately decided to side with "convenience and utility," reasoning "that
a city is to be composed principally of the habitations of men, and that
strait sided, and right angled houses are the most cheap to build." Were
they to be asked why they adopted the grid plan, the answer was simple:
"it appeared to be the best; or, in other and more proper terms, attended
with the least inconvenience." That was of course not to say very much.
They were a bit more expansive regarding the lack of open space, which
they admitted might be a "matter of surprise" to some. Here they observed that unlike Paris or London, New York did not rest beside "a
small stream." The reality was that "those large arms of the sea which
embrace Manhattan Island, render its situation, in regard to health and
pleasure, as well as to convenience of commerce, peculiarly felicitous."
And with the price of land "uncommonly great," they seemed to have
no room to spare. The grid plan's main goal was to provide for New
York's move from the "rank of cities of the second order" into the top tier
of most populous. The commissioners ventured that in fifty years' time,
New York would be "closely built" to about Thirty-Fourth Street, with a
population approaching four hundred thousand.[49]

It has been argued that the grid plan was the product of the political
culture of the time. The divvying up of the land into rectangles was a
gesture toward the republican vision that informed the early national
period. No longer, the grid plan seemed to imply, would a social system
founded on special privilege alone rule Manhattan. With its more than
two thousand rectangular boxes, the architects of the grid threw their
support behind the seeming neutrality of the market and sought a way
for New Yorkers to carve out the urban equivalent of idyllic Jeffersonian
lives. While it seems like a stretch to imagine a bunch of Federalists at
work on such a project, it is possible that the men had by this point made
their peace with the importance of individual ownership to the concept

of freedom. Whatever the case, the grid's meaning went well beyond the world of political rivalry.[50]

Seen from a landlubber's perspective, the grid appears to be about streets and terrain. In fact, the surrounding waters shaped the logic of the grid. Given the historic importance of the waterfront, it could not be otherwise. The profusion of cross streets looks from one angle like the work of republicans and from another like the work of merchants desperate to open as much access as possible to New York's premier resource. More than a third of the roughly eleven thousand acres planned were earmarked for streets. Of that figure, the area devoted to east-west traffic amounted to well more than twice the quantity allotted for transportation in a north-south direction. If the commissioner's grid plan meant to aid in the disposal of land, it also anticipated the need for universal access to the waterfront. Street planning and waterfront development operated as two sides of the same coin. It could hardly be a coincidence that the legislation enabling the street commissioners included a provision expanding the city's underwater estate. Nor was it an accident that the grid plan encroached on both the East and Hudson Rivers. Twelfth Avenue, as Gouverneur Morris and his colleagues explained, "runs from the wharf at Manhattan Ville nearly along the shore of Hudson's River, in which it is finally lost." Lost at the time, but destined to be found by virtue of various landfill projects later in the century. If the gridiron plan spoke to the preoccupation of the Revolutionary generation with ensuring freedom through an equal distribution of property, it also had at least one foot in the past, in the older heritage of colonizing underwater land stretching back at least to the time of John Montgomerie.[51]

Much has been made of the commissioners' lack of concern for the "contours of the land." There is certainly no denying the drive, even the arrogance, of the plan. Nor is there any doubting that some were awestruck by the grid's scorched-earth proposal to "spare nothing that bears the semblance of a rising ground." Even so, some natural features of the island proved too daunting and thus escaped the commissioners' orthogonal logic. Wetlands seemed especially problematic. The Haerlem Marsh, for example, resisted the advances of the grid. The commissioners' grid plan, in all its neat right angles, halted at 106th Street, before the largest wetland complex on the island. The wetlands in this area made up, by one estimate, a total of about 370 acres. A brook, variously called Haerlem Creek or Pension's Creek, extended from north of what is now Central Park to the East River. So many otters congregated along the south bank that the Dutch named the spot Otterspoor.[52]

Farther south, the commissioners found another large salt marsh that left them scratching their heads. This was the Stuyvesant Meadows. It too remained outside the grid's embrace. The commissioners instead harked back to a past Dutch tradition in urban planning. They proposed a canal with the intent of turning the area into a public market. Before the word *market* took on its abstract meaning connoting the "boundless and timeless phenomenon" of exchange, it referred to actual physical places. These places were typically located in marches, or natural frontiers often found along the coast, where the dirty work of exchange could

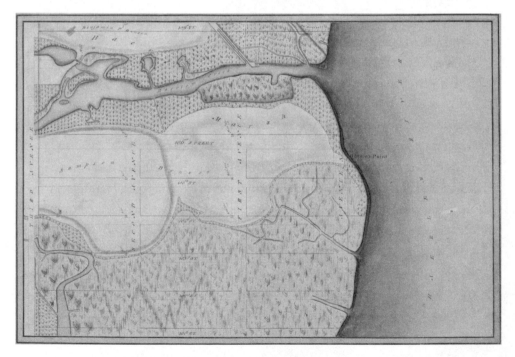

A salt marsh surrounding Haerlem Creek, a substantial body of water in its own right, escaped the rectilinear logic of the grid.

unfold on neutral territory. Precisely a place like the Stuyvesant Meadows. Rather than representing an outright denial of topography, the grid yielded before the swamps of New York.[53]

Even more interesting, for all its seeming hubris, the grid actually underestimated the growth of New York. Though Morris and company predicted a city of four hundred thousand stretching uptown to Thirty-Fourth Street in fifty years' time, the population on the eve of the Civil War was, in fact, twice that amount, and development had surged all the way to Forty-Second Street.[54]

If the grid's architects fell short in the domain of prophecy, their forecast about New York's growth did demonstrate one thing: "closely built" living, as they put it, was their goal. It was not the logic of real estate that was the driving force behind the 1811 plan so much as the philosophy of high-density development. Although we may never know exactly what the commissioners were thinking, the reality is that they emphasized issues of population, growth, and housing in their remarks. Their plan was not primarily about giving realtors the tools they needed—though it did, of course, inject a good measure of predictability into the market in land. It was mainly about accommodating economic and population growth in an island environment where land was the limiting factor. In the end, there was nothing inevitable about the idea of squeezing hundreds of thousands of people into a relatively small island. But when the grid was thrust upon the land, it represented the opening act of New York's unique version of urban development and consequently set the stage for the greatest transformation in New York Harbor's ecological history.[55]

4 ADVENTURES IN DRAINAGE

By 1821, the tenth anniversary of the grid, New York had, as planned, grown in size, but not enormously so. It was a city of a bit more than 120,000 people; another 11,000 lived in neighboring Kings County. From the standpoint of world history, New York was still small, and that, for once, was a good thing. For on September 3, 1821, the most powerful hurricane in the recorded history of the area, a Category 1 storm with howling winds estimated to be as high as seventy-eight miles per hour, raged through New York Harbor. "What a lesson this to proud and presuming man," was how one correspondent sized up the effects of the storm's fury.[1]

In the annals of hurricane history it is a curious storm, almost completely forgotten by students of New York. Had it happened a generation later, after the Erie Canal and the subsequent demographic upsurge in the city, it would doubtless rank as one of the most significant hurricanes in US history. Coming as it did in 1821, with New York's economic glory days still off on the horizon, the disaster has been reduced to little more than a footnote.[2]

Drenching rain and thunderstorms pummeled New York on the weekend before the hurricane, with the wind shifting "to almost every point of the compass." Then about five o'clock on Monday afternoon, the gales whipped up and continued "with all the violence and fury of a hurricane" for the next four hours, "throwing down chimnies, unroofing buildings, and prostrating trees in various directions." The storm made landfall near Jamaica Bay. The sloop *Glory Ann* and three other vessels set sail on Monday from Brookhaven, on the south shore of Long Island, headed for New York. But the ferocious winds caught up with them, tearing their sails to shreds and driving the ships aground. Of the eighteen mariners aboard the boats, only one survived.[3]

The center of the hurricane tracked to the west of New York. That meant that the city experienced the weather system's fastest winds and a pounding storm surge, subsequently reckoned at ten to eleven feet above normal. "The tide, although low water when the gale commenced, rose to an unusual height, overflowing all the wharves and filling the cellars of all the stores on the margin of the East and North rivers." Waves crashed over the streets along the East River, battering them so badly that it was "dangerous for carts to venture on them." Gusting winds blew down factories and stripped off roofs. The land on the lower part of Paulus (Powles) Hook (Jersey City) "was carried away" and its dock "nearly ruined." At Hoboken, "the wharves and bridges were entirely destroyed." Altogether, the hurricane "did more damage in this city and vicinity, than was ever before witnessed."[4]

As stunning as the hurricane was, what happened next was even more dumbfounding. For the next six and a half decades, no major low-pressure systems to speak of struck New York City. During the lull, New York rose to supremacy in trade and finance, and its population exploded. The calm would last all the way until 1888, when a severe extratropical storm with sixty-mile-per-hour winds dropped more than twenty inches of snow and paralyzed the city. Even that storm, though intense, was not as fierce as the one that swept through in 1821. It would be more than halfway through the twentieth century before a hurricane came even close to rivaling it. By the time that happened, New York had eclipsed London as the linchpin of the world economy.[5]

What approach did New York and neighboring Brooklyn take to the land during the calm? Though it would be a mistake to read back into the past our current knowledge about coastal flooding, the inescapable reality is that, in the forty years after the grid, development unfolded in harm's way. This period is defined by the furious efforts to transgress the natural limits to the land, to drain the soil, plow under wetlands, and build in the floodplains. New York, in other words, exchanged its varied natural topography for a far more standardized and vulnerable one.

Even into the nineteenth century, the landscape of lower Manhattan still bore the direct effects of its former life as a swamp. The Dutch hydraulic engineer Andries Vierlingh, over a century earlier, had the right idea when he wrote, "Water will not be compelled by any 'fortse' [force], or it will return that force onto you." It was a point that New Yorkers were coming to learn well.[6]

Throwing dirt at the problem only took the city so far. The Collect was a case in point. Life at the former pond remained waterlogged for quite a while. Then the water moved on into the groundwater flow, and the erstwhile pond began to resemble the surrounding terrain, which happened to be a wetland and thus not that much better from the standpoint of real estate development. One perceptive observer wrote that "by spreading a coat of loose earth over the swamp I speak of, the marshiness may be concealed from view and the surface made to appear dry at times as in Water and Front streets. It is not the less true, that the marsh below and in the bottom of the Collect *exists.*" Workers could cart dirt into the Collect, but that alone failed to "prevent the water in the surrounding hills from following the channels which nature formed for it." In the end, there was no escaping the realities of hydrology. The Collect "will still be a *Collect (of water and filth)* as truly as if it had been filled up with paving stones instead of earth."[7]

By 1812, the Collect had dried out enough for the city to convey thirty-four building lots on the newly made land. To help hurry development along, the Common Council followed through on the old reclamation plan of Anthony Rutgers. It had an open ditch dug through Lispenard Meadows to the Hudson. We know the old trench today as Canal Street. The adventure in drainage cleared the way for what has been described as "the most notorious neighborhood in nineteenth-century America": Five Points, after the five corners of its main intersection. At midcentury, it was the densest ward in New York and possibly (with some exceptions in London) the world.[8]

African-Americans and Irish immigrants began taking up lodging in the two-and-a-half-story wooden tenements and by the 1820s had already started to dominate in proportions that far outstripped their share of the general population. "Something ought to be done for the honour of the city," urged an 1826 report, "if for no other reason than to render the place less disgusting and pernicious." But little was done, and the defenseless poor were left to fend for themselves in one of the most poorly drained parts of New York, where basements flooded and houses sank into the muck.[9]

While the Collect was morphing into Five Points, another drainage work on a far more Homeric scale was taking place in New Jersey. The chief figures behind these reclamation exploits were the Swartwout brothers: John, Robert, and Samuel. The men's ancestors emigrated from the Netherlands to America in the seventeenth century. After the Revolution, the three brothers moved to New York City. The eldest, John, lived on Water Street and worked in the dyewood trade before going into state politics. Robert also toiled away in the family mercantile business and in 1808 was residing at 24 Duane Street, on the edge of the ephemeral Collect Pond. Samuel was a confidant of the mercurial politico Aaron Burr.[10]

The Swartwouts had a penchant for gunplay. In a sense, they were the opening act for the duel—known to every student of American history—between Aaron Burr and Alexander Hamilton. In 1802, across the Hudson in Hobuck (Hoboken), John Swartwout, who like his brother Samuel was a supporter of Burr, fought De Witt Clinton, then a US senator, after Clinton, according to Swartwout, took "very unwarrantable liberties with my character . . . too gross to be repeated." The duel ended badly for John, who left the grounds with two bullets lodged in his ankle. The following year, Robert Swartwout returned to Hobuck to have it out with Richard Riker, an assistant to Clinton. Robert (also a

Burrite) dispatched Riker with a wound to his right leg, though rumor had it that Riker—apparently no great marksman—shot himself by accident.[11]

When the United States declared war on Great Britain in 1812 to protest interference with its shipping and the impressment of its sailors, all three brothers reported for duty. John was a general in the state militia and was based on Staten Island. Samuel fought with the Irish Greens, flamboyant soldiers who wore green coats and white pantaloons. Robert, for his part, was appointed by James Madison as quartermaster general of the army. It was about this time that the Swartwouts decided to take their aggression out on a different kind of enemy.[12]

Drawn perhaps by their Dutch heritage to underwater real estate, the three men set their sights on a marsh complex about seven miles west, as the crow flies, of Midtown Manhattan—a wetland so vast it made New York's meadows look puny by comparison. Here in New Jersey, they found a morass that covered forty-two square miles, or about twice the land area of present-day Manhattan. The New Jersey Meadows—now commonly known as the Meadowlands—arose on the remains of a giant glacial lake.[13]

A forest of white cedar still dominated when the Swartwouts stumbled upon it, though the need for timber to build ships and plank roads had probably put a good-sized dent in the woods by then. The place was an excellent habitat for beavers and muskrats. In the sultry days of August, ripening green stands of wild rice attracted flocks of black-and-white bobolinks, the males with yellow heads, and sora rails, belting out a high-pitched call. Northern water snakes, thick-bodied and ranging as long as three feet—some brown, some red, some gray—slithered along the water's edge in search of worms. Not for nothing is a nearby town named Secaucus, a word derived from *siskakes*, or "place where the snakes hide." Back in the seventeenth century, the Duke of York conveyed the meadows along with a giant swath of land in eastern New Jersey to Sir George Carteret. (The town of Elizabeth, New Jersey, was named for his wife.) Carteret died in 1680, and the land eventually came into the hands of Newark farmers who divided it up and carved ditches into the ground to help with drainage and etch out property lines. Their goal was to harvest the salt hay for winter forage, although the crop turned out to be too coarse for consumption by livestock.[14]

The plucky Swartwouts took the drainage of the meadows much more seriously. Starting in 1813, they began accumulating several thousand acres of New Jersey mire. The reclamation of such a vast marsh when the city of New York itself could barely manage to tame a few hundred acres in southern Manhattan seemed like madness at the time. Nevertheless, in 1816, a year after they had set to work improving the property, one newspaper reported, "The *Swartwouts* have pushed their experiments on a bold and generous scale." They had, in just a short time, erected a seven-mile "dyke along the margin of the Hackensack, (which excludes the ocean-tide)." The men complemented the dike with sixty or seventy miles of ditches, traversing "the vast meadow in regular lines, enclosing convenient squares, and intersecting each other at right angles." And on this nice little grid, exclaimed the paper, "potatoes have been raised where salt-grass was mowed last year!" Normally, the report continued, labor and capital increase the value of land. But in this case, labor and capital "seem to have *created* it."[15]

By this point, improvement was truly in the air. John Swartwout had made up with his former dueling opponent De Witt Clinton and agreed to accompany him on a committee established to "promote a Canal Navigation between the great Western lakes and the tide waters of the Hudson." The canal in question was the famous Erie Canal. Feeling that the time was ripe for reclamation projects, the Swartwouts petitioned the New York Common Council in 1816 for financial assistance. In the marsh between the Passaic River and the lower reaches of the Hackensack, the Swartwouts claimed to have enclosed twenty-three hundred acres of land with embankments. More than that, over 50 percent of the girdled land had been drained using ditches, and of that amount, three hundred acres were already "under the most promising cultivation." The levees kept out the salt water harmful to crops; the ditches, dug in the process of building the bulwark, drained the soil.[16]

When they began the project, even their friends were dubious. But they noted in their appeal to the Common Council, "the inexperienced and the sceptical if they will take the trouble may find innumerable instances on record of the recovery of immense tracts of land from the ocean itself." Furthermore, the project would give employment to the poor and comfort to the rich. Even "recovered nature will rejoice."[17]

That the city even entertained the Swartwouts' proposition reveals just how thoroughly the idea of developing low-lying land dominated the thinking of New York's leaders at this time. The sympathetic Common Council acknowledged the value of the project in turning the New Jersey Meadows with its "coarse hay of inferior quality . . . rushes and other useless plants" into fertile terrain that could benefit New York with a new source of vegetables and fodder. It recognized the "great anxiety" and all the money that had already been expended on the project. It viewed the Swartwouts' brainchild as "public-spirited." But in the end, it denied the request for financial aid. The city already had considerable debt and feared the example that would be set by loaning money "for the purpose of encouraging undertakings commenced not only beyond the boundaries of the City but beyond those of the State." Besides, New York had its own meadow problems to deal with.[18]

The month following the Common Council's negative decision in August 1819, unusually high tides got the best of the Swartwouts' dikes. Some believe muskrats also undermined the integrity of the structures, allowing salt water to intrude and no doubt killing whatever was growing on the land. Moving on, the Swartwouts tried to borrow money in Holland, their ancestral homeland, where reclamation was something of a national religion. But it was to no avail. Nor did the hurricane of 1821 help. The Swartwout reclamation, according to one account, "was considerably injured." In 1823, with John Swartwout now dead, Robert and Samuel began to quarrel. Samuel's interests strayed from the vast New Jersey marshland, but Robert seemed unable to get the place out of his mind.[19]

"The project of reclaiming the marshland in the valley of the Hackensack, I have long had upper most at heart," Robert wrote his brother in 1837, "and [it is] one which until it is accomplished will continue to receive my undivided attention." In the end, the marshland would triumph over Swartwout's obsession. Despite the strength of his determination, despite the dike, the embankments, the ditches, despite the years of grinding work, Robert could never figure out a way to shut out "the frequent overflow of the salt water." A report from the 1830s would confirm these fears, describing the property as being "in a dreary, sunken, and desolate situation, subject to the inundation of every tide from the River, and totally destitute of cultivation." He died in 1848 in Derby, Connecticut, far from the land he loved, his heart broken by the relentless tide of the sea.[20]

"We are rapidly becoming the London of America," wrote the prominent New York merchant John Pintard in 1826. That same year, the state of New York finished the work John Montgomerie had started roughly a century earlier. It ordered that letters patent be conveyed for underwater land extending four hundred feet beyond the low-water mark the rest of the way along the Hudson and East Rivers to as far north "as Spytden Duyvel creek, otherwise called Harlaem river." With the opening of the Erie Canal the year before, the city's control over trade and finance, and the resulting population growth, there came yet more building in low-lying land.[21]

Even before the canal opened, the task of tackling the largest single unified salt marsh in the city had begun. This was the Stuyvesant Meadows. It extended to a width of over twenty-five hundred feet and occupied almost a mile along the East River. It took its name from Peter Stuyvesant, who owned a home there. This part of New York was so swampy that high tides severed a one-acre piece of land, unimaginatively named Manhattan Island, from the city. In 1811 Gouverneur Morris and his associates on the grid plan had recommended turning part of the salt marsh into a public market by running a canal from the East River through its center. That seemingly Dutch-inspired plan had faded by the 1820s, buried like the old Heere Gracht under Broad Street or the unrealized plan to build navigation canals at Collect Pond. Instead, the Stuyvesant Meadows, like the Lispenard Meadows, came under the improving hand of a city that now viewed the waterfront as the appropriate locus for trade and internal land as the proper domain of speculative real estate.[22]

In 1823 street commissioners appointed under a state law began the process of "regulating" the Stuyvesant marsh with the intention of furthering private development. An enormous amount of earth was required to obliterate the wetland. This was in large part because the land in question, from the Bowery to the East River, required a high enough slope to carry off water, especially now that the state (in 1826) granted the city title to underwater land even farther into the river. Other plans called for sewers or open canals to drain the land, which would have considerably reduced the amount of earth. But substantial prejudice existed at the time against drains of any kind, above or below ground. The disinclination was not entirely misplaced in that, to this point, New York's drains were poorly graded and tended to clog with filth, a situation not helped by the dead animals and other debris tossed in. In any case, landowners on higher ground, seeking to avoid a tax assessment, rejected all such plans as simply a subsidy to those with low land who wanted to avoid the expense of filling up the ground to grade. The highlanders, in other words, wanted to simply see dirt thrown at the problem.[23]

If only there was enough dirt. The Common Council rejected the various drainage plans and the lowlanders scrambled for soil to fill their property. By 1831, the surrounding hills, wrote those with property in the marsh, had "gradually disappeared" and all the city had to show for it were a couple of streets and one main thoroughfare. "From the neighborhood it cannot be hoped that sufficient earth can be procured, as all the high grounds within the radius of a mile from the centre of the property have been levelled."[24]

Among the lowlanders with property in the Stuyvesant Meadows was John Jacob Astor. Born near today's Heidelberg, Germany, Astor, the son of a butcher who went on to achieve stupendous wealth, had dabbled in Manhattan properties between 1789 and 1791. But it was in the early nineteenth century that he began amassing his main real estate holdings. One of the beneficiaries of the city's expanding underwater empire, Astor accumulated six water lots. He was also notorious for failing to develop his underwater land, often relying on others to make the necessary improvements, as seemed to be the case at the Stuyvesant

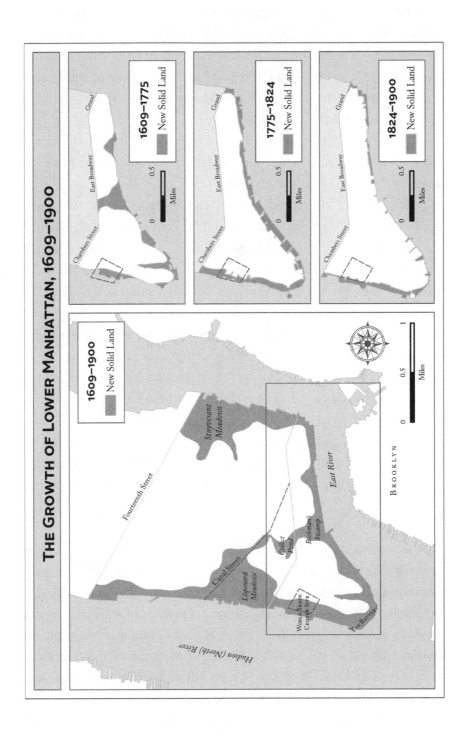

THE GROWTH OF LOWER MANHATTAN, 1609–1900

Meadows. As one of his biographers has written, in an otherwise ha-giographic portrait of the man, "Astor was by no means so eager to do his part in the improvement of the city as he was to acquire all the public lands which the corporation could give him." Astor's career highlighted the rise of real estate as a form of capital accumulation that would soon rival trade and finance in importance.[25]

It seems likely that in their haste to spread the cost of reclaiming the meadows, lowlanders like Astor exaggerated the shortage of fill. In any case, by the 1830s, workers drove piles and buried the Stuyvesant Meadows in endless cartloads of dirt. In 1834 part of the salt marsh opened as Tompkins Square Park, named for Daniel D. Tompkins, a for-mer governor of the state and James Monroe's vice president, who had helped finance the reclamation of part of the meadows. And two years later, Peter Stuyvesant's grandson, who like Astor and others owned land in the marsh, gave up on the prospect of an elaborate drainage project to benefit his private property and offered the city some of the soggy ground for use as a public space. Stuyvesant Square was the result.[26]

By early the following decade, the Stuyvesant Meadows were little more than a memory. On the beach where one student of the island's geology had ventured to catch *Cicindela*, spectacular beetles colored me-tallic green, purple, or iridescent blue, there was now the New-York Dry Dock Company. Old Manhattan Island and the Stuyvesant Meadows were "almost all filled over with the earth of the surrounding hills, and built upon."[27]

It is customary, especially among those inclined to see New York's rise as geographically predestined, to accord a major role to the Erie Canal. There are good grounds for such an interpretation, for there is no doubt-ing the importance of the canal in lowering the cost of shipping western produce and timber down the Hudson River to Manhattan. But the un-remitting focus on the canal has tended to overshadow an underwater discovery of great consequence. Though not as flashy as the Erie Canal, the unearthing of a new channel in the harbor also played a significant role in the rise of the port of New York and led to still more development in the floodplain, especially along the newly blossoming water-front across the East River in Brooklyn.[28]

Next to Thomas Dongan and John Montgomerie, perhaps no figure looms as large in New York's underwater history as Thomas Gedney. The man is hardly a household name and is almost never mentioned in histories of the city. And yet what he discovered while cruising the waters of New York Harbor one day in 1835 would earn him what the historian Robert Albion—one of the few twentieth-century students of New York to mention him—dubbed "a lasting place in the port charts." Gedney made underwater history when he happened upon a deeper channel through Sandy Hook at the entrance to New York Harbor.[29]

A port is only as good as the depth of its main channel. Before the Civil War, vessels powered by sail or steam drew a maximum of twenty-three feet of water. For the largest ships, when fully loaded, the entrance to New York Harbor could represent a white-knuckled experience. Seemingly, several miles of open water ran from Sandy Hook, a barrier spit, across to Coney Island. In fact, a minefield unfolded below. A huge sandbar, intersected here and there by channels, extended across the entrance to the harbor. To survive the trip into port required a good pilot. Accepting this fact, the colony of New York complied in 1694 with an "Act for settling Pylotage for all Vessels that shall come within sandy Hook." Even so, the wrecks continued.[30]

Just how delicate an operation entering the harbor could be is nicely revealed in Edmund M. Blunt's *The American Coast Pilot* (1822). The directions for entering Sandy Hook begin with the advice to "keep 3 miles from the shore to avoid the Outward Middle," the name for one of the many bars. The instructions then continue: "In approaching the lighthouse [on the shore of Sandy Hook spit], you must not haul too nigh the shore, on account of the False hook—by keeping a mile from the beach you will avoid that shoal." Blunt then warns the would-be pilot "not [to] be deceived with respect to Brown's hollow." Eventually the navigator observes "two hummocks of land, each forming as it were a saddle, like thus: ‿‿⁄ The easternmost of the two is the mark for coming up the channel, so as to avoid the Upper Middle." The complexity of the approach, needless to say, created a brisk business for knowledgeable guides.[31]

The depth in the main ship channel at low water was twenty-one feet. The harbor sported pilots an additional four to five feet during high tide, a fact that sometimes kept fully loaded vessels waiting out at sea until they could muster the requisite draft. Into these waters, in 1835, sailed Lieutenant Thomas Gedney, who was working for the US Coast Survey.

In 1807, the year the state authorized the grid that some claimed ate Manhattan's landscape, Thomas Jefferson and his colleagues at the American Philosophical Society finally succeeded in getting Congress to authorize an agency to bring a similar level of order to the sea. Under the law, the Coast Survey was to chart "the islands and shoals, with the roads or places of anchorage, within twenty leagues of any part of the shores of the United States."[32]

The organization was under the command of Ferdinand Rudolph Hassler. He'd come to the United States in 1805 to flee the turmoil of French-occupied Switzerland. His calling was geodesy: that is, applying mathematical precision to the earth's size and shape. Bilked out of money by a corrupt land agent, Hassler eventually landed in Philadelphia, where he encountered Jefferson and the members of the American Philosophical Society—men with a penchant of their own for measuring the earth. Jefferson, after all, was the architect of the grid pattern that guided the sale of western lands. Measuring being the order of the day, New York's Common Council, in 1806, had even tried to prevail on Hassler to make "a correct Map of this Island." But Hassler became ill in the interim, sparing New York, perhaps, from an even more precise grid at the hands of one very meticulous fellow. Instead, in 1807, with the support of his patrons in Philadelphia, who sought to protect maritime commerce and military interests by collecting detailed knowledge of land under water, Hassler was chosen director of the Coast Survey. He proposed to measure the Atlantic Coast through a process of triangulation, but the War of 1812 intervened, and then Congress, in a moment of austerity, cut the funding for the survey. Hassler was eventually rehired in 1833, and the survey began in earnest. Known for his painfully exacting standards—he once worked forty-three days measuring a single nine-mile baseline—Hassler began plans for soundings in New York Harbor. He chose Gedney to carry out the work.[33]

Gedney was a Southerner who joined the navy after the end of the War of 1812 and made the rank of lieutenant a decade later. He is best known for his role in the seizure of the slave ship *Amistad* in the waters off of Long Island. Four years before he encountered that ship with its mutinous slaves, Gedney drifted into New York Harbor and found a hitherto unknown channel leading to what was fast becoming one of the most important cities in the world. The channel was a full twenty-three feet deep, two feet more than the old main ship channel. Soon known as Gedney's Channel, the new passage also offered mariners a shorter approach to the city. What Gedney had done was to temporarily liberate New York commerce from tidal action. It was no longer necessary to yaw and slew at sea waiting for the moon and sun to line up to raise the water on the Sandy Hook bar. "There is water enough in this channel to float a vessel as large as old Noah's," wrote one correspondent. "No large vessel now attempts any other passage, and its discovery has, by diminishing the risk and delay that previously existed, enhanced the value of every dollar's worth of property that crosses the bar," read one glowing report on the discovery. It was an improvement that had it been "effected by art" would have cost millions.[34]

New York City presented Gedney with a pricey silver service for his troubles, which he accepted, acknowledging with modesty the role played by his crew and, of course, by Hassler. Even Hassler, a man not known for his humility (he once requested a salary commensurate with that of Secretary of the Treasury Levi Woodbury, noting that while "There are plenty of Voodburys . . . there is only one, *one* Hassler"), had to admit that Gedney's venture had "succeeded even beyond my expectations."[35]

New York was booming. Its economic prospects buoyed by the Erie Canal and Gedney's Channel, the city experienced staggering growth in the second quarter of the nineteenth century. By 1830, no other city in the nation could rival it in population. The landscape reeled under the weight of the numbers. "The face of the island," explained an 1836 gazetteer, "was originally uneven and rough." But the frenzied pace of building—more than twelve hundred new structures went up in 1835—paralleled the closing of old streets and the opening of new ones following the 1811 grid plan, a process that tended to level the Manhattan landmass. Undeterred by a devastating fire on December 16, 1835, the real estate boom led inevitably, given the waterfront's importance to commerce, to still more development in the floodplain. In the southern part of the city, hills "have been levelled, and the swamps and marshes filled up. Many creeks and inlets on the margin of the rivers, have also disappeared."[36]

Events along the waterfront were the driving force behind the changing face of the island. Results tabulated for a day in 1824 showed a total of 324 vessels weighing anchor off the city's shores. But on a comparable day in 1836, a stunning 921 ships were tied up along the East River alone. Several hundred more docked on the Hudson River. The latter became even more central to economic life in the wake of the Erie Canal, a fact apparent as early as 1828, when the city received the state's permission to alter the grid plan and extend West Street farther into the river. The climactic moment in the city's domineering approach toward the sea came in 1837. Just as economic panic set in, the state of New York sanctioned yet another encroachment, conveying title to underwater land beyond the four-hundred-foot mark from Hammond Street (West Eleventh Street) north to 135th Street. Out of this underwater land, Thirteenth Avenue would rise. The logic behind Thirteenth Avenue rested on the idea that New York would need a place to deposit all the fill from the highlands running north of Forty-Eighth Street to Spuyten Duyvil Creek. But the economic downturn of the late 1830s and later restrictions by the state turned Thirteenth Avenue into little more than a pipe dream. Only fragments of it ever materialized (in Greenwich Village and Chelsea).[37]

Even Brooklyn, which had thus far been outshined by the great city, was coming to life. New York's dense pattern of development left little room for storage, and this is where Brooklyn came in. It was close by, and would serve as a giant warehouse for various bulk commodities such as lumber, coal, and grain. In the thirty years following 1820, Brooklyn's population surged from 7,175 to 96,838. Like New York, it also colonized various underwater reaches, thereby extending the contours of the floodplain.[38]

Brooklyn started out under New York's thumb. Crown and state charters had given New York extensive rights not just around York Island, but along the shores of "Nassau Island" as well. Under a 1708 charter confirmed by Governor John Montgomerie in 1731, New York received ferry privileges that in turn gave it a claim on land from Wallabout Bay all the way around "the West side of the Redd hook comonly called the fishing place." But development of the underwater resource was slow to happen. It was 1764 before New York conveyed its first grant.[39]

In the early nineteenth century, an underwater discovery brightened Brooklyn's maritime prospects. As tensions with the British mounted in 1807, and New York contemplated wooden underwater obstructions to defend itself, Colonel Jonathan Williams was sent to survey the harbor. He found evidence of significant environmental change between Governors Island and Brooklyn, a reach known as Buttermilk Channel. "There are people now living who remember when the channel between Governor's island and Long Island was fordable," he wrote, "and I have the best authority for saying that about fifty years ago, the gardener of the then Governor used to pass and repass in a canoe, without a paddle, by merely a push with his foot at setting out." By 1776, a chart revealed that the channel had deepened in its shallowest points to a full three fathoms, or eighteen feet. Another assessment completed in 1798 showed the same spot measuring a depth of five fathoms, and by the time that Williams got around to measuring it in 1807, he discovered "seven fathoms of water at low tide."[40]

How did a channel passable on foot become more than forty feet deep in just fifty years? Williams believed the change had come from "the cast given to the East river ebb tide, by the docking out on that side of the city." He was correct that the filling in of underwater land in southern Manhattan and the consequent narrowing of the East River upstream contributed to the change. But it was not the ebb tide that drove the deepening process. By constricting the river, New Yorkers had effectively put their collective thumb over the opening of a giant hose. They inadvertently called forth a jet of water that eroded the seabed and turned what had once been not much more than a tidal mudflat into a bona fide navigation channel.[41]

In a sense, the more New York built, the more Brooklyn benefited. After the War of 1812, when ferry service began between the island and Manhattan, Brooklyn began taking its first tentative steps to wade out into the water. Between 1815 and 1818, New York City made eighteen water-lot grants in Brooklyn. The village of Brooklyn (Brooklyn Heights), incorporated in 1816, began to thrive, as did the land north of Wallabout Bay where the US Navy built a shipyard. This area was named for Jonathan Williams, the surveyor who laid it out. In 1818 David Dunham, the "father of Williamsburgh," initiated a ferry to York Island, and in 1827 the place solidified into an incorporated village. By the 1830s, the town had fanned out to absorb additional land, and wharves had been constructed along the East River. Growth had even compelled the opening of yet more ferry service to the lower part of Manhattan.[42]

To the south, Red Hook experienced its own makeover. Once known for its shad, Red Hook (originally Roode Hoek and famous for its red-colored soil) evolved in a more speculative direction, capitalizing on the unintended geographical effects of New York's growth. "There is very little doubt, but that Governor's Island was formerly connected with Red Hook point in this town," declared one local historian in 1824. The land bridge across which cattle were once driven was now the deepening Buttermilk Channel, and Brooklyn, incorporated in 1834, adapted as large vessels churned through.[43]

While this was happening, a merchant named Daniel Richards was making his way to New York. Richards hailed from upstate and made a name for himself developing Richfield Springs, a sulfur spring located on the hills overlooking the Mohawk River valley. In 1827, however, he decided for some reason to give up the cool mountain breezes for the damp salt air of New York City. When cholera broke out in 1832, he relocated again, this time crossing the East River to Brooklyn, where, smelling a promising business opportunity, he developed an interest in land along Buttermilk Channel. In 1840, under his leadership, the Atlantic Dock Company was formed. Its directors were none other than some of New York's most prominent merchants, including James De Peyster Ogden, Nathaniel L. Griswold, and Henry Grinnell, a partner in the prominent shipping firm Grinnell, Minturn & Co.

Berthing space was at a premium at the time. On just a single day in October 1836, the harbor played host to "101 ships, 22 barques, 93 brigs, and 41 schooners; about 65 steam boats, 30 tow boats, 41 tow barges, a large number of sloops, market boats, canal boats, and other small craft, besides rafts and other things requiring slip room." It was not uncommon for vessels to weigh anchor and wait as many as ten days before unloading, subjecting them in winter to the perils of floating ice. This holdup was what the company set out to solve. Capitalized with one million dollars, it had the power to erect docks, bulkheads, and warehouses "within the line established by law." That line fell a bit short of the aspirations of these investors. Established in the 1830s, the pier line cut them off from the deep water they coveted. So they lobbied to change the line, and succeeded in 1841, over the objections of the government of New York City.[44]

The dredging of some of the more shallow areas along the shore eventually produced a forty-acre basin backed by numerous warehouses. Grain would be the dock's stock-in-trade. The invention of the marine leg in the early 1840s, a steam-powered device for retrieving grain from a ship's hull and depositing it in silos, transformed the Atlantic Docks into a bustling seaport. "The immense storehouses on the interior of the dock," Walt Whitman wrote later, "would have answered for Joseph to store the grain of Egypt, preparatory to the year of famine." But for the dialectics of nature and history upstream in New York, and the consequent deepening of Buttermilk Channel, the Atlantic Docks would likely never have happened.[45]

The channel's enhanced navigational prospects hastened development throughout South Brooklyn. In 1846 Brooklyn's Common Council zeroed in on the Gowanus Creek marshlands as the city continued to pursue its role as a warehouse for its big-city neighbor. A West Point

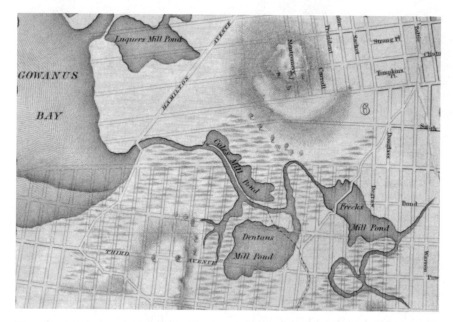

The Gowanus area, with a grid plan superimposed, before the canal. Bergen Hill is shown (labeled "Montgomery") before it was leveled to help create land at the Atlantic Docks.

engineer named Major David B. Douglass was engaged to draw up a plan to drain "the Gowanus Meadows." The marshes, of course, had a history, though it has been somewhat obscured over time. Once the head of the Gowanus Creek hosted an Indian village named Werpos. An echo of its rich marine life is caught in Dutch missionary Jasper Danckaerts's 1679 report of eating "roasted, a pail-full of Gouanes oysters, which are the best in the country." Later on, the English colonists harvested the carpet of salt hay, set back from the creek, for forage.[46]

Douglass set in motion a new, less pastoral chapter in the Gowanus Creek's history. The surrounding region, he noted, was "capable of accommodating a population of 200,000 inhabitants." Dismissing the idea of simply turning the place into solid ground, Douglass came up with two plans, including one that involved building a connection with Wallabout Bay. His ideas remained on the shelf, but the same year that Douglass published them, Daniel Richards received permission to build docks and wharves "on the land under water" adjoining his property at

Gowanus Bay. Richards put forward a new plan to build a roughly one-mile-long canal. He further proposed the use of timber piling to raise up a bulkhead; dredged spoil (earth and rock) shoveled in behind it would form land for warehouses. The Brooklyn Common Council approved the plan in 1849. A month later, the state authorized "a canal . . . to be called the Gowanus canal." The Gowanus opened in 1854, but it later turned out that the bulkhead could not stop the surrounding meadows from washing "mud into the canal at stormy seasons" and causing it to become "so choked as to be practically useless except at high water." [47]

These feverish attempts to renovate the floodplains of South Brooklyn had their detractors. The most famous was Walt Whitman, who thought it was a pity to sacrifice the bluffs of Brooklyn for waterfront development. "It is a sad thing to lose this beautiful bluff," Whitman wrote about a headland that once nudged into Gowanus Bay. "They fill up the shores with it, preparatory to running out piers and wharves." Whitman had moved to Brooklyn in 1823 when he was four and spent his childhood immersed in coastal life: digging clams, sailing, catching eels. Over the next quarter century, he watched as that world was replaced with a more commercial one that brought the city of Brooklyn farther out into New York Bay. [48]

The breakneck pace of landscape change, especially the efforts to turn marsh and water into dry land, did lead to some calls for reform. No one thought more deeply about the consequences of perishing water from the land than Egbert Ludovicus Viele. Viele came from a family with a long history in the city. His ancestors lived in the prosperous port town of Hoorn in the Netherlands and arrived in New Amsterdam sometime in the early seventeenth century. Viele's father, John L. Viele, was an Albany attorney and a friend of De Witt Clinton's. Egbert Viele was born in 1825 in Waterford, New York. He attended West Point, completing the prescribed course of study in 1847, and then served as an officer in the Mexican-American War. By middle age, he was balding with a big, bushy handlebar mustache and was known for being intemperate—he swore up a storm—and idiosyncratic. So it was that he distinguished himself not in military affairs or even engineering but in the more arcane realm of lost landscapes.[49]

In 1855 Viele sat down with a map of New York Harbor drawn a hundred year earlier. "The dense forests that covered the area drained by these rivers," he reflected, "served to retard the melting of the snows, the rapid dissolution of which, has since proved so injurious by the annual freshets, not only in immediate damage but in future consequences." He then unfurled a map of the harbor published in 1853 showing "the changes created by man, and by nature in her struggles with his innovations." What he discovered was that "the original shore line has, in a great measure, disappeared; at some points it has given place to wharves and piers; at others, dense blocks of houses now stand where vessels once floated." New York had gained significantly on the sea, upsetting the prevailing drainage system. While most of the topographic modifications had come in New York, even New Jersey had flirted with the idea of infringing on the ocean. Viele's main concern arose from his view that "nature, ever true to her laws, maintained an equilibrium." To interfere with that steady state, he argued, would have consequences. As he put it, "with regard to rivers, nature acts by certain fixed laws. . . . Man cannot change them; all his efforts to do so, have but produced modifications; the evil he attempts to remove, reappears with greater force at another point."[50]

Viele further made clear his views when he was hired to shape Central Park, where he worked as chief engineer starting in 1856. The idea for the park arose from a serious lack of open space brought on in part by the conversion of the very few public areas designated on the grid plan (such as a promenade, from Twenty-Third to Thirty-Fourth Streets, known as the Military Parade) into private property. Unsurprisingly, the park wound up situated in the center of the island, on land that the market had rejected—rugged and swampy terrain that squatters had come to inhabit. Like a good Dutchman, Viele paid special attention to drainage, proposing a plan that called for maintaining "the original water courses, wherever they exist, as permanent drains." He worked within a naturalistic framework that tended to minimize the transformation of land out of respect for its topography. As it turned out, by 1857, Viele's plan had been cast off like an old piece of driftwood. Viele was a political appointee, and he lost his job when the Republican-controlled legislature deputized a new reform-minded Central Park commission. The men he lost out to? Calvert Vaux and Frederick Law Olmsted.[51]

If Viele was largely concerned with topography and drainage, the focus of Olmsted's and Vaux's "Greensward" plan was considerably more ambitious. They too had a drainage plan—a far more extensive one. Central Park ascended into a massive testament to the control of nature. It involved, in five years' time, the excavation and transport of two and a half million cubic yards of soil and stone, an amount of material equivalent to roughly 390 football fields, each filled three feet high. Workers blasted ridges. They filled in wetlands. They planted more than a quarter million trees and bushes. And by the end of 1858, they had installed enough drainage pipe to cross from the northern to the southern tip of Manhattan and two-thirds of the way back again.[52]

It was as if Olmsted and Vaux were trying to immortalize the more prominent physical formations of the island. So brooks bored them. "Mere rivulets are uninteresting, and we have preferred to collect the ornamental water in large sheets, and to carry off through underground drains the water that at present runs through the park in shallow brooks." Water became a design tool. Their plan transformed a bog into a twenty-acre pond, excavated to a depth of just four feet for the sake of ice-skater safety. More than a generation since Bunker Hill had disappeared into Collect Pond, an artificial lake went in on the low-lying land in the southeast part of the park.[53]

Bitter at being passed over, Viele eventually volunteered for service during the Civil War. But when he returned from battle, he still could not get the lost New York landscape out of his head. He drew a topographic map of the city that amounted to a cartographic return of the repressed. It rendered clear, explained one account, "the water courses, streams, meadows, marshes, ponds, ditches, canals, & c., that existed and now exist." Like many Victorian urbanists, including Olmsted, Viele expressed his displeasure with the 1811 grid plan. But Viele's main complaint hinged on the grid's disrespect for hydrology. He criticized the laying out of the city into a "rectangular system of streets" because it interfered with the island's "original drainage-streams" and led to "the collection of large bodies of water all over the island." The city's plan for dealing with water, in other words, did not seem to extend much beyond the use of landfill. The result: large areas of stagnant water, made worse by the filling in of seven hundred acres of underwater land around the perimeter of the island "where the tide once flowed." In Viele's view, the only solution to the drainage woes was to respect hydrology while raising the grade where possible and appropriate.[54]

To the end, Viele battled the hydrologic denial that had taken hold of the city. If the water could not be made to go away, as he maintained, at least it could be catalogued. In his work, Viele tried to etch the former waterscape into geographic consciousness. He reminded people of the stream that once coursed through Maiden Lane and the Collect Pond, "now disappeared from view, but . . . more or less present in the soil." He mentioned Old Wreck Brook, leading from the Collect to the East River, Lispenard Meadows, Minetta Water, and on up the island. "I know that it is generally supposed," Viele wrote presciently, "that when the city is entirely built upon, all that water will disappear; but such is not the case." Therein lies a dark secret. Buried in lower Manhattan, in South Brooklyn, and all across the New York area where building has infiltrated the floodplain, the water remains—forever there to haunt the city like one grotesque postdiluvian torment.[55]

5 THE REVENGE OF THOMAS DONGAN

George Washington would never have believed his eyes. The New York Harbor to which he had made his triumphant return in 1789 was, sixty years later, a vastly different place.

There were no longer any marshlands to speak of in the southern part of Manhattan Island. The dense stands of grass had given way to a city of more than half a million people. Gone were the Lispenard Meadows, and, across town, the Stuyvesant Meadows too had knuckled under to development. Not cordgrass but building lots sprouted—thirty-five hundred below Thirty-Fifth Street alone. Close to seven hundred acres of land had been conquered from the East and Hudson Rivers. Wall Street, where the Founding Father had once disembarked, now extended a full city block farther into the harbor. The East River had grown so congested, so filled with solid earth and cluttered with wharves and slips, that the increased velocity of the current downstream from these protrusions made it difficult for large vessels to turn without the aid of auxiliary steam power. "The changes which our harbor has undergone, even within the memory of persons now living," reads an 1853 report, "are most extraordinary."[1]

New York was bulging at the seams and in the throes of its first real environmental crisis. Treating land as a means of wealth accumulation had placed a premium on terra firma at the expense of the sea. This trend combined with the realities of high population on a small island to give rise to a hypertrophic version of New York.[2]

One witness to the changes declared, "The Harbor is emphatically one God has given to man, and the improvement he has made, or commenced, has been almost exclusively individual in character, and for single personal ends." What he seemed to mean was that the invisible hand of self-interest had arisen to dominate relations with land and water. Put more strongly, New York Harbor had come face-to-face with the full fury of the Scottish philosopher Adam Smith's ideas.[3]

What, alas, had Thomas Dongan done when he started the city down the path of gaining on the sea? It was a question that recurred from time to time as those invested in finance and trade faced off against the world of speculative real estate. On the one hand, the merchants of New York strove to preserve the "natural advantages" of the harbor, the source of their fabulous wealth. On the other, a burgeoning real estate industry, increasingly organized to profit from the city's explosive growth, sought to impose farther on the surrounding waters in the quest for building lots, venturing so far out that it looked to some as if the East River might just disappear. Then there was Brooklyn to contend with. It too had ambitions as a port and a desire to reach farther offshore and thereby capitalize on the nice, deep stretch of water at Buttermilk Channel that the building of New York had in part delivered to its doorstep.[4]

Out of these struggles came a new metropolitan vision, as well as the dawning realization that there were some natural constraints on the pursuit of unfettered growth.

One of the earliest flash points in the battle for New York Harbor involved the Battery in lower Manhattan. Originally called Capske Hook—Native American for "rocky ledge"—it took its name from the gun emplacements the British installed in the seventeenth century. In 1788 Fort George (initially Fort Amsterdam) was torn down and the rubble thrown into the water, beefing up the land. The Battery was one of the few open spaces in the densely settled southern part of the island

and, as a result, it evolved into a promenade for genteel New Yorkers and, later on in the nineteenth century, a working-class haunt. By the 1840s, as the built-up waterfront encased the city and blocked off views of the harbor, support for more open space gained momentum. One solution latched onto, in these days before the idea of Central Park had surfaced, was to enlarge the Battery with landfill. The city had earlier acquired Castle Clinton, a circular structure built in 1811 a couple hundred feet from shore (and named for De Witt Clinton); the plan called for filling in the water and absorbing the castle into the island. The southern tip of Manhattan had a flat edge at the time, and the idea was to expand out into the water. This would not only add more land but also form a rounded tip and thereby create more waterfront vistas. The widening of streets in lower Manhattan recently approved by the city was expected to generate significant surplus earth, necessitating "some convenient and accessible dumping place upon our own island, instead of building up and making land at Brooklyn and New Jersey, out of the limits of our own city."[5]

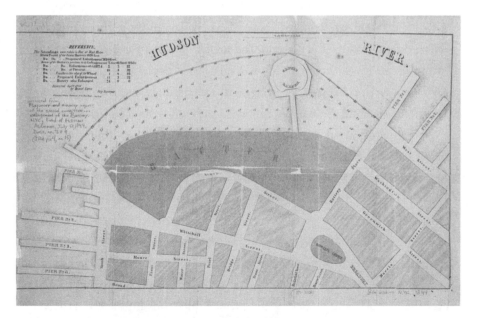

The 1849 plan to enlarge the Battery with landfill.

Granted, the prospect of an enlarged Battery jutting out into an already crowded harbor where it could imperil navigation might have on its own caused the merchant elite to object. But the planned expansion came shortly after the city had taken steps to impinge significantly on the East River. By midcentury, the Common Council was no longer the private preserve of the merchant class. Petty entrepreneurs and craftsmen had gained control. These were people with a very keen sense for the market value not simply of the city's assets but of estates that New York did not even own. Ordinances passed in 1850 opened the way for building in the area between Thirteenth and Twenty-Third Streets some one thousand feet beyond where the state (in 1826) had granted the city underwater land. New York, in other words, was trespassing on state property.[6]

This thrust outward, combined with the prospect of still more solid land at the Battery, led the merchant class to advocate for a line in the sand. One dispatch cried out, "The harbor of New York is already too small for its increasing commerce." The report went so far as to question the very legitimacy of the Dongan and Montgomerie Charters, dredging up a letter written by Governor William Cosby in 1733 in which he pointed out to the home government that it had "passed away grants of a very extraordinary nature." In the end, the article pleaded for a survey of the harbor, under the authority of the federal government, before undertaking any more "encroachments," a word that, interestingly, had cropped up in the sixteenth century in conjunction with the enclosure of common lands.[7]

No institution raised a bigger fuss over the intrusions than the New York Chamber of Commerce, the city's first and most powerful business lobbying group. In 1851 its members came together to object that the new and improved Battery would "result in an injury to the navigation of those noble rivers which are now the pride of our city, avenues of wealth to our population." The group recruited Lieutenant Maxwell Woodhull of the US Navy to offer an expert opinion on the matter. He was in complete agreement that further encroachment could injure the harbor. Woodhull took pains to note that earlier expansions into the East River had transformed Buttermilk Channel to such an extent that it now measured "7 fathoms in place of what was formerly a marsh," redounding—it now hardly needed to be said—to the commercial advantage of New York's rival across the river. It is not difficult to appreciate why, given this history of channel change, Gotham's merchant elite would be wary of any further efforts to displace water.[8]

But the group had another reason to resist the creation of more land. Somehow Sandy Hook, at the entrance to the harbor, seemed to be growing longer, raising the prospect that if it extended too far into the channel it would block the entrance to the port. Over the course of eighty-seven years (1761–1848), the sandbar had grown nearly a thousand yards into the shipping channel. Not knowing that the movement of coastal sediments (littoral drift), not the city's love affair with underwater land, was behind the growth of Sandy Hook, the merchant elite worried that any more filling in of water would limit the scouring effects of the tide's ebb and flow, cause Upper New York Bay to silt up, and "destroy in time one of the best harbors now known to commerce."[9]

By the 1850s, the harbor was feeling the effects of more than the generosity of New York's colonial governors. Changes in the law had laid the foundation for a more speculative approach to waterfront land. The notion of absolute property captured in the writing of the eighteenth-century English jurist William Blackstone was slowly fading before a dynamic understanding of land under water. A leading New York case from 1829 concerned the construction of a pier that destroyed access to an already-existing wharf. The owner of the wharf had received his grant from the state's land office. But the legislature, seeking to advance "a great public improvement for the benefit of commerce," subsequently authorized a new pier that effectively destroyed much of the older wharf's value. In the old days when Blackstone's ideas held sway, such a naked gambit to compromise property in the name of development would likely have been rejected. The majority in the case did not see it this way. In the brave new world of waterfront real estate, the wharf owner's loss was ruled *damnum absque injuria*: that is, no *legal* injury. The owner was barred an action for damages.[10]

An even finer point was put on the matter in a case sanctioning the destruction of the public's navigation and fishing rights in the Hudson River, provided it was "essential to the public welfare." The "public welfare" in this case meant the right of a railroad to build an embankment that prevented boats from entering a channel and accessing a farm. The same prejudice favoring new capital over old also informed an 1853 opinion involving the city of New York. Just a few pages was all it took for the court to establish the transitory quality of waterfront in mid-nineteenth-century America. Making a water-lot grant short of the four-hundred-foot mark, the ruling held, did not deprive the city from later conveying residual underwater land to others, cutting off the earlier grantee from the water. As Karl Marx and Friedrich Engels expressed it so famously in 1848, "All fixed, fast-frozen relations, with their train of ancient and venerable prejudices and opinions, are swept away."[11]

New York's merchant elite must have felt even uneasier about a change in waterfront policy. Originally, underwater grants made by the state land office allowed merely for the erection of docks and wharves and the collection of associated fees. No underwater land was actually conveyed. But in 1850 the land office received authority to make grants for "beneficial enjoyment." This type of grant handed over underwater land "in perpetuity" and thus permitted the grantees to go beyond docks and wharves to build warehouses and other structures. Described by one legal authority as a "radical departure," the new grants offered further encouragement to the speculative forces eager to cash in on the harbor.[12]

But one need not ascend to the rarified domain of the law to profit so long as one was patient. Over time the slips along the southern part of Manhattan made the transition from water to dry land on their own, like some kind of slow-motion magic trick. Stone ballast was pitched into them in these days before ships turned to water as a counterweight. "Hundreds of tons" of cinders were dumped from steamships daily in the stretch between the Battery and Corlear's Hook alone. Hay, bricks, and coal unloaded from vessels inadvertently fell overboard. Oyster shells were jettisoned in such quantities that once a layer some ten feet deep was dredged out between Fulton and Dey Streets. Night soil—that is, human excrement—was tipped. Sewage coursed in, as did sediment that washed into the estuary from ocean waves and tidal currents. Some of the sediment traveled a long way, cascading off the Adirondack Mountains upstate. By 1850 New York had cleared more acres of forestland, it is not irrelevant to note, than any other state in the nation. Removing woodland raised the risk of floods and increased erosion, thereby adding even more particulate matter to an estuary already brimming with it.[13]

The pileup at the bottom of the harbor could, of course, be addressed. People have been dredging harbors since the Phoenicians, but, not surprisingly, it was the Dutch who invented (in the seventeenth century) an early version of the clamshell bucket. The technology was available to New Yorkers but not always the will. Although the need to cleanse slips of "Filth And Dirt" was noted as early as 1745, it was only after the Revolution that New Yorkers began to seriously affect the water near to shore. In 1787 the Common Council received word of the construction of "a Vessel with a Machine for clearing the Slips & Docks of the Mud & Filth." A few years later, the street committee made use of a Dock Drudge for deepening public slips. Some twelve to thirteen scow loads of muck per day were being dredged out of the river by the 1820s. By early the following decade, an astonishing thirty thousand tons of material was "taken out by the mud machine, in one season." In 1834 it had become necessary to lobby the state for a law compelling riparian landowners to deepen the waters near to shore.[14]

A perverse incentive kept the scouring of the harbor bottom from happening as often as it should have. Wharfage rates in New York remained low relative to other ports, and the merchant elite wanted to keep the fees this way to attract business. (In part the low rates stemmed from the narrow tidal range in New York Harbor.) Ships entering and clearing New York at midcentury paid a fraction of the fees charged vessels calling at London, Liverpool, and Amsterdam. The low rates led wharf owners to defer on maintenance. In addition, let the slip fill in enough and eventually there might arise the prospect of a new wharf and building lot. The *Times* put it this way: "The difference between the value of a water-lot occupied by a wharf, and the same when filled and built over with capacious warehouses, is prodigious; and capital is perpetually tempted to obtain the privilege of making land farther and farther into the river."[15]

What would have come of the western part of Long Island had New York not helped, with its land-making adventures, is hard to say. But one thing is certain: a thriving port bent on its own incursions into the East River was beginning to take hold there by the middle of the century. As urbanization worked its way up the island of Manhattan it forced the shipyards that once lined the East River south of Fourteenth Street out of its path. Across the river was a peninsula blanketed with green grass. It was called, naturally enough, Green Point. Led by a shipbuilder and industrialist named Neziah Bliss, the shipyards migrated across the river to this part of Long Island in what was then the town of Bushwick. In 1849 Bliss and several other shipbuilders, including David Provost, a descendant of one of the original Huguenot settlers, received permission "to erect and fill in, keep and maintain a bulkhead, docks and wharves" in front of their land and "lying in the East river." The improvements could extend all the way to a line in the river drawn on an official map. To understand how burning the impulse was to conquer water, it is helpful to understand that the line was penciled through a section of river no less than fifty feet deep. Because it would take literally a mountain of material to build new land at that depth, the shipbuilders only filled out into eighteen feet of water, though even that was a substantial invasion of the channel.[16]

The transgressions continued. In 1852 a cunning New York lawyer named Henry Ruggles—the younger brother of the better-known Samuel Ruggles, who masterminded Gramercy Park—applied for and received a water-lot grant from the state land office. The grant was for land under water in Brooklyn and incorporated the new "beneficial enjoyment" clause, giving Ruggles the right to fill in the lands for purposes other than waterborne commerce. It was an unusual situation. Ruggles owned land on the margin of the East River, and the grant was supposed to afford him the opportunity to improve the submerged land in front of his lot. But the boundaries given in the grant referenced underwater property that was actually in front of his *neighbor's* lot. His neighbor happened to be the US Navy Yard. An injunction was issued to stop Ruggles—who may have been trying to extract a settlement from the US government—from moving forward. If nothing else, the episode highlighted the pulsating entrepreneurialism pressing in around the edges of the harbor.[17]

A kind of antebellum equivalent of modern-day gridlock had taken hold of the waters surrounding New York, and the situation threatened to worsen. In 1853 Brooklyn prevailed on the state to grant those with bulkheads on the East River the right to extend piers beyond a "permanent line" established in 1836. Brooklyn seemed determined to follow in New York City's footsteps, cluttering the river, as one report put it, "under the pretence of accommodating commerce, that bulkheads and building lots might follow."[18]

The new state law, needless to say, was not appreciated by New York's merchant elite. Even less so when, a few weeks later, Brooklyn received permission from the state to merge with Bushwick and Williamsburgh, a union that, by 1855, caused the city's population to double to over two hundred thousand people, making it, by the Civil War, the third largest city in the nation.[19]

The merchants of New York responded by inviting none other than the fourteenth president of the United States, Franklin Pierce, to come take a look for himself at how the harbor was "rapidly being destroyed by the encroachments upon its navigable waters." In town to pay a visit to the New York Crystal Palace—built to one-up the British, who in 1851 had erected their own such showplace of the same name in London—Pierce boarded a steamer packed shoulder to shoulder with the city's most powerful merchants, including Walter R. Jones, president of the New York Board of Underwriters, and Pelatiah Perit, president of the Chamber of Commerce. The boat circled Governors Island and then churned toward Hurl Gate. The destination was not chosen randomly.[20]

Hurl Gate was an area of tumultuous waters in the upper reaches of the East River near Long Island Sound. In reality, the sixteen-mile East River is not a river at all. It is a tidal strait connecting the sound with New York Bay. The operative word here is *tidal*. Two different currents—one from the sound and one from the bay—met up at the doorstep of the East River to form the most turbulent stretch in all of New York Harbor, if not the entire Atlantic Coast. The Dutch called the spot Hellegat, meaning "passage to Hell." In the early nineteenth century, as the wealthy filed into the vicinity and built country estates, the name Hurl Gate materialized, presumably so as not to offend the delicate sensibilities of the new residents. But the truth is that the waters were hellish. Two different tidal rhythms with their ebbs and flows came together with a raft of huge rocks to create one giant maritime nightmare—geology's answer to Scylla and Charybdis. According to a 1789 account, "The adamantine shore, the insulated rocks, the narrowness of the channel, the rapidity of the current, the whirl, the roar, the boiling of the water," made Hell Gate a most fearsome place. A British frigate carrying gold and silver that went down in its rampaging waters during the Revolution was just one of many wrecks. So many rocks dotted the waters that mariners had to give them names to distinguish them all: Pot Rock, Gridiron, Frying Pan, Bread and Cheese, Flood Rock, Hog's Back, Bald Headed Billy. The rocks stood in between New York and a valuable additional route to the sea. New York's merchant class wanted the rocks removed.[21]

By the time Pierce and his hosts steamed toward Hurl Gate, various stabs had been made to tame these roiling waters. Some of New York's leading insurers, for example, mounted an effort to recruit Congress to help cut a canal across an outcropping of land in Queens so that ships could avoid the tempestuous stretch. In 1832 the state empowered a railway company "to dig and construct a canal ... so as to enable vessels to reach the railway without passing through Hurlgate." Nothing came of any of these efforts, and the seething waters thundered on as the economy slumped. Then manufacturing began to take off in Harlem, and once again the rocks became a hot topic. The navy surveyed the area several times in the late 1840s and recommended the blasting of Pot Rock, Frying Pan, and Way's Reef. In 1850 Lieutenant Woodhull of the

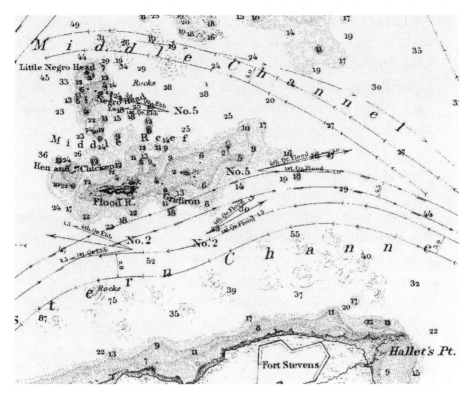

An 1851 Coast Survey map of Hell Gate showing water depths and some of the rocks that mariners had to skirt.

Coast Survey created "a very curious and valuable plan of the bottom of the East river at Hell-gate." The elaborate papier-mâché model, some four feet square, made the case that simply removing "two or three of the most dangerous rocks in the channel" would improve navigation.[22]

By 1849, an enterprising New Yorker named Ebenezer Meriam was corresponding with Benjamin Maillefert, a gritty French engineer who specialized in underwater blasting. He had formerly been employed in the Bahamas by the British to blow to smithereens rocks in Nassau, New Providence. Meriam took up subscriptions to help bring Maillefert's expertise to bear at Hurl Gate, securing financial support from, among others, Henry Grinnell, a principal in one of New York's most important shipping firms. Maillefert initially agreed, in exchange for six thousand dollars, to lower Pot Rock to achieve a mean low-water depth of twenty-four feet.

In 1851, two years before Pierce visited the area, Maillefert set to work. The blasting went well at first. "You can now erase the rock 'Bald-headed Billy' from the chart of Hell Gate," reported Lieutenant Washington Bartlett late in 1851. Then, a few months later, Maillefert acted out a death wish. He accidently switched wires, setting off an explosion that killed two of his men and nearly drowned himself. At the time of the blast, Bartlett reported that Pot Rock, one of the most substantial rocks, had been reduced to "*[t]wenty and a half feet*, at the shoalest part." The news induced Grinnell to pay off his subscription and Congress (later that year) to appropriate twenty thousand dollars toward the further streamlining of these waters. There was only one problem. A subsequent and more accurate survey revealed just a bit over eighteen feet of water on the rock. The expenses continued to mount while Pot Rock lived on and Hurl Gate remained, to quote Maillefert himself, "a terror to navigators." Eventually Congress tired of the project and cut off funding, leaving the score at Pot Rock one, New York zero.[23]

The removal of the rocks at Hurl Gate was of a piece with the merchant community's larger effort to guard the harbor "from ruinous encroachments," as Meriam put it. That explains why President Pierce cruised up the East River, sailing under the flags of James G. King—a former president of the Chamber of Commerce—and Walter Jones. The two honorees had ponied up money to clear the rocks from the bedeviled stretch of water. After a "sumptuous collation" on board and various toasts, US Attorney General Caleb Cushing rose from his seat to point out that once "the barometer of the financial atmosphere of the globe was suspended in Threadneedle street." But now New York seemed destined to cause a shift from the London Stock Exchange to Wall Street, where "shall beat the heart of the universe." There was no way that New York's mercantile community was going to let such a prospect slip away. So the merchants were delighted that Pierce endorsed the idea of having a commission draw a "permanent line" beyond which no more land would rise, a move designed to thwart any further efforts to imperil New York's financial lifeblood.[24]

The idea of a limit on the expansion of land was not altogether new.

As far back as 1824, New York's governor, Joseph Yates, tried unsuccessfully to prevail on the city to lay down its shovels. By midcentury, however, the rise of Brooklyn and the escalating real estate economy had made New York's merchants nervous and increasingly eager to put some limits on any further incursions. Trends in naval architecture complicated the situation still more. In the 1820s, the largest ships had a carrying capacity of about six hundred tons. Thirty years later, vessels built for long-distance sailing to the West Coast or China ranged from eighteen hundred to twenty-five hundred tons. The largest ships traveling from New York to Europe could transport as much as twice that. A ship with cargo weighing five thousand tons drew about twenty-three feet of water, which was the depth, at low water, on the bar at Sandy Hook. If New York City could not accommodate the largest class of vessels, it verged on an underwater disaster.[25]

It would have been common knowledge among the merchant elite that ports rise and fall. The fates of ports in the English maritime counties of Cornwall and Devon are a case in point. In the sixteenth century, tin mining caused them to silt up with earth and stone. Once able to accommodate ships of eight hundred tons, the harbors filled to the point where vessels just a fraction of that capacity could barely navigate through at low water. What tin mining was to Cornwall, underwater mining of a different kind was to New York.[26]

Under the leadership of Mayor Fernando Wood, the city of New York took another stab at carving more land out of the harbor. Wood was just the man to attempt it. He excelled at speculation and was once convicted of bilking gold rush investors. He speculated in so much real estate that even the swaggering political boss William M. Tweed said of him, "I never yet went to get a corner lot that I didn't find Wood had got in ahead of me." In the winter of 1855, Mayor Wood asked the legislature to legalize ninety lots' worth of underwater land on the Hudson River. He would later claim not to know "the extent of our boundaries" on the West Side of the city. The gift of Thomas Dongan just kept giving.[27]

Before Manhattan could become any larger, New York's governor,

Myron Clark, stepped in. A member of the Whig Party and thus inclined to favor government intervention to achieve commercial power, Clark acceded to the demands of New York's merchants and barred any more underwater grants. He also appointed a commission to consider whether "any further extension of piers, wharves or bulkheads, into the said harbor, ought to be allowed." Heading up the commission was George Washington Patterson, born just a month before his namesake died in 1799. With his white, tousled hair and serious demeanor, Patterson was a career politician who had recently served as lieutenant governor of New York.[28]

He was joined by four other men, the most prominent of whom was Preston King, a portly fellow who, like Patterson, had gravitated by the 1850s toward the Republican Party. Melancholic and obviously deeply troubled, King would one day buy a twenty-pound bag of lead shot, tie it around his neck, and plunge off a ferryboat into the Hudson River. His partially decomposed body was later found floating in Buttermilk Channel. King claimed that he was never consulted about his appointment to the harbor commission—that he read about it in the morning paper.[29]

That may have been because the real work of the committee was carried out by some far more knowledgeable scientific authorities. These included Joseph Totten, a sad-faced, hollowed-eyed hero of the Battle of Plattsburgh (War of 1812), who had helped with the construction of fortifications at the Battery and Governors Island. In 1838 he was appointed commander of the US Army Corps of Engineers and occupied the post for a quarter century. Also included among the science advisors was Charles Henry Davis, a trim, fastidious-looking navy man and graduate of Harvard College who, as part of his work for the Coast Survey, had studied the tides of New York Harbor and prepared a special plan to improve Hell Gate. But the most important man of science involved in the project was Alexander D. Bache, who, upon Ferdinand Hassler's death in 1843, replaced him as head of the Coast Survey.

Born in 1806, Bache had grown up in a well-to-do Philadelphia family before entering West Point at age fifteen, where he received one of the finest scientific educations available. A studious man of formidable intellect, he finished first in his class. Bache embraced a practical vision of science, taking a page, as it were, out of the book of his great-grandfather, who happened to be none other than America's most famous scientist: Benjamin Franklin. With his high forehead and full beard, Bache, as one student of his life has written, looked to "rationalize the natural world." He took over the Coast Survey at precisely the time when ocean shipping, now liberated from the earlier economic downturn, needed reason and planning the most.[30]

In this New York Harbor project, Bache and the Coast Survey had the vigorous support of the Chamber of Commerce. For Bache's goal was not simply to study the coast but also to rule over it. As he once explained regarding the ocean bottom, "[I]f all the conditions of the movement and deposit of sandbars and banks are carefully studied the position of bars may also be controlled." Above all, Bache recognized one of the most important aspects of life in the city of New York: that the fates of land and sea were intertwined. Raising a glass in a toast before the Chamber of Commerce, he declared: "*The prosperity of the New York of the land—the New York of the sea*—one and indivisible." It was a savvy tribute that highlighted the shared interests of real estate and commercial capital.[31]

Bache put the hydrographer Edmund Blunt on triangulation duty in the harbor. What John Randel did for the land, Blunt did for the sea. In 1816, while Randel was off slapping down the gridiron on Manhattan, Blunt, who was working for Hassler, sailed out into New York Harbor to establish the first set of common reference points, allowing future maps of the ocean to be in alignment. When Bache appointed him, it was thought that, given all the time the Coast Survey had already spent in the area, little in the way of such work would be necessary. In fact, Blunt had his work cut out for him. As Bache explained, "hills had been cut down and radical changes of all sorts had been made so as to render almost an entire new triangulation indispensable." New Yorkers were so busy reorganizing land and water that they made earth measuring into a cottage industry.[32]

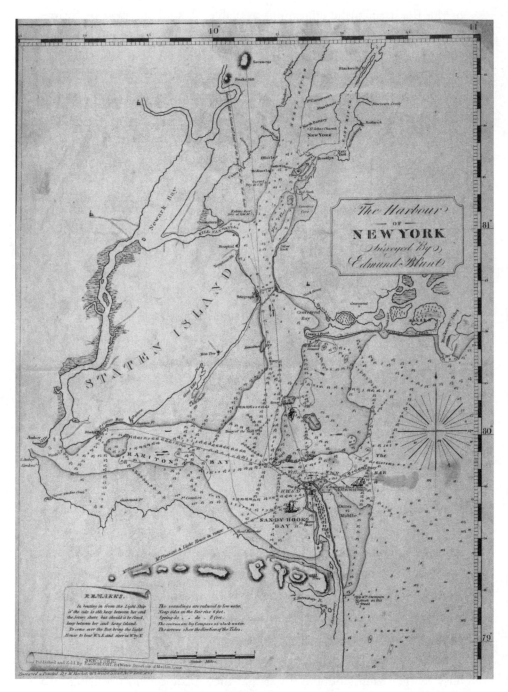

This map of the soundings of New York Harbor was published by Edmund Blunt and his brother George and was likely sold at their store on Maiden Lane.

Bache and his team, meanwhile, reviewed harbor surveys completed between 1835 and 1848 to see how the underwater landscape had changed. They found that Gedney's Channel had lost some capacity because of shifting sands, while Buttermilk Channel had increased. New York Harbor remained as dynamic as ever—even more so, they believed, because of the implacable speculative ethos that had descended like a dark cloud over it. It was nothing less than astonishing, wrote Bache and his colleagues, that "the chief depot of all the commerce of the United States, should have been utterly abandoned, sometimes to the hands of ignorance and sometimes of cupidity." At a minimum, the changes to the waterfront had increased the velocity of the East River and imperiled navigation, especially in the stretch downstream from Corlear's Hook. But with all of that said, it would be wrong, they thought, "to treat all invasions of the water area as positively injurious." As they concluded, "To regret that we have not the shore line of 1750, is to wish away the commerce, the wealth, the wonderful growth of the city."[33]

These men were realists who recognized that New York's geographic endowment, as substantial as it was, could be undermined by further efforts to transform water into land. Hence, they recommended a set of exterior lines that largely ratified the existing contours of the Manhattan and Long Island shores. One could say that they put the landscape on ice.

Menacing news coming out of the Isle of Dogs, in the East End of London, influenced their thinking. There, on marshland along the Thames River that Dutch dike masters once fought to reclaim, Scottish naval engineer John Scott Russell and his partner, Isambard Kingdom Brunel, the mastermind behind Britain's Great Western Railway, were at work on a new project. Brunel had an infatuation with the monumental. In the 1830s, he aspired to build the world's largest steamship, the SS *Great Western*. On April 23, 1838, it came sailing into New York Harbor, an event that, according to one report, worked to "abridge, as it were, time and space." A man of infinite ambition, Brunel teamed up with Russell in the early 1850s on a new contribution to transatlantic shipping, a boat christened *Leviathan*. The ship was described as being "a furlong in length, and has a greater capacity than the larger estimates of

Noah's ark." It claimed room for four thousand passengers and enough coal to cruise completely around the world without refueling. It was of a size the likes of which New York Harbor had never seen. "[A] vessel," Bache and his team wrote breathlessly, "which cannot enter the harbor of New-York, *because there is not water enough on the bar at Sandy Hook.*"[34]

If ever there was a time to open the back door to New York Harbor, this was it. Hell Gate had to be rendered a navigable passage into the city. A new and larger, more "systematic" plan for New York was paramount lest it become what they termed "a second class port."[35]

George Washington Patterson and his colleagues also found themselves thinking big. Theirs was a metropolitan vision. They conjured up a harbor that would one day collect commerce from across the globe "in its capacious waters and make New-York the commercial capital of the world." Nature had conferred on New York "a harbor unrivalled in geographical position, in immediate proximity to the ocean, and sheltered on every side from the influence of storms." To preserve these "advantages of inestimable value," however, required some reform. They indicted the liberal terms of the grants made to New York, going back to Governor Thomas Dongan and continuing into the nineteenth century when "[t]he State has been still more liberal." The time had come to end the underwater land rush and adopt the exterior lines recommended by their science advisors.[36]

The move did not exactly make anyone's day in Brooklyn. After all, it was only after the 1853 law that conveyed the right to Brooklyn to build piers out beyond the established bulkhead line that concern with the fate of the harbor welled up in New York City. New York had, of course, conquered acres of the harbor compared to what some described as mere rods of ground in Brooklyn's case. "Brooklyn has to pay enormous sums to New York *for every foot* of her own shore, between high and low water mark, merely for her natural right of access to the East river," the *Brooklyn Daily Eagle* lamented, referring to New York's crown-granted rights to a significant part of Long Island's foreshore, "and now her attempt to participate in the commerce of the Empire State is 'Encroachments on the Harbor of New York.'" Nor were Brooklyn merchants and developers the only ones upset. Before the lines could go into place, New York's Common Council made a last-ditch and ultimately futile attempt to wrest another several hundred feet from the East River between Seventeenth and Thirty-Eighth Streets.[37]

The Common Council's endgame came after the political winds had shifted dramatically in Albany. Fernando Wood's days as mayor were numbered. John Alsop King, a representative of the newly formed Republican Party, had been elected governor in the fall of 1856. The same election put the Republicans in the majority in the state assembly as well. Coalescing around opposition to the expansion of slavery on the national level and to the special privilege garnered by New York City on the local, the Republicans forced Wood, a Democrat, to his knees and made him submit to reelection. The newly empowered Republicans undercut New York City's status as a municipal corporation with independent powers and its own massive underwater empire. The state, in other words, began poking its nose into the city's business. It was the perfect context for the state-appointed harbor commissioners to finish their work.[38]

Under the pretext of saving New York from encroachment, the commissioners put forward one of the most audacious plans on record for reshaping its waters. It amounted to the start of an entirely new conception of the metropolis. With the harbor lines now settled and out of the way, the commissioners launched into a plan of needed improvements to the waterfront. Warehouses were too distant from the piers and theft rampant. A new system of wet basins would solve these problems. The federal government, they argued further, should be recruited to help liberate Hell Gate from its geological past and give the city the thirty-plus-foot depth that the largest vessels would soon be commanding. Harlem River—described as "an important and neglected passage between the Hudson and East rivers"—ought to be made navigable. Across the Hudson, the Jersey Flats, mudflats off of Jersey City, could be profitably improved with wet basins. It was a bold plan for the redevelopment of the port, but who would carry it out? Anticipating the rise of Greater New York, they wrote: "That the control of the harbor should be committed to one body, in whatever manner it may be expedient to organize it, is obvious."[39]

If New York's merchants failed to act immediately on such high-minded thinking, in the short run the elite received what it wanted: a set of limits on future underwater development. In 1857 Moses H. Grinnell, of Grinnell, Minturn, the brother of the aforementioned Henry, organized a meeting on Wall Street to discuss the fate of the harbor. The men decided to form a committee and send it to Albany to lobby in favor of the new harbor lines. Just about every powerful merchant in the city lined up for duty, from tobacco magnate Peter Lorillard to Pelatiah Perit, the president of the Chamber of Commerce. And in the end, the bankers and merchants succeeded. The harbor lines became state law, placing land making in check. New York's richest men had triumphed, and one can only guess how much champagne they spilled celebrating.[40]

Hindsight allows us to see that the lines turned out to be just a footnote. In the long run, it was the larger metropolitan vision that would triumph as all kinds of lines were crossed in the pursuit of growth.

By 1860, New York had come a long way from the days of George Washington's inaugural trip to the city. Every decade, with one exception (the 1810s), saw the population explode by over 50 percent. New York was not just the largest and most significant city in the United States, leading its closest rival, Philadelphia, by nearly a quarter million people. It was arguably, especially if it was considered in metropolitan terms and included Brooklyn, now contending with the largest cities in the world: London and Paris. There was no telling where all this growth would stop.[41]

The crisis of the 1850s is important, however, because for the first time there was a recognition of limits. These nineteenth-century men were conscious of the fact that they were changing the natural world and that doing so could have consequences. Growth was not, for them, open-ended. They had a keen sense of the unpredictable, as the struggle over the changing underwater geography demonstrated. What happened at Buttermilk Channel, after all, could happen elsewhere. This they understood. They did not take the control of nature for granted the way that planners down the road would.

6 THE OPEN LOOP

In the 1850s, a long-haired French socialist named Pierre Leroux stepped forward to propose a new approach to man's relationship with the earth—a brazen plan that was essentially built on a pile of shit. Leroux postulated that hunger could be eradicated if human waste found its way back to the land as plant food (the case in China and India). Seeing a down-and-out Londoner bearing a shovel on which had been scratched "worker seeking labor," Leroux reckoned that "every last one of these poor wretches could live off his own manure." As one student of his ideas explained, Leroux "argued that the proper use of human excrement could effectively replace money and release humans from enslavement to the wage-based economy." Such thoughts sound to us today like those of a madman. But in the mid–nineteenth century, great cities such as London, Paris, and New York were still relatively new phenomena, and it struck some people as insane that the large stock of fertilizing content present in urban areas should gush forth wasted into the surrounding waters.[1]

George Washington, had he been around, may well have agreed with Leroux. In his day, a much more economical relationship existed with respect to the waste products of the city. Washington observed this husbanding of resources firsthand in the spring of 1790 when he decided to get out a little and smell the country, leaving his home in Manhattan and heading for Long Island. As an agricultural improver who decried the soil exhaustion of postrevolutionary farms, the Founding Father took note as follows: "Country in a higher State of Cultivation & vegitation of Grass & grain forwarded than any place else I had seen—occasioned in a great degree by the Manure drawn from the City of New York."[2]

The president witnessed a city locked into a close relationship with the surrounding countryside: an organic city. Manure passed out of New York and food and fodder returned in exchange. In the process, nutrients journeyed back to the soil in what today is sometimes called a closed ecological system. But with the growth of New York in the first half of the nineteenth century, this closed network began to open up. New York became a more linear entity as an explosion in population led to the overproduction of waste. Eventually this shift helped to precipitate a profound transformation of the waters of New York Harbor.

The thinker who best articulated the essence of the urban-rural network Washington observed was a man by the name of Johann Heinrich von Thünen. Born in 1783, von Thünen gave manure intellectual respectability. In 1803, while studying near Hamburg, Germany, he discovered that farms near the town used manure to nourish crops and increase yields. Delicate, more perishable products, he later concluded, would be grown near towns, with the lands beyond differentiating into concentric zones each specializing in its own set of products. The calculus of transportation cost and the price the goods could command in urban markets determined the product mix in each zone. Manure was the key determinant in dividing the first ring of market gardens growing produce, milk, and hay from the second ring, covered with timber. The first belt's ability to buy "most of the manure it uses from the Town" was what put it "so far ahead of all the rest." City and country came together to advance economically and to maintain soil fertility—the foremost goal of any method of farming—with manure acting as the lifeblood of the system.[3]

New York offered a textbook case in this early form of closed-loop recycling. "The city of New-York affords great quantities of manure from ashes, street dirt, stable dung, and earth taken from under old buildings," explained Ezra L'Hommedieu, a member of the Continental Congress who, by the 1790s, had become something of a manure aficionado. "These different kinds of manure are in great demand, and consequently have become very dear." In Queens County, across the river from New York, L'Hommedieu found von Thünen's model in action. He observed a world of market gardens underwritten ecologically by the nutrients contained in "a large pile of manure . . . brought from New-York." Yale College president Timothy Dwight toured Long Island in 1804 and found similar evidence of the enduring bond between country and city. "The country between Jamaica and Brooklyn," he pointed out, "being generally owned by persons who have grown rich with the aid of New York, and being manured from the streets and stables of that city, is under high cultivation."[4]

What was good for the country was also good for the city. New York even made money on the deal. In 1799 the city gave the green light to a plan "to Collect the Street Dirt and Manure at their own expense and sell the same." When the so-called superintendent of scavengers tallied up his accounts in 1803, he discovered that manure sales boomed so fabulously that they not only covered but actually outstripped the cost of cleaning the streets and dredging slips.[5]

It is no mere hyperbole to say that urban manure had morphed into a form of brown gold. When the city privatized its garbage collection in 1806, contractors cherry-picked the manure and left what remained. The heaps of garbage mounted so high that in 1810 New York was forced to reenter the disposal business. Seeking to reform garbage collection, the city now required that its trash superintendents hire scavengers with two dedicated carts: one for manure and one for the rest. Not just anyone could collect the precious manure; only those charged with the task, which was a sign of its value. As was the fact that the cherry-picking continued.[6]

Nineteenth-century New York overflowed with "the wastes of an intensely animal world." Though solid figures on the demographics of the horse population do not exist, it is known that horse-drawn traffic caused bottlenecks on Broadway as early as the 1820s. Later that decade, the omnibus appeared on the scene. This was a large stagecoach that seated upward of ten people and ran on a regular schedule. Given its weight, the omnibus required the power of three or four horses. In the 1830s came the horsecar—an equine-powered trolley car with two or three times the capacity of an omnibus—to whisk passengers along rails, not cobblestones. With horses at the focal point of the New York transit system, a word about the animal's toileting habits is in order. Each one produced a titanic thirty to fifty pounds of dung per day. Because of its pure quality, stable manure proved so valuable that it offset the cost of purchasing a horse within five or six years. Much of the excreta was bound for Long Island, where farming had evolved—especially in the wake of the Erie Canal—much along the lines that von Thünen had predicted. The canal brought western grains into the city and encouraged Long Island farmers to specialize in the hay and oats essential to feed the burgeoning city horse population.[7]

Back in the colonial period, manure functioned to transport nutrients from one part of the farm (a meadow or pasture) to another (tilled fields). But the rise of the traffic in urban manure extended the reach of this recycling system. As a result, farmers allowed barnyards—where they husbanded manure in advance of spreading it on tillage—to languish. A report from Long Island noted that Queens County "depends essentially upon a supply of the richest manures, from the cities and towns on the North and East Rivers, which is brought by water and railway to the nearest points where it is required; and the farmers of this county proceed . . . upon the principle, that it is better and more profitable to sell the corn and the oats, the straw and the hay, for cash in the market, and with it, to purchase the manures required for the growth of their crops."[8]

With horses, not to mention hogs, roaming through the streets in search of food and leaving behind their own contributions to the compost pile, New York had matured, in the words of one historian, into "a veritable manure factory." By the time of the Civil War, one gentleman farmer on Long Island described the amount of manure streaming into Kings and Queens Counties as "almost incredible." "Every day in the year," reported the journal *American Agriculturalist* in 1861, "long lines of wagons loaded with New-York stable manure may be seen crossing the ferries to Long Island, there to be manufactured into vegetables, grain, and hay for the City market."[9]

Nevertheless, supply eventually outstripped demand. As the population of Manhattan swelled from 123,706 in 1820 to 813,669 on the eve of the Civil War, the horse traffic grew accordingly. As a result, the recycling network began to break down. The precise timing of the decline is difficult to fathom. What we do know is that by 1835, the city's manure dealers found themselves running short of space to store the steaming heaps. A few years later, Gotham's aldermen, desperate to solve the problem, recommended a railroad to expand the market for all the droppings. New York was slowly entering the world of scatological excess.[10]

Human waste, on the other hand, had a more profligate history. It seems unlikely that much human excrement traveled back to the soil in the colonial period in light of all the available land. As late as 1700, it was simply dumped into the streets. But then a change set in. An ordinance tried to put a stop to the spilling of "Tubbs of Odour and Nastiness" by making the official resting place "the River & no where Else." The reform and, indeed, the very idea of locating settlements along rivers, was likely inspired by a recognition of the self-cleansing capacity of running water. That unique quality derived from two traits: turbulence, which introduces oxygen, and the chemistry of the freshwater-saltwater interface, which causes impurities to drop out of the water. Though the science behind this purifying power may have been unknown back then, the sanitizing effects of estuaries had likely become evident.[11]

So-called night men or necessary tub men—a *necessary* was an old word for privy, or outhouse—hauled the unmentionable away in the dead of night. This was a job that seems to have devolved to African-Americans. Naturally enough, the night men drank, perhaps to help overcome the stench, and sometimes disturbances broke out. "These persons scream through the streets all hours of the night with such vociferation," wrote some artisans in 1817, "as to disturb everyone within reach of their detectable cries." Not only that, "the first shilling they earn is commonly spent on rum and before their work is over they are generally in a state of intoxication owing to this or from carelessness they sometimes drop their loads where it is left overnight and for many hours of the morning to poison all in its vicinity." But even these malcontents were forced to admit that the night men "are employed in a work that cannot be dispensed with."[12]

Human waste eventually took the name night soil. The phrase entered the language in the eighteenth century. Use of the term exploded in the century that followed, corresponding with human manure's transformation into a commodity. In 1837 night soil was made into a product called *poudrette*. The technique for deodorizing human waste and refining it into fertilizer began in France; hence the name, which translated as "very fine dust." The most successful New York area firm set up shop in 1839 on the Hackensack River as the Lodi Manufacturing Company. The company soon obtained a contract from New York City to remove night soil and shipped it across the harbor to its plant, though it is thought that peat from the Hackensack Meadows, next door to the factory, was the primary ingredient in the product. Scavengers also made money from night soil. The magazine *Working Farmer* observed that night men would "empty their carts into a canal boat for 12½ cents per load, instead of throwing their contents into the river."[13]

How much night soil was produced is impossible to say exactly, though an 1831 study by the Lyceum of Natural History estimated that New Yorkers generated an amount equivalent to "about 100 tons of excrement every 24 hours." "The nearest dock or pier is generally selected as the place of deposit for the load of the cart," wrote city inspector John Griscom some years later. It sometimes happened that in dumping a load in the river after dark, night men failed to notice small boats below. The sorry fate of such vessels was to be "either wholly or partially filled, and instances are said to have occurred of their being carried to the bottom with their unnatural load." The story is perhaps apocryphal, but the filling of slips with night soil is beyond question. In 1843 the law required night men to deposit their loads at the end of piers, but as Griscom was quick to note, "the slip being the nearest, is too often the receptacle." Again, in the realm of "excrementitious matter" precision in numbers is elusive. According to one estimate, 750,000 cubic feet of night soil was removed annually from the slips, or only about half what the Lyceum had calculated. New York was defecating itself into a corner.[14]

While there was certainly no shortage of effluvium streaming into the rivers adjoining New York, nothing the night men did could come close, in the long run, to the opening of the Croton Aqueduct in terms of its ecological impact on the harbor. The aqueduct began on the Croton River at Garretson's Mill in Westchester County, north of New York City—a few miles upstream from its confluence with the Hudson— and ran south for forty miles, ending at a distributing reservoir built at Murray Hill, a wooded knoll on Fifth Avenue that is now home to the New York Public Library. The conduit was a response to a problem diagnosed as early as 1831 by a committee of scientists who concluded about Manhattan *that no adequate supply of good or wholesome water can be obtained on this island, for the wants of a large and rapidly increasing city like New York.* For the first time, New York tapped a source located outside of the island: the sparkling waters of the sixty-mile Croton River. This development had three main consequences. First, it vastly increased the carrying capacity of the land and satisfied a chief precondition for further population growth; second, it set the stage for indoor plumbing and a labyrinth of pipes that put the night men out of business; and third, it led to improved sanitation, but at enormous cost to New York Harbor's plant and marine life.[15]

The new supply of freshwater was meant to address the notoriously poor-quality well water. New Yorkers, explained one 1810 account of the wretched domestic supply, were literally "drinking a proportion of their own evacuations." Ten years in the making, the aqueduct represented one of the great engineering feats of the era, nearly on a par with the Erie Canal. A fifty-foot-high dam was stretched across the Croton River, flooding four hundred acres of land. Every day, millions of gallons of water would exit the reservoir and head south through a forty-one-mile pipe lined with brick and stone that brought the Croton straight to York Island. On October 14, 1842, the city celebrated the start of its new supply with a five-mile-long parade that trooped through town as water shot fifty feet into the air from a fountain at City Hall Park.[16]

The Croton system severed the connection that New Yorkers had with the island's wells and springs and made possible spectacular demographic growth. But New Yorkers did more than simply survive off the new supply. They were awash in water. Under today's standards, approximately thirteen gallons a day per person is necessary to take care of basic human needs (drinking, sanitation, bathing, cooking). In 1850 New Yorkers consumed nearly six times that amount—over seventy-seven gallons per day. That translated into forty million gallons of water sloshing through the city.[17]

Initially, New York's network of sewers could not handle what the Croton system dished out. Moreover, the city had long struggled to deal with the consequences of building in a swamp, and the introduction of Croton water combined with the abandonment of public wells—there were 238 public pumps as of 1808—worsened the drainage predicament by raising the water table and flooding cellars.[18]

Underground New York got off to a rocky start. The first sewers had been constructed to handle storm-water runoff, though the grade was often inadequate, so they clogged with a nauseating array of filth. The Common Council occasionally granted industry the right, for a fee, to tie into a sewer. But the city had grown to the point in 1841 where it was necessary to revoke the variances. Then in 1845 the authorities changed course and began permitting waste—animal, vegetable, and human—to enter the growing subterranean world. Before too long, the city found itself overwhelmed with requests from property owners to hook into the pipes, now channeling both storm water and household waste. Some people believed the sewer outfalls ought to terminate at the piers to help protect the slips. But no action was taken and the slips turned into giant latrines as the length of sewer line increased dramatically following the outbreak of cholera—perhaps the most dreaded disease of the mid–nineteenth century—in 1849. Though just a little over three miles of sewers were built in the cholera year, over time workers eventually rammed through a network that, by 1856, was over 150 miles long.[19]

New York was by this point in the thick of its first real waste climacteric. In 1853 the city inspector reported "thousands of loads of street, stable and other manure and filth on the docks . . . and the dumping of night soil from the docks into the East and North rivers." Population growth had overwhelmed the recycling network formed to send manure out to the country. Large amounts of nutrients, contained in both the night soil and sewer pipes, hurtled toward the harbor.[20]

The same year that Pierre Leroux promoted manure as the savior of the working class, a visionary lawyer and landholder from upstate in the Hudson valley named Robert L. Pell called attention to the waste of "town sewerage." He calculated that the yearly loss of nitrogen in New York City was enough to raise 480 million pounds of wheat. But instead, this valuable fertilizer was being "lost in the rivers encircling New York city." [21]

A discovery made in 1840 underpinned this critique. The German scientist Justus von Liebig determined that human waste could serve as a medium for recycling nutrients back to the soil. Building on this insight, the champion of London's poor Edwin Chadwick had envisioned a form of city life that collected waste and, instead of allowing it to menace the underprivileged, channeled it onto the land. Across the Atlantic, the grid maven John Randel took up the charge, designing a contraption for collecting New York's sewerage, disinfecting it, and returning the nutrients back to the countryside. Meanwhile, another New Yorker named James Jay Mapes, whose ancestors had been farming on Long Island since the seventeenth century, was following these developments. Mapes was a chemist and an agricultural reformer who longed for some way of distilling out the valuable fertilizing component. "Could the Common Council of New York but be induced to examine this subject, and then legislate like philanthropists, the farmers of the surrounding country could hope to vie with their southern competitors in the production of early crops." Nothing remotely close to this utopian ideal came to be.[22]

Perhaps no one objected more eloquently to the open loop than George Waring, a protégé of Mapes. In 1867 Waring proposed a Battery tunnel to conduct wastewater away from Manhattan and help nourish the "sandy soil on the south side of Long Island." Like a pool of water on a melting hot day, the idea evaporated. Though there were quite a number of efforts made to utilize bodily waste for purposes of agriculture in Europe, the concept failed to catch on in New York. The island geography made the prospect of boring a tunnel to transport the water prohibitively expensive, and, in any case, the land near the city was increasingly converted into real estate by the third quarter of the nineteenth century. Instead, a new word—coined in the 1830s—described a product now rarely viewed as having any connection with land at all: *sewage.*[23]

Robbing from the land to give to the sea had ecological consequences. They began to materialize as early as the 1850s. Consider the sea worm (probably *Teredo navalis*), a brown creature about two-thirds of a foot in length that feeds mainly on wood. Not native to North America, it must have hitched a ride in the ballast of a ship sailing for New York. Although described as worms, they are actually burrowing mollusks with the ability to damage ships, dikes, and wooden pilings. For this reason, they are sometimes called shipworms. An 1833 report mentioned that timber piers and wharves "are temporary, and generally endure only from fourteen to seventeen years before they are destroyed by worms." But by midcentury, the animals no longer caused much trouble. In 1856 a wharf owner on the North River observed that "since the construction of the sewers and the introduction of the Croton water, they have almost disappeared from the New-York shores or have ceased to commit serious depredations." Put simply, the colonists inadvertently brought a nonindigenous species to New York that their nineteenth-century descendants unwittingly managed to slaughter. The low oxygen and salinity levels found at sewage outfalls that likely contributed to their destruction no doubt meant that much of the other marine life nearby the island had met a similar fate.[24]

In more technical terms, New York Harbor was likely undergoing "eutrophication." The nitrogen in the night soil and sewage increased the nutrient load funneled into the harbor and sparked a chain reaction. More nutrients led to more plant growth or, in the language of the ecologist, heightened "primary production." The main beneficiary of this trend was the phytoplankton—algae and other minuscule plants—found floating in the water. More phytoplankton might sound like a benign or even a positive development, but it is not. When the planktonic species swell in numbers and then die, they are broken down by bacteria in a process of decomposition that robs the water of oxygen. Then there is the sewage that is not converted into a form that the plankton need. Instead, it simply settles to the bottom of the harbor where again bacteria set to work sucking up yet more oxygen in the process.[25]

Although the sewage churning in the harbor played a key role, it was not the only factor in the overfertilization of the water. Nutrient loading of the Hudson River estuary was high even prior to European settlement. Geography explains why. The size of the Hudson River watershed dwarfed the estuary proper by a factor of over two hundred. In addition, deforestation of the Hudson watershed peaked in the mid–nineteenth century, assuming New York State followed a pattern similar to what unfolded, for example, in nearby New England. The denuding of woodland tended to increase erosion and delivered more phosphorus—another nutrient that lowered the oxygen level—downstream.[26]

Numerous forces, in other words, were nourishing the harbor to death. New York was fast becoming one giant shoe with an expanding ecological footprint.

Though no one in the 1850s understood the fine points of eutrophication, the clash over the future of New York Harbor drove home the limitations on its waters. But that did little to slow the calls for more economic expansion. By the third quarter of the nineteenth century, precisely as the real estate economy came of age with the birth of a central salesroom and trade journal, boosters advanced the idea that New York's genius lay in its potential for phenomenal growth, particularly in land values and population. The real estate lawyer William Martin put a very fine point on the matter and thus stood out as one of the leading promoters of the growth imperative.[27]

In the opening line of his 1865 work titled *The Growth of New York*, Martin argued that "the concentration of population in great cities . . . appears to be so constant and to be due to such general and permanent causes, that it may be regarded as a fixed tendency and law of growth." The broader idea that economic growth was a limitless proposition had taken root as early as the 1830s. Martin built on this earlier understanding by applying the onward and upward vision to an urban environment, and went so far as to argue that the people of New York had an obligation "to prepare the place for the million more who are coming."[28]

It should not surprise us that Martin held a boundless view of natural resources to go along with his mighty vision of the city's economic future. As he wrote, "There is no spot in Christendom where Nature has been more lavish of her gifts or promises for a great city than the site where New York stands." A proponent of the geography-is-destiny school of thought, Martin titled this section of his treatise "The Natural Site for a Great City." He then expounded on New York's natural endowment: its location on a "wide and deep bay"; access to the Hudson River; proximity to "fruitful" Long Island; and, to the west, "the fertile fields and meadows of New Jersey." Though the Hackensack Meadows had languished since the forays of the Swartwouts, Martin made it seem as if their conquest was only a matter of time. But what he failed to explore was the reverse question: was this great city suited to its natural site? As a result, the natural environment's limiting factors were passed over in silence.[29]

Chief among these was the availability of water. Consider Brooklyn, which Martin included in his vision of metropolitan New York without examining the hard realities bound up in furnishing water to its vaulting population—on yet another island, no less. Like New York, Brooklyn had initially relied on springs and wells when incorporated in 1834. But as its population exploded more than tenfold over the next thirty years, the quality of the well water declined, prompting Walt Whitman to bemoan the fact. "With all the vaunted beauty and wholesomeness of Brooklyn, as a place of residence," he wrote in 1851, "our having no water better than pump-water, is enough to put us down below twenty other places."[30]

Brooklyn had initially considered teaming up with New York to draw on the Croton River but engineers thought the supply would be inadequate to quench the thirst of two cities lusting after urban dominance. In 1850 a plan surfaced to siphon, for the very first time, the streams of eastern Long Island, though it took nearly a decade to figure out how to organize the waters into a supply system. Nine years later, Brooklyn staged a celebration, just as New York had in 1842, to inaugurate its new public works project fed by the crystalline waters of Jamaica Creek, Hempstead Creek, Springfield Brook, and other waterways located farther east on Long Island.[31]

Before the next decade had even ended, Brooklyn was already looking to conquer more water. Not only was the population growing rapidly, per capita consumption surged upward from twelve gallons in 1860 to forty-seven in 1870. The following year, the state authorized construction of the Hempstead storage reservoir, completed in 1877. Even that supply proved inadequate as Brooklyn barreled past the half-million mark in population (1880). "If the subject of a further extension of the works is held in abeyance from year to year in the future, as it has been in the past," the commissioner of public works felt compelled to warn, "we may well be held to account by the people for deeds of omission and gross neglect of a great public trust."[32]

When it came to building a sewer system to handle the torrent of wastewater, Brooklyn was more systematic than New York. Early on, it devised a plan to divide the city into drainage districts and began laying sewer pipe. The amount of pipe increased from 5 miles in 1857 to just shy of 150 by 1870. By the end of the 1870s, the city had at least eighteen sewer outfalls emptying somewhere between forty to fifty million gallons of water a day into the bay. But in all the glorification of Brooklyn's progress, some smelled a rat. "Brooklyn claims to be [the] most perfectly sewered city in the Union," declared the *Brooklyn Daily Eagle* in 1871. "But our plan goes no farther than delivering the wastes of the city into the waters that surround it." In effect, the city turned "to the ocean to swallow up what belongs to the land."[33]

A great transformation was playing out across New York Harbor.

Around the city of New York alone, the amount of material entering the waters had grown precipitously in the generation since the harbor commissioners conducted their investigations in the 1850s. Back then the slips along the East River filled at a rate of "one-half to one foot per annum." A reform in 1857 proscribed steamboats from casting cinders into either the Hudson or East Rivers; it also barred night soil and rubbish from being tossed into slips. But the failure to provide adequate enforcement meant that the slips continued to shoal. By the late 1870s, the slips silted up at a rate of three to four feet per year. The city responded to the siltation problem in 1871 by adopting a reform suggested a generation earlier: relocating sewer outfalls to the end of piers. But the legacy of decades of misuse remained. Borings made in 1879 at the West Thirteenth Street outfall passed through a stunning 175 feet of muck en route to the bottom of the harbor.[34]

Further complicating matters was the disposition of bones, butcher's offal, and carrion, a not insignificant issue in a city still so dependent on animals for transportation and food. Bones presented a particular opportunity for profit, like copper piping today. They had value, and not just as fertilizer. Bone black, a charcoal made by burning animal bones, worked for making pigment and for filtering and refining sugar (a major industry in New York). Marrow could be made into tallow. Hooves could be converted into gelatin. Anything left over was fed to the hogs rooting around on places like South Brother Island, at the entrance to Long Island Sound, where such a resource-recovery operation sprawled out in the 1850s. At least, that was the theory. In practice, the garbage business was suffused with graft, and most everything with the exception of the valuable bones was pitched into the water.[35]

Defenders of the harbor had no doubt that abandoning the remains of the day at sea harmed navigational interests. Harbor commissioner George Blunt, whose brother Edmund worked for Alexander Bache to set the harbor's 1856 exterior lines, blamed corruption and economic self-interest. And his protestations seem to have been heard. In 1871 a state law regulated the casting of "carrion, offal, or dead animals" into the North and East Rivers or, for that matter, into New York Bay or Raritan

Bay. The law, which provided for an inspector who issued permits, had at least two results. First, it helped direct some of the offal to Barren Island, in Jamaica Bay, where it was rendered into commercial fertilizer; and, second, it shifted the dumping grounds from the upper to the lower bay. That move kept dead animals from bobbing off the shores of New York but left the harbor still subject to untold amounts of organic matter. It also left places like Coney Island—by then a resort—to fend for itself. "It is not pleasant when you are tumbling in the surf," wrote one reporter in a moment of tremendous understatement, "to have a decayed cabbage stalk or the carcass of a dead cat strike you full in the face."[36]

Compounding the problem of excessive harbor nutrients was the steady loss of wetlands. A cleansing action that can help ward off eutrophication takes place when water is circulated through the vegetation found in salt and freshwater marshes. In short, wetlands act like giant water filters. In light of this, the filling in of the largest wetland complex on Manhattan is worthy of note. By 1875, the Harlem Flats, described as "salt marshes and low lands in the upper portions of New York city," had evolved into "the dumping place of garbage and other refuse." Another marsh for filtering nutrients had made the journey into the world of solid ground, joining the old Lispenard and Stuyvesant Meadows.[37]

If there was ever any chance of building a closed-loop system between country and city, it was all but lost by the 1870s. An island with a population of New York's size surrounded by land increasingly caught in the grip of real estate development would never, with the then-prevailing technology, be able to ship manure back to the soil in any meaningful way, no matter what utopians like Leroux thought. Nor did boosters like William Martin believe there was any future for sewage farming in New York, advocating instead "the best modern scientific methods of disposing of sewerage," which meant, of course, simply flushing wastewater out to sea. Moreover, a growing recognition of the relationship between filth and disease, brought on by experiences in both the Civil War and the 1866 cholera epidemic, gave birth to new standards of hygiene that only escalated the demand for water, and inadvertently sent yet more nutrients on a one-way journey to the bay.[38]

This 1879 bird's-eye view of New York depicts how thoroughly the landscape had been transformed and the sheer impossibility of a closed-loop system.

Hence, New York had at least two very good reasons to expand its water supply. First, to underwrite its relentless quest for growth; and, second, to ensure better sanitary conditions. It took less than a decade after the launching of the Croton system in 1842 before the search was under way for a place to build another storage reservoir to fend off the effects of drought. The resulting reservoir of nearly a hundred acres, completed in 1862 and built in Central Park, was dubbed by Mayor Daniel Tiemann the "new lake of the Manahatta." The name, of course, recalled the old Indian word for the island. Tiemann was quick to note that the new lake "will far surpass the dimensions of the old kolch"—that is, Collect Pond, which was a good thing in light of the frenzied development that would take place in the city once the Civil War had ended. Surveyors had already fanned out over Putnam County, north of Westchester County, looking for yet more water. In 1865 the city received permission to place the West Branch of the Croton River under its control.[39]

As a dam was thrown across the river's path, a new city charter in 1870 gave William M. "Boss" Tweed of Tammany Hall—the quintessential well-oiled political machine—the kind of power he dreamed of. He used it to follow through on William Martin's paean to growth, a vision of awe-inspiring expansion shared by developers such as Samuel Ruggles, who earlier in the century had drained marshland to create Gramercy Park, and politicos like Fernando Wood. Tweed ignited one of the city's most spectacular building booms. He ended up opening large stretches of the less rugged (compared with the West Side) terrain along the East Side of Manhattan to development. Macadam avenues, made from broken stone held together with tar, were pushed through north of Fifty-Ninth Street. Alongside them arose new buildings with indoor plumbing and water courtesy of the new and improved Croton system. In 1875 New York's population broke through the one million mark, and water amounting to ninety-five million gallons a day—equivalent to a football field flooded to a height of over two hundred feet—went coursing out to sea, taking the dreams of Pierre Leroux with it.[40]

7 THE EXPLODING METROPOLIS

In the realm of water, what Moses was inclined to part, an engineer named James E. Serrell resolved to move. An Englishman who came to the United States as a child, Serrell began working as a surveyor for the city of New York in 1845. By the time of his death, he was said to have taken the measure of more Manhattan property than any other human being (save perhaps John Randel). After serving in the Civil War, Serrell arrived back in New York with a big plan that went like this: thus far, he argued, New York had been subject to development for "single personal ends." Now the time had come "to inaugurate a grand and comprehensive system of improvements." In what was surely one of the more lavish topographic fantasies in New York's history—maybe in US history— Serrell proposed "cutting a New East River" through Queens and filling up the old channel, thereby consigning the cursed stretch of water at Hell Gate to the hereafter. The project would add thousands of acres, more than making up, he pointed out, for the land lost in building Central Park. The end result would be a new and improved entrance to the port and, of course, a much bigger city, extending to "cover seven times as much ground as *now*." Serrell's plan was so vast and monumental, it made Baron Georges-Eugène Haussmann's modernization of Paris in the mid–nineteenth century seem like mere child's play.[1]

Was Serrell out of his mind? Not quite. Serrell was a product of his time. As he came of age, a new approach to geography was already in the air. How else to explain, for example, an 1857 editorial entitled "What Shall Be Done with the East River?" It was a question that rested on a strong dose of instrumentalism vis-à-vis the natural world. To the *New York Evening Post*, rivers were no longer natural boundaries to be endured, but impediments standing in the way of civilization. At least three plans had cropped up by the 1850s to transcend the East River. John Roebling, an engineer who invented a sturdy wire cable, broached the idea of building a bridge across it. Others aspired to dam it off between Blackwell's Island and lower Manhattan, creating a wet basin for shipping. For his part, Serrell called for a tunnel. But the Civil War intervened, and somehow Serrell began thinking even more boldly.[2]

On the one hand, it seems difficult to square Serrell's Magna Geographica with the geographic determinism of the times. Since the eighteenth century, New York's stunning success as a port had seemed to rest on the island's superior natural advantages. In response to the Serrell plan, the *New York Herald* declared it "involves a violation of the laws of nature which have given Manhattan Island its present shape, and of those laws, almost equally fixed, which regulate the growth of all great cities, and which have made New York gradually reach its present expansion." Serrell's urban renewal project, in other words, ran afoul of the longstanding assumption that nature had ordained New York's commercial greatness. Only a crank would want to fool around with that.[3]

But on the other hand, Serrell's daring proposal seemed to fit neatly within the can-do geographic climate taking root. Where New York began was clear: the island of Manhattan. Where it would end, no one could say for sure. As the booster William Martin wrote, "A growing city expands on all sides for five or ten miles." The *Real Estate Record*, a weekly report of building activity in the city and surrounding areas, made the same point. "Nothing is more clearly written in the book of Fate," it editorialized, "than that, to meet the constant increase in our population and resources, we *must* go on building, and rapidly too, until we have not only covered every square foot of Manhattan Island, but laid tribute [to] the opposite shores of the East and Hudson Rivers for our overflowing numbers."[4]

Nothing could be allowed to stand in the way of the city's manifest destiny, certainly not the bordering marshlands. "This city is surrounded by a line of marshes, the drainage of which the necessities of its increasing population will in a very few years eventuate," declared the real estate paper. And sure enough, the Central Railroad Company of New Jersey was already filling in the sweeping green marshes and prolific oyster beds along the Hudson. While ecological change descended on the Jersey waterfront, there rose up in Queens in the swamps along the East River a new city called Long Island City. That development set off yet more change, as the wetlands farther inland along Newtown Creek were turned into solid land, most famously at the hands of the Standard Oil Company. Even a new East River materialized, though admittedly not the one that Serrell had in mind. New York was living through "the age of capital," and as the city solidified its place at the economic heart of the nation it pioneered a more dynamic geographic ethos less mindful of the limits of the natural world. Out of this new understanding of the landscape came a new chapter in the history of the region. We know it today as Greater New York.[5]

With the exception of the maniacal, if underfunded, work of the Swartwout brothers, New Jersey was slow to capitalize on its waterfront along New York Harbor. Bergen Neck is illustrative. This was a peninsula of land that intervened between Newark Bay and Upper New York Bay. The Kill Van Kull separated it from Staten Island to the south. The Dutch name for this peninsula was Oesters Eylandt, or Oyster Island, a name that gives a sense of what the colonists found attractive about the property. A 1777 map drawn by the British labeled the waters off of Bergen Neck as "Oyster Banks." Even as late as the mid–eighteen hundreds, with New York now an urban juggernaut, Bergen Neck (also known as Old Hackensack Neck), was renowned for its fisheries, not for its piers and wharves, despite being surrounded by navigable water on three sides.[6]

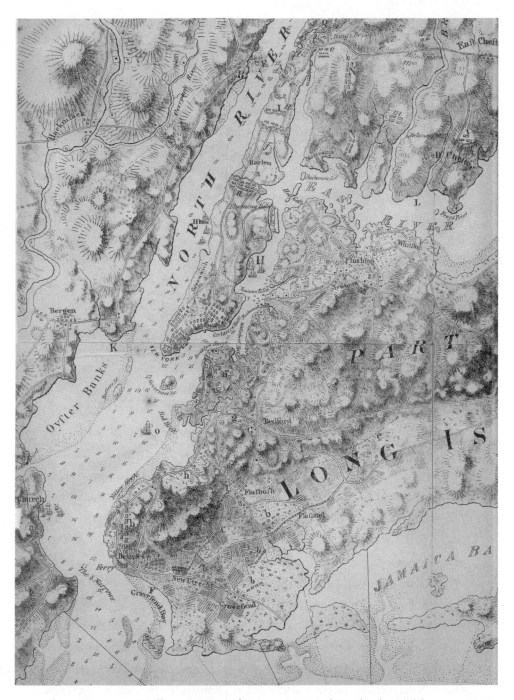

The oyster grounds off Bergen Neck, from a 1777 map drawn by the British.

Although little touched by the hand of improvement, Bergen Neck had nevertheless lost its innocence. It had once been a long stretch of tidewater marsh, back bays, and quiet coves that spread out over the Hudson River side of the landmass. But that was all changing in the nineteenth century as a result of the torrent of sediment that came barreling down the Hudson and East Rivers, especially the former. Downstream from the relentless deforestation of the Hudson watershed and the sewer outfalls of the nation's largest city, Bergen Neck (much like the spot across the bay at Gowanus) took on tons of silt and mud. Over time, certainly by the middle of the nineteenth century, the cascade of alluvium had sketched out a new landform on the western edge of Upper New York Bay: the Jersey Flats.[7]

To this point, virtually all the development along the Bergen Neck waterfront had taken place at Paulus Hoeck, the eventual site of the City of Jersey, better known as Jersey City. This tidal island had been part of a tract once under the control of Michael Pauw, a rich merchant who had purchased it from the Lenape. It seems that Pauw had an agent named Michael Poulaz (or Paulusson), who traded with the Indians, and it is after him that Paulus Hoeck derived its name.[8]

The Dutch dubbed the place a *hoeck,* or spit, but it is best thought of, until the end of the eighteenth century at least, as a kind of island or, more precisely, a set of small hills jutting out into the Hudson. It was surrounded by the waters of Communipaw Cove to the south, Harsimus (Ahasimus) Cove to the north, and, to the west, a long ribbon of spongy marsh linking these inlets. When high tide rolled in, a boat could glide seamlessly from one cove to the other.[9]

The British found Paulus Hoeck so conducive to security that they made it their headquarters, digging a moat through the soft mud of the marsh to secure the perimeter. Even as late as 1804, by which point a New York lawyer named Anthony Dey had acquired the bluff and ferry privilege, a third of the spit's seventy-three acres remained covered with water. Nevertheless, by the middle of the century, the morass had evolved into a small independent city of a little less than seven thousand people. By then, twelve underwater acres had been wrested from the sea. That was an accomplishment, to be sure, but it was a meager one in light of the waterfront development that had taken place in New York and Brooklyn. Why was there so little underwater improvement along the Jersey shore?[10]

One answer is that New Jersey had no cities sitting atop a vast store-house of underwater wealth, as was the case in New York, where Thomas Dongan and John Montgomerie and their grants had blazed the way for a new land of opportunity. But there is far more to the story than simply the lack of special privileges.

New Jersey's antidevelopment atmosphere derived from a strong commons tradition, defined as "the theory that vests all property in the community and organizes labor for the common benefit of all." The provenance of this impulse remains somewhat murky. But there is little question that the idea of a commons in underwater land had the force of Jersey law behind it well into the nineteenth century. A leading 1821 case involving oyster reefs known as the Great Beds, located between Staten Island and the Raritan River, held that lands under water were "common to all the citizens, and . . . each has a right to use them accord-ing to his necessities." The lawyer for the winning side even invoked the Magna Carta, arguing that the legendary 1215 document protecting "common law and common right" was as relevant on the shores of New York Bay as it was at Runnymede. Although this understanding of the law did not go unchallenged, even a generation later New Jersey still had a soft spot in its heart for the commons. How else to explain that as late as 1847 the state still hewed to the old English common-law view that those with land on the bank of a river owned only to the high-water mark. It followed therefore that so-called riparian landowners "can have no rights either to the flats or to the land covered with water."[11]

Nevertheless, by the middle of the nineteenth century, things were beginning to change. In 1848, property owners who had built beyond the high-water mark felt the need for some reassurance, and the legislature complied. The rights of dock and wharf owners to remain in control of their improvements and to continue to collect revenue from them were reinforced. In other words, the law evolved to reflect the fact that land-owners had been wharfing and docking out beyond the high-water mark since early in the state's history, "filling in and reclaiming the ground from the dominion of the water." Now the legal authorities ruled that the English common law did not apply in New Jersey, that riparian own-ers could transcend the high-water mark and extend wharves and fill in land to low water so long as they did not endanger navigation. The com-mons still had its defenders, including one dissenting judge who argued that the new legal rule imperiled "public oyster grounds or the flats in the vicinity of large cities." These areas, he intoned, now would be threatened by the "stimulated vigilance of private enterprise."[12]

In 1851 the New Jersey legislature put a fine point on the privat-ization of the underwater world. It passed a "wharf act" that quickened development along the shore. The legislation empowered riparian own-ers to make improvements all the way to the low-water mark and even beyond if they received a license.[13]

No one played a bigger role in the passage of the law than Abraham Oothout Zabriskie. Born in 1807 in Millstone, New Jersey, Zabriskie was the son of a Dutch Reformed minister. A big bear of a man, excep-tionally learned, a graduate of Princeton University, Zabriskie projected a sense of power. Described as having matured among an "agricultural people, who held on to the traditions of the past," Zabriskie moved on to a career in law and rose into the ranks of New Jersey's managerial elite. But when he moved to Jersey City and came to represent Hud-son County in the state senate, he apparently felt the need to overturn those old traditions. As he traveled increasingly in real estate and rail-road circles, he became convinced of the need to further private rights to underwater land at the expense of the commons.[14]

One can reasonably ask how it is that violating a customary law be-came grounds for overturning that very law. But that was not something asked by the state's highest court. Apparently operating in the same log-ical universe as Zabriskie, it ruled in 1852 that "where a shore owner has filled in on the shore opposite his lands with the acquiescence of the state, *he owns it.*"[15]

For those with an interest in land development, the trend at mid-century could not have looked more auspicious. For those, on the other hand, who depended on the commons and its marine life, the picture was grim. Not only the custom of the commons had been swept aside. In addition, sediment pouring down from the Hudson and gushing out of New York City was burying the oyster beds. In 1857 New York City aggravated the problem. It dredged spoil out of its slips and hauled the material to "a point between Ellis Gibbet island and Bedloe's island," the former named for Samuel Ellis, who once owned the land, and a gibbet, or gallows, on which a black sailor was hanged in 1824. We know it today for its famous inspection station. Before the island went into the immigration business, it was known for its oysters. Thus New York's special delivery led to an outcry and the decision to relocate the dumping ground to a sandbar known for its shellfish, two miles from the New Jersey shore. The move precipitated, predictably enough, a complaint about "the destruction of an oyster bed located there."[16]

By the time of the Civil War, the coves along the eastern shore of Bergen Neck—now looking increasingly like mudflats—were on the cusp of even more radical change. Railroads were the driving force.

Leading the way was the Central Railroad Company of New Jersey. The company traced its roots back to 1831. It was established to capitalize on the rich coal deposits of Pennsylvania and aspired to compete with the Morris Canal, which carried coal all the way from the Delaware River to Jersey City on the Hudson. In 1849 the company changed its name from the Somerville and Easton Railroad Company to the Central Railroad Company, a sign that it aspired to transcend mere local ambition and turn itself into one of the most important common carriers in the state. As part of that new, more ambitious agenda, the railroad appealed to the state legislature to expand its reach, gaining permission in 1854 to build wharves and piers in Elizabeth. But the company's president, a New Yorker named John Taylor Johnston, had a bolder plan in mind, one that would place the railroad closer to the big city. A handsome, immaculate man, raised amidst wealth, with a shock of dark hair, and an eye for aesthetics (he was a founder of the Metropolitan Museum of Art), Johnston, in 1860, pushed for the right to extend the railroad "to some point or points on New York Bay, in the County of Hudson, at or south of Jersey City." In other words, Johnston imagined building a railroad terminal directly across from New York, north of Elizabeth.[17]

Eventually, after paying the state handsomely for the rights to underwater land, the company began expanding from the Jersey Flats into New York Bay. It started by building a bulkhead, reclaiming underwater land, and then constructed piers over four hundred feet out into the harbor. To supplement the silt that had poured down from upstream, the company turned to New York City street sweepings, offal, and garbage, provoking an outcry from the citizens of Jersey City that reached a fevered pitch after cholera arrived in the spring of 1866. The company's sprawling terminal complex (located roughly at the site of today's Liberty State Park) would eventually wipe the oyster grounds of Communipaw Cove from the map.[18]

The work of the Jersey Central inspired another business enterprise, the New Jersey Railroad and Transportation Company (in coordination with other railroads) to repeat the same feat north of the new terminal at Harsimus Cove, a place "once famed for its oysters and fishing." Even before the New Jersey Railroad began filling in the cove, it was described as once a "deep indentation of the shore" but now "in a great measure obliterated." By the time of the Civil War, it had already silted up considerably, offering the builders of the terminal a head start. Not only did the coves and oyster beds of Bergen Neck disappear, but also there was even a plan floated to fill in the flats all the way east to a line extending from the islands off of Jersey City south to Robbins Reef lighthouse. It was the kind of reclamation project likely to impress the James Serrells of the world.[19]

The years after the Civil War were heady times indeed. In 1867, as Serrell released his swashbuckling plan for a new East River and with the railroads imposing their own geography on Bergen Neck, a scheme was hatched to conquer the Hackensack Meadows, or at least a part of them, and thereby pick up where the Swartwouts left off. The key figure here was Spencer Bartholomew Driggs, who was born in Ypsilanti, Michigan. A man who was good with his hands, Driggs, in his thirties, had worked on pianos and registered at least one patent. By the 1860s, he was living in New Brunswick, New Jersey, not too far from the Hackensack Meadows. He resolved to vanquish the marshland. His plan involved the use of iron dikes for drainage, dikes so impenetrable that even the muskrats would not be able to gnaw through them. Driggs purchased roughly three thousand acres of land once owned by the Swartwouts (and held at one point by Anthony Dey, who was instrumental in the rise of Jersey City). But unable to secure title to all the land he desired, Driggs recruited a rich Cincinnati distiller named Samuel N. Pike to his crusade. Together they formed the Iron Dike and Land Reclamation Company.[20]

Driggs sold most of his land to Pike and agreed, in return, to convert it into arable property. Where Swartwout once dreamed of an agricultural paradise, and the *Real Estate Record* imagined market gardens and even tulips, the Iron Dike Company envisioned something significantly less pastoral. Pike's goal was to build "docks, warehouses, and other buildings, and then apply to the legislature to have the new-made tract incorporated as a township." By 1868, a substantial length of dikes jutted up from the banks of the Hackensack River. Workers then sunk down iron plates in the drainage ditches (from which the earth to build the embankments came) "reaching down below the low water mark to prevent the burrowing of muskrats." But the dreams of the Iron Dike Company were dashed. As the water seeped off the meadows, the land subsided, and that, in turn, caused the drains to fail. Pools of water accumulated on the sunken land. In 1872 Pike suddenly died, leaving the Hackensack Meadows once again to the rodents.[21]

If the animal world still reigned over the majestic meadows, the same could not be said for the oyster beds off of Bergen Neck. A vast tidal marsh once extended from Castle Point (opposite Fourteenth Street in New York) south down the coast to the Kill Van Kull, some fifteen hundred acres in all. An 1879 report observed that this "extended and tortuous line of tidal swamps has been invaded, and, at various places, partially filled in by demands of trade and the speculative control of proprietors."

By that time, the area known as Hoboken—originally an island with a handsome expanse of marsh separating it from the mainland—had been blanketed with earth and converted into building lots. But the real action took place to the south in Jersey City, where the sea of grass surrounding two islands as well as Paulus Hoeck had been absorbed into Bergen Neck. The population, meantime, exploded from under seven thousand in 1850 to over eighty-two thousand in 1870, a twelvefold increase. In Jersey City, no less than its near neighbor, the growth imperative went from land making, to population, back to more land making. The result was that crowds of people replaced the enormous biological productivity that had inspired the colonists to inscribe the word *oyster* into the region's cartography.[22]

How Bergen Neck burgeoned into a convex landform is not a simple story. The lay of the land had a great deal to do with the change, especially its position downstream from the Hudson River watershed and the sediment-laden water funneled to this point in the harbor. But the silt created only flats, not terminals and solid land. That change happened because of a shift in thinking about land and sea, one nicely summed up in the life of a New Jersey lawyer named Cortlandt Parker. A native of Perth Amboy and the grandson of one of the proprietors of the colony of New Jersey, Parker came from the Abraham O. Zabriskie school of underwater law. Which is to say that he was bent on speeding the development of the tidelands. As he put it in 1864, the state must use its power to see that these lands were "rescued from the sea, creating a commercial city, where it finds useless sand, and, perhaps, at farthest, a shad fishery."[23]

Geography in Parker's hands was a very malleable concept. A few years later, he reflected on New York's rise to power, noting how "the great city of the continent expands itself with a rapidity unexampled and limitless." There was only one problem with New York's imperial ambitions: "Manhattan Island is far too small." This is where New Jersey came in. It contained miles of valuable waterfront and would host its own "densely populated" cities someday. But only if places such as the Jersey Flats were filled in so that shippers could reach the navigable wa-

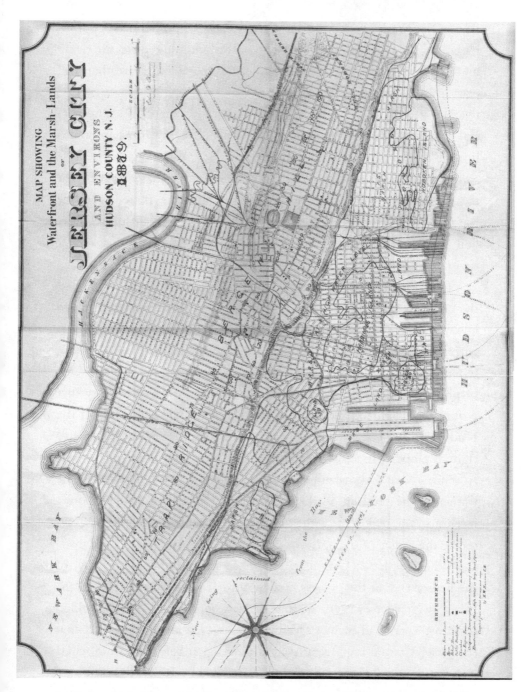

An 1879 waterfront map showing the islands that became Jersey City and Hoboken.

ters of New York Harbor. "[T]he useless flats," he pronounced approvingly, "are daily becoming wharves and basins, and warehouses are rising upon them, to become the dwelling place of more commerce than will exist in New York itself."[24]

Not if New York had anything to do with it. New York's commercial community was not particularly keen about these various efforts to intrude on the harbor's waters. The port of New York was slowly blossoming into the Port of New York and New Jersey and, fearful of what that might mean for the city, not to mention the state, there began one last desperate effort to try to recover the old glory days of John Montgomerie, when New York had a monopoly over the harbor's underwater treasure.

The Montgomerie Charter was nothing if not generous. It granted the city of New York expansive powers, including territorial control "to low water mark on the west side of the North [Hudson] river." In 1827, with John Montgomerie moldering in his grave, the state of New York reiterated its intention to continue to honor that old colonial claim. Unsurprisingly, New Jersey objected and in 1833 negotiated a treaty that moved the boundary line between the two states to the middle of the Hudson River. The document reserved for New Jersey "the exclusive right of property in and to the land under water lying west" of the line. In return, New York received "exclusive jurisdiction of and over all the waters" in the Hudson on the theory that, as the dominant economic interest in the region, it ought to have primary responsibility for overseeing the waters of the port as a whole.[25]

When the Jersey Central carved more than a hundred acres out of the harbor and, in the process, waded out beyond even the lines established by New Jersey itself, the state of New York went to court. Seeking to stop the railroad in its proverbial tracks, New York submitted that the Jersey Central required the city's permission before it could wharf out. But the days of special privilege had faded by 1870, when the case went to trial. Even the highest court in the state of New York was unsympathetic. It instead embraced a maximizing ethos and found that what the Jersey Central had done was not an "encroachment" but "really works and improvements . . . obviously designed, to promote and facilitate trade, commerce and navigation." [26]

At least the merchants of New York City could smooth the edge off the disappointment by taking solace in a new construction project moving forward that promised to open the harbor's back door.

When we last left Hell Gate, the flamboyant Frenchman Benjamin Maillefert had nearly killed himself trying to put its waters on an even keel, leaving the rocks to stay, the costs to mount, and Congress to cut off his funding. But the subsequent Civil War expanded the power of the federal government and prompted it to take charge of local matters. Moreover, the importance of supplying the Union troops had demonstrated the value of a good transportation network. So when the war ended, the Army Corps of Engineers put a forty-four-year-old lieutenant colonel named John Newton in charge of the Hell Gate improvement. Handsome, bearded, and trim, Newton had fought gallantly against Confederate forces and now resolved to distinguish himself on a very different kind of battlefield. [27]

At the time Newton assumed command of the project, it took a very strong wind to escape the currents at Hell Gate, and even with a good blow, it was easy for a vessel to wind up smashed against one of the many rocks that dotted the river. By 1868, Newton had decided to take aim at Hallett's Point Reef, off the coast of Queens, a move supported not just by mercantile interests but also by the real estate community, which expected land values to rise precipitously in the vicinity. Named after William Hallett, a seventeenth-century English settler, the reef extended across three acres. Newton intended to turn it into a giant piece of Swiss cheese, so that when an explosion was touched off, the rock would collapse. A herculean underground mining project ensued involving the boring of seven thousand feet of tunnels, replete with trains to cart the debris to derricks so that it could be hauled up to the surface. [28]

As the project went forward, New York's center of gravity seemed to be shifting north in Newton's direction. In 1868 a visionary urban reformer named Andrew Haswell Green had raised the possibility of clearing out the obstructions in the Harlem River and the adjoining Spuyten Duyvil Creek so as to make navigation possible between the Hudson and East Rivers. Forty-eight years old, with a full beard, and small, penetrating eyes, Green was the human embodiment of the growth imperative—a man bent on transcending boundaries. Scrupulously honest, Green was born in Worcester, Massachusetts, came to New York in 1835, and went on to practice law with Samuel J. Tilden, a corporate lawyer, later elected governor of New York State, who saw it as his duty to clean up Tammany corruption so that the educated upper crust could hold office. Green would come to be viewed as the father of Greater New York.

Even at this early date (1868), Green was thinking big. Making the Harlem River navigable could not be accomplished in piecemeal fashion, he reckoned, but would require "one authority," implying that southern Westchester ought to merge with New York, which is precisely what happened in 1874. But Green did not stop there. After all, a population of more than 1.5 million people resided within a short radius of the city. New York, Kings, and parts of Westchester, Queens, and Richmond Counties, he reasoned, could all fall "under one common municipal government." Somewhat ahead of his time, Green was nevertheless intent on thrusting New York in a northern direction.[29]

The planned pulverization of Hallett's Point Reef was of a piece with this northern shift in thinking about the city's economic geography. There was even speculation that the principal entrance to the port would shift from Sandy Hook—where littoral drift (still as yet not fully understood) caused sediments to threaten to blockade the harbor—to Long Island Sound. "It has been prophesied," read one report in a building trade magazine, "that the success of this enterprise will turn New York upside down, making Harlem, Randall's and Ward's Islands, with the new annexed wards in Westchester county, the main centers of trade."[30]

This upside-down trend seemed to find expression a little south of where Newton prepared to blow his holes, along the Long Island waterfront at the entrance to Newtown Creek. Wending its way along a four-mile course through swampy forest into sleepy lowlands, marsh grass dancing in the breeze, the creek met up with the more powerful waters of the East River, which forced the shallow brook out of its banks. The Indians named the creek Mespat, or "overflowing tidal stream." The wet, boggy land at the mouth of the creek was one of four salt marshes (including Gowanus, Wallabout Bay, and Bushwick Creek) that formed pockets along the Brooklyn coastline. Country estates once lined Newtown Creek, which was famous for its fish and oyster beds. But by the middle of the nineteenth century, the character of the place began to change. Where the creek debouched into the East River was called Hunter's Point, after George Hunter, who had inherited a tract of land from his father-in-law. Hunter died in 1825, and his estate eventually came under the control of a group of real estate developers. In 1855 two improvers received a grant of land under water at the junction of the creek and the East River, having already demolished some sand hills and filled in marsh.[31]

Around the same time, the Flushing Railroad laid tracks alongside the waterway, the only good level ground it could find as it forged a connection between Hunter's Point and Flushing. As the Civil War began, the Long Island Railroad decided to open a terminal as well at Hunter's Point to capitalize on the ferry service to New York (started in 1854). The move underwrote the birth, in 1870, of Long Island City, encompassing the land north and east of the creek all the way to Bowery Bay, facing Rikers Island. At the time, a local historian described Hunter's Point as "no better than a raw frontier town in the mid-West." But that was before a tenacious man named James Thomson realized the enormous opportunity that could be had in dirt.[32]

Thomson speculated that the extensive marshlands would need to be filled in and graded to create a street system for the new city. So in 1874 he purchased a nearby thirty-acre farm with the intention of harvesting soil from the uneven terrain. Using steam shovels, he excavated, it is estimated, some one million cubic yards of earth and sold it to the city. That was roughly the same amount of fill that was later mined to build the World Trade Center. The ambition behind the high-flying revamping of the landscape found expression in the new city's name, which was deliberately chosen to compete with its counterpart across the East River.[33]

Urbanization set in motion yet more change upstream along New-town Creek, where the second industrial revolution—technological change underwritten by mechanization, fossil fuel, and expanded markets—came hard and strong. Oil and lumber companies filled in along the banks. In 1871 alone, the year after the incorporation of Long Island City, the state granted seven pieces of underwater land along the creek. The most famous industrial enterprise in the area was John D. Rockefeller's Standard Oil Company. At this time, New York already hosted several gas works—factories that converted coal into kerosene for illumination purposes. With the prospect of foreign oil sales on the horizon, the company found the port of New York attractive, especially with the government now working to improve navigation prospects at nearby Hell Gate. In 1874 Rockefeller surreptitiously purchased Charles Pratt's Astral Oil Company in just one of his many legendary efforts to squeeze out the competition. By early the following decade, Rockefeller had ruthlessly pulled ahead of his competitors and stood in command of over a hundred stills on Newtown Creek. Each week, the refineries hummed with the bustle of two thousand workers transforming three million gallons of crude oil into kerosene. Newtown Creek had ascended into the crossroads of the oil world.[34]

As the marshlands around Hunter's Point and Newtown Creek fell victim to industry, the tunneling at Hallett's Point Reef moved forward. In 1876, with all the necessary excavation completed, the final explosion was scheduled for a Sunday in September. Newton's two-year-old daughter set off the explosive device, perhaps making a point about how future generations would benefit from the blast. The Chamber of Commerce declared in the wake of the successful detonation: "The Centennial year will be for ever known in the annals of commerce for this destruction of one of the terrors of navigators." It took years to clean up all the debris. But by 1881, ships finally glided through the now-tamed passage without the aid of a pilot.[35]

Even before the completion of the work at Hallett's Point, Newton had taken on another challenge: a nine-acre reef that went by the name of Flood Rock. This rock was three times larger than the reef scheduled to be blown to smithereens. Again, Newton planned to tunnel his way to success. The project required drilling four miles of underground caverns. Roughly eighty thousand cubic yards of rock had to be quarried, enough to fill a football field to a height of over thirty-seven feet. In 1885 it was time to bring in the explosives, as well as his daughter to detonate them again. Dignitaries such as abolitionist preacher Henry Ward Beecher and Union general Philip Sheridan were on hand to witness the event, said to be the strongest planned blast on record prior to the dropping of the first atomic bomb.[36]

The environmental significance of the reshaping of the East River is something that must be inferred. Some at the time predicted that the removal of the rocks at Hell Gate would cause the bar at Sandy Hook to silt up. But there was no truth to the claim as far as modern physical oceanography goes. More likely, the demolition of the reefs caused a change in fauna. The rocks and strong currents were the right habitat for various invertebrates such as bryozoans (moss animals that inhabit rocky surfaces), sea anemones, and starfish. In its pre-explosion days, the turbulent stretch of water must have been a great place for catching bass and bluefish. The large rocks also gave rise to eddies and quieter spots for fish to hide in during the different phases of the tidal cycle. This rich habitat succumbed to Newton's underwater blasting.[37]

In 1871 *Harper's Weekly* magazine played George Washington for a day. It published an article and accompanying map titled "Eighteen Miles around New York." Emboldened by New York's seemingly unstoppable growth, *Harper's* ventured far beyond the York Island landscape that President Washington had come to know on the quaint fourteen-mile exercise jaunts he took north along old Bloomingdale Road. Indeed, Manhattan is not even at the center of the map. That honor went to New York Bay. The map purports to give a bird's-eye view of the area within an eighteen-mile radius of the metropolis. It contrasts the vastness of the still untamed Hackensack and Newark Meadows with the changes along the Jersey Flats, showing the Jersey Central's embankment along the bay. Like James Serrell's vision for the East River, the map (published just a few years after) was the product of the same boundary-breaking impulse. "The map illustrates the growth of New York," writes the author, "and indicates what would have been the territorial extent of the metropolis of the Western world but for its cramped position between two wide and deep rivers." The use of the conditional perfect tense could be taken at face value were it not for the claim that the surrounding areas "in reality belong to New York."[38]

It took a budding professional geographer to place New York in its proper natural setting. In 1873 a German pharmacist turned naturalist turned geographer named Friedrich Ratzel, age twenty-eight, sailed for New York. He steamed into New York Harbor on a clear day, spotting Sandy Hook to his left. The ship then skirted Staten Island before forging through the Narrows into the shelter of Upper New York Bay. Ratzel found the "natural contours" of southern Manhattan, which he understood once consisted of "a number of swamps as well as a deep pond," to be "hard to recognize." There he encountered a city that was bigger than the sum of its political parts. He saw a metropolis—not just New York but also Brooklyn, Jersey City, and Hoboken—crowded around what he called the *Hudsonmündung*, or the Hudson River estuary. The estuary linked New York with the adjoining network of cities and provided the geographic basis for what Ratzel predicted would be a new era in the region's political life. "If one speaks of the development, significance, or future of New York," he wrote, "one does not think of the city of one million inhabitants, which actually carries that name, but of the entire urban complex around the Hudson estuary, which soon will have a population of two million, and will one of these days probably unite to form the political unit that the nature of things already seems to have predestined."[39]

Why did a new, more expansive view of the city take root in the last quarter of the nineteenth century? It is easy to imagine New York City as the urban equivalent of a colonial power, conquering lands and adding them to its empire much as the British accumulated countries across the globe (or, closer to home, as the United States itself did beginning in the 1890s). On the other hand, the various places that would make up New York City had reasons of their own to want to be part of a larger enter-

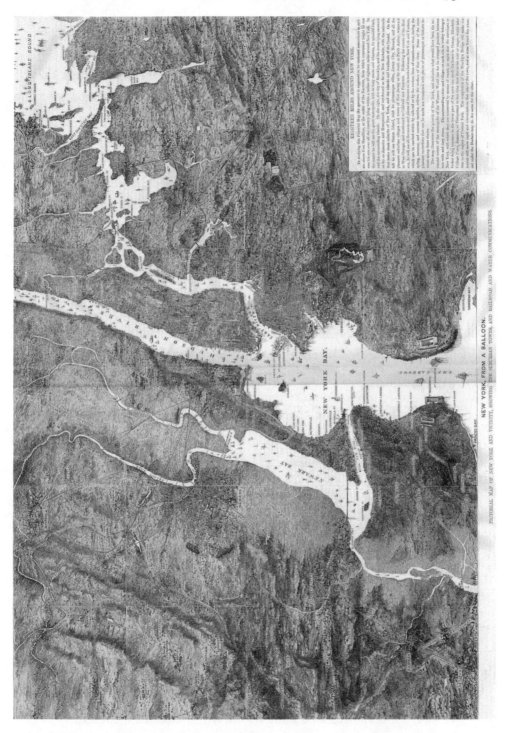

The *Harper's Weekly* map published May 6, 1871.

prise, not the least of which was access to New York's impressive supply of Croton River water. But the one factor often missing in the story of Greater New York is the role that the harbor played in fostering the interdependence of the communities that lived along its shores. In this sense, Gotham's Gilded Age geography grew out of a recognition that in New York all roads really led to the sea.

There was nothing new about the commercial elite's concern for the harbor. That had been an anxiety since the 1850s, if not before. But the evolving impact of high-density development, with its rampant population growth and overproduction of waste, demonstrated even more clearly by the last quarter of the nineteenth century the conflict between land and water. Concern for the harbor's future was heightened by an 1871 investigation that uncovered some obstruction of the main shipping channel. The inquiry tied the trouble to shoaling near the Jersey Flats, though the blame cast on the land-making exploits of the Jersey railroads was likely misplaced. The harbor system had only so much capacity to transport sediment, and by this point in New York Bay's history, more deposits from deforestation, sewage, ashes, and other refuse poured in than the ebb tide could send out. Simply burying garbage farther out beyond the entrance to the harbor was tempting, but also costly and time consuming. Nor was there any waste separation program in place to help with the problem. In 1879 the Chamber of Commerce called for such a program so that rotting garbage could be separated from ashes and the latter used to work "some pecuniary return to the city." But it would be years before the idea of separation took hold, briefly, and in the meantime, the rise of the open-loop system continued to haunt the harbor.[40]

The evolution of New York into the main headquarters of corporate capitalism further complicated life for these waters. Major corporations, following the example set by Standard Oil, relocated to the city to gain access to the capital of its investment banks as well as expert legal advice. The demand for office space to supply these companies and their support staffs spurred a building boom, with hundreds of structures exceeding nine stories in height going up in Manhattan by the close of the century. The word *skyscraper* took on new meaning. Originally, the term referred to the uppermost sail in a square-rigged vessel, but by the 1880s, it had made the journey from sea to land and had come to denote a tall building. Laying the foundations for the structures required excavation, and that in turn produced enormous quantities of *cellar dirt*: excavated soil and rock. Reports of corruption popped up as building contractors (including one involved in erecting the United States Electric Lighting Company Building at Avenue B and Seventeenth Street) tried to unload the surplus earth by prevailing on the Street Cleaning Bureau to haul it away to sea at public expense, taxing the harbor still further.[41]

Midway through the 1880s came more bad news. A report surfaced that the bar at Sandy Hook had risen a full foot in one year "due to the dumping of refuse matter, street sweepings &c." It was the kind of news that caused the merchant elite to lie awake at night. The Chamber of Commerce had already issued a call for federal intervention to police the waters. Complicating matters, the major steamship lines ratcheted up the pressure on the port with a cri de coeur for a thirty-foot channel. They fretted over the time lost waiting for the tide to rise so that ships could cross the bar at Sandy Hook. This was, after all, the era that witnessed the development of standard time (superseding an older temporal understanding rooted in seasonal tasks). The steamship lines no longer wanted to be constrained by the natural rhythms of the tides.[42]

In 1888 the federal government finally stepped in. A supervisor was appointed to oversee the harbor. He soon established two dumping sites (one for mud including stone, earth, and spoil; one for refuse such as street sweepings, garbage, and offal) a few miles south of the entrance to Rockaway Inlet, where Henry Hudson began his fabled journey. But the supervisor had too few ships under his command to carry out his duty properly. The clandestine tipping continued. Even a change in the law to make it easier to prosecute offenders failed to halt what the Chamber of Commerce described as "this great and crying evil." The amount of refuse produced by urban development was simply mind-boggling. In

1893 alone, the supervisor issued legal dumping permits for nine million cubic yards* of material.[43]

Taking some of the pressure off the harbor was a plan, that same year, by the New York Department of Docks to put garbage to better use. The department built a retaining wall off a small island nestled in the East River between the Bronx and Queens. This was Rikers Island. The city had acquired it in 1884 from the descendants of Abraham Rycken, a seventeenth-century Long Island colonist, and made it into a prison farm. But the garbage sent to expand the island was not separated, and because it included everything from ashes to food scraps, the move amounted to more of an exercise in fermentation than in land making. As New York grew, the problem only became worse.[44]

It would be reductive to argue that illegal dumping was what jolted Greater New York to life. But there is no question that, by 1890, the subject was on the mind of the man most instrumental in New York City's consolidation. Andrew Haswell Green decried "[t]he rogueries of garbage and mudscow boatmen" for defiling the waters of New York Harbor from Sandy Hook all the way to Yonkers in Westchester County. "Every little district has its marauders, who by encroachment, appropriation, and misuse deplete the general system, to transfuse its vitalities into some niggard scheme or individual profit."[45]

Green was a big-picture man. The waters of New York, he had come to realize, had gone from being "bonds of union" to a source of division. A byzantine set of counties, cities, and states sliced up the land surrounding New York Harbor like the result of some deranged feudal lord divvying up his fief. To correct the situation, he determined, required a new geographic understanding: "The various rivers, estuaries, streams, straits, and inlets which thread our situation here were once the frontier lines of barbaric jurisdictions of a vanished race." These old boundaries simply would not do. New York started out small, confined below "the Canal Street estuary." But that natural feature of the land had fallen as New York advanced uptown, subduing the Collect and the adjoining

---

*   The largest Dumpster on the market today can hold sixty cubic yards of refuse.

wetlands, and eventually heading clear across the Harlem River to bring southern Westchester into its orbit. As Green pointed out, New York's island geography was "peculiar" among the largest cities in the world: "Our narrow island, bounded on each side by the rivers which serve our commercial business so well, is hemmed in by natural moats more effective than any which military skill could construct." It was time, in other words, to conquer nature in the quest for urban growth. New York could not let mere water stand in its way.[46]

On January 1, 1898, Green's dream for a greater New York came to fruition with the consolidation of all five boroughs. The result was an urban leviathan that was vast in size, dense in population (eleven thousand people per square mile), and endowed with a staggeringly long waterfront. The new city was over three hundred square miles in extent, or nearly a third the size of the entire land area of the state of Rhode Island.[47]

Development brought with it significant paving over of the soil. Indeed, there was so much impervious ground cover at the dawn of the new century—buildings, roads, and roofs—that it changed the city's very climate, producing an urban heat-island effect (the temperature difference between dense cities and sparsely settled hinterlands) of at least one degree Celsius. What happened was that heat-trapping buildings and asphalt streets replaced vegetation, which has a moderating effect on temperature (through evaporation and transpiration). Even worse, by preventing water from percolating through the soil, the impervious surfaces contributed to eutrophication as runoff streamed over the warmed hardscape, picking up manure and other debris and sending it into the surrounding water— where it lowered oxygen levels and harmed marine life.[48]

New York was indeed unique. Compared with its rivals—London, Paris, Berlin—New York evinced astonishing population growth. But unlike these other cities, where, as one report noted, "the bodies of water that separate the different sections are comparatively narrow," Greater New York was a full-fledged island environment surrounded by sizable bodies of water not easily spanned. Altogether, the myriad islands, rivers, bays, and inlets gave rise to a sweeping expanse of waterfront, a full 578 miles in all, or roughly the distance, if it were to be unfurled into one

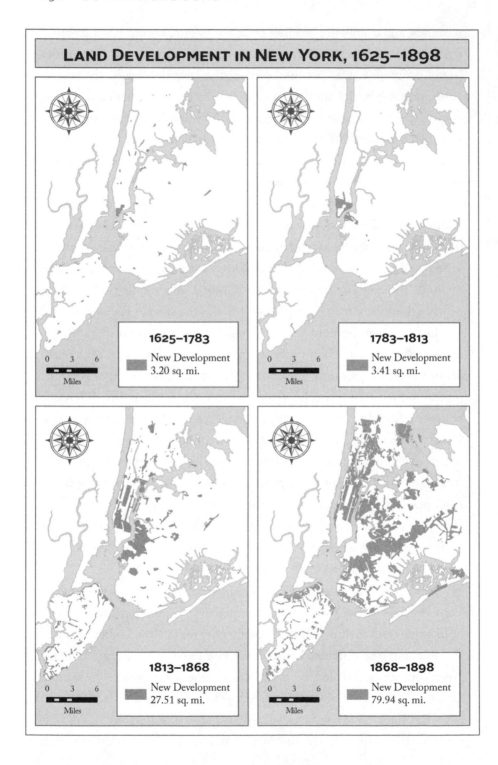

LAND DEVELOPMENT IN NEW YORK, 1625–1898

1625–1783
New Development
3.20 sq. mi.

0   3   6
Miles

1783–1813
New Development
3.41 sq. mi.

0   3   6
Miles

1813–1868
New Development
27.51 sq. mi.

0   3   6
Miles

1868–1898
New Development
79.94 sq. mi.

0   3   6
Miles

long line, from Wall Street all the way to Toledo, Ohio. This "immense water frontage," the *Real Estate Record* prophesied, would underwrite significant landscape change in the years ahead as "the natural features are one by one destroyed." In return there would materialize a truly great city "capable of supporting an incalculably increased population, the greatest in the world."[49]

8 TWO-DIMENSIONAL GOTHAM

It is no exaggeration to call James Reuel Smith the most accomplished spring hunter in the history of the world. With an anal-retentive vigor that would have terrified even Sigmund Freud, Smith bicycled about turn-of-the-century New York photographing and measuring each and every last little fountain that had managed to somehow survive the fight with the all-consuming, desiccating march of progress. The resulting book, titled *Springs and Wells of Manhattan and the Bronx New York City at the End of the Nineteenth Century* (1938), is by all accounts the definitive work on the topic. Why would someone find it necessary to devote such energy to a monumental exercise in ecological antiquarianism?[1]

It goes without saying that Smith had a lot of time on his hands. An ample inheritance allowed for a life of leisure and time for hobbies. The grandson of a prosperous New York merchant, Smith is shown in one photograph looking melancholic, with worried eyes. He lost his mother at the tender age of five and was raised by his father's cousin in New York City. Erudite, educated in classical and biblical literature, Smith was a great lover of books who died with a personal library of four thousand volumes. A biographer observed: "He delighted in arranging and cataloguing everything about him according to an exact decimal system, and all his notes and clippings and photographs were in meticulous order."

Not surprisingly, Smith was also the author of *Springs and Wells in Greek and Roman Literature, Their Legends and Locations* (1922), a stunningly thorough book of some seven hundred pages and with no fewer than three different indexes. But the New York literary scene was not nearly so rich as the classical one, leaving Smith at a loss for the narrative thread required to write up his Gotham water story. In the end, the treatise had to be published posthumously. We are left, then, with a very curious book: an inventory of New York's land and waterscape at one of the most important moments in its environmental history.[2]

Smith marveled at how much Manhattan had changed in the generation before his pilgrimages. In the fall of 1898, as New York City agglomerated, Smith biked to a spring located at 122nd Street and the Hudson River. Reflecting on the shorefront extending south, Smith pointed out that even "[a]s late as 1880, the entire tract down to 72nd Street was a forest in a primitive state." Indeed, "a black snake six feet long was killed on Riverside Drive a few hundred feet from the spring." But by the time of Smith's visit, the old-growth forest—oak, chestnut, hickory—had given way to Riverside Park, an area of "asphalt walks and close-cropped open lawns" masterminded by Frederick Law Olmsted in the 1870s.[3]

The only significant trace of old Manhattan was in Washington Heights. There Smith stumbled upon a deep well near Fort Washington Avenue and today's 171st Street. "In a distance of fully two miles north from here," he wrote, "there is an almost unbroken woods, up hill and down dale, interspersed with deep ravines, with numerous noisy brooks, rocks, a fallen tree, and all the wildness of a place far out in the country." Only the occasional wealthy estate interrupted the sylvan expanse. On an earlier visit, Smith found a chestnut tree where someone had thoughtfully nailed a shelf on which a glass was kept "for those who know of the spring's whereabouts." A spring in the woods, on an island with a population approaching two million people, was a rare sight indeed.[4]

Smith's book can be read as one man's attempt to immortalize Gotham's lost landscape. Writing about his excursions, Smith lamented that "especially during the last decade [circa 1906 to 1916], springs and other natural features of the landscape are disappearing from sight with such celerity that it is merely a matter of months when there will be none whatever left in view upon Manhattan Island." In the decade or so that had elapsed since Smith's journeys, many of the springs and wells he had visited had indeed disappeared "out of sight, their former pleasant woodland homes being now covered with the stone and metal hives of humanity."[5]

Smith took his jaunts about the city at the high point of topographic consciousness. This was a period when the grid plan came in for some of its worst bruising—pilloried for robbing Manhattan of its ponds, streams, and rugged terrain. As Thomas Janvier wrote in his book *In Old New York* (1894), the grid commissioners had "decided that the forests should be cut away, the hills levelled, the hollows filled in, the streams buried; and upon the flat surface thus created they clapped down a ruler and completed their Bœotian [dull, stupid] programme by creating a city in which all was right angles and straight lines." So deeply ingrained was the trauma of the grid on middle-class consciousness that when Isaac Newton Phelps Stokes, perhaps the city's most famous historian, published his six-volume magnum opus *The Iconography of Manhattan Island, 1498–1909,* he chose to use the 1811 plan as a dividing point in his chronology and pledged to pay special attention to Manhattan's "topographical features."[6]

If Smith launched his spring inventory as part of a more general concern with landscapes lost, he also did so in response to a more obvious development: the changing nature of the water supply. The more water that came from off the island of Manhattan, the more superfluous its springs and wells. But more was at stake in the development of an off-island water system than the simple ushering of the springs of New York down the road to the curiosity shop. New rivers of water underwrote the incredible population growth of New York and Manhattan in particular. In 1910 the latter reached its highest population ever: more than 2.3 million people packed onto a twenty-odd-square-mile landmass. Altogether, the water, in combination with the quest for more growth, would so thoroughly alter New York Harbor that in some parts its once bountiful marine life would almost completely perish.[7]

• • •

At the time that James Smith climbed aboard his bicycle, New York had already humbled the wild tributaries of the Croton River to assume control of enough river water to flood Manhattan to a depth of almost eight feet. How was it that New York took such liberties with the Croton watershed?[8]

In the 1870s, drought, high per capita consumption, and the impact of the vast Tweed-inspired street projects (and the speculative building boom they brought to life) joined to intensify the demand for water. A drought in 1876, the likes of which had not been seen in a half century, scorched the Croton watershed. "The Croton River itself has dwindled to the dimensions of a mere brook," wrote the commissioner of public works. Meanwhile, daily per capita consumption more than doubled between 1842 (when the Croton first came online) and 1875, from thirty-eight to ninety-one gallons. The *Herald*, writing during the 1876 "water famine," explained the root of the problem as follows: "The trouble is that the men who projected the Croton Aqueduct never dreamed that within so brief a period as twenty-five years the city would demand such a vast increase in its water supply." The architects of the water system had figured on forty gallons a day per person, "but we have got extravagant in water as well as in everything else, and now each of us, it seems, is put down for ninety-five gallons a day—enough for an elephant to swim in." Selling water on the "frontage system"—not according to the amount used—helped kindle such Brobdingnagian thirst. This method involved a formula that calculated the building height, the number of plumbing fixtures, and street frontage. Needless to say, ignoring actual usage did nothing to curtail consumption. Nor were there any water meters to speak of.[9]

The commissioner of public works concluded the 1876 shortage was nothing that control of more water could not solve. First came the move to master the Bronx and Byram Rivers with dams and a fifteen-mile pipeline. Then came what would turn out to be the longest and largest aqueduct in the history of the world. The idea behind the New Croton Aqueduct project was to capitalize more fully on the runoff available in the watershed and store it in reservoirs before delivering the water by gravity through a new conduit.[10]

The man behind this plan was Isaac Newton, a tall, balding forty-three-year-old bachelor who seems to have suffered from paranoia and depression. Born in New York City, Newton studied civil engineering at the City University of New York. During the Civil War, he helped to design the USS *Monitor*, the first ironclad US warship. After the war ended, he worked for coal and railway companies in the United States and Canada before his appointment in 1881 as chief engineer of the New York Department of Public Works. It took him only a little more than a month on the job to conclude that New York required a new aqueduct to deliver more water. "A liberal supply of pure water," he wrote, "is as important as sunlight, and I believe it is the sense of the community that such a supply should be led into the City as soon as it is possible to do so." He went on to broach a plan for a water tunnel capable of delivering 250 million gallons a day—about two and a half times the amount then available to New York. But he did not live to see his ambitions realized, because in 1884 he stole away into a closet at his Union Square apartment and slit his throat.[11]

Newton's grand plan seemed to reinforce the ambitions of those who believed in the limitless growth of the city. As Mayor Abram Hewitt vouched, New York's "imperial destiny as the greatest city in the world is assured by natural causes." Of course, that such assurance was felt necessary likely bespoke some doubt about New York's natural predisposition to greatness.[12]

Work on the New Croton Aqueduct began in 1884 and finished in 1890. Ninety-two men died while building the thirty-one-mile pipeline. When the tap was turned on, water use in New York (Manhattan and the Bronx) swelled from roughly 105 million gallons a day to 153 million by the following year. The aqueduct set the stage for yet more domination over distant waters. In 1891 the city built a reservoir to capture the East Branch of the Croton River and Bog Brook. Two years later, it completed the largest reservoir in New York's water supply system, a seven-hundred-acre reserve on the Titicus River, a tributary of the Croton River. Two years after that, the West Branch of the Croton River yielded before eighteen feet of masonry to create just shy of one thousand acres of water. And in 1897 the Muscoot River, another Croton tributary, succumbed to New York's designs to bring on another six-hundred-acre sheet. The peaceful waters of this tributary watershed of the Hudson River, fanning out to the northeast of Sing Sing prison, had been reworked into the linchpin of jam-packed New York as its population ballooned from less than a million in 1870 to over 2.5 million in 1890.[13]

But even water enough to drown all of Manhattan seven feet deep was not adequate to satisfy the powers that be. Fourteen years in the making, the New Croton Dam was finally completed in 1906. At nearly three hundred feet, it was the tallest masonry dam on earth at the time and nearly doubled the city's water storage capacity. To gain that supply required remaking the narrow Croton River into a nearly two-thousand-acre lake, nineteen miles in length. Bearing witness to life in the river valley back when there was still a river, the civil engineer Edward Wegmann testified that "[i]t was anything but waste land when we came here to claim it." There were four towns and three railroads. "All had to be removed or destroyed," he explained matter-of-factly, "to give room for New York's water supply."[14]

A similar story of mounting water consumption unfolded across the East River in the nation's fourth largest city. While New York had ventured north to the Croton to furnish its supply, Brooklyn stuck somewhat closer to home. It continued to rely on Long Island through the end of the nineteenth century. But by the 1890s, the faucet seemed to be drying up, as demand outstripped supply. In the generation leading up to 1895, Brooklyn's average daily water consumption had increased eightfold to more than seventy-five million gallons. Having already drawn on western Long Island, the city in 1893 began considering sources farther east. And as it set its sights on these more distant sources in Suffolk County, it began to run into trouble. Baymen who survived off the surrounding oyster beds and relied on freshwater to "fatten" the shellfish before sale convinced the legislature in 1896 to grant the county's board of supervisors the right to preempt Brooklyn from infringing on its streams and ponds. Unable to overcome the Suffolk opposition, even the most independent-minded Brooklynites could see that consolidation, if nothing else, would at least keep the water flowing.[15]

By the turn of the century, with Brooklyn pumping away and the Croton system working at full throttle, the now consolidated New York City consumed enough water on a daily average basis to fill the entire Empire State Building one and a third times. Where did all the water go?[16]

The short answer is that it is hard to say. John Ripley Freeman, one of the most respected civil engineers of his time, estimated that roughly half or more of the water delivered to Manhattan was wasted, disappearing from countless cracks and leaks in the service pipes. About 20 percent of it went to manufacturing and commercial establishments for things such as generating power, including the muscle to pump water up to the top floors of tall buildings. These skyscrapers soaked up considerably more water than the buildings they replaced. (The American Tract Society Building on Nassau Street in lower Manhattan, to take one example, consumed almost ten times that of the structure it supplanted.) The remaining 30 percent went to supply domestic needs. But even here, New York was exceptional in its water use, at least when compared with foreign cities such as Berlin, which employed meters to maintain very low rates of per capita consumption. New understandings of cleanliness as a moral imperative also played a role. Flush toilets date from 1809, but they became common only in the latter part of the nineteenth century, as hygiene turned into a full-fledged American obsession. As one civil engineer put it in 1906: "[P]erhaps in no large city in the world is the proportion of fixtures to population as great as in New York."[17]

The growth imperative at the heart of New York's thirst for water seemed almost impossible to tame. It was abundantly clear that installing water meters curbed consumption, but the law required only business establishments to have them. As late as 1900, only about a third of the taps—mainly in industrial operations—had meters. Although the engineering community believed that metering domestic consumers would postpone the need for further expansion of the water supply, landlords fought such measures vigorously. Landlords opposed it because water being sold on the frontage system saved them the trouble and expense of repairing or upgrading leaking fixtures. In 1910 the real estate lobby, with support from Mayor William Gaynor, beat back an effort to install meters in residential structures. "We believe that water should be as free as the air," said a lawyer for the Harlem Property Owners' Association, "that water should be supplied by the city to its inhabitants not only in sufficient quantity but in over-abundance."[18]

There is perhaps no stronger testament to the preoccupation with the limitless consumption of nature than New York's early fixation on waters even farther afield than Westchester County. Before the 1870s had even closed—while workers fitted the Croton with a new set of pipes—the Department of Public Works had completed a preliminary survey of New England's Housatonic River. The idea was to turn the plentiful waters of the Housatonic watershed into the Croton River. In 1895, with the New Croton Aqueduct completed and storage basins taking command of the landscape, the aqueduct's chief engineer, Alphonse Fteley, acknowledged the inevitability of further expansion. The city of New York, he explained, "with its habits of wasteful water consumption, and with its fast growing population, including its prospective expansion of 'the Greater New York,' will necessarily have to look for more water when the present supply has reached its limits."[19]

Instead of forging northeast, the city turned to the northwest, setting its sights on the Catskill Mountains. In 1887 a private company, by virtue of a corrupt political deal, received special powers and thereby cornered the market in upstate water. The ruse placed New York City at the company's mercy. To sell the project to the locals, the company, according to a *Times* report, presented its plan as an opportunity to turn the region into "a second Switzerland." But the civil engineer John Freeman, for one, had his doubts (and, in any case, the legislature revoked the company's charter in 1901). Freeman did not believe the plan to control the waters of Esopus Creek and thereby destroy life in "the thriving village of Shokan" would yield a sufficient supply of water. But ironically, his remarks on the Esopus piqued the curiosity of the Department of

Water Supply, Gas, and Electricity, which sent out crews to assess its potential. With the idea of out-of-state sources exposed as legally problematic and opposition surfacing from counties nearer to New York to any further water control, the city seemed to have little choice but to venture northwest to slake its thirst. Before long, New York's business class—from the Chamber of Commerce, to the Brooklyn League, to the New York Board of Fire Underwriters—lined up behind the Catskills scheme. The project also had the backing of the mayor of New York: George B. McClellan Jr., the son of the Civil War general. Although opposition ran high in upstate areas, newly passed state laws cleared the way for yet another massive alteration of a distant watershed. The Catskills would change dramatically and, as it turned out, so would New York Harbor, the final stop on the water's journey from the mountains.[20]

On June 20, 1907, McClellan departed the Battery in a steamer and chuffed up the Hudson to take part in the groundbreaking. For the occasion, the New York jeweler Tiffany & Company had crafted a special spade inlaid with silver and replete with a mahogany handle designed to look like a cross section of the planned aqueduct. McClellan turned over the first piece of sod, and as he did so, he effectively issued a declaration of ecological independence. The Catskills further liberated New York from the constraints imposed by island life and cleared the way for urbanization to flourish on an archipelago that could never—with its local water supply—have supported such multitudes.[21]

On April 30, 1889, the newly elected president, Benjamin Harrison, followed in George Washington's footsteps and commemorated the centennial of the Founding Father's historic journey. Harrison boarded a train in Washington that rattled along headed for Elizabethport, New Jersey. The president, who had celebrated his own inauguration in a terrible downpour the month before, then stepped aboard a steamship that, under beautiful blue skies, sailed down the Kill Van Kull before dropping into Upper New York Bay. Throngs of people scrambled atop the seawall lining the Staten Island shore. With red, white, and blue bunting everywhere, and whistles screaming, the steamship sliced through the freezing, steel-gray water on its way to the East River. After the vessel moored alongside Wall Street, some old codgers from the Marine Society of New York (a couple of them over eighty)—the same organization that had ushered Washington into town—dusted off their oars and prepared a launch to barge Harrison ashore. The *Boston Evening Journal*, in its report on the centennial, called New York Harbor "the most beautiful of American bays."[22]

That was then. It is no exaggeration to say that in New York Harbor there was no more sudden and significant environmental change than the decline in oxygen levels that began at the turn of the twentieth century. In the world of coastal ecosystems, dissolved oxygen is the currency of life. Marine animals are highly dependent on it for growth and survival. Below 55 percent saturation, the abundance and number of fish species begin to drop. When the oxygen saturation falls under 30 percent, the water is said to be hypoxic. Hypoxia has been shown to cause significant changes in the coastal benthos. Crustaceans are especially sensitive to oxygen depletion. The waters immediately surrounding Manhattan Island likely experienced hypoxia (caused by a nutrient overdose) as early as the 1850s. It is even possible that some areas had already become completely bereft of oxygen (a condition known as anoxia). But what had been a localized problem evolved into a systemic one shortly after consolidation. The harbor underwent a literal sea change.[23]

The dark side of the waterscape first manifested itself in New Jersey's Passaic valley. The Passaic River had come a long way from the days when George Washington and his army took time off from battle to visit the majestic basalt rocks and thundering waters of Great Falls in Paterson. Back then shad and sturgeon still swarmed up the serpentine river to spawn before being stopped by the massive lava rocks at the foot of the waterfall.[24]

Overpowering change came to pass beginning in the mid–nineteenth century. A railroad made solid land of the water between Green Island off of Newark (a great spot for catching shad and smelt) and the west bank of the Passaic. Then in 1858 a dam built downstream from Great Falls delivered the coup de grâce to the spawning runs. In the period after the Civil War, the lower reaches matured into an early version of a giant, grimy industrial park. So much refuse and sewage poured into the river that in the 1870s, a drought joined with hot weather to induce eutrophication, bringing on the first fish kills. Efforts to crack down on the paper mills and other factories discharging waste initially inspired hope, but the sheer scale of the population growth and the sewage continued to befoul the once crystal-clear river. By the 1880s, the water had deteriorated to the point where the city of Hoboken, which relied on it for drinking, tapped the Hackensack River instead. In 1889 Newark—notorious for its poor sanitation, epidemic disease, and high death rate—also abandoned the river. By the end of the century, the only fish left in the Passaic River were the few that could tolerate the poorly oxygenated water and the degraded wetlands that flanked it.[25]

In 1902 the state of New Jersey pondered the lower river's despoiled condition and organized the Passaic Valley Sewerage District to address the issue. By then, an idea was circulating that would make the tainted stream New York's problem. As it happened, Newark Bay was far from the ideal place to be sending sewage. It was very shallow, not well flushed with water, and susceptible to high summertime water temperatures—precisely the conditions favorable to eutrophication. So the new agency aspired to build a sewer to reroute all the organic matter straight into Upper New York Bay instead. The Passaic watershed and its population (in 1900) of nearly a half million people would be delivering a little present to the big city to the east, right on the western edge, no less, of the harbor's main ship channel.[26]

New York's business class, naturally enough, did not look kindly on the plan. It was one thing to allow sewage to run into New York Bay from the adjacent land. That had been the custom for a very long while. But shipping it by trunk line—annihilating space with sludge, if you will—made the Chamber of Commerce (already concerned about New York's dwindling share of foreign trade) fear even more for the harbor's future. "Why not dump it into Newark Bay?" asked a merchant named Welding Ring about the Passaic plan to provide some rudimentary treatment. "We don't want it over here. If it is not a bad thing, let them keep it."[27]

The state of New York took legal measures to stop the scheme. But it lost in the end when it failed to show that the New Jersey sewage shuffle differed in any significant way from the longstanding New York practice of sending vast amounts of organic matter into the harbor. Federal law supported that conclusion. After all, the Refuse Act of 1899 barring the jettisoning of detritus into the nation's navigable waters included an exemption for sewage. Indeed, it is a little hard to escape the conclusion, given the timing, that the loophole in the 1899 law emboldened the Passaic authorities to build the trunk line in the first place.[28]

The struggle with New Jersey caused the waters of New York Harbor to be scrutinized more carefully than ever before. Several water quality studies took place during the first two decades of the twentieth century. The results showed significant ecological change. As New York completed the expansion of its Croton system, sewage deluged the harbor. Over seven hundred million gallons a day of it coursed in by 1910, filling the water with sediment particles and drifting plankton feeding off the nutrients in the waste matter. The waters around New York grew murkier. Speaking of the East River, one person recalled its earlier, more limpid state: "I remember the time, gentlemen, when you could go in twelve feet of water and you could see the pebbles on the bottom of this river." The darkening of the waters was not just an aesthetic issue but also a biological one. The lowered light conditions contributed to the loss of subaquatic vegetation such as sea grass. This was no ordinary grass. Ecologists consider it an "ecosystem engineer"—a life-form that sculpts a habitat for other plants and animals.[29]

Sewage, like night soil, is loaded with nitrogen. It thus played an important role in fostering plant growth. But when the plant matter died, photosynthesis went into reverse, as bacteria broke down the organic matter with the aid of oxygen. In 1909 levels of dissolved oxygen in New York Harbor began trending downward and continued on that course for over two decades. At first, the lower oxygen levels affected primarily the harbor north of the Narrows. What happened to Gowanus Creek in Brooklyn was emblematic of the trend.[30]

A physician recalled life along the creek in the 1850s as follows: "I lived within a stone's throw from the canal in those years when on the right bank entering the canal it was marsh land, it was not a basin in the sense that it is today [1911], and fishing right in that neighborhood and around was a daily occurrence. I remember treading for clams right near where Hamilton Avenue is passing over from Smith Street to Third Avenue, and my remembrance of the water in those days was that of being clean, pure salt water, with abundance of fish and fish food." But with the completion of the Gowanus Canal, factories and sewer outfalls filed in and oxygen levels slumped. A fifteen-foot relief sewer finished in 1892—designed to ease the effects of flooding likely brought on by the increasingly impermeable ground cover—played a particularly devastating role. As early as 1906, a water sample taken from the Gowanus Canal revealed an oxygen saturation of 0 percent. The Gowanus had reached rock bottom.[31]

Three years later, Newtown Creek fell into the same abyss. The Passaic River near Newark had just a 7 percent reading, and the Harlem River and the lower part of the East River also showed signs of distress, with average dissolved-oxygen levels below 65 percent. There is little question that all the water spewing into the city from the Croton watershed was driving the decline. The Harlem River's troubles are especially easy to explain. By 1909, Manhattan alone had 172 sewer outfalls, though roughly two-thirds of all the discharge flowed through just 29 outlets. Of these, 6 emptied into the Harlem River. The Harlem, moreover, had a surface area that was a mere fraction the size of the Hudson and East Rivers.[32]

But even the waters of the East River had deteriorated, indeed, to the point where the New York Aquarium no longer trusted them. Opened at the Battery in 1896, the aquarium instead serviced its exhibits with water brought by tanker all the way from Sandy Hook. "I am convinced from looking over certain old natural history books of this region," declared the director, Charles Townsend, "that a considerable portion of the aquatic life of the New York Bay region has disappeared." As an example, he mentioned the sea horse (*Hippocampus erectus*), a fish species at one time so common in New York Harbor that it was mistakenly given the scientific name *Hippocampus hudsonius*. However, by Townsend's day, the sea horse had been turned into a museum piece for exhibit at the aquarium. And in a sign of the ramifying effects of ecological change, the zoologist William Hornaday reported that osprey, which once nested on the rocks of the Palisades, had, by 1909, fled. New York Bay, he surmised, "no longer furnishes good fishing-ground for them." [33]

In 1909 New York celebrated the three hundredth anniversary of Henry Hudson's discovery. This was a highbrow affair organized by the elite to mark the ascent of New York into one of the most important and populous cities in the world. It was the booster celebration to end all booster celebrations: two weeks of parades beginning in Manhattan and extending out to the boroughs and up the Hudson River. But urban growth had its costs, a point that may have dawned on some of the revelers. George Frederick Kunz of the American Scenic and Historic Preservation Society, for one, was at some pains to highlight how human density had altered the natural kind. "[I]n our admiration of the beauties of the Hudson," Kunz reminded those at the dedication,

> we must not forget the practical problems that offer themselves in the case of a river that receives the drainage of a great city. The immense populations dwelling in New York city and its vicinity are pouring into the Hudson two million tons of sewage materials annually. This means that an enormous amount of valuable fertilizing material, derived from the products of the farms of the country, is irreparably lost in the sea, killing the fish, polluting the water. . . . If this two million tons of material annually wasted could be taken to some vacant land on Long Island, this would mean a great saving for the people, and would stop the drain upon the richness of the land.

As Kunz recognized, the path of organic matter had changed. Instead of a nutrient cycle, along the lines of the urban-rural network that George Washington observed, New York had gravitated toward an export economy. The open-loop system, in other words, had come to New York Harbor with a vengeance.[34]

By the First World War, with the city poised to eclipse London as the center of global capitalism, New York's world-historical significance rested on two pillars: finance and filth. As Sigmund Freud once wrote, "In reality, wherever archaic modes of thought have predominated or persist . . . money is brought into the most intimate relationship with dirt." There must have been a great deal of archaic thinking happening in New York. For never did the phrase "filthy lucre" seem so apt in describing the essence of a metropolis.[35]

The prospect of war distracted the attention of New York's progressive reformers; their concern for the fate of the harbor—expressed in thousands of pages of investigative reports testifying to collapsing oxygen levels—ended up in a filing cabinet somewhere. No action was taken on a comprehensive waste management plan for another seventeen years. Although a handful of rudimentary treatment plants went online beginning in 1884, they managed only to remove grit. Flushing remained the preferred mode for dealing with the nosedive in water quality, a point driven home by the opening in 1911 of a tunnel to send water from the head of the Gowanus Canal to Upper New York Bay—the public works equivalent of a giant enema.[36]

It did not help that the escalating nutrient load delivered to the harbor coincided, roughly speaking, with another important ecological shift: the plunge in the once prolific populations of oysters and menhaden, the latter a small, toothless, silvery fish with a big head and oily flesh. These two filter-feeder species sift suspended matter that blocks sunlight from reaching oxygen-producing marine plants. They are the "ocean's kidneys," removing excess nitrogen and phosphorus from the water.* Two of New York's most prolific filter feeders, both species feed

---

* Oysters will purify—assuming an average three-inch size—between ten and one hundred gallons of water a day; a single adult menhaden can filter an estimated four gallons in just a minute.

on something that the nutrient-rich harbor excelled at producing: *phytoplankton*, a word that comes from Greek meaning "drifting plant matter." The booming human population, prodigious water supply, and consequent rise in nutrient-rich liquid caused a corresponding explosion in this passively floating life-form. These microscopic organisms include blue-green algae, a bacteria and ancient form of life; diatoms, largely nonmotile organisms with handsome silica shells; and dinoflagellates, unicellular organisms with tails to propel themselves along. Without the oysters and menhaden around to eat them, the phytoplankton died after just a few days and settled to the ocean floor where they contributed to lower oxygen levels as they decomposed.[37]

Hundreds of square miles of oyster beds once lined the harbor. And the benefits extended beyond the health of New York's water life. The *Independent Reflector* in 1753 called the oyster "the daily Food of our Poor." Pehr Kalm, an eighteenth-century Swedish naturalist famous for his travels around America, pointed out that "there are poor people who live all year long upon nothing but oysters and a little bread."[38]

Despite its impressive size, the evidence suggests that the colonists may have endangered the oyster stock not long after they first arrived. As we have seen, in 1658 the Dutch felt compelled to ban digging for oysters in the waters around lower Manhattan. The colonists made lime and paved streets with the shells, apparently with such abandon as to elicit this early conservation measure. By 1715, the colony passed An Act for Preserving of Oysters. Fifteen years later came An Act for the *Better* Preservation of Oysters. This law singled out slaves for raking oysters all throughout the year and bringing them to market "in Such great Quantities that the Oyster banks are Like to be soone Destroyed." None of these measures did much good, and sometime in the first third of the nineteenth century, oystermen embraced artificial methods, transplanting young oysters from the remaining robust beds to the now depleted ones.[39]

Artificial cultivation and the continued existence of substantial natural seedbeds (Newark Bay, Raritan River) jump-started the oyster trade. By the early 1850s, fifty square miles of water off Staten Island's south shore had reopened for business. Nearby was the free-black community of Sandy Ground. Many of these African-Americans had fled Chesapeake Bay because of a restrictive Maryland law requiring a white person to vouch for them before receiving a license to operate an oyster sloop. Together the African-American oystermen, who likely enjoyed the independence offered by maritime pursuits, developed a set of customary practices for staking out claims to beds. They also invented a philosophy of the commons founded on the freedom of anyone to harvest natural oysters (those not planted and staked). Oystering remained a small-scale, artisanal pursuit even through the Civil War. By then, the oyster had emerged as the quintessential New York food. In 1869 so many oyster shops lined the streets that one reporter exclaimed, "New York without oysters would cease to be New York!"[40]

That New York began to vanish in the last quarter of the nineteenth century. Dredgers now operated on steam power, nurturing a vast expansion in the acreage planted with oysters. The oyster trade, in other words, matured into a capital-intensive enterprise. The most important company, at least with respect to the waters of Staten Island, was J. and J. W. Ellsworth, a Manhattan-based operation started in 1873. Ellsworth would eventually control hundreds of acres in Prince's Bay with a workforce numbering 250 men. The advent of refrigerated railroad cars enabled the firm to ship seed oysters to places as far away as Sacramento Bay—110 carloads in 1901 alone.[41]

The small-scale oystermen hung on, but just barely. As the industry grew more concentrated, the Staten Island baymen who worked the natural beds cried out. In 1905 they protested the state's leasing of beds to the "oyster trust." State law had once limited how much acreage could be leased and restricted planting to those beds that no longer produced oysters naturally. "Under the law," explained a lawyer for the baymen, "the natural oyster beds are common property, where any one may fish, and they cannot be leased." But the truth was that these earlier laws had been watered down. The acreage limitation had been set aside. And the stipulation that the natural grounds must contain no oysters before being leased had been qualified. Now they just had to be devoid of bivalves for five years.[42]

As late as 1905, naturally occurring oysters cloaked the bottoms of Newark Bay, the Arthur Kill, and even the Jersey Flats. But over the next two decades, the beds experienced a frontal assault as four different trends came together. First, the large-scale oyster companies such as Ellsworth, unlike the Sandy Grounders, shunned self-regulation. They produced for markets across the United States and Europe, and thus operated as floating factories, with dredgers clanking away as they scraped the beds clean. Such an operation was a long way from the slow, moiling work of the old oystermen who raked the last of the natural beds with long, wood-handled tongs. We know the species must have been feeling the effects of overharvesting because of bans on steam-powered dredging that went into effect.[43]

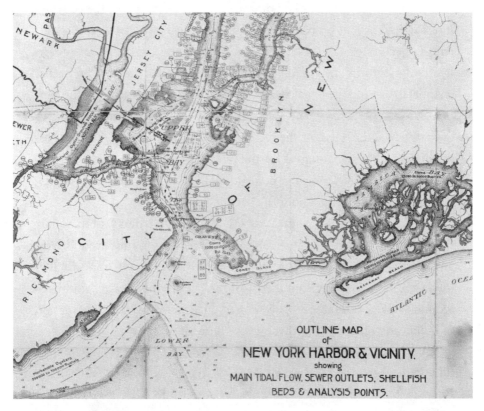

This 1905 map shows the hundreds of sewer outlets serving New York's population interposed with the remaining shellfish grounds.

Second, contamination cropped up as an increasingly serious problem. Because they are filter feeders, oysters concentrate whatever is in the water, including bacteria found in sewage and toxic metals, as well as toxins from harmful algal blooms. The sweeping beds off of Staten Island (Prince's Bay) were implicated in typhoid fever and shut down in 1916. Factory waste also imperiled them. By the early 1920s, the New York metropolitan area had soared into the largest center for oil refining in the world. The state of New York, it is true, banned the discharge of acid oil waste. But corporations such as Standard Oil found a much more congenial legal climate in New Jersey, where a laissez-faire approach to factory pollution prevailed to the detriment of oyster beds, especially those surrounding Staten Island.[44]

Third, in the generation following 1880, dredgers gouged out channels to improve navigation and destroyed many oyster beds. The passages into the harbor had been deepened in 1884 to thirty feet to accommodate larger vessels. In 1898, the year New York consolidated into its five-borough form, the Chamber of Commerce called for an even deeper channel to cater to the larger steamships being built at the turn of the century such as the *Oceanic*. The resulting Ambrose Channel, cut to a depth of forty feet and named for the engineer John W. Ambrose, who spent his dying days lobbying Congress for the money, was authorized in 1899 and completed in 1914. To further accommodate the larger vessels, dredging projects multiplied throughout the harbor.[45]

And fourth, as the natural seedbeds gave out, planters had to go farther afield for oysters to transplant to the depleted grounds around New York. By the early 1920s, even the seed grounds of distant Connecticut—the last good remaining source for spat to supply the dredged-out beds around New York Harbor—succumbed, victimized by the construction of bulkheads, channel "improvements," and factory waste.

A remarkable change had occurred. Oysters had once been so plentiful and inexpensive that simply raking them up was considered déclassé. Even as late as the turn of the century, bountiful supplies inspired the rich to gorge themselves in oyster-eating competitions. (In 1898 a Wall Street insurance man named Thomas G. Greene stuffed down 228 oysters in just half an hour.) And perhaps the wealthy continued to indulge in such conspicuous consumption. But not the poor. In a 1920 report on the decline of the oyster industry, the New York State Conservation Commission predicted, with great accuracy, the oyster's journey from poverty into the world of haute cuisine: "Whereas oysters were once plentiful, and were food for the common people, the present conditions are forcing them gradually to become classed as luxuries. With a further depletion of the natural growing areas, the food will be further removed from the people, and oysters will become a delicacy."[46]

The ecological impact of the flagging beds was equally significant. Extracting oysters from the ecosystem allowed more plankton to settle to the bottom of the harbor, where it broke down and exacted a toll in yet more precious oxygen. Bottom fish such as flounder and striped bass swam toward the surface to breathe; lobsters and crabs crawled out of their burrows toward shallow spots where predation befell them; and dead zones sprang up as summer rolled around and temperatures rose, stratifying the water into a warm top layer that trapped a dense, cold, toxic bottom one largely devoid of life.[47] It is not too much to say that the waters surrounding New York had been turned upside down.

It would have helped if at this point the huge schools of menhaden—or mossbunkers, as the Dutch colonists called them—had been around to aid in the harbor's ecology. But here too factory fishing had driven this dull but indispensable animal from the inshore waters.

Back in the colonial period, the Indians harvested menhaden that swam close to the coast to help fertilize the soil. The colonists continued the practice. In the middle of the nineteenth century, experimentation revealed that a little industry could render oil from the fish. Menhaden factories set up shop off of Gardiners Bay on the eastern end of Long Island, and also at Barren Island in Jamaica Bay. One of Jamaica Bay's largest landmasses, Barren Island contained a nice-sized, green salt meadow. Easily accessible from the mainland at low tide, it made for attractive grazing land. Beginning in the last third of the nineteenth century, however, the island earned a reputation in what today is called resource recovery. Dead animals, offal, and menhaden harvested from the bay entered the factories, and out came two principal commodities: fertilizer and fish oil. It was not a particularly inviting environment. One garbologist called Barren Island "the largest, most odorous accumulation of offal, garbage, and alienated labor in the history of the world."[48]

After boiling down the fish, the menhaden factories pressed out the valuable oil for use in tanning leather, fueling lamps, paint, and lubricant. In the 1870s, the largest mossbunker company on Long Island—Hawkins Brothers—opened a factory on Barren Island. J. W. Hawkins, who plowed the proceeds of his fish venture into supporting his political ambitions as a New York state senator, lobbied so hard for his business that he came to be known as Mossbunker Hawkins.[49]

Menhaden swim in schools, and colonial farmers, seeking fertilizer, snagged them with simple fishing nets right from the shore in astonishing numbers: twenty oxcarts' worth in a single haul, by one 1795 account. (It took a massive eight thousand menhaden to manure just a single acre.) In the mid–nineteenth century, the invention of the purse seine—a giant drawstring pocketbook for fish—made it possible for fishermen to capture entire schools in offshore waters. Mechanization then followed. Steam-powered hoists emptied the purse seines automatically and put still more pressure on the menhaden stocks. The once vast numbers of menhaden that thronged the coast from Florida to Nova Scotia showed signs of overharvesting. Maine passed a law in 1865 prohibiting purse seining "within three miles of the shore." While it was not then known that menhaden grazed on phytoplankton, it was evident that the fish fed on "unutilized organic matter." Equally important, the fish are a critical link in the food chain in that they serve as prey for bluefish, weakfish, and striped bass, which don't eat plankton. The fate of one of the most important fish in the sea was on the cusp of great change.[50]

By the 1870s, inshore waters around New York no longer swarmed with menhaden as they once had. Fish populations fluctuate naturally from season to season and year to year because of shifts in ocean temperature and larger changes in climate. But there is little doubting the ecological impact of industrial fishing as steamer after steamer unfurled its seines (harming biodiversity by accidentally snaring six thousand sharks off New Jersey in one four-month period) in the quest for maximum yield. A Raritan Bay fisherman recalled in 1884 seeing "one hundred acres of these menhaden flapping their tails and making the water fly. But now we would hardly see any." Another noted that the menhaden furnished subsistence for the poor. "[I]f the Government only gave them the privilege of using guns off here to shoot these fellows," he said about the baymen and their murderous rage for the so-called menhaden pirates, "they would do it free gratis."[51]

William Brown, a notary public from the fishing community of Point Pleasant, New Jersey, deplored how the "natural rights" of the people for "food and sustenance" had been sacrificed to the interests of "foreign fish marauders." "Year by year," exclaimed an 1882 jeremiad, "our fishermen have seen the supply of food fishes on our coast grow smaller and smaller." Brown put his finger on the essential issue when he pointed to the pitched battle between "organized capital, to the amount of millions of dollars, against unorganized and poor fisherman." Much as Brown predicted, Mossbunker Hawkins and his business associates prevailed on Congress not to intervene to restrain the factory fishing. No significant check was ever placed on the purse seiners.[52]

Although some half measures took hold on the state level—New York banned purse seining in Raritan Bay in 1888 but repealed the law four years later—the menhaden fishery continued its inexorable decline. Toward the end of the nineteenth century, a shakeout began as the collapsing fish population sent the industry reeling. A period of consolidation ensued. A combined British and American enterprise called the American Fisheries Company gobbled up factories and vessels. The venture even recruited Standard Oil, which aspired to blend the fish oil with factory waste to produce an alternative fuel for lighting fixtures. But shortly after its incorporation in 1898, American Fisheries shuttered its factories on Barren Island as the fishery shifted out to the high seas. Thus did the loss of the menhaden coincide with the decline of the once equally prolific oyster, depriving New York Harbor of two of its best defenses against eutrophication—and at the worst possible time.[53]

• • •

It is easy to make the mistake of assuming that the decline of the once oxygen-rich waters of New York Harbor was somehow inevitable. But in reality, this great transformation happened because high-density development in Gotham rested on limitless growth and resource use. The idea of New York as an open-ended proposition shaped the city's imperial approach to water and seemed to discourage efforts to grapple with the intensifying pollution—or at least made the question of how to deal with it difficult to address. This was a point made by an English engineer named John D. Watson in 1913. "If there were any prospect of limits being set to the bounds of New York," he wrote, ". . . the disposal of the sewage—vast as the volume of that is—would be comparatively easy. But it is quite otherwise."[54]

Among the great cities in the Western world, New York stood out in two respects: per capita water consumption remained uniquely high, and little attention was paid to the ultimate fate of the sewage. That left the city in the unenviable position as the wastewater capital of the planet. As one 1914 report concluded, "It is probable that there is no other city in the world within whose crowded districts so much sewage is discharged."[55]

Things were different in Europe. There the per capita rate of water consumption in cities was half that in the United States. In part because of the smaller amount of water consumed, the utilization of sewage for farming purposes in a closed-loop system proved more viable. Take Berlin. In the early twentieth century, the city had more than forty thousand acres of land dedicated to so-called sewage farms that raised everything from cabbages and potatoes to beets and rye. According to one account, "The Berlin farms are the most extensive and perhaps the best managed in the world." Nor was Berlin alone. Paris also made substantial use of such farms beginning in the latter half of the nineteenth century, as did Britain, where over two hundred were in operation in 1883. Nor was the idea unknown in the United States.[56]

New York City, on the other hand, entertained only briefly the idea of channeling nutrients to farmland on Long Island. Ultimately, the sheer volume of water and the high transportation costs caused the plan to be dismissed. To be fair, there was little scientific support for the closed-loop system. As one Harvard professor put it in 1910, "The primary question is no longer how to extract the small amount of fertilizing matter it contains, with the idea of making a fortune by sewage farming or a valuable artificial manure, but how to rid ourselves of the sewage that it may do the smallest amount of harm at the least possible cost."[57]

In fact, when these words were written, New York City was causing the most amount of harm in the least possible time. An argument has been made that the oxygen decline in New York Harbor happened very suddenly. Although the waters around Manhattan likely experienced hypoxic conditions by the 1850s, the harbor as a whole was largely unaffected by the increase in population and the consequent organic pollution load. This was because of the continued existence through most of the nineteenth century of privies and cesspools, which kept organic matter from ending up at sea. Added to this was the presence of healthy populations of oysters and menhaden. But as the use of water closets and indoor plumbing increased—as it did beginning in the late nineteenth century—and the population density of filter feeders declined, the nutrient load increased dramatically. It is conceivable that in the span of just sixteen years (1900 to 1916), the waters surrounding New York went from close to an average of 100 percent oxygen saturation to less than half that amount. The key shift, populationwise, occurred when the number of people flushing into sewers rose from 2.5 million to 3.5 million, causing dissolved-oxygen levels to plunge to 47 percent. Thus the natural limit to New York City, it can be argued, occurred precisely in the early twentieth century when the integrity of the harbor was compromised. Put another way, from a marine-life perspective, New York needed to stop growing in population at almost exactly the point, ironically, when it enacted its bold, boundary-breaking plan for Greater New York.[58]

Needless to say, restraint was not foremost on the minds of those who ruled the city. Continued growth through the acquisition of a vast water supply was their main preoccupation, a point underscored in 1917 when the Catskill system came online. More people died in the construction of the 120-mile aqueduct—237—than perished while building Hoover Dam on the Colorado River. The Ashokan Reservoir, located seventy miles north of New York City in the Hudson valley, would eventually feed the tunnel more than half a billion gallons each day, but at the cost of dislocating nearly two thousand people in the Catskills. The reservoir forced them out of the fertile bottomland condemned by the city and onto less desirable clay soils in the nearby hills. Eight communities eventually disappeared.[59]

When it came to water, New York was the new Rome. In 1917 Edward Hagaman Hall of the American Scenic and Historic Preservation Society, founded in 1895 to protect natural scenery and landmarks, observed that even "[t]he greatest of the famous Roman aqueducts was only half as long as this one, and in technical difficulty was, in comparison, like building houses with children's 'blocks.'" George McClellan, the former mayor, argued that the Panama Canal—opened in 1914—for all its hardships, did not compare with the aqueduct, which he dubbed "the greatest piece of water supply engineering, if not the greatest engineering achievement of any kind, in the world." But looked at from a different perspective, the aqueduct served as an immense nutrient pipeline. In the New York metropolitan area as a whole, untreated sewage increased from 622 million gallons a day in 1910 to 739 million gallons in 1920. The nitrogen loading to the Hudson-Raritan Estuary in the period between 1880 and 1920, it is estimated, grew more than five times to over twenty-eight thousand metric tons, or more than half the peak reading (which came in 1970) for this crucial element. Nor were there any signs that the Catskills project had done anything to quench the city's thirst. In fact, between 1916 and 1920, the annual rate of increase in demand for water stood at forty-two million gallons a day, nearly three times the rate at the turn of the century.[60]

By the twenties, New York Harbor had a raging oxygen disaster on its hands. The problem, of course, was not all New York's fault. Communities from Westchester to Newark had built sewers routing nutrients to the surrounding waters. Commercial fisheries in Newark Bay and the Passaic River all but ceased to exist by the early twentieth century, and avian populations declined. One study concludes that "the mid-1920s probably represented a significant low point in the health of the ecology of the estuary." To put the problem in ecological terms, a positive feedback on oxygen had begun. In a context of imperiled oyster and menhaden fisheries, increasing amounts of organic matter in particulate form entered the harbor and settled to the bottom. That initial disturbance led to a drop in dissolved oxygen, a condition that further compromised the future of these two filter feeders because they had evolved in a more aerated environment. Without these species grazing on phytoplankton, more organic matter filled the waters. That led to still less dissolved oxygen, as bacteria set to work decomposing the surplus organic input. It was the kind of inadvertent, runaway ecological dilemma that can happen in a complex system like New York Harbor.[61]

Once the population tributary to the harbor crossed the threshold of 3.5 million people, one study concluded, average dissolved-oxygen levels remained steady in the 40 percent range despite increasing demographic growth. But the average figures obscure the stunning change that had come over these troubled waters. In 1926 the Harlem River's average summer oxygen saturation plummeted to just 14 percent. Oxygen in the lower East River fell to 13 percent—too low for most fish to survive. According to an Army Corps of Engineers report, in the waters north of the Narrows, there was not "enough oxygen during one third of the year to permit active fish to live and the remainder of the time it is impossible for even sluggish varieties to thrive." While the city had spent roughly two hundred million dollars accumulating a water supply that would have made the Romans envious, it had done virtually nothing to address the Goliath flushing problem that had devastated the marine environment.[62]

As a result, natural population densities declined, and biodiversity suffered. Consider shad, one of the most significant fish species in the New York area. The amount caught in the Hudson increased until 1901, when the catch stood at seventeen million pounds a year; three years later, the haul amounted to less than a third that amount. Whatever else might be said about the slump, the enhanced nutrient load was bound to have played a key role.[63]

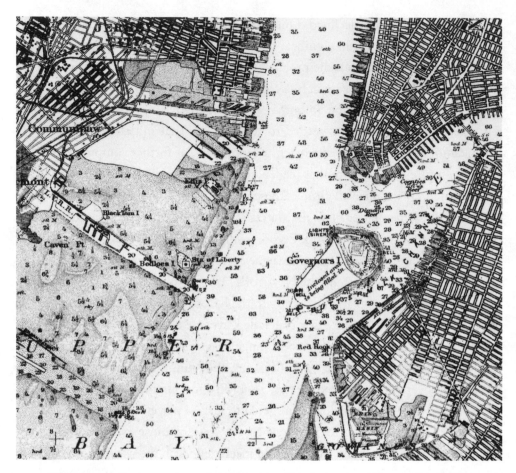

This 1910 nautical map shows the dense development encroaching on the harbor after a decade-long population surge of 1.3 million people—demographic growth that contributed to the transformation of water quality. Governors Island is shown being filled in with rock excavated in building New York's first subway.

Likewise, an inventory of mollusks compiled in the late nineteenth century uncovered significant species diversity, but then things changed. By 1920, fourteen out of a total of fifty-seven species in the waters surrounding Staten Island had become either rare or especially rare. Some of the mollusks relied on subaquatic vegetation for habitat. But with all the particulates coursing into the harbor (sewage and sediment), the underwater greensward suffered as turbidity increased and the grass was forced to compete for light with phytoplankton. Another threat to the sea grass came from dead algae. A brown blanket of partially decomposed matter covered the grass leaves, reducing the available light and, thus, photosynthetic potential and oxygen produced. And as the habitat became degraded, marine life struggled. The decline of the oyster beds, in particular, had ramifying effects. Oyster reefs are important nursery grounds for fish, including shad. The compromised reefs impacted all kinds of life-forms—from sponges and anemones to barnacles and worms—that glommed on to the shell substrate etched across the bottom of the harbor.[64]

As New York above ground grew demographically and exploded into three dimensions—giving birth to its iconic skyline—the surrounding waters flattened like a pancake. Though not widely recognized as such, the dense complexes of plants and animals found along the coast are as biologically rich as forests or savannas. Only the viscosity of seawater relative to air, some ecologists have argued, keeps us from realizing this elemental fact. The hard truth was that by early in the twentieth century, New York's coastal waters had experienced an extraordinary transformation. In the language of ecology, New York Harbor went "from complex and diverse 3-dimensional biological habitats to simple 2-dimensional sediments and rocky surfaces populated by scattered organisms."[65]

In 1911, on the hundredth anniversary of the proverbial grid that had paved the way for high-density development, there was no celebration. And given what is now known about the legacy of New York's mushrooming growth on the harbor, perhaps that was just as well.[66]

PART 3

NIGHT COMES TO THE MARSHES

1900–1980

9 THE ROAD TO HERMITVILLE

While it is often said that New York is one of the most highly engineered environments on the face of the earth, what is even more remarkable is that this massively altered landscape arose in the middle of
what was, just a hundred years before, a swamp. Or, to use more precise
terminology, Greater New York materialized out of a system of tidal
wetlands, a sprawling delicate green world of marsh grass that sheltered
box turtles, garter snakes, Fowler's toad, and spring peeper tree frogs, a
world suffused with the high-pitched sounds of the spotted sandpiper
and the tinny rapping of the clapper rail, a world of ocean breezes and
salty smells. On Long Island, these soggy marshes extended along the
south shore from Jones's Island through to Jamaica Bay and Coney Island. On the north, in the borough of Queens, unfolded the Flushing
Meadows, shot through with lazy brooks. Staten Island had its Great
Kills and Fresh Kills: wide-open marshes crawling with raccoon and
mink searching for clams. There were the wetlands of the eastern Bronx
and, of course, the massive Hackensack Meadows—a dense hinterland
of majestic Atlantic white cedar, marsh grass, and sedge overseen by
hawks, harriers, and osprey; a place that had thus far thumbed its nose
at each wave of conquerors. By one calculation made early in the twentieth century, some three hundred square miles of wetland blanketed the

ground within a mere twenty-five-mile radius of New York's city hall. That was an area more than thirteen times the size of Manhattan, and much of it was about to wind up buried beneath asphalt and concrete.[1]

If the deoxygenating effect of urban growth defined ecological history in the nineteenth century, the reform of this once breathtaking expanse of wetlands came to distinguish the period that followed. By 1897, New Jersey was already contemplating a "comprehensive public improvement" of the Hackensack Meadows that would leave "the whole tract of marsh land . . . wiped out at one stroke." A slightly later account—citing the nearly three million cubic yards of material (imagine a giant box, 432 feet on each side) placed from 1902 through 1905 in marshes spanning all the way from Newark to Staten Island to Newtown Creek—concluded that "[t]he possibilities of this reclamation are almost boundless."[2]

How did these dreams become a reality? The short answer is that the quest for urban growth spread out beyond the initial core in Manhattan and Brooklyn, and as it did so, the original marshlands declined by nearly 80 percent. But, of course, that simply raises the question of why urban development dispersed across the metropolitan area in the first place.[3]

It turns out that by the early twentieth century, New York had run into a problem with its geography. New York City was slipping as a port; the problem was logistical.[4]

The major railroads doing business in the region tended to locate their terminals in New Jersey (between Greenville and Weehawken), while the shipping lines operated on the New York waterfront. Transporting goods from the rail terminals to the marine ones proved awkward and rested on a fleet of lighters: large barges for transferring cargo. A veritable armada—as many as two thousand lighters at times—packed the harbor. During the First World War the congestion, especially during the dead of winter, when cold and ice slowed down waterborne traffic, backed up freight trains all the way to Pennsylvania.[5]

Nearly everyone agreed that to resolve New York's geographic dilemma, the metropolis should be expanded. Once again, destiny demanded density. Thurlow Weed Barnes, the grandson of the political boss

Thurlow Weed, captured the concurrence when he said, "[W]e cannot have too much of New York City." The problem confounded solutions. "Greater New York is in the position of a giant bound by iron bands," declared Marcus M. Marks, Manhattan borough president, in 1914. Since the eighteenth century, New York had been in the habit of dealing with congestion along the waterfront by simply tearing down old piers and wharves and nosing out farther into the harbor. But the controversy over

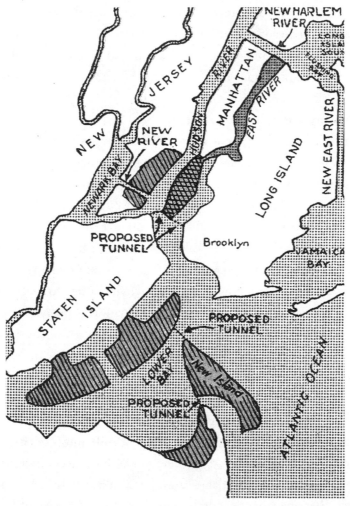

Thurlow Weed Barnes was responding to ideas like this one put forth in 1914 to reclaim some fifty square miles of land from the harbor. Similar kinds of plans persist to this day.

these encroachments in the nineteenth century, followed by federal intervention in 1888 limiting any further colonization of the navigation
channels, had the city hemmed in.[6]

By the early twentieth century, in an effort to accommodate larger
steamships, there began the construction of the Chelsea Piers, a project
that forced the city to turn inward and condemn a block of land. With
the piers completed in 1910, the city began a similar project farther north
along the Hudson. In other words, New York was being forced to canni-
balize itself. As one publication explained, "the City found that it could
push out its pierheads no farther, and in a condition of real extremity
it began that recent project of desperation and prodigious expense—
the extending of piers and slips inland into Manhattan waterfront—the
most valuable land in the world."[7]

Inevitably the question was raised: Should New York continue in
the port business? New York's mercantile community began to realize
that one way out of the dilemmas posed by the decline of the port was to
reach across the waters to New Jersey. The Chamber of Commerce began
to voice the idea of a regional authority that would be free of Tammany
politics and other petty provincialisms to conduct the work necessary to
revitalize the entire lower Hudson River's economic potential. In 1917 a
joint harbor commission was formed to address the problems raised by
New York's unique geography. "Physically we find a territory very much
cut up by waterways," the commission explained. It initially endorsed a
kind of giant conveyor belt designed to haul freight from the railroads
in New Jersey under New York Bay to marine terminals in Manhattan. It also called for more transformation of marshland into port space,
replicating developments at the new Port Newark Terminal, where, by
1915, five hundred acres of solid ground had been reclaimed from marsh
and swamp forest and a channel driven a half mile into the city. What
happened at Newark was to be the new model for a decentralized port
involving the conquest of wetlands from Jamaica Bay to the Hackensack
Meadows. Regionalizing the port would open the way for Manhattan to
specialize in its new métier: real estate and finance.[8]

In 1921 the Port of New York Authority was founded to address the growing pains of this island community. The port district spanned from Long Island to eastern New Jersey and from Sandy Hook all the way up the Hudson River into Westchester. The authority was charged with devising a unified system to solve the port's logistical problem. Its mission came down to figuring out how to move freight efficiently—a core precept of the Progressive Era—across the expansive waters of New York. Its goal, in other words, was nothing less than to overcome New York's geography. Building on earlier ideas, the authority developed a comprehensive plan that would have warmed the heart of any model-train enthusiast, aspiring to wrap the metropolitan area in a massive transportation network involving fifteen rail lines and twelve freight terminals. It was a train system that would have done a railroad tycoon like Cornelius Vanderbilt proud. But it never made it past the blueprint stage because the railroad companies refused to go along. Never mind that this was hardly a time of excess faith in government power.[9]

What to do with New York emerged in the 1920s as the single most important question in urban planning circles. There were all kinds of ideas afloat, including one that combined an expansive notion of a greater New York with the Port Authority's interest in tunnels. "New York City, now credited with being the most populous city in the world, must find more territory," declaimed one magazine in touting the idea. The project would add six square miles to Manhattan and tie the metropolitan area together with tunnels between New Jersey, Staten Island, and Brooklyn. The new landmass would absorb Governors Island and even Bedloe's Island, where the Statue of Liberty stood guard. "[N]o longer will Liberty cast the rays from her light over the stagnant waters at her feet. Instead they will illuminate the roofs of high office buildings." These were heady days indeed.[10]

Less radical in its intentions was the Regional Plan Association (RPA) formed in 1922 and funded by the Russell Sage Foundation. The group espoused the virtues of the growth imperative. As its economic director put it, "Instead of explaining why so large a portion of the population is found in the urban areas, one must give reasons why that portion is not even greater." But unlike earlier growth advocates in New

York, who took a laissez-faire approach to the issue, the RPA believed that density necessitated control and proper planning. Firmly set within the Progressive Era mold, the group tried to develop a landscape plan that would allow New York to proceed efficiently in executing its mission as the rising capital of capitalism. "The raison d'être of a city is to carry on business," its general director, Thomas Adams, once explained. It was growth or die at the hands of one's competitors—a prospect as compelling for those in real estate as it was for those who ruled the city and worried that New York might lose ground to another urban area.[11]

The idea was to spread urban cores over the landscape in an orderly manner, to "bring the place of work closer to the home of the worker." Congestion was to be addressed through a coordinated approach to transportation and a regional park system to deal with the shortage of open space. The plan called, in other words, for continued growth of the metropolitan area, arguing for spreading industrial development out around new cores beyond Manhattan. It foresaw "vast schemes of reclamation" in the marshlands and even raised the possibility of "a new city development" on the mudflats off the Bayonne Peninsula (Bergen Neck).[12]

A rival group, including the landscape architect Henry Wright and the philosopher Lewis Mumford, put forth a more measured approach to growth, though it gained little traction. Mumford would go on to offer one of the most devastating critiques of a growth plan ever written. The RPA's guiding assumption, which held "the extension and the congestion of the metropolitan area as inevitable," he wrote, was flawed. The plan was not all that different from the 1811 grid in that both met "the interests and prejudices of the existing financial rulers." Moreover, both plans "believed in the Manifest Destiny of New York. One saw Manhattan Island, the other the metropolitan region, as a limited area, waiting to be filled up." What Adams and his colleagues concocted, Mumford called "nothing bolder, more stirring, more radical if you will, than an orderly dilution of New York over a fifty-mile circle with double its present load of humanity."[13]

Whatever else might be said about the plans of the RPA and its rival, both, to one degree or another, made the obligatory nods toward more growth. In the long run, it was the RPA's plan that would have more impact on the landscape. As a result, marshlands across the New York metropolitan area would no longer be seen as unique, individual places but as a collective resource awaiting the hand of development. The man most firmly attached to that hand was Robert Moses.[14]

Born in 1888 in New Haven, Connecticut, Robert Moses was nine when the family moved to a brownstone located immediately off of Fifth Avenue in Manhattan. Moses grew up amidst substantial privilege, surrounded by cooks, maids, chauffeurs, walnut paneling, and framed Rembrandt prints. The money to support this lifestyle came from Moses's maternal grandfather, a German immigrant who was sent by his parents to New York and achieved great success—first as an importer, then in real estate—and from his father himself, who owned a department store. The product of Yale, Oxford, and Columbia, Moses measured a notch above six feet, and was powerfully built, dark complexioned, and blessed with a winning smile. He was also arrogant, condescending, bullying, not to mention devious, vindictive, and hardly above smearing his detractors. He kept himself in impeccable physical condition and was known to change into his swimming trunks in his limousine, dive straight into the Atlantic Ocean, and make a beeline for the horizon. The sea occupied a special place in his heart.[15]

Moses began his rise to power under Al Smith, the cigar-chomping, expectorating Tammany governor of New York. Smith actually supported the plan put forth by Mumford and his colleagues. But when Smith elevated Moses to power—appointing him president of the Long Island State Park Commission in 1924—he ceded control over the state's landscape to a man who would largely accept the boundless approach to growth outlined by Adams and the RPA. Though never elected to a public office, Moses was a genius at amassing power and holding on to it. For over four decades in his various appointed capacities, he built in New York like no one ever had—bridges, tunnels, parkways, and expressways that took an archipelago and made it into a unified city, unlocking the wilds of Long Island and Staten Island along the way—before being shunted aside at eighty years of age after clashing with activists who feared his projects would harm their communities.[16]

Moses was a virtuoso at building public works, but as a recent history of his life's work concludes, "Moses the visionary was second rate." One sociologist has put it even more bluntly: "Moses simply poured the concrete on the dotted lines indicated in the [RPA's] plan." Farseeing or not, by following through on the RPA's ideas, his building program would deeply impact the wetlands of New York.[17]

The role Moses played in sculpting the New York landscape has caused at least one student of his life to equate him with some monumental natural force, implying that the master builder was comparable in impact to the great glacier of thousands of years ago. Though there is some merit in this line of argument, it is wrong to attribute too pronounced a role to Moses in the landscape's transformation. The fundamental change to the region's wetlands that would define the ecological history of the twentieth century was not—indeed, could not be—the work of any one man. Moses represented a difference of degree, not of kind. He certainly poured a lot of concrete, but, of course, Moses had a lot of concrete to pour. Put a caravan of cement mixers in the hands of his nineteenth-century booster counterparts, and how many ponds and wetlands would have disappeared under the tide of pavement is hard to say. It must be emphasized that the growth imperative had been at work swallowing land and sea for decades by the time Moses assumed power.[18]

In the end, the rollback of the marshlands had three important effects. First, it helped bring more development close to the sea, while eliminating the very wetlands that served as storm buffers. Second, revamping wetlands into upland changed the nearshore habitat and contributed to the emergence of flora and fauna uniquely suited to live in close proximity to a large concentration of people. And third, the old customs of the marshlands (haying, hunting, foraging) died out. The result was the New York landscape we know today.

. . .

At the dawn of the twentieth century, the south shore of Long Island was a vast in-between—not quite land, but not quite water, either—of salt meadow, cordgrass marsh, beach, and white cedar swamp rent by tidal inlets driven through in storms. In the spring, flocks of shorebirds visited, searching for something to eat en route to breeding grounds in the Arctic, and found eggs spawned by the legions of hulking horseshoe crabs crawling up from the ocean floor. The birds were not the only visitors. Hunters and collectors also felt the attraction of this place. The hunters came for the ducks and snipe. More difficult to imagine are the collectors bent on pursuing what one historian (who studied the Middle Ages) has called "the primeval instinct of foraging." The south shore was not just an intermediary between land and sea but a commons: a place for gunning, for cutting salt hay for winter forage, and for collecting wild berries and mushrooms. A growing tide of real estate and recreational development, however, would put an end to these age-old traditions.[19]

The overturning of this way of life had its roots on Coney Island. Although now notorious for its crowds, Coney Island started out as a very lonely place. Geologically speaking, it was an outwash plain formed when silt and sediment from the melting Wisconsin ice sheet cascaded in. Then sea level rose, and sediment coursed westward along the coast (littoral drift) to create a barrier island. By the nineteenth century, the southern part of the island had evolved into a landscape of dunes—as high as thirty feet—and drifting sand. On the western third, colonial farmers once cut down cedar trees for posts. Most people recognized it as a very changeable place, where water enough to float a fifty-ton vessel eventually dried out into solid ground. A tidal creek—originally broad but considerably narrowed by the 1830s—snaked through a salt marsh and cordoned off the island from the mainland. Into the early twentieth century, leather-faced fisher folk were still setting nets in the creek to catch eels and flounder.[20]

In 1824 a man named John Terhune tried to bring the island into New York's orbit by building a bridge across Coney Island Creek so that stagecoaches could deliver guests to a sleepy inn with a superb ocean view. Within a generation, the island had garnered a reputation for "sea bathing and fishing." It was the railroad, however, that after the Civil War cleared the way for it to earn a spot among New York's most famous destinations. No fewer than five railways eventually knitted the barrier island together with Brooklyn. More land development ensued as the island amalgamated with the urban world on the other side of the creek.[21]

In the 1870s, and perhaps even later, a part of Coney Island lingered on as common property. The very idea of exclusive ownership of land remained a somewhat tentative proposition. Even as late as 1885, the *Real Estate Record* pointed out, "No practical man, much less a student of social science, will deny that the private ownership of the soil may be replaced by some better social arrangement." Thus when a hotel developer built a bulkhead and proceeded to turn the beach into private property, blocking the local people's customary access to the grounds, the commoners took offense. The resort responded by building a fence and hiring a security detail.[22]

In the early twentieth century, Coney Island Creek still separated the island from the mainland. Technically speaking, the creek was a tidal strait that ran between Gravesend Bay and Sheepshead Bay, the latter named for a fish that preyed on oysters and clams. The story of Coney Island's trip down the peninsular road begins with an enterprising young businessman by the name of Milton Kennedy, who devised a scheme for ridding Brooklyn of waste by employing out-of-service trolley cars in the dead of night. Kennedy had the foresight to also acquire a number of dumps in close proximity to the trolley lines. But what Kennedy did not foresee was the rapacious strivings of Anthony N. Brady, a financier and traction magnate who controlled the Brooklyn Rapid Transit Company and went on to amass spectacular wealth in the merger-and-acquisition business. Brady initially provided capital to Kennedy, but he then managed to co-opt the naïve businessman into a buyout. The really big loser was the city of New York, which overpaid Brady's consortium Brooklyn Ash Removal for hauling away coal and incinerator waste. By 1906, the ash had been used to fill in Coney Island Creek and the surrounding tidal lands. More than a hundred carloads a day, on average, made the trek to Coney Island. "The enormous quantity of material deposited," read a report in the *Times*, "is rapidly filling in the unsightly marsh." The newly made land—valued at five thousand dollars an acre—helped turn Coney Island into a misnomer.[23]

Robert Moses's Belt Parkway, designed to present motorists with scenic views of the sea, finished the job. Coney Island Creek had to be filled in farther to build the support structure for the road. Today two inlets are all that is left of it. But we get ahead of our story.[24]

In the 1890s, research established a link between the mosquito and malaria. This medical breakthrough turned out to dovetail nicely with increasing fears that nettlesome swarms of mosquitoes undercut property values. These developments in turn led those in real estate circles to conclude that Long Island's great swathes of salt marsh required a good drying out. A leader in this effort was a man named Henry Clay Weeks. Unlike his namesake, the antebellum Kentucky statesman Henry Clay, who was famous for his compromising stances, Weeks took a brass-knuckles approach to salt marshes. He wanted them gone. Under the assumption that land in dehydrated Manhattan was worth infinitely more than land just a few miles away in the "New Jersey swamps," Weeks, in his position as sanitary inspector for New York City's Department of Health, put together a power bloc to force the retreat of the marshes. To his cause he enlisted, for example, blue bloods such as William C. Whitney, the horse-racing financier who endured clouds of mosquitoes at his summer home on Sheepshead Bay. Weeks also conscripted a representative from Anthony Brady's Brooklyn Rapid Transit Company, as well as one from the Long Island Railroad. The latter had been trying to sell the island as a vacationland since the nineteenth century. They closed ranks behind Weeks's scorched-earth approach, aspiring to eradicate every last drop of water from the land.[25]

Weeks carried on his extermination campaign along Long Island's Gold Coast. Made famous by F. Scott Fitzgerald in *The Great Gatsby*, this was where the private estates of the Morgans, Pratts, and Phippses, and their polo fields and golf courses, gilded the landscape. In the employ of the North Shore Improvement Association, Weeks (and some colleagues) conducted a survey along Long Island Sound between Manhasset and Huntington Bays. Not much in the way of actual landscape change came out of the project. But the guiding logic behind it was nicely summarized by one Weeks disciple who predicted that a radical reshaping of the land would soon take place: "Piece by piece marsh and meadow land will be taken up and made mosquitoless, drained, and dyked. . . . All this spells improvement, the adding of large values to property very plainly."[26]

In fact, something less dramatic took place. Experiments on the Newark Meadows had shown that mosquitoes could be controlled with less radical measures than the complete annihilation of marshland. Simply digging ditches and ridding the land of pools of water would help. Moreover, the ditches created aquatic habitat conducive to killifish, a species that preys on mosquito larvae. With these ideas in mind, the city of New York took on the vast, muggy marshlands of Jamaica Bay, a morass of water, green islands, tortuous channels, and oyster reefs extending to close to twice the land area of Manhattan. "Tuesday will go down in the history of this war as 'Salt Marsh Day,'" said Charles F. Bolduan of the New York Department of Health in 1916. "Work will then begin on the ditching of the salt marsh areas adjoining Jamaica Bay."[27]

By the end of the year, workers opened a "miniature 'western front'" on the bay, carving ditches through an area the size of half of Manhattan. Over 1.7 million feet of ditches had gone in as New York waged its own little version of the Battle of Verdun, being fought in France that very year. More broadly speaking, in the five boroughs as a whole, over thirty thousand acres of freshwater and salt marsh came under the thumb of some kind of drainage scheme. Workers fired up newly invented ditch-digging machines to cut two-foot-deep trenches into the marshland. Sometimes they sprayed oil—creating a film that suffocated mosquito larvae—on ponds farther inland. "It is extremely gratifying to report that the only remaining large salt-marsh breeding place in the Borough of Brooklyn (that of the meadows in Dyker Beach Park) is to be taken care of permanently by the Park Department of that borough," crowed the sanitary engineer Eugene Winship. Dyker Beach had been an important habitat for migratory waterfowl as they flew between South America and the Arctic.[28]

What those who made their living in the salt marsh felt about the ditching is largely unknown. Hay cutters may have resented the interference with the flow of water, especially if it made it more difficult for them to harvest the meadow grass. The changes in the land, and more specifically, the tendency for ditched marshes, as one study put it, "to have fewer ponds than unditched marshes," may have reduced habitat for waterfowl and diminished hunting prospects. We know the tradition of the commons was in operation along parts of the Long Island shore (as at Coney Island), and it seems almost certain that it must have prevailed along other portions of New York's expansive network of tidelands. There may even have been resistance to the ditchdiggers, a whiff of which is caught when Winship wrote, "The hay cutters, the small boy, the waterfowl hunters and tidal influence will all contribute to place obstructions in the ditches, but will not completely block them."[29]

Modern scientific research allows us to feel more certain of the ecological impact. The ditching and draining lowered the water table and resulted in a change in vegetation, as salt marsh cordgrass found in low-marsh habitats yielded to high-marsh species more likely to thrive on the now better-drained soil, such as salt hay and marsh elder. Wading birds and waterfowl accustomed to shallow water more or less tapered off as tidal pools and mudflats disappeared. Marshes that underwent ditching also hosted fewer ponds than untouched ones, making them less hospitable to bird life. Overall, however, the trenches meant more aquatic and less terrestrial habitat. That change benefited some intertidal species such as fiddler crabs but dampened prospects for semiaquatic organisms like dragonflies, which, paradoxically, prey on mosquitoes.[30]

Like a giant army of moles, the ditchdiggers had orders to proceed east through the chain of salt marsh that stretched out along Long Island's south shore from Jamaica Bay to Great South Bay. A large section of the meadow on the eastern fringe of Jamaica Bay fell under the political jurisdiction of Nassau County. Originally part of Queens, this section of Long Island wound up outside the boundaries of the 1898 New York City consolidation arrangement. So, the following year, Nassau County was formed. In 1915, after a season of drenching rains, some of the wealthier property owners and the summer rental crowd established the Rockaway Peninsula Mosquito Extermination Association. But the group lacked any legitimate governmental power, a problem addressed the following year by Thomas A. McWhinney, a Brooklyn-born plumber turned Republican lawmaker from Nassau County. McWhinney introduced legislation officially declaring "[a]ny accumulation of water in which mosquitos are breeding" a nuisance. The move opened the way for entry onto "any or all lands within the county for the purpose of draining or oiling."[31]

In 1916, as New York City began to tackle the Jamaica Bay marshlands, the Rockaway Peninsula Association began ditching forty-two hundred acres of meadow abutting the bay in Nassau County. From there over 140 islands dotted the landscape east along the shore, many still wild and not even named. The islands varied in size from less than an acre to as much as a few hundred, and their importance to animal life is hard to overstate. On these nurturing lands, marine species from shrimp to sea horses to sea bass got their start. Egrets and herons flocked there in search of food. On the sandbars and mudflats in the middle of the complex of bays, clammers from the villages of Freeport and Baldwin dug for steamers and took them away by the boatload. Into this rich environment—a hunter's paradise of shorebirds and waterfowl—came the mosquito exterminators determined to carry out trench warfare, and, like twentieth-century conquistadores, they helped themselves to naming rights.[32]

One island was named for Ronald Ross, the Englishman who uncovered the mosquito's role in the transmission of malaria, one of the greatest advances in medical history. Another was named for Leland Howard, an entomologist who pioneered the use of oil as a larvicide. Yet another for Thomas Headlee, who, in his capacity as New Jersey's state entomologist, wore himself out trying to drum up support for mosquito extermination commissions like the one in Nassau County. And, of course, one went to honor Eugene Winship, who spearheaded New York City's drainage campaign. By the end of 1917, the Nassau swamp busters planned to have half of the south shore's thirty square miles of salt marsh under control. Early in the following decade, more than five million feet of drainage ditch sprawled out from the city line east to Seaford Creek.[33]

Over the course of just twenty years, the island's marshes underwent a profound change. The breeding habitat of the mosquito declined, while other species, including killifish and some crustaceans (fiddler crabs, for example), derived an advantage from the new environment. There is little question that the change cleared the way for development by reducing infectious disease. In 1921 malaria in Kings County, which killed at a rate of twenty-seven per ten thousand in 1871, had been eradicated.[34] If the transformation of the coast had ended when the last ditchdigger retired his shovel and the marshlands had been subjected to only a simple mosquito-control plan, the New York metropolitan area would be a much different place today. But in the supercharged economy of the 1920s, with the automobile casting its shadow over urban growth, Robert Moses had some far more ambitious ideas in store for Long Island's waterfront.

Back in the days of the Welshman Thomas Jones, the island set to host the most famous state park in the New York metropolitan area rested just a couple of feet above sea level. Jones had fought in the Battle of the Boyne on the east coast of Ireland (1690) on King James II's behalf and later was commissioned a privateer in reward for his courage. Jones's relationship with this salt-sprayed land fronting the Atlantic began after he married a woman named Freelove Townsend. Sometime in the latter part of the seventeenth century, his father-in-law gifted him an expanse—once the domain of the Massapequa Indians—along Long Island's south shore. Then, in 1710, Governor Robert Hunter made Jones the "rainger generall" of Nassau, a post that put him in charge of a whale fishery. But whatever the virtues of whaling, they lasted only three years before Jones died. Chiseled into his tombstone are these words about the land he had come to inhabit: "From Distant Lands to This Wild Waste He Came, This Seat He Chose, And Here He Fixd His Name."[35]

It is hard to say whether the person who chose those words chose them carefully. For the sake of argument, let us say that they did. The word *waste*, by the time of Jones's death in 1713, denoted a "wild and desolate region." But it also had legal meaning, signifying uncultivated land "not in any man's occupation, but lying common." As it turned out, the land whipped into shape for Jones Beach State Park belonged to the Town of Hempstead's stock of common land. Much of it was meadow located on small islands with names that have fallen off the map: Middle Crow Island, Petit Marsh, False Channel Meadow. The town leased the meadowland to husbandmen who headed out at sunup in the waning days of summer in search of fodder to winter their cows.[36]

A local named Daniel M. Tredwell, writing in 1912, described a landscape that was "perfectly level and is interspersed by creeks running in every conceivable direction." This land "produces a salt grass very healthful for cattle and sheep. And it being common land of the town, any townsman may harvest as much as he pleases." The unique environment gave rise to an important agricultural ritual: a custom called "marshing," or hay cutting. Farmers ditched the sodden ground to give it enough integrity for them to step on, mowed the hay, and carted it home. Marshing made ecological sense: the salt hay provided the nutrients that eventually gravitated back to the soil in the manure spread over the land. The salt hay grew naturally, without cultivation, and Tredwell, who was born in 1826, recalled heading down every summer to Mud Hole Hassock on Shell Creek, slightly west of today's Jones Beach State Park, to harvest it. One can only imagine what it was like for Tredwell out on a foggy morning, grass buffeted by a fitful wind, surrounded by a cacophony of bird life: yellow rail, sandpiper, godwits, mockingbirds, black-bellied plover. Tredwell remembered eating eels, clams, flounder, and fluke, and at times "indulging in the luxury of such game as snipe and duck." But by the time he published his reminiscence, the custom of marshing on the coastal common lands was drawing to an end. Suburban development had begun its brisk march across Long Island. "All is now passed and oblivion is fast closing over even the memory of these interesting local institutions."[37]

It was this low-lying terrain that Robert Moses would eventually come to see as crucial to a new vision of Long Island—indeed, of New York. In 1925 Moses, just settling into his job as president of the Long Island State Park Commission, wrote the Town of Hempstead as follows: "The rapid and continuing increase in the population in the metropolitan area, particularly in the Counties of Queens and Nassau is a well known fact; suffice it to say that in the county of Nassau alone, the number of motor cars has trebled in the last four years." The people in this new automobile age, Moses maintained, demanded not just parks but parks located along the shorefront. "In the County of Nassau," he helpfully pointed out, "there fortunately remains undeveloped a stretch of ocean beach extending from Jones' inlet to and beyond the Nassau-Suffolk County Line to the east, of sufficient size for development as an ocean park which would provide recreational enjoyment for many thousand people daily." The "plain or common lands" he had in mind had escaped development, and the point of his letter was to ask whether the town would hand over the property.[38]

Looked at from the ground up, what Moses did on Jones's Island was in some ways simply an extension of the earlier mosquito war. He saw a landscape in need of reform, just as the mosquito men did. Indeed, some of the very same people involved in the earlier drainage crusades helped Moses with his plan for Jones Beach. He yearned for a new environment along the shore just like the earlier generation of ditchdiggers, even if he was more inclined toward parks than real estate. He even once referred to himself, later in his life while defending himself against charges of power brokering, as simply a "ditchdigger." Of course, Moses never lifted a shovel. But from an ecological perspective, the long shadow he cast over the landscape is perhaps best conceptualized as emanating from one giant drainage plan. When he was finished with Jones's Island, the landmass had been liberated from the grip of the ocean and now sat elevated fourteen feet above the sea.[39]

The transformation of Long Island in part grew out of a shortage of open space. According to Moses's calculations at least, relative to the other boroughs (leaving aside sparsely settled Staten Island), by the 1920s Brooklyn and Queens retained the smallest percentage of park- and forestland: a mere 4.5 percent for the former and a miserable 1.5 percent for the latter. Manhattan, for all its density, still had a stock of 13 percent, and the Bronx slightly more. Of course, those with access to automobiles could flee the city and venture off to, say, Palisades Interstate Park (masterminded by Moses's friend George W. Perkins), but there was still no escaping the crowds, with park attendance up almost twenty-five times since 1915. Public space remained at a premium, and yet without it, as one conservationist argued, "the common people couldn't get out and wash themselves in the living waters of nature, or enjoy the beauties of nature without trespassing on somebody's private property." The commoners had lost their common rights to land, and, whether out of paternalism, shame, civic duty, or some combination of these, Robert Moses was determined to do something about it. Only what he did ended up alienating some people even further from the land.[40]

It was no accident that Moses chose Long Island as the laboratory for his first experiment in power brokering. Long Island is the largest island in the continental United States. By the time Moses showed up, it had been through a long era of conquest. Its waters had been tapped by the city of Brooklyn. With the consolidation of New York in 1898, its crystal ponds, lakes, and streams fell into the hands of the city. Its forests had long since been denuded to supply fuel to New York or burned up in the fires sparked by railroads chugging along. Cutover and bilked of its water, the island could justly be called a colony. Robert Moses would build on this earlier history.[41]

The island's geopolitics emanated from one simple fact: it was a cul-de-sac ending at the Atlantic Ocean. If its geography made it inhospitable to port development, and it did, its vast natural resources could still play a role in urban growth now that the city had turned upstate for its water. As Moses realized, Long Island possessed nearly all New York State's seashore. That long shorefront could furnish New York City— half the population of which lived on the landmass—with an escape from the hurly-burly of daily life. But as Moses saw it, Long Island had evolved much along the lines of the old 1811 grid plan, thwarting the people's journey to the salt air and sea. The grid plan had famously rationalized the lack of attention to open space by highlighting the bounteous surrounding waters. But, of course, Gouverneur Morris and his associates, as Moses was quick to interject, "did not anticipate then New York City would have a population of about 6,000,000 in 1925." It never dawned on the 1811 commissioners that there would be any need to preserve shorefront. Nor had the thought crossed anyone's mind on Long Island. Until Moses.[42]

It was hard to quarrel with such logic when one journeyed through the well-appointed private estates on the island's north shore, with their polo fields and butlers. But the story at Jones's Island and vicinity was a bit more complicated. There were no mansions here to speak of. The land for the beach and parkway that Moses dreamed of remained the common land of the towns, a place people went to camp or to shoot waterfowl. In 1924 Moses tried to prod the town of Babylon into putting the matter of surrendering its oceanfront to a vote. His efforts went nowhere. The *Babylon Leader*, arguing that the land was already a "natural park," urged that it be kept "as a heritage for its children." Another paper feared what a state park would bring: "lawns planted and fences erected and 'Keep off the Grass' signs stuck up where now folks may enjoy picnics." The town's baymen, who made their living raking clams, would not hear of it.[43]

Nor was Moses any more successful in the other towns, though he did eventually manage to get a referendum to cede the common lands on the ballot in Hempstead. It failed miserably at the polls. The opposition, it turned out, proposed more local control and spurned the roadside landscaping that Moses had favored. In this sense, the opposition was ahead of its time in backing what was essentially an expressway. Their approaches may have differed, but both sides still agreed on the wisdom of developing Jones's Island. While these events unfolded, Moses received the backing of the Regional Plan Association, fearful that unplanned speculation would hamper its vision of urban growth. At this point, all Moses had to do was to figure out a way to soften up the voters on Long

Island. He turned to local veterans of the mosquito war: Hempstead real estate men who were no strangers to reclamation projects (including Thomas McWhinney). Together they prevailed on the state to back the formation of the Hempstead Planning Commission, a front for Moses and his grand plans, but a move that nonetheless conveyed the impression to the locals that home rule was in operation. The newly formed commission recommended that the town grant several hundred acres of common lands to build a beach and causeway. This time the voters of Hempstead approved the measure.[44]

Like all barrier islands, Jones's Island was a changeable environment. It owed its existence to littoral drift, the process whereby wave action carried sand west from the eroded headlands on Long Island's eastern end. Storms also affected the landmass. One such storm plowed through and created Zach's Inlet, after an obscure man named Zachariah James of Seaford, New York. The inlet dated from 1880, but by the time the area showed up on Moses's radar, it had been closing. In 1926 it disappeared altogether, uniting Short Beach with Jones's Island. Swirling inside Moses's head was a plan to put an end to these migratory habits and place the island on a more stable footing.[45]

Standing in Moses's way was a little community called High Hill Beach, a recent addition to Jones's Island. This was a small summer colony—small because until 1929 the only access was via ferry. In 1905 four cottages nestled on the secluded windswept terrain. Twenty years later, about a hundred families summered there. The permanent residents included the nation's most famous hermit, Will Cuppy, a curmudgeon and satirist who blamed Manhattan's hustle and bustle for his lack of writerly success and who retired to a tar paper shack on the island in 1921, calling his little abode "Tottering-on-the-Brink." A bay named after Zachariah James lay just behind the barrier island, and it was here that the community of High Hill took root. High Hill's name derived from the "[h]igh sand dunes, covered with wild shrubbery, beach flowers and grasses" that circled the bay. The fishing was spectacular, the waters brimming with untold numbers of bluefish, weakfish, flounder, and fluke. A huge sandbar in Zach's Bay, recalled a man who grew up visiting High Hill, was jam-packed with soft-shell clams, "so prolific that commercial clam diggers from Freeport and Baldwin came every day when the tide was out to dig boatloads of the bivalves."[46]

The beginning of the end for High Hill came when the first dredgers were cranked up to start work on a causeway out to Jones's Island in 1927. In the end, the Town of Hempstead, from which everyone at High Hill leased, refused to renew, and the houses were either destroyed or moved. Even Cuppy, whom Moses considered a deeper nature thinker than Henry David Thoreau, had to go. "They were, and still are, as I pen these words," Cuppy scoffed in his book *How to Be a Hermit*, "engaged in pumping up sand to build a road, with bridges, across the bay, so that thousands upon thousands of utterly delightful people can drive their automobiles right out to Jones's Island and up and down the length of same on a concrete boulevard."[47]

The road that destroyed Hermitville on the Atlantic was called the Jones Beach Causeway. It began in the village of Wantagh and eventually spanned the marshlands behind Jones's Island, forging through Great Island across a channel and then to Low Island, over Goose Creek to Cross Teal Island, Flat Island, and on to Long Meadow before ending on the beach at a point just west of Zach's Bay. The steam dredge ships included the aptly named *New York*, which Sidney Shapiro, the engineer in charge of the project, said was "reputed to be the largest of its kind in the United States."[48]

One hundred twenty men worked around the clock, and by the end of 1927 had excavated more hydraulic fill than was dug out of the earth to build the World Trade Center (over 1.3 million cubic yards), piling it up into a long plateau so that the road would not wash out. Streams in the construction site threatened to wreck the new tableland running down the island, so workers simply closed them up. Sometimes they went in the other direction, enlarging waterways such as Flat Creek into navigation channels. Even more stunning was the change that swept over Zach's Bay. Dredgers sucked up five World Trade Centers' worth of fill (6 million cubic yards), sent it through pipelines, and spewed it across

Jones's Island. "The bay bottom," one resident recalled, "was pumped up through the pipe at considerable speed, and the noise of the clams and other hard objects racing through the pipes shattered the quiet of High Hill Beach." Like a magical levitation act, the earthmoving left Jones's Island fourteen feet above sea level. That was high enough to build a road—the Ocean Parkway—and bathhouses. A native New Yorker captured the spirit of the place perfectly: "[N]ature here appears with an abstract horizontal purity and a luminous clarity that only culture can create." [49]

When a man described as "the greatest builder in American history" comes to a dynamic natural environment like Jones's Island, there is almost inevitably an ecological toll. Which is not to say that High Hill beachgoers did not change the environment. They must have trampled dune vegetation and set the stage for blowouts: depressions in the landscape sculpted by the wind. They also changed the flora from its native form (dominated by beach grass, salt hay, bayberry, and a pretty wildflower called sea rocket) by importing various flowering plants and perennials, especially blackberries, which multiplied prodigiously. But what Moses did was several orders greater. The landscape architect Clarence Combs, who worked on the Jones Beach park, and painstakingly employed native plantings where he could, summed up the alterations this way: "Over the intensely developed portions of Jones Beach whatever of value or beauty that existed in the original landscape was unavoidably obliterated by the hydraulically placed sand fill and other construction necessary to fit the area for active recreation by large numbers of people." [50]

The two most important ecological changes resulting from the park were the breaching of the primary dune and the dredging of Zach's Bay. To offer visitors a dramatic, clear sightline between the East Bathhouse and the crashing waves of the Atlantic, the primary dune and native beach grass had to go. The bay side of Jones's Island, explains one ecological history of the park, "was dredged and re-formed, destroying the breeding grounds for the shellfish, finfish, and waterfowl that inhabited the area." Looking back on his accomplishment in 1938, Moses made the astonishing claim that he had not touched the meadowlands. "One of the things that has made Jones Beach what it is," he reveled, "is the fact that we have left the meadow lands precisely as nature made them." That was, of course, simply not true.[51]

Jones Beach State Park opened on a warm Sunday, August 4, 1929. The timing of the celebration could not have been worse. For on that day nature struck back. In a preview of the infamous Dust Bowl—when dust storms raked the southern plains—Jones's Island put on a sand-storm of its own. The two disasters shared a common causal thread. The proximate cause of both was the destruction of the land's natural vegeta-tive cover. Of course, on Long Island, the driving force behind the 1929 sandstorm was not the quest to grow wheat for profit along the lines of what happened in Kansas. Its roots were more complicated, resting on the need for some mass-produced version of nature to serve as a recre-ational escape from the sweltering asphalt streets of urban life. But it shared with the Dust Bowl the same relentless drive to denude the land-scape. "[S]and fill [blew] over everything and everybody," remembered Raymond P. McNulty, the lawyer for the Park Commission. "It drifted across the roads to such an extent that they became dangerous for driv-ing, it filled eyes and ears and noses; got into the carburetors of cars and stalled them; chipped the paint off mudguards and license plates, and generally played such havoc that the critics who said 'it couldn't be done' had a grand holiday." To combat the storm, workers eventually planted beach grass, Japanese rose, bayberry, and beach plum.[52]

Franklin Roosevelt, the governor of New York, and former governor Al Smith both showed up for the festivities and joked about the "social-istic" aspects of the Moses-made beach. There was, of course, nothing particularly socialist about what Moses had done. But that the gover-nors jested about the supposed radical politics of the beach reclamation reflected a level of discomfort with the expansive state power that was brought to bear. After all, the Jones Beach project unfolded before the New Deal—which tackled the Great Depression with federal economic programs—had legitimized such an approach to governance.[53]

Others had a more serious complaint. They decried the park's threat to the freedom that once ruled the south shore common lands. A man named Clarence Boudreau of Hempstead found "a beautiful park built by the tax money of the ordinary or even common people—but now that it was built—they are excluded from it. They want to enjoy the privileges of a public park, the ocean breezes but not at '50 cents' for a few minutes." Moses charged for parking, even though he had earlier suggested that he wouldn't. Boudreau went so far as to ask whether he was living "in Italy where Mussolini rules with iron hand?" Josephine Roettinger of Baldwin felt much the same way. "Jones Beach is the bunk," she scolded. "There are always people like myself who detest crowds and enjoy a little freedom." She apparently had trouble finding it at Jones Beach. There were police to tell her to leash her dog, so she left the hound behind. Then she pulled out some sandwiches and a root beer. "My career of crime commenced at once. I started to put up a small tent in violation of the Constitution and got promptly subdued by a policeman." There was no camping on the beach. "Well so long, Jones Beach," she bitterly concluded, "you will never see us again."[54]

Moses responded by declaring that the Park Commission "makes no apologies for catering to all classes of people." Never one to mince words, he glowered as he said, "It is a stupid and vicious thing, in our opinion, to advocate that great public parks in the suburbs shall be only for the poor." In fact, his park at Jones Beach was very much a bourgeois extravagance. It took a car to visit (easily, at least) and money to park, and while one can argue that it was better than orchestrating another commercialized Coney Island, the disagreeable truth is that the park was designed to encourage a certain class of visitor—no disorderly littering types, please—and was run at the expense of the freedom that once sprawled across the shifting sands of these common lands. Further, harvesting vegetation on that land now became a criminal act; the evil work of "shrubbery thieves" in Moses's words. Yet couldn't it be that those in the business of "contraband greenery," as Moses put it, operated in a different legal universe, where the rules of the commons still held sway? Is it not conceivable that some of the supposed thieves saw the landscape as wild and felt justified in taking it, just like the oysters once found in the natural beds surrounding New York Harbor? It is more than a little ironic that, two years after Jones Beach opened, a New York court eclipsed the public's right to forage along the foreshore (in this case, for bait worms). The court arrived at this conclusion in light of the "shore front playgrounds which are freely placed at the disposal of all the people."[55]

Reflecting on what was perhaps his greatest public works project, Moses portrayed the barrier island as a wasteland creeping with "vicious wild cats and dogs, scores of rabbits, and one family of red foxes. Not to speak of clam diggers, most of whom had not seen New York in twenty years and had no idea of ever returning." It was this supposed wild stretch of New York that Moses set out to improve, justifying his conquest in much the same way that the colonists had—a people who arrived in North America more than three hundred years earlier to misconceive the Indians' peripatetic relationship with the land, and who saw the ground as simply vacant and in dire need of the ownership and improvement they intended to carry out. It is no accident that a 1924 Long Island State Park Commission map labeled the island "Jones Beach" and not Jones's Beach, after the landmass's most famous bayman. Moses and his men had so thoroughly altered this land that they robbed it of every last vestige of its past, including its apostrophe.[56]

10 THE LANDSCAPERS OF QUEENS

It is bewildering to learn that Robert Moses—for all his various road-building exploits—never learned to drive. But perhaps we should be even more surprised that he never learned to fly. Moses's preferred vantage point was from on high. Not for nothing did he employ aerial photography liberally in his work.* Looking down from overhead, Moses embraced a unified view of New York, not a set of discrete neighborhoods, boroughs, or, for that matter, watersheds and marshes. Moses missed the forest *and* the trees. What he saw from up above was a large city set in an island environment in urgent need of unification; a Greater New York that could be made even greater if its various regions could be bridged and consolidated into one smoothly functioning metropolis. Perhaps this is what Iphigene Ochs Sulzberger, matriarch of the *Times*, was getting at when she told Moses's biographer, "He saw Nature as a whole."[1]

Moses did not operate in a vacuum. He was hardly the only or even the first person to conceptualize the need for a comprehensive plan for the entire metropolitan area. That idea arose as far back as the 1850s, in the midst of the struggle to deal with the various invasions of New

---

* The first aerial photographs of New York City were taken in the 1920s.

York's waters. It surfaced again in the early twentieth century in the debates over how to handle the deoxygenated water conditions. And it was later embodied in the work of the Regional Plan Association. Not only did Moses derive many of his ideas straight from the pages of RPA guides, he shared the group's sense that growth in the estuary was inevitable. "It seems unlikely," Moses once wrote, "that a stop can be put to the massing of population at great natural harbors."[2]

Nevertheless, Moses distinguished himself with respect to New York's environmental history in some crucial respects. In place of local ecological regimes (baymen raking oysters, farmers and foragers trudging through marshlands), he helped to invent a new urban ecology that was regional in scope. He took what he called New York's "islandic geography" and reformed it by mounting a sweeping infrastructure campaign—indeed, the most massive crusade to build parkways, tunnels, bridges, and expressways that the city had ever known. By the end of the 1930s, he had united Long Island with the rest of New York like never before, building the Triborough Bridge (opened in 1936), the Bronx-Whitestone Bridge (1939), the Grand Central Parkway (1936), the Interborough Parkway (1936), the Whitestone Parkway (1939), and the Cross Island Parkway (1940). If many of his ideas derived from the work of others, there is little question that Moses managed to knit together a "sprawling city of islands," as he put it, into an integrated metropolitan region.[3]

But Moses's impact did not stop there. This new regional ecology was based on a different approach to the natural world, and especially wetlands. Moses took the stylistic, streamlined stance toward nature he pioneered at Jones Beach—where he turned a low-lying barrier island into a sweeping expanse of beautiful white sand, graced with pink petunias and green lawns—and in the 1930s vowed to thrust it more widely across the landscape. On the west side of Manhattan, for example, Moses seized hold of an embattled ribbon of waterfront along the Hudson and made it into what the *Times* called "the most extensive alteration of Manhattan's topography in recent history." He created 132 acres of man-made land, leveled bluffs to provide nice, even approaches to Riverside Drive, and put in playgrounds and lawns on the brand-new terrain. In the process, he managed to bulldoze his way through one of the last remnants of primeval forest at Inwood Hill Park—known for its stately tulip trees—even though a more circuitous route had been proposed to avoid the woodland gem. At Pelham Bay in the Bronx, he hauled in sand from the Rockaways to build 115 acres of new land and linked together Hunter Island with Rodman's Neck to the south, creating a smart-looking crescent at Orchard Beach.* And he also proposed consolidating Randall's Island in the East River with a wetland positioned just to the east called Sunken Meadow. He later dismissed the meadow as "a geological slopover."[4]

In other words, Moses had little patience for the irregularities of the natural world. He and his colleagues in the planning establishment made their mark tidying islands and wetlands into trim, well-groomed landscapes. Their loyalties were less to the landscape than to *landscaping*, the latter a far more instrumental approach to the natural world than existed back in Frederick Law Olmsted's day. Strictly speaking, nature to these pioneers of twentieth-century modernity was a set of resources meant to serve practical ends such as roads and parks, so that New York could continue to grow, yes, but in a way that made urban living palatable to the millions. They were seeking to dominate nature in much the same way that others of their generation were doing along the Colorado River, most famously at Hoover Dam (1935). And as they subjugated the land in the name of maximum growth, they managed to consolidate their power not simply over the region but also over the common people, who had a more direct and intimate relationship with the open tidal marshes of New York.[5]

The purest expression of this new managerial relationship with the land came about in a Queens salt marsh called the Flushing Meadows. The story begins with moving a mountain.

---

* In 1947 the Twin Islands were also absorbed into the beach complex.

• • •

Back in the year of his inauguration, George Washington paid a visit to Flushing to have a look at a nursery famous for its mulberry, fig, almond, and cherry trees. It was said that over the next century and a half, little about Flushing had changed since the Founding Father's visit. The slow pace of development can likely be traced to the sizable salt marsh, a low-lying sweep of cordgrass roughly three miles in length and a mile in width, crawling with fiddler crabs and burrowing ribbed mussels, spread along Flushing Creek. Only one part of the wetland had been caught in the grip of urban growth, the northerly portion where a mountain of ashes had arisen like a hulking volcano to loom over Queens.[6]

The mountain arrived courtesy of Anthony Brady's Brooklyn Ash Removal Company. In 1909, after the real estate potential of Coney Island Creek had been maximized, Brooklyn Ash began shipping cinders—coal being the dominant heating source—in trams north to Queens. The final destination was a place called Corona, once known as West Flushing. A developer had renamed the area in 1872 to advertise it as the crown jewel of Long Island villages. Instead, the place was destined to be crowned king of all ash heaps.[7]

In the 1910s, Queens arrived more squarely in Manhattan's orbit, after the Pennsylvania Railroad dug tunnels beneath the East River to connect Long Island with its new Beaux Arts Pennsylvania Station. As the tunnels went in, the contractor Michael Degnon, known for his work on the Williamsburg Bridge and the New York subway system, began accumulating land along Flushing Creek. A huge man with a bushy handlebar mustache, Degnon had spent most of his adult life building railroads and other transportation projects, and in Flushing he saw great potential along these same lines. He dreamed of one day presiding over a great port on Flushing Bay, the creek's final destination. To achieve his goal, he organized two subsidiaries to fill in the wetland, while also recruiting the corrupt Tammany-indentured outfit Brooklyn Ash to his cause. Legend has it that its treasurer, John A. "Fishhooks" McCarthy, earned his nickname for being so tightfisted that it took a fishhook to extract money from him. Brooklyn Ash sent its forty-foot railroad cars loaded with ash north to Flushing Meadows. The train became known as the "Talcum Powder Express" because the company was notorious for neglecting to cover the ash with tarpaulins before setting off in a cloud of smoke. "In this way," explained one Queens historian, "Degnon was in effect setting up a vast conveyor belt for the refuse of an entire borough to be dumped in Corona." [8]

Over the years, ashes and cellar dirt piled up along Flushing Creek as the quest to reclaim the land persisted. But all the dirt-moving would prove for naught. Degnon could never pry loose the government support he needed, because the industrial base simply was not there to compel federal intervention. With Degnon's hopes for a port dwindling, the supply of ash escalated as the city—the prospect of resource recovery receding—began building municipal incinerators. And with the port out of the picture, there wasn't any incentive to lay additional railroad tracks so that trams could deliver ash to bury more marshland. Instead, Brooklyn's cinders ended up all piled into one three-hundred-acre site in Corona. As the heap grew skyward—ultimately reaching ninety feet—it took the name "Mount Corona." [9]

At the time that Moses was zeroing in on Jones's Island, F. Scott Fitzgerald immortalized this part of Queens in *The Great Gatsby*. He called it the "valley of ashes." In this dale, he wrote, "ashes grow like wheat into ridges and hills and grotesque gardens." This marsh encumbered with the remains of urban life apparently made so deep an impression on Fitzgerald that he even thought of calling his novel *Among Ash-Heaps and Millionaires*. Meanwhile, in nonfictional Queens, the real ash heap generated enough smoke and dust that traffic cops had to be deployed on nearby streets to direct motorists through the dense fog. [10]

Nor was Mount Corona the only mountain in this neck of New York. Not too far away in the East River sat Rikers Island. Rikers took over this stretch of river in much the way that crabgrass spreads over a lawn, growing from under a hundred acres to over four hundred today. Early in the twentieth century, convict labor hauled in ashes to expand the island. Then in 1925, city officials announced a plan to build a prison to replace the one bulging at the seams at Welfare (now Roosevelt) Island. As the second quarter of the century opened, the waste stream had ballooned to where New York requested permission from the federal government to extend Rikers farther into the water. Space was one problem, rodents another. The Rikers rat population surged to such an extent that one New Yorker pledged to organize a hunting party to tramp around the island slaying them. This was after the failure of "poison gas, poison baits, ferocious dogs and pigs."[11]

Mayor Jimmy Walker, a flamboyant, wisecracking songwriter turned lawyer known for his efforts to legalize prizefighting, anticipated that the prison would put an end to "the garbage heap of this island." But the rats lived on, as did the phosphorescent fires (caused by spontaneous combustion), some of which had been burning for years. In 1934 the penitentiary's warden painted a picture of the island: "At night it is like a forest of Christmas trees—first one little light . . . then another, until the whole hillside is lit up with little fires. When it was covered with snow during the Winter, the fires burned just the same. It was beautiful." Not everyone, of course, had quite the same aesthetic sensibilities. Once a small island in the East River, Rikers had, by 1934, accreted into a grotesque tribute to the dark side of urban growth: a monstrous, rat-infested inferno, with some peaks as high as 130 feet.[12]

Into this bleak expanse forged Robert Moses and his Grand Central Parkway. Begun in the early 1930s, the Grand Central brought about the expansion of the western edge of Flushing Bay with sand barged from the waters off Brooklyn. The buried waterfront was likely a mudflat brimming with mud snails and marine worms and an important feeding ground for shorebirds.[13]

To complete the parkway, it was imperative that Moses control a strip of Brooklyn Ash's empire of cinders for a legal right-of-way. By this point, the company, in response to growing resentment in Queens over serving as the burial ground for Brooklyn's waste, had made some concessions. In 1931, for example, it opened a golf course described as "smooth and green as an English Park." In 1933 the opportunistic Samuel Rosoff (aka Subway Sam), a millionaire who made his fortune building subways and hauling Manhattan's unending waste, underbid the company for the city's removal contract. A strike, meantime, idled Brooklyn Ash's five incinerators, and as raw garbage streamed into the Corona ash heap, the Queens borough president cried out. Also in that year, Republican Fiorello La Guardia, running an anticorruption campaign, defeated the incumbent Tammany Hall candidate, John O'Brien (who'd succeeded Jimmy Walker in 1932 after he resigned under mounting charges of corruption). La Guardia's victory spelled reform, and together with the incinerator strike and the pressure from Rosoff, Brooklyn Ash was left without a contract. In 1934 the city bought out the company, and Moses had his parkway right-of-way—albeit one that abutted an ash heap. Next door was a far-flung salt marsh of wind and tide, grass, birds, and fish.[14]

The year 1935 would turn out to be one of the most fateful in the history of the Flushing Meadows. New York City was still groping its way through the throes of the Depression and its business leaders, looking to stimulate a recovery, stumbled on the idea of sponsoring a World's Fair. The hope was to duplicate the huge financial success Chicago had with its 1933 exposition. The salt marsh would never be the same.

The leaders of what became the 1939 New York World's Fair were bankers, corporate executives, and Wall Street lawyers, though representatives of state and local government and labor received some token representation in the deliberations. Apart from Moses, the three most influential people involved were Percy Straus, Grover Whalen, and George McAneny. The son of Isidor Straus, the Jewish department store magnate and *Titanic* victim, Percy Straus was president of the retail giant R. H. Macy & Co. He was also a director of the Regional Plan Association, the group that saw it as the business of the city to do everything it could for business. His obituary nicely summed up his motivations as far as the fair was concerned: "His analysis of trends in the city from 1930 to 1935 led him to the belief that New York stood in need of a substantial project for stimulating a new inflow of commercial and cultural activities." Straus, in other words, believed that the fair would revitalize the prospects for urban growth during the Great Depression.[15]

Grover Whalen was the most colorful figure in the group. Named for President Grover Cleveland, who was married on the day his namesake was born, Whalen came of age on the Lower East Side. He went on to fill various positions in the administration of Mayor John F. Hylan, who was uneasy in public and who relied on the irrepressible Whalen to handle things at welcoming events. Debonair, square shouldered, and handsome, Whalen ascended to the position of city police commissioner and gained notoriety for his anticommunism and vindictiveness. With his good looks and flamboyance, however, Whalen was better off in public relations than police work. Realizing Whalen's true talents, La Guardia appointed him the city's official greeter. It is fair to say that no one was better suited than the glad-handing, silver-tongued Whalen to sell the World's Fair to the world, a point borne out by all the foreign nations he inveigled into opening pavilions on the grounds.[16]

McAneny was the most important figure of the three. Then in his sixties, George McAneny was an uninspiring, boyish man, slight of build, with straight, neat, dark hair parted a little off center. Erudite and earnest, he had a mind for facts and figures. His reputation for incorruptible efficiency was second to none. A reformer and disciple of the Republican political activist Carl Schurz, who, with other liberals of the time, worried about the effects of spoilsmen on democracy, McAneny had given considerable thought to New York's future. He had, after all, served in many different capacities: Manhattan borough president, president of the Board of Aldermen, executive manager of the *Times*, commissioner of sanitation, and president of the Regional Plan Association, a post he held from 1930 until he died in 1953. He was influential in the creation of New York's pacesetting 1916 zoning ordinance, famous for favoring offices over manufacturing space in Manhattan and ramping up the real estate economy. "We must have vision enough to see the wonderful growth of our city in the years to come," said the forward-thinking McAneny, "and wisdom enough to pave the way for that growth along sane and rational lines."[17]

McAneny was familiar with the Flushing Meadows from his days as sanitation commissioner, when he helped put an end to Brooklyn Ash's

mountain-making escapades. Nevertheless, there was nothing foreordained about the choice of the meadow as the home of the fair. Busi-
nessmen in Canarsie, Brooklyn, had lobbied for Jamaica Bay, with its
"cooling ocean breezes." The chairman of a Manhattan neighborhood
association insisted on the West Side: "on the beautiful shores of the
historic American River on which the greatest City in the World is situated." Even an old plan to extend Manhattan with landfill six miles
south of the Battery was put forward as a possible site. None of these
various boosters could fathom the appeal of Flushing Meadows, belit-
tling the Queens site as "bog lands" and a "bottomless swamp." As one
Jamaica Bay booster complained, "[H]ow anomalous it seems for New
York to hold its World's Fair along a narrow creek when it boasts to the
World of its incomparable Waterfront and Port facilities."[18]

So how did the fair wind up at Flushing Meadows? In a word: speculation. Unlike the West Side of Manhattan or Jamaica Bay, where the
city retained extensive landholdings, the Flushing Meadows enjoyed one
main advantage, and that was that landlords and brokers would make a
killing on the purchase of private property with public funds. Queens
realtor and commissioner of public works John J. Halleran, for example,
would profit enormously. Halleran hardly tried to hide his intentions. He
anticipated "a most noticeable enhancement in land values" in the wake
of the fair. The idea was for the fair to establish a foothold in the region
and thereby lay the groundwork for a park once the exposition closed.
Gentrification would ensue, following, roughly speaking, what had happened with Central Park. Robert Moses, who built his reputation on
creating recreational space, strongly backed the park idea. The collective
wish of the Queens-based fair and park boosters was to launch a new
kind of Times Square outside Manhattan, to spread high-density development more broadly over the land, precisely as the RPA proposed.[19]

In the crisp days of fall 1935, Moses, in his capacity as New York
City park commissioner, a post he had been appointed to the year before, sent a photographer zooming off in a plane to take images of the
site. The photographs revealed something that Moses already knew: the
backdrop for the fair would be pyrotechnic Rikers Island. Some called

the place "Sanitation's Eternal Lights." As Moses would go on to explain, "New York City cannot afford to offend World's Fair visitors with the burnings of refuse at Rikers Island in connection with an obsolete system of garbage and refuse disposal." Moses recommended ending the dumping at Rikers, but, failing that, he pressed for a ridge with plantings to mask New York's trash nexus.[20]

As it turned out, Rikers Island was cannibalized to fill two hundred acres in the East River in connection with the opening in 1939 of North Beach Airport (later named La Guardia). Trucks lumbered over a temporary trestle linking the two sites, adding millions of cubic yards of fill to the airport and decapitating the 130-foot-high "East River Vesuvius." Moses later recounted, though perhaps the story is apocryphal, how he once witnessed a sixteen-foot lamppost sink into the muck at the airport, purportedly while William Carey, the city's sanitation commissioner, "was expatiating on his filling operations and on the firm foundation underneath." If nothing else, the story reflected the perils of building on one of Long Island's sprawling wetlands, a problem that Moses would confront firsthand at Flushing Meadows.[21]

Although people such as Grover Whalen would disparage Flushing Meadows as "a mosquito-infested swamp," in fact, it is more complicated. The Brooklyn Ash property, with its Mount Corona and rats, made up only a little over three hundred acres of the sprawling meadow. Much of the remaining land was wild and bursting with cordgrass, cattails, waterfowl, turtles, snakes, chipmunks, frogs, and, yes, mosquitoes. Though the World's Fair boosters thought of the site as virgin land, the truth was that the communal customs of trapping and timber collection had long held sway. Urban fur trappers, for example, snared muskrats in Flushing Meadows and sent the pelts to St. Louis. Of course, muskrats alone did not begin to convey the richness of the animal life found at the fair site, which included ducks, rabbits, puff adders, and owls. Apart from trapping, people collected firewood and raised vegetables—even on the ash heap itself, where tomatoes and radishes were said to ripen more quickly than normal because of the heat. In one section of the meadows around Maspeth, squatters moved in, this being the Great Depression.[22]

In 1936 this way of life came to an end. The city acquired or condemned the necessary land, and soon the sheriff arrived to evict people, destroying what remained of an old working-class Italian community. Flushing Meadows, in other words, witnessed its own little Trail of Tears. "At least half a dozen ancient nags were hitched to old wagons, which probably are on their last 'wheels,' to move everything . . . ," read one report. "The World's Fair may turn out to be wonderful," sighed Mary Kopp, a sixty-five-year-old widow, "but it's certainly a heartache to me." As bulldozers crept across the landscape, the holdouts—those who lacked the resources to move—saw their former way of life vanish before them. The landscape was smashed right down to the bocce courts. Property owners received handsome advances from the city on the assessed valuation of condemned lands; renters and squatters received nothing.[23]

Before gentrification could justify the boosters' speculative ambitions, the looming Mount Corona had to be disposed of. Moses and his parks department supervised the initial grading and improvement of the site, aspiring to relocate the mountain of ashes into the meadows. It was not an easy job. At high tide, workers wrestled with waves of mud as truck tires, their weight bearing down on the swampland, caused geysers to shoot up into the air. Elsewhere, dust storms kicked up and traffic ground to a halt. Just over six months later, the ash heap had vanished, just as surely as a magician's cage of doves. An elaborate system of floodlights dubbed the "white way" lit up the marsh so that work could take place around the clock. Men hacked away at the native vegetation to make way for landscaping. By the time the contractors were through, they had "completely changed the geography of the section between Kew Gardens and Corona." Seven million cubic yards of material had been redistributed over the Flushing Meadows, enough, it was said, "to pave a broad four-lane highway extending from New York to Daytona Beach, Florida."[24]

The result was an entirely new topography. Gone was the old Flushing Meadows, the legacy of age-old geological forces, and in its place arose a new, more solid landscape punctuated by two new lakes: Meadow and Willow. Only the names of the lakes were left to testify to the landscape's buried history. Part of the appeal of the Flushing Meadows site, as McAneny once noted, was that this watery world was conducive to the making of lagoons. It was Moses's intention to go a step further and turn the site into "a people's Versailles"—a garden paradise for the masses.[25]

The two lakes served as the centerpieces of this new land ethic. This act of topographic wizardry—and Moses's work was often viewed as magical—involved gouging out the old Flushing Creek and meadowland for the lake beds and moving, as well as straightening, the stream itself. One news report read: "The geography of an expanse extending more than three miles and almost a mile wide has been completely changed during the last few months. What was water prior to the starting of operations is now land and what was land is now water."[26]

The new ecological chapter in the history of Flushing Meadows was the most significant landscape change in this corner of the planet since the retreat of the Wisconsin ice sheet. So perhaps it was fair to compare Moses, as his biographer has, "to some elemental force of nature."[27]

As the lakes materialized and the meadows underwent the change into dry land, the perennial question of drainage cropped up. The borough of Queens had long centered its water management plans on Flushing Creek. Now, with the eyes of the entire world trained on the World's Fair site, a flood was out of the question. Two enormous sewers were plunged through the ground on the eastern and western margins of the fair. Built to about the size of one of the Holland Tunnel tubes (which linked the West Side of lower Manhattan with Jersey City, New Jersey, and was finished in 1927), the sewers were said to be the largest in the world at the time. A local paper reassured its readers, "While it may seem to some, and particularly to the taxpayer that these storm water sewers are excessively large, when one stops to think that the City is doing away with Flushing River and taking the flow from this natural valley into artificial channels confined and entirely underground, then the attempt to improve on Nature can be realized and the magnitude of the job visualized." The troubled history of sewers in Queens made such assurance necessary. As late as 1931, former Queens borough president

Maurice Connolly was still serving time on Welfare Island for having rigged sewer contracts. The gargantuan trunk lines made Flushing drier as the various tributaries of Flushing Creek (Horse Kill, Kill Jordan) and the waters of the adjacent marshlands disappeared into the giant pipes.[28]

The name Flushing was an English corruption of Vlissingen, a Dutch port on the North Sea. By the mid–nineteenth century, the word *flushing* had attained its modern meaning, denoting a cleansing by rushing water. And that seemed like an appropriate name for a place that, by the 1930s, had found itself on the receiving end of technocrats pursuing a man-made hydrology. The immense plumbing job undertaken to divert storm water away from the fair site was just the beginning. The effects of the tide made the water too brackish to support the range of ornamental plant life that Moses had in mind to surround the new set of man-made lakes. Nor did he want visitors to the fair to have to endure the odor and sight of the lake bottom exposed during the rise and fall of the tide. So Moses installed a gate and dam to defeat the tide and keep the salt water at bay. Flushing Meadows now sported two new bodies of freshwater.[29]

It was a clever piece of handiwork, but not without an ecological price. Problems with eutrophication surfaced as early as 1938, when microorganisms turned the lake water "decidedly green and turbid." The green algae flourished as the salt marsh buried under the lake began to decompose, releasing nutrients in the process. Although wetlands can filter phosphorus from the water, flooding them tends to liberate the stored nutrient. Sewage further exacerbated the problem. Then in the melting heat of the summer of 1938, clouds of midges descended on the shores of the lakes. The tiny insects forced motorists "to stop about every fifty feet to wipe off their windshields in order to see." The official Latin name for this family of nonbiting flies is *Chironomidae*. They are early colonizers of newly created habitats high in sediment and organic matter; precisely the environment created at the new lakes. The fair corporation eventually sprayed to control the problem. As the fairgoers approached the gates on April 30, 1939, they entered a prefabricated world graced with what was now New York City's largest lake—Meadow

Lake—a man-made body of water built, fittingly enough, by the master builder himself.[30]

On April 16, 1939, George Washington, decked out in a homespun suit and tricornered hat, set off from Mount Vernon en route to his inauguration in New York City. Not the real Founding Father, of course, but an actor impersonating him. The three-hundred-mile trip was made by horse-drawn coach until inclement weather forced the faux Washington and his retinue to step aboard a Greyhound bus, strapping the old coach on behind. Somewhere around the Mason-Dixon Line, the bus pulled over, and an elderly woman stuck her head in and asked, "General, where's the horses?" Back in his coach, the general forged toward Elizabeth, New Jersey, where his party scrambled aboard a retrofitted navy sailer with a high prow manned by eight oarsmen schooled in the Portuguese gig-stroke. They skimmed down the Kill Van Kull and into New York Bay, and, with tug whistles screaming, Washington and his entourage put into port at the Battery. The George look-alike then clattered up Broadway—doffing his hat along the way—to city hall, where he met Mayor Fiorello La Guardia. A few days later, on April 30, 1939, Washington, the sound of drums echoing across the grounds, took the oath of office on the revamped Flushing Meadows.[31]

When the real George Washington galloped into Flushing back in 1789, he came to visit William Prince's nursery. The Prince nursery strove to collect all known trees, plants, and shrubs of horticultural value and eventually made Flushing something of a legend in gardening history. A generation and a half after Washington's reception, the nursery imported from Europe what became New York City's most famous tree, *Ailanthus altissima*, the so-called tree of heaven. It is one of the most invasive tree species in the world and can thrive in some of the poorest soils imaginable. It was the perfect tree for the tough streets of New York.[32]

By the time the make-believe George Washington rumbled into town in the spring of 1939, the Flushing Meadows had experienced the effects of what *Popular Science* magazine described as "the greatest transplanting operation ever undertaken." In 1937 the great migration began when three sycamores, wrested from a Pennsylvania tobacco farm, made the journey to the big city. Elms and maples, pin oaks and honey locusts uprooted from Virginia, Maryland, New Jersey, and Connecticut went on to shade the grounds in Queens.[33]

Commemorating Washington's inauguration was hardly the exposition's only mission. "The Fair is, above all," *Life* magazine proclaimed, "a magnificent monument by and to American business." After all, the city did serve as headquarters to some of the nation's most powerful corporations. Amidst the privation and hardship of the Depression, the corporate-inspired fair strove to offer a glimmer of hope. Its organizers thus billed the fair as the "World of Tomorrow." This new world unfolded in a city—indeed, in a city within a city—as a jaunt over to the Democracity exhibit confirmed. There visitors could see firsthand the look of a future metropolis, with its urban core surrounded by industry and suburbs—a city, as the Regional Plan Association put it, that "has been planned throughout in advance of any presumed growth." This was not just any old plan but one that anticipated that the growth imperative would produce a boundless city spanning eleven thousand square miles, or about twice the size of the entire state of Connecticut.[34]

Making the most of New York, in turn, involved a different approach to the land itself. In this sense, Flushing Meadows was no longer a landscape per se. It had been turned, instead, into something far removed from its salt marsh roots: into *landscaping*, a noun that does not appear to have been in use in the English language before 1930. Formerly, landscapes just *were*. Now human beings laid them out. In the brave new world of the fair, the land came made to order, gussied up with exotic plants and trees with no natural ties to the soil at hand. A functioning ecosystem at the Flushing Meadows—and later an urban commons hosting fur trappers and "bumper garden crops raised by squatters behind fences of discarded bed springs"—had been reinvented as a novelty item available to anyone willing to pay the price of admission. What Arthur Pound wrote in 1935 in his history of Manhattan land values, *The Golden Earth*, applied to the city as a whole: "[L]and has become progressively too valuable for trees except as embellishment for real estate."[35]

The landscaped grounds embodied one of the fair's most important visual themes: color. Unlike the "chromatically dull" expositions of the past, as a writer for the *New Republic* put it, the New York fair brought forth a kaleidoscope of light and color. The idea of borrowing from the plant world to paint a colorful picture on the land was not new. Jones Beach had a designer who did "nothing but color planning." The fair at Flushing Meadows, however, took color to new heights. Expert botanists conducted tests on plants that had never been grown before in Flushing to figure out the exact hue they would give off. "The function of the extravagant use of color at the Fair was not only to produce an atmosphere of gaiety, but to provide a contrast to the drabness of the cities from which some visitors came," one fair historian would later observe. By day, color-coded avenues radiated out from the towering Trylon, a three-sided modernist spire, and its counterpart, the Perisphere, a massive man-made globe, at the heart of the fairgrounds. At night, in-ground mercury vapor lights illuminated the plants, causing the leaves to give off a "shimmering, luminous green." The plant world, in other words, now served aesthetic ends.[36]

Around Willow Lake, the land moved in a much less formal direction, though even here the ground that visitors set foot on was engineered. Landscape architects had paid heed to what was described in the promotional literature as an "ecological system" in which "special consideration will be given to the mutual relations between plants and their environment." The goal, however, was not to organize plants into groupings by species (like a typical botanical garden) but to create a set of "landscape effects." The landscaping at Willow Lake was thus done with an eye toward giving it the appearance of a wildlife sanctuary to compensate for a nearby refuge lost to development. The idea was to fabricate a stopover location for migrant waterfowl, in effect manufacturing a habitat akin to the lost Dyker Meadows off of Gravesend Bay.[37]

The fair landscape was designed to look as natural as possible. The thousands of large trees shipped to the site were meant to impart the impression that "they had matured there during the years," explained one magazine article. The resulting landscape went off into the realm of interchangeable space. Habitats were losing their connection to place now that they could be manufactured at will at any location. In the past, New Yorkers were in a battle to wrest more land from the sea. But what happened in the 1930s went beyond such struggles to change how the very natural world was conceived. It was now taken for granted that land and sea were malleable, changeable, and there to serve humankind. To venture forward into the confident future advertised by the fair was to gravitate toward a world alienated from the natural environment itself.[38]

The most telling evidence of this estrangement was directly underfoot. Ex-wetlands make bad building sites. That fact compelled the fair organizers to import yet another forest to solidify the terrain with an in-ground sea of wooden pilings. Workers drove thousands of Douglas fir timbers (each nearly a hundred feet in length) from the Pacific Northwest into the muck. "An entire forest was destroyed," the fair's promotional literature announced proudly, "to convert the Flushing marsh into solid foundation."[39]

In 1938 Moses sat down to reflect on the history of the Flushing Meadows, in an essay for the *Saturday Evening Post* titled "From Dump to Glory." As Moses told it, once upon a time the Flushing Meadows "was a typical unspoiled bit of Long Island landscape—a tidal marsh covered with salt hay through which a stream flowed into an unpolluted bay." Then came its downfall at the hands of unseemly contractors and politicians who built a steaming pile of ash that stimulated the imagination of F. Scott Fitzgerald. But by the early 1930s, redemption was around the corner. After all, events had transpired to place the meadow in an auspicious location. "The Flushing meadow was almost the exact geographical and population center of the city," Moses wrote, again bending facts to assist in an assertion. Development, in other words, was Flushing's true destiny. As a result, planning began for a road to connect the Triborough Bridge with the parkways of eastern Long Island. "The route led inevitably along Flushing Bay, through the Flushing meadow and the middle of the Corona dump." Inevitable in the sense that this was "the logical place" for such a road, assuming "a general reclamation of the entire surrounding area."[40]

By Land, By Sea, By Air
ALL ROADS LEAD TO
NEW YORK WORLD'S FAIR 1939

Aerial view of Greater New York showing the fair's so-called auspicious location. The Hackensack Meadows can be seen, undeveloped, almost dead center in the map.

In fact, there was nothing inescapable about the road or the reclamation, though it did have a certain logic. A triangulated bridge helped to counteract New York's geographic disadvantages as an island community. From that bridge ran the roadways that subverted local ecologies in the name of a regional one. In the new regional system, landscape evolved (to use Moses's language) into *landscaping*—the ecological corollary to life in a world where place did not matter so much anymore. And as the century progressed, the landscapers would break out their shovels and start digging even more furiously across Greater New York.

11 THE WILDS OF STATEN ISLAND

In the shadow of the newly completed Empire State Building, a mere five miles from throbbing lower Manhattan, there was an island; a place drifting along as a rural backwater, a land of hybrid oaks with magical acorns—no two alike—a place of forested wetlands filled with black willow, sweet gum, and red maple; a world of oozing springs and gurgling brooks, carpeted with salt marsh, tidal mudflats, swamps, and vernal pools; a place alive with spotted salamanders, snapping turtles, bullfrogs, muskrats, cottontails, deer, and red-winged blackbirds nesting in reeds; a place where one could still quietly withdraw from civilization and, in the stillness of the morning, watch majestic great egrets—pristine white with yellow bills—let out a croak and then take flight.

It was nearly 1930 before it was even possible to reach Staten Island in anything other than a boat. Despite a flurry of bridge building that began in 1928, spanning both the Arthur Kill and the Kill Van Kull and thereby connecting the island with mainland New Jersey, Staten Island remained largely outside the orbit of the urban thicket that was New York. More than half the island had yet to be settled. Wetlands cloaked over five thousand acres, and the biodiversity of the enclave was remarkable, with more than thirteen hundred plant species still in existence as late as the Great Depression. The natural richness and open space gave rise, understandably enough, to a tradition of commoning—hunting, fishing, trapping, foraging—that persisted well into the twentieth century. Not until the Great Depression did Staten Island begin to make the shift from its own unique local ecology with its custom of the commons to the new regional ecology based on parks, private property, and landscaping. In light of Robert Moses's reputation as a power broker, it would be easy to assume that he alone brought the island more squarely into line with the big city's new approach to the land. But it would be wrong. In fact, it was the burgeoning conservation movement that forged the way.[1]

William Thompson Davis was Staten Island's answer to Henry David Thoreau. He was born on October 12, 1862, just a few months, as it turned out, after Thoreau died. It was an interesting case of timing, given Thoreau's own ties to Staten Island: he'd lived briefly in the Dutch Farms section, tutoring for the family of William Emerson, Ralph Waldo's brother. (Dutch Farms went on to be named Concord, in tribute to these New England visitors.) According to his biographer, Davis spent nearly his entire life "within 200 feet of the spot where he was born." That was an exaggeration, as no one seemed to have a better sense of the entire Staten Island landscape, its marshlands in particular, than William Davis.[2]

As Davis came of age, the island's landscape evolved along industrial lines. The mining of clay, for example, began before the middle of the nineteenth century and was made famous by a German named Balthasar Kreischer, who manufactured bricks on the Arthur Kill at the eponymous Kreischerville. Workers dug the clay by hand and shoveled it into wagons; donkeys pulled the loads along rail lines crossing the clay pits. Over time the clay pits were dug so deep that some of the rail spurs had to be turned into tunnels. Mechanized excavation in the 1880s left gaping wounds in the earth that eventually filled with water and turned into ponds and sometimes swamps—places with names such as Red Lake, Long Pond, Cape Henlopen, False Pond, and, predictably, Clay Ponds (now Clay Pit Ponds). In other words, in the last quarter of the nineteenth century, the island moved in precisely the reverse direction of Manhattan: that is, toward moister, not drier, conditions.[3]

Davis, meantime, went to work at the New York Produce Exchange, a commodities market and leading exporter of items such as wheat and flour. In 1884, however, Davis displayed ambivalence about his decision to join this distinguished organization, confiding in his diary his yearning to assume "my desired occupation as a future tramp." It was this craving to get out and about that motivated Davis to publish, at age thirty, a book he titled *Days Afield in Staten Island*. "Perhaps the chief value of going afield," he wrote in language reminiscent of Thoreau, "is that we are judged by a true standard—a dollar isn't worth a cent there." Among other things, what he discovered in his travels around the island in the 1890s was that by this point a "purely natural" brook was "a great rarity."[4]

There was, to be sure, still plenty of wild land on Staten Island; places such as the marsh at Old Place Creek, where Davis "spent many hours." But the changes in the land evident by the 1890s compelled Davis to produce a catalogue reminiscent of our old spring-hunting friend James Reuel Smith, a detailed list of every last spring, kill, creek, brook, hill, reef, and cove. His point was "to preserve the old, so that even the ever changing maps, that also fall within the laws of evolution, cannot make us forget Duxbury's Point or the Watering Place."[5]

In 1909, while still in his forties, Davis left his job in the business world. The future tramp had received his main chance "to ramble afield at any time I so desire." But rambling was not what it was. Thoreau's old stomping ground in Concord, Staten Island, was a case in point. As late as 1891, a map showed something on the order of fifty ponds in the area. Within five years, Radcliff's Pond had already been drained, and Cherry Pond too had nearly vanished. Mosquito control likely claimed them. By the turn of the century, New York City turned to the Standard Oil Company, with its nearby refinery in New Jersey, for oil to eradicate the menace. At Muller's (Miller's) Pond, a magazine article noted, mosquitoes confronted "a miniature Hunter's Point," a reference to the factory-dominated waters found along Newtown Creek in Queens. "Muller's pond," the article continued, "was never a beautiful sheet of

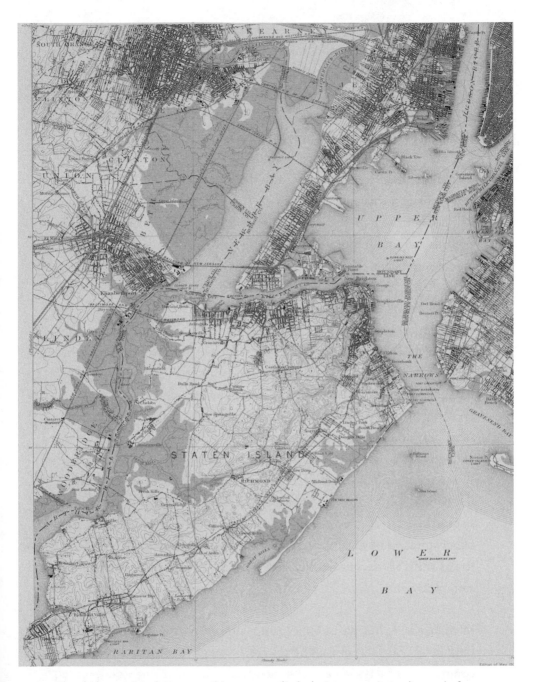

The darker, striated areas on this 1902 geological map represent salt marsh, featuring the Newark Meadows at the top south through the Elizabeth Meadows and Fresh Kills. Great Kills is pictured on the south side of Staten Island. The Old Place marsh is east across the Arthur Kill from Linden, New Jersey.

water. It is now like a bit of the Dead sea." It was less costly, however, to ditch and drain the marshes than to spread oil over them. By 1930, four million feet of trenches crisscrossed the island. Davis was undeterred. Balding, slight in stature, bespectacled, and with an easygoing smile, Davis, decked out in boots and straw boater, binoculars and butterfly net in hand, tramped through the remaining marshlands.[6]

In 1937 Davis published a second edition of his natural history. During the nearly half century since the initial publication, he reflected, "great changes have taken place in old Staten Island." For one, the island had become drier, more susceptible to wildfire, and less characterized by salt marshes and mosquitoes. In 1931 a merciless drought scorched the land. More than a third of the island—some twenty square miles—went up in flames. Mosquito control, meanwhile, had "made Staten Island livable." People flocked there. The greatest demographic gains of the twentieth century came between 1910 and 1930, when the ditching and draining intensified. From Davis's perspective, however, livability had its costs. "Devilopments" is the word he concocted to describe the shift from marshes and woodlands to housing lots.[7]

Despite the changes, Davis was still able to take pleasure in reporting "that only about 45 per cent of the land is occupied, and that there are still large areas of woodland and wide stretches of salt meadow." Elsewhere he wrote that "counting domestic animals and cultivated plants, our natural history is about as rich now as it ever was before, except perhaps in insects." As late as the Great Depression, Staten Island remained largely intact ecologically, a point confirmed by botanical data.[8]

It was this rich ecological heritage that Davis was determined to save at all costs.[9]

William Davis was part of a growing conservation movement founded on a bourgeois land ethic. These were people who saw no role for the commoning of days gone by. No place for those who cut wood, picked wild plants, hunted, or trapped on the open lands of Staten Island. Which is to say that they helped to further the regional ecology unfolding across the metropolitan area. This new conversation with the land was more firmly centered on public parks (like the ones Moses was building on Long Island), the rigid enforcement of property boundaries, and landscaping. The groups promoting this new relationship had differences. Robert Moses favored landscaping, while Davis and his compatriots derisively called it "landscraping." Both sides, however, shared a belief in private property, both revered order and control over the landscape, and both craved regulations, fences, and keep-off-the-grass signs.

The parks movement in Staten Island arose in tandem with Progressivism, a reform movement that, among other things, cracked down on hunting and collecting. By the turn of the century, disdain among the elite for the hunting of the poor and working class was palpable. In 1901, for example, the *Times* called for more game protectors on Staten Island (and throughout the metropolitan area) to combat the "[e]arly risers among the Italians" who were "raising havoc with the robins of those localities." It is no accident that the paper singled out ethnic Italians. Billions of birds typically surge up the Mediterranean flyways en route from Africa to breeding grounds in Eurasia every spring. Trapping songbirds has long been a deep-seated tradition not just in Italy but also in Malta and Cyprus. "[T]he Italian is a born pot-hunter," declared William Hornaday, the conservationist and director of the New York Zoological Park (Bronx Zoo) in 1913, "and he has grown up in the fixed belief that killing song-birds for food is right!"[10]

In 1916 the Staten Island Association of Arts and Sciences (founded in 1881 by natural historians and now the Staten Island Museum) tried to establish a bird sanctuary but found the custom of hunting on open land a problem. Hunters caught violating state game laws managed to escape prosecution when magistrates refused to hold them for shooting in sparsely settled areas. For generations, the island served as one of the city's best hunting grounds, a largely rural and wild place where gunfire generally caused no harm. But as the real estate market came to life in the early twentieth century, custom began to give way to rule of law. Holding poachers to account "tends to further the observance of order in the borough and will be welcomed not only by the householder but by the real estate operator," reported the *Staten Islander*. By the Progressive

Era, New York City had enacted ordinances forbidding the discharge of small firearms, with exceptions for the various shooting clubs still around. When, in 1916, the Board of Aldermen tried to buck the trend by sanctioning small firearms, Mayor John Purroy Mitchel—called the "boy mayor" after assuming office at age thirty-four—would have none of it. Mitchel, an anti-Tammany reformer, declared, "It is my opinion that Staten Island has gone beyond the point where it can be used as a hunting preserve." He refused to sign off on the ordinance.[11]

Staten Island conservationists viewed hunting, cutting wood, trapping, and otherwise exploiting the use-value of the land as vandalism. They likewise despised the groomed world of lawns and hedges and built on an understanding of nature that came of age with the city itself. To their eyes, nature was something that existed beyond urban life proper— an untouched domain best cordoned off. Hornaday was Davis's comrade in arms in this crusade. A cantankerous former taxidermist turned zoo-keeper who was unapologetic about his decision to put an African man on display in the monkey house, Hornaday went on to become one of the most influential conservationists of his time. When he landed on the Bronx Zoo site in 1896, it was "virgin forest" and he tried to keep it "in as natural a condition as possible," calling for special park police to guard it. Nature, in this view, was a land apart. As one bird club publication observed, "Many have the mistaken idea that nothing is of value that does not show human effort; they think that Nature as is, can be of no account, is crude and uninteresting. This of course is far from the truth, and is really disproved by the thousands who visit the forested areas of Bronx Park." Of course, there was nothing any more "natural" about fencing the area off into a park than leaving it open to the public to harvest its fruits.[12]

The "natural state" of Hornaday's Bronx creation stood in sharp contrast with the landscaped parks being built elsewhere in New York. While Robert Moses played an important role in turning landscape into landscaping, he did not singlehandedly give birth to the trend. On Staten Island, the interest in creating perfectly groomed parks had taken root in the twenties as the opening of both the Outerbridge Crossing and the Goethals Bridge to New Jersey improved access to the island.

Sensing an opportunity, realtors sold the connection between the preservation of parkland and the escalation of land values. The Staten Island Chamber of Commerce also backed the idea of devoting fully 10 percent of the island to parks. In 1930 the organization teamed up with the Park Association of New York City, headed by millionaire philanthropist Nathan Straus Jr., to promote that ambition. As a result, plans went forward for a marine park at Great Kills on the south shore, replete with a yacht basin. The city parks department also gained control of marshland at Wolfe's Pond and Willowbrook, the latter a valued hideout for American soldiers during the Revolution. Richmond Park Commissioner John O'Rourke planned to transform the 106-acre Willowbrook marsh into athletic fields. The project also resulted in the island's first man-made lake—that is, if one excludes the unintended impact of mining clay.[13]

Landscaped creations such as Willowbrook drew the ire of natural parks enthusiasts like Davis. What they aspired to was a park system made up of urban wild land. Certainly that was the goal of W. Lynn McCracken, another Staten Island conservationist who considered himself "a self-appointed Attorney for the Birds, the Water Fowl, the Trees, and all manner of creeping Wildflowers." It was McCracken who decried what he called the "misguided 'landscraper.'" McCracken recalled some renegades coining the word while condemning "the overtaming process now going on in some of the city parks." Nevertheless, the landscapers and those like Davis and McCracken who opposed their stylized version of the natural world did come together on one important issue: the need for control over the island's common lands.[14]

Although Robert Moses is often portrayed as a dictatorial figure, the truth is that the city had already criminalized customary behavior before his term as park commissioner began in 1934. In 1931, for example, park-goers could not "go upon any lawn or grassplot" without a permit. Nor was any woodcutting tolerated or the "[p]icking of wild flowers." (Davis was on record already against the "thoughtless plucking.") Nor the hunting and trapping of "any animal, bird or reptile." What the Moses administration did do was take a more aggressive approach toward the preservation of land and animal life. In 1938, new rules prevented park-goers from removing not just trees or wildflowers, but "any growing thing." Firearms were now banned in the parks. The regulations also imposed a much stricter code of personal conduct: no expectorating, littering, or glass bottles in bathing areas. A set of bourgeois values now governed the parks, though as late as 1932, no special police existed to enforce them.[15]

The changes were not beyond controversy even within the ranks of the middle class itself. Gretchen Ernst, a woman from polite society circles, spoke to the provisional nature of the newly emerging rules governing open space on the island. The prospect of "East Side peddlers and their children littering up the grass" drove her fellow conservationists—known for their efforts to preserve the "pristine beauty" of Staten Island—mad. But Ernst sided with the working class, who "worship Nature, and love trees, birds and grass" just as much as the conservationists. In her view, keeping the woods open to those of limited means involved rolling back some of the authoritarian logic that guided relations with the land. It meant, in other words, embracing a more democratic impulse. If not exactly a defender of the commons, Ernst had room in her heart for the common people and their right to commune with the natural world.[16]

The decline and fall of the Staten Island commons happened at a time of significant social and ecological dislocation. The Great Depression hit the city of New York hard, with unemployed workers tripling between 1930 and 1933. Hospitals began seeing cases of death by starvation; the poor—desperate for food—raided stores and even delivery trucks. At one time, the dispossessed could at least fill up on oysters, freely harvested from the prolific beds around the harbor, a practice dating back to the Indians. But the vertical integration of the oyster trade in the late nineteenth century made it hard even for small-scale oyster planters to survive off the local beds. And, in any case, the reefs off of Staten Island had been shut down by 1927 and remained closed until 1939. In short, by the Depression, the great transformation had taken place and marine life was severely compromised. It remains speculative as to how an intact set of marine resources might have aided the underprivileged as they struggled through hard times.[17]

Nevertheless, the summer of 1932 offered a textbook lesson in the significance of the commons. Crowds swarmed the waterfront early in August as vast schools of Atlantic mackerel came racing into the inner harbor. What explained this unprecedented fish run remains a mystery, though such banner years for mackerel had happened before. (In 1813 "the bays, creeks, and coves were literally alive with them," recalled an authority.) One skipper with some half century of experience in New York Bay claimed that "hungry schools of bluefish" had chased the mackerel into port. Whatever the explanation, the fish so darkened the water that infantrymen at Staten Island's Fort Wadsworth, positioned at the Narrows, were reportedly spearing them with bayonets. "Men, gaunt, unemployed and unable to find work by which they could buy food for their tables," clustered along the waterfront. Hundreds of people "are driven by their desperate poverty to this means of obtaining free food." The fish run virtually depopulated the interior of the island, as people flocked to the ocean commons in search of a safety net.[18]

Given the evident needs, the attack on the Staten Island commons launched in the name of conservation could not have come at a worse time for the poor. It is easy to forget that as late as the 1930s, the underprivileged depended on public land not just for food but also for fuel. It was even parks department policy to deliver firewood to those in need after cutting down dead street trees. In the brisk days of fall 1932, the Democratic Staten Island park commissioner, John O'Rourke, put out a call for five hundred men to thin the forests and deliver the firewood to the needy. The move drew predictable criticism from conservationists.[19]

By the following year, all the tree felling brought forth warnings of a "treeless Staten Island." Conservationists viewed woodcutting and other acts of so-called vandalism in the island's parks as an argument for a special park police. But the call went unheeded: it was not until 1981 that such a force was established. As the Depression ground on, the poor continued their depredations, even onto privately owned land. Island conservationists in 1933 tried to make an example out of a group of seven men, all ethnic Italians, who mowed down a grove of half-century-old oaks on private property. Two were so poor that upon conviction they couldn't pay the twenty-five-dollar fine and ended up in jail. Nature lovers, led by McCracken, went so far as to propose a ban on all tree cutting—applicable to both public and private property—done without a license. "If the householder is permitted to invade private property to fill his woodbox," went one argument, "he should also be permitted to break into grocery stores to replenish his larder."[20]

Of all the commoners' common rights, it was hunting and trapping that hung on the longest. According to the new middle-class view of the land, what was hunting to the common man was poaching to the conservationist. An allowance was made for the "true sportsman," class realities being what they were. But not for those who "belong to the tribe of those who neglect to put back the gate bars on a farm or do their gunning within range of farm buildings." These people were the modern equivalent of wild Indians—and with as little right to "invade" Staten Island's parks as the Native Americans had to reclaim the island. Moses put a finer point on the issue. "The talk about shooting by poor people for food is twaddle," he condescended. "After a man gets through paying for a license, buying a gun and ammunition and otherwise equipping himself for hunting, he might be better off going to the local butcher or grocer and buying himself something to eat like any other civilized person living within the city limits." The day after Moses explained his position, police found a man, who described himself as a caulker, outside a city park "carrying a gun and a dead rabbit."[21]

A conflict of laws complicated the hunting issue. As late as 1940, the New York Conservation Department continued to sell hunting licenses on Staten Island even though discharging a firearm was illegal under the city code. It was an old problem that Davis had wrestled with by collecting signatures on a petition that read in part, "[A] slaughter of song birds often takes place by actions of persons permitted to carry guns under hunting licenses, which persons also often invade private property." To remedy the problem, legislators in Albany introduced a bill, at the request of Robert Moses, to ban urban hunting. Though sportsmen pushed back, conservationists lined up behind the measure, making a distinction between sportsmen and pothunters. While the word *pothunter* dates to the late sixteenth century and originally meant a parasite, it had come to mean someone out for food or monetary reward, not sport. The disdain shown so-called pothunters on the island was demonstrable. Hunting near increasingly populated areas was, of course, an understandable concern. But to describe the lingering commoners as lacking "common sense" was to justify the alienated landscape as the product of reason. The fact remains that by seeking to put an end to the customary right to hunt, the conservationists worked to transform the city into a simple public-private expanse, devoid of any true commons where those of little means could harvest the fruits of the earth.[22]

Although the state passed a law in 1940 that criminalized "hunting with a dangerous weapon" in Staten Island, the ban was by then all but irrelevant. Hunters likely already felt frustrated. "The coming of the apartment house and the golf course, the miles of paved highway and the offices of real estate men, has sounded the swan song of the old-time hunter," declared a 1931 report. An island once rich in deer, foxes, opossum, and wolves had slowly been turned over to squirrels, chipmunks, mice, Norway rats, and other species better adapted to the new urban ecology taking root. And yet, as great as the ecological changes that wracked the island were, more radical upheaval lay ahead.[23]

12 THE MASSIFS OF FRESH KILLS

The Dutch colonists called it Todt Hill—that is, Death Hill. Its elevation is 412 feet, making it the highest point on the Atlantic Coast from
southern Maine to Florida. As best as anyone can tell, the name for this
outcropping derived either from a Moravian cemetery; or an Indian war
that evidently did not go well for the white settlers; or its steep grade.
For all of Staten Island's recorded history, Todt Hill loomed over New
York Harbor. Then, after the Second World War, it ran into some competition as the city of New York made a molehill into a mountain. Or,
put more technically, a tidal marsh into a mountain range better known
as Fresh Kills, the most notorious landfill in American history.[1]

The name Fresh Kill (no *s* initially) comes from the British name for
a waterway that the Dutch called Kleine Kill. Two streams feed it: Main
Creek and Richmond Creek. As the Fresh Kill flows toward the Arthur
Kill, it forks to pass around the Isle of Meadows. In the colonial period,
salt marsh swept back from the edges of these waters, purifying them
and keeping sediment from spoiling the feeding grounds of American
eels and Atlantic silversides. This land, which even in William Davis's
day was rich with ducks, herons, and bitterns, with barn swallows and
northern harrier gliding above, the air ringing with the distinctive *witch-
ity* call of yellowthroat, underwent one of the most profound face-lifts

in the entire New York metropolitan area. What the slump in oxygen levels was to the harbor, the rise of the Fresh Kills mountains was to the land. Neither change seems plausible outside the context of high-density urban development. Both changes led to a new biota: an explosion in phytoplankton in the one case, and of gulls and Phragmites (common reed) in the other.[2]

Fresh Kills started out under one big legal cloud. Colonial land governors doled out grants, but the marsh they conveyed had imprecise boundaries, complicating title issues and thus development. In the early twentieth century, the area came under increased scrutiny as a possible site for resource recovery. Plants located at Jamaica Bay's Barren Island had serviced this need, but the stench and the tendency for explosions thwarted real estate and especially the interests of the flamboyant William H. Reynolds, who was once to suburban development what Donald Trump later was to the world of hotels and towers. The city's policy of entering into short-term contracts with waste handling firms discouraged investment in upgrades to plants and equipment and contributed to the nuisance. In 1916 the Board of Estimate, in a concession to Reynolds, approved the idea of locating a new plant at the "Fresh Kills meadows."[3]

Just about every imaginable business interest in Staten Island denounced the idea, on the sound theory that it would negatively impact land values. There then ensued a struggle between local real estate interests and the outside garbage contractors. Various parts of Fresh Kills were occupied or invaded by one or the other side. At one point, the real estate operators built a shack and stationed two men on nearby Prall's Island to stake a claim. The garbagemen responded by sending armed thugs to kidnap the watchmen. The other side then sent out a derrick and boom and picked up an entire structure built by the garbage boosters—with six people inside—and loaded it onto a waiting vessel. But by that point, the city had already given its approval to a new garbage reduction plant at Lakes Island, so named because it presumably was inundated by the Isle of Meadows high tide. (Back in the 1840s, Thoreau reportedly collected arrowheads there.) The Metropolitan By-Products Company opened in

1917. In the fall mayoral campaign, John F. Hylan, Tammany's nominee, cleverly made an issue of the plant by daring Mayor John Mitchel to change the name of Staten Island to Barren Island. "They have already given you the smell," Hylan said, "and they may as well give you the name."[4]

Malodorous the plant may well have been, but it did manage to engage in some impressive resource recovery. It turned out that the closed loop made a bit of a comeback in the Progressive Era under the leadership of George Waring. A tidy man with a long, protruding mustache, Waring liked to put things in their place. Early in his career, he was charged with turning soggy Central Park into dry, manicured lawns and nicely sited ponds. In 1895 he focused his attention on waste manage-

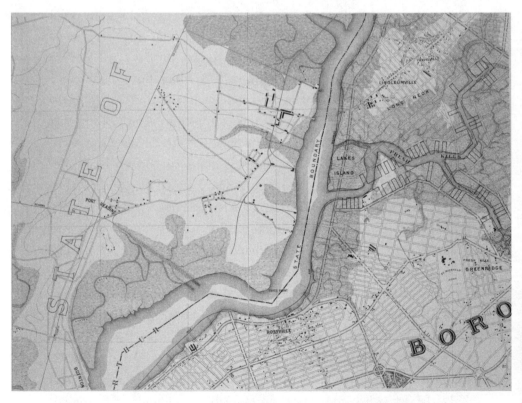

A 1901 view of Fresh Kills showing the island where Thoreau wandered. The only substantial development before the landfill was the town of Linoleumville (now Travis), home to a flooring factory.

ment as the newly appointed street-cleaning commissioner. Waring, who was famous for making garbage collection into a martial art of sorts and forcing his employees to dress up in white suits, put in place a garbage separation program. Separating the waste stream into its various components allowed for the recovery of grease, fertilizer, metals, and other valuables. Though Waring held office just a short while, the legacy of his reforms lived on. They shaped developments at Fresh Kills, where the controversial waste recovery facility produced nitrogen for use in explosives, and phosphoric acid and potash to make commercial fertilizer. Several factors, including rising labor costs and resource shortages associated with the First World War, worked to put an end to the plant. In 1918 the New York City Board of Health declared the factory a nuisance and shut it down for good. It was as if New York were making a mockery of old George Waring, who valiantly tried to give the closed loop a second life.[5]

The rise of mass consumption in the 1920s complicated the garbage situation in two ways. First, the physical volume of goods produced grew by an unusually large amount in the first three decades of the twentieth century. Second, the rise of marketing led to innovative packaging materials, many of them synthetic and designed to be thrown away. Both trends tended to undermine the profitability of resource recovery, while increasing the amount per capita of waste discarded.[6]

That left fast-decomposing items such as food to deal with. As in the past, the bulk of it continued to be barged out to sea. In 1922 the city had to purchase twelve garbage scows to supplement the seven it already had just to keep up. Unsurprisingly, the *Times* reported, "[I]t is no uncommon thing to bump into melon rinds and grapefruit while in bathing." So much refuse defiled the shores surrounding the harbor that the courts eventually banned the practice of ocean dumping as a nuisance. New York had until 1934 to put a stop to the practice.[7]

Nowhere was the effect of the decision felt more profoundly than at Rikers Island, which now was forced to take on 1.5 million cubic yards of ashes, or more material than was later dug out of the ground to build the World Trade Center, that would have been shipped out to sea in 1933.

Rikers already had twelve mountains of garbage varying in elevation from 40 to 130 feet. Capacitywise, the island was nearing its saturation point. To solve the problem, the city asked the federal government for permission to expand the island by moving out its pier lines. The government complied, and New York received another sixty-five acres of space. But what the federal government gave, Robert Moses took away when he objected to the smoldering Rikers as a backdrop to the World's Fair. Before too long, New York was in the market for a new burial ground for its trash.[8]

The man charged with figuring out the new site was Sanitation Commissioner William Carey, whom Robert Moses once called a "big international dirt mover and builder." Carey had indeed moved a lot of dirt. He put his back into building railroads, bridges, a power dam, and an indoor arena. He had a hand in the Chicago Drainage Canal, the Panama Canal, the dredging of the Salish Sea (Port Angeles, Washington), and North Beach Airport (La Guardia). In 1936 Mayor Fiorello La Guardia picked Carey, a pugnacious, clean-shaven fifty-seven-year-old, to head the New York City Sanitation Department. Without him, the mountains of Fresh Kills would likely not exist.[9]

With Rikers Island's long-term future as the city's garbage cemetery terminated by the World's Fair, Carey took a step back into the past and dredged up an old plan to build a major port at Jamaica Bay, a scheme that at least in one incarnation had involved reclaiming fifteen thousand acres of marshland. Carey's plan brought forth an outcry from conservationists, residents—one community group called the idea a return to the "Dark Ages"—and, most famously, from Robert Moses himself. Moses was appalled by the thought of an industrial port rising along the shores of an island he had long dreamed of making into a suburban recreational paradise. Instead, Moses pledged his allegiance to preserving Jamaica Bay "in its natural state" and vowed to turn it into New York City's very own Jones Beach. "Having spent millions to remove two great dumps at Flushing Bay before the World's Fair," an amazed Moses asked, "are we so stupid as to fill up the middle of Jamaica Bay with garbage, rubbish and ashes, carted around the rough waters of Coney Island by way of the Atlantic Ocean and Rockaway Inlet, with the fantastic accompaniment of fire, smell and smoke to harass nearby residents on the mainland and the beach?" That, to Moses, was an unnatural act. But by the fall of 1938, Carey backed down. Decrying what he described as Moses's narcissistic building shenanigans, he announced plans to turn to Fresh Kills instead to deal with New York's garbage woes.[10]

What Carey had planned for Fresh Kills was a long way from the closed-loop ambitions of George Waring. Carey pioneered what in 1939 was called "the land-fill method" for disposing of waste, a phrasing that highlighted the apparent novelty of his approach. The idea was to take a new, more sanitary stance on waste management by layering the refuse much as one would in baking a cake: a layer of garbage, followed by a layer of ashes, then more garbage, and soil after that to curb the odor. The British invented the method; Carey put it into practice in New York. As best as anyone could tell in the 1930s, landfills caused no risk to public health. They also had the virtue, as the *Times* pointed out, of adding "much new, valuable, taxable real estate." The city's sanitary code was reformed accordingly (limiting the depth of the refuse layer, requiring earth to be used as cover, and so forth), thereby launching what one geologist has called "the most prolific era of land reclamation with solid waste in New York City history."[11]

The effect on the salt marshes cannot be overstated. Unlike fresh-water wetlands located in uplands, tidal salt marshes were far more extensive and perfectly suited to be landfills. In 1935 it was estimated that roughly twenty-nine thousand acres of salt marsh still sprawled across New York City. That was an area of land about twice the size of Manhattan. In just a little more than one decade, a dramatic change unfolded as residential refuse reached its peak for the entire twentieth century (940 kilograms per capita) in 1940. By 1947, the acreage of salt marsh had shrunk by about half. In other words, salt marsh equivalent to about the size of Manhattan had disappeared in just over a decade to make way for not only garbage but also the World's Fair, North Beach (La Guardia) Airport, Idlewild (Kennedy) Airport in Queens, and Orchard Beach in the eastern part of the Bronx, as well as roads galore—highway building being one of Robert Moses's major preoccupations.[12]

On Staten Island, Robert Moses proposed building a park modeled after Jones Beach. In 1940, over the objections of Staten Island conservationists, who argued for a wildlife sanctuary, he recommended a massive filling project. It required that millions of cubic yards of sand be sucked from New York Harbor and deposited at Great Kills, a salt marsh on the island's south shore. To tame the marshlands, in 1944 Moses contrived to have sanitation fill barged in, primarily from Manhattan, a convenient arrangement in that the Rikers Island landfill had closed down for good the year before. In all, 467 acres of marsh and underwater land was nullified so that Great Kills Park could open in 1949. Moses had put the "great" back in Great Kills, or so he argued.[13]

If Great Kills Park came at the expense of salt marsh, it came in a borough with still plenty to spare. Staten Island hosted about 65 percent of the city's remaining marshland (in 1947), including New York's last major wetlands complex at Fresh Kills. Not content to stop with Great Kills Park, Moses resolved to conquer yet more of Staten Island. In 1945 he prevailed on the state to convey title to property at Fresh Kills, an area that he characterized as "unimproved and unused since colonial times."[14]

An initial attempt by the New York City Planning Commission (established in 1936 to oversee zoning and development) to fund the project went down in defeat. Stoking the opposition was what even Moses called the "disgraceful condition" of the Great Kills operation. Equipment problems, in large part the result of wartime constraints, had left several acres of garbage uncovered. As far as four miles away, homeowners told of invading rats. Understandably, the prospect of another much larger landfill garnered little political support. Protesters packed a City Planning Commission meeting. "Don't send us your garbage!" one yelled as the crowd egged him on. "[W]e don't want it; we won't have it."[15]

Nevertheless, the plan eventually gained the backing of Cornelius Hall, Staten Island's new borough president. In his earlier capacity as public works commissioner, Hall had initially opposed the landfill. But when his new position put him more squarely in charge of the island's economic destiny, he had a change of heart. "I am firmly convinced that a limited landfill project can be undertaken at Fresh Kills," he announced, "a project which would prove of great value to the island through the reclamation of valuable land from now worthless salt marshlands." The landfill would be the first step in an ambitious land development scheme "to build a belt highway along the west shore of the island and open vast acreage to industrial development." On this issue at least, Hall and Moses agreed completely. "The logical place for industry is on your west shore, opposite the heavy industrial area of New Jersey," Moses declared. "You have an immense acreage of meadow land in this locality which is presently valueless." Fresh Kills had made the leap from a wild and untamed marsh into a place of no earthly use whatsoever, a move that consigned the vast wetland to the dust heap of history before the first garbage scow had even arrived.[16]

There was a veneer of inevitability imparted to the decision to bury Fresh Kills. Moses articulated the "logical" nature of industrial geography on Staten Island's west shore, but he also understood the logic behind the unnatural needs of high-density urbanism. Since the federal courts had banned dumping at sea, and with New York's incinerator program starved for funds, there was really very little choice or, as he put it, "no other way" of dealing with the rising waste stream. To Moses, reclamation was destiny. Fresh Kills was just another salvage project in a long list: Orchard Beach (198 acres), Soundview Park (159 acres), and Van Cortlandt Park (74 acres) in the Bronx; Flushing Meadows (1,100 acres), Juniper Valley Park (51 acres), and Baisley Pond Park (24 acres) in Queens; and Canarsie (61 acres) and Dyker Beach Parks (31 acres) in Brooklyn. According to New York City Department of Parks calculations, Moses and his men had, with a wave of the hand, changed (or were in the process of changing) useless waste into park real estate amounting to more than 2,600 acres with an assessed value of twenty-three million dollars.[17]

Fresh Kills was more than simply a way to wring yet more value from the land. To Moses, it was the key to the growth of Staten Island

and the linchpin of a grand scheme to expand parkland, push through a major highway, and perhaps even build an airport and thereby bring the island more in line with his regional vision of the landscape. "We have pushed back the sea and filled in the swamp for parks and airports," crowed the *Times* in an editorial embracing the Fresh Kills Landfill. A "bigger future" lay ahead for Staten Island. And waste disposal was at the heart of it.[18]

While Moses was keen to invest the Fresh Kills enterprise with a false air of fatalism, there was no escaping the reality that even if the city revved up its incinerator program and managed to cut its waste stream in half, there would still be thousands of tons of unburnable waste—ash residue, bottles, cans—in need of burial somewhere. As it was, New York's municipal incinerators peaked in capacity in 1937 (with twenty-one plants) and declined dramatically during the Second World War, when salvage and conservation programs put a serious dent in combustibles. The result was the closing of nine of the city's incinerators and a free fall in the combustion of refuse by 1944. By 1946, only ten incinerators were in operation, with a capacity just half that in 1937. That meant even more solid waste for the city's eight landfills to handle. Of these, the two in Brooklyn and the two in the Bronx had, respectively, just one and two years of capacity. Only one landfill in the entire city—Edgemere in Queens—had anything approaching a long-term future. Some alternative site had to be found.[19]

That Fresh Kills was a choice, not an inevitability, is visible in the recognition that filling in the wetland could impact avian life. Staten Island's Republican congressman, Ellsworth B. Buck, pointed out that, although a part of New York, Fresh Kills "remained relatively untouched by the city's growth and development," and called for the federal government to intervene to help preserve the wetland in its "natural state." Buck speculated that the opening of the landfill could "conceivably have serious detrimental effect to the migratory wild fowl of the Eastern Seaboard." This was a plausible claim in light of New York's position on the Atlantic Flyway, the bird migration route linking eastern Canada and the Gulf of Mexico. For its part, the US Fish and Wildlife Service found that the fate of Fresh Kills took on larger significance, given its proximity to Long Island, where salt marshes had already come under heavy assault; the agency publicly stated its preference that the Staten Island wetland remain untouched. But just a few days later, the New York City Council forged ahead and, in a narrow vote, funded the Fresh Kills project. William Powell, who replaced Carey at the helm of the Sanitation Department, vouched for the necessity of the venture and gave his word that increased incineration would within two years reduce the need for landfills.[20]

There seemed to be no stopping the Fresh Kills project. Not even the cries of those who urged Staten Island to secede from New York, or the passage of state legislation (later vetoed by the governor) requiring all garbage to be incinerated before being placed in a landfill, seemed to slow the momentum. Responding to the pressure of Staten Islanders, however, Mayor William O'Dwyer announced suddenly that another site was under consideration. The location turned out to be a four-hundred-acre marshland in the Bronx along the Hutchinson River. But the Hutchinson was too narrow and meandering to allow ship traffic to proceed simultaneously in both directions, and in any case, the location was vastly smaller than Fresh Kills. It was said to have just a year and a half of useful life as New York's primary landfill. Fresh Kills, on the other hand, had at least a full decade's worth of space. The big city needed a big dump.[21]

Before the winter of 1947 was out, plans went forward to dredge at Fresh Kills to clear a path in advance of the heavily loaded garbage scows. The work took place near the old Metropolitan By-Products Company buildings, constructed thirty years earlier and still standing as a vestigial symbol of an older world centered not on warehousing garbage but on resource recovery. By the time the first scows approached in 1948, the City Planning Commission had approved the expansion of the site into a massive thirteen-section, twenty-six-hundred-acre complex that was about the size of a large ski resort. The stage was set for what would one day be described as "the world's largest waste disposal facility."[22]

. . .

Sometime around 1950, a man from the swamps of North Carolina named Joseph Mitchell set up a rendezvous with a man from the swamps of Staten Island named Andrew Zimmer. Mitchell was working as a reporter; Zimmer as shellfish protector for the state of New York Conservation Department. Born in 1901, Zimmer grew up on Old Stone Road at the edge of Fresh Kills on a farm owned by his father, John, an immigrant from Germany. In his childhood years, Zimmer wandered the marshes spearing eels and digging for steamers. He also raked oysters in Prince's Bay, at least until state health officials closed down the beds in 1916. When primary sewage treatment plants came online in New Jersey in 1940, the clam beds in the bay were reopened. So Zimmer spent his time pursuing poachers who crossed state lines.[23]

Zimmer sometimes forsook his trusty skiff and took a tour of duty plodding across the marshes. He found them teeming with crows, hawks, snakes, and pheasants. He also discovered an entire world of marsh people. Staten Island had attracted a large Italian population—the result of migration patterns during the Progressive Era—and they descended on Fresh Kills in the fall to collect mushrooms. Spring brought them back for dandelion to put in their salads. In the summer, they returned to harvest mud shrimp for *frittura di pesce*, an Italian fish fry. Others came in search of wild grapes to make jelly; some to harvest the watercress alongside freshwater creeks; and farmers to cut the immense stands of salt hay. Come Judgment Day (Hoshana Rabbah), Jews took to Fresh Kills to root around for weeping willow branches to beat the ground with and help perish all sin. As Zimmer perambulated Fresh Kills, he grew depressed about its dismal future with the dumping now under way. The city, Mitchell wrote plaintively, would eventually get around to "fill[ing] in the whole area, and then the Department of Parks will undoubtedly build some proper parks out there, and put in some concrete highways and scatter some concrete benches about." Zimmer glimpsed the world of tomorrow, and what he saw was a lot of pavement.[24]

It helps, in appreciating Zimmer's gloom, to understand something about the larger environmental context surrounding Fresh Kills and, in particular, Staten Island Sound, or the Arthur Kill, as it had come to be known, on which it was situated. In the preceding thirty years, the Arthur Kill had evolved into the most industrialized section in the entire port. Oil and chemicals formed the basis of the industrial florescence. The Arthur Kill itself accounted, in tonnage, for almost 40 percent of the commerce of the Port of New York and New Jersey. Some 138 piers alone jutted into the waterway. By 1951, the Arthur Kill had risen into the top ranks of industrial centers, discharging the greatest amounts of oxygen-depleting waste into the harbor (joining the Kill Van Kull, Newtown Creek, and the East River). To accommodate all that industry, the Army Corps of Engineers launched a multimillion-dollar project to deepen the middle of the waterway. The Corps dumped the spoil at Fresh Kills marsh.[25]

Robert Moses strove to take this gritty history into account as he tried to force Staten Island to relinquish its insularity. Initially, the Fresh Kills Landfill was sold to Staten Islanders as a temporary expedient while the city spent three years (starting in 1948) overhauling its decaying system of incinerators. But by 1951, the city had little to show for its efforts. So Moses, Cornelius Hall, and the new city sanitation commissioner, Andrew Mulrain, resolved to make the landfill a more permanent enterprise. First, they reviewed the role that landfill had played in New York, most famously at Flushing Meadows. Then they asked, Why could not the same kind of transformation that happened in Queens happen out on the meadows of Staten Island? Instead of the Grand Central Parkway, Staten Island could have a West Shore Expressway. Instead of Flushing Meadows Park, Staten Island could double its parks through reclamation around Fresh Kills. Their vision of the future was to take the world of the marsh wanderers—a world they viewed in 1951 as "fallow and useless"— and reclaim it for highways, parks, and nearly nine hundred acres of industrial and commercial development. The Fresh Kills Landfill was not simply a garbage dump. "We believe," they intoned, "that it represents the greatest single opportunity for community planning in this City." All they asked for was time—until 1968—to finish the project.[26]

In the meantime, the waste would continue to arrive at Fresh Kills from Manhattan and the northwestern section of Brooklyn, where no room remained for landfills. Even the most conservative estimate placed the amount of refuse buried in the meadows in its first few years at six million cubic yards, or more than four Empire State Buildings' worth of material. The refuse equivalent of roughly 85 percent of the fill used to reclaim Flushing Meadows was now being deposited at Fresh Kills *every year*.[27]

While the waste came from other boroughs, the topsoil—required by the city sanitary code to cover the trash—came from closer by. To get to that soil, the Sanitation Department looked to fill in the nearby Clay Pit Ponds so that it could have better access to the earth on the high ground beyond. The man-made ponds had become a habitat for least bitterns, pied-billed grebes, and wood ducks, as well as a considerable population of muskrats and thus a source of livelihood for trappers. When a Columbia University graduate student investigated Fresh Kills in the early 1950s for his master's thesis, he came face-to-face with this wildlife and the vibrant trapping economy it supported. "West of the farmlands," which families like Zimmer's still worked, "in the waving marsh grass and the inlets leading up from Arthur Kill, some of the best fur trapping along the East Coast is to be found," he wrote. "Sixty licensed trappers run their lines in this area and average about 200 muskrats apiece each year, and occasionally a mink." Some of the ponds, however, would have to go, not simply because the city needed the earth beyond them, but also because the West Shore Expressway was slated to bisect them.[28]

Ecological change was set to explode with a vengeance on William Davis's beloved island, especially on the salt marshes that had once made up one-seventh of its land area. As the postwar economic boom unfolded and the city prospered, Manhattan became top heavy with speculative office buildings, all the while sending its waste—the detritus on which the world economy turned—out to Fresh Kills for burial. The reclamation, in combination with the ditch digging to rid Staten Island of mosquitoes, dried out the landscape. The shift in habitat in turn affected the flora and fauna. If postwar Staten Island had been a state, the state bird would have been the herring gull, and the state "flower," the Phragmites.

Herring gulls fed on the fish, marine invertebrates, and insects found in the intertidal marshes. Unlike some birds, such as piping plovers, for example, which are fussy eaters, gulls are opportunists. Landfills presented them with a sprawling picnic, a point evident as early as 1946 when a bird census conducted at Great Kills found six thousand herring gulls. "The gulls have never had it so good," one Staten Island naturalist explained years later. The birds "are drawn to the table spread by the 'world's greatest garbage dump.'"[29]

The herring gull's counterpart in the plant world was the prolific Phragmites, a grass that thrives in disturbed environments. Ditch digging for mosquito control and the rise of the Fresh Kills Landfill created a literal field day for this plant. The Muhammad Ali of the grass world, the common reed is an invasive plant that is so aggressive and grows so densely that it shuts down the ability of native salt marsh vegetation like cattails (and an indigenous version of Phragmites) to survive. It can grow to twice the height of a basketball hoop and has been known to result in such thick stands that even deer cannot penetrate it. Altogether, the gulls and Phragmites gave rise to a new high-density ecology that paralleled the booming human population, which in 1950 surpassed ten million and made the New York City region the world's first megacity.[30]

There was more, of course, to landscape change in Staten Island than simply the great reclamation projects. Real estate development in anticipation of the Verrazano-Narrows Bridge (completed in 1964) also played a role in reducing the amount of marshland and the overall drop in biodiversity. Reclamation also affected wildlife prospects in the remaining marsh by blocking out the ocean tide and causing the water to stagnate, making it inhospitable to waterfowl. "Staten Island," the state game protector Sergius Polevoy said in 1960, "is being written off as a wildlife refuge." Across the island, "garbage is literally taking over."[31]

A generation after Lewis Mumford criticized the Regional Plan Association for aspiring to dilute high-density New York over a fifty-mile radius, the prediction seemed to be coming true. Even before the opening of the Verrazano-Narrows Bridge, remote Staten Island had a density (in 1960) approaching four thousand people per square mile. And in the world of planning, the concept of New York remained a big, sprawling one still largely centered on the reclamation of marshland.[32]

In 1957 the City Planning Commission announced an epic scheme to reclaim twenty thousand acres of salt marsh and land under water in all the boroughs save Manhattan. The man behind this idea was James Felt, who is best known for championing zoning reform. Felt gave new meaning to the term "city booster." He once went so far as to say that "if there was ever a place where the conscience of the world has reposed, it's New York." The 1957 plan offered a little more room for that conscience: an area of newly made land a third larger than all of Manhattan. Most of it would be located in Brooklyn, Queens, and Staten Island. The driving force behind this capacious vision was the need, it was said, for industrial parks in the outlying boroughs. Planners still operated, that is to say, within the very same extensive approach to the land that Mumford railed against twenty-five years before.[33]

The idea flopped. The future of New York real estate, it would turn out, was not in industrial parks but in speculative office buildings. By this point, David Rockefeller, the grandson of the oil magnate, had leapt at the opportunity to construct what would become the largest bank building the world had ever known: One Chase Manhattan Plaza. It was to rise near Wall Street and involve the creation of a new superblock out of the bulldozed remains of old city streets. The sixty-story building would signal the final phase of lower Manhattan's redevelopment from blue-collar port to center of finance, insurance, and real estate. Not factories and warehouses but office buildings were coming to define the economic base, a point made evident in a 1961 zoning resolution limiting manufacturing, especially in Manhattan. New York, in other words, was moving from an extensive relationship with the land to an intensive one. The modus operandi of high-density development was evolving away from the horizontal world of reclamation toward a vertical world aimed at centralizing economic activity around an urban core.[34]

What, then, was in store for Fresh Kills in light of the assumption among the planning establishment that New York would continue to grow in population? After all, there was still the question of how to handle the resulting solid waste.

Or not. In 1968 the Regional Plan Association put forth a second blueprint asserting that "waste disposal problems need not require limiting population growth in order to protect the quality of the environment." The growth of the New York metropolitan area, in the RPA's view, was in effect limitless. All that was required was some "efficient waste management." Not that the Second Regional Plan found no merit in the land reclamation that made Robert Moses famous. The plan extolled the virtues of Flushing Meadows Park and Great Kills. Indeed, the RPA seemed bent on taking the Moses model even further afield. An arresting photograph of the Hackensack Meadows found in one RPA publication has a caption noting that the far-reaching marsh is "only a short distance from Manhattan and Newark" and "untouched by development." The RPA, in short, was still thinking within the old extensive framework for marshland and employing an even wider lens.[35]

Nevertheless, the planning association concluded that to intrude further on this resource was to risk the ire of conservationists. It is perhaps this new environmental consciousness that in part explains why the City Planning Commission, now under the chairmanship of Donald H. Elliott, proposed a more intensive solution. "Existing landfill sites can be mounded," it wrote in its 1969 *Plan for New York City*, the only master plan ever produced by the city itself (and a document destined for irrelevance because real estate worried that it might limit growth). The commission also had some very particular advice with respect to Fresh Kills. "At Fresh Kills landfill on Staten Island, for example, it might not be impractical to start building a small mountain for skiing. In time, as a matter of fact, it may be impractical *not* to build one."[36]

With the climate for developing wetlands becoming less hospitable, it was time for Robert Moses to exit the stage, a move ushered along by the community outrage over his various building projects. In 1968 Governor Nelson Rockefeller demoted him while absorbing the Triborough Bridge and Tunnel Authority—Moses's base of operation—into the Metropolitan Transportation Authority. After more than forty years, his career was over. It may have been just as well for the great builder, because the days of grandiose reclamation, at least in New York City, seemed at an end. Notwithstanding the aspirations of the real estate elite, there were indeed limits to growth, and by the late 1960s, the city had run full force into some of them. Chief among these was what to do with New York's staggering waste stream—estimated in 1969 to be about seven million tons a year—as the remaining landfills ran out of room. The idea to heap the trash ever higher came just a short time after Mayor John Lindsay's sanitation commissioner, Samuel Kearing, calculated just eight years of life left in the city's seven remaining landfills. (Lindsay changed sanitation commissioners like other people changed shirts, with nine different men serving in the post during his eight years in Gracie Mansion.) Worse, though the official forecast was for eight years, the unofficial forecast was for just half that. "We were building mountains out there while I was in office," said Kearing, who, by 1969, had resigned from his post, "and they're still doing it."[37]

Arguably, the mountain building began twenty years before, when, shortly after the opening of Fresh Kills, the decision was made to increase the final elevation of city landfills to ten to fifteen feet above sea level. By the latter part of the 1950s, in response to apprehension over available disposal space, the permissible elevation rose to twenty to forty feet. By the 1960s, most of New York's tidal marshes had been filled, and, as a result, the disposal of solid waste began encroaching on underwater land. In 1969 city officials spoke euphemistically of "contouring" to further extend the useful life of its landfills. The following year, the City Planning Commission shifted to a more honest term: *mounding*. At Fresh Kills, it now recommended a final elevation somewhere between fifty and one hundred feet. The idea was to buy the city more time while it explored other waste disposal options that, the Planning Commission said, "will not endanger the environment." Fresh Kills became a sacrificial landscape.[38]

Two factors stood behind the landfill space shortage and the decision to look upward for a solution. The first was declining incinerator capacity. Despite the checkered history of burning waste, by the 1960s,

New York City had still managed to marshal what one authority called "arguably the largest refuse incineration infrastructure ever assembled in a city." At that time, New York operated eleven municipal incinerators and (because of a 1951 law requiring new apartment buildings in excess of three stories to have onsite incineration) a stunning seventeen thousand smaller units. Gotham had engineered itself into the crematory capital of the world. Roughly 40 percent of the garbage was being reduced to ash. That saved landfill space, but at the cost of a significant decline in air quality, a problem addressed in the early 1960s after evidence surfaced linking air pollution to lung cancer and respiratory disease.[39]

In 1966 the city passed a set of reforms requiring the oldest incinerators to be either upgraded with scrubbers or shut down. Incinerators built after 1951 would eventually have the option of substituting trash compactors for scrubbers. Within four years, particle emissions declined by almost 25 percent. The city itself had not built a new municipal incinerator since Brooklyn's Hamilton Avenue facility in 1962. In 1972, in response to the decision to end operations at Manhattan's Seventy-Third Street incinerator, Sanitation Commissioner Herbert Elish said, in a telling juxtaposition, "We are merely trading cleaner air for less room in our landfills." Or, more precisely, trading New York's last remaining significant wetland for fresh air.[40]

The second, and perhaps less obvious, factor behind New York's increased reliance on landfills arose from the workings of mass consumption. Sanitation Commissioner Kearing was one of the few officials in New York courageous enough to go on record about the problem, though admittedly it was after he had retired from office. Kearing blamed the lack of regulation at the federal level, which left US industry free to simply produce things and, rather than arrange to receive them back at the end of their useful lives, to thereby benefit from a de facto policy of allowing "anything at all to be buried in the ground." This approach "encourages, indeed makes inevitable, the practice of built-in obsolescence and disposability in everything from automobiles and furniture to clothing and containers. It eliminates craftsmanship while destroying the countryside."[41]

In fact, Kearing's analysis did not go far enough. Since as far back as the mid-1950s, US corporations had been engineering an ethic of personal responsibility that put the onus on individual New Yorkers themselves—indeed, on all Americans—to cope with the problem of solid waste. It was at this time that the word *littering* began to enter public discourse as part of a moral crusade.* A nonprofit organization called the Citizens Committee to Keep New York City Clean, founded in 1955, did more than any other group to foster the idea that individuals ought to be personally responsible for litter. The group's motto was "A Cleaner New York Is Up to *You.*" Like the better-known Keep America Beautiful organization, many of the sponsors of Keep New York City Clean were major corporations, including the American Can Company and Continental Can Company. These were companies that, of course, had a vested interest in pushing the cost of disposal onto the public sector, especially so in light of the surge in residential waste production that took place from 1963 through 1973 as the economy thrived. In other words, the campaign to clean up New York was brought by some of the very same companies that helped to create the solid-waste problem in the first place.[42]

In the context of continued urban growth, these two trends (declining incinerator capacity and increasing consumption) caused the garbage mounds at Fresh Kills to creep higher and higher. The final date for closing the landfill was repeatedly pushed off. Moses had estimated that the end would come in 1968. But 1968 came and went, and eventually the end was extended to 1975. In 1969 the city signaled its intention to keep the landfill in operation for an additional two to as many as five years past even that date. The scale of the solid-waste stream was simply staggering. By the early 1970s, New York produced enough in a single year to fill both towers of the newly finished World Trade Center.[43]

Barely a generation was all it took for an orgy of growth to transmogrify the biodiverse wildlands of Fresh Kills into an impoverished world of gulls and Phragmites. Fresh Kills had mutated into New York's

---

*   The word had once simply meant the act of furnishing an animal with a layer of bedding, but by the middle of the 1950s had come to mean the act of "throwing or dropping litter."

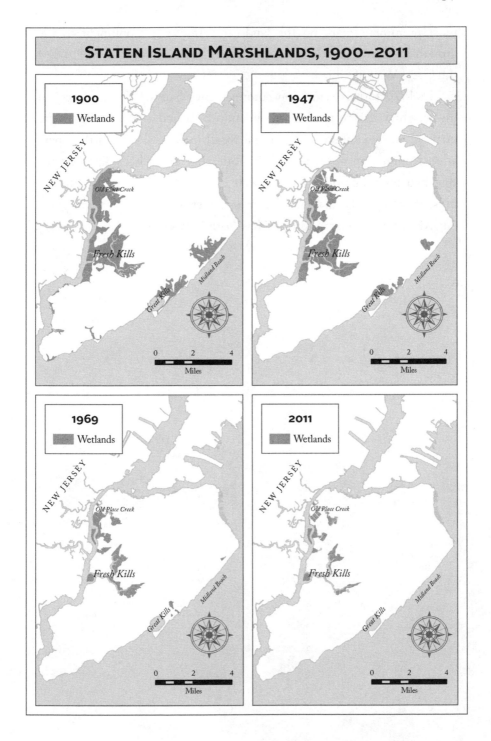

STATEN ISLAND MARSHLANDS, 1900–2011

1900
Wetlands

NEW JERSEY
Old Place Creek
Fresh Kills
Great Kills
Midland Beach
0   2   4
Miles

1947
Wetlands

NEW JERSEY
Old Place Creek
Fresh Kills
Great Kills
Midland Beach
0   2   4
Miles

1969
Wetlands

NEW JERSEY
Old Place Creek
Fresh Kills
Great Kills
Midland Beach
0   2   4
Miles

2011
Wetlands

NEW JERSEY
Old Place Creek
Fresh Kills
Great Kills
Midland Beach
0   2   4
Miles

most prominent mark on the landscape. It was a monument to the growth imperative that would one day (in 1991) exceed the volume of the Great Wall of China.[44]

In 1970 former sanitation commissioner Samuel Kearing recalled his very first visit to the legendary landfill. "It had a certain nightmare quality," he remembered. "I can still recall looking down on the operation from a control tower and thinking that Fresh Kills, like Jamaica Bay, had for thousands of years been a magnificent, teeming, literally life-enhancing tidal marsh. And in just twenty-five years, it was gone, buried under millions of tons of New York City's refuse."[45]

13 THE GREAT HACKENSACK DISAPPEARING ACT

If the wilds of Staten Island had William T. Davis, the Hackensack Meadows had a more hardscrabble group of spokesmen, including people such as Jacob Kraft. Born in the waning years of the nineteenth century, Kraft grew up hunting ducks and rabbits, and trapping muskrats, raccoons, weasels, and mink. He angled for catfish, shad, and striped bass, and harvested the stands of cedar and salt hay found near his home on Paterson Plank Road in New Jersey's Hackensack Meadows.* "My father brought me out here when I was eleven months old," Kraft recalled in the 1950s. "He paid twenty-five dollars for a half-acre of virgin swampland and built a house. He lived off the meadows the same as I always have." A day would come when Kraft would be known as the "Mayor of the Meadows." There was nothing remarkable about his life scraping by on the marshes except one thing: he lived within sight of one of the most densely packed islands in the world, a mere ten miles from Times Square.[1]

---

* This chapter focuses mainly on the Hackensack Meadows, the largest wetland in the New Jersey Meadows, which also included the Newark and Elizabeth Meadows. Figures on the overall size of the New Jersey Meadows can be found in appendix E.

A map published in 1896, the year Kraft was born, shows the Hackensack Meadows sprawling out over more than twenty thousand acres. The meadows began on the north roughly a few miles west of where Columbia Presbyterian Medical Center is today and extended south—straddling the Hackensack River—to the shores of Newark Bay, at about the same latitude as Governors Island. It was by all accounts a magnificent expanse of marshland. But by roughly the time that Kraft died in the early 1970s, it looked as if Harry Houdini had figured out a way to transpose his legendary vanishing-elephant trick out in New Jersey. By 1976, the Hackensack Meadows, once the New York metropolitan area's largest wetland and home to both nesting and migratory species such as herons, raptors, shorebirds, and rails, had shriveled to seventy-six hundred acres, a mere two-fifths of their size in 1889. And it all happened over the course of a single man's lifetime.[2]

Although most of the retreat of the meadows came to pass near the end of his life, Kraft concluded that significant ecological changes had swept over the landscape in the early years of the twentieth century. Kraft's father worked as a hay and cedar dealer, so the changes affected him directly. The hay supplied bedding for animals; it also helped to pack ice harvested from ponds in the days before refrigeration. The cedar found its way into everything from fence posts to poles for hanging clotheslines. In 1910 Kraft's father identified himself as a tinsmith, perhaps a sign that he had already begun to turn to scrap collecting for subsistence in response to the decline of the salt hay and cedar trees.[3]

What was happening in the Hackensack Meadows during the early twentieth century that would have compromised the hay and cedar so dear to the Krafts? Mosquito control and dam building. Both involved grappling with water, and both led to a significant alteration in plant life.

In some measure, the mosquito problem was a self-inflicted calamity caused by the building of railroad embankments, roads, and other projects, which, in the words of one exterminator, "destroyed the excellent drainage system established by nature." Artificially induced or not, the insect was understood to negatively affect property values. As happened

An 1896 map showing the Hackensack Meadows north of Newark Bay, as well as the Newark and Elizabeth Meadows on the bay's western shore.

elsewhere in the metropolitan area, officials ordered drainage ditches to be dug, allowing the tide to penetrate the marshes and bringing killifish to prey on the mosquitoes. In the first decade of the twentieth century, workers carved about 180 miles of trenches through the counties making up the Hackensack Meadows. But none in Bergen County, where the Krafts lived. Then in 1911 drought followed by heavy rains and high tides produced a perfect storm of mosquitoes in Jersey City, Newark, and Elizabeth. The following year, New Jersey governor Woodrow Wilson signed a law making it the duty of every county to establish a commission empowered "to eliminate all breeding places of mosquitoes." Two decades later, Bergen County alone had over four hundred miles of drainage ditches, more than any of the other counties making up the Hackensack Meadows. The ditching tended to dry out the ground, and as the drier conditions prevailed, salt hay gave way to Phragmites.[4]

With the twenties about to begin, the spirit of improvement stalked the land. "In the case of the Hackensack marsh," explained a 1919 account, "drainage ditches have helped considerably in the amelioration of the wild marsh conditions. This land has become extremely valuable for railroad terminals and factory sites, as much as $4,000 per acre having been paid for some of it." By the second decade of the century, dikes thoroughly dried out the terrain slightly south at the Newark Meadows. The diking, combined with the filling of land to create space for Port Newark and (later in the 1920s) Newark Airport, led to the disappearance of nearly a quarter of the wetlands around the lower Passaic River and Newark Bay between 1905 and 1932.[5]

Neither the ditching nor the diking was good news for those who, like the Krafts, lived off the salt hay. In addition, the rise upstream of the Oradell Dam directly affected the other main component of their living: harvesting cedar trees from a forest that, when the colonists arrived, likely covered as much as a third of the meadows. The cutting of trees for shipbuilding and roads (like Paterson Plank Road, where Kraft grew up) had already had a significant impact on the woods. But the coup de grâce for the cedars was the Oradell Dam. The dam was the work of the Hackensack Water Company, established in 1869 to supply the town of the same name. Over the course of time the company branched out to supply water to various municipalities, including the city of Hoboken. Finding that demand necessitated more reservoir capacity, the company demolished an old timber dam upstream on the Hackensack River and erected a new twenty-two-foot concrete structure, flooding neighboring land. The new dam delivered water to a long list of cities and towns and helped underwrite the real estate boom in Bergen County that began in 1927 with the construction of the George Washington Bridge.[6]

It also transformed the ecology of the Hackensack Meadows. By significantly reducing the flow of freshwater, the dam lowered the water table along the southern part of the river, and salt water from Newark Bay intruded farther upstream. The landscape below the dam, in other words, evolved from a lowland cedar forest dominated by freshwater into one long brackish estuary. Or, more accurately, a beleaguered estuary. Fourteen sewage treatment plants eventually stood along the banks below Oradell Dam, to say nothing of the waste brought to the meadows from Newark Bay as the tide rolled in.[7]

These were perfect conditions for Phragmites to flourish. Common reed does exceeding well in disturbed environments and has a high tolerance for pollution. It is unusual among grasses in that it can survive in both fresh and brackish water. By the early 1930s, the phragmites had spread like spilled ink. Indeed, the reed became so prolific that it eventually walled off the meadows from the very mosquito exterminators charged with overseeing the entire operation in the first place. Not for nothing is the plant's name derived from the word *phragma*, or Greek for "fence." Hacking away at the stands only seemed to make them denser. "Constant cutting of the reeds," explained one mosquito authority, "had the same effect as repeated cutting of a lawn, namely, bigger and deeper roots and a more luxuriant growth."[8]

As the Hackensack Meadows turned into the marshland equivalent of the suburban lawn, so did the life of Jacob Kraft take a more domesticated course. In 1916 there were not enough cedars around to bother with anymore, and Kraft took a job as a ditchdigger with the Bergen County Mosquito Extermination Commission. The more he dug, the more the Phragmites thrived. As a food source, the reed is not particularly liked by wildlife, with one main exception: muskrats. In the winters when he was not swinging a shovel, Kraft trapped. "Mostly muskrat," he remembered, "sometimes a mink." Even the bounteous waterfowl of the Hackensack Meadows must have felt the impact of the systematic drainage plan, if the nearby Newark Meadows are any guide. A 1935 report described the Phragmites crowding out "most of our native salt-marsh bird life" and the ditching as making large expanses no longer suitable for breeding. If he was not exactly digging his own grave, Kraft was certainly helping to bury the world of his father (who died in the 1918 flu pandemic) and replace it with a narrower biota largely dominated by killifish, muskrats, and the proliferating Phragmites. Little wonder that an image of the reed eventually got stamped right onto the New Jersey state license plate.[9]

During the twenties and thirties, extravagant plans to reclaim the Hackensack Meadows, including one that called for factories, suburbs, and a large park, all shot through with canals—akin to an American version of Italy's Venice—and requiring almost twenty-five times the fill used at Flushing Meadows, came to naught. If no great plans were put into action, at least the meadows had a highway spanning them that allowed automobiles to rumble freely from Manhattan clear to Newark and beyond. Opened in 1932, the road would eventually be called the Pulaski Skyway to honor Casimir Pulaski, a Polish nobleman turned mercenary who acquitted himself brilliantly during the American Revolution's Battle of Brandywine. The story of the skyway starts in 1927, when the Holland Tunnel between Manhattan and New Jersey opened. The tunnel was one thing, but once New Jersey–bound motorists emerged from it, they found themselves faced with congested local roads that left them slogging through a swamp on the way to Newark. The drive could take hours. It was this problem that the Pulaski Skyway was designed to address.[10]

The skyway was so named because it combined an elevated highway with a series of bridges over both the Hackensack and Passaic Rivers.

Moving people more quickly past the meadows, however, did nothing to curb the desire to conquer them. "A great deal has been said about reclaiming the meadow swamps that separate Newark from Jersey City," the *Times* observed before making the following prophecy. "The day is no doubt coming when the mosquito-infested jungle of rank vegetation will be only a memory of the oldest inhabitants of Secaucus and Kearny."[11]

In fact, another generation passed before the subjugation of the wilds of Jersey. Indeed, even as late as the early 1950s, there were still over thirteen thousand acres of marsh left in the Hackensack Meadows, down significantly from the twenty thousand that existed in 1889 but still a major presence. The sheer scale of the wetlands, together with their organic soils and thus very poor drainage, seemed to insulate them—if not from the mosquito exterminators, then at least from the calculating plans of those eager to erect a vast city atop them.[12]

If anything, the Hackensack Meadows seemed to be regressing. A nor'easter on November 25, 1950, ploughed through the New York metropolitan area with sustained winds clocked at more than eighty miles per hour, buffeting Newark.* This was not just any old storm. It was the most powerful extratropical disturbance to strike the harbor since March 1888, when a blizzard with high winds so paralyzed New York City that the authorities ordered that overhead wires be buried. Indeed, the 1950 nor'easter is rated as an even more severe disturbance than its nineteenth-century precursor. The storm affected the entire United States east of the Mississippi River, bringing record low temperatures, snow, and high winds. It killed approximately three hundred people. In the New York area, all three airports closed. Flushing Bay overwhelmed the runways at La Guardia. Large parts of Long Island lost power. Long Beach, New York, a barrier island, was cut off when the Atlantic Ocean came crashing over the two bridges connecting it with the mainland.

The sea gushed into the tubes linking Manhattan and New Jersey, the latter of which was especially hard hit. The swollen waters of the

---

*   Four years later, Hurricane Carol struck New York City and brought gusts of 125 miles per hour.

Hudson, Hackensack, and Passaic Rivers spilled into the streets. An amphibious vehicle had to be sent to Sea Bright to evacuate people after water cut off the old fishing community. Roughly a third of Newark went dark. There was water two feet deep in the streets of Jersey City, and gale-force winds snapped a church steeple and left it dangling. Railroad cars in Hoboken stood in three feet of water as strong onshore winds brought the sea surging in.[13]

In the North Arlington section of the Hackensack Meadows, the storm completely washed out three tide gates and six thousand feet of dikes. Unable to afford the expense of rebuilding the water control structures, the Bergen County Mosquito Commission left the area to revert to its former life as an open meadow. Ironically, letting the dikes languish may have been the most effective move the commission took in pursuit of mosquito control. The dikes had kept the killifish at bay, eliminating a primary predator of mosquito larvae. Moreover, the diking had created a habitat for the house mosquito, an insect that thrived on the freshwater that pooled behind the embankments after it rained. When the storm breached the dikes, the marsh's ecology went into reverse. The omnipresent Phragmites lost ground to salt marsh cordgrass. And as the vegetation changed, so did the bird life, shifting from rails and red-winged blackbirds—species that thrived in the Phragmites—to coots, grebes, and gallinules. Mudflats returned and so did migrating species of shorebirds. The fate of the Hackensack Meadows in 1950, in other words, was up in the air as the marshes escaped from under the thumb of human control.[14]

Scrutinizing the numbers, one finds a significant change in the meadows taking place in the early 1950s. For more than half a century beginning in 1889, the wetlands disappeared at a rate of about one hundred acres per year. Then the figure on annual wetland loss jumped to well over two hundred acres. What happened to cause this doubling in the rate of change?[15]

The beginning of the end likely began with the building of the New Jersey Turnpike. In 1949 the state of New Jersey, sandwiched between New York and Philadelphia and thus subject to considerable traffic, established a turnpike authority to relieve congestion and capitalize on the flow of goods. Conveniently, during the administration of Franklin Roosevelt, the US Bureau of Public Roads had already sketched out a path through the state. In 1949 ground was broken for the turnpike. Three years later, it was largely finished and included a ten-mile stretch that forged through the Hackensack Meadows en route to the George Washington Bridge. More than 5.6 million cubic yards of rock and sand disappeared into the marsh, including a portion of the only hill of any stature in the meadows, an outcropping in Secaucus called Snake Hill—which Progressive Era reformers changed to Laurel Hill in order to enhance the city's image. In the ten-mile section built across the meadows, the turnpike crossed seven waterways, including the Hackensack and Passaic Rivers as well as brooks such as Penhorn Creek, which drained through the marshland around Secaucus. As a *Times* report on the progress of the project put it, a caravan of more than two hundred trucks rumbled on "in a seemingly endless procession as formerly useless marshland is transferred into a solid base for the multi-lane roadway." Of course, modifying the word *marshland* in this way tended to pave over the world treasured by meadow men such as Jacob Kraft.[16]

At a minimum, the turnpike's embankments divided up the eastern portion of the Hackensack Meadows and impeded the estuary's tidal action. But the indirect environmental effects of the road proved even more consequential.[17]

The new turnpike attracted the attention of a farmer's son turned entrepreneurial trucker named Malcolm McLean, who owned a large fleet of vehicles for hauling textiles and cigarettes from North Carolina to cities in the North. Concerned about highway congestion and looking for a way to save costs in a tightly regulated industry, McLean masterminded a plan to use ships to transport the containers. The idea was to unload from ships directly to tractor-trailers and thereby avoid highway traffic altogether. In 1953 McLean began to zero in on Port Newark as a possible place to buy terminal space. He found the port's proximity to the turnpike attractive. Better yet, the Port Authority offered to float the bonds to develop the site and then simply lease the space to McLean, saving him the trouble of raising a vast amount of capital. McLean would eventually call his company Sea-Land Service.[18]

This new vision of the land's relationship with water had its most profound impact on the marshlands around Elizabeth (south of the Hackensack Meadows and Port Newark). The success of McLean's Newark operation inspired the Port Authority in 1955 to put forward a plan to build the nation's most ambitious port project to date. Port Elizabeth would have enough berth space for twenty-five containerships, with plenty of room alongside the vessels for storing the big shipping boxes. It would initially encroach on 450 acres of meadowland and put the last of the salt hay farmers out of business. Sea-Land was able to open in 1962; the marine complex was expanded to over seven hundred acres later in the decade. What eventually became known as the Port Newark–Elizabeth Marine Terminal constituted the finishing blow to the Elizabeth Meadows.[19]

To the north, the turnpike launched the Hackensack Meadows on its career as one of the most famous dumping grounds in the country. It is often forgotten that before hills of garbage adorned the land, the meadows played host to a kind of urban factory farming. Secaucus was the epicenter. Telling the story requires dropping back in time nearly a century.

In the 1860s, the New York City Board of Health closed down factories for boiling swill (scraps of food mixed with water) near Fifty-Second Street and Seventh Avenue. Instead, swill collectors began delivering refuse from hotels and restaurants by ferry to piggeries in New Jersey. It is hardly romanticizing to point out that, if nothing else, the sixty or so pig farms and hundreds of thousands of porkers, while they certainly transformed various creeks into their own private toilets, also managed to recycle garbage into usable food. The turnpike, however, dealt the closed loop a blow. The road took the land of eleven of fifty-five farms. The national attention the Secaucus piggeries gained when one of their own, a man named Henry Krajewski, ran for president ("The Democrats have been hogging the Administration at Washington for 20 years, and it's about time the people began to squeal") didn't help. By 1953, Secaucus, in response to complaints about the awful odors, banned any new piggeries. Concerns about trichinosis and a swine virus only added to the pig farmers' woes; eventually the state cracked down and forced them, under court order, to close up shop. The farms had all been driven from Secaucus by 1961.[20]

But the metropolis's waste had to go somewhere, and as the farms wound down their operations, the landfills ramped up theirs. Altogether, the number of landfills in New Jersey rose from just 10 in 1954 to 141 six years later. The marshes suffered accordingly. A 1957 report on the East Rutherford Meadows (near the family home of the Krafts) found that bulldozers filled in roughly five to six acres of marsh *every month*.[21]

By the 1950s, the Hackensack Meadows was slowly becoming *The Meadowlands*—the last extensive stretch of meadow in Greater New York. Resting a short distance from the world's greatest monument to speculative real estate, the Meadowlands had emerged as one giant anomaly just crying out for development. "That the meadows, wild, seemingly boundless, and so often beautiful beyond description, should remain as they are within this, the greatest urban concentration on the face of the earth, is in itself a curious thing," wrote the novelist (and native New Yorker) Howard Fast in 1958. The Meadowlands ran against the grain of history. Fast had no doubt that within a decade, the meadows would be diked off and reclaimed. "For these fifty square miles are potentially the most valuable unbuilt area of its kind in the whole world," he concluded. "Consider it, an area larger than Manhattan Island, paralleling Manhattan Island, and less than five miles away—and empty." The *Times* agreed that the place was one great wilderness adventure that could not last. Shortly after New Jersey's governor Robert Meyner (echoing Fast) declared it "potentially the most valuable acreage in the world," the paper put a very fine point on the entire matter. "The city and its environs are bursting at the seams. The meadows must go."[22]

Continuing in this same vein, a geographer named Charles Morrison, who had worked for the Regional Plan Association, an organization that had been eying the developmental potential of the Meadowlands for some three decades, called the sweeping marshlands in 1961 "a land use anomaly." Given that the Meadowlands had a permanent population of just over six hundred people, Morrison felt justified in calling it essentially vacant. There was, to be sure, some industrial development in the meadows: about a thousand acres devoted to chemical factories and other manufacturing concerns. The turnpike, meanwhile, had attracted warehouses and truck terminals, almost fifty of them, to the marshlands. Then, of course, there were the garbage dumps. And Morrison did acknowledge that the meadows were being "used"—a word he qualified with scare quotes—by ordinary people. There were those seeking to commune with nature, those on a quest for recreation, and the meadow men and mosquito exterminators, callings that came together in the life of Jacob Kraft.[23]

With development staring this real estate no-man's-land in the face, the world of the meadow men came increasingly to light. One of the interesting aspects of this world was its fluid sense of property. Interviewed in a 1957 article in the *New Yorker*, Kraft admitted that he and his fellow meadow comrades had no "exclusive rights on any land except what we owned." Another trapper, Charles Lanza, seemed to treat the Meadowlands as a commons, not knowing whose land he trapped on and, in the words of the reporter, saying he "didn't give a hoot." How widespread this freewheeling understanding of the land was is hard to say. A Jersey City trapper named Jack Churuti interviewed in 1959 claimed that he had been picking huckleberries, collecting cattails, and hunting muskrats using clubs in the Bergen County marshes for fifty years, presumably on land he had no ownership stake in at all.[24]

As the 1960s drew to a close, the Meadowlands had solidified its reputation in two main areas: as an urban wilderness and as the solid-waste capital of the state. In 1968 it absorbed nearly thirty thousand tons of garbage per week. That calculated out to about nine million cubic yards of refuse a year, or enough to fill the Washington Monument three hundred times. Over a hundred municipalities in New York (principally New York City) and New Jersey disposed of the remains of the day in these once magnificent marshlands. Domestic waste made up a third of the trash stream, industrial waste another third, and demolition debris—including parts of old New York landmarks such as Penn Station (demolished in 1963) and the Ziegfeld Theater (razed in 1966)—the remainder. Landfills had thus far reclaimed roughly fifteen hundred acres of marsh. On the recouped land were everything from diners, to gas stations, to a par-three golf course and, of course, roads such as the New Jersey Turnpike to help shuttle people to these commercial strips. Eleven active landfills operated on an additional eleven hundred acres.[25]

Sometimes ecological change took an unexpected turn. Consider the canary. Pet lovers fed their canaries seed derived from marijuana, and then cleaned out the birdcages and threw the droppings in the garbage, which were duly trucked off to landfills. Marijuana takes well to water, and eventually the Hudson County portion of the Meadowlands turned into a kind of cannabis plantation. In 1968 the state's drug czar lobbied for helicopters. "We could defoliate the place à la Barry Goldwater," he said. One part wilderness, one part transportation corridor, and one part Wild West show, the Meadowlands muddled on—a strange, liminal place on the edge of one of the most intensely developed pieces of land in the world.[26]

In 1966, though the Hackensack Meadows had been slimmed down to a little over half its late-nineteenth-century size, there still remained more than ten thousand acres of marsh hovered over by rough-legged hawks. It was a world of nesting bitterns; of black skimmers with stunning red and black bills knifing through the water looking for fish; of noisy killdeer letting out plaintive calls; of blue crabs, striped skunk, and snapping turtle. This was Willie Royka's stomping ground. Royka hailed from Little Ferry, located in Bergen County, near where the Krafts also lived. A 1965 photograph of him at the age of forty-six shows a hard-bitten, scrappy-looking, stubble-cheeked man wearing waders and a torn sweatshirt standing in a reed-flanked creek. In each hand he is holding a dead muskrat, as if to say to the viewer, "These little creatures are my life"—which they were. For twenty-five years, Royka had been trapping muskrats and shooting ducks to make a living off the land, supporting his family with what he could kill with his bare, half-frozen hands. If history had ended here, a marsh about three-quarters the size of Manhattan would rest on the western flank of the New York metropolitan area.[27]

The future of the meadows could not have looked more uncertain. First, there was the laissez-faire approach to development. With no state income tax, the municipalities that made up the meadows longed for a revenue stream to help lower property taxes, and found it in the form of various industries eager to set up business in the marshlands. Those who favored turning over the meadows to development in the relentless pursuit of more tax dollars, and watched merrily as it was paved over, came to be known in some circles as "the cement people." The result was a helter-skelter approach to planning. Second, a countervailing force helped to slow down piecemeal reclamation of the meadows and made it hard for anyone to imagine the future. A 1960 legal ruling had thrown into question the entire idea of private property in the meadows. The decision concerned the old "tidelands doctrine," which came originally from English common law dating back to the fifteen hundreds and established that title to land washed by the tide belonged to the monarchy. Ownership of the tidelands eventually devolved to the individual states that made up the United States. But the 1960 legal rule applied the doctrine to *marshland* that was not necessarily on or even near the coast at all. As the state began asserting claims to hundreds of parcels of land, the Hackensack Meadows became a legal quagmire overnight.[28]

The Hackensack Meadowlands Development Commission (HMDC) was established to create order out of this chaos. The agency was the brainchild of three men: New Jersey's governor, Richard Hughes, a confidant of Lyndon Johnson's, who, like the president, was known for his high-pressure tactics; Paul Ylvisaker, an urban planner who served on President Johnson's Task Force on Cities; and Fairleigh Dickinson Jr., a Republican businessman born in the Hackensack Meadows town of Rutherford (named for John Rutherfurd of 1811 grid fame), who was eager to halt the descent of the marsh into the New Jersey equivalent of Fresh Kills. Together they fought for state legislation, passed in 1968, creating the new commission. The act referred to the area as "the Hackensack meadowlands" (not The Meadowlands), an overwhelmingly natural entity awaiting the transformation that would bring with it the capitalization of the site's name. The new law applied to roughly twenty-one thousand acres of land in fourteen municipalities in Bergen and Hudson Counties, a low, wet region notable for its unplanned development and thus in danger of losing an "incalculable opportunity." The commission amounted to a zoning and planning agency with two responsibilities: systematic development and the management of the vast quantity of solid waste streaming into the meadows. Although centered on civilizing the marsh, the commission was charged as well—this being after Rachel Carson helped launch the environmental movement with *Silent Spring* (1962)—with preserving "the delicate balance of nature."[29]

Ecologically speaking, at the time the commission took charge, the Hackensack Meadows had hit rock bottom. There was still some functioning cordgrass marsh east of the new turnpike spur (completed in 1971), but the diversity of the estuary—from oysters and razor clams, to green crabs and periwinkles—had vanished. Now four main life-forms dominated: Phragmites, muskrats, killifish, and waterfowl. The biota was the result of an ecological history dating back three generations—of the ditches, dikes, and dams that had transformed the hydrology. Gone were the wild rice and bur marigold once found in tidal freshwater marshes, where the incoming salt water was overwhelmed by the flow from upstream. Only a few remnants of cedar swamp survived, clinging to life in Little Ferry and Moonachie. As the commission concluded, "[A] wholly new ecology, that of the urban estuary, has been formed."[30]

At the time the commission took over, the growth imperative was also under assault on several fronts. It had pushed the land about as far as it could go, the environmental movement was gearing up, and the era of grand public works projects in the Robert Moses mold was coming to a close. But the commission was stuck in the past and felt itself drawn to some kind of boundless urban vision. The planners seemed for some reason to have Italy in mind. At Berrys Creek, for example, the commission proposed a residential and office complex situated along an already existing canal. "The center should have all the charm of Venice's San Marco Plaza." Apart from the meadow men, the wetland had never been home to many people. This state of affairs the commission strove to change. It envisioned island communities sprouting in the meadows housing a population of 185,000. The houses would be located near new marshland conservation areas and parks. Other parts of the meadows would, under the commission's master plan, see more traditional kinds of development such as rail and truck terminals, as well as manufacturing and light industrial activity, the stock-in-trade of the Hackensack Meadows. In the background, trucks would be humming away, tending to the twenty-six thousand tons of solid waste a week, the minimum that the law required the commission to take responsibility for in perpetuity.[31]

The logic behind the plan went as follows. Building high-density housing developments along the Hackensack River would spur the cleanup of the waters and make the new homes attractive. The housing would in turn generate a tax base to support more sewage treatment plants and thus further boost water quality. An aide to the HMDC's executive director put it this way: "To the messianic ecologist who asks, 'Are you going to put *anything* there?' the answer is, 'Of course we are.'" A dense population had been thought of as a threat to the natural environment. The commission turned this idea on its head, arguing, in effect, that more growth was the best way to safeguard ecology.[32]

Like every one of their predecessors dating back to the Swartwouts, the planners had their hopes dashed. One almost has the feeling that the Hackensack Meadows would have reduced even a Baron Haussmann or a Robert Moses to tears. Objections to the master plan cropped up almost immediately. Editorials took aim at the idea of an urban utopia when hard-pressed cities, including nearby Newark, had decayed into smoldering ruins. Others damned the commission's logic as illogical. "There is no instance in man's history where the development of a new city has benefited nature in any way," read one. "We do not need another city in northern New Jersey," proclaimed a conservationist. Another pointed out that the population density around the meadows rivaled that of Hong Kong. Leave the marshes be! went the cry. This philosophy, put forward by environmentalists, questioned the older, extensive approach to urbanization, going back a century, as a boundless, open-ended proposition. The environmental community, in short, wanted to limit growth to the existing urban cores and thereby spare open wetland from development.[33]

Before the HMDC plan even received much of a hearing, it was overshadowed by the prospect of a giant sports complex to be built on the Walden Swamp, just south of Paterson Plank Road in East Rutherford. More than anything else, it was the transformation of this erstwhile cedar swamp into a sports and exposition center that solidified the reputation of the area as *The Meadowlands*—no longer a generic complex of marshland but a tourist and entertainment destination. The Meadowlands Sports Complex, located on land set aside by the HMDC, would host Giants Stadium and a racetrack. Access to the facilities would come via the new western spur of the New Jersey Turnpike, finished in 1971, a roadway that funneled eleven million cubic yards of fill into the marshlands and buried old haunts like Doctor's Creek. The sports facility would sprawl across 750 acres of what had been protected wetland. Indeed, the authority empowered to build the project was given, as one legal commentator put it, the "freedom to disregard environmental standards." In the end, the sports complex accounted for fully 12 percent of the wetlands lost during the two decades following 1966.[34]

Jersey real estate deal makers such as Charles Klatskin could hardly control their enthusiasm. "If all goes well," exclaimed Klatskin, "many of us will live to see the creation of a magnificent metropolis which will rival New York City and in many ways surpass it." Realtors anticipated soaring land values. By the fall of 1971, twenty-five hundred acres of land under the control of the Hackensack Meadowlands Development Commission was, as the name implied, open for development, including a 720-acre tract in Secaucus on which the real estate arm of Hartz Mountain Products, better known for its pet food, built industrial and commercial space. "Things were helter-skelter until the commission came in and laid down rules," one Hartz Mountain spokesperson pointed out. "Now everyone knows that if they want to build they have to take care of the land." The HMDC had indeed brought order to the development process. It saw to it that buildings went up at the proper elevation and with adequate sewage disposal. The laissez-faire approach to the Hackensack Meadows had vanished just as surely as the cedar swamps had. "I get a sense after two years," said satisfied HMDC executive director Clifford A. Goldman, "that the attitude that the meadowlands is a place to get rid of your junk is over."[35]

As the sports complex went up, so did land values, doubling between 1970 and 1974. Klatskin was so smitten with the Meadowlands that he held his fortieth birthday party in a vacant warehouse out in the reeds. "The hottest area in the US used to be Houston," he raved. "Now it's the Meadowlands." Klatskin said that developers had the HMDC to thank for taking "'politics' out of the land development." What he meant was that before the commission undertook its work, petty rivalry among towns stymied real estate deals. Now land development could proceed with fewer restraints. Between 1966 and 1976, the Meadowlands experienced the most unsparing attack in its recorded history, an onslaught that diminished the marshes by more than three hundred acres a year.[36]

Piecemeal development combined with increasing solid-waste disposal to chip away relentlessly at the Meadowlands, replacing the natural density of the marshland with a new urban ecology thick with people, highways, and industry. Improvement had some unforeseen results. Willie Royka found it simple to catch muskrats now that reclamation had narrowed down their habitat. As he worked the wetlands, he watched as development rushed in. "All this building makes it much easier for me," he explained in 1978. "I get the rats in a bunch now." When he wasn't trapping muskrats, Royka collected scrap metal, barely getting by with his family. By the 1970s, Royka had become something of an urban sensation: a poor trapper who, despite his proximity to the big city, still managed to scrounge a living from the Meadowlands. Why the attention showered on Royka? It may have been a reflection of just how alienated from the natural environment urbanites had become. As the veteran nationally syndicated news reporter Tom Tiede put it in a 1972 feature article, Royka was "perhaps the only man left in the megalopolis who manages to survive off what remains of the land."[37]

Nevertheless, it would be a mistake to conclude that the ecological history of the Meadowlands was simply one long, descending curve. Environmental reforms, beginning with the 1972 Clean Water Act, had a positive impact. In 1978 the US Environmental Protection Agency described the Meadowlands as "a water-quality success story." Fish kills in the Hackensack River estuary had fallen dramatically since earlier in the decade, as the HMDC collaborated with the EPA to increase dissolved-oxygen levels. Most spectacularly, the marshland along Saw-mill and Kingsland Creeks, flooded during the 1950 storm, had regenerated by the 1970s into an intact stretch of cordgrass marsh (in what was, admittedly, a vast sea of Phragmites). Development could work in unexpected ways. Even severely disrupted drainage systems, like the marsh-land near the New Jersey Turnpike, evinced enormous productivity. By chance, the highway combined with the failure of a pumping system to transform the area into a freshwater ecosystem with several substantial ponds. Although dominated by Phragmites, the 342-acre marsh con-stituted prime waterfowl habitat with "a phenomenal waterbird density and diversity unparalleled by any other fresh water marsh in the state," according to Richard Kane of the New Jersey Audubon Society. More than two hundred different species of birds—pied-billed grebes, gull-billed terns, black-crowned night herons, and scores of others—roosted and fed on the marsh, while just a short distance away, traffic whizzed along at seventy miles per hour. These gains, however, were, of course, offset by the dramatic decline in wetlands acreage from over twenty thousand in 1889 to a bit over fifty-seven hundred in 1985—a more than 70 percent drop.[38]

By this point, the geography of the modern Meadowlands was all but complete. An entire armamentarium of federal agencies, including the Army Corps of Engineers, the US Fish and Wildlife Service, the Federal Emergency Management Agency, and the National Marine Fisheries Service had converged to improve the ecology of the marsh-land. The EPA played the most important role, holding up even small projects by strictly applying Section 404 of the Clean Water Act, de-signed to regulate the discharge of fill into waterways. "At some point there's got to be a limit to development before you get real ecological

damage in that area," explained one EPA administrator in capturing the
spirit of the agency's mission. By the mid-1980s, development of the
Meadowlands ground to a halt, much to the chagrin of Hartz Mountain, which had expanded its real estate holdings and had accumulated
so much money building there that some joked that HMDC stood for
Hartz Mountain Development Commission. The Meadowlands had
largely assumed its current topography. In the decade after 1985, annual
wetlands loss plunged to just twenty acres a year, the lowest level of loss
in a century.[39]

If the Meadowlands, like most wetlands in the New York metropolitan area, had been reduced to a fraction of its former size, it also came to
resemble other one-time marshlands in its mountainous terrain. When
the HMDC first began its work, roughly an acre a day of wetland was
lost to the garbagemen. More than one hundred municipalities sent trash
to the landfills, where it was bulldozed into the marshes. Undeveloped
marshland saved on costs because under the law, sanitary landfills had to
be covered with earth; otherwise soil would have to be trucked in from a
distance. Plans for a super-incinerator to offset the dumping and provide
ash fill for more development—the HMDC being first and foremost
a development authority—stalled, because even the largest furnaces in
the world could not handle the volume produced in New Jersey. By the
early 1970s, roughly forty-two thousand tons of waste a week streamed
into the landfills, a more than 60 percent increase over the twenty-six
thousand tons the HMDC was obligated to provide for under the law.
It was a matter of losing the wetlands entirely or building them up. The
reformers at the HMDC chose the latter tack.[40]

In 1987, landfill operations that had once extended over twenty-five
hundred acres of wetland had been reduced, under the guiding hand of
the HMDC, to just a tenth of that. Consolidation had left three large
mountains, each over a hundred feet in height. At the imposing Bergen
County landfill in Lyndhurst, the trash had piled up so high that a garbage truck lost control and went careering down the slope, landing right
in front of the HMDC's headquarters.[41]

In the space of just fifty years, the major wetlands in the New York

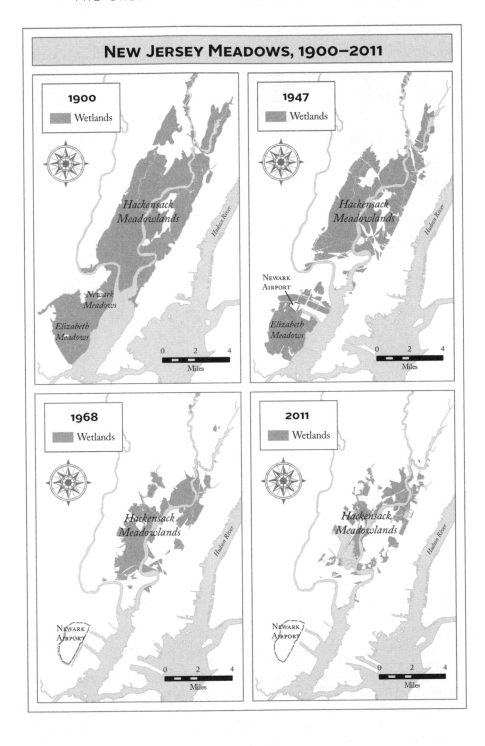

NEW JERSEY MEADOWS, 1900–2011

metropolitan area had not only been filled. Some had been made into mountains.* The transformation of this land brought with it a new high-density biota of gulls, pigeons, and Phragmites that was able to adapt and flourish in disturbed habitats with a dense human population. Altogether, less than a quarter of the original marshland around the harbor remained intact by the 1980s. Put differently, an expanse of marsh four times the size of Manhattan had retired from sight. Night had come to the meadows.[42]

---

* Although the data are sketchy, one estimate suggests that in the twentieth century, an estimated 50 percent of the marshland across the globe had been sacrificed to make way for agriculture and more megacities such as New York. Dhaka, Bangladesh, with over fourteen million people, lost more than 50 percent of its wetlands between 1968 and 2001 alone.

PART 4
THE GREEN COLOSSUS

1960–2012

14 THE AGE OF LIMITS

The hypertrophic approach to landscape reached its zenith in the early 1970s. Along the Hudson in southern Manhattan, one of the most dramatic topographic changes in the recorded history of the island was taking shape: a ninety-one-acre land-making project named Battery Park City. And that was not all. Along the East River a planned expansion—encompassing the very spot where George Washington set foot—dubbed Manhattan Landing was anticipated to swell the island by over a hundred acres. "We are not satisfied with the size of the island we bought," declared Mayor John Lindsay, whose patrician upbringing instilled in him a sense of limitless ambition.[1]

It is not every day that a mayor wakes up and decides his quarters are too small. But then it is not every city that has been so intoxicated with expansion. Perhaps the purest expression of that impulse came at the hands of the Regional Plan Association in its second blueprint, released in 1968. Fully cognizant, of course, of the New York metropolitan area's status as the largest urban agglomeration in the world, the RPA asked, "How big should an urban region grow?" The answer echoed down the centuries: "[T]he urban region has lost its boundaries and should be considered an open-ended system." Population growth within an urban core was "both logical and desirable." There were, in other words, no true limits to growth. "The acceptance of large metropolitan size," explained the RPA, "is not simply bowing before the inevitable; it is a recognition that the great city is one condition of man's fulfillment in the modern world."[2]

Around the same time that Lindsay expressed his disaffection with Manhattan's size, the New York Convention and Visitors Bureau summoned forth the moniker that remains in place to this day: the Big Apple. A jazz term, the phrase captured the sense in musical circles that performing in New York meant playing in the big time. City boosters, naturally enough, rarely suffer from a deficit in overweening pride, but the point stands that New York's leaders longed to inflate both the city's image and its physical reality. Who at the time would have dreamed that, despite the power and allure of this expansionary impulse, the Big Apple had grown about as big as it would get?[3]

Battery Park City turned out to be the last major expansion of Manhattan Island. By the 1970s, the growth imperative was under attack, a trend nowhere more apparent than in the battle over Westway, an extravagant land-making plan set to rise along the Hudson River on Manhattan's West Side. New York was entering an age of limits founded on a new approach to the natural world that, while still deeply oriented toward real estate development, was more constrained in its stance toward the surrounding waters.

Nevertheless, the new, gentler approach to the waterfront did little to change the *kind* of boundary found where land and sea met. The expansion of Manhattan had proceeded in lockstep with the hardening of its shoreline, a process that involved replacing wetlands and mudflats with bulkheads, turning the island into a fortress of sorts. But the safety the bulkheads seemed to afford was an illusion. By allowing building to take place directly in the floodplain, they actually made the island more vulnerable to storm damage. The walls also had some inadvertent ecological consequences that fit with the pattern of the metropolitan area's more recent natural history. By disposing of the shallow habitat adjacent to Manhattan, the hardened shoreline created an open-water environment hospitable to a smaller range of life-forms. And the fish species that did flourish flourished like mad, producing a high-density biota that was a kind of marine equivalent to the ubiquitous Phragmites. If New York's human population was known for its density and diversity, its plant and animal population tended more toward the former at the expense of the latter. A kind of cookie-cutter ecology had taken hold.

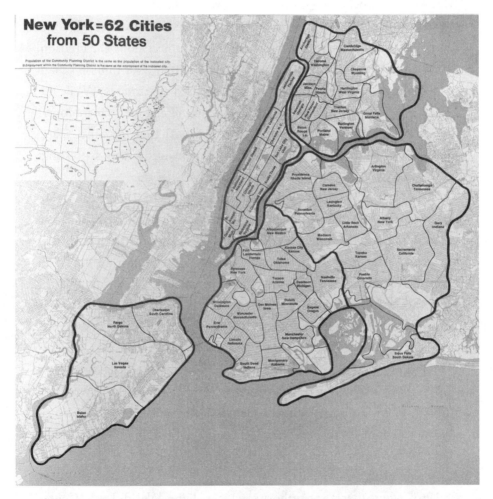

New York = 62 Cities from 50 States

This 1969 City Planning Commission map, published at the height of the hypertrophic approach to landscape, valorized New York's high human population density. A high-density biota came along with all the people.

• • •

It is a historical justice of sorts that Battery Park City went up in the section of Manhattan that served as the birthplace of the city's underwater adventures. Originally referred to simply as the Hudson River Landfill Project, the Battery Park City development was dreamed up by the New York City Department of Marine and Aviation. Its most powerful backer, however, was an organization called the Downtown-Lower Manhattan Association (DLMA), the brainchild of David Rockefeller, the grandson of the famed oil magnate and president of Chase Manhattan Bank. The plan for a sixty-five-acre landfill project along the Hudson, broached in 1962, called for six pier slips, more than four million square feet of commercial space, and forty-five hundred apartments. While the DLMA approved of the plan, it deemed commercial piers "inappropriate." Rockefeller preferred a waterfront ringed with housing, office space, and esplanades, the last a concept so unfamiliar in the early sixties that he was asked by one radio host what it meant.[4]

The New York waterfront was in transition. In 1960 Manhattan and Brooklyn together accounted for more than three-quarters of all the cargo shipped through the port. But just six years later, with the containerport in Elizabeth, New Jersey, now in operation, almost a third of all cargo flowed through facilities in the Garden State. The crumbling of New York City's maritime economy was a complex process, but there was nothing inevitable about it. Indeed, Rockefeller and the DLMA seemed hell-bent on ushering along this transformation and, in the process, reinventing lower Manhattan. As early as 1959, Rockefeller called the New York waterfront "inadequately utilized." Two years later, the city pushed through a new zoning ordinance that radically reduced the amount of allowable manufacturing space, especially in Manhattan. The deindustrializing ethos at the heart of the new zoning impacted the island's East River side nearer the financial district more than the Hudson side. But in 1961, when the Port Authority relocated the World Trade Center project—another Rockefeller-inspired venture originally planned for the East River—to the Hudson River (to convenience New Jersey commuters on the newly created PATH—Port Authority Trans-Hudson—transit system), the stage was set for a radical remaking of lower Manhattan's western shore.[5]

In the spring of 1966, David Rockefeller's brother Nelson, then the governor of New York, announced a plan to build office and recreational space, housing, and even some light industry on a ninety-eight-acre landfill in the Hudson River. Nelson Rockefeller envisioned a city within a city: hence the name Battery Park City. The project was of a piece with the monumental trend in architecture then dominating lower Manhattan, the most massive of which were the twin towers backed by David and Nelson Rockefeller and planned to rise just a short distance away.[6]

Ground was broken for the towers that summer, as workers dug a hole roughly seventy feet deep—the so-called bathtub—in order to lay the foundation. The Port Authority had initially planned to simply deposit the excavated material at sea. But under an agreement worked out between the agency and the city, the fill instead went to reclaim 23.5 acres of land in the Hudson River (most of which fell within the confines of the old Montgomerie grant, extending four hundred feet from the low-water mark). "The landfill will further fatten Manhattan Island," read a report in the *Times* referencing the three-hundred-year history of land making. Robert Moses, never shy about giving his opinion, offered that the newly made land should house the New York Stock Exchange but found little support for the idea. This was one instance where those in authority backed a plan that was bolder than the one posed by New York's boldest builder.[7]

No shortage of grand plans for lower Manhattan existed in the hustling real estate market. Perhaps the grandest of all was the Lower Manhattan Plan released in 1966. While Rockefeller and Moses were off eying the waterfront near the rising World Trade Center complex, the City Planning Commission and the DLMA set to work on what started out as a traffic study to solve lower Manhattan's congestion problem. But after seeing the opportunity created by the proposed World Trade Center and its excavation, as well as Rockefeller's plan for a small city, the authors put forward a more brazen scheme. Hailed at the time as the most important planning document since the 1811 grid, the Lower Manhattan Plan aspired to crack the traffic problem, extend the island 190 acres into the Hudson and East Rivers, forge highways beneath the fill, and erect housing and plazas above. At the time, the plan's "readiness to reshape the Hudson River" so offended Ian McHarg, one of the landscape architects involved and a founding father of ecological planning, that he quit. But what was taking place went beyond the substance of a single development plan. In effect, Robert Moses was reluctantly passing the baton to a new group of planners who married commercial interests and citizen interests to spur a new round of public-private projects with far-reaching ecological implications.[8]

There was no moving forward with any of these schemes without first confronting the specific legal context. Two issues presented themselves. First, the city's charter prohibited it from leasing land near the shore for a period of more than thirty years, hardly long enough to interest investors in financing elaborate waterfront projects. Second, the US government, under its power to regulate navigable waterways, had the right to condemn any landfill or platform built in coastal waters. To solve the first problem, in 1968 the state created a so-called public-benefit corporation called the Battery Park City Corporation Authority and made it responsible (in conjunction with the city and private interests) for improving the "blighted area" near the tip of the island. The state legislature granted the new authority a property tax exemption and amended the city's administrative code to allow the Board of Estimate to lease the newly made land to the authority for up to ninety-nine years. To handle the marine-travel issue, in 1968 Congress simply declared the waters in question "nonnavigable." The result: an agency unanswerable to the electorate with the power to oversee what was now its own little private domain along the Hudson.[9]

In 1969 the city and state released a joint plan to fill in almost seventy football fields' worth of the Hudson River; housing, office buildings, and plazas would arise on top of the newly made ground. Longshoremen responded by launching a last-ditch effort to derail the project. A spokesperson for the International Longshoremen's Association said the venture would "destroy the means of livelihood of many thousands of longshoremen and other citizens." Civil rights leaders such as Bayard Rustin objected that the plan gave short shrift to low-income housing. Manhattan borough president Percy Sutton called the proposal "the Riviera of the Hudson." A dissenter on the City Planning Commission, which approved the project, simply characterized it as "speculation at its most blatant." [10]

But to its supporters, the Battery Park City project embodied the best in urban planning. The efficiency-minded Citizens Budget Commission, representing the city's largest taxpayers, called it a "most dramatic illustration of the use of landfill" that offered "more of what is the scarcest commodity." It touted the project as "free of relocation headaches," which, regardless of the argument's merit, was a powerful tack to take with memory still fresh of the pitched battles over Robert Moses's various highway adventures. The architecture critic Ada Louise Huxtable raved about the project, heaping praise on its scale, comprehensiveness, and ingenuity in "making its own land." To critics concerned that the city's densest section would grow even more jam-packed, she responded that concentration, if well handled, "is a proper urban answer, not an unqualified enemy of the human condition." Even the Park Association of New York City, despite professing a concern for conservation, called the decision to fill the Hudson with the excavated remains of the World Trade Center foundation and develop it "both sound economics and good planning." [11]

Battery Park City seemed doubly sound in the context of the time. The pace of growth in the late 1960s was like nothing New York had seen before. With office construction booming and infrastructure improvements such as a third water tunnel on the drawing board, excavation was fast becoming a way of life. As Merril Eisenbud, an environmental protection administrator for New York City, put it in 1968, "We are going to be taking more hard rock out of the ground in the next few years than anyone has done any place in the world." Rather than view the rock as a simple externality, Eisenbud considered the rubble an opportunity and floated the idea of "building a two-thousand-foot mountain for skiing at

Fresh Kills on Staten Island." It sounds silly to our ears today, but Eisenbud did not seem to be kidding. Battery Park City, in other words, came about during a building boom that, as a practical matter, required some place to deposit the remains of all the creative destruction.[12]

To bring about the makeover of the waterfront demanded escaping the strictures imposed on the shore by the city's past life as a port. Even as late as 1940, the law was settled that New York City was authorized to administer the waterfront only for "navigation and commerce"—that is, for public use, not "for private business purposes." John Lindsay set out to change that, prevailing on Governor Rockefeller to sign a bill in 1970 that "will allow development of recreation facilities, housing, and business uses of underutilized or vacant waterfront properties." The new law, by clearing the way for private business ventures, set off a kind of waterfront gold rush. A year after the bill was passed, the *Times* reported, "There are signs now that a new chapter in the expansion of Manhattan is beginning."[13]

No one could top the gusto of Charles Urstadt when it came to waterfront landfill ventures. Urstadt was the first chairman of the Battery Park City Corporation Authority. Like his colleague in the world of underwater enterprise Robert Moses, Urstadt loved to swim, starting out in the waters off of City Island in the Bronx. When he wasn't donning his swimming trunks, Urstadt helped out in his family's real estate business, collecting rents in preparation for his own career in the field under the tutelage of the real estate deal maker William Zeckendorf, whom Urstadt later admiringly called "the Donald Trump of his time." In 1971 he also held a position as Rockefeller's housing commissioner and helped push through a law—notorious among housing-rights advocates—that preempted New York City from toughening its rent control ordinance.[14]

Perhaps New York's most militant landfill enthusiast, Urstadt saw Battery Park City as part of a New York tradition dating back to the seventeenth century, when the Dutch first set foot on the island. Manhattan had grown 47 percent larger since that time, he said, and though his figures were off (20 percent between 1609 and 2010 is more accurate), his point was to justify the Hudson River Landfill Project on customary grounds. "We are merely following what has been going on for hundreds of years," he explained. But unlike those earlier projects or the works carried out by Robert Moses, Urstadt sat atop a quasigovernmental authority with the power to create enormous profits in the speculative realm of real estate. Urstadt himself said that creating land for roughly fifty dollars a square foot in the midst of New York's real estate economy was "like finding gold in the streets."[15]

Urstadt worked in a different context from Robert Moses, one where endless growth was under attack from a beefed-up environmental movement coming off the success of Earth Day, an event in 1970 that laid the groundwork for a new green generation. He had to adapt the growth imperative to the new conditions. One way that the booster Urstadt did this was to argue—as would those in real estate for the foreseeable future—that growth was justified on the grounds that it put the waterfront within easier reach of the public. It was a clever perversion of the commons tradition that titrated access to a resource once unreservedly open to all. Urstadt also pledged to accomplish all this in an environmentally sound fashion. As he explained, "At Battery Park City we will prove that it is possible to add to our physical properties without destroying the environmental features that we have inherited." This too was a shrewd move. By "inherited," he meant the state of things as of the 1950s. And against that ecological reference point—as opposed to, say, the one Henry Hudson observed—building anything was not just possible but also environmentally virtuous.[16]

Urstadt's coconspirator in shifting forward the ecological baseline for judging the impact of the Battery Park project was the Army Corps of Engineers, which had to sign off on the new landfill. In 1971 the Corps issued an environmental statement focused on the ninety-one acres of water slated for conversion to land. In the course of its investigation, the Corps took note of Manhattan's three centuries of land making and derived from this history that the current shore constituted "man-made phenomena rather than a natural river-front." The island had expanded at the expense of "old marshlands and tidal flats," and as a result of this "long history of man-made intrusion," there existed an "almost total absence of indigenous fishlife, shellfish, crustaceans, wildlife and migratory birds." As best the Corps could tell, "There is no question of disturbing, displacing, or destroying a viable wild environment." In a mere fifty-odd pages, the Corps determined that there would be "no adverse effect on the already low value of the area as a fish and wildlife resource." In short, the agency concluded that the waters off lower Manhattan had so hopelessly declined that any improvement would be an improvement.[17]

The completion in 1976 of Battery Park City offered the strongest evidence yet of New York's status as a boundless proposition; a place that could seemingly go on forever. To construct housing on the freshly made land, Urstadt recruited Samuel J. LeFrak, who had just finished the massive city in Queens that bears his name and knew something about building cities within cities. To its critics, however, the project was a boondoggle designed to pave over the river, when the money could have gone to benefit the dispossessed—ultimately a valid criticism in light of the fact that under the pressure of the 1970s fiscal crisis, mixed-income housing was jettisoned to build an upscale community on the site. "It's the kind of contempt for the poor and just plain greed," said Democratic congressman Herman Badillo, who was running for mayor in 1977, "that could lead them to create landfill all the way to London to build so-called middle-class housing which will have to be subsidized with money that should have gone to the slums." If landfill all the way to England seemed far-fetched, this was still, after all, the Big Apple, and without the advantage of hindsight, there was no saying at the time how much larger the city would get.[18]

Even as late as 1974, New York's ambitions were of biblical proportions. "Perhaps the most interesting advance in architecture and urban design in this city," declared the architect Peter Blake, "is that we are learning to walk, as it were, on water." As the story goes, even Saint Peter couldn't do that.[19]

The city was barreling forward with yet more grandiose schemes to trespass on the sea. Exhibit A was a proposed 234-acre landfill in the Hudson River—replete with a highway sent through concrete tubes below—hatched to rejuvenate lower Manhattan's western edge and named Westway. No project tested the limits of the growth imperative more. If not for a serious case of bad timing—New York would soon be poised to declare bankruptcy—there is almost no question that the Big Apple would have grown bigger.[20]

Westway dovetailed with other major public works projects that preceded it in the twentieth century—many of them built, of course, by Robert Moses. These sweeping ventures tended to dislocate people and turn a blind eye to custom and tradition; indeed, to the past more generally. While the claim was made that Westway would not lead to the kind of social dislocation that Moses was notorious for, it certainly did not lack ambition. The project was so expensive that estimates for the four-mile highway were often broken down not by the mile or even the foot. One estimate put the cost at $15,782 per inch, a hair-raising amount made more comprehensible by the realization that, because the highway was designated as an interstate, the federal government would be absorbing 90 percent of the cost. The project called for 11.3 million cubic yards of fill, most of which likely would have come from the bottom of Lower New York Bay. That was enough material to bury all of Central Park to a depth of more than eight feet.[21]

A scheme this vast could not be built without significant ecological impact. Or so one might think. But the stretch of river north of Battery Park City was by some accounts so deracinated that it did not have far, if anywhere, to fall. One environmental impact statement depicted the inshore area slated to be filled as largely devoid of fish and invertebrates. Another, issued in 1977, called the inshore "biologically impoverished." A technical report simply dubbed it a "biological wasteland."[22]

These characterizations, however, directly contradicted the portrayal of the lower Hudson presented by the journalist Robert H. Boyle. "As of now," he wrote in his 1969 classic *The Hudson River: A Natural and Unnatural History*, "the biological productivity of the lower Hudson is staggering." He called the millions of fish jamming the waters for feeding, spawning, and nursing, "the greatest single wildlife resource in New York State." Although conceding that the Hudson was "a mess" as it coursed past Manhattan, he found the available conditions with respect to dissolved oxygen adequate to support "numerous species of fishes." Angling for striped bass right off the shores of the West Side was by no means uncommon.[23]

No fewer than three government agencies lodged objections with the Army Corps of Engineers, the government entity responsible for issuing the dredge-and-fill permit required under the 1972 Clean Water Act. It turned out that Boyle's rendering was to a large extent correct. There were significant quantities of fish, especially during the wintertime. But in the end, the Corps blundered ahead and in 1981 issued a permit anyway. This was an agency, after all, that had left an indelible imprint on the eastern half of the country, transforming millions of acres of wetlands into arable property. What was a few hundred acres off of Manhattan, especially in light of the money to be gained by making more of some of the most high-priced real estate in the world?[24]

In 1981 Westway may have looked unstoppable. The project had a long list of powerful allies behind it, from the Oval Office (Ronald Reagan) and Capitol Hill (New York senator Daniel Patrick Moynihan), to Albany (Governor Hugh Carey) and city hall (Mayor Ed Koch). It had the support of business, including the Downtown-Lower Manhattan Association, and labor, eager for all the jobs. The fourth estate backed it, including the newspaper of record, the *New York Times*. But despite such an impressive roster of allies, Westway never left the drawing board. Environmentalists were appalled and went to court to stop it. Although much has been said about the project, there has been little consideration of the larger historical forces that were at work.[25]

Two developments structured the debate. The first was a shift in understanding of nearshore habitats. The evolving federal Clean Water Act imposed a high standard for issuing dredge-and-fill permits. No land-making projects could take place if they threatened an "unacceptable adverse impact" on aquatic life. This reform intersected with the changing ecology of New York. With the filling in of the wetlands, the area around piers began to emerge as a prime habitat for fish, waterfowl, and even migratory bird life. The piers slowed the river currents and in some ways functioned like the marshes they replaced. Altogether, ecological change and emerging environmentalism combined to focus increased attention on interpier locales like the one at issue in Westway.[26]

The second and arguably more influential trend was economic. By the 1970s, the so-called golden age of postwar American capitalism had come to an end. Battered by inflation, slow growth, and an energy crisis, the US economy veered off course. In 1975 New York City was running out of cash to pay its bills. As it happened, the solution settled on—though by no means an inevitable one—involved cutting services and laying off city workers, thereby weakening the power of unions. No wonder labor stood by Westway. Moreover, this was the context for city housing commissioner Roger Starr's notorious concept of so-called planned shrinkage. Starr advocated reducing services to the poor to help lessen the need for taxes on the grounds that cities like New York could no longer serve as a land of opportunity. Ironically, Starr, who clung to Westway like a barnacle to a pier, did not quite grasp that the shrinkage he had in mind could be transposed onto projects he supported. As political theorist Marshall Berman has put it rather bluntly, "[T]he modern societies of the 1970s were forced to live in the shadow of the speed limit and the stop sign."[27]

The conjunction of these two trends at the dawn of the Reagan era left the future of Manhattan an open question. Was the island on the cusp of the largest single expansion in its history, or was it poised to begin a humbler chapter in its relations with the earth?

The battle over Westway would turn on fish; indeed, just one fish: the striped bass. The Chesapeake Bay was at this time the largest source of striped bass in the Atlantic fishery, but the Hudson River was second in rank and rising as the productivity of the Chesapeake declined. Striped bass qualify as charismatic megafauna; glamorous animals that, like timber wolves and bald eagles, resonated in the 1970s as supporters of the Endangered Species Act enlisted them in their cause. The striped bass was a sympathetic victim and had been previously recruited by Albert Butzel, lead counsel in the Westway litigation, to good effect in blocking a project at Storm King Mountain, located fifty miles up the Hudson, by the Consolidated Edison energy company.[28]

The fundamental legal issue was this: Would the Westway landfill degrade the aquatic habitat and cause harm to the fishery? One report expressed concern over the cumulative impact of Westway in light of its planned location north of Battery Park City. "The Battery Park landfill is of special concern here since its habitat loss effectively removed any respite displaced fish might have found before leaving the river for the stressful and unfamiliar marine-like environment of Upper New York Bay or Long Island Sound." The document concluded that filling in the Hudson would cause "a significant adverse impact" to the striped bass. In issuing a dredge-and-fill permit, the Corps tried to finesse this conclusion and claim that the word *significant* was invoked in its statistical sense, as opposed to its common, everyday meaning. An appeals court later called out the agency for its "Orwellian-like 'doublespeak.'"[29]

The long legal battle over Westway eventually brought to light the essential truth about the venture: it was a landfill development masquerading as a highway. The documentation and court proceedings proved it. The environmental impact statement, on which the Corps based its decision to grant a dredge-and-fill permit in 1985, conceived of the project as having a "basic transportation purpose." Transportation had to be the goal because the agency was collaborating with the Federal Highway Administration (FHWA), which was, of course, in the business of overseeing highways. The Corps, for its part, was quite aware that there was absolutely no need to build a two-hundred-plus-acre landfill in the Hudson to satisfy the need for basic transportation along the West Side. There were at least five other less ecologically intrusive highway plans—sans landfill. Indeed, under federal guidelines, the Corps was required to reject an application for a landfill permit if less environmentally adverse alternatives existed.[30]

To resolve the dilemma, the Corps defined Westway as "a 'redevelopment' project." By formulating the project in development terms, the Corps found no possible alternatives because the environmental impact statement on which it rested its decision had considered only *transporta-*

tion options, not fallback real estate ones. One does not have to have majored in analytical philosophy to see what had gone wrong here. As the district judge in the case observed, the environmental impact statement "defined the project one way to suit the needs of the FHWA, and the Corps decision defined the project another way in granting the landfill permit." [31]

With this tortured logic now out in the open, Congress took up the fate of Westway. While there remained a number of diehard Westway supporters, a surprising number of congressmen rose to denounce the ruse of conceptualizing a development project as a road. Westway, said one congressman, "is really a real estate development posing as a highway." Another referenced Westway's "unsavory history" and made the same point. Yet another pointed out that the highway trust fund was not supposed to be used for "paving over the Hudson River." Congress blocked the use of highway funds for landfill on the very day in 1985 that a federal appeals court affirmed (largely) the district court's decision invalidating the Corps's dredge-and-fill permit. There would be no Westway. [32]

Westway's downfall represented a blow to the never-ending vision of New York. It did not, though, put an end to expansionary schemes along the waterfront. The growth imperative was alive and well and living in New York, and it could be made to adapt to the new circumstances. There was, however, a shift in methods: from landfill to platforms. Platforms built along the rivers surrounding Manhattan did not completely bury habitat the way that landfill did. [33]

By the mid-1980s, with the economy now growing after a downturn earlier in the decade, the waterfront was humming with development. The Koch administration had put coastal real estate affairs (non-maritime-related) in the hands of the Public Development Corporation (PDC), organized in the 1960s to manage the sale and lease of city-owned property. The head of the agency, James P. Stuckey, felt that the state of New York, as a whole, lagged behind other states in "aquatic construction." To rectify this lapse, the PDC was working to develop thirteen platform-based waterfront projects extending out into the Hudson and East Rivers. One project in the West Thirties would perch on a thirteen-acre platform in the Hudson River. Another on the East River (Sixteenth to Twenty-Fourth Streets) would sprawl across twenty-seven acres of overwater platforms.[34]

The sheer audacity of the ventures virtually assured scrutiny. One report in 1987 counted no fewer than fifty-nine projects (either planned or in progress) on the shores of New York and New Jersey. The New York City Council decided to investigate the shock therapy being administered along the coast, and what came back was a long list of concerns: whether "meaningful public space" was falling victim to private development; the environmental impact of the switch from landfill to platforms; and the PDC's "reputation for developing projects with little or no public input." Unlike landfill, platform development did not require Corps approval. Only decks that ventured into navigable waters did. Of course, in Manhattan's case, portions of the surrounding waters had been declared nonnavigable, allowing some platforms to skirt federal review. With the ecological impact of platforms unclear, the City Council panel called for a halt pending further research.[35]

Opposition to aggressive waterfront development continued to mount as a bill worked its way through Albany that would have banned any more building in the Hudson from Chambers Street all the way to Forty-Second Street. Opposed by Stuckey and Koch, the bill did not pass, but in an effort to preempt further controversy, the West Side Waterfront Panel, a group charged with determining how to develop the Hudson waterfront after the collapse of Westway, went on record opposing landfill. Michael J. Del Giudice, an investment banker at Lazard Frères & Company who was appointed by Governor Mario Cuomo to serve on the panel, put it this way: "What we're saying is, 'Forget it. Ain't no way it's going to happen.'"[36]

Del Giudice's announcement represented an adaptation to the antidevelopment climate but did not lack ambition. An earlier task force, established by the governor and the mayor, had recommended a modest roadway and public esplanade for the stretch below Fifty-Ninth Street.

Del Giudice's West Side Waterfront Panel had a bolder plan to kindle gentrification: not a simple esplanade but a park—indeed, a park that would be the largest open-space project in Manhattan since the building of Central Park. They called their creation Hudson River Waterfront Park. In place of the "deteriorated, lifeless place," they proposed thirteen publicly accessible piers that would span four miles from Battery Park City to Fifty-Ninth Street. This "band of green" was designed to reclaim the Hudson River for New Yorkers. Further, the panel pledged to respect the ecology of the river not only through the ban on landfill but also "by restricting additional pier coverage." [37]

On the surface, the park sounded a whole lot better, ecologically speaking, than Westway. But the composition of the panel, filled as it was with Wall Street financiers and others keen to develop the island, raised eyebrows among environmentalists. And, sure enough, the panel did endorse "[n]ew commercial or residential development" so long as it occurred in only "limited areas." Just as significantly, the panel put forth, in its list of planning principles, a preference for "[w]ater-related" uses. The term sounded innocuous enough, but, in fact, it represented a retreat from the stricter water-*dependent* standard that had been articulated in the city's waterfront revitalization plans going back to 1982. [38]

Critics pointed out that the river already belonged to the people "for free." Another felt that it was hardly necessary to "approve significant housing and commercial development in the park" to give the public access. The historian Kirkpatrick Sale, who in 1990 had written an un-flattering portrayal of Columbus and the impact of his voyage, dubbed the panel a "charade" and recommended spending a modest sum on re-storing the wetlands to something approaching their original state. "That is what the river would ask of us," he intoned, as if the river were begging for mercy. Another person pointed out that the plan seemed to be over-looking the needy, who still fished the waters and frequented the fifteen tackle shops listed in the yellow pages. "I would just remind you," said this advocate for the poor's access to the commons, "that when George Washington came to New York to be inaugurated, he came in a small boat." [39]

Whatever the faults of the park proposal, the need to bring a little green spirit to bear on the western edge of Manhattan was underscored shortly thereafter when the New York City Department of City Planning, which regulated development and worked alongside the City Planning Commission, put forth a comprehensive plan for the waterfront. The department studied what seemed like every last inch of the city's 578-mile shoreline. Along the east side of Manhattan, it found that "[a]lmost nothing remains of the original natural waterfront except for the river." Bulkheads, riprap, piers, and platforms had so thoroughly walled off the island's western edge that the only "original shoreline" still in existence was a sliver at the end of Thirty-Fourth Street that had somehow escaped the concrete hand of development. For example, between 1870 and 1936, the Department of Docks encased a nearly five-mile stretch of the West Side north of the Battery. Manhattan looked like a fortress.[40]

Moreover, the idea of building a "band of green" on the island's coast meshed with the planning department's larger waterfront philosophy. For example, the comprehensive plan expanded the opportunities for development along the shore by supplementing the old "water-dependent" standard with a less restrictive phrase it called "water-enhancing." The latter would include everything from restaurants and bars to theaters and miniature golf courses and was only slightly more restrictive than the "water-related" standard put forth by the park's proponents. The revised plan, eventually codified in a zoning resolution, also sanctioned the use of new piers and platforms, while at the same time reining in the no-holds-barred approach to the waterfront made famous by Donald Trump (whose initial plans for the West Side included a scheme to harvest the development rights to underwater land in the Hudson River and transfer them to dry ground in order to realize a multimillion-square-foot mini-city to be named after himself). In short, agreement among those who ruled New York seemed to be coalescing on the need for commercial development within a green corridor along the Hudson.[41]

To advance that goal, Governor Cuomo and Mayor David Dinkins entered into an agreement in 1992 to create a subsidiary of the Urban Development Corporation (UDC) called the Hudson River Park Conservancy. Del Giudice was made the chairman. But the antidevelopment fringe of the environmental community filed suit to dismantle the conservancy unless it complied with state law and produced an environmental impact statement, an argument that a court would throw out in 1995. The conservancy, meantime, drew up a Disneyesque plan that included everything from bike paths and ball fields, to water taxis and ice-skating rinks, to an artificial beach and even "a high-tech golf driving range."[42]

The main stumbling block to the park's realization was the widespread distrust of the conservancy's status as a subsidiary of the UDC—an agency that had strayed far from its original mission to honor Dr. Martin Luther King Jr. by building housing for the poor. That problem was solved, however, by the formation in 1996 of the Hudson River Park Alliance, an umbrella organization made up of numerous environmental groups. The alliance, founded by Albert Butzel, a lawyer who opposed Westway, embraced the idea of allowing some of the profits from private development to help subsidize the expansion and maintenance of open space. Butzel, who had close ties to the administration of Mayor Rudolph Giuliani, helped shepherd through Albany legislation that banned the use of landfill, platforms, or piling in the Hudson, while also creating yet another institution to oversee the park's creation—a trust that people could presumably trust.[43]

With the founding of the Hudson River Park Trust in 1998, New York seemed to fulfill a promise that some believed dated all the way back to 1811. That was when the grid's fathers justified the lack of open space by arguing that the surrounding rivers would render the island's "health and pleasure ... peculiarly felicitous." Best of all, in the minds of the park's supporters, commercial development would underwrite maintenance and operating expenses, and thereby allow this new addition to the city to "forever pay its own way." As one observer exclaimed in the *Times* about the new recreational prospect, "It could do for New York in the twenty-first century what Central Park did in the nineteenth."[44]

To critics, however, the park remained deeply problematic. Granted, the park included a special estuarine sanctuary for the "water section" of the property. But excluded from the so-called water section were the numerous piers along the waterfront, which, of course, extended out over the water. The piers, in other words, were outside the sanctuary and thus open to more strenuous development even though they encroached on the river. For example, the planks on old, dilapidated piers could be re-placed under the law, a move that would cast a shadow over the water. That sounds like a small change, except that research was beginning to emerge that shaded areas made for poor habitat, especially for win-ter flounder and juvenile weakfish. Only species such as American eel, which does not rely entirely on its vision to forage, managed to thrive in the shade under the piers. Nor did it bode well for the vast range of fish that the park act allowed up to eight acres in the sanctuary to be "covered or altered by floating structures."[45]

By the millennium, work on the park proceeded in earnest, though it turned out that this portion of the Hudson waterfront was not exactly the "lifeless place" the West Side Waterfront Panel made it out to be. At least six homeless encampments were in need of "relocation." In ad-dition, a group called the Floating Neutrinos had camped out in a large raft named *Town Hall* (and other vessels) located at Pier Twenty-Five. They too were slated for removal. The group was the brainchild of David Pearlman, a drifter and free spirit who called himself Poppa Neutrino and who later built a boat out of timbers he found floating in New York Harbor and sailed all the way to Europe in it. Neutrino was as fleeting as the subatomic particle from which his name derived, but more than that, he was the personification of all that New York was not: antimate-rialistic, opposed to landlords, and inclined to see the entire world as a commons. As he once put it, the whole earth was his garden, though he had no formal legal attachment to it.[46]

The Giuliani administration described the Floating Neutrinos as squatters, but a more sympathetic rendering was offered by the Work-ing Waterfront Association, founded to show that the future park was "not just a wasteland." It instead portrayed them as a "communal group." In 2000, while Neutrino and his wife Betsy Terrell were away working on an idea for a floating orphanage, the Floating Neutrinos received a midnight visit from a contractor, who, after detaining the vessel's master, hoisted the *Town Hall* out of the water only to drop and destroy it while loading it onto a barge. "Blighted"—to use the language of the Hudson River Park Act—the waterfront may have been, but to the Floating Neutrinos, it was not just home but a part of the ocean commons.[47]

Hudson River Park—550 acres of bike paths, basketball courts, restaurants, minigolf, and open grass—stands as a monument to the market-oriented environmental protection that has emerged in response to life in an age of limits. Although the economics of allowing profit-making enterprises in the park to help pay maintenance costs was called into question, the Hudson River Park private-public template inspired other such ventures, including the nearby Brooklyn Bridge Park.[48]

The value of a green ribbon ringing the city was accepted by supporters of the new park model and even by critics, including one who called it "a good idea" while decrying it as a "bribe for unbounded highrise development." But from the standpoint of aquatic life, it is not the green strip but the nature of the border between land and water that matters more. The hard-boundary ethos that undergirded the 1998 Hudson River Park Act conflicted with the prevailing wisdom in ecology, in which a sloping interface between land and sea was known to encourage species diversity. Wetlands or mudflats, instead of a hard wall, mean a diversity of wildlife, from marsh wrens, to swamp sparrow, to blue crab, and, farther upland, diamondback terrapin, mink, and raccoon. The eclipse of Manhattan's shallow shoreline by bulkheads would also eventually be shown to have resulted in a "malformed community of fishes"—that is, fish selected for open coastal waters and not the shallow, vegetated habitat that once lined the shore. In other words, extremely large populations of a handful of species—anchovy, Atlantic herring, blueback herring, striped bass—dominated, eclipsing the biodiversity that preceded the hardening of the shoreline. The picture we have in our mind of Manhattan must be revised. From an ecological perspective, it is even more crowded and less diverse than is commonly thought.[49]

15 THE BIG APPLE BIOME

By about the time that the four hundredth anniversary of Henry Hudson's voyage rolled around, New York City—the concrete colossus, the human artifact nonpareil—had come to be viewed in some circles as the best thing to happen to environmentalism since John Muir.

To mark the occasion of Earth Day in 2007, Mayor Michael Bloomberg announced the most far-reaching environmental plan in New York's history. He called it *PlaNYC: A Greener, Greater New York*. Largely the work of the management-consulting firm McKinsey & Company, the blueprint included a list of no fewer than 127 initiatives. These dealt with everything from congestion pricing* and tree planting, to the introduction of mussel beds and vegetated ditches (to reduce impervious ground cover), to a curb on the idling time of taxicabs.[1]

In announcing the plan, Bloomberg highlighted that there were now more New Yorkers than ever: 8.2 million people crammed into the five boroughs, and all of them locked into a "collision course with the environment" unless the city took steps to foster sustainable urbanism. By the year 2030, the population was projected to surge past the 9 million mark,

---

* This involved a surcharge imposed on Manhattan roadways designed to encourage people to use mass transit.

a demographic boost that would be roughly the equivalent of all the residents of San Francisco packing their bags and moving to the City That Never Sleeps. Yet by implementing the environmental reforms called for in the plan—especially by tackling traffic congestion and increasing the energy efficiency of power plants and buildings—the city's actual carbon footprint would decline. "Counterintuitive though it may be," declared the mayor, "by absorbing nearly a million more residents by 2030 into one of the world's most efficient places to live, we will prevent more than fifteen million metric tons of greenhouse gases from being released into the atmosphere each year." New York's high population density had, in the context of the emerging problem of global warming, become an environmental virtue. As the plan explained, "[G]rowing New York is, itself, a climate change strategy."[2]

Retreat was off the table. Rather than call for some limits on growth in the face of the challenges posed by what Bloomberg himself admitted was an "unstable and uncertain" environment, the administration instead made population density the centerpiece of its urban vision. The growth imperative, in other words, had evolved into environmental reform.[3]

The idea that high-density life could form the basis for a sustainable future gained further credence when *New Yorker* staff writer David Owen published *Green Metropolis* (2009). Building on the work of the urban activist Jane Jacobs, who died in 2006, Owen challenged the idea that crowded urban life is somehow inherently out of balance with nature. Although it might seem that sparsely settled areas were more ecologically benign, Manhattan, with 1.5 million people all shoehorned into twenty-three square miles, was actually a lot greener than some small bucolic town in Vermont. Manhattan's compact structure led to a host of resource efficiencies, as urbanites eschewed cars for mass transit and energy-efficient apartments.[4]

Owen traced New York's extraordinary population density to a string of "serendipitous historical accidents," including its location on an island and its 1811 grid plan. "No one today," he wrote, "would lay out such a large inhabited area with such a paucity of open space, but the relentlessness of the street plan is actually one of the keys to the city's continuing vitality—and to its greenness." Moreover, it turns out that Greater New York is overflowing with dense environments. New York City as a whole ranks fifth in density among incorporated places nationwide, trailing four municipalities in neighboring New Jersey: Guttenberg, Union City, West New York, and Hoboken. With density like this, it could be argued, who needs the Sierra Club?[5]

While hardly the first person to call attention to New York as an ecological role model, Owen did offer the most thorough case to date for the benefits of a world chock-full of Manhattans. But his work does beg the question: How did what Owen himself described as "one of the most thoroughly altered landscapes imaginable" evolve into one of the most sustainable ones? And precisely what kind of ecology has high-density life produced? The ecological impact of the compact New York metropolitan area turns out to be more complicated than either supporters or detractors of the big city might think.[6]

The idea that the densely packed metropolis constituted an efficient, green machine began to take root in elite planning circles in the 1990s. But its roots go further back. High-density life had long been justified on efficiency grounds and, more specifically, as a way of saving space. The Regional Plan Association, in its second plan, had made precisely this point. "A technologically advanced society," the association wrote in 1967, "is finding it more efficient to group its population in a few large, select, highly accessible areas, leaving most of the rest of the continent available for mechanized crop cultivation, conservation, recreation or other non-urban purposes." Note the emphasis on advanced technology to describe what the planners aspire to as a society.[7]

A generation and a half later, the RPA put forward a third blueprint for the New York area. This one was founded not on technology but ecology. If the explosion in automobile use inspired the First Regional Plan in the 1920s, and the perils of suburban sprawl the second one in the 1960s, it was the threat posed by the economic downturn in the late 1980s that stirred the planners to emphasize not "managing growth" but forestalling its decline. Significantly, the focus on ecology in the 1996 plan arose in a context bent on stimulating development. Thus the Third Regional Plan endorsed the entrepreneurial model of the Hudson River Park Conservancy, noting that the success of reclaiming the waterfront for visitors hinged on the need for "active and appropriate commercial uses." The heart of the plan was a call for sustainable growth of regional centers in New York City, and Manhattan in particular, for the purpose of "restoring and improving the great urban ecosystems."[8]

The plan's ecological emphasis can in part be explained by a larger scientific trend: the increasing appreciation of the relevance of the ecosystem concept for cities. A body of evidence was slowly demonstrating the biological importance of densely populated areas, New York included.[9]

Broader trends in popular culture also spurred the reinvention of New York as a green metropolis. None was more important than the return of nature to the city. Of course, the plants and animals never left. What returned was the *idea* of nature. That point was underscored when the writer Robert Sullivan set off on a journey through the Meadowlands reminiscent of Henry Thoreau's legendary trip along the Concord and Merrimack Rivers. As he recounts in his 1998 book *The Meadowlands: Wilderness Adventures at the Edge of a City*, Sullivan paddled his way to the aptly named Walden Swamp, near the sports complex, and managed to make one of the most denatured environments imaginable seem like a pristine world lurking within earshot of the New Jersey Turnpike. Going in search of nature, a few found it a marvel that there was still some to find.[10]

By the turn of the century, the nature writer Anne Matthews, author of *Wild Nights: The Nature of New York City*, found herself standing amidst "the planet's most profoundly developed real estate" listening for birdsong. Even on Wall Street, one could hear the rush of migrating birds in the fall and spring, though admittedly the glass towers and light disoriented the animals. (Some twenty-three hundred birds turned up dead or injured near the World Trade Center in the four and a half years prior to the September 11 attacks.) Regardless of whether or not one viewed New York as an example of ecological overreach, there was no denying that, in a very real way, nature—the idea—had returned.[11]

The return of nature reached a climax in a thought experiment cooked up by the journalist Alan Weisman, who imagined Bloomberg's (or any mayor's) worst nightmare: a New York completely devoid of people. In such a depopulated environment, the rivers take back the land, waterlogging the foundations of skyscrapers and causing them to topple like long rows of dominoes. "Gradually," Weisman wrote, "the asphalt jungle will give way to a real one," as Central Park reverts to marshland and, with its tunnels now flooded and bridges slowly rusted away, Manhattan reappears as an island once again, the home of moose and bears. Weisman's book—published, ironically, the same year that Bloomberg released his plan to accommodate a major jump in population—was called *The World Without Us*. But, of course, one way to interpret the book was that in the "world with us," there was no escaping the natural environment, no ignoring the water seeping into the basements of buildings, even the towering Empire State Building—built near the remains of an old pond. Nature was not gone, just repressed. And if this was true, then perhaps New York was not quite as thorough a human artifact as it was sometimes made out to be. Perhaps in the world with us, there was some room for nature after all.[12]

The radical changes to the estuary and land around New York Harbor dating back to the early nineteenth century had given rise two centuries later to a recognition that the metropolis had produced not just a towering monument to the human control of nature but also a fundamentally new ecology. As one study explained, "[T]he natural environment of the area has been so extensively modified by human activities as to have become a kind of ecosystem of its own." Call it the Big Apple Biome.[13]

The most monumental aspect of this biome is the new plumbing system put in place across the region. The new man-made hydrology was the result of several trends: the rollback of wetlands; the dredging of the harbor bottom; the rise of what was effectively a new river of water from outside watersheds to supply domestic needs; and a system of sewage treatment plants to replace the filtration of water once carried out by the marshlands. These developments completely transformed the distribution and movement of water. The physical features of the harbor thus changed considerably. Newark Bay, for example, has diminished by a third since 1845, mainly as a result of the rise of the containerports at Newark and Elizabeth. Similarly, Upper New York Bay contracted by 26 percent because of the addition of thousands of acres of landfill between 1845 and 1989. And while the bays shrunk in area, they increased in volume—in Newark Bay's case, by a stunning 50 percent—as dredgers were cranked up to deepen the harbor for shipping.[14]

Perhaps the most dramatic changes occurred at Jamaica Bay, where Henry Hudson first came calling back in 1609. As late as 1904, the bay was described as "so full of marsh islets and islands as to render its navigation utterly impossible except to very light-draft vessels with local pilots on board." At that time, the marshlands of Jamaica Bay extended over twenty-five square miles. Then, beginning in the 1930s, the main ship channel into the bay was deepened to thirty feet, swallowing up several islands. In 1931 Barren Island was connected with Brooklyn in order to build Floyd Bennett Field, the city's first municipal airport. Later in the decade, bulldozers at the sanitary landfills along the bay's northern perimeter began to fill in still more marshland. In 1941 the city eyed the wetlands on the eastern side for a new airport. Concerned about congestion at the Flushing Meadows airport that would eventually bear his name, Mayor Fiorello La Guardia oversaw the purchase of more than forty-five hundred acres for the new aviation hub, originally named Idlewild after the golf course on the site. It was later renamed to honor John F. Kennedy after his assassination in 1963.[15]

To build Kennedy Airport, huge intake pipes vacuumed sand out of the bay and spewed it onto the marsh. "We had so many dikes and canals we began to look like Holland, but with a difference," said one employee. "We had to prevent the land from flowing into the sea instead of the sea flowing over the land." By 1971, Jamaica Bay's once majestic expanse of sixteen thousand acres of marshland had shriveled to just four thousand—a wetland nearly the size of all Manhattan dredged and filled out of existence. What's more, the bay's average depth swelled from three to sixteen feet. The change in depth meant that it now took

three times as long—more than a month—for the tides to flush pollut-
ants out of the bay; no small point, given the sewage treatment plants
discharging millions of gallons a day. "These alterations to the original
pattern of freshwater discharge," one biologist has written, "have been so
radical that the watershed of Jamaica Bay is sometimes referred to as a
'sewershed'—a distinctly urban concept."[16]

The dramatic decline of the Jamaica Bay wetlands paralleled the
broader trend during the postwar economic boom. More than one-fifth—
some seventeen thousand acres—of the tidal marsh estimated to be present in the estuary in the mid–eighteen hundreds vanished in just twenty
years (1953 to 1973), most of it swallowed up to make room for housing, office construction, airport expansion, and landfills. The postwar
economic boom, in other words, was especially hard on the marshlands
of Greater New York. At Jamaica Bay, 30 percent of the marsh around
in 1900—nearly eight square miles—was wiped out between 1947 and
1969. Altogether, an area of wetland equal to nearly one and a half times
the size of the island of Manhattan disappeared at Jamaica Bay, Staten
Island, Flushing Meadows, and the Meadowlands during this thriving
twenty-year period.[17]

The dwindling of the wetlands, though remarkable, constituted just
one of the major changes made to the region's plumbing. Perhaps even
more stunning was the rise of what was effectively an entirely new river
born of New York's desire for escalating growth. During the affluent two
decades after the Second World War, New York City followed through
on its quest to tap the waters of the Delaware River watershed, a project first broached in the 1920s in response to skyrocketing population
growth. By 1967, the construction of four reservoirs and an accompanying eighty-four-mile aqueduct had doubled the amount of water available to the city.[18]

There were more conservation-minded plans afloat. In 1950 the efficiency gurus at the Citizens Budget Commission lobbied for a plan to
build a pumping and filtration system directly upstream on the Hudson
River instead of going far afield. The virtue of the Hudson River plan
was that it would curb water consumption because the costs of operat-

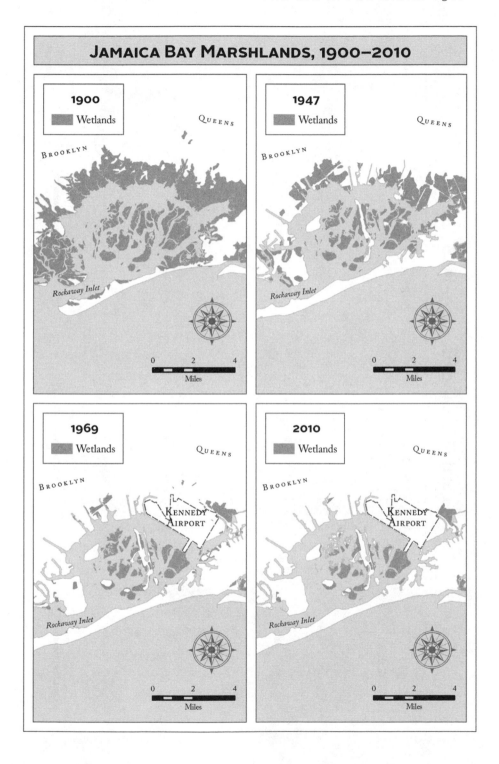

JAMAICA BAY MARSHLANDS, 1900–2010

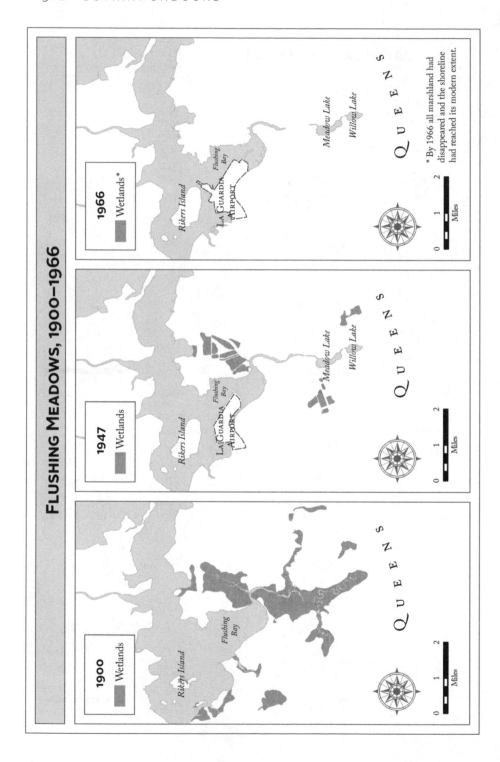

FLUSHING MEADOWS, 1900–1966

1900 — Wetlands

1947 — Wetlands

1966 — Wetlands*

* By 1966 all marshland had disappeared and the shoreline had reached its modern extent.

ing the filtration facility would increase with the amount of water consumed. But preying on concerns (largely unfounded, as it turned out) about the purity of the Hudson supply (Robert Moses argued, repeating a Dutch maxim, that drinking water, like Caesar's wife, should be above suspicion), Mayor Vincent Impellitteri scuttled the plan. The move to continue the tradition of building reservoirs upstate worked to uncouple consumption from cost, and as a result, per capita water use peaked during the 1980s at over two hundred gallons per day—or fifteen times the minimum amount required for domestic use. The absolute amount of water consumed reached its zenith in 1991 at a daily value of nearly 1.5 billion gallons, which, for purposes of comparison, was about eight hundred million gallons short of the Hudson River's minimum discharge. In other words, the idea that New York's population ought to move in only one direction—upward—resulted in the birth of a kind of miniature Hudson River.[19]

To deal with purifying all the water coursing into the harbor, sewage treatment plants—fourteen in New York City alone by the 1990s—replicated the role once played by wetlands and streams.* To say that these plants were taxed is to understate the case. The plants handled wastewater, but because roughly four-fifths of the city operated on a so-called combined sewage system, they also dealt with a large amount of storm water as well. Storm-water runoff increased markedly over the course of the twentieth century as a result of more impervious ground cover, which bars water from penetrating the soil (and recharging the groundwater supply). Population density, it turns out, is correlated with an increase in impermeable surfaces. About three-quarters of New York (circa 1992) consisted of such impervious material. During a heavy rain, the combined sewer systems overflowed into the estuary, discharging both storm water and raw sewage. Currently there are more than 450 of

---

* An alternative treatment model can be found today in India's East Kolkata wetlands, where roughly twenty thousand families recycle sewage into vegetable patches and fish ponds, improving water quality by converting nutrients into biomass and making a substantial contribution to the city's food supply.

these events in New York a year, releasing billions of gallons of noxious water and floating debris. Moreover, the high population density and rampant colonization of the underground for transportation, electric, natural gas, and other utilities have left little room to build overflow canals or subterranean storage systems to stem the tide.[20]

The scale of the hydrological transformation boggles the mind. The quest for distant sources of water underwrote population density, which in turn led to more pavement, which resulted in billions of gallons of wastewater discharged into the estuary (2.75 billion gallons a day by 1987). It is true that in recent years the city has curbed its water use by introducing metering and a low-flow toilet program—deemed the "porcelain revolution" by one historian. None of these measures, however, substantially challenged the overarching growth imperative that has guided development since the nineteenth century. Indeed, it is arguable that the need to preserve growth, not stem it, spurred these conservation measures. The city, for example, made installing water meters in some areas a priority only after the state threatened to impose a building moratorium because the rush of wastewater had outstripped the capacity of the local sewage treatment plants.[21]

The sobering reality is that even with all the wastewater management, the harbor has been irrevocably changed. Overfertilization became a way of life. Despite all the improvement that has followed in the wake of the Clean Water Act, the amount of nitrogen discharged into New York Harbor in 1999 was 40 percent above the level released at the turn of the twentieth century. Phosphorus levels were 100 percent higher. These trends remain a pressing concern in light of the threat the nutrients pose to biodiversity. More than anything else, it is this overdose of nutrients that stands in the way of those eager to see the return of the harbor to the days of Henry Hudson.[22]

If high-density living has produced New York's labyrinthine plumbing system, it has also fashioned a unique set of simplified habitats, the second defining feature of the Big Apple Biome. Biodiversity has suffered accordingly.

A recent review of trends in species richness uncovered depressing news. An analysis of twenty-six studies focused on terrestrial, freshwater, and marine habitats within a hundred miles of Midtown Manhattan found that seventeen of them showed declines. The downward trend was likely related to anthropogenic factors such as "development, exotic species, changes in land use, chemical contamination and recreational use of natural areas." In other words, as a whole, the tendency over time has been toward a simplification of the ecological order.[23]

Anthropogenic change has also tended to shape the kinds of wildlife that by the second half of the twentieth century (if not before) had come to dominate the region. "Only those species tolerant of human activities can persist," explained one study of the estuary, "for there is no wilderness here." By "here," the authors refer to the nearshore habitat consisting of tidal marshes, mudflats, and oyster beds. Barely a fifth of the tidal marshland estimated to be present in New York Harbor when Henry Hudson voyaged to the region remained by the last part of the twentieth century, and, even more stunning, an expanse of underwater land about the size of Staten Island had been filled in across New York and New Jersey. Animal life evolved in tandem with the transformation of the nearshore habitat and the rapid population growth and density. Instead of bats, weasels, and foxes—secretive species—the region hosted "urban generalists" such as gray squirrels and raccoons. Pigeons, gulls, and crows—so-called adaptable avian species—also responded very well to the changing state of the estuary's habitat.[24]

Some species actually developed a dependency on the human modification of the landscape. The prolific herring gulls present at landfills are the definitive example. And what happened on land also happened at sea. For example, the final resting place for sewage sludge from waste treatment plants was a site twelve miles from New York City in the Christiaensen Basin. This spot in the New York Bight remained the primary disposal site from 1924 until it was closed in 1987, and as the sludge piled up, it led to organismic change, as pollution-tolerant worms crowded out other marine species.[25]

This is not to say that there is some iron rule that all alterations of the harbor diminished biodiversity. Take the borrow pits dug to produce the millions of cubic yards of sand hauled off to create Battery Park City and other land-making projects. They have been found to support a large range and population of fish, more than in unmined areas. Digging the borrow pits apparently complicated the topography of the sea floor, creating more habitats and thus the possibility of more species. More broadly, as a whole, water quality in the harbor has improved significantly since the 1930s, especially so since the Clean Water Act of 1972, when pollution-control plants were forced to upgrade to secondary treatment standards. Dissolved oxygen has rebounded to levels that have led to the return of pollution-sensitive creatures such as the shipworm (*Teredo*), a bivalve that thrives on the submerged wooden structures built along the waterfront. Oxygen saturations have even (with the help of the Marine Mammal Protection Act of 1972) created conditions favorable to the reappearance of sea turtles, dolphins, and seals.[26]

The return of these marine species, though a positive trend to the extent that it contributed to increased complexity, underscores just how profoundly the harbor has changed since the days of Henry Hudson. The growth of the seal population, for example, may be a reflection of the animal's close relationship with human beings, a species New York has no shortage of. Reports in the early twenty-first century of a seal colony on Swinburne Island, located off of Staten Island's eastern shore, or the existence of seal-watching tours are a result of the animal's capabilities as an adaptable generalist. They flourish in the presence of people. What raccoons are to the suburbs, seals are fast becoming to the water around New York, as the animal and plant worlds evolve in tandem with the bulging human population. Put simply, the Big Apple Biome is, ecologically speaking, a world apart from life pre-Hudson, and there could be no turning back the clock.[27]

Management of the high-density, simplified ecology was the only real option. Nothing did more to advance that end than the preservation of open space, which provides important habitat for both plant and animal life. And, as it happens, New York has a significant amount of it.

Seventeen percent of the city (as of 1990) was devoted to parkland, and it is arguable that high-density life created the context for some of this free space. But how much of this land is actually of ecological importance? Fragmented parkland or land with a high ratio of circumference to interior area tends to be of little value, at least from an environmental perspective. Strictly speaking, only about a quarter of the parkland could reasonably be expected to contain habitat conducive to biodiversity.[28]

Thirty-odd parks made the list of those with significant amounts of natural area. The largest of these was Gateway National Recreation Area, a constellation of open space throughout the region. The most sweeping Gateway park is located at Jamaica Bay. In addition, noteworthy environmental reserves have been established in Staten Island and the Meadowlands. Altogether, the undeveloped land in these three locales has created an ecologically significant open-space effect. How did these preserves come to be?[29]

In the early 1970s, the future of Jamaica Bay hinged on three proposals. The first was a Port Authority plan to expand Kennedy Airport and tackle airspace congestion by building additional runways at the expense of the bay. A second plan by the Army Corps of Engineers—responding to two powerful storms in 1960 and 1962 that precipitated high tides—called for building a hurricane barrier across Rockaway Inlet. The Corps envisioned an imposing structure designed to protect the city from a storm with only a one-in-a-thousand chance in any given year, which is to say an extremely powerful storm. A third idea was to launch a national recreation area. It required the city to transfer the land it owned at Jamaica Bay to the federal government, so it could be combined with other lands at Breezy Point, Sandy Hook, and Great Kills to form a string of parks. Various interests, including a community group called Gateway Citizens Committee and the Regional Plan Association, lobbied for it. But a national study group made up of scientists and policy makers, concerned about the ecological impact of the various proposals, dismissed both the runway extension and the storm barrier (noting that "[h]urricanes are rather rare in the New York area"). While the group was also negatively inclined toward the park idea, this resulted mostly from the US National Park Service's own ambivalence about running an urban park. Congress, in any case, chose to move ahead with the Gateway park in 1972.[30]

Described as "an ecological Fort Knox," the Jamaica Bay segment ran up against considerable concrete. Just as had happened in Manhattan, tributary streams were dredged and bulkheads built, converting natural watercourses into concrete channels for carrying storm water and waste. With four sewage treatment plants spewing three hundred million gallons a day (1985) of effluent into the bay, surplus nutrients were a particularly invidious problem. Even today, despite efforts to stem the tide, eutrophication continues. Nor has the conservation of open space forestalled the decline of the bay's marsh islands. The rate of marshland loss was seventeen acres per year between 1951 and 1974; eighteen acres per year in the following fifteen years; and thirty-three acres between 1989 and 2003.[31]

This gloomy news was offset by evidence (in the 1980s) of a considerable number of different species of finfish and shellfish beds that continued to offer "subsistence to a significant number of local people." Furthermore, the conjunction of the man-made freshwater ponds (which Robert Moses sandbagged the New York City Transit Authority into building in return for land for a viaduct) and the saltwater bay fostered significant avian biodiversity: ducks, shorebirds, terns, gulls, egrets, geese, grebes, cormorants, and skimmers. By the turn of the century, the Jamaica Bay Wildlife Refuge played host to more than three hundred different bird species and was a pivotal stopover on the Atlantic Flyway.[32]

The Jamaica Bay open-space initiative was followed by the creation of the Staten Island Greenbelt. The roots of the Greenbelt extend back to 1963, when the Girl Scouts looked to profit in the turbocharged real estate market sparked by the impending Verrazano-Narrows Bridge. The scout leadership sold its small woodland camp to developers intent on building garden apartments. But the intervention of a conservationist named Gretta Moulton—and of Robert Moses, who saw the camp as integral to a parkway—led the city of New York to condemn the bulk of the land, paying off the developers. In 1965 the city dedicated the modest High Rock Park (about seventy acres), which was expanded into one of the largest green spaces in all of New York.[33]

The city officially recognized the so-called Staten Island Greenbelt, made up of various public parks and privately owned land, in 1984. A decade later, the Greenbelt encompassed nearly twenty-five hundred acres, an expanse just shy of three times the size of Central Park. The acreage included a rare remnant forest of sugar maple, basswood, and ash. In its forests could be found wood thrush, common screech owl, downy woodpecker, northern harriers, and red-tailed hawks. Significantly, the weasel, a secretive species rarely found in the Big Apple Biome, had cropped up in the belt of open space. The Greenbelt also offered a habitat to Staten Island's embattled amphibian and reptile species, including the Fowler's toad, spring peeper, diamondback terrapin, and northern water snake. In 1998 a naturalist argued that the wildest place in all of New York City—defined as the piece of land "most remote from streets or homes"—was located in the Greenbelt.[34]

The Greenbelt takes on even more weight when understood in the context of a later open-space effort: the companion Bluebelt. Its story began when the escalating real estate market driven by the construction of the Verrazano-Narrows Bridge outstripped the public sector's ability to build sewers.

By the latter part of the 1980s, flooding had reached a flashpoint, and after roughly a decade and a half filled with calls for a more modest role for government, environmental officials managed a small victory by resurrecting a suggestion made in the 1960s by the landscape architect Ian McHarg. Under the leadership of the Department of City Planning and the New York City Department of Environmental Protection, a program of land acquisition began in 1991 that eventually resulted in the twelve-thousand-acre Staten Island Bluebelt.[35]

The idea was simple. The bulk of New York City's freshwater wetlands sprawled across the southern end of Staten Island, and the thought was to put them to use controlling floods and improving water quality. The Bluebelt performed brilliantly during the nor'easters and tropical storms that battered the city during the first decade of the twenty-first

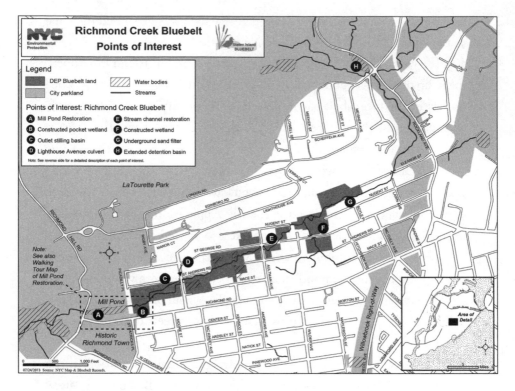

Driving tour of a portion of the Staten Island Bluebelt.

century. Altogether, the Greenbelt and Bluebelt represent a retreat from the rising tide of impervious ground cover that defined New York's approach to the land during the twentieth century.[36]

There is one more aspect of the open-space picture on Staten Island worthy of note: the return of osprey and red-tailed hawks to Fresh Kills. As late as the 1980s, it was nearly impossible to imagine encountering osprey or, for that matter, American goldfinch or northern snapping turtles at the monumental landfill. The sanitation department had even floated a "500-foot-high 'fill and landscaping' plan" for the area. In 1985 the closing of the extensive Fountain Avenue facility in Brooklyn left Fresh Kills to take care of 90 percent of the city's solid waste. When the Edgemere Landfill in Queens shut down in 1991, Fresh Kills became New York's only remaining disposal site. Fiscal pressures, environmental regulations that made operating landfills more complicated and expensive, and community opposition to next-generation incinerators like the one proposed for the Brooklyn Navy Yard, all conspired to leave Fresh Kills the last landfill standing. It might still be in operation but for the elections of Rudolph Giuliani and George Pataki, who yielded in 1996 to Staten Island borough president Guy Molinari's longstanding plea. Apparently, the closing of Fresh Kills was something the three Republicans could all agree on.[37]

Inclined toward the virtues of the free market, they favored hiring private waste haulers to ship the trash out of state, especially in light of the unfavorable economics that marred the waste-to-energy sector. Between 1997 and 2000, the share of total municipal waste exported rose from zero to nearly half. The vast bulk of the solid waste went to landfills in Pennsylvania. A much less significant portion was packed off to New Jersey (where most of it was incinerated), Virginia, and Ohio. It turned out that the invisible hand of the market shuffled solid waste from states with higher population densities and per capita incomes to those with lower ones. Those on the receiving end had no power to block the trash from entering because of a 1978 US Supreme Court decision that protected the interstate waste trade under the Constitution's commerce clause. The closing of Fresh Kills, in other words, was underwritten by the transformation of trash into a freely circulating commodity. The shuttering of the landfill also set the stage for Freshkills Park.[38]

Projected for completion in 2037, the park is dominated by four mountains filled with everything from decomposing watermelons to soiled diapers. The man-made mountains have been sealed off with various layers of soil and drainage material as well as a thick plastic membrane. They also include a set of pipes to harvest the landfill gas. To help encourage improvement at a site as disturbed as Fresh Kills required planting native flora, with the hope that it would attract birds. The birds would aid in seed dispersal and help propagate still more indigenous plants. Hopes were raised when the city parks department claimed that more than two hundred different species of wildlife had been observed at the budding park during 2010 and 2011, including American kestrel, turkey vulture, ring-necked pheasant, red-winged blackbird, and tree swallow. At a bit over two-and-a-half times the size of Olmsted's Manhattan gem, Freshkills Park, with its burgeoning wildlife populations and plans for still more native grasses and wildflowers, has been described as "the planet's greatest act of ecological atonement." Such a positive assessment, however, does not account for the environmental impact of relocating the waste out of state, where others are left to deal with the leachate (garbage juice) and greenhouse gases (carbon dioxide and methane) generated by the Big Apple's trash. But in New York, the park is having a very positive effect—helping to create a solid block of almost eight square miles of open space in the borough often written off as a laughingstock.[39]

It was perhaps only a matter of time, given the trend toward reincarnating erstwhile dumps as open-space refuges, before the largest, most subjugated, and defiled part of Greater New York experienced a similar face-lift. As late as 1970, development of the Meadowlands was on track to pare down what had been almost twenty-four Central Parks' worth of wetlands by a crushing 93 percent. But then history out on the embattled meadows took a U-turn. Over the next generation and a half, the meadows decline came to a halt, and in 2004 a new master plan preserved eighty-four hundred acres—that is, ten Central Parks' worth of open water, wetlands, and abandoned landfills.[40]

How did this open-space reserve come about? Although the pace of annual marshland loss slowed considerably in the decade between 1985 and 1995 to just twenty acres per year—down from over two hundred acres per annum in the preceding decade—the quest to conquer this land continued as if there were no tomorrow. Developers cleverly promised to restore despoiled wetlands if the authorities would allow them to fill in and build on even more degraded parts of the Meadowlands. The idea of re-creating long-lost habitat came to be known as wetlands mitigation. Those eager to profit from northern New Jersey's high-density demographics embraced it, and none more so than the Mills Corporation, a real estate investment trust. In the 1990s, Mills, which viewed this part of the metropolitan area as "undermalled," pledged to restore four hundred acres of wetland in Carlstadt, New Jersey, if it were allowed to build a megamall on another two hundred acres of what the company believed was even more degraded habitat.[41]

The battle lines were drawn. On one side were environmentalists who thought the last thing that New Jersey needed was another shopping mall and who came to the defense of the remaining open land—Phragmites and all—arguing that just bulldozing barriers and letting the water take over was human intervention enough. On the other side were the developers and their enablers who wanted to annihilate the exotic Phragmites—"very tall lawns," said one—and turn back the clock on the meadows by restoring an older version of the ecosystem, while building a mall along the way: Henry Hudson meets Louis Vuitton.[42]

The Mills mall project, meanwhile, because it involved the filling of wetlands, required the approval of the Army Corps of Engineers. Over nine thousand letters poured into the Corps's New York office—more than any project since Westway. Four-fifths of those who wrote objected to the proposed two-million-square-foot mall. Perhaps sensing the changing political currents, in 2001 the Hackensack Meadowlands Development Commission had changed its name to reflect a less business-oriented mission. It dropped the word *Development* to become the blander New Jersey Meadowlands Commission (NJMC). The newly named commission later teamed up with the Corps and endorsed a plan to study the possibility of restoring the ecology of the Meadowlands. The Mills Corporation, perhaps with knowledge of the study, backed off its plan for a mall in Carlstadt. Then, in 2004, the NJMC released its new master plan providing for eighty-four hundred acres of wetlands and open water. Included in this expanse was the Carlstadt land that Mills had been after. In return, Mills entered a deal to build a new mall at the Meadowlands Sports Complex, replete with a twenty-story indoor ski mountain with lifts.[43]

There is no questioning the ecological importance of the Meadowlands. This open space remains the largest brackish tidal wetland system within a twenty-five-mile radius of the Statue of Liberty. Its position on the Atlantic Flyway, and the inclusion of some very large unitary wetlands such as the 753-acre Sawmill Wildlife Management Area, set the stage for a great deal of biodiversity. Sawmill Creek alone provided habitat for diamondback terrapin, common moorhen, fiddler crabs, osprey, and least bittern, among other wildlife.[44]

The moral of this story is that there is no recovering the biological glory of Henry Hudson's day or even George Washington's. Twenty-first-century New Yorkers live in a "now" closed off to a "then." The only relevant question is how to manage the land to increase diversity and ecological complexity as much as possible in a profoundly human-dominated environment.

Nevertheless, efforts to recover the lost world of pre-grid New York live on. Consider Governors Island, a small landmass that through the centuries had been bulked up, under the supervision of the military, into 172 acres lying off Manhattan's southern flank. In 1995 the Coast Guard announced the closing of its operation on the island, and the prospect of a significant addition to the city's stock of open space materialized.[45]

The federal government eventually sold the island for one dollar to the Governors Island Preservation and Education Corporation (GIPEC), a partnership between New York City and the state set up to manage the land. Under the terms of the agreement, at least ninety acres were made off-limits to real estate speculation and had to be developed to advance some "public benefit." A design competition for the forty-acre park to be located on the far side of the island took place, and the winning design dreamed up by a Dutch architecture firm consisted of stylized vertical landforms, some of which were to stretch nearly two hundred feet into the air and given names such as "Babylonic Hill."[46]

With the southern and western parts of the island located in a FEMA-designated *V* zone, meaning that it was subject not simply to a 1 percent chance of flood in a given year but to a velocity hazard resulting from storm-induced wave action as well, one can appreciate the appeal of a proposal focused on elevation. The design, according to the firm's lead architect, Adriaan Geuze, was meant to "dramatize the landscape through topography," while helping to "heighten the experience of the harbor." The Dutch plan, which included the restoration of a wetland, gave a nod to the city's buried ecological past. "We wanted to give it the attitude of a national park," explained one partner at the Dutch firm, "one with primal nature, robustness, where you don't feel the hand of man." Only in New York would people think to take an island, 60 percent of which is man-made, with a shoreline described in a 1998 environmental impact statement as "entirely man-altered," and turn it into Gotham's answer to Yellowstone National Park.[47]

Of course, if the goal was to achieve a landscape untrammeled by human action, one obvious approach was to let the island be. Governors Island was a far better candidate for this kind of treatment than, for example, Fresh Kills Landfill, which required human management to deal with the toxins leaching out of it after a half century of solid-waste disposal. That this kind of "world-without-us" approach received no serious discussion, especially in light of the island's vulnerability to natural disaster and the documented ecological virtues of large, unified areas of open space, suggested just how much the growth imperative had come to dominate New York's conversation with the land. The Gotham frontier, it would seem, must be closed.[48]

16 THE FUTURE OF NEW YORK

For some two hundred years, writers, artists, and filmmakers have dreamed of the destruction of what is one of the most engineered spots on the planet. Popular culture, as it turns out, has had an easier time picturing New York City's destruction than its developers. The cataclysmic imagination seems to know no bounds: earthquake, flood, meteorite, atomic bomb, and even Martian invasion have been broached. Notions of New York succumbing to a "watery death," as one historian has put it, seem to have played an outsized role. If nothing else, the images of New York's demise suggest that if the metropolitan area is one gigantic human artifact, it is at best a very tentative one, a point driven home in 2012 by Hurricane Sandy. High-density living, it must be said, has resulted in a high-risk landscape.[1]

It is only very recently, however, that planners have homed in on the threats posed by natural hazards. Not until the last third of the twentieth century did the realization dawn that squeezing masses of people into the floodplain, plowing under wetlands, and rolling out impervious ground cover had produced a landscape prone to natural disaster. Struck, it seems, by the heavy damage in various urban catastrophes around the world, New York officials finally responded to the threats of earthquake, heat wave, and, most importantly, coastal flooding. In 2009 the city released its first full-fledged natural-hazards mitigation plan. It was as if the city, having survived four hundred years, was finally declaring its intention to make it another four hundred intact—an unqualified human good for those of us who love New York.

Of all the natural hazards, the threat of earthquake has been the one most subject to denial, a peril stuffed away in the deep recesses of city government's inner self like some dirty secret that everyone would just as soon forget about. Although the National Earthquake Hazards Reduction Program (established by Congress in 1977), sensing the potential for damaging seismic shocks in the metropolitan area, increased the recommended lateral load requirements for buildings in 1985, New York procrastinated a full decade before taking any real action. With the city biding its time, a 1989 report noted that while seismicity remained low, a magnitude 6.0 earthquake centered off of Rockaway Beach and roughly seventeen miles from city hall would generate more than eleven billion dollars in damage, or a bit less than half the insured losses in the 9/11 attacks. Rockaway Beach was not chosen randomly. In 1884 an earthquake there estimated at magnitude 4.9 caused shocks to be felt all the way from Vermont to Maryland and created quite a stir in New York City, though damage was minimal.[2]

In 1989 increasing concern over the threat of an eastern earthquake impelled New York's building commissioner to form a committee to revamp the building code. But it took two major California convulsions (Loma Prieta in 1989 and Northridge in 1994) and one in Japan (Kobe in 1995) to drive home the risk. The City Council finally responded by promulgating New York's first seismic building code in 1995. The move forward was tempered, however, by the one-year grace period built into the measure. Developers rushed to file for building permits in the final days before the code became law. Donald Trump's massive Riverside South towers, for example, built partly on soil prone to liquefaction (a condition where saturated soil loses its strength under stress), alone received seven permits right before the law took effect.[3]

Though unquestionably a step forward, the code still left the city, according to an important study, "ill prepared" to deal with the moderate magnitude 5 temblors that, if history is any guide, strike about once a century. Such an event would produce debris on the order of the World Trade Center attack. But a stronger earthquake, roughly comparable to the Loma Prieta, would result in an estimated sixty-seven hundred deaths, most of them "concentrated in the densely populated New York City metropolitan area" where there are still legions of vulnerable un-reinforced masonry buildings. Which is to say that while New York's seismic *hazard* remains low because damaging earthquakes occur infrequently, its seismic *risk* is high because of the concentration of people and property, and the profusion of unreinforced structures.[4]

The increasing acknowledgment of the seismic risk paralleled a growing recognition of yet another natural hazard: heat waves, or, as they are known in the scientific literature, extreme heat events. Although New York had suffered through extreme heat, including a stretch in 1896 when the temperature at city hall reached 112 degrees, killing as many as thirteen hundred people in New York and Brooklyn, the issue has shown up only recently on the radar of policy makers. It took a lethal 1995 Chicago heat wave—believed to have claimed a minimum of 485 and perhaps over 700 lives—to focus attention on the issue. Shortly thereafter, scientific evidence indicated excess deaths from heat during an average New York City summer ranged in the neighborhood of three hundred, or over seven times the number of New Yorkers who died in Hurricane Sandy.[5]

In part, the urban heat-island effect was to blame. As we have seen, by the beginning of the twentieth century, New York City already had warmed by at least one degree Celsius relative to the surrounding countryside. Over the course of the century, there was more modest growth of approximately a half degree. It is worth noting, however, that the rise combined with the more general global warming trend resulted in a not-insignificant three and a half degree Celsius increase in New York City's annual average temperature, a trend that only aggravated the problem of heat-related mortality.[6]

The deaths of an estimated fifteen thousand people in France alone during a 2003 Western European heat wave drew more attention to the problem. Although the catastrophe was extraordinarily unusual, scientists used the episode to extrapolate excess death figures to get a sense of the effects of such a hot spell in New York. They found, again, that the city demonstrated a great deal of sensitivity—mortalitywise—to extreme heat. It was postulated that the reason for the city's atypical response could rest with the built environment—the many brick high-rises found in poor areas, for example—as well as the high population density.[7]

Despite mounting evidence of the heat problem, New York public-health officials indulged in denial. Other cities, such as Philadelphia and Chicago, had spent the 1990s broadening their definition of heat-related deaths to more accurately reflect the magnitude of the problem. In Philadelphia, for example, an overly stringent definition that required evidence, before death, of a body temperature in excess of 105 degrees was replaced with a definition of heat-related death that took into consideration whether the body was found in an enclosed environment with a high temperature and no cooling system present. New York, however, clung to a very narrow reading of the problem. As late as 2006, the city's chief medical examiner, when questioned about broader so-called heat-related deaths replied, "We don't use that term." Later that same year, in a sign of change, the city's Department of Health and Mental Hygiene for the first time made a calculation using excess deaths to better understand the impact of a heat wave the previous summer. The official death toll had been placed at forty. But the new calculation showed that the heat had claimed more than three times that number.[8]

Climate change will only aggravate the problem. By the middle of the twenty-first century, premature death from heat could increase on average 70 percent over the mortality rate in the 1990s. New York City was singled out as particularly vulnerable because of the urban heat-island effect. As one study pointed out, "[T]hose counties currently experiencing the hottest summers are the highly urbanized counties in and around New York City, which also have the greatest population density, thus exposing millions of residents to periodic summer heat stress." More premature heat-related deaths will be the result, a problem that will fall the hardest on the city's tens of thousands of homeless people.[9]

As troubling as the threats from earthquake and heat are, it is flooding that has evolved into the most pressing concern. Recent storms have highlighted the paralyzing effects of floods on the city's monumental economy, which a 2010 estimate reckoned was over 4 percent of the entire economic output of the United States. New York is, of course, not just a dense metropolitan area but a dense *coastal* metropolitan area. In the three and a half decades following 1965, coastal population in the tristate region increased roughly 17 percent. In addition, a vast and complex infrastructure system—sewage treatment plants, bridges, tunnels, airports—had developed along the waterfront. In 1990 it emerged that Greater New York was at risk of a much higher hurricane storm surge than previously thought. A storm surge involves an abnormally high, wind-driven gush of water over the land; it represents a grave threat to people and property. What happened in 1990 is that a new computer model took into consideration the city's location at the apex of the New York Bight, where the coastline bends, and found that the shoreline configuration in conjunction with the depth of the water was destined to intensify the effects of a storm surge.[10]

Two years later, a nor'easter swept through the metropolitan region, much of which is situated less than 16.4 feet above average sea level. The storm generated flood conditions that had not been experienced in four decades and led to the shutdown of the PATH and New York City subway systems. The Battery Tunnel filled with six feet of water. And yet this was only a moderate nor'easter.[11]

In 1995 the Army Corps of Engineers, while studying the time necessary to evacuate New York, employed the new computer model mentioned above to estimate the maximum storm-surge heights from a Category 3 hurricane. The results proved alarming. The Corps study showed that the abnormal elevation of the water level caused by such a storm would be twenty-four feet at the Battery Tunnel and twenty-five feet at Kennedy Airport. The normally staid Corps employed the term "dire significance" to describe what would have happened if the 1992 nor'easter had instead been a moderate to severe hurricane. The short answer is that New York would have drowned in a storm surge it estimated as ranging from sixteen to thirty feet above normal. "The possibility of voluminous flood waters rapidly filling several roadway tunnels and a large percentage of the rail tunnel network," the report concluded ominously, "raises a specter of catastrophe."[12]

It is important to keep in mind that high-density life has unfolded in New York during a period of relative quiescence in intense hurricane activity. Recall that before the Erie Canal even opened, when the city's population was just 124,000, an 1821 hurricane (Category 1) scored a direct hit on the city. Significant destruction resulted because of the hurricane's high forward speed (increasing wind and surge damage) and its track along a path, roughly speaking, through Newark, New Jersey—which placed the population center in New York on the dangerous right side of the storm. The hurricane produced an estimated ten-to-eleven-foot storm surge and caused lower Manhattan to flood as far north as Canal Street. As of the twenty-first century, most of the seawall encasing Manhattan measured barely five feet in height. While subsequent storms in 1893, 1903, 1938, and a spate in the early 1950s buffeted the region, the sporadic occurrence of hurricanes led the city to spend most of the twentieth century planning for snowstorms (like the devastating 1888 blizzard) and garden-variety floods.[13]

Not until 1960 did a storm comparable to the 1821 hurricane in terms of its effect on the tide strike the city. Hurricane Donna, which made landfall on Long Island and caused the wind to gust to ninety-three miles per hour at La Guardia Airport, resulted in a total water level as measured at the Battery of 13.3 feet, the second highest level ever recorded at the site. The scale of the flooding caused by Donna prompted consideration of a proposal to build hurricane barriers. The plan was to place them at the entrance to Lower New York Bay (between Sandy Hook and Breezy Point, Queens) and at Throgs Neck in the Bronx to safeguard the city from the Long Island Sound. No such elaborate plan was ever carried out, though in 1965 the Army Corps of Engineers did recommend that an eighteen-foot-high hurricane barrier be built across Rockaway Inlet. The cost was enormous, and, in any case, the project ran into trouble from the burgeoning environmental movement because it would aggravate Jamaica Bay's already considerable pollution problem. New York passed on these measures.[14]

While plans to up the level of protection were being mulled over, the surface of the sea cooled off, helping to spare the region from major hurricanes. The climatic change at issue is known as the Atlantic Multidecadal Oscillation (AMO), a periodic cycle of warming and cooling of surface temperatures in the North Atlantic. During the warm phase of the cycle (coincident with the 1938 hurricane, the flurry of storms in the 1950s, and Hurricane Donna), there is an increased chance that weak storms will evolve into more intense hurricane systems. But after 1965, the cycle shifted into its cooler phase, working to insulate New York. The hurricanes that did make contact turned out to be relatively anemic. Interest in hurricane preparedness and protection waned as Hurricane Gloria in 1985 and Hurricane Bob in 1991 petered out as they neared New York. In 1999 the metropolitan area again escaped disaster when Hurricane Floyd, downgraded to a tropical storm as it reached the city, arrived in time for low tide. Floyd failed to inflict any significant flooding.[15]

Then the climate changed again. The warm phase of the AMO returned in the middle of the 1990s, and with it came the prospect for more major storms. New York's vulnerability led a group of scientists at Stony Brook University in 2004 to dredge up the old plan for storm-surge barriers. The proposal called for three barriers to be positioned to protect "valuable real estate around the edges of lower Manhattan, low-lying areas in Brooklyn and Queens, western Staten Island, Jersey City and Hoboken." The barriers were to be located at critical junctures (the Narrows, the southern entrance to the Arthur Kill, and the intersection of the East River and Long Island Sound) and were modeled on similar projects in England and the Netherlands. The project's leader likened the barrier scheme to the building of Hoover Dam. Critics noted that the barricades left portions of the city, such as the southern parts of Brooklyn and Staten Island, unprotected. (A fourth barrier across Rockaway Inlet was proposed later.) They even worried that such a Maginot Line might create a false sense of safety that would only tend to green-light further development. And they also raised concerns about the eco-logical effects the barriers would have on fisheries, sediment transport, and salinity levels in the harbor.[16]

Chastened by Hurricane Katrina, the Bloomberg administration put in place a new evacuation plan in 2006. Though criticized for its hands-off approach to nursing homes and hospitals struggling with how to deliver patients to safety, the plan was still a major step forward and wel-come news in the Big Apple Biome. For the numbers did not look good. In 2006 Max Mayfield, the director of the National Hurricane Center, said, "It is not a question of *if* a major hurricane will strike the New York area, but *when*."[17]

New York, even with its new evacuation plan, was not entirely ready for such an eventuality. A 2008 study of coastal flooding caused by storm surge, conducted by the Organization for Economic Co-operation and Development (OECD), examined the exposure for 136 port cities around the world; the results made for very depressing—frightening—reading. Greater New York was one of four cities in the top ten ports in terms of both population and assets exposed.* Also, New York was sec-ond only to Tokyo on the list of ports most vulnerable to wind damage from cyclones.[18]

Examining exposure to coastal storms is not the same as studying the actual risk of impact from this type of geophysical extreme. When the study examined the latter issue, what it discovered was even more startling. Even though New York's gross domestic product surpassed that of London, Tokyo, and Amsterdam, it lagged well behind in terms of its level of defense against coastal flooding. While these three cities and even Shanghai, China, all had substantial protections in place to defend against at least a one-in-a-thousand-year storm, New York was shielded to just a tenth of that level. "New York," the OECD pointed out, "has rather low defences for such a rich city." More worrisome still was a subsequent study examining the physics of hurricanes and storm surge. According to its findings, Gotham's risk of experiencing "a cata-

---

* The other three were Miami, Osaka-Kobe, and New Orleans.

strophic coastal flood event" was higher than had been thought (higher than the normal distribution, in the language of statistics). In trading in its tidal wetlands for land development, the city had denied itself a frontline defense against storm surge that, if the sedimentary record is any guide, kept all but the most vicious flooding at bay.[19]

By the time the city released its natural-hazards mitigation plan in 2009, a new problem had emerged: flash floods. While the plan acknowledged the threats posed by earthquakes, heat waves (admitting that New York's figures for heat-related deaths tended to be "substantially lower from what other cities report"), and hurricanes, it also called attention to flash floods resulting from the "dense population and abundance of impervious surfaces." Two years earlier, a largely unpredicted storm deposited between one and a half and nearly three and a half inches of rain in just a couple of hours. With the city's drainage systems equipped to deal with only one and three quarter inches per hour, the storm threw the transportation network into chaos.[20]

Climate change threatened to further complicate the natural-hazards profile, accelerating rates of sea level rise and making the metropolitan area even more vulnerable than it was already to coastal storm surge and flooding. "Concentration of high population densities in vulnerable areas will pose serious problems in the event of evacuation during major storms," one study warned, "in as much as many evacuation routes lie close to present-day storm flood levels." This forecast was particularly bad news for New York's dispossessed, since minorities living in the floodplain (where much of the city's public housing is located) tended to be undercounted and thus were at a disadvantage with respect to plans for emergency preparedness and relief.[21]

For all the hype about the destruction of New York depicted in Hollywood movies, it is remarkable how fortunate the city has been in dodging hurricane disaster, at least until very recently. Even as late as 2011, the city emerged from Hurricane Irene looking like a lucky gambler holding a royal flush. The hurricane had weakened on arrival, though it would have taken only a slight increase in wind speed or a somewhat different arrival time (when the tide was higher) to have caused the subway and the Battery Tunnel to flood. New York City also now had a solid evacuation plan in place, though it was criticized for not including Rikers Island—the bulk of which is landfill and home to ten jails—in its calculations. If the logistical issues involved in evacuating close to four hundred thousand people living in the zone most at risk of flooding— on an archipelago, no less—seemed to call into question the wisdom of limitless growth, no one in the corridors of power seemed to have second thoughts about business as usual in the floodplain.[22]

Despite the above projections, the idea of hyperdensity not only survives but also thrives. Consider, for a moment, the changing fortunes of the grid plan, perhaps one of the best ways of charting density's recent re- vival. The disdain for the grid on the part of Victorian urbanists such as Frederick Law Olmsted prevailed for the bulk of the twentieth century. Which is to say that the simplistic understanding of the grid as a ruth- less display of economic calculation persisted. The negativity surround- ing the grid, however, began to fade by the end of the 1970s, when the Dutch architect Rem Koolhaas published his brash treatise, *Delirious New York*. The timing of the grid's rehabilitation is worth noting. New York had just suffered through its worst fiscal crisis, a set of economic woes that was solved by redistributing power away from the municipal unions and working class toward the financial elite. If the city was no longer supposed to function as the land of opportunity for the little guy, what was its raison d'être?[23]

Congestion, Koolhaas explained, was its reason for being. As he had it, the 1811 grid plan was the driving force behind one giant mob scene and the source of all that was good about New York. Calling the Manhattan grid "the most courageous act of prediction in Western civ- ilization," Koolhaas noted, with approval, that "the subjugation, if not obliteration, of nature is its true ambition."[24]

During the decade that followed Koolhaas's book—a period known for the premium it placed on entrepreneurialism—the grid staged a re- surgence. Far from being dismissed as a mercenary effort to retrofit the natural environment of Manhattan, the grid was resuscitated by one historian as the consummate expression of republicanism; an ingenious response to the limits placed on public authority during the period in which it was born. Another historian wrote that if the grid "left New Yorkers free to crowd their properties and to ravage the landscape, it above all provided them with a predictable future and a guaranteed order within which they could carry on their myriad acts of development." The iconoclast John B. Jackson, who found beauty in even the ugliest everyday landscapes, and the sociologist William H. Whyte, who in 1968 wrote a book defending urban density to save more open space, both endorsed the principles of the grid. By the 1990s, during an exhibition of the Dutch painter Piet Mondrian's work at the Museum of Modern Art, it almost seemed as if gridded New York was being proclaimed a kind of work of art. Adding to the excitement was Manhattanhenge, the twice-yearly phenomenon when the sun sets in perfect alignment with the grid pattern. In the early twenty-first century, New Yorkers jostled for position to watch as the dazzling gaseous sphere lingered on the horizon, lighting up the sky in a blaze of red, orange, and copper, and illuminating all the island's cross streets in a light show that seemed to immortalize the city's true genius.[25]

When the grid's two hundredth birthday arrived (by which point Koolhaas had put his imagination to work on a grid plan for Dubai that put a little New York density in the Arabian Desert), the mood was nearly all celebration. The Museum of the City of New York hosted an exposition on the 1811 plan that tended to glorify it. What else to make of an exhibit titled *The Greatest Grid*? Amanda Burden, the director of city planning, said the grid was responsible for Manhattan's vibrancy. Scott Stringer, the Manhattan borough president, mentioned its role in making the city intrinsically navigable. The *Times* architecture critic Michael Kimmelman paid tribute by calling it "deeply subversive" and "oddly beautiful" and largely responsible for Manhattan's unique "urban theater." A writer on the paper's opinion page went so far as to argue, based on circumstantial evidence, that the commissioners, in designing the grid, "made prescient and wise use of the city's natural environment."

He had in mind the grid's alignment with the east-west compass points (responsible for Manhattanhenge) and the numerous cross streets that he claimed allowed floodwaters to ebb more quickly. The grid, in this understanding, was no mere "primal topographic curse," as the novelist Henry James had put it in 1906, but an example of people "working with nature."[26]

There were, to be sure, a few contrarians. The writer Tony Hiss worried that the grid distanced New Yorkers from their "natural surroundings." The Bronx-born tour-bus guide Timothy "Speed" Levitch advocated blowing up the grid, calling it "some real estate broker's wet dream." But otherwise the grid had been vindicated. New York, because of its hyperdensity, had come to represent one of humanity's greatest triumphs.[27]

There is no doubt a good deal to admire in the richness, diversity, and vibrant face-to-face interactions that characterize dense urban life in New York. And there is little questioning, at least in principle, the natural-resource efficiencies, especially with respect to energy consumption. But to turn around and argue, as the Bloomberg administration and others have, that hyperdensity is also an environmental strategy is problematic for three reasons. First, to single out places such as Manhattan, Shanghai, and London as "the real friends of the environment," in the words of economist Edward Glaeser, risks reflexively endorsing the growth imperative despite what it might mean for habitat loss or eutrophication. Second, his assertion that "there is nothing greener than blacktop" in an odd way places too much emphasis on carbon emissions and the consequent global warming. Of course, climate change is important, but it is not the only ecological issue that New York—much less the world—faces. For at least from a natural-hazards perspective, there is something greener than blacktop: the wetlands that ward off the prospect of floods, for one. And third, density tends to alienate people from the land while obscuring the connections to the distant places and resources that they depend on for survival.[28]

• • •

This map was created in an effort to reconnect people with the environment of the Gowanus area. The Gowanus Canal, Newtown Creek, and the Hudson River have been designated by the EPA as Superfund sites.

A planner for the city of New York was once asked whether there was any limit to the number of people who could live in Manhattan. "The natural limits of density?" he responded. "That's a subject that we don't really think about at City Planning." But there are, in fact, some natural limits to density, and we can find no better example than in the area of airline transportation.[29]

In New York, airports are to wetlands what gulls are to landfills. All the major ones are located atop them: Newark Liberty at the old Newark Meadows, La Guardia at Flushing Meadows, and Kennedy at Jamaica Bay. The airports are found in places that were slow to be developed. But they also sprung up where there was room to expand runways into the open water.

Over time the growth of the metropolitan area tended to increase airport congestion, as those involved in finance and corporate management, plus all the tourists, boarded planes to reach the city. Greater New York required another airport, but there was no room for one within a forty-mile radius of Manhattan.[30]

So that left expanding one of the current airports with landfill as a main option. A 2011 study by the Regional Plan Association considered the prospects for combatting airport congestion and proposed four plans to enlarge Kennedy Airport. Three of them involved the use of landfill, ranging from two hundred to nearly four hundred acres. The land would come at the expense of Jamaica Bay.[31]

The idea of building with landfill was complicated by Jamaica Bay's precarious ecology. The bay had been losing land at a rapid rate, with half its tidal wetlands disappearing between 1924 and 1999. Moreover, the rate of marsh loss accelerated over the course of the twentieth century. In 2001 the New York State Department of Environmental Conservation estimated that if the bay's marshes continued to decline at the rate of forty-four acres per year (as they had in the 1990s), they would vanish completely by 2024. With the marsh in crisis, New York City passed legislation requiring the Department of Environmental Protection to create a comprehensive plan to improve the bay's "ecological integrity." A later analysis employing aerial photography proved even more alarming, showing that the marsh islands were eroding more rapidly than was previously thought and predicting an earlier demise.[32]

The case of Jamaica Bay's vanishing wetlands was complicated; the precise reason for the decline unclear. The list of possible causes spanned everything from sediment loss, to water pollution, to overgrazing of salt marsh cordgrass by geese. A leading theory held that the marshes were fading away because the sediment load had declined with the building of bulkheads on the bay's perimeter and the channelization of its erstwhile freshwater streams. In addition, Grassy Bay, which was radically deepened during the construction of Kennedy Airport, acted as a sink for sediments, keeping such material from nourishing the bay's islands. But whether filling in Grassy Bay—as called for in the airport expansion— would slow marsh loss and benefit the ecology was an open question. "Anytime you push out any runways into the bay, you have a problem," said Don Riepe of the American Littoral Society. "At some point you have to think about limits and directing people to other airports." How the future of Jamaica Bay is handled may answer the question of whether the exponents of high-density living are willing to admit to some checks on the urban form.[33]

One of the clearest indicators of what those who rule New York have in store for the natural environment can be found in the city's plans for its premier resource: the waterfront. It was here that the trends toward hyperdensity and climate change came together to shape the Bloomberg administration's *Vision 2020* plan. The new plan was centered on many of the same goals that the city had been pursuing since the 1990s: public access, economic development, and environmental protection. *Vision 2020*, however, waded into new territory with its pledge to improve water quality, restore degraded waterfront habitats, and address the anticipated effects of climate change.[34]

There is no question that what the *Times* called "necessary growth" remained the major thrust of the city's image of the future. Since 1992, more than twenty thousand units of residential housing went in along the waterfront, and as of 2011, there were another six thousand units in the offing. Dozens and dozens of rezonings affecting roughly three thousand acres had taken place since the early 1990s. Approximately half of these changes spurred development by, for example, allowing for a shift from low-density to high-density building. Noting that population was projected to increase to over nine million by 2030, the *Vision* plan argued that development of the waterfront would help ease the need for housing.[35]

The *Vision* blueprint contained some important ecological interventions. So, for example, the plan mentioned the success of the Staten Island Bluebelt in addressing flood control and water quality. It referenced the city's purchase of a few hundred acres of wetlands. It pointed to the remediation of hundreds of acres of land around Jamaica Bay (including two former landfills), to the planting of tens of thousands of trees, to the creation of coastal grassland, and to efforts to restore oyster reefs. And it touted the success of three Special Natural Waterfront Areas (established in 1992) at Jamaica Bay, northwest Staten Island, and along the Upper East River and Long Island Sound, the last including Robert Moses's old stomping grounds at Willow and Meadow Lakes.[36]

All were undeniably important habitats. The Staten Island section included Shooter's Island, Prall's Island, and the Isle of Meadows. As of the 1990s, these islands provided nesting sites for numerous wading birds, including great egret, glossy ibis,* and black-crowned night herons.[37]

But plans to improve the ecological integrity of the Big Apple Biome ran up against the constraints imposed by the guiding growth ethos. Even the Bloomberg administration's PlaNYC initiative admitted that, whatever the success of the Bluebelt program, the city's "ability to replicate this process across the city is limited due to our dense development." As for the Special Natural Waterfront Areas, they are not formally incorporated into the city's zoning resolution, likely because they have the potential to jeopardize future residential and commercial plans.[38]

The authors of the *Vision* plan considered landscape change—in particular the various shoreline expansions that took place over the course

---

* The glossy ibis is actually a southern species, unknown in Henry Hudson's time, that owes its existence in Greater New York to global warming.

of several centuries—to be at the heart of New York's ecological success. New York's pioneering role in the creation of high-density life—which paved the way for a very large population and significant economic activity in a small area—"is one of its greatest contributions to the environment." The reference was to the role that hyperdensity played in low per capita carbon emissions and "the preservation of open space and natural resources elsewhere," though the latter was more of an assertion than a data-driven finding. It was the first claim, however, that was given more prominence. "The continued growth of New York City itself," the plan concluded, "is a mitigation strategy for climate change."[39]

Whatever the validity of the claim that compactness tempers climate change, the latter clearly carries threats to high-density life. A city task force made up in part of climate scientists found that the past record would be of little help in this regard. "Historical climate precedents are no longer valid for long-term environmental planning," it declared in a 2010 report. By the 2050s, average temperatures in New York City might be in line with those in Norfolk, Virginia. In all likelihood, heat waves will become more frequent and longer lasting. Sea level is expected to increase eleven to twenty-four inches, though possibly as high as thirty-one inches. That trend in turn would increase the severity of coastal flooding associated with storms. A one-in-a-hundred-year flood, that is, an inundation with a magnitude that today (2014) has a 1 percent chance of occurring in a given year, will become five times as likely to happen by midcentury if sea level indeed rises to the highest projected level. Were a Category 3 hurricane to strike New York City, similar to the 1938 storm that slammed into Long Island fifty miles to the east, the insured property losses alone would total almost three times those experienced in Hurricane Katrina.[40]

Given the stakes, some kind of adaptation strategy was in order. Realizing that mitigation alone—efforts to reduce the magnitude of greenhouse gas emissions—would not be adequate to safeguard the city, New York began considering what could be done to adjust to the inevitable changing climate. On the positive side, the task force found that the city already had in place "an effective approach to climate change adaptation." It praised the city's "proactive leadership" and the efforts to link climate change to the broader sustainability initiative embodied in PlaNYC. But sometimes the task force seemed more interested in reinforcing the high-density paradigm than in reducing vulnerability. For example, one part of the study noted that while "[i]ncreased intensity or density of development" in low-lying areas raised the flood risk, it could be offset with "flood-resistant construction, even at higher densities" and possibly abated through the installation of "shoreline protection measures." Such a statement legitimized further high-density growth while relying on technology that may not prove effective during a future coastal storm. "The risks posed by climate change," this section of the report concluded, "do not necessarily dictate that the city should retreat from highly populated and developed areas or avoid all development in areas where flood risks exist."[41]

Beginning on October 29, 2012, the sea paid a little visit to New York. In the space of just a few hours, it had thrown history into reverse, sabotaging several hundred years' worth of hard-won and fabulously expensive reclamation. New York seemed, for a brief moment, to have wound up nearly back where it started.

Jones Beach, Robert Moses's handiwork, which he so carefully elevated out of harm's way, took a terrible beating. Crashing waves reduced the wooden boardwalk to splinters. Lifeguard shacks were tossed around like toys. Metal highway signs snapped, underpasses flooded, and the amphitheater dramatically perched on the edge of Zach's Bay took on several feet of water. The storm left such a powerful statement in its wake that even Donald Trump—a man who seems to have the growth imperative imprinted on his very genetic makeup—sat up and took notice. Hurricane Sandy put the kibosh on his plan for eighty-six thousand square feet of development on the beach. Trump on the Ocean became Trump in the Ocean.[42]

Next door at Long Beach, a barrier island briefly cut off from the mainland in the 1950 nor'easter, water surged over the sand dunes holding back the sea and rose five to ten feet high in the streets. Houses burned, and basements filled with sewage. It was as if a miniature version of Colorado's Great Sand Dunes National Park and Preserve had opened at the City by the Sea.* With residents forced to turn to bottled water and portable toilets because of the utility damage, one person described the conditions as "very nineteenth century."[43]

And so it went on west down the shore: the storm threatened to turn the tarmac at Kennedy Airport into its older life as mushy meadow muck and put fifteen feet of water in an AirTrain connector to a Delta Airlines terminal. What was left of Coney Island Creek after all the filling in was enough to overflow with such a vengeance that it nearly killed a group of city utility workers trapped by the rising waters. Floodwater gushed into the former marshlands along the Gowanus Canal—coating the neighborhood in an oily sheen, mangling metal security doors, and tearing down walls. And in Red Hook, water from Buttermilk Channel and Gowanus Bay surged into row houses built in old marshlands, filling the homes almost ceiling high.[44]

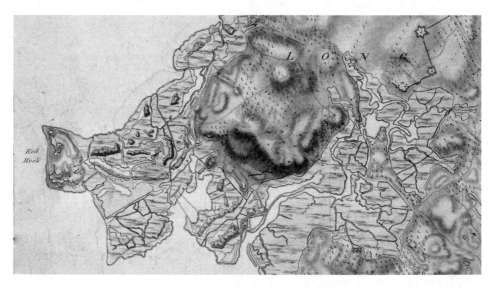

A portion of the 1782 British Headquarters Map showing Brooklyn's former marshlands, an area hit hard by Hurricane Sandy.

---

*   In the cleanup afterward, the sand would be bulldozed into a mound aspiring to the Great Pyramid of Giza except for the American flag flapping in the wind on its peak.

Across the harbor in Staten Island, the storm's impact was particularly deadly. More people died in the borough (twenty-one) than died in the states of New Jersey, Connecticut, and Pennsylvania combined. The carnage took place along the flood-prone outwash plain near Great Kills on the south and east shores of the island located at the crest of the New York Bight, where geography funneled the ocean's angry waters. The force of the water tore houses from foundations and, in one case, sent a home flying into a sea of Phragmites. Back in William Davis's early life, this land was a desolate, tide-swept marsh. But then came its paving over in houses and roads. When Hurricane Sandy whipped through, the sea returned to the neighborhood. At Midland Beach, eight people in a little stretch of just eight blocks drowned. The highest water levels in all New York occurred, sure enough, on the island, at nearly eight feet above ground level. The death and destruction, however, have not slowed plans near the ferry terminal to Manhattan for the world's tallest Ferris wheel, accompanied by a hundred-store outlet mall, to be built close to where the storm drove thirty-foot-long dock pilings through the ground floor of an apartment complex (where the author once lived).[45]

North along the onetime tidelands fronting the Hudson shore of Bergen Neck, the ocean breached seawalls, and water poured into the streets of Hoboken and Jersey City. When the water receded from the backyard of one Jersey City home, it left its calling card: a brown watermark on a basketball-hoop backboard. People slogged through the thoroughfares of Hoboken, breathing in the fumes from the toxic brew that had made the very streets themselves slippery. Roughly half the city of Hoboken was flooded, and when the storm surge peaked, fully twenty thousand people found themselves completely surrounded by water. Hoboken started out as an island, and so, briefly, did it return to one.[46]

As went Hoboken, so went the southern tip of Manhattan. The hardest hit areas were where John Montgomerie granted New York title to land under water. What Montgomerie conveyed, Hurricane Sandy took away. Cars floated through lower Manhattan near where George Washington once stood. The Battery Tunnel filled to the hilt—all two miles of it. The East River broke through a bulkhead and poured into the city, reclaiming the Lower East Side and other parts of southern Manhattan built on landfill. Floodwater traveled almost half a mile down the aptly named Canal Street. The storm put Hudson River Park under almost four feet of water and knocked out the electrical system, though to the south, Battery Park City, because of its elevation, escaped relatively unscathed. At the old World Trade Center site, where a museum commemorating the September 11 attacks was being built below ground, the steel-reinforced concrete bathtub, there to keep the Hudson River—less than two hundred feet away—at bay, gave ground to the storm as well. The wall had held during the 2001 catastrophe, prompting one architect to remark that it symbolized the city's "indomitable spirit." Sandy, however, menaced New York's soul, as the sea rose up to overwhelm the concrete wall—a reminder that the control of nature is an illusion.[47]

Then, in the middle of all the pandemonium, with the limits to growth staring the city straight in the eye, something right out of a Hollywood movie took place: an explosion at a Consolidated Edison substation in the East Village that lit up the night sky in green and knocked out power to lower Manhattan.

But even with all the water surging and the darkness descending, the City That Never Sleeps was up late. A beacon of light radiated out in the black at 200 West Street, once a stretch of open water before its rise into a vibrant seaport and later its decline via landfill into an old Battery Park City parking lot. Now it was the site of a gleaming forty-three-story tower, the home of none other than Goldman Sachs. Here was the citadel of capitalism weathering the storm, barricaded behind hundreds of sandbags, equipped with a backup generator, showing the world who was boss in a tower erected to gold-rated green-building specifications and located, ironically enough, smack in what was once the Hudson River.[48]

Hurricane Sandy was, barometrically speaking, an extremely intense storm, though the 1938 Great New England Hurricane was likely more powerful. The wind field (the extent of strong winds) was immense: three times Hurricane Katrina's. Hurricane Sandy was somewhat unusual in that rather than taking a traditional northeasterly path, it hooked to the west, placing the city on the dangerous right side of the storm, where

This 2007 FEMA map places Sea Gate on the western tip of Coney Island almost completely outside the flood-hazard zone, as depicted by the lighter gray.

Despite its name, Sea Gate proved no match for Hurricane Sandy, as shown by the darker shading. What remained of Coney Island Creek rose up and closed down the original Nathan's Famous store on Surf Avenue for more than half a year.

onshore winds drove water toward the coast. Nevertheless, the 1950 nor'easter took a similarly "anomalous" path, which is to say that Sandy was not entirely unique. And, moreover, in all the puffing up of nature's fury, it is often overlooked that on landfall in New Jersey, the storm had weakened and was no longer a hurricane at all but a posttropical cyclone.[49]

Predictably, what seemed to impress those in power in the immediate wake of the tragedy was the sheer dominance of the natural world. President Barack Obama said, "All of us have been shocked by the force of Mother Nature." The governor of New York, Andrew Cuomo, added, "This was a major, major assault by Mother Nature that we went through, and it's not going to be a one- or two- or three-day situation." Discussing the loss of life, Mayor Michael Bloomberg pointed out that, "sadly, nature is dangerous, and these things occur." Steven Spinola, president of the Real Estate Board of New York, quipped, "The city can't control Mother Nature."[50]

There is, of course, no denying the magnitude of this low-pressure system. Sandy caused the storm tide at the Battery to reach its highest level—14.06 feet—since the start of record keeping at the site in 1920. What's more, although flood-insurance maps drawn by the federal government beginning in 1983 determined that thirty-three square miles of land in New York City remained at risk of a one-in-a-hundred-year flood, Sandy resketched the maps and proved that, in fact, a remarkable fifty-one square miles of land—17 percent of the city—was in jeopardy. And yet to interpret the calamity as an act of nature is to make it seem as if the disaster came out of nowhere. Invoking Mother Nature risked leaving the impression that the long history of land making and building in the floodplain had little to do with the catastrophe. In fact, this was a self-inflicted calamity.[51]

Thus it is all the more important to draw the connections between the storm and long-term historical developments. Three trends are worthy of note. First, New York has been thumbing its nose at the ocean for over three hundred years. The Dutch took some tentative steps into the floodplain of the East River back in the seventeenth century, but it was the English who invented, as we have seen, a whole new form of property—land under water—that allowed building to go forward in harm's way. Still, it was only in the nineteenth century that the idea of New York as a limitless proposition led to the extensive development of coastal areas. That move came at the expense of the wetlands and mudflats that once safeguarded the shoreline and helped to mitigate the effects of storm surge. In the period since the 1930s, the marshlands at Flushing Meadows, Newark Bay, and Jamaica Bay capitulated to roads and airport tarmac. And eventually real estate development took over the waterfront, as gentrification spilled out across lower Manhattan and the West Side, along the East River in Queens and Brooklyn, and on Staten Island's eastern shore, turning run-down warehouses and piers into sleek towers of glass and steel.

Just weeks before the storm struck, the geophysicist Klaus Jacob, who had been urging New York to deal more aggressively with the threat of natural hazards for a generation, noted that the city had been "extremely lucky." He added that he was "disappointed that the political process hasn't recognized that we're playing Russian roulette." The blind spot to which he referred has come about because of the sway of the growth imperative—that is, the idea of New York as an infinitely expanding entity in terms of its population, economy, and relations with the land. It was this vision that drove the relentless development of land at the expense of the sea. It was this vision that drove the makeover of the floodplain, first to serve maritime interests, and, later, as the city grew in every direction, to house the real estate, roads, landfills, and airports that have made New York the place it is today.[52]

It is too early to tell how the storm will shape the future of New York. A climatologist at Columbia University called for putting "managed retreat" from the shore on the table. But water was still sloshing around in the Battery Tunnel when the advocates for Gotham unbound spoke up in favor of yet more untrammeled growth. Vishaan Chakrabarti, director of Columbia's Center for Urban Real Estate, an organization behind the idea to vastly expand lower Manhattan with yet more landfill all the way to Governors Island, acknowledged that the promotion of waterfront development had put people into the path of danger. Still, he made clear his intention to foster more growth, holding up the Dutch reclamation efforts as a model.

"They really don't treat the water in this kind of eggshell kind of

way that they do in the United States," Chakrabarti remarked about the
Dutch. "They reclaim the land, use dredging material, do a whole variety
of things to reshape the shoreline, like we first did when we were New
Amsterdam." To characterize as hesitant what has gone on in the way of
wetland loss and land making in Greater New York is, at best, a gross dis-
tortion of the historical record. Moreover, nothing the Dutch colonists
did at New Amsterdam comes even remotely close to the transformation
of land and water that has happened since the nineteenth century. And
that is still happening at places such as Manhattan's West Side, where
Hurricane Sandy did nothing to dampen the spirits for a twenty-six-
acre real estate development called Hudson Yards, much of which is set
to rise directly in the one-in-a-hundred-year storm floodplain. If New
York wants to return to the days of Petrus Stuyvesant, it should dig a
canal down Broad Street, modeled on the old Heere Gracht, and call it
a day.[53]

The second historical trend necessary to understanding Hurricane
Sandy's significance involves changes in the natural environment itself.
Consider something as simple as the water level at the Battery. Accurate
records exist all the way from 1856, when New York Harbor was locked
in a battle ignited by those bent on filling it in, to the present. If we examine just the top ten high-water episodes for that century-and-a-half
period, what we find is startling. All of them have occurred since 1960,
and nine of the ten have happened since 1984 alone. Over roughly the
same period, sea level rose nearly 1.5 feet. A repeat of the 1821 hurricane
would involve not only a higher storm surge than Hurricane Sandy's (10
to 11 feet versus 9.4 feet) but also the need to accommodate, currently,
close to an additional 1.5 feet of water—indeed, at least 4 to 8 inches
more than even that, if current predictions for the 2020s stand. It need
hardly be pointed out that, unlike in 1821, there are now six million people living on the most destructive right side of such a storm.[54]

Finally, one last historical force helped determine the scale of the
disaster: a failure of political will. The drive for growth so overshadowed
relations with the natural environment that it caused a near total lapse
in concern for the hazardous consequences of building on low ground.

How else to explain that while the land around Upper New York Bay has long been home to millions of people and to extraordinary wealth, it has never been the subject of a full-scale flood-protection study? Only in 2013, in the wake of the ravaging effects of Hurricane Sandy, did Congress authorize such a step. With more people living in the floodplain of New York than in any other US city, the authorization came not a moment too soon.[55]

If the swashbuckling hub of advanced capitalism has seemed a bit blasé about its future, perhaps it is because those who have run the city have tended to indulge too often the maximizing strategies at the heart of the growth imperative and have thus taken an arrogant stance toward land and sea. From the perspective of four hundred years of history, the prospect of more environmental machismo, of growth for the sake of growth, should give us all pause. Cities, it is true, do indeed encourage energy efficiency. They can also create vibrant, accessible public spaces that are potentially more liberating than the manicured, resource-intensive sprawl of suburbia.[56] Nevertheless, there are limits to urbanism. There are constraints where growth means encroaching yet farther on the scant, buffering marshlands to build, say, more airport runways. And, of course, there are limits to piling more people—an additional one million? two? three?—onto a low-lying island environment in a world of rising seas.

New York's ecological history teaches us a moral lesson. Namely, that port cities across the world—from Shanghai to Mumbai, Tokyo to Bangkok—need to preserve as much wetland and unfragmented open space as possible. There must be a less rigid and less militantly developmental approach to life on the edge of the ocean. We must even seriously entertain the idea of retreat. What's more, those questing for more growth bear the burden of addressing a city's true ecological footprint: the waste stream's effects on life near and far and the danger that large numbers of people concentrated in one spot pose to biodiversity. There must be, in short, some owning up to the limits imposed by life in an estuary. And that, in turn, requires not just absorbing the history told in these pages but escaping it.

It is not for the historian of Greater New York to conjecture about what lies over the horizon. That job falls most heavily on Greater New Yorkers, who, knowing their estuary's ecological history, can rightly ask: Will those in charge of the real estate capital of the world, forever bent on increasing the value of land at all costs, find a way to adapt to the high water ahead? Or will those who profess to love New York, as the booster saying goes, love it to death?

PERCENTAGE OF LARGEST CITIES LOCATED IN ESTUARIES, 1800–2010

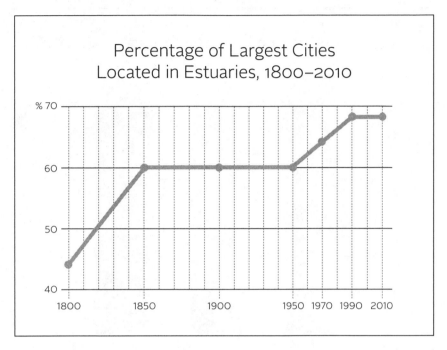

SOURCES: The top twenty-five cities from 1800, 1850, and 1900 are compiled from Tertius Chandler, *Four Thousand Years of Urban Growth: An Historical Census* (Lewiston, N.Y.: St. David's University Press, 1987), 485, 490, 492. The top twenty-five from 1950, 1970, 1990, and 2010 are from the Population Division, Population Estimates and Projections Section, of the United Nations Department of Economic and Social Affairs, *World Urbanization Prospects, the 2011 Revision*, http://esa.un.org/unup/index.html.

SOCIAL STATUS OF WATER-LOT GRANTEES, 1686–1818

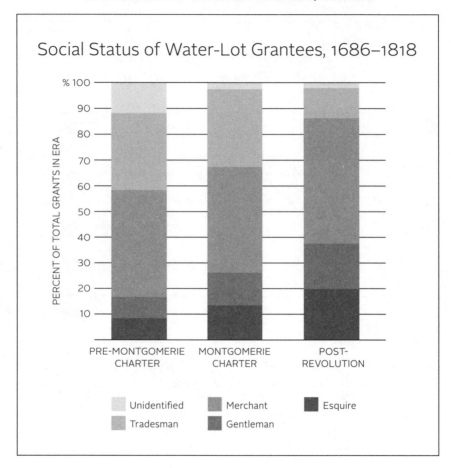

Social Status of Water-Lot Grantees, 1686–1818

SOURCES AND NOTES: The sources for the bar graphs are Corporation of the City of New York Grant Books A–F, Finance Department, Division of Real Estate, City Grant Series, New York Municipal Archives. The source for the pie chart is Grant Book E, pp. 81–254. The "tradesmen" category includes occupations such as baker, black-smith, boatman, cooper, cordwainer, joiner, mariner, miller, painter, shipwright, shoe-maker, and smith. In addition to members of the British gentry, the "esquire" category includes lawyers, doctors, clergy, and military officers. About 80 percent of grantees are identified by status or occupation in the grants themselves. When a grantee's status was not identified in the grant, a search was conducted using various sources, including the published Common Council Minutes; the New-York Historical Society *Abstracts of Wills* series; the Historical Society's *Burghers of New Amsterdam and the Freemen of New*

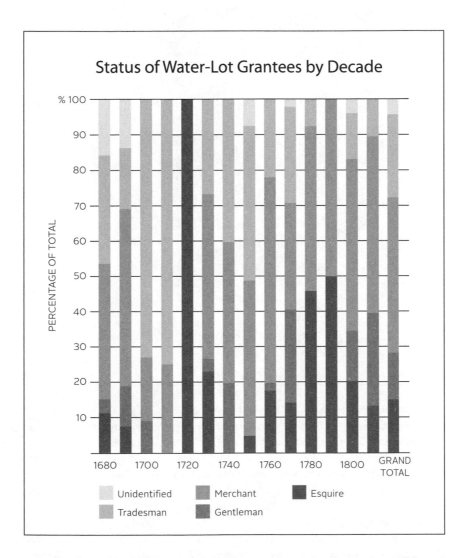

York, 1675–1866 (New York, 1885); *The New York Genealogical and Biographical Record*; and a number of published biographical and genealogical compilations, such as John Austin Stevens Jr., *Colonial New York, Sketches Biographical and Historical, 1768–1784* (New York, 1867); Walter Barrett Scoville, *The Old Merchants of New York City* (New York, 1885); Whitehead Cornell Duyckinck and John Cornell, *The Duyckinck and Allied Families* (New York, 1906); and William B. Aitken, *Distinguished Families in America, Descended from Wilhelmus Beekman and Jan Thomasse Van Dyke* (New York, 1912).

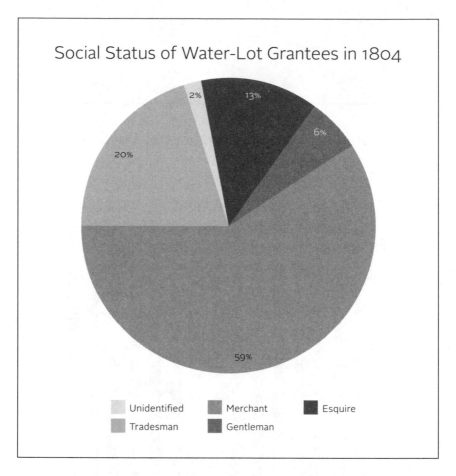

Tradesmen were treated as being part of a more "middling" class. But it must be said that some tradesmen, especially if they were involved in the maritime trade, could be quite prosperous and rightly be considered part of the merchant elite. For example, the shipwrights Stephen Crossfield and Joseph Totten, who received grants in 1766, were technically tradesmen. But they apparently ran in elite circles, as evidenced by a large purchase they made in the Adirondacks in 1771. It is also important to realize that some tradesmen (or their sons) over time became merchants.

Finally, not reflected in the graphs and chart above is the fact that the key years, in terms of the merchant elite's evolving dominance over the water-lot grants, are 1772 and 1804. There was a nearly equal balance between tradesmen, merchants, and gentlemen/esquires in 1772, but in 1804 merchants dominate. The Common Council was relatively inactive with respect to the grants after 1775 and before 1804.

SALT MARSH IN THE NEW JERSEY MEADOWS BY COUNTY

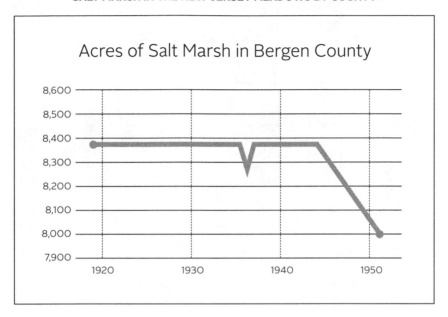

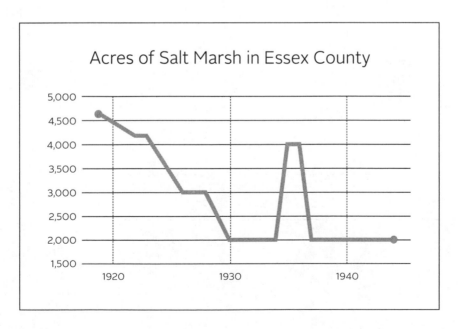

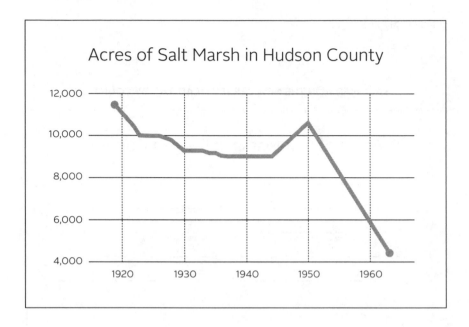

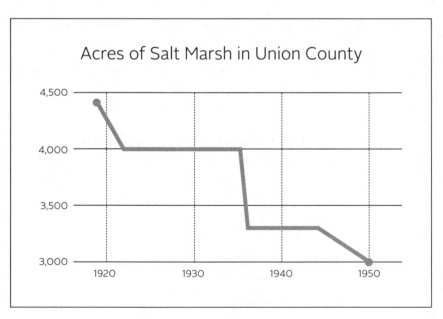

NEW DITCHING IN THE NEW JERSEY MEADOWS BY COUNTY

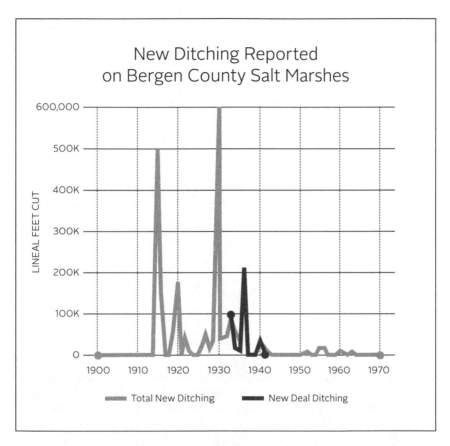

New Ditching Reported
on Bergen County Salt Marshes

SOURCES FOR APPENDIXES C AND D: John B. Smith, *Report of the New Jersey Agricultural Experiment Station upon the Mosquitoes . . .* (Trenton, N.J., 1904), 51; John B. Smith, "Report of the Mosquito Work in 1907," in *Twenty-Eighth Annual Report of the New Jersey State Agricultural Experiment Station and the Twentieth Annual Report of the New Jersey Agricultural College Experiment Station for the Year Ending October 31st, 1907* (Trenton, N.J., 1908), 496; John B. Smith, "Report of the Mosquito Work for 1908," in *Twenty-Ninth Annual Report of the New Jersey State Agricultural Experiment Station and the Twenty-First Annual Report of the New Jersey Agricultural College Experiment Station for the Year Ending October 31st, 1908* (Paterson, N.J., 1909), 381; John B. Smith, "Report on the Mosquito Work for 1911," in Smith, *Report of the Entomological Department of the New Jersey Agricultural College Experiment Station for the Year 1911* (Trenton, N.J., 1912), 506; Thomas J. Headlee, "Report on the Mosquito Work for 1912," in *Thirty-Third*

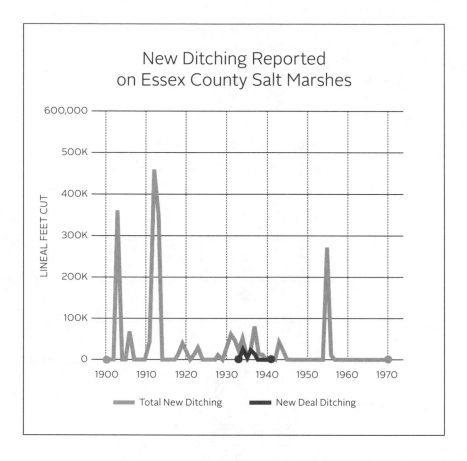

Annual Report of the New Jersey State Agricultural Experiment Station and the Twenty-Fifth Annual Report of the New Jersey Agricultural College Experiment Station for the Year Ending October 31st, 1912 (Union Hill, N.J., 1913), 461; Robert F. Engle, "Status of Mosquito Control in New Jersey," *Proceedings of the Fifth Annual Meeting of the New Jersey Mosquito Extermination Association* [hereinafter *NJMEA*] (Trenton, N.J., 1918), 52, table 2; *Proceedings of the Sixth Annual Meeting of the NJMEA* (New Brunswick, N.J., 1919), 33; *Proceedings of the Seventh Annual Meeting of the NJMEA* (Somerville, N.J., 1920), 9, table 1; *Proceedings of the Eighth Annual Meeting of the NJMEA* (Somerville, N.J., 1922), 28, 35, 41; *Proceedings of the Tenth Annual Meeting of the NJMEA* (New Brunswick, N.J., 1923), 110; *Proceedings of the Eleventh Annual Meeting of the NJMEA* (Newark, N.J., 1924), 89–90; *Proceedings of the Fourteenth Annual Meeting of the NJMEA* (Somerville, N.J., 1927), 38, table 2; *Proceedings of the Sixteenth Annual Meeting of the NJMEA* (New Brunswick, N.J., 1929), 34; *Proceedings of the Eighteenth Annual Meeting of the NJMEA* (New Brunswick, N.J., 1931), 82, table 1; *Proceedings of the Nineteenth Annual Meeting of the NJMEA* (New Brunswick, N.J., 1932), 42, table 1; *Proceedings of the Twentieth Annual Meeting of the NJMEA* (New Brunswick, N.J., 1933), 56, table 17; *Proceedings of the Twenty-First Annual Meeting of the NJMEA* (New Brunswick, N.J., 1934), 31, table 19; 32, table 20;

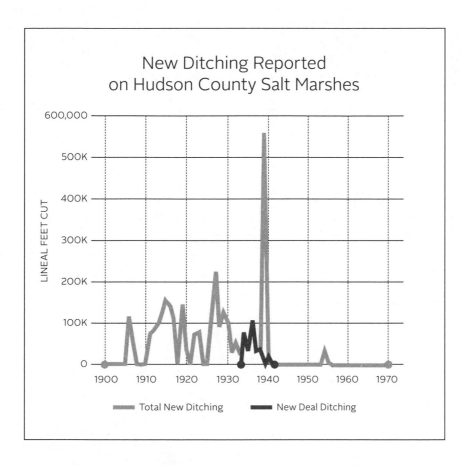

New Ditching Reported on Hudson County Salt Marshes

LINEAL FEET CUT

600,000 — 500K — 400K — 300K — 200K — 100K — 0

1900 1910 1920 1930 1940 1950 1960 1970

━━ Total New Ditching   ━━ New Deal Ditching

35, table 24; *Proceedings of the Twenty-Second Annual Meeting of the NJMEA* (New Brunswick, N.J., 1935), 28, table 19; 40, table 1; *Proceedings of the Twenty-Third Annual Meeting of the NJMEA* (New Brunswick, N.J., 1936), 40, table 22; *Proceedings of the Twenty-Fourth Annual Meeting of the NJMEA* (New Brunswick, N.J., 1937), 42, table 3; *Proceedings of the Twenty-Fifth Annual Meeting of the NJMEA* (New Brunswick, N.J., 1938), 16, table 17; *Proceedings of the Twenty-Sixth Annual Meeting of the NJMEA* (New Brunswick, N.J., 1939), 47, table 1; *Proceedings of the Twenty-Seventh Annual Meeting of the NJMEA* (New Brunswick, N.J., 1940), 59, table 3; *Proceedings of the Twenty-Eighth Annual Meeting of the NJMEA* (New Brunswick, N.J., 1941), 75, table 2; *Proceedings of the Twenty-Ninth Annual Meeting of the NJMEA* (New Brunswick, N.J., 1942), 90, table 22; *Proceedings of the Thirtieth Annual Meeting of the NJMEA* (New Brunswick, N.J., 1943), 142, table 2; *Proceedings of the Thirty-First Annual Meeting of the NJMEA* (New Brunswick, N.J., 1944), 96, table 4; *Proceedings of the Thirty-Second Annual Meeting of the NJMEA* (New Brunswick, N.J., 1945), 164, table 2; *Proceedings of the Thirty-Eighth Annual Meeting of the NJMEA* (New Brunswick, N.J., 1951), 76; *Proceedings of the Thirty-Ninth Annual Meeting of the NJMEA* (New Brunswick, N.J., 1952), 181; *Proceedings of the Fortieth Annual Meeting of the NJMEA* (New Brunswick, N.J., 1953), 202–3; *Proceedings: Forty-Second Annual*

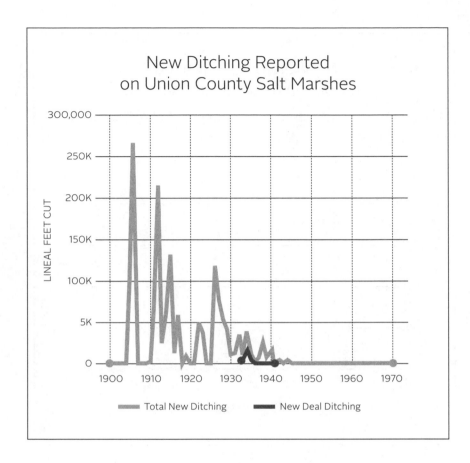

Meeting, NJMEA (Atlantic City, N.J., 1955), 157; *Proceedings: Forty-Third Annual Meeting, NJMEA* (Atlantic City, N.J., 1956), 192, 197, 199; *Proceedings: Forty-Fourth Annual Meeting, NJMEA* (Atlantic City, N.J., 1957), 177, 182; *Proceedings: Forty-Eighth Annual Meeting, NJMEA* (Atlantic City, N.J., 1961), 218; *Proceedings: Forty-Ninth Annual Meeting, NJMEA* (Atlantic City, N.J., 1962), 208; and *Proceedings: Fifty-First Annual Meeting, NJMEA* (Atlantic City, N.J., 1964), 170, 185.

APPENDIX E

COMBINED TOTAL MARSHLAND IN THE NEW JERSEY MEADOWS, FLUSHING MEADOWS, STATEN ISLAND, AND JAMAICA BAY

YEAR	SQUARE MILES	% OF MARSH
1900	79.22	100
1947	48.95	62
1966–1969	18.88	24
2010–2011	11.12	14

New Jersey Meadows
(Hackensack, Newark, and Elizabeth Meadows)

YEAR	SQUARE MILES	ACRES	% OF MARSH
1900	42.29	27,066	100
1947	29.37	18,797	69
1968	11.88	7,603	28
2011	6.72	4,301	16

Flushing Meadows

YEAR	SQUARE MILES	ACRES	% OF MARSH
1900	3.76	2,409	100
1947	0.91	584	24
1966	0.00	0	0

Flushing Made Land
(including La Guardia Airport and Rikers Island)

YEAR	SQUARE MILES	ACRES
1900–1947	1.19	760
1947–1966	0.18	117

Staten Island Marshlands

YEAR	SQUARE MILES	ACRES	% OF MARSH
1900	7.97	5,099	100
1947	6.08	3,893	76
1969	2.35	1,502	29
2011	1.35	865	17

Jamaica Bay Marshlands

YEAR	SQUARE MILES	ACRES	% OF MARSH
1900	25.21	16,134	100
1947	12.58	8,051	50
1969	4.66	2,982	18
2010	3.04	1,946	12

SOLID LAND IN MANHATTAN
Entire Island

YEAR	SQUARE MILES	ACRES
1609	17.74	11,351
2010	21.31	13,636
Total Made Land	3.57	2,286

Below Chambers, East Broadway, and Grand Streets

YEAR	SQUARE MILES	ACRES
1609	0.60	384
1775	0.72	458
1824	0.89	568
1900	0.98	624

Above Chambers, East Broadway, and Grand Streets but Below Fourteenth Street

YEAR	SQUARE MILES	ACRES
1609	2.13	1,362
1900	2.96	1,896

Total Below Fourteenth Street

YEAR	SQUARE MILES	ACRES
1609	2.73	1,746
1900	3.94	2,520
Total Made Land	1.21	774

A NOTE ON SOURCES

The following essay is meant to give readers a sense of those sources that figured most prominently in my thinking about ecological issues in the New York metropolitan region.

We begin with a brief tour through the field of urban environmental history. The starting point must be William Cronon, *Nature's Metropolis: Chicago and the Great West* (New York: W. W. Norton, 1991), a landmark study that examines commodity flows to show the linkages between the country and the city. Joel A. Tarr, "Land Use and Environmental Change in the Hudson-Raritan Estuary Region, 1700–1980," in *The Search for the Ultimate Sink: Urban Pollution in Historical Perspective* (Akron, Ohio: Univ. of Akron Press, 1996), 36–76, was important in helping me conceive of the New York area as an estuary. Likewise, the work of Mike Davis, especially *City of Quartz: Excavating the Future in Los Angeles* (London: Verso, 1990), *Ecology of Fear: Los Angeles and the Imagination of Disaster* (New York: Metropolitan Books, 1998), and *Planet of Slums* (London: Verso, 2006), is essential reading for those seeking to understand urban issues.

For works that adopt a case-study approach to the role of the natural world in cities, see Andrew Hurley, *Environmental Inequalities: Race, Class, and Industrial Pollution in Gary, Indiana, 1945–1980* (Chapel Hill: Univ. of North Carolina Press, 1995); Matthew Gandy, *Concrete and Clay: Reworking Nature in New York City* (Cambridge, Mass.: MIT Press, 2002); Ari Kelman, *A River and Its City: The Nature of Land-*

scape in New Orleans (Berkeley: Univ. of California Press, 2003); Jared Orsi, *Hazardous Metropolis: Flooding and Urban Ecology in Los Angeles* (Berkeley: Univ. of California Press, 2004); Craig E. Colten, *An Unnatural Metropolis: Wresting New Orleans from Nature* (Baton Rouge: Louisiana State Univ. Press, 2005); Harold L. Platt, *Shock Cities: The Environmental Transformation and Reform of Manchester and Chicago* (Chicago: Univ. of Chicago Press, 2005); Matthew W. Klingle, *Emerald City: An Environmental History of Seattle* (New Haven, Conn.: Yale Univ. Press, 2007); Michael Rawson, *Eden on the Charles: The Making of Boston* (Cambridge, Mass.: Harvard Univ. Press, 2010); Sarah S. Elkind, *How Local Politics Shape Federal Policy: Business, Power, and the Environment in Twentieth-Century Los Angeles* (Chapel Hill: Univ. of North Carolina Press, 2011); and Matthew Morse Booker, *Down by the Bay: San Francisco's History Between the Tides* (Berkeley: Univ. of California Press, 2013). Booker's work is perhaps the most like my study of New York in its conceptualization of the city as an estuary. For a stimulating discussion of the crusades to control ragweed in New York City, a development that occurred at roughly the same time as the movement in favor of mosquito extermination, see Zachary J. S. Falck, *Weeds: An Environmental History of Metropolitan America* (Pittsburgh: Univ. of Pittsburgh Press, 2010), 92–132.

Introductions to the Hudson River include Tom Lewis, *The Hudson: A History* (New Haven, Conn.: Yale Univ. Press, 2005); and Stephen P. Stanne, Roger G. Panetta, and Brian E. Forist, *The Hudson: An Illustrated Guide to the Living River*, 2nd ed. (New Brunswick, N.J.: Rivergate Books/Rutgers Univ. Press, 2007). An excellent guide to ecological issues in New York Harbor is John Waldman, *Heartbeats in the Muck: The History, Sea Life, and Environment of New York Harbor*, rev. ed. (New York: Empire State Editions, 2013). Those interested in a more technical discussion of the ecology of the harbor should begin with the essays in Jeffrey S. Levinton and John R. Waldman, eds., *The Hudson River Estuary* (Cambridge, UK: Cambridge Univ. Press, 2006); and Garry F. Mayer, ed., *Ecological Stress and the New York Bight: Science and Management* (Columbia, S.C.: Estuarine Research Federation, 1982). On

Long Island Sound, see Tom Andersen, *This Fine Piece of Water: An Environmental History of Long Island Sound* (New Haven, Conn.: Yale Univ. Press, 2002).

On the broader ecological history of oceans, see Callum Roberts, *The Unnatural History of the Sea* (Washington, D.C.: Island Press/Shearwater Books, 2007). A great interdisciplinary work combining the efforts of historians and marine ecologists is Jeremy B. C. Jackson, Karen E. Alexander, and Enric Sala, *Shifting Baselines: The Past and the Future of Ocean Fisheries* (Washington, D.C.: Island Press, 2011). A painstakingly researched and beautifully written book about the history of the northwest Atlantic is W. Jeffrey Bolster, *The Mortal Sea: Fishing the Atlantic in the Age of Sail* (Cambridge, Mass.: Belknap Press of Harvard Univ. Press, 2012).

There is not room here to discuss all the great books written about New York City. I relied heavily on the definitive history of the city, Edwin G. Burrows and Mike Wallace, *Gotham: A History of New York City to 1898* (New York: Oxford Univ. Press, 1999). Another precious source was Kenneth T. Jackson, ed., *The Encyclopedia of New York City*, 2nd ed. (New Haven, Conn.: Yale Univ. Press, 2010). I found the following important studies particularly helpful in writing about the city's early environmental history: Robert Greenhalgh Albion, *The Rise of New York Port, 1815–1860* (1939; repr., Boston: Northeastern Univ. Press/South Street Seaport Museum, 1984); Edward K. Spann, *The New Metropolis: New York City, 1840–1857* (New York: Columbia Univ. Press, 1981); Elizabeth Blackmar, *Manhattan for Rent, 1785–1850* (Ithaca, N.Y.: Cornell Univ. Press, 1989); Anne-Marie Cantwell and Diana di Zerega Wall, *Unearthing Gotham: The Archaeology of New York City* (New Haven, Conn.: Yale Univ. Press, 2001); and Russell Shorto, *The Island at the Center of the World: The Epic Story of Dutch Manhattan and the Forgotten Colony That Shaped America* (New York: Doubleday, 2004).

On the city's later development, I was fortunate to be able to rely on David C. Hammack, *Power and Society: Greater New York at the Turn of the Century* (1982; repr., New York: Columbia Univ. Press, 1987); Roy Rosenzweig and Elizabeth Blackmar, *The Park and the People: A History of Central Park* (1992; repr., New York: Henry Holt, 1994); Max Page,

The Creative Destruction of Manhattan, 1900–1940 (Chicago: Univ. of Chicago Press, 1999); Marc Linder and Lawrence S. Zacharias, *Of Cabbages and Kings County: Agriculture and the Formation of Modern Brooklyn* (Iowa City: Univ. of Iowa Press, 1999); Jameson W. Doig, *Empire on the Hudson: Entrepreneurial Vision and Political Power at the Port of New York Authority* (New York: Columbia Univ. Press, 2001); David M. Scobey, *Empire City: The Making and Meaning of the New York City Landscape* (Philadelphia: Temple Univ. Press, 2002); and Keith D. Revell, *Building Gotham: Civic Culture and Public Policy in New York City, 1898–1938* (2003; repr., Baltimore: Johns Hopkins Univ. Press, 2005).

For works that deal specifically with the city's waterfront, see Ann L. Buttenwieser, *Manhattan Water-Bound: Manhattan's Waterfront from the Seventeenth Century to the Present*, 2nd ed. (Syracuse, N.Y.: Syracuse Univ. Press, 1999); Kevin Bone, ed., *The New York Waterfront: Evolution and Building Culture of the Port and Harbor*, rev. ed. (New York: Monacelli Press, 2004); and Phillip Lopate, *Waterfront: A Walk Around Manhattan* (2004; repr., New York: Anchor, 2005). The only environmental history of a New York City river (apart from the Hudson) that I am aware of is Maarten de Kadt, *The Bronx River: An Environmental and Social History* (Charleston, S.C.: History Press, 2011).

On the natural history of New York, see John Kieran, *A Natural History of New York City: A Personal Report After Fifty Years of Study and Enjoyment of Wildlife Within the Boundaries of Greater New York* (Boston and Cambridge, Mass.: Houghton Mifflin/Riverside Press, 1959); Bruce Kershner, *Secret Places of Staten Island: A Visitor's Guide to Scenic and Historic Treasures of Staten Island* (Dubuque, Iowa: Kendall/Hunt Publishing, 1998); Betsy McCully, *City at the Water's Edge: A Natural History of New York* (New Brunswick, N.J.: Rivergate Books of Rutgers Univ. Press, 2007); and Leslie Day, *Field Guide to the Natural World of New York City* (Baltimore: Johns Hopkins Univ. Press, 2007).

For a fascinating book by a landscape ecologist that employs computational geography to reconstruct the landscape at the time of Henry Hudson's voyage, see Eric W. Sanderson, *Mannahatta: A Natural History of New York City* (New York: Abrams, 2009). Although one can question how complete the lists of species are, or the perils of a two-point analysis (juxtaposing the landscape in 1609 with 2009), the book is a wake-up call for those inclined to take New York's current ecology for granted. For commentary on Sanderson's project (and the earlier cartography of John Randel), see Marguerite Holloway, *The Measure of Manhattan: The Tumultuous Career and Surprising Legacy of John Randel Jr., Cartographer, Surveyor, Inventor* (New York: W. W. Norton, 2013).

The most systematic examination of geography's role in New York's rise to dominance is Edward L. Glaeser, "Urban Colossus: Why Is New York America's Largest City?" in *Federal Reserve Bank of New York Economic Policy Review* 11 (Dec. 2005): 7–24. See also his *Triumph of the City: How Our Greatest Invention Makes Us Richer, Smarter, Greener, Healthier, and Happier* (New York: Penguin, 2011). More generally, environmental determinism experienced a revival in the late 1990s with the publication of David S. Landes, *The Wealth and Poverty of Nations: Why Some Are So Rich and Some So Poor* (New York: W. W. Norton, 1998); and Jared Diamond, *Guns, Germs, and Steel: The Fates of Human Societies* (New York: W. W. Norton, 1997). An important critique of these books is James M. Blaut, "Environmentalism and Eurocentrism," *Geographical Review* 89, no. 3 (1999): 391–408. For a book that casts a critical eye on commonly assumed geographical divisions, see Martin W. Lewis and Kären E. Wigen, *The Myth of Continents: A Critique of Metageography* (Berkeley: Univ. of California Press, 1997).

The idea of cities as so-called growth machines is developed in Harvey Molotch, "The City as a Growth Machine: Toward a Political Economy of Place," *American Journal of Sociology* 82, no. 2 (Sept. 1976): 309–32. See also John R. Logan and Harvey L. Molotch, *Urban Fortunes: The Political Economy of Place* (1987; repr., Berkeley: Univ. of California Press, 2007). The geographer David Harvey has spent much of his career theorizing about the capitalist city. See, for example, *Social Justice and the City* (Baltimore: Johns Hopkins Univ. Press, 1973); *The Urbanization of Capital: Studies in the History and Theory of Capitalist Urbanization* (Baltimore: Johns Hopkins Univ. Press, 1985); and *The Urban Experience* (Baltimore: Johns Hopkins Univ. Press, 1989).

The best discussion of New York City's water-lot program can be found in Hendrik Hartog, *Public Property and Private Power: The Corporation of the City of New York in American Law, 1739–1870* (1983; repr., Ithaca, N.Y.: Cornell Univ. Press, 1989). For a nice introduction to the Dongan Charter, see Leo Hershkowitz, "The New York City Charter, 1686," in *The Roots of the Republic: American Founding Documents Interpreted*, ed. Stephen L. Schechter, Richard B. Bernstein, and Donald S. Lutz (Madison, Wis.: Madison House, 1990), 83–89. Copies of both the Dongan and Montgomerie Charters are available in Jerrold Seymann, *Colonial Charters, Patents and Grants to the Communities Comprising the City of New York* (New York: Board of Statutory Consolidation, 1939). I gained an increased understanding of title to underwater land from reading Murray Hoffman, *Treatise Upon the Estate and Rights of the Corporation of the City of New York, as Proprietors*, 2nd ed. (New York, 1862); J. W. Gerard Jr., *A Treatise on the Title of the Corporation and Others to the Streets, Wharves, Piers, Parks, Ferries, and Other Lands and Franchises in the City of New York* (New York, 1872); George Ashton Black, *The History of Municipal Ownership of Land on Manhattan Island*, 2nd ed. (New York, 1897); Thomas Carmody, *Grants of Land Under Water by State of New York, with History and Interpretation Thereof and Other Opinions as to State Water Powers* (Albany, N.Y.: J. B. Lyon, 1913); Charles G. Stevenson, "Title of Land Under Water in New York," *Yale Law Journal* 23, no. 5 (Mar. 1914): 397–414; and Anson Getman, *Principles and Sources of Title to Real Property as Between the State and the Individual and the Relative Rights of Individuals* (Albany, N.Y.: Matthew Bender, 1921). Those interested in the actual water-lot grants themselves can find them at the New York Municipal Archives. For archival materials relating to underwater land in New York State, the best source is the New York State Archives, Albany, New York.

There is an extensive literature on the Manhattan grid, but the best place to start is with Hilary Ballon, *The Greatest Grid: The Master Plan of Manhattan, 1811–2011* (New York: Museum of the City of New York/Columbia Univ. Press, 2012). Other important works on this topic include Alan Trachtenberg, "The Rainbow and the Grid," *American Quar-*

terly 16, no. 1 (Spring 1964): 3–19; John W. Reps, *The Making of Urban America: A History of City Planning in the United States* (Princeton, N.J.: Princeton Univ. Press, 1965); Rem Koolhaas, *Delirious New York: A Retroactive Manifesto for Manhattan* (New York, 1978); Peter Marcuse, "The Grid as City Plan: New York City and Laissez-Faire Planning in the Nineteenth Century," *Planning Perspectives* 2, no. 3 (1987): 287–310; Edward K. Spann, "The Greatest Grid: The New York Plan of 1811," in *Two Centuries of American Planning*, ed. Daniel Schaffer (Baltimore: Johns Hopkins Univ. Press, 1988): 11–39; Reuben Skye Rose-Redwood, "Re-Creating the Historical Topography of Manhattan Island," *Geographical Review* 93, no. 1 (Jan. 2003): 124–32; and Rose-Redwood and Li Li, "From Island of Hills to Cartesian Flatland? Using GIS to Assess Topographical Change in New York City, 1819–1999," *Professional Geographer* 63, no. 3 (2011): 392–405.

One aspect of New York City's environmental history has received a fair amount of attention: the water supply. Early works include Nelson Manfred Blake, *Water for the Cities: A History of the Urban Water Supply Problem in the United States* (Syracuse, N.Y.: Syracuse Univ. Press, 1956); and Charles H. Weidner, *Water for a City: A History of New York City's Problem from the Beginning to the Delaware River System* (New Brunswick, N.J.: Rutgers Univ. Press, 1974). More recent works include Diane Galusha, *Liquid Assets: A History of New York City's Water System* (1999; repr., Fleischmanns, N.Y.: Purple Mountain Press, 2002); Gerard T. Koeppel, *Water for Gotham: A History* (Princeton, N.J.: Princeton Univ. Press, 2000); and David Soll, "Watershed Moments: An Environmental History of the New York City Water Supply" (PhD diss., Brandeis Univ., 2009), since published as a book titled *Empire of Water: An Environmental and Political History of the New York City Water Supply* (Ithaca, N.Y.: Cornell Univ. Press, 2013). A stimulating exploration of the relationship between New York City and the Catskill Mountains that goes beyond the issue of water to consider broader ideas about nature can be found in David Stradling, *Making Mountains: New York City and the Catskills* (Seattle: Univ. of Washington Press, 2007).

An excellent place to begin with respect to sanitary issues is John

Duffy, *A History of Public Health in New York City, 1625–1866* (New York: Russell Sage Foundation, 1968). A brilliant early work that has significant material about New York is Charles E. Rosenberg, *The Cholera Years: The United States in 1832, 1849, and 1866* (Chicago: Univ. of Chicago Press, 1962). Also essential reading are the various essays dealing with waste issues in Joel Tarr, *The Search for the Ultimate Sink: Urban Pollution in Historical Perspective* (Akron: Univ. of Akron Press, 1996); and Martin V. Melosi, *The Sanitary City: Urban Infrastructure in America from Colonial Times to the Present* (Baltimore: Johns Hopkins Univ. Press, 2000). For a look at the politics of sewer construction in New York, see Joanne Abel Goldman, *Building New York's Sewers: Developing Mechanisms of Urban Management* (West Lafayette, Ind.: Purdue Univ. Press, 1997). Valuable works on the broader topic of human waste are Dominique Laporte, *History of Shit*, trans. Nadia Benabid and Rodolphe el-Khoury (1978; repr., Cambridge, Mass.: MIT Press, 2000); Jamie Benidickson, *The Culture of Flushing: A Social and Legal History of Sewage* (Vancouver: UBC Press, 2007); and Rose George, *The Big Necessity: The Unmentionable World of Human Waste and Why It Matters* (New York: Metropolitan Books, 2008). For an excellent analysis of sewage treatment plants as industrial ecosystems that widens to examine questions of nature and culture, see Daniel Schneider, *Hybrid Nature: Sewage Treatment and the Contradictions of the Industrial Ecosystem* (Cambridge, Mass.: MIT Press, 2011). On New York solid-waste issues, the work of Daniel C. Walsh was especially helpful. See, for example, Daniel C. Walsh, "Urban Residential Refuse Composition and Generation Rates for the 20th Century," *Environmental Science & Technology* 36, no. 22 (Nov. 2002): 4936–42.

The best overall book on solid waste in New York is Benjamin Miller, *Fat of the Land: Garbage in New York; The Last Two Hundred Years* (New York: Four Walls Eight Windows, 2000). Also very helpful is Steven Hunt Corey, "King Garbage: A History of Solid Waste Management in New York City, 1881–1970" (PhD diss., New York Univ., 1994); and Daniel Eli Burnstein, *Next to Godliness: Confronting Dirt and Despair in Progressive Era New York City* (Urbana: Univ. of Illinois Press, 2006).

On the disposal of waste at sea, see Donald F. Squires, *The Ocean Dumping Quandary: Waste Disposal in the New York Bight* (Albany, N.Y.: State Univ. of New York Press, 1983). Excellent more general treatments of the subject are William L. Rathje and Cullen Murphy, *Rubbish! The Archaeology of Garbage* (1992; repr., New York: HarperPerennial, 1993); and Susan Strasser, *Waste and Want: A Social History of Trash* (New York: Metropolitan Books, 1999).

Those interested in learning more about the biology of filter-feeder species such as oysters should consult Paul Simon Galtsoff, *The American Oyster: Crassostrea virginica Gmelin* (Washington, D.C.: G.P.O., 1964); and Victor S. Kennedy, Roger I. E. Newell, and Albert F. Eble, *The Eastern Oyster: Crassostrea virginica* (College Park: Maryland Sea Grant College, 1996). For a very readable and entertaining history of oysters in New York, see Mark Kurlansky, *The Big Oyster: History on the Half Shell* (2006; repr., New York: Random House, 2007). On oysters and the issue of common property, the most important book is Bonnie J. McCay, *Oyster Wars and the Public Trust: Property, Law, and Ecology in New Jersey History* (Tucson: Univ. of Arizona Press, 1998). See also, John M. Kochiss, *Oystering from New York to Boston* (Middletown, Conn.: Mystic Seaport/Wesleyan Univ. Press, 1974). For oystering on Staten Island, see William V. Askins, "Sandy Ground: Historical Archaeology of Class and Ethnicity in a Nineteenth Century Community on Staten Island" (PhD diss., City Univ. of New York, 1988). An excellent introduction to menhaden is H. Bruce Franklin, *The Most Important Fish in the Sea* (Washington, D.C.: Island Press/Shearwater Books, 2007). Also of value is G. Brown Goode and W. O. Atwater, *A History of the Menhaden* (New York, 1880). For a broader study of marine life in New York Harbor, see Clyde L. MacKenzie Jr., *The Fisheries of Raritan Bay* (New Brunswick, N.J.: Rutgers Univ. Press, 1992).

Excellent introductions to the subject of wetlands include John Teal and Mildred Teal, *Life and Death of the Salt Marsh* (Boston: Little, Brown, 1969); and Judith S. Weis and Carol A. Butler, *Salt Marshes: A Natural and Unnatural History* (New Brunswick, N.J.: Rutgers Univ. Press, 2009). Two important books on the history of wetlands are Ann Vileisis, *Discovering the Unknown Landscape: A History of America's Wetlands* (Washington, D.C.: Island Press, 1997); and Nancy Langston, *Where Land and Water Meet: A Western Landscape Transformed* (Seattle: Univ. of Washington Press, 2003). A good starting place for those interested in New York's wetlands is Elizabeth Barlow, *The Forests and Wetlands of New York City* (Boston: Little, Brown, 1971). Two engaging books on the Meadowlands are John R. Quinn, *Fields of Sun and Grass: An Artist's Journal of the New Jersey Meadowlands* (New Brunswick, N.J.: Rutgers Univ. Press, 1997); and Robert Sullivan, *The Meadowlands: Wilderness Adventures at the Edge of a City* (New York: Scribner, 1998). For a great essay on the history of the Meadowlands before 1969, see Stephen Marshall, "The Meadowlands Before the Commission: Three Centuries of Human Use and Alteration of the Newark and Hackensack Meadows," *Urban Habitats* 2 (Dec. 2004), www.urbanhabitats.org/v02n01/3centuries_abs.html. See also Timothy J. Iannuzzi et al., *A Common Tragedy: History of an Urban River* (Amherst, Mass.: Amherst Scientific, 2002), which is a historical ecology of the lower part of the Passaic River.

In charting the modification of the Greater New York landscape, I had the benefit of Donald F. Squires, "Quantifying Anthropogenic Shoreline Modification of the Hudson River and Estuary from European Contact to Modern Time," *Coastal Management* 20, no. 4 (1992): 343–54; Ralph W. Tiner, *Wetlands of Staten Island, New York: Valuable Vanishing Urban Wildlands* (Hadley, Mass.: US Fish and Wildlife Service, 2000); and Ralph W. Tiner, John Q. Swords, and Bobbi Jo McClain, *Wetland Status and Trends for the Hackensack Meadowlands: An Assessment Report from the US Fish and Wildlife Service's National Wetlands Inventory Program* (Hadley, Mass.: US Fish and Wildlife Service, 2002). The impact on wildlife of shoreline changes can be surveyed in D. F. Squires and J. S. Barclay, *Nearshore Wildlife Habitats and Populations in the New York/New Jersey Harbor Estuary* (report for the New York/New Jersey Harbor Estuary Program, 1990). Another important work is M. Llewellyn Thatcher and Cesar Mendoza, *Hydrologic Modifications* (report prepared for the New York/New Jersey Harbor Estuary Program, 1991).

Robert Moses was one of the most significant figures in the transformation of the region's wetlands. The starting point for those interested in Moses is Robert Caro, *The Power Broker: Robert Moses and the Fall of New York* (1974; repr., New York: Vintage, 1975). Caro offers a very critical portrayal of Moses, one that some historians have been at pains to correct by offering a balanced rendering of his life and achievements. Important works in the new Moses scholarship include Joel Schwartz, *The New York Approach: Robert Moses, Urban Liberals, and Redevelopment of the Inner City* (Columbus: Ohio State Univ. Press, 1993); and Hilary Ballon and Kenneth T. Jackson, eds., *Robert Moses and the Modern City: The Transformation of New York* (New York: W. W. Norton, 2007). See also the essays in Joann P. Krieg, ed., *Robert Moses: Single-Minded Genius* (Interlaken, N.Y.: Hearts of the Lakes Publishing, 1989), as well as Anthony Flint, *Wrestling with Moses: How Jane Jacobs Took On New York's Master Builder and Transformed the American City* (New York: Random House, 2009). Those interested in consulting the papers of Robert Moses will find them at various institutions, including the New York Municipal Archives; the New York Public Library; the New York State Office of Parks, Recreation and Historic Preservation, Long Island Region, Babylon, New York; and Yale University.

My discussion of the commons tradition in Greater New York is based on a rich secondary literature. The work of the great British social historian E. P. Thompson remains the starting place for those interested in the history of this subject. See E. P. Thompson, *Whigs and Hunters: The Origins of the Black Act* (New York: Pantheon, 1975); and Thompson, "Custom, Law and Common Right," in *Customs in Common: Studies in Traditional Popular Culture* (New York: New Press, 1991), 97–184. Other important works on the subject are Douglas Hay, Peter Linebaugh, John G. Rule, E. P. Thompson, and Cal Winslow, *Albion's Fatal Tree: Crime and Society in Eighteenth-Century England* (New York: Pantheon, 1975); Karl Jacoby, *Crimes Against Nature: Squatters, Poachers, Thieves, and the Hidden History of American Conservation* (Berkeley: Univ. of California Press, 2001); and Peter Linebaugh, *The Magna Carta Manifesto: Liberties and Commons for All* (Berkeley: Univ. of California Press, 2008).

Trends in real estate and their social impact over the last forty years are covered in Robert Fitch, *The Assassination of New York* (London: Verso, 1993); Eric Darton, *Divided We Stand: A Biography of New York's World Trade Center* (New York: Basic Books, 1999); and Kim Moody, *From Welfare State to Real Estate: Regime Change in New York City, 1974 to the Present* (New York: New Press, 2007). The response by progressives to developments in the real estate economy is examined in Julie Sze, *Noxious New York: The Racial Politics of Urban Health and Environmental Justice* (Cambridge, Mass.: MIT Press, 2007); and Tom Angotti, *New York for Sale: Community Planning Confronts Global Real Estate* (Cambridge, Mass.: MIT Press, 2008).

HISTORICAL GEOGRAPHIC INFORMATION SYSTEMS SOURCES

General Note

Using ArcGIS, historic maps were manually georeferenced by comparing them with 2010-, 2011-, and 2012-edition USGS 7.5-minute series topographic maps. On each map, the shoreline and marshland boundary were manually digitized by creating polygons. The area figures presented in appendixes E and F were then calculated from these polygons.

MANHATTAN

The 1609 and 1900 estimated solid-land boundaries were drawn from the Brooklyn and Staten Island "Surficial Geology Sheets" in Frederick J. H. Merrill, *New York City Folio* (Washington, D.C.: US Geological Survey, 1902), 30, 31. The 1775 estimated solid-land boundary was drawn from John Montrésor, *A Plan of the City of New-York & Its Environs* . . . ([London], 1775). The 1824 estimated solid-land boundary was drawn from William Hooker, *Hooker's New Pocket Plan of the City of New York* . . . (1824). These historic maps were manually georeferenced by comparing them with 7.5-minute USGS topographic maps for Jersey City (2011) and Brooklyn (2010).

NEW JERSEY MEADOWS

The 1900 shoreline and marshland were drawn from the Paterson and Staten Island "Surficial Geology Sheets" in Merrill, *New York City Folio*, 28, 30, and compared with *Map of the Hackensack Meadows to Illustrate Report on Drainage* in New Jersey Geological Survey, *Annual Report of the State Geologist of New Jersey for 1896* (Trenton, N.J.: 1897); Donald F. Squires, "Quantifying Anthropogenic Shoreline Modification of the Hudson

River and Estuary from European Contact to Modern Time," *Coastal Management* 20, no. 4 (1992): 343–54; and Regional Plan Association, *Waste Management: Generation and Disposal of Solid, Liquid and Gaseous Wastes in the New York Region* (New York, 1968), 62, 63. The 1947 shoreline and marshland were drawn from 1947-edition 7.5-minute USGS topographic maps of Elizabeth, Jersey City, Orange, Weehawken, and Yonkers, and the 1940-edition 7.5-minute USGS topographic map of Hackensack (1940). The 1968 shoreline and marshland were drawn from 7.5-minute USGS topographic maps of Elizabeth (1969), Jersey City (1969), Orange (1972), Weehawken (1968), and Hackensack (1972). The 2011 shoreline was drawn from the 2011-edition 7.5-minute USGS topographic maps of Elizabeth, Jersey City, Orange, Weehawken, Paterson, and Hackensack, and the 2011 marshland was drawn from these maps after comparing them with aerial photographs from Google Maps and Ralph W. Tiner, John Q. Swords, and Bobbi Jo McClain, *Wetland Status and Trends for the Hackensack Meadowlands: An Assessment Report from the US Fish and Wildlife Service's National Wetlands Inventory Program* (Hadley, Mass.: US Fish and Wildlife Service, 2002), 18.

FLUSHING MEADOWS

The 1900 shoreline and marshland were drawn from the Harlem and Brooklyn "Surficial Geology Sheets" in Merrill, *New York City Folio*, 31, 32, and compared with Squires, "Quantifying Anthropogenic Shoreline Modification of the Hudson River and Estuary," 343–54; and Regional Plan Association, *Waste Management*, 62, 63. The 1947 shoreline and marshland were drawn from 1947-edition 7.5-minute USGS topographic maps of Flushing and Jamaica, and the 1966 shoreline and marshland were drawn from 7.5-minute USGS topographic maps of Flushing (1966) and Jamaica (1969).

STATEN ISLAND

The 1900 shoreline and marshland were drawn from the Staten Island "Surficial Geology Sheet" in Merrill, *New York City Folio*, 30, and compared with Squires, "Quantifying Anthropogenic Shoreline Modification of the Hudson River and Estuary," 343–54; and Regional Plan Association, *Waste Management*, 62, 63. The 1947 shoreline and marshland were drawn from 1947-edition 7.5-minute USGS topographic maps of Perth Amboy, Keyport, Arthur Kill, the Narrows, Elizabeth, and Jersey City; and the 1943-edition 7.5-minute USGS topographic map of South Amboy. The 1969 shoreline and marshland were drawn from 1969-edition 7.5-minute USGS topographic maps of Arthur Kill, the Narrows, Elizabeth, and Jersey City, and the 1968-edition 7.5-minute USGS topographic map of the Narrows. The 2011 shoreline was drawn from 2011-edition 7.5-minute USGS topographic maps of Perth Amboy, South Amboy, Keyport, Arthur Kill, the Narrows, Elizabeth, and Jersey City, and the 2011 marshland was drawn from these maps after comparing 1969 maps and aerial photographs from Google Maps.

JAMAICA BAY

The 1900 shoreline and marshland were drawn from the Brooklyn "Surficial Geology Sheet" in Merrill, *New York City Folio*, 31, the 1903-edition 15-minute USGS topographic map of Hempstead, and the 1900-edition 15-minute USGS topographic maps of Oyster Bay, and compared with Ellen Kracauer Hartig et al., "Anthropogenic and Climate-Change Impacts on Salt Marshes of Jamaica Bay, New York City," *Wetlands* 22, no. 1 (Mar. 2002): 71–89; Squires, "Quantifying Anthropogenic Shoreline Modification of the Hudson River and Estuary," 343–54; and Regional Plan Association, *Waste Management*, 62, 63. The 1947 shoreline and marshland were drawn from 1947-edition 7.5-minute USGS topographic maps of Jamaica, Brooklyn, Coney Island, Far Rockaway, Lawrence, and Lynbrook, and the 1969 shoreline and marshland were drawn from 7.5-minute USGS topographic maps of Jamaica (1969), Brooklyn (1967), Coney Island (1968), Far Rockaway (1971), Lawrence (1968), and Lynbrook (1972). The 2010 shoreline was drawn from 2010-edition 7.5-minute USGS topographic maps of Jamaica, Brooklyn, Coney Island, and Lynbrook, and the 2012-edition 7.5-minute USGS topographic maps of Far Rockaway and Lawrence. The 2010 marshland was drawn from these maps after comparing aerial photographs from Google Maps and Hartig et al., "Anthropogenic and Climate-Change Impacts on Salt Marshes of Jamaica Bay, New York City," 71–89.

LAND DEVELOPMENT IN NEW YORK

The area of development was drawn from New York Department of City Planning, "Urban Development of the City of New York, 1625–1988" (1988).

NEW YORK HARBOR

The historical GIS analysis conducted for *Gotham Unbound* focused on the five geographic areas noted above. In the text, figures for the entire harbor were drawn from Squires, "Quantifying Anthropogenic Shoreline Modification of the Hudson River and Estuary," with one exception. A study of the low-lying areas along the New Jersey shoreline, conducted for *Gotham Unbound*, revealed that there is not room for more than about 30,000 acres of underwater land to have been filled between the George Washington Bridge and the Raritan River. Thus, Squires's estimate that 293,000 acres of underwater land had been filled along this section of the New Jersey shoreline is too high by a factor of ten. Comparison with the results of the GIS conducted for *Gotham Unbound* confirms Squires's other findings and suggests that the best estimate for the amount of underwater land filled across the entire harbor since European settlement is 37,800 acres.

ART CREDITS

PAGE

13   [Joan Vinckeboons], *Manatvs gelegen op de Noot* [*sic*] *Riuier* [1670s?], Library of Congress, Geography and Map Division

29   *A New Map of the Harbour of New-York by a Late Survey* (1735), Butler Library, Columbia University

35   John Montrésor, *A Plan of the City of New-York & Its Environs* ... ([London?], 1775), Library of Congress, Geography and Map Division

45   British Headquarters Map (1782), National Archives, MR 1/463

54   New York Municipal Archives, Corporation Grant Book E, 293

64   Randel Farm Map no. 55 (1820), City of New York and the Office of the Manhattan Borough President

84   J. H. Colton & Co., *Topographical Map of the City and County of New-York, and the Adjacent Country* (1836), Library of Congress, Geography and Map Division

91   Daniel Ewen, *Proposed enlargement of the present Battery* [1849?], Lionel Pincus and Princess Firyal Map Division, New York Public Library

99   Survey of the Coast of the United States, *Hell Gate and Its Approaches* (1851), Historical Nautical Charts Collection, National Oceanic and Atmospheric Administration

104 Edmund and George W. Blunt, *The Harbour of New York* (1827), Library of Congress, Geography and Map Division

124 Will L. Taylor, *The City of New York* (1879), Library of Congress, Geography and Map Division

129 Joseph F. W. Des Barres, *A Sketch of the Operations of His Majesty's Fleet* ... (1777), Jersey City Free Public Library

137 E. W. Harrison, *Map Showing Waterfront and the Marsh-Lands of Jersey City and Environs, Hudson County, N.J.* (1879), Jersey City Free Public Library

145 "Eighteen Miles Around New York," *Harper's Weekly*, supplement, May 6, 1871, pp. 420–21, HarpWeek, 1999

169 New York Bay Pollution Commission, *Outline Map of New York Harbor & Vicinity:*

Showing Main Tidal Flow, Sewer Outlets, Shellfish Beds & Analysis Points (1905), Lionel Pincus and Princess Firyal Map Division, New York Public Library

178 Coast and Geodetic Survey, *New York Bay and Harbor* (1910), Historical Nautical Charts Collection, National Oceanic and Atmospheric Administration

185 T. Kennard Thomson, *A Really Greater New York* (1914), 3

225 New York World's Fair Inc., *By Land, By Sea, By Air: All Roads Lead to New York World's Fair 1939* (1938), New York World's Fair 1939–1940, Manuscripts and Archives Division, New York Public Library, Astor, Lenox and Tilden Foundations

229 Frederick J. H. Merrill, *New York City Folio* (Washington, D.C.: US Geological Survey, 1902), 22. Digitized courtesy of Texas A&M University Libraries

240 New York Topographical Bureau, *General Map of the Borough of Richmond (Staten Island) in the City of New York* . . . (1901), Lionel Pincus and Princess Firyal Map Division, New York Public Library

261 *Map of the Hackensack Meadows to Illustrate Report on Drainage* in New Jersey Geological Survey, *Annual Report of the State Geologist of New Jersey for 1896* (Trenton, N.J., 1897). Digitized courtesy of the Meadowlands Environmental Research Institute Library

285 Material entitled "New York=62 Cities from 50 States," used with permission of the New York City Department of City Planning. All rights reserved.

320 New York Department of Environmental Protection, *Richmond Creek Bluebelt Points of Interest* (2004). Used with permission of the City of New York and the NYC Department of Environmental Protection

338 Eymund Diegel, *The Gowanus Canal Canoeing & Superfund Tourism Map* (2011).

344 British Headquarters Map (1782), National Archives, MR 1/463

347 Jeff Larson and Al Shaw, ProPublica, 2013

ACKNOWLEDGMENTS

"New York," the master-builder-cum-power-broker Robert Moses once declared, "is just too big, too complex to be covered by any one writer."* The old man had a point. To tackle New York, you have to have help.

My first debt is to a younger generation—Samuel Duncan, Jon Hazlett, Joshua Palmer, Jesse Tarbert, and Jonathan Wlasiuk—who not only helped me in ways too numerous to list but also inspired me as well. Jesse Tarbert deserves a special mention for all the hours he put in working on the appendixes and the historical GIS that helped to show the changing land and waterscape. I don't believe I have ever met anyone with quite the same combination of sharpness of mind and discipline.

Those who generously took time out of their lives to read the manuscript include: Daniel Berick, the only corporate lawyer I know who can polish off a seven-hundred-page manuscript in a week; Michael Clark, who for twenty-nine years has talked ideas with me and worked tirelessly to promote my work to a wider audience; Daniel Cohen, whose high spirits, attention to details, and incredible clarity of thought I greatly admire; Robert Hannigan, my teacher and friend, who has done me more good turns than I can possibly count; Kenneth Ledford, who never tires of bailing me out of trouble and who would give William Strunk Jr. a run for his money; Peter McCall, who patiently taught me more about the world of science than anyone on the planet; Jim O'Brien, who read

---

* Robert Moses, *Public Works: A Dangerous Trade* (New York: McGraw-Hill, 1970), 2.

multiple drafts and delivered his criticism with the kind of good humor that makes him a tribute to humanity; Adam Rome, who pushed me harder to figure out what I was trying to say; Jonathan Sadowsky, my great Queens friend, who read an early draft that, I fear, must have bored him to death, but stuck with me all the same; and Nathan Steinberg, who read the manuscript aloud to me with precision and verve. He'll probably never really know how much his help meant to me.

Historians who have helped me include: John Broich, Vera Candiani, Maarten de Kadt, Brian Donahue, Seth Fein, David Hammack, Hendrik Hartog, Stephen Marshall, Clay McShane, Alan Rocke, Peter Shulman, David Stradling, Joel Tarr, and Donald Worster. I also had assistance from experts, scholars, and friends outside of the field of history, including: James Carlton, Amy Cherry, Eymund Diegel, Mitch Feuer, Jeffrey Levinton, Dorothy Merritts, Bruce Mizrach, Paul Robbins, Dan Rosenberg, Catherine Scallen, Mano Singham, David Strayer, Dennis Suszkowski, Ralph Tiner, John Waldman, Peter Whiting, and Martha Woodmansee. Additional research and editorial support was provided by several excellent high school, undergraduate, and law students, including Laura Gates, Devin Herlihy, Ryan Isenberg, and Mimi Woelper.

These are perilous times for all universities, so it is nice to be able to take refuge in a community of scholars like the Case Western Reserve University Department of History, which, under the leadership of Jonathan Sadowsky, has become a great place to work. I thank him and all my colleagues for enriching my intellectual life.

In the History Department and at the School of Law, I have had the pleasure of working with Phyllis Banks, Jennifer Hines, Iwona Hrelja, Marissa Ross, Emily Sparks, Deborah Turner, Kallisto Vimr, and Elizabeth Weiss.

Funding for university libraries is hardly a priority these days, but notwithstanding the declining resources, the staffs of the Judge Ben C. Green Law Library and the Kelvin Smith Library acquitted themselves with an unparalleled level of skill and professionalism. There is no way I can possibly repay the following individuals: Megan Allen, Kathleen Carrick, William Claspy, Andrew Dorchak, Deborah Dennison, Mark

Eddy, Donna Ertin, Mary Finan, Sharlane Gubkin, Brian Hanna, Ann Holstein, Judith Kaul, Carl Mariani, Patricia Marvel, Robert Myers, Lisa Peters, SaraJean Petite, Andrew Plumb-Larrick, and Karen Thornton.

Libraries and archives tend to be wonderful places to work in large part because of the first-class support to be found at such institutions. I thank Kenneth Cobb at the Municipal Archives of the City of New York, especially for arranging for the microfilming of the water-lot grant books; Shawn Purcell at the New York State Library; Christine Bruzzese at New York's City Hall Library; Jim Folts and Bill Gorman at the New York State Archives; Tammy Marshall at the Meadowlands Environmental Research Institute; John Beekman at the Jersey City Free Public Library; John Hyslop at the Queens Borough Public Library; Joy Holland and Olivia Morales at the Brooklyn Public Library; Peter Sattler of the Interstate Environmental Commission; Cara Dellatte at the History Archives and Library of the Staten Island Museum; Geri Solomon at Hofstra University's Long Island Studies Institute; Mark Rothenberg at the Patchogue-Medford Library; Michelle Somma at the New York State Office of Parks, Recreation and Historic Preservation; Ted O'Reilly at the New-York Historical Society; Alan Bauder at the New York State Office of General Services; Brooke Baldeschwiler at Columbia University's Avery Library; Tara Craig at Columbia University's Rare Book and Manuscript Library; Emily Holmes and Erik Sommer at Columbia University's Preservation & Reprography Department; Thomas Lannon, Tal Nadan, Megan O'Shea, and Laura Ruttum at the Manuscripts and Archives Division of the New York Public Library; David Klaassen at the Social Welfare History Archives of the University of Minnesota; Glenn Friedman and James Splendore at the New York City Department of City Planning; Alison Gilgore at the New York City Department of Environmental Protection; and Hector Rivera, Binchan Luo, and Jimmy Yan at the Manhattan Borough President's Office.

My gratitude as well goes out to the Adeline Barry Davee family, who endowed the chair I currently hold, for their generous support.

Cyrus Taylor and Gary Simson both saw the value of this book and helped provide the time off necessary to complete a project on this scale.

Lawrence Mitchell at the School of Law has continued this tradition of support. Nor would I have ever had the help of the law school in the first place were it not for Robert Strassfeld. I am grateful to all four of them, as I am to Elliott West and Richard White, who wrote letters that helped me gain support from the National Endowment for the Humanities. It should go without saying, but I'll say it anyway because I must: any views, findings, conclusions, or recommendations expressed in this book do not necessarily reflect those of the National Endowment for the Humanities.

Joe Veltre, the most genial man I have ever met, has a magic touch, and so does Thomas LeBien, who offers an unparalleled, gold-standard level of editorial service with few rivals in the publishing world. His un-bridled enthusiasm for this project from day one has been a source of con-stant joy to me, as was working with his colleague Brit Hvide. The same goes for Jonathan Evans, the only production editor I know with a sense of humor about compound adjectives. Phil Bashe is an extremely careful reader who forced me to explain myself in the clearest possible language. Michael Accordino, Nancy Singer, and Kris Tobiassen together produced a simply gorgeous book. Jeff Ward drew the overview map of the harbor, achieving his usual level of clarity and beauty. Stephen Bedford, Maureen Cole, Julia Prosser, Richard Rhorer, Elisa Rivlin, and Elina Vaysbeyn are a tribute to their employer, Simon & Schuster, itself a superb publishing house, which I am proud to have worked with on this project.

Lewis Stein provided the wheels and Helen Steinberg the meals that kept me going on those dog days fighting it out on the Belt Parkway.

No one has paid more dearly for this book than my family: my two sons and my in-house counsel, Maria Del Monaco. I hope they think the end result was worth the Double Happiness that was sometimes sacrificed.

I dedicate this book to a hard-nosed group from Brooklyn who had something money cannot buy: a sense of community nurtured by people like Henchie, the mayor of 603, who clawed out a life for her family while selling bras and girdles. Rippy I leave out because of the terror he instilled, though I recently learned that this ferocious dog was actually named—by one very clever resident of this apartment house—for the great tragedian Euripides.

NOTES

Legal cases, state session laws, federal and state legislative documents, and city ordinances are provided below in the style recommended by *The Bluebook: A Uniform System of Citation*, published by the Harvard Law Review Association, and which includes a comprehensive list of legal abbreviations.

Abbreviations

REPOSITORIES

LISI	Long Island Studies Institute, Hofstra University, Hempstead, N.Y.
MERI	New Jersey Meadowlands Commission, Environmental Research Institute Library, Lyndhurst, N.J.
NYCMA	New York City Municipal Archives
NYPLMA	Manuscripts and Archives Division, New York Public Library, Astor, Lenox, and Tilden Foundations
NYSA	New York State Archives, Albany
NYSL	New York State Library, Albany
SIM	Staten Island Museum History Archives and Library, Staten Island, N.Y.
THA	Town of Hempstead Archives, Hempstead, N.Y.

MANUSCRIPT COLLECTIONS

CCP	Papers of the New York City Common Council, NYCMA
CG Book	Corporation of the City of New York Grant Books, Finance Department, Division of Real Estate, City Grants series; letters refer to the individual volumes with books A–C (available on master negative

35932); books D–E (master negative 35933); and F–G (master negative 35934), NYCMA.

DLMAP	Downtown-Lower Manhattan Association Papers, series 2.3, Rockefeller Archive Center, Sleepy Hollow, N.Y.
EC	Environment Collection, SIM
EKP	Edward I. Koch Papers, NYCMA
EML	Ebenezer Meriam Letters re Hell Gate, 1848–54, folder 2, New-York Historical Society, New York
GMP	George McAneny Papers, Mudd Manuscript Library, Princeton Univ., Princeton, N.J.
HHP	Helen Hall Papers, Social Welfare History Archives, Univ. of Minnesota, Minneapolis
NYCCR	New York Chamber of Commerce and Industry Records, Rare Book and Manuscript Library, Columbia University, New York
NYCDPGF	New York City Department of Parks, General Files, Administration, NYCMA
NYCDPOC	New York City Department of Parks, Office of the Commissioner (Robert Moses), NYCMA
NYWFR	New York World's Fair 1939 and 1940 Incorporated Records, 1935–45, MssCol 2233, NYPLMA
PC	Parks Collection, SIM
PS	Park Series, THA
RMP	Robert Moses Papers, NYPLMA
RGP	Rudolph W. Giuliani Papers, NYCMA
RSP	Robert Swartwout Papers, NYPLMA
TLS	Town Land Series, THA
WTDC	William T. Davis Collection, SIM

NEWSPAPERS

BE	*Brooklyn Daily Eagle*
DNI	*Daily National Intelligencer* (Washington, D.C.)
DN	*Daily News* (New York)
DSG	*Daily State Gazette* (Trenton, N.J.)
EP	*New-York Evening Post*
FMI	*The Flushing Meadow Improvement*
GNY	*Greater New York: Bulletin of the Merchants' Association of New York*
JoC	*New York Journal of Commerce*
LIP	*Long Island Daily Press* (Jamaica, N.Y.)
LIS	*Long Island Daily Star* (Long Island City, N.Y.)
NDR	*Nassau Daily Review* (Nassau County, N.Y.)

NSJ	*North Shore Daily Journal* (Flushing, N.Y.)
NSN	*North Shore News* (Flushing, N.Y.)
NSDN	*Newark (N.J.) Sunday News*
NYG	*New-York Gazette*
NYH	*New York Herald*
NYT	*New York Times*
NYTr	*New York Tribune*
NYHTr	*New York Herald Tribune*
NYWT	*New York World-Telegram*
NYWTS	*New York World-Telegram and Sun*
Record	*The Record* (Bergen County, N.J.)
RERBG	*Real Estate Record and Builders' Guide*
SI	*Staten Islander*
SIA	*Staten Island Advance*
SL	*Star-Ledger* (Newark, N.J.)
WF	*Working Farmer* (New York)
WH	*Weekly Herald* (New York)

PUBLIC DOCUMENTS

Cong. Rec.	*Congressional Record*
Fed. Reg.	*Federal Register*
N.J. Laws	*Laws of New Jersey*
N.Y. Laws	*Laws of New York*
Pub. L. No.	Public Law Number
Stat.	*US Statutes at Large* (1874–present)
Stat at Large of USA	*Public Statutes at Large of the United States of America, 1789–1873*

PUBLISHED PRIMARY SOURCES

ARCCNY	*Annual Report of the Corporation of the Chamber of Commerce, of the State of New-York*; also *Annual Report of the Chamber of Commerce of the State of New-York*
Black	George Ashton Black, *The History of Municipal Ownership of Land on Manhattan Island to the Beginning of Sales by the Commissioners of the Sinking Fund in 1844*, 2nd ed. (New York, 1897)
DBA	*Documents of the Board of Aldermen, of the City of New York*, 35 vols. (New York, 1834–1868)
DBA&A	*Documents of the Board of Aldermen, and Board of Assistants of the City of New-York*, 3 vols. (New York, 1831–1834)
DRCHNY	*Documents Relative to the Colonial History of the State of New-York;*

	Procured in Holland, England and France, ed. John Romeyn Brodhead, Berthold Fernow, and E. B. O'Callaghan, 15 vols. (Albany, N.Y., 1853–1887)
GWD	George Washington, *The Diaries of George Washington*, ed. Donald Jackson and Dorothy Twohig (Charlottesville: Univ. of Virginia Press, 1976–1979)
Jameson	J. Franklin Jameson, *Narratives of New Netherland, 1609–1664* (New York, 1909)
MCC, 1675–1776	Herbert L. Osgood, Austin Baxter Keep, and Charles Alexander Nelson, *Minutes of the Common Council of the City of New York, 1675–1776*, 8 vols. (New York, 1905)
MCC, 1784–1831	Arthur Everett Peterson, *Minutes of the Common Council of the City of New York, 1784–1831*, 19 vols. (New York, 1917)
Seymann	Jerrold Seymann, *Colonial Charters, Patents, and Grants to the Communities Comprising the City of New York* (New York: Board of Statutory Consolidation, 1939)
Van der Donck	Adriaen van der Donck, *A Description of New Netherland*, ed. Charles T. Gehring and William A. Starna, trans. Diederik Willem Goedhuys (Lincoln: Univ. of Nebraska Press, 2008)

PUBLISHED SECONDARY SOURCES

Albion	Robert Greenhalgh Albion, *The Rise of New York Port, 1815–1860* (1939; repr., Boston: Northeastern Univ. Press/South Street Seaport Museum, 1984)
ANYAS	*Annals of the New York Academy of Sciences*
BAMS	*Bulletin of the American Meteorological Society*
BTBC	*Bulletin of the Torrey Botanical Club*
Burrows & Wallace	Edwin G. Burrows and Mike Wallace, *Gotham: A History of New York City to 1898* (New York: Oxford Univ. Press, 1999)
Duffy	John Duffy, *A History of Public Health in New York City, 1625–1866* (New York: Russell Sage Foundation, 1968)
NYFedEPR	*Federal Reserve Bank of New York Economic Policy Review*
Hartog	Hendrik Hartog, *Public Property and Private Power: The Corporation of the City of New York in American Law, 1730–1870* (1983; repr., Ithaca, N.Y.: Cornell Univ. Press, 1989)
Jackson	Kenneth T. Jackson, ed., *The Encyclopedia of New York City*, 2nd ed. (New Haven, Conn.: Yale Univ. Press, 2010)
Klawonn	Marion J. Klawonn, *Cradle of the Corps: A History of the New York District, US Army Corps of Engineers, 1775–1975* (New York: US Army Corps of Engineers, New York District, 1977)

Levinton   Jeffrey S. Levinton and John R. Waldman, eds., *The Hudson River Estuary*
& Waldman   (Cambridge, UK: Cambridge Univ. Press, 2006)
LIF   *Long Island Forum*
MPB   *Marine Pollution Bulletin*
Miller   Benjamin Miller, *Fat of the Land: Garbage in New York; The Last Two
               Hundred Years* (New York: Four Walls Eight Windows, 2000)
NCHSJ   *Nassau County Historical Society Journal*
PS   *Popular Science Monthly*
PNAS   *Proceedings of the National Academy of Sciences of the United States of
               America*
PNSASI   *Proceedings of the Natural Science Association of Staten Island*
PSIIAS   *Proceedings*, Staten Island Institute of Arts and Sciences
Revell   Keith D. Revell, *Building Gotham: Civic Culture and Public Policy in
               New York City, 1898–1938* (2003; repr., Baltimore: Johns Hopkins
               Univ. Press, 2005)
Rosenwaike   Ira Rosenwaike, *Population History of New York City* (Syracuse, N.Y.:
               Syracuse Univ. Press, 1972)
Rosenzweig   Roy Rosenzweig and Elizabeth Blackmar, *The Park and the People: A
& Blackmar *History of Central Park* (1992; repr., New York: Henry Holt, 1994)
Sanderson   Eric W. Sanderson, *Mannahatta: A Natural History of New York City*
               (New York: Abrams, 2009)
Sanderson   Eric W. Sanderson and Marianne Brown, "Mannahatta: An Ecologi-
& Brown   cal First Look at the Manhattan Landscape Prior to Henry Hudson,"
               Northeastern Naturalist 14, no. 4 (2007): 545–70
Stokes   I. N. Phelps Stokes, *The Iconography of Manhattan Island, 1498–1909*,
               6 vols. (1915–1928; repr., New York: Arno Press, 1967)
TASCE   *Transactions of the American Society of Civil Engineers*
Weidner   Charles H. Weidner, *Water for a City: A History of New York City's
               Problem from the Beginning to the Delaware River System* (New
               Brunswick, N.J.: Rutgers Univ. Press, 1974)

COMMISSION AND AGENCY NAMES

BPCCA   Battery Park City Corporation Authority
HMDC   Hackensack Meadowlands Development Commission
MSC   Metropolitan Sewerage Commission of New York
NJMEA   New Jersey Mosquito Extermination Association
NOAA   National Oceanic and Atmospheric Administration

MISCELLANEOUS

Assem.	Assembly
comm.	committee
mn.	master negative
J	Joint
Rep.	Report

Introduction

1. Sanderson, 10, 78, 92, 139, 269, 284–89.
2. On land use on Manhattan Island, see Sanderson & Brown, 552–53, table 2. The population of Manhattan in 2010, according to the US Census, was 1,585,873. The acreage of Manhattan was 14,610, or 22.83 square miles. See New York City Department of City Planning, "Table PL-P5 NYC: Total Population and Persons Per Acre, 2000 and 2010," www.nyc.gov/html/dcp/download/census/census2010 /t_pl_p5_nyc.xlsx. The five densest incorporated places in 2010 were: Guttenberg (55,880 people per square mile), Union City (51,918), West New York (49,216), and Hoboken (39,066), all in New Jersey, and New York City (27,013). I calculated these densities using US Census Bureau, State and County QuickFacts, http:// quickfacts.census.gov/qfd/index.html.

    In London, population density in the mid–nineteenth century was one hundred thousand people per square mile in some parts of the city. See Dale H. Porter, *The Thames Embankment: Environment, Technology, and Society in Victorian London* (Akron, Ohio: Univ. of Akron Press, 1998), 12. The highest population density ever recorded is said to be in Kowloon Walled City in Hong Kong. See Ritchie S. King and Graham Roberts, "Manhattan's Population Density, Past and Present," *NYT*, Mar. 1, 2012, www.nytimes.com/interactive/2012/03/01/realestate/manhattans -population-density-past-and-present.html?ref=realestate.
3. These figures are derived from the historical GIS carried out for this project. For more on the method and sources employed, see the back matter section titled "Historical Geographic Information Systems Sources." Central Park is 843 acres.
4. Few scholars in the area of urban environmental history have chosen to make the concept of the estuary the main basis of their analysis. Two notable exceptions are Joel A. Tarr, "Land Use and Environmental Change in the Hudson-Raritan Estuary Region, 1700–1980," in *The Search for the Ultimate Sink: Urban Pollution in Historical Perspective* (Akron, Ohio: Univ. of Akron Press, 1996), 36–76; and Matthew Morse Booker, *Down by the Bay: San Francisco's History Between the Tides* (Berkeley: Univ. of California Press, 2013).
5. According to the 2010 US Census, the New York–Northern New Jersey–Long Island Metropolitan Statistical Area had a population of 18.9 million people. The total US population was 308.7 million. See US Census Bureau, *Population Distribution and Change: 2000 to 2010* (2011), 1, 6, table 3, www.census.gov/prod/cen2010 /briefs/c2010br-01.pdf.
6. Stokes, 1: xxix; Edward L. Glaeser, "Urban Colossus: Why Is New York America's

Largest City?" *NYFedEPR* 11, no. 2 (Dec. 2005): 7; and Ric Burns and James Sanders with Lisa Ades, *New York: An Illustrated History* (1999; repr., New York: Knopf, 2008), 6.

7. An estimated 56,000 acres of marsh were filled or dredged in New York Harbor between the early 1800s and 1980. See Donald F. Squires, "Quantifying Anthropogenic Shoreline Modification of the Hudson River and Estuary from European Contact to Modern Time," *Coastal Management* 20, no. 4 (1992): 347, table 1; and M. Llewellyn Thatcher and Cesar Mendoza, *Hydrologic Modifications* (report prepared for the New York/New Jersey Harbor Estuary Program, 1991), 5. The historical GIS conducted for this book, after comparison with Squires's study, suggests that an estimated 37,800 acres of underwater land were filled. The amount of open water developed was equal to 2.78 times the current size of Manhattan Island (13,636 acres). Altogether, 93,800 acres of tidal marsh and underwater land were developed, or almost half the current size of New York City (195,072 acres).

8. Steven Stoll, *The Great Delusion: A Mad Inventor, Death in the Tropics, and the Utopian Origins of Economic Growth* (New York: Hill and Wang, 2008), 59; and Tom Angotti, *New York for Sale: Community Planning Confronts Global Real Estate* (Cambridge, Mass.: MIT Press, 2008), 39.

9. Most narrative studies of New York City have relatively little to say about the role of land, water, plants, animals, and climate in the city's history, though there is more extensive coverage of the geography and water supply. See, for example, Burrows & Wallace, 3–5, 334–36, 359–62, 594–95, 625–28, and the brief discussion of the marshes and hills of Red Hook on 582.

10. On the New York Bight, see Donald F. Squires, *The Bight of the Big Apple* (Albany, N.Y.: New York Sea Grant Institute, 1981); and Jack B. Pearce, "The New York Bight," *MPB* 41, nos. 1–6 (Jan.–June 2000): 44–55. The bight is part of the Northeast US Continental Shelf: Large Marine Ecosystem #7, one of sixty-four such coastal ecosystems throughout the world. See NOAA, "Large Marine Ecosystems of the World," 2013, www.lme.noaa.gov/.

11. On the return of avian life to the Arthur Kill off of Staten Island, see Wehran-New York, *Draft Environmental Impact Statement for the Fresh Kills Ash/Residue Landfill, Staten Island, New York* (report for the New York Department of Sanitation, Middletown, N.Y., 1991), III-35.

12. Overall, the Atlantic Coast is not in such bad shape, ecologically speaking, when compared with the coasts of Europe. See Heike K. Lotze et al., "Depletion, Degradation, and Recovery Potential of Estuaries and Coastal Seas," *Science* 312, no. 5781 (June 23, 2006): 1807, fig. 1E, doi:10.1126/science.1128035. This study examined twelve coastal ecosystems in North America, Europe, and Australia, and found that the most degraded ones in terms of species abundance were the Adriatic, Wadden, and Baltic Seas.

13. Mark Kurlansky, *The Big Oyster: History on the Half Shell* (2006; repr., New York: Random House, 2007), xv.

14. U.N. World Health Organization, Global Health Observatory, "Urban Population Growth," www.who.int/gho/urban_health/situation_trends/urban_population _growth_text/en/index.html. For more on the ecological virtues of New York and specifically on how Manhattanites today use less per capita energy than people

living in rural areas, thus producing a correspondingly smaller carbon footprint, see David Owen, *Green Metropolis: Why Living Smaller, Living Closer, and Driving Less Are the Keys to Sustainability* (New York: Riverhead Books, 2009), 1–48. On New York as the first megacity, see Tertius Chandler, *Four Thousand Years of Urban Growth: An Historical Census* (Lewiston, N.Y.: St. David's Univ. Press, 1987), 507, table.

15. Gilbert Millstein, "Architectural Extravaganza," review of *Delirious New York: A Retroactive Manifesto for Manhattan*, *NYT*, Dec. 24, 1978.

1. Entrepôt

1. Jameson, 17 ("drowned Land" quotation); Douglas Hunter, *Half Moon: Henry Hudson and the Voyage That Redrew the Map of the World* (New York: Bloomsbury, 2009), 16; D. F. Squires and J. S. Barclay, *Nearshore Wildlife Habitats and Populations in the New York/New Jersey Harbor Estuary* (report for the New York/New Jersey Harbor Estuary Program, 1990), 10 ("drowned estuary" quotation); and John Waldman, *Heartbeats in the Muck: The History, Sea Life, and Environment of New York Harbor*, rev. ed. (New York: Empire State Editions, 2013), 8–10.

2. Jameson, 17 ("three great Rivers" quotation); Hunter, *Half Moon*, 149–50; Waldman, *Heartbeats in the Muck*, 8; and Squires and Barclay, *Nearshore Wildlife Habitats*, 11.

3. Jameson, 17 ("many Salmons" quotation), 18 ("went on Land"). On the salmon issue, see Waldman, *Heartbeats in the Muck*, 19; and Sanderson, 293. For Beeren Eylant, see Hunter, *Half Moon*, 152. For the changing nature of Jamaica Bay, see Ellen Kracauer Hartig et al., "Anthropogenic and Climate-Change Impacts on Salt Marshes of Jamaica Bay, New York City," *Wetlands* 22, no. 1 (Mar. 2002): 74. This study estimated Jamaica Bay's marshlands in 1907 at 6,549 hectares (16,183 acres) and 1,620 hectares (4,003 acres) in 1970, for a decline of 75 percent. The historical GIS conducted for this book found a slightly greater decline between 1900 and 1968 of 82 percent. See appendix E.

4. On the emergence of the salt marshes, see Anne-Marie Cantwell and Diana di Zerega Wall, *Unearthing Gotham: The Archaeology of New York City* (New Haven, Conn.: Yale Univ. Press, 2001), 87. Lucianne Lavin, "Coastal Adaptations in Southern New England and Southern New York," *Archaeology of Eastern North America* 16 (Fall 1988): 108 ("most productive" quotation). Lavin was referring to New England's marshlands.

5. The Canarsie and the archaeological record are discussed in Hunter, *Half Moon*, 160. On the Lenape as a coastal people, see Sanderson, 119. The "great store of Maiz" quotation is from Jameson, 18. On the rich natural environment and the Lenape's strong sense of place and community, see Cantwell and Wall, *Unearthing Gotham*, 113, 115. On the poor soil and evidence for the low productivity level of maize grown in the New York area, see Sanderson, 119–23. See also Robert E. Loeb, "Evidence of Prehistoric Corn (*Zea mays*) and Hickory (*Carya* spp.) Planting in New York City: Vegetation History of Hunter Island, Bronx County, New York," *Journal of the Torrey Botanical Society* 125, no. 1 (1998): 74–86, www.jstor.org

/stable/2997233, which examines the fossil pollen records and finds evidence of corn planting between 1075 and 1285, at which point it ceased.

6. Jameson, 18 ("sound the other River" quotation), 19 (all remaining quotations). For a discussion of the *vlieboat*, biographical information on Colman and details of his journey, see Hunter, *Half Moon*, 60, 81, 165.

7. On the extent of the Hackensack and Newark Meadows, see Timothy J. Iannuzzi et al., *A Common Tragedy: History of an Urban River* (Amherst, Mass.: Amherst Scientific, 2002), 50–52, which indicates that they extended over 27,000 acres, or 42.2 square miles. The historical GIS conducted for this book found 42.29 square miles of marsh in 1900. For the white cedar swamp and wildlife, see Kevin W. Wright, *The Hackensack Meadowlands: Prehistory and History* (report no. 1988-039, MERI, 1988), 6, 8–9. More on changing vegetation during the Little Ice Age and the era of European colonization can be found in Dee Cabaniss Pederson et al., "Medieval Warming, Little Ice Age, and European Impact on the Environment During the Last Millennium in the Lower Hudson Valley, New York, USA," *Quaternary Research* 63, no. 3 (May 2005): 238–49, doi:10.1016/j.yqres.2005.01.001. For a study that examines a sediment core from the Hackensack tidal marsh and charts "changes in land-sea relationships" over the last twenty-six hundred years, see Dorothy Peteet Carmichael, "A Record of Environmental Change During Recent Millennia in the Hackensack Tidal Marsh, New Jersey," *BTBC* 107, no. 4 (Oct.–Dec. 1980): 514–24.

8. Jameson, 19 (quotation).

9. Hunter, *Half Moon*, 171–72. Others have argued that Coney Island was named by the Dutch for its wild rabbits, known as *konijn* in Dutch. See Elizabeth Bradley, "Coney Island," in Jackson, 299.

10. Jameson, 20 ("good Harbour" quotation). On the narrowing of Upper Bay, see Hunter, *Half Moon*, 179. Walt Whitman, "A Letter From Brooklyn," in *The Uncollected Poetry and Prose of Walt Whitman*, ed. Emory Holloway, 2 vols. (Garden City, N.Y.: Doubleday, Page, 1921), 1:239.

11. For more on oysters, see Hunter, *Half Moon*, 180; and Mark Kurlansky, *The Big Oyster: History on the Half Shell* (2006; repr., New York: Random House, 2007), 12, 35. Kurlansky writes that some biologists estimate that "New York Harbor contained fully half of the world's oysters." This statement, however, is likely an exaggeration. Oysters grew up and down the East Coast of the United States and in Europe, and there were numerous estuaries—Long Island Sound, Chesapeake Bay, the Gulf of Mexico—that together would have almost certainly held more than half.

12. The botanical names for the grasses mentioned are: *Spartina alterniflora* (salt marsh cordgrass), *Spartina patens* (salt meadow hay), *Distichlis spicata* (spike grass), *Panicum virgatum* (switchgrass), *Scirpus* (rushes), and *Zostera marina* (eelgrass). For more on marsh grasses, see Judith S. Weis and Carol A. Butler, *Salt Marshes: A Natural and Unnatural History* (New Brunswick, N.J.: Rutgers Univ. Press, 2009), 21–27. On the likely presence of these plant species in 1609 (with *Spartina patens* somewhat less likely), see Sanderson, 276.

13. That the ecosystem was largely intact at the end of the eighteenth century is a conclusion that can be drawn from a stunningly detailed map drawn by the British

in the early 1780s and that Sanderson relied on to compute the landscape at the time of Henry Hudson. See Sanderson, 40–43. Coastal waters, however, experienced some significant change. Along the coast from Maine to Delaware Bay, the colonists killed no fewer than twenty-four hundred right whales in the period from 1696 to 1734. See W. Jeffrey Bolster, *The Mortal Sea: Fishing the Atlantic in the Age of Sail* (Cambridge, Mass.: Belknap Press of Harvard Univ. Press, 2012), 70. On the name *Manna-hata*, see Jameson, 27.

14. Audrey M. Lambert, *The Making of the Dutch Landscape: An Historical Geography of the Netherlands* (London: Seminar Press, 1971), 1; Johan van Veen, *Dredge, Drain, Reclaim: The Art of a Nation* (The Hague: Nijhoff, 1948), 18; Simon Schama, *The Embarrassment of Riches: An Interpretation of Dutch Culture in the Golden Age* (New York: Knopf, 1987), 38; Immanuel Wallerstein, *The Modern World-System II: Mercantilism and the Consolidation of the European World-Economy, 1600–1750* (New York: Academic Press, 1980), 40; and Eco W. Bijker, "History and Heritage in Coastal Engineering in the Netherlands," in *A History and Heritage of Coastal Engineering*, ed. Nicholas C. Kraus (New York: American Society of Civil Engineers, 1996), 395 ("Don't fight" quotation).

15. Hunter, *Half Moon*, 279–81; Michael Kammen, *Colonial New York: A History* (1975; repr., New York: Oxford Univ. Press, 1996), 26; and Jaap Jacobs, *The Colony of New Netherland: A Dutch Settlement in Seventeenth-Century America* (Ithaca, N.Y.: Cornell Univ. Press, 2009), 28, 30. The Dutch expected to find a climate approximating Madrid's, a city on roughly the same latitude. A winter or two in North America disabused them of this notion. See Benjamin Schmidt, *Innocence Abroad: The Dutch Imagination and the New World, 1570–1670* (Cambridge, UK: Cambridge Univ. Press, 2001), 214. On Governors Island, which the Indians called Pagganck, meaning Nut Island, see Hunter, *Half Moon*, 179.

16. On the decision regarding where to locate, see Adriana E. van Zwieten, "'A Little Land . . . To Sow Some Seeds': Real Property, Custom, and Law in the Community of New Amsterdam" (PhD diss., Temple Univ., 2001), xvii–xxi. Quotations regarding location are from A. J. F. van Laer, trans. and ed., *Documents Relating to New Netherland 1624–1626 in the Henry E. Huntington Library* (San Marino, Calif.: Henry E. Huntington Library and Art Gallery, 1924), 47, 89. Verhulst's character is mentioned in Burrows & Wallace, 21. The Schaghen quotation is from "Translation of Pieter Schaghen's 1626 Letter, Which Mentions the Purchase of Manhattes (Manhattan)," New Netherland Research Center, last modified Jan. 26, 2010, www.nysl.nysed.gov/newnetherland/schaghentrans.htm.

17. Burrows & Wallace, 19; and Charles Gehring, "Peter Minuit's Purchase of Manhattan Island—New Evidence," *De Halve Maen* 55 (Spring 1980): 6–7.

18. On behaving honorably with the Indians, see Schmidt, *Innocence Abroad*, 247. Russell Shorto, *The Island at the Center of the World: The Epic Story of Dutch Manhattan and the Forgotten Colony That Shaped America* (New York: Doubleday, 2004), 56–57, argues that the Manhattan purchase "was roughly in line with other prices paid to Indians" and "in the same ballpark" as sales made between the Dutch. For another side to the debate, see James W. Loewen, *Lies My Teacher Told Me: Everything Your American History Textbook Got Wrong* (1995; repr., New York: Touchstone, 1996),

122, which argues (on the basis of very slim evidence) that the Dutch paid the wrong group of Indians for Manhattan. The historian quoted is Stuart Banner, *How the Indians Lost Their Land: Law and Power on the Frontier* (Cambridge, Mass.: Belknap Press of Harvard Univ. Press, 2005), 76–77.

19. On the Indians and their inexperience in land sales, see Banner, *How the Indians Lost Their Land*, 57, 76; Van der Donck, 103 (quotation); and Robert S. Grumet, "The Selling of Lenapehoking," *Bulletin of the Archaeological Society of New Jersey* 44 (1989): 3. For more on the history of usufruct among North American indigenous peoples, see William Cronon, *Changes in the Land: Indians, Colonists, and the Ecology of New England* (New York: Hill and Wang, 1983), 62–67.

20. Grumet, "The Selling of Lenapehoking," 2–5.

21. My discussion of real property is based on Van Zwieten, "'A Little Land,'" 1–2, 12–14. Van Zwieten notes that in 1628 there was at least one instance of a settler seeking a land grant, which the West India Company promised to make. See also, Burrows & Wallace, 35. On the high level of urbanization found in the Netherlands, see Schmidt, *Innocence Abroad*, 7.

22. On Minuit and rivers, see Oliver A. Rink, *Holland on the Hudson: An Economic and Social History of Dutch New York* (Ithaca, N.Y.: Cornell Univ. Press, 1986), 85. Regarding the composition of the forests of Manhattan, see Sanderson, 27. According to Sanderson & Brown, 552, table 2, 77 percent of Manhattan Island was covered with forest and shrubbery in 1609. On *Gänóno*, see Shorto, *The Island at the Center of the World*, 42. The founding of the various New York towns is documented in Harrington Putnam, "Origin of Breuckelen," in *Historic New York: Being the Second Series of the Half Moon Papers*, ed. Maud Wilder Goodwin, Alice Carrington Royce, Ruth Putnam, and Eva Palmer Brownell (New York: G. P. Putnam's Sons, 1899), 387–88, 396; William C. Morey, *The Government of New York: Its History and Administration* (New York: Macmillan, 1902), 230; Burrows & Wallace, 67, 69–70; and Dorothy Valentine Smith, *Staten Island: Gateway to New York* (Philadelphia: Chilton, 1970), 24.

23. On Van der Donck, see Shorto, *The Island at the Center of the World*, 103–4. With respect to free trade, see Rink, *Holland on the Hudson*, 136–37; and Schmidt, *Innocence Abroad*, 248–49.

24. Hugo Grotius, *The Jurisprudence of Holland*, 2nd ed., trans. Robert Warden Lee, 2 vols. (1953; repr., Aalen: Scientia Verlag, 1977), 1:230, 231 (proverb quotation); and Shorto, *The Island at the Center of the World*, 212–13. Canals and urban life are discussed in Josef W. Konvitz, *Cities and the Sea: Port City Planning in Early Modern Europe* (Baltimore: Johns Hopkins Univ. Press, 1978), 31, 36, 65.

25. Van der Donck, 18, 133, 7, 11, 14, 15.

26. On the landscape in 1609, see Sanderson & Brown, 552, table 2. For beaver, see Gerard T. Koeppel, *Water for Gotham: A History* (Princeton, N.J.: Princeton Univ. Press, 2000), 10; and Van der Donck, 117–18, 120–21. Van der Donck describes the animal life he discovered in detail on 47–62. The quotation is from 55. On the depletion of Europe's estuaries and coastal waters, see Bolster, *The Mortal Sea*, 23–34.

27. Jacobs, *The Colony of New Netherland*, 5; Van der Donck, 8, 9; and Jan de Vries and Ad van der Woude, *The First Modern Economy: Success, Failure, and Perseverance of*

the Dutch Economy, 1500–1815 (Cambridge, UK: Cambridge Univ. Press, 1997), 357–62.

28. De Vries and Van der Woude, *The First Modern Economy*, 33; and "Ordinance of the Director General and Council of New Netherland against cutting Sods or dredging Oyster shells on Manhattan Island . . . ," Apr. 11, 1658, in *Laws and Ordinances of New Netherland, 1638–1674*, comp. and trans. E. B. O'Callaghan (Albany, N. Y., 1868), 347. For the larger ecological meaning of the law, see Michael Xavier Kirby, "Fishing down the Coast: Historical Expansion and Collapse of Oyster Fisheries Along Continental Margins," *PNAS* 101, no. 35 (Aug. 31, 2004): 13096–99, doi:10.1073/pnas.0405150101. "Convenient entrepôt" is from Burrows & Wallace, 48. On the West India Company's triangular trade involving the shipment of Dutch goods to Africa, slaves to North America, and sugar back to Europe, see De Vries and Van der Woude, *The First Modern Economy*, 396–402.

29. Jonathan Israel, *The Dutch Republic: Its Rise, Greatness, and Fall, 1477–1806* (Oxford, UK: Clarendon, 1995), 328–29; and Van der Donck, 2, 15.

30. For Stuyvesant's career, see Burrows & Wallace, 41–42; Shorto, *The Island at the Center of the World*, 151; and Jacobs, *The Colony of New Netherland*, 80. On the pier, see O'Callaghan, *Laws and Ordinances of New Netherland*, 69. "Water and morass" quotation is from Berthold Fernow, ed. *The Records of New Amsterdam from 1653 to 1674 Anno Domini*, 7 vols. (New York, 1897), 7:171. For more on Stuyvesant's improvements, see Stokes, 1:67, 123.

31. "Foot shorter" quotation is from Jameson, 343. Burrows & Wallace, 62–63, discusses the circumstances surrounding the decision to form a municipal government. On the financial problems with the West India Company, which set the stage for that decision, see De Vries and Van der Woude, *The First Modern Economy*, 401–2. On the Heere Gracht, see Stokes, 1:62. The pier at Moore Street is mentioned in Burrows & Wallace, 46. For a discussion of the Stadhuis, see Dennis J. Maika, "Commerce and Community: Manhattan Merchants in the Seventeenth Century" (PhD diss., New York Univ., 1995), 162; and J. H. Innes, *New Amsterdam and Its People: Studies, Social and Topographical, of the Town Under Dutch and Early English Rule* (New York: Charles Scribner's Sons, 1902), 185–86.

32. De Vries and Van der Woude, *The First Modern Economy*, 409.

33. De Vries and Van der Woude, *The First Modern Economy*, 409–10; Burrows & Wallace, 68–72; and Kammen, *Colonial New York*, 71.

34. Burrows & Wallace, 72–73; and Kammen, *Colonial New York*, 71–72.

35. Kammen, *Colonial New York*, 84. For a brief discussion of the word *kill*, see Barry Lopez, ed., *Home Ground: Language for an American Landscape* (San Antonio, Tex.: Trinity Univ. Press, 2006), 199.

36. Arthur Everett Peterson and George William Edwards, *New York as an Eighteenth Century Municipality*, pt. 1 (New York: Longmans, Green, 1917), 93 ("rubbish, filth" quotation); and Berthold Fernow, ed. and trans., *Minutes of Orphanmasters Court of New Amsterdam, 1655–1663* (New York, 1907), 2:176 ("very foul" quotation). It was longstanding tradition in Amsterdam to require homeowners along a canal to dredge the area fronting their houses to a depth of three feet; that custom seems to have been carried over to New Amsterdam. See Van Zwieten, "'A Little Land,'" 104.

Konvitz, *Cities and the Sea*, 65, argues, mainly by deduction, that the English could not have filled the canal because it was pestilential. The stench, he claims, was not something that bothered people until the nineteenth century. It also was not that the British were thumbing their noses at the Dutch in nationalist pique. The problem was that if the canal had been extended, it would have interfered with private property and required condemnation through eminent domain. New York under British rule, he argues, was too democratic to allow such condemnation, and that presumably meant an end to the canal. The stench may have seemed unremarkable in the seventeenth-century context. It was not until the late eighteenth century that a more refined sense of smell developed, at least if patterns in France are any guide. See Alain Corbin, *The Foul and the Fragrant: Odor and the French Social Imagination* (Cambridge, Mass.: Harvard Univ. Press, 1986).

37. Peterson and Edwards, *New York as an Eighteenth Century Municipality*, 76 ("cleansing" quotation); and *MCC, 1675–1776*, 1:19 (1675) ("Liueing" quotation). Peterson is the historian mentioned, and the quotation is on 77.

38. For a discussion of the Andros era, see Burrows & Wallace, 84–85. Early efforts to make the waterfront more accessible are discussed in Peterson and Edwards, *New York as an Eighteenth Century Municipality*, 106–7. The Great Dock is covered in Stokes, 4:308 (entry for Jan. 10, 1676), 311 (entry for Nov. 10, 1676). The quotation is from a letter in the Winthrop Papers, Massachusetts Historical Society and quoted in Stokes, 4:310 (entry for Sept. 12, 1676).

39. Burrows & Wallace, 87.

2. George Washington Stepped Here

1. E. B. O'Callaghan, ed., *Calendar of Historical Manuscripts in the Office of the Secretary of State, Albany, N.Y.*, part 2, (Albany, 1866), 138 ("wolves" quotation). The classic discussion of the ecological impact of colonial agriculture is found in William Cronon, *Changes in the Land: Indians, Colonists, and the Ecology of New England* (New York: Hill and Wang, 1983), 127–56.

2. Van der Donck, 21. Between 1609 and 2010, the island of Manhattan grew by 2,286 acres to total 13,636 acres. See appendix F. An American football field is 1.32 acres. Dividing the numbers results in 1,732 football fields of new land.

3. John H. Kennedy, *Thomas Dongan, Governor of New York (1682–1688)* (1930; repr., New York: AMS Press, 1974), 14; Leo Hershkowitz, "The New York City Charter, 1686," in *The Roots of the Republic: American Founding Documents Interpreted*, ed. Stephen L. Schechter, Richard B. Bernstein, and Donald S. Lutz (Madison, Wis.: Madison House, 1990), 86–89; and Cathy Matson, *Merchants and Empire: Trading in Colonial New York* (Baltimore: Johns Hopkins Univ. Press, 1998), 92–93. The actual charter is reproduced in Seymann, 216–36, and the quotations are from 220 and 233.

4. For more on the Massachusetts ordinance, see Mark Cheung, "Rethinking the History of the Seventeenth-Century Colonial Ordinance: A Reinterpretation of an Ancient Statute," *Maine Law Review* 42, no. 1 (1990): 115–58.

The space between the high- and low-water mark, known in the law as the foreshore, had only emerged as a form of property in the late sixteenth century, when Europe's forays into the Americas and the resulting shift toward a world economy centered more on trade brought the coast increasingly into consciousness. A complex struggle between the English Crown and those landholders asserting a right to the shore ensued. Given how fraught and confused the entire tideland subject was in Anglo-American law, one can appreciate why New York would want some clarification on the issue, and why Dongan would want to provide it if he wished the city to prosper as a port. See Patrick Deveny, "Title, Jus Publicum, and the Public Trust: An Historical Analysis," *Sea Grant Law Journal* 1 (1976): 27, 41–42. The classic work on the legal history of the foreshore is Stuart A. Moore, *A History of the Foreshore and the Law Relating Thereto* . . . (London, 1888), xxviii, xxxvi, 180. See also Royal E. T. Riggs, "The Alienability of the State's Title to the Foreshore," *Columbia Law Review* 12 (May 1912): 398, 400.

5. Anne-Marie Cantwell and Diana di Zerega Wall, *Unearthing Gotham: The Archaeology of New York City* (New Haven, Conn.: Yale Univ. Press, 2001), 226, 239; Nancy S. Seasholes, *Gaining Ground: A History of Landmaking in Boston* (Cambridge, Mass.: MIT Press, 2003), especially 3 on wharfing out. The Dutch may have been less aggressive than the English with respect to encroaching on the surrounding waters. The evidence is scanty, but it seems that Dutch deeds from the 1650s made grants that extended only to the high-water mark. See Black, 13.

6. On the high proportion of slaves in the East Ward because of all the work required at the port, see Thelma Wills Foote, *Black and White Manhattan: The History of Racial Formation in Colonial New York City* (New York: Oxford Univ. Press, 2004), 79. The "Dock Mudd" quotation is from a 1692 grant in CG Book A, 70. On the word *dock*, see Seasholes, *Gaining Ground*, 22. The *Oxford English Dictionary*, however, notes that *dock*, referring to "an artificial basin excavated, built round with masonry, and fitted with flood-gates," had been in use since the fifteenth century. See "dock, n.3," *OED Online*, www.oed.com. A great discussion of the archaeology of the waterfront is found in Cantwell and Wall, *Unearthing Gotham*, 227–34.

7. *MCC, 1675–1776*, 2:103 (1700); Cadwallader Colden to Dr. John Mitchell, Nov. 7, 1745, in *Collections of the New-York Historical Society* 67 (1937): 329 ("filth" and "smell" quotations); and Richard Bayley to Richard Channing Moore, July 20, 1796, in Samuel L. Mitchill, Edward Miller, and Elihu H. Smith, *The Medical Repository*, 3rd ed. (New York, 1804): 1:120 ("dead horses" quotation).

8. The ninety-four water lots are in CG Book A, 4–395, and CG Book B, 2–95. On the Van Cortlandts and Frederick Philipse (1627–1702), the latter the colony's wealthiest individual in 1674, see Patricia U. Bonomi, *A Factious People: Politics and Society in Colonial New York* (New York: Columbia Univ. Press, 1971), 60–63. Philipse received two grants. So did two members (Gerardus and Johannes) of the prominent Beekman family. Also on the list of grantees are some of the wealthiest traders in the city, including Miles Forster, Jacob Kip, Brandt Schuyler, and Philip French. Corporation grants to Jacob Kip, Apr. 21, 1692; Frederick Philipse, Apr. 21, 1692; Brandt Schuyler, Sept. 7, 1692; and Miles Forster, Oct. 12, 1694, CG Book A, 72–74, 80–82, 87–88, 124–28, 183–87. Corporation grants to Philip French and

Brandt Schuyler, Aug. 21, 1702; Johannes Beekman, Sept. 8, 1719; and Gerardus Beekman, May 22, 1722, CG Book B, 33–42, 70–76, 83–95.

On the wealth of the city's top traders, see Matson, *Merchants and Empire*, 354n64. On the occupational groups that made up the city's middle ranks, see Bruce M. Wilkenfeld, "The New York City Common Council, 1689–1800," *New York History* 52 (July 1971): 255. About one-third of the grantees were tradesmen. Eleven grantees were unidentified in terms of social rank. Although it is true that by selling water lots the city financed public improvements, including the construction of a Battery on the southern part of the island, the city seemed to go out of its way to cater to the needs of the wealthy with respect to underwater resources. Merchants tended to be represented in numbers exceeding their proportion in the population on the Common Council, the institution which governed these decisions. See Wilkenfeld, "The New York City Common Council," 262. On the use of water-lot proceeds to finance improvement at the Battery, see Black, 22.

9. John Romeyn Brodhead, *Documents Relative to the Colonial History of the State of New-York*, 15 vols. (Albany, N.Y., 1853), 3:261 ("smale shipps" quotation). According to Matson, *Merchants and Empire*, 50, in 1694, "there were 40 ships, 62 sloops, and 62 riverboats registered to New Yorkers." The demolition of the palisade is discussed in Burrows & Wallace, 109–10. For more on New York outstripping Boston in commercial strength, see Matson, *Merchants and Empire*, 3.

10. On the state of the foreshore, see Black, 24. My discussion of economic history is based on Michael Kammen, *Colonial New York: A History* (1975; repr., New York: Oxford Univ. Press, 1996), 152, 161–62; and Burrows & Wallace, 116, 120–22.

11. Stokes, 1:239, 243; and *MCC, 1675–1776*, 3:276, 274 (1721).

12. Rosenwaike, 8, table 1; *Boston News-Letter*, Aug. 15–22, 1723 ("Wharffs" quotation); and *MCC, 1675–1776*, 3:326 (1723) ("Intirely Ruined" quotation). Black, 26, discusses the storm's impact on the city's budget surplus.

13. The "four hundred feet" quotation is from "Petition of the Mayor, Aldermen and Commonality of the City of New York, for a Confirmation of Their Charter, and the Enlargement of Their Bounds, to Comprehend 400 Feet Below Low Water Mark," Aug. 13, 1730, Applications for Land Grants, Land Papers, series A0272, 10:130, NYSA. This document is the original handwritten copy of the petition. A printed copy can be found in *MCC, 1675–1776*, 4:18–22 (1730). The sand hills are mentioned in Stokes, 4:384, and "Mannette" and "Devil's Water" quotations are from 6:157. For more on these various physical features of the land, see Sanderson & Brown, 556, 559. The acreage figures are from "Description of a Survey of the Same, Containing about 210 Acres, Cadwallader Colden, Survr. Genl.," Sept. 2, 1730, Applications for Land Grants, Land Papers, ser. A0272, 10:129, NYSA. The Montgomerie Charter is reproduced in Seymann, 248–335, and the quotations are from 252 and 271. On the issue of municipal land ownership in US versus European cities, see Harold S. Buttenheim and Philip H. Cornick, "Land Reserves for American Cities," *Journal of Land and Public Utility Economics* 14, no. 3 (Aug. 1938): 254–65, www.jstor.org/stable/3158681.

14. Black, 27 ("history branches" quotation). On the issue of the grants being made in fee, see S. Stevens to James M. Brown, May 6, 1885, 5, NYCCR, ser. VII.3, box 229.

15. On the Bradford map being bound together with a copy of the Montgomerie Charter, see Stokes, 1:263. The John Peter Zenger edition of the charter is catalogued as *The Charter of the City of New-York* (New York, 1735). The historian Michael Kammen notes that the Bradford map was "the first engraved map of New York's harbor." See Kammen, *Colonial New York*, 292n.

16. Burrows & Wallace, 168–72.

17. The *Independent Reflector* essay was published in two parts, only the second of which is of interest to me here. See "The Consideration of the Natural Advantages of New-York, Resumed and Concluded," no. LII, Nov. 22, 1753, in William Livingston et al., *The Independent Reflector Or Weekly Essays on Sundry Important Subjects More Particularly Adapted to the Province of New-York*, ed. Milton M. Klein (Cambridge, Mass.: Belknap Press of Harvard Univ. Press, 1963), 433–34. For a modern essay that echoes these same sentiments, see Edward L. Glaeser, "Urban Colossus: Why Is New York America's Largest City?" *NYFedEPR* 11, no. 2 (Dec. 2005): 7–24. The *Independent Reflector* was the work of a group of men associated with what is sometimes called the "landed interest"—that is, the wealthy landowners living in the Hudson valley and their supporters. The "landed interest" and the opposing "mercantile interest" are explained briefly in Burrows & Wallace, 116–17. For a more extended discussion, see Bonomi, *A Factious People*, 60–75.

18. Hartog, 48.

19. Kammen, *Colonial New York*, 278–81. The classic account of artisans as a class is Gary B. Nash, *The Urban Crucible: Social Change, Political Consciousness, and the Origins of the American Revolution* (Cambridge, Mass.: Harvard Univ. Press, 1979). For a more detailed discussion of the social status of the water-lot grantees, see appendix B.

20. The phrase "quiet enjoyment" is from Morton J. Horwitz, *The Transformation of American Law, 1780–1860* (Cambridge, Mass.: Harvard Univ. Press, 1977), 36. The English jurist William Blackstone would later capture the idea that gave rise to legal doctrines such as preemption when he wrote, "There is nothing which so generally strikes the imagination, and engages the affections of mankind, as the right of property; or that sole and despotic dominion which one man claims and exercises over the external things of the world, in total exclusion of the right of any other individual in the universe." See William Blackstone, *Commentaries on the Laws of England*, 4 vols. (1766; repr., Chicago: Univ. of Chicago Press, 1979), 2:2. The *Independent Reflector* ran critiques of the idea of preemptive rights along the waterfront in "Remarks on a Petition, Preferred to the Corporation in the Year 1748; Lately Revived, and Now under Consideration" and "Remarks on the Water Lots, Continued," nos. IV and X, Feb. 1, 1753, and Mar. 1, 1753, in Livingston et al., *The Independent Reflector*, 118–27, 151–56. Quotations are from 155. On the elite dominating the Common Council, see Wilkenfeld, "The New York City Common Council," 263–64.

21. For biographical material on Walton, see Burrows & Wallace, 123, 177; and John Austin Stevens Jr., *Colonial New York, Sketches Biographical and Historical, 1768–1784* (New York, 1867), 55–68. "Swamp" quotation is from "The Walton Mansion-House—Pearl-Street," *New York Mirror*, Mar. 17, 1832. For Rotten Row's wretched state, see

"New-York," *NYG*, Apr. 4, 1757. On market boats and coasters, see Hartog, 119. The petition of Walton and others is in *MCC, 1675–1776*, 5:453 (1754).

22. "Lands under Waters of the Harbor or East River, in front of Queen Street," Mar. 27, 1717, Letters Patent, ser. 12943, 8:172, NYSA; and Letter to the Editor, *NYG*, June 10, 1754. On the absence of a commons in New York, see Hartog, 27–28 ("exclusive" quotation); and Burrows & Wallace, 140–41.

23. New York Chamber of Commerce, "Inaugural Meeting Minutes," in Columbia Univ. Libraries Exhibitions, Item #2661, https://ldpd.lamp.columbia.edu/omeka /exhibits/show/nyccc/founding/item/2661. William Walton Jr. and his brother Jacob Walton were two of the twenty founding members of the Chamber of Commerce and present at the first meeting on Apr. 5, 1768. Gerrard Walton, a brother of William Jr., and Jacob, was elected a member of the organization at the second meeting. See John Austin Stevens Jr., *Colonial Records of the New York Chamber of Commerce, 1768–1784, with Historical and Biographical Sketches* (New York, 1867), 8. Another brother, Thomas Walton, was elected a member on Feb. 7, 1769. See Stevens, *Colonial Records*, 36. And yet another brother, Abraham Walton, was elected July 4, 1780. See Stevens, *Colonial Records*, 234. These five men—William Jr., Jacob, Gerrard, Thomas, and Abraham—were all nephews of William Walton and sons of Jacob and Maria (Beekman) Walton. The grant to William Walton's nephew, Jacob Walton, is in CG Book D, Feb. 15, 1769, 5–12; and the grant to William Walton, another nephew, is in CG Book D, Feb. 15, 1769, 13–20. The language granting limited public access reads as follows: "reserving for the use of the publick a Slip on the East and West Sides thereof." See CG Book D, Feb. 15, 1769, 8.

24. For more on the social status of the water-lot grantees, see appendix B. Hartog has argued that the water-lot program, which required grantees to fill in the water and build wharves at their own private expense, amounted to a clever "planning tool." In other words, the city authorities' approach to the shore allowed it to develop the waterfront while continuing to abide by the central tenets of eighteenth-century political culture, a world premised on the idea that government ought to have little role in society. In this interpretation, the water-lot grants, even though they went to affluent families, had a redistributive effect, causing wealth to trickle down to the community at large and improve the overall prospects for the port. There is significant merit to placing New York's water-lot sales in their proper historical context. Notwithstanding the considerable value of Hartog's argument, he does sometimes seem to make the granting of water lots seem rational without considering the role that power played in the management of this valuable resource. See Hartog, 48, 61–62, 65–66.

25. See CG Book D, Aug. 12, 1772, 160; and Karl Marx and Frederick Engels, *The Communist Manifesto: A Modern Edition* (1998; repr., London: Verso, 2012), 38.

26. Sanderson & Brown, 552, table 2.

27. The quotation is from John Montrésor, *A Plan of the City of New-York & Its Environs* . . . ([London?], 1775). The seventy-four-acre figure is from appendix F. The densely settled portion of the city in 1695 was eighty acres. See Nan A. Rothschild, *New York City Neighborhoods: The 18th Century* (San Diego: Academic Press, 1990), 8.

28. *MCC, 1675–1776*, 1:146 (1683); Gary B. Nash, *The Urban Crucible: The Northern Seaports and the Origins of the American Revolution* (Cambridge, Mass.: Harvard

Univ. Press, 1986), 158; David M. Ludlum, *Early American Winters, 1604–1820* (Boston: American Meteorological Society, 1966), 61 (Watts quotation, citing J. Watts, *Letter Book*, 331); and Paul E. Cohen and Robert T. Augustyn, *Manhattan in Maps, 1527–1995* (New York: Rizzoli, 1997), 88. See also Michael Williams, *Americans and Their Forests: A Historical Geography* (Cambridge, UK: Cambridge Univ. Press, 1989), 78. One student of the Manhattan forest has estimated consumption patterns for firewood and concluded that the bulk of the island was deforested sometime between the late seventeenth century and the early eighteenth century. See Richard Howe, "Notes on the Deforestation of Manhattan Island," *Gotham History Blotter*, 2012, www.gothamcenter.org/blotter/?p=690.

29. Ludlum, *Early American Winters*, 115; George Washington, *Writings*, selected by John H. Rhodehamel (New York: Library of America, 1997), 440; and Sanderson & Brown, 558.

30. *MCC, 1784–1831*, 2:138 (1795).

31. GWD, 5:445.

32. Rosenwaike, 16, table 2. For details of Washington's travels see Frank Monaghan, "Notes on the Inaugural Journey and the Inaugural Ceremonies of George Washington as First President of the United States" (MS prepared for New York World's Fair, 1939, New York Public Library), 14–39, 38 ("God Save" and "porpoises" quotations). New York's population in 1790 was 33,131. See Rosenwaike, 16, table 2. As for the area of New York, I used Sanderson & Brown, 552, table 2, who list it in 1782 as 4,944 hectares, which is equal to 19.1 square miles. Thus the population density of New York at roughly the time of the inauguration was 1,735 people per square mile. I derived the population density of Ketchikan (1,851 people per square mile) from US Census Bureau, State and County QuickFacts, http://quickfacts .census.gov/qfd/index.html.

33. See Cronon, *Changes in the Land*, 76–81.

3. The Reticulation

1. Vincent Scully, *American Architecture and Urbanism* (New York: Praeger, 1969), 76; [Clement Clarke Moore], *Addressed to the Proprietors of Real Estate, in the City and County of New-York* (New York, 1818), 24, 23, 49–50; Joseph Jay Rubin, *The Historic Whitman* (University Park: Pennsylvania State Univ. Press, 1973), 338; Frederick Law Olmsted, *Frederick Law Olmsted: Landscape Architect, 1822–1903*, ed. Frederick Law Olmsted Jr., and Theodora Kimball, two volumes in one (1922; repr., New York: Benjamin Blom, 1970), 2:46; Henry James, "New York Revisited," *Harper's Monthly Magazine*, May 1906, 900; and Stokes, 1:407, 408.

2. Stokes, 5:1532. A good image of Manhattan's pre-grid topography is found in Reuben Skye Rose-Redwood, "Re-Creating the Historical Topography of Manhattan Island," *Geographical Review* 93, no. 1 (Jan. 2003): 128, fig. 2, www.jstor.org/stable/30033893.

3. David Owen, *Green Metropolis: Why Living Smaller, Living Closer, and Driving Less Are the Keys to Sustainability* (New York: Riverhead Books, 2009), 32–34, argues that Manhattan's density is the product of an island geography and the grid-based street plan.

4. For biographical information on William Beekman, see Philip L. White, *The*

Beekmans of New York in Politics and Commerce, 1647–1877 (New York: New-York Historical Society, 1956), 53–54. A very helpful rendering of the physical features of southern Manhattan is available in Rebecca Yamin and Joseph Schuldenrein, "Landscape Archaeology in Lower Manhattan: The Collect Pond as an Evolving Cultural Landmark in Early New York City," in *Envisioning Landscape: Situations and Standpoints in Archaeology and Heritage*, ed. Dan Hicks, Laura McAtackney, and Graham Fairclough (Walnut Creek, Calif.: Left Coast Press, 2007), 82–85.

5. Yamin and Schuldenrein, "Landscape Archaeology in Lower Manhattan," 82–83, gives the Collect's waters as "reaching depths in excess of 15 metres."

6. "Affidavit in Support of Captain Rutgers' Petition," in *DRCHNY*, 5:917; and Sanderson & Brown, 562.

7. For more on African-Americans at the Collect, see Yamin and Schuldenrein, "Landscape Archaeology in Lower Manhattan," 77. On the cemeteries, see Burrows & Wallace, 133, 249, and the map on 206. Berthold Fernow, ed. *The Records of New Amsterdam from 1653 to 1674 Anno Domini*, 7 vols. (New York, 1897), 2:201 ("kiss" quotation), 5:93 ("hanged" quotation). *MCC, 1675–1776*, 1:20 (1676).

8. *DRCHNY* 2:441 (quotation). On the lack of ammunition and guns, see Burrows & Wallace, 73. Gerardus Comfort built a pump to tap into the spring near the Hudson River. Slaves trudged back and forth to the well to retrieve water for their masters. See Jill Lepore, *New York Burning: Liberty, Slavery, and Conspiracy in Eighteenth-Century Manhattan* (2005; repr., New York: Vintage, 2006), 133–36.

9. *DRCHNY*, 5:915, 916 ("standing water" and "Bushes" quotations), 917 (on cattle getting lost); and "Certain Swamp & fresh pond called the fresh water," Dec. 31, 1733, Letters Patent, ser. 12943, 11:127 ("Certain swamp"), 129 ("undrayned" and "Noysom"), NYSA.

10. Ernest H. Crosby, *The Rutgers Family of New York* (New York, 1886), 3–5.

11. Duffy, 42. Quotations are from *MCC, 1675–1776*, 4:177–78 (1733), 216–17 (1734).

12. *MCC, 1675–1776*, 4:209–10 (1734).

13. Yamin and Schuldenrein, "Landscape Archaeology in Lower Manhattan," 84, relying on eighteenth-century maps, chart the historical geography of the pond.

14. *MCC, 1675–1776*, 5:118, 119, 121 (1744). The ordinance banning tanners south of the Collect granted an exception to "Pitts in the place Commonly Called Beekman Swamp." See *MCC, 1675–1776*, 5:121 (1744). On the tanneries, the changing state of the Collect area, and yellow fever, see "The Pearl Street Tanneries," Five Points Archeology Project, http://r2.gsa.gov/fivept/mccarts.htm; Yamin and Schuldenrein, "Landscape Archaeology in Lower Manhattan," 84–85; and Gerard T. Koeppel, *Water for Gotham: A History* (Princeton, N.J.: Princeton Univ. Press, 2000), 26. While the city's elite had sought out land at higher elevations, New York's black households wound up in low-lying areas such as the Sixth Ward, which, as one historian has noted, "had never been securely reclaimed from marshes, springs, and the Collect." See Elizabeth Blackmar, *Manhattan for Rent, 1785–1850* (Ithaca, N.Y.: Cornell Univ. Press, 1989), 98, 99.

15. *MCC, 1784–1831*, 1:523 (1790), 642 (1791), 701 (1792). On the 1795 yellow fever outbreak, see Duffy, 101–4 and Burrows & Wallace, 357. The Common Council appointed a "Committee on the Subject of a Canal." It is also interesting to note

that the Common Council minutes for 1796 use the name "fresh Water Pond," but the name "Collect" is written in above it. See *MCC, 1784–1831*, 2:282 (1796).

16. Nan A. Rothschild, *New York City Neighborhoods: The 18th Century* (San Diego: Academic Press, 1990), 9; "Petition for filling up the whole or Pond of Magazine St. to the foot of Potbakers Hill," June 7, 1797, CCP, box 18, folder 516, Reports; and *MCC, 1784–1831*, 2:352, 356 (1797), quotation is from 356.

17. "[Illegible] for getting clean cool uncontaminated Water into New-York," *Commercial Advertiser* (N.Y.), Sept. 5, 1798 ("leakings" quotation); and Henry Wansey, *An Excursion to the United States of North America, in the Summer of 1794*, 2nd ed. (London, 1798), 219.

18. Sanderson & Brown, 556; "[Illegible] for getting clean cool uncontaminated Water" ("shocking hole" quotation); and *Proceedings of the Corporation of New-York, on Supplying the City with Pure and Wholesome Water: with a Memoir of Joseph Browne, M.D. on the Same Subject* (New York, 1799), 15, 17. Not much is known about Browne. See Koeppel, *Water for Gotham*, 69; and Duffy, 202–4. The 1798 yellow fever epidemic is discussed in Duffy, 105–9.

19. Browne was appointed street commissioner on Sept. 13, 1802. See Duffy, 184. His report to the Common Council is available at *MCC, 1784–1831*, 3:137, 136–39 (1802), quotation is from 137. Another report pointed out that the pond, which once reached as much as fifty feet or more in depth, was now just twelve feet deep. See "To the President and Directors of the Manhattan Company," *Commercial Advertiser*, Apr. 19, 1799. A committee appointed to evaluate a canal made a report that can be found at *MCC, 1784–1831*, 3:218–20 (1803).

20. Reclamation of the Collect would come at the expense of "a high hill" found on city-owned land, supplemented with soil excavated to build the foundation for a new city hall. See *MCC, 1784–1831*, 3:253 (1803); Issachar Cozzens Jr., *A Geological History of Manhattan or New York Island* (New York, 1843), 22n ("delight" quotation), 28n; Burrows & Wallace, 359; and "The Comptroller Report on the presentment of Peter Schermerhorn, for damages sustained in his Ropewalk," Mar. 3, 1806, CCP, box 28, folder 787, Finance.

21. Rebecca Shanor, "New York's Paper Streets: Proposals to Relieve the 1811 Gridiron Plan" (master's thesis, Columbia Univ., 1982), 51. While New York was encroaching on the sea, Europeans began to discover the virtues of coastal environments for recreational purposes. See Alain Corbin, *The Lure of the Sea: The Discovery of the Seaside in the Western World, 1750–1840*, trans. Jocelyn Phelps (Berkeley: Univ. of California Press, 1994). For a more general survey of coastal history, see John R. Gillis, *The Human Shore: Seacoasts in History* (Chicago: Univ. of Chicago Press, 2012).

22. Albion, 7–8; and Rosenwaike, 16, table 2.

23. The best introduction to these distant processes is Phil Stoffer and Paula Messina, "Geology and Geography of New York Bight Beaches," www.geo.hunter.cuny.edu /bight/index.html, especially the page titled "The Transient Atlantic Shoreline." On the change in vessel size, see Burrows & Wallace, 334.

24. This description of the port of New York is based on James Morris, *The Great Port: A Passage Through New York* (New York: Harcourt, Brace & World, 1969), 11–13; Donald F. Squires, *The Bight of the Big Apple* (Albany, N.Y.: New York Sea Grant

Institute, 1981), 31; and Burrows & Wallace, 334, who write: "The bottom-line case for New York was simple: larger cargoes could move in and out more rapidly and surely than elsewhere."

25. The most sophisticated geographic-based interpretation of New York's economic success does not mention the tidal-range issue. See Edward L. Glaeser, "Urban Colossus: Why Is New York America's Largest City?" *NYFedEPR* 11, no. 2 (Dec. 2005): 7–24. The definitive narrative history of the city does offer a brief mention of the matter in a footnote. See Burrows & Wallace, 435n–436n. Squires, *The Bight of the Big Apple*, 28, notes that "because New York did not have to contend with the high tidal ranges so often encountered in European ports, its docks were simple affairs." The mean tidal range at the Brooklyn Bridge is 4.51 feet. See "Datums for 8517847, Brooklyn Bridge NY," NOAA, last modified Oct. 15, 2013, tidesandcurrents.noaa .gov/datums.html?id=8517847. The tidal range in London on the Thames River increased significantly during the nineteenth century. For an analysis of these trends, see A. J. Bowen, "The Tidal Régime of the River Thames; Long-Term Trends and their Possible Causes," *Philosophical Transactions of the Royal Society of London, Series A, Mathematical and Physical Sciences* 272, no. 1221 (May 4, 1972): 187–99, www.jstor .org/stable/74029. In 1889 the mean tidal range at London Docks was reported to be 20.75 feet. See Lords Commissioners of the Admiralty, *North Sea Pilot: Part III, East Coast of England*, 5th ed. (London: Hydrographic Office, Admiralty, 1889), 360.

26. This discussion is based on an analysis of the grants found in CG Books D and E, NYCMA.

27. Rosenwaike, 31, table 4; for grants in 1804, see CG Book E, 81–254; for grants from 1734–1803, see CG Book B, 125–525; CG Book C, 7–593; CG Book D, 1–648; and CG Book E, 1–80, NYCMA; and Samuel Miller, "A Discourse Designed to Commemorate the Discovery of New-York by Henry Hudson," *Collections of the New-York Historical Society for the Year 1809* (1811), 1:28.

28. Isaac Weld Jr., *Travels Through the States of North America, and the Provinces of Upper and Lower Canada, During the Years 1795, 1796, and 1797*, 2 vols. (London, 1807), 1:265. "Dock Drudge" quotation is from Sidney Irving Pomerantz, *New York: An American City, 1783–1803; A Study of Urban Life*, 2nd ed. (Port Washington, N.Y.: I. J. Friedman, 1965), 271. Burling Slip quotation is from John Oothout (health commissioner) to James Kent, July 17, 1797, CCP, box 17, folder 510, Health Committee. Old Slip quotation is from "Petition and Remonstrance," June 1796, CCP, box 16, folder 487, Petitions. On the need to widen the slips to allow boats to dock, see Hartog, 120.

29. *MCC, 1784–1831*, 2:138–39 (1795), 214–15 (1796); Act of Apr. 3, 1798, ch. 80, 1798 N.Y. Laws 255 (concerning streets, wharfs, and piers in New York City), 256 ("curving" quotation); and Hartog, 120.

30. See, for example, Corporation Grant to Henry Cruger, Nov. 8, 1773, CG Book D, 417–22; and Corporation Grant to Peter Schermerhorn, Jan. 3, 1804, CG Book E, 81–83, NYCMA.

31. "Nincompoop" quotation is from Benjamin Wright to John B. Jervis, Jervis Papers, quoted in Gerard T. Koeppel, *Bond of Union: Building the Erie Canal and the American Empire* (Cambridge, Mass.: Da Capo Press, 2009), 287.

32. Marguerite Holloway, *The Measure of Manhattan: The Tumultuous Career and Sur-prising Legacy of John Randel Jr., Cartographer, Surveyor, Inventor* (New York: W. W. Norton, 2013), 20–21, 24, 30, 44, 97.

33. "Gunning" quotation is from Petition, 1811, CCP, box 44, folder 1123, Laws, Or-dinances, Resolutions. There is a brief discussion of the Zantberg in "Yes and No," *New Yorker*, May 1, 1978, 33. See also Nick Paumgarten, "The Mannahatta Project," *New Yorker*, Oct. 1, 2007, 49. Quotations are from John Randel, "City of New York, North of Canal Street, in 1808 to 1821," in *Manual of the Corporation of the City of New York* (New York, 1864), 547, 549.

34. Hilary Ballon, ed., *The Greatest Grid: The Master Plan of Manhattan, 1811–2011* (New York: Museum of the City of New York/Columbia Univ. Press, 2012), 48–55, reviews the various precedents for the Manhattan grid throughout the world. On the Goerck Plan, see Ballon, ed., *The Greatest Grid*, 22–23; and John W. Reps, *The Making of Urban America: A History of City Planning in the United States* (Princeton, N.J.: Princeton Univ. Press, 1965), 296.

35. *MCC, 1784–1831*, 2:411 (1797), 4:398 (1807), which discusses the terms of the 1797 contract for a new city map. "Metropolis of commercial world" quotation is from "Engineers Project for Making a Bason or Dock at the Fresh Water Pond," Feb. 15, 1796, CCP, box 16, folder 489, Reports.

36. The 1803 Mangin-Goerck Plan is discussed in Paul E. Cohen and Robert T. Au-gustyn, *Manhattan in Maps, 1527–1995* (New York: Rizzoli, 1997), 96–98, quota-tion from 96; and Ballon, ed., *The Greatest Grid*, 23–24, which includes a brief but very helpful essay by Koeppel. For brief biographical information on Joseph François Mangin, see Koeppel, "Joseph François Mangin," in Jackson, 785–86.

37. See Augustyn and Cohen, *Manhattan in Maps*, 97–98; "regulation, n. and adj." and "regulate, v.," *OED Online*, www.oed.com; Ballon, ed., *The Greatest Grid*, 23–24; and *MCC, 1784–1831*, 3:404 (1803).

38. *MCC, 1784–1831*, 4:368 (1807).

39. Act of Apr. 3, 1807, ch. 115, 1807 N.Y. Laws 125 (concerning improvements to streets and roads in New York City).

40. Reuben Skye Rose-Redwood, "Rationalizing the Landscape: Superimposing the Grid upon the Island of Manhattan" (master's thesis, Pennsylvania State Univ., 2002), 44; Eric Foner, *Give Me Liberty! An American History*, 2nd ed. (New York: W. W. Norton, 2009), 250–51; and Gouverneur Morris, *Notes on the United States of America* (Philadelphia, 1806), 22.

41. T. Romeyn Beck, *Eulogium on the Life and Services of Simeon de Witt . . .* (Albany, N.Y., 1835), 4, 5–6, 12 (quotations); Holloway, *The Measure of Manhattan*, 36–37; Hildegard Binder Johnson, *Order upon the Land: The U.S. Rectangular Land Survey and the Upper Mississippi Country* (New York: Oxford Univ. Press, 1976), 42; and Ballon, ed., *The Greatest Grid*, 51.

42. Ballon, ed., *The Greatest Grid*, 48.

43. Raymond Williams, *Keywords: A Vocabulary of Culture and Society*, rev. ed. (1983; repr., New York: Oxford Univ. Press, 1985), 160–61. For more on the word *im-provement*, see Carol Sheriff, *The Artificial River: The Erie Canal and the Paradox of Progress, 1817–1862* (New York: Hill and Wang, 1996), 25.

44. Simeon De Witt, *The Elements of Perspective* (Albany, N.Y., 1813), ix. See also, Rose-Redwood, "Rationalizing the Landscape," 71–72.

45. De Witt, *The Elements of Perspective*, xiv, xx, xxix. My discussion of art and nature is based on Paul E. Johnson, *Sam Patch: The Famous Jumper* (New York: Hill and Wang, 2003), 56–57.

46. Holloway, *The Measure of Manhattan*, 33, 43–48, 51–52, 84. On the landscape that Randel found, see Rose-Redwood, "Rationalizing the Landscape," 51–52. Quotations are from Randel, "City of New York, North of Canal Street," 850, 847.

47. Randel, "City of New York, North of Canal Street," 848, 849; and Act of Mar. 21, 1809, ch. 103, §§ 16, 17, 1808 N.Y. Laws 475, 480 (respecting streets in New York City). The classic work on the mill acts is Morton J. Horwitz, *The Transformation of American Law, 1780–1860* (Cambridge, Mass.: Harvard Univ. Press, 1977), 47–53.

48. On the size of the actual map, see Ballon, ed., *The Greatest Grid*, 32. New York's population in 1810 was 96,373. See Rosenwaike, 18, table 3. London's population in 1800 was roughly 861,000. See Tertius Chandler, *Four Thousand Years of Urban Growth: An Historical Census* (Lewiston, N.Y.: St. David's Univ. Press, 1987), 485.

49. "Ruthless" quotation is from Burrows & Wallace, 420. The authors continue on 421 to write that the grid "enshrined republican as well as realtor values." "Real estate logic" quotation is from Ballon, ed., *The Greatest Grid*, 39. For a critique of the interpretation of the grid as having the effect of neutralizing space and "rendering it [urban space] void of any meaning beyond the utilitarian calculation of its exchange value as commodity," see Reuben S. Rose-Redwood, "Mythologies of the Grid in the Empire City, 1811–2011," *Geographical Review* 101, no. 3 (July 2011): 398, doi:10.1111/j.1931-0846.2011.00103.x. Remaining quotations are from the remarks of the commissioners in William Bridges, *Map of the City of New-York* (New York, 1811), 24, 25, 26, 27–28.

50. For an excellent discussion of the grid as an expression of "republican simplicity," which worked to reinforce "the market as a neutral social mechanism," see Blackmar, *Manhattan for Rent*, 94–96.

51. Turpin C. Bannister, "Early Town Planning in New York State," *New York History* 24, no. 2 (Apr. 1943): 194. Edward K. Spann, "The Greatest Grid: The New York Plan of 1811," in *Two Centuries of American Planning*, ed. Daniel Schaffer (Baltimore: Johns Hopkins Univ. Press, 1988), 19–20, is dubious about the role that access to the waterfront played in the thinking of the commissioners, arguing that the grid "was intended to facilitate land development." David M. Scobey, *Empire City: The Making and Meaning of the New York City Landscape* (Philadelphia: Temple Univ. Press, 2002), 143, argues that the grid had the effect of "nullifying New York's most important topographic endowment (generalized access to water transport) and accentuating its primary disadvantage (a long, narrow landmass)." On the expansion of the city's underwater estate from Bestevar's Killitie on the Hudson River around the tip of Manhattan Island north to Corlear's Hook on the East River, see Act of Apr. 3, 1807, *supra* note 39, § 15, 129–30. Quotations are from the remarks of the commissioners in Bridges, *Map of the City of New-York*, 31.

52. "Contours" quotation is from Reps, *The Making of Urban America*, 298. See also Rem Koolhaas, *Delirious New York: A Retroactive Manifesto for Manhattan* (1978;

repr., New York: Monacelli, 1994), 20, which mentions the grid's "indifference to topography." "Spare nothing" quotation is from [Moore], *Addressed to the Proprietors of Real Estate,* 49. Hartog, 163, makes the point that people were in awe of the grid plan. On Harlem, see Rose-Redwood, "Rationalizing the Landscape," 46–48, especially the map on 47; Sanderson & Brown, 557, on the size of the wetlands near Harlem; and Ballon, ed., *The Greatest Grid,* 70. On Otterspoor, see Paumgarten, "The Mannahatta Project," 50, 52.

53. Bridges, *Map of the City of New-York,* 27–30, 37; and Jean-Christophe Agnew, "Threshold of Exchange: Speculations on the Market," *Radical History Review,* Fall 1979, no. 21: 100, 109 ("boundless" quotation). See also, "march, n.3," *OED Online,* www.oed.com. The grid's actual effects on the ground are, by one account, surprising. Two geographers have argued that "topographic variation has remained largely constant for nearly the past two centuries." See Reuben Rose-Redwood and Li Li, "From Island of Hills to Cartesian Flatland? Using GIS to Assess Topographical Change in New York City, 1819–1999," *Professional Geographer* 63, no. 3 (2011): 403, doi:10.1080/00330124.2011.574090.

54. Rosenwaike, 36, table 6, indicates that New York's population in 1860 was 813,669. On development to Forty-Second Street by the mid-1850s, see Scobey, *Empire City,* 66.

55. On the lack of records with respect to the creation of the grid, see Gerard Koeppel, "Who Were the Commissioners?" in *The Greatest Grid,* 47.

4. Adventures in Drainage

1. Rosenwaike, 18, table 3; 31, table 4. The 1821 hurricane, according to a 1963 report, "caused the highest storm surge on record in the harbor," estimated to be ten to eleven feet. See Samuel Gofseyeff and Frank L. Panuzio, "Hurricane Studies of New York Harbor," *TASCE* 128, no. 4 (Apr. 1963): 396–97; Nicholas K. Coch, "Hurricane Hazards Along the Northeastern Atlantic Coast of the United States," *Journal of Coastal Research,* special issue no. 12 (1994): 130, 136, fig. 23, www.jstor.org/stable/25735594; and "The Hurricane," *NYG,* Sept. 5, 1821.

2. The 1821 hurricane is not mentioned in Burrows & Wallace. Nor does the hurricane surface in other survey histories of the city, such as François Weil, *A History of New York,* trans. Jody Gladding (New York: Columbia Univ. Press, 2004), or George J. Lankevich, *American Metropolis: A History of New York City* (New York: New York Univ. Press, 1998). The storm does, however, receive mention in David M. Ludlum and John Rousmaniere, "Weather," in Jackson, 1389.

3. "Tremendous Gale," *EP,* Sept. 4, 1821 (all quotations); and "The Late Hurricane," *NYG,* Sept. 6, 1821.

4. On the storm surge, see Gofseyeff and Panuzio, "Hurricane Studies of New York Harbor." "The tide" and "dangerous" quotations are from "Tremendous Gale." All other quotations are from "The Hurricane," *NYG,* Sept. 5, 1821.

5. After 1821, the next major storm to strike the area around New York Harbor was the blizzard of March 1888. The next "unusually severe" *hurricane,* however, did not occur until Hurricane Donna in 1960, with the better known 1938 hurricane rated

just "severe" according to the categorization employed in the best historical hurricane study available. See Gofseyeff and Panuzio, "Hurricane Studies of New York Harbor," 397, table 1. The population of New York surpassed Mexico City in the second quarter of the nineteenth century, making it the largest city in the Western Hemisphere. See Rosenwaike, 33.

An analysis of sediments from western Long Island has concluded, "There is little evidence of intense hurricane landfalls in the region for several hundred years prior to the late 17th century A.D." There followed a period of intense storms in 1693, 1788, 1821, and 1893 (the latter a storm that was only rated as "severe" by Gofseyeff and Panuzio). See Elyse Scileppi and Jeffrey P. Donnelly, "Sedimentary Evidence of Hurricane Strikes in Western Long Island, New York," *Geochemistry, Geophysics, Geosystems* 8 (June 2007): 1, doi:10.1029/2006GC001463.

6. Johan van Veen, *Dredge, Drain, Reclaim: The Art of a Nation* (The Hague: Nijhoff, 1948), 33 (quotation). On the former life of Manhattan, see "Letters Concerning the General Health, No III," *NYG*, Oct. 19, 1805. In its "natural state," reads this report, the island had been "broken into steep hills and declivities," with "little level ground, except in the marshes." But through the expenditure of "immense labour, both now and for many years past, hills have been taken down and vallies filled, and a dead level or sluggish descent produced where Providence had kindly shaped the surface unequal enough to lead the waters rapidly away."

7. "Letters Concerning the General Health, No. VII," *American Citizen*, Oct. 31, 1805.

8. CG Book F, 100–111, 115–44, 147–62, 165–74; *MCC, 1784–1831*, 7:388–90 (1813); N.Y. State, *Journal of the Assem. of the State of New-York*, 36th Sess., at 541 (1813); and Tyler Anbinder, *Five Points: The 19th-Century New York City Neighborhood That Invented Tap Dance, Stole Elections, and Became the World's Most Notorious Slum* (2001; repr., New York: Plume, 2002), 1 (quotation), 14, 16, 19, 75.

9. Anbinder, *Five Points*, 16; and Cornelius, "For the New York Evening Post," letter to the editor, *EP*, Sept. 21, 1826.

10. Arthur James Weise, "The Swartwout Chronicles: Preface," http://swarthoutfamily .org/Genealogy/chronpref.html; and Walter Barrett, *The Old Merchants of New York City*, 5 vols. (New York: Thomas R. Knox, 1885), 4:248–51.

11. John Swartwout letter, *American Citizen and General Advertiser*, Aug. 4, 1802; "Hobuck," *New Jersey Journal* (Elizabethtown, N.J.), Aug. 3, 1802; and *NYG*, Nov. 15, 1803. On Riker shooting himself, see John Brooks, "The Meadows–I," *New Yorker*, Mar. 9, 1957, 107.

12. Barrett, *The Old Merchants of New York City*, 4:252.

13. See Sanderson & Brown, 552, table 2, which indicates a total, in 1782, of 447 hectares of fresh and saltwater marsh in Manhattan, or 1.7 square miles. On the size of the New Jersey Meadows, see the table in appendix E.

14. Brooks, "The Meadows," 104, 105, 106; and Stephen Marshall, "The Meadowlands Before the Commission: Three Centuries of Human Use and Alteration of the Newark and Hackensack Meadows," *Urban Habitats* 2 (Dec. 2004): www.urban habitats.org/v02n01/3centuries_abs.html. On the poor quality of the hay, see Robert Sullivan, *The Meadowlands: Wilderness Adventures at the Edge of a City* (New York: Scribner, 1998), 37; and *MCC, 1784–1831*, 10:519 (1819).

15. "Triumphs of Industry," *Albany (N.Y.) Advertiser*, Aug. 31, 1816. The article was reprinted from the *New-York Columbian*.

16. "Grand Canal," *Otsego Herald* (Cooperstown, N.Y.), Jan. 11, 1816; and Swartwouts to Corporation of the City of New York, July 22, 1816, CCP, box 59, folder 1414, Letters.

17. Swartwouts to Corporation of the City of New York, July 22, 1816.

18. *MCC, 1784–1831*, 10:519, 520 (1819).

19. Brooks, "The Meadows," 108; and "The Hurricane," *NYG*, Sept. 5, 1821.

20. Robert Swartwout to Samuel Swartwout, Dec. 8, 1837, RSP, box 1 ("project of reclaiming" quotation); "To the Honorable Council and General Assembly," [1835], RSP, box 2 ("frequent overflow" quotation); "Report on the Meadows," Apr. 23, 1833, RSP, box 2; and "Connecticut, Deaths and Burials Index, 1650–1934," www.ancestry.com.

21. John Pintard, *Letters from John Pintard to His Daughter, Eliza Noel Pintard Davidson*, 4 vols. (1816–33; repr., New York: New-York Historical Society, 1940–41), 2:265; and Act of Feb. 25, 1826, ch. 58, 1826 N.Y. Laws 43 (regarding improvements in New York City).

22. Sanderson & Brown, 557, describe the Stuyvesant Meadows as "[t]he largest single wetland on the island," though there were wetland complexes that were bigger. For the actual physical dimensions of the meadows, see Issachar Cozzens Jr., *A Geological History of Manhattan or New York Island* (New York, 1843), 34–35. On Manhattan Island and the two streams that crossed the Stuyvesant Meadows, see George Everett Hill and George E. Waring Jr., "Old Wells and Water-Courses of the Island of Manhattan," in *Half Moon Series: Papers on Historic New York*, ed. Maud Wilder Goodwin, Alice Carrington Royce, and Ruth Putnam, 1st ser., 2 vols. (New York: G. P. Putnam's Sons, 1897), 1:344–45.

23. Edward K. Spann, "The Greatest Grid: The New York Plan of 1811," in *Two Centuries of American Planning*, ed. Daniel Schaffer (Baltimore: Johns Hopkins Univ. Press, 1988), 25; Act of Apr. 10, 1823, ch. 128, 1823 N.Y. Laws 146 (providing for the regulation of New York City streets); and Act of Apr. 13, 1826, ch. 166, 1826 N.Y. Laws 155 (amending Act of Feb. 25, 1826, regarding New York City improvements). One estimate placed the amount of earth at 14.5 million cartloads assuming nine cubic feet per load, though this was probably an exaggeration. See *Reports and Documents Relative to the Stuyvesant Meadows, from the Year 1825 to 1831, Inclusive* (New York, 1832), 27, and 3–24, on the various plans put forth. For a discussion of the prejudice against sewers, see Duffy, 405–6.

24. *MCC, 1784–1831*, 16:394–95 (1827); and *Reports and Documents Relative to the Stuyvesant Meadows*, 42–43.

25. Kenneth Wiggins Porter, *John Jacob Astor: Business Man*, 2 vols. (Cambridge, Mass.: Harvard Univ. Press, 1931), 2:910, 919. Astor received ten water-lot grants, but three were corrected versions of previous grants, and one was an extension of a previous grant. Four of the six grants were along the Hudson. See CG Book E, 237, 256–68, 400–416, 445, 476–79; CG Book F, 35–48, 66–73, 267–72; CG Book G, 402–4, NYCMA. A nice, brief discussion of the rise of real estate can be found in Hilary Ballon, ed., *The Greatest Grid: The Master Plan of Manhattan, 1811–2011* (New York: Museum of the City of New York/Columbia Univ. Press, 2012), 87.

26. Ballon, ed., *Greatest Grid*, 103, 106; Act of May 11, 1835, ch. 268, 1835 N.Y. Laws 309 (concerning the right to alter the New York City street plan); and Lisa Keller, "Stuyvesant Square," in Jackson, 1257.

27. Cozzens, *A Geological History of Manhattan*, 34–35.

28. Edward L. Glaeser, "Urban Colossus: Why Is New York America's Largest City?" *NYFedEPR* 11, no. 2 (Dec. 2005): 7–24, which argues strenuously for the importance of geography, mentions the canal four times. On the canal's economic impact, see Burrows & Wallace, 431; and Carol Sheriff, *The Artificial River: The Erie Canal and the Paradox of Progress, 1817–1862* (New York: Hill and Wang, 1996), 95.

29. Albion, 233. Burrows & Wallace, the definitive history of the city, does not mention Gedney by name, but on 822 does note that the federal government, under the auspices of the US Coast Survey, underwrote channel explorations in New York Harbor.

30. Albion, 17–19, 23; and Charles Z. Lincoln, William H. Johnson, and A. Judd Northrup, *The Colonial Laws of New York from the Year 1664 to the Revolution*, 5 vols. (Albany, N.Y., 1894), 1:324. For more on ships encountering the shoals, see Jeannette Edwards Rattray, *Perils of the Port of New York: Maritime Disasters from Sandy Hook to Execution Rocks* (New York: Dodd, Mead, 1973), 2, 54.

31. Edmund M. Blunt, *The American Coast Pilot . . .* (New York, 1822), 208.

32. Act of Feb. 10, 1807, ch. 8, 2 Stat. 413 (providing for coastal surveys).

33. The discussion of Hassler is based on Hugh Richard Slotten, *Patronage, Practice, and the Culture of American Science: Alexander Dallas Bache and the U.S. Coast Survey* (Cambridge, UK: Cambridge Univ. Press, 1994), 43, 44; Andro Linklater, *Measuring America: How the United States Was Shaped by the Greatest Land Sale in History* (2002; repr., New York: Plume, 2003), 189, 191–92, 194; and Gerard Koeppel, "The Legacy of the Mangin-Goerck Plan," in *The Greatest Grid*, ed. Ballon, 24. "Correct Map" quotation is from *MCC, 1784–1831*, 4:238 (1806). On Hassler's activities in New York Harbor and his work with Gedney, see US Coast Survey, *Principal Documents Relating to the Survey of the Coast of the United States Since 1816* (New York, 1834), 111, 163–64, 176.

34. "Survey of the Coast," *Sailor's Magazine and Naval Journal* 8 (1835): 134–35, is one of the first reports of Gedney's discovery. Albion, 25, 233, discusses the new channel but gets the discoverer's name wrong, calling him "R. T. Gedney." "Gedney's Channel," *Morning Herald* (N.Y.), Nov. 23, 1837 ("Noah's" quotation); and "The Gedney Channel," *DNI*, Dec. 18, 1838 (remaining quotations).

35. "Service of Plate to Lieut. Gedney," *New-York Spectator*, Aug. 6, 1838; Slotten, *Patronage, Practice, and the Culture of American Science*, 53 ("Voodburys" quotation); and "The Gedney Channel," *DNI*, May 8, 1839 ("succeeded" quotation). At one point, some New York pilots disputed that Gedney discovered the channel, claiming that it had been known to them for some time as "the old north channel." See "Gedney's Channel," *Sun* (Baltimore), Sept. 6, 1838.

36. Black, 58; and Eugene P. Moehring, *Public Works and the Patterns of Urban Real Estate Growth in Manhattan, 1835–1894* (New York: Arno, 1981), 5. On Manhattan's changing topography, see Reuben Skye Rose-Redwood and Li Li, "From Island of Hills to Cartesian Flatland? Using GIS to Assess Topographical Change

in New York City, 1819–1999," *Professional Geographer* 63, no. 3 (2011): 392–405, doi:10.1080/00330124.2011.574090. Quotations are from *A Summary Historical, Geographical and Statistical View of the City of New York; Together with Some Notices of Brooklyn, Williamsburgh, &c., in Its Environs* (New York, 1836), 13.

37. Burrows & Wallace, 435; Act of Mar. 31, 1828, ch. 149, 1828 N.Y. Laws 163 (regarding improvements to West Street); and Act of Apr. 12, 1837, ch. 182, 1837 N.Y. Laws 166 (regarding an exterior street along the North or Hudson River). On the logic behind Thirteenth Avenue, see New York State Commissioners on Encroachments, *Report of Commissioners Relative to Encroachments in the Harbor of New-York*, S. 80–40, at 54 (1857). In 1857 the harbor commissioners established exterior lines, which prohibited the building of the avenue.

38. Rosenwaike, 31, table 4.

39. The "Cornbury Charter for New York City" is reproduced in Seymann, 241–47, and the quotations are from 242 and 243. The 1764 grant of land under water fronting "Nassau island" was to the merchant Philip Livingston. See CG Book C, 281–85.

40. The tensions with the British are discussed in Burrows & Wallace, 410–11. Williams's letter is available in *MCC, 1784–1831*, 4:531–39; quotations are from 532.

41. *MCC, 1784–1831*, 4:532 (quotation). In 1854, in the thick of an outcry over encroachments in New York Harbor, a letter appeared questioning whether Buttermilk Channel was once only a shallow creek, saying that the evidence was from a 1741 trial in which two elderly people, one of whom was eighty-four and another seventy-seven, testified to the channel's shallow depth. See "Encroachments on the Harbor," *NYT*, Jan. 20, 1854.

42. The eighteen grants are in CG Book F, 441–48, 451–58, 477–81, 483–90, 493–500, 508–11, 525–32, 552–53, 555–56, 558–60, 565–68, 571–74, 587–89; and Judith Berck and Cathy Alexander, "Williamsburg(h)," in Jackson, 1403.

43. On the shad and other fish at Red Hook, see Henry R. Stiles, *A History of the City of Brooklyn*, 3 vols. (Brooklyn, N.Y., 1870), 3:519n. On the naming of Roode Hoek, see Ellen Fletcher and John J. Gallagher, "Red Hook," in Jackson, 1090. Quotations are from Gabriel Furman, *Notes Geographical and Historical, Relating to the Town of Brooklyn, in Kings County on Long-Island* (Brooklyn, N.Y., 1824), 7–8. For a brief discussion of the bulldozing of the hills of Red Hook into the marshlands, see Burrows & Wallace, 582.

44. Stiles, *A History of the City of Brooklyn*, 3:578n; *Prospectus of the Atlantic Dock Company* (New York, 1840), 3, 7, which provides a list of the directors of the company and indicates that it was not unusual for a vessel to wait fifteen days before it could find a berth; "Report of the Committee on Wharves Relative to the Erection of a Great Pier in the North River," *DBA*, 3:438, 440 ("101 ships" quotation) (1837); Act of May 6, 1840, ch. 215, 1840 N.Y. Laws 164 (incorporating the Atlantic Dock Co. and "within the line" quotation); J. W. Gerard Jr., *A Treatise on the Title of the Corporation and Others to the Streets, Wharves, Piers, Parks, Ferries, and Other Lands and Franchises in the City of New York* (New York, 1872), 52, which discusses the pier line confirmed in 1839; and Act of May 26, 1841, ch. 268, 1841 N.Y. Laws 253 (amending Act of May 25, 1836, authorizing Henry Patchin and others to build structures in the East River).

45. Stiles, *A History of the City of Brooklyn*, 3:576n; and Walt Whitman, "A Letter from Brooklyn," in *The Uncollected Poetry and Prose of Walt Whitman*, ed. Emory Holloway, 2 vols. (Garden City, N.Y.: Doubleday, Page, 1921), 1:239. Whitman's letter was published in the *EP*, Mar. 21, 1851. In 1848, when Lieutenant David Porter of the navy steamed through, he called Buttermilk Channel "the deepest, most direct, and the clearest channel in the East river." Porter's report, dated Sept. 23, 1848, is extracted in New York State Commissioners on Encroachments, *Report of Commissioners Relative to Encroachments and Preservation of the Harbor of New-York*, Assem. 79–8, at 91 (1856).

46. David Bates Douglass, *Major Douglass' Report on the Drainage and Graduation of That Part of the City of Brooklyn Which Lies Over, and Adjacent to, the Gowanus Meadows* (Brooklyn, N.Y., 1847), 1; and Jasper Danckaerts, *Journal of Jasper Danckaerts, 1679–1680*, ed. Bartlett Burleigh James and J. Franklin Jameson (New York: Charles Scribner's Sons, 1913), 53. On the aboriginal people and the colonists' reliance on the salt hay, see James Lee, Patrick Harshbarger, and Richard Hunter, *Archaeological Sensitivity Study, Gowanus Canal, Brooklyn Borough, City of New York, Kings County, New York* (draft report prepared for the US Environmental Protection Agency, 2011), II-3.

47. Douglass, *Major Douglass' Report*, 3 ("200,000" quotation), 8, 9; Act of May 5, 1847, ch. 202, 1847, vol. 1, N.Y. Laws 194 (authorizing Daniel Richards and others to build structures in Gowanus Bay); Lee, Harshbarger, and Hunter, *Archaeological Sensitivity Study*, R-32–R-33; Act of Mar. 6, 1849, ch. 79, 1849 N.Y. Laws 112 (authorizing the construction of a canal in Brooklyn); and "The Gowanus Canal Improvement," *BE*, Feb. 17, 1868 ("mud" quotation).

48. Whitman, "A Letter from Brooklyn," 1:239; and Norman Foerster, "Whitman as a Poet of Nature," *PMLA* 31 (1916): 737.

49. Kathlyne Knickerbocker Viele, "Aernout Cornelisen Viele," *New York Genealogical and Biographical Record* 44, no. 3 (July 1913): 232–33; Kathlyne Knickerbocker Viele, *Viele 1659–1909: Two Hundred and Fifty Years with a Dutch Family of New York* (New York: Tobias A. Wright, 1909), 106; and "Egbert Ludovicus Viele," in *Dictionary of American Biography*, Allen Johnson et al., 20 vols. (New York: Charles Scribner's Sons, 1928–36), 19:267.

50. *Report of the Joint Comm. of the Senate and General Assem. of the State of N.J. on the Encroachments upon the Bay and Harbor of New York, with the Report of Egbert L. Viele, State Topographical Engineer* (1855), 22, 23, 24.

51. According to a law passed in 1829, the parade "shall cease to be considered as a parade." See Act of Apr. 25, 1829, ch. 269, 1829 N.Y. Laws 400 (altering the plan of New York City). On the Jones Woods, see Rosenzweig & Blackmar, 20–22, 44–45, 50–53, and 63–91, on the people who inhabited the area of Central Park before it became a park. The "original water courses" quotation is from Egbert L. Viele, *First Annual Report on the Improvement of the Central Park, New York* (1857; repr., Washington, D.C.: McGrath/National Recreation and Park Association, 1974), 13. On the events leading up to Olmsted and Vaux's winning plan, see Ian R. Stewart, "Central Park, 1851–1871: Urbanization and Environmental Planning in New York City" (PhD diss., Cornell Univ., 1973), 149–59.

52. On the physical transformation of the area, see Rosenzweig & Blackmar, 150, 164;

and Frederick Law Olmsted, *The Papers of Frederick Law Olmsted*, vol. 3, *Creating Central Park 1857–1861*, ed. Charles E. Beveridge and David Schuyler (Baltimore: Johns Hopkins Univ. Press, 1983), 214.

53. Olmsted, *The Papers of Frederick Law Olmsted*, vol. 3, *Creating Central Park 1857–1861*, 151 (quotation); Stewart, "Central Park, 1851–1871," 191–92; and Rosenzweig & Blackmar, 164–65.

54. "The Public Health," *NYH*, Nov. 3, 1865 ("water courses" quotation); and Egbert L. Viele, *The Topography and Hydrology of New York* (New York, 1865), 6, 7, 11–12.

55. Viele, *The Topography and Hydrology of New York*, 7–8, 10.

5. The Revenge of Thomas Dongan

1. Rosenwaike, 16, table 2. According to a statement made in 1854 by the scientist James Renwick, 321 acres of land had been gained from the East River and 390 acres from the North (Hudson) River. More than one thousand buildings had gone in on the made land between Whitehall Street and Corlaers (Corlear's) Hook, and another twenty-five hundred buildings between the hook and Thirty-Fifth Street. See "Statement of Professor Renwick in regard to encroachments," in New York State Senate Comm. on Commerce and Navigation, *Report of the Majority and of the Minority of the Comm. on Commerce and Navigation on the Encroachments upon the Harbor of New-York*, S. 77–49, at 27 (1854). On the difficulty of vessels seeking to turn, see New York State Commissioners on Encroachments, *Report of Commissioners Relative to Encroachments and Preservation of the Harbor of New-York*, Assem. 79–8, at 45 (1856) [hereinafter *Assem. Report on Encroachments*]. "For the Journal of Commerce," *JoC*, June 29, 1853 (quotation).

2. It was the "great value of the land in New York city" that had "induced owners, in the course of time, to fill up land under water to a considerable extent," explained the Coast Survey. See "Extracts from the Report of A. Boschke, Esq., U.S. Coast Survey, to Professor A. D. Bache, Superintendent," Feb. 1857, in N.Y. State Harbor Commissioners, *Report of the Harbor Commissioners in Relation to Gowanus Bay*, S. 80–126, at 33 (1857).

3. David Everett Wheeler, *The New York Harbor and the Improvements Necessary for Its Accommodation of Commerce, and the Removal of the Dangers at Hell Gate* (New York, 1856), 12. It is worth noting that Smith believed that the mechanism of the market needed to operate in a way that promoted the common good, lest there be a descent into moral corruption.

4. J. Smith Homans and J. Smith Homans Jr., *A Cyclopedia of Commerce and Commercial Navigation*, 2nd ed. (New York, 1859), 1434 ("natural advantages" quotation).

5. Jonathan Kuhn and Kate Lauber, "Battery Park," in Jackson, 102–3; Rosenzweig & Blackmar, 43; and "Enlargement of the Battery," *JoC*, June 6, 1851 (quotation).

6. For a discussion of the changing shape of municipal government, see Burrows & Wallace, 822–25. On the overreach by the Common Council, see *Assem. Report on Encroachments*, 35.

7. "New York Harbor," *JoC*, June 10, 1851. The article quotes Cosby's 1733 letter. The full text of Cosby's letter is in "From the Archives of British Board of Trade: Broad-

head Papers," *Municipal Gazette*, July 27, 1846, 582. On the etymological issue, see "encroachment, n.," *OED Online*, www.oed.com.

8. Quotations are from "Chamber of Commerce," *JoC*, June 16, 1851. For more on the extension of the Battery, see *Report of a Special Committee of the Chamber of Commerce of the State of New-York, on the Battery Extension*, which is reprinted in *Seventh ARCCNY, for the Year 1864–'65* (New York, 1865), 105–20.

9. "Encroachments Upon the East River: Correspondence of Walter R. Jones, Esq., President of the Board of Underwriters of the City of New York, with Major Richard Delafield, of the United States Corps of Topographical Engineers, in Relation to the Encroachments upon the East River," *JoC*, June 26, 1851. New York, relative to Boston for example, was more prone to a scouring effect from the tides, but even so, there is no question that littoral drift was responsible for the changes to the land at issue at Sandy Hook. For a discussion of tidal scour in Boston Harbor, see Michael Rawson, *Eden on the Charles: The Making of Boston* (Cambridge, Mass.: Harvard Univ. Press, 2010), 224–31.

10. *Lansing v. Smith*, 4 Wend. 9, 23, 27 (N.Y., 1829).

11. *Gould v. Hudson R. R. Co.*, 6 N.Y. 522, 543 (1852); *Furman v. Mayor, etc., of New-York*, 10 N.Y. 567 (1853); and Karl Marx and Frederick Engels, *The Communist Manifesto: A Modern Edition* (1998; repr., London: Verso, 2012), 38.

12. Thomas Carmody, *Grants of Land Under Water by State of New York, with History and Interpretation Thereof and Other Opinions as to State Water Powers* (Albany, N.Y.: J. B. Lyon, 1913), 21, 22, 24, 11.

13. New York State Commissioners on Encroachments, *Report of Commissioners Relative to Encroachments in the Harbor of New-York*, S. 80–40, at 311 ("hundreds" quotation), 264, 288 (1857) [hereinafter *S. Report on Encroachments*]. A report from the 1840s reads, "A considerable portion of the forest which once covered the water shed of the Hudson River has already disappeared and the effect of such destruction is already apparent." See [J. D. P. Ogden], Notes on Hudson Watershed, [1845], NYCCR, ser. VII.3, box 231. By this point, the Hudson River watershed had been so denuded in response to the demand for lumber that the merchant elite (fearing the result would be reduced stream flow) raised the prospect of making hundreds of thousands of acres in the Adirondacks into a preserve. On deforestation in New York, see Michael Williams, *Americans and Their Forests: A Historical Geography* (Cambridge, UK: Cambridge Univ. Press, 1989), 119, fig. 5.1.

14. *MCC, 1675–1776*, 5:141–42 (1745); *MCC, 1784–1831*, 1:301 (1787), 646–47, 651 (1791); John Eveleth to Mayor and Corporation of the City of New York, Oct. 25, 1824, CCP, box 94, folder 1913, Wharves, Piers, and Slips; Report of the Street Commissioner, Apr. 15, 1833, *DBA&A*, 2:479–80 (1833); Act of Apr. 26, 1834, ch. 186, 1834 N.Y. Laws 245; and Act of Apr. 20, 1835, ch. 122, 1835 N.Y. Laws 107 (both state acts authorizing the deepening of the waters adjacent to New York City).

15. *Assem. Report on Encroachments, supra* note 1, at 8, table; *S. Report on Encroachments, supra* note 13, at 281, and 17–18, on the low wharf rate; and "Harbor Encroachments," *NYT*, Feb. 16, 1854. See also, "From Albany," *NYT*, Feb. 25, 1854; and "Wharf Dues and Harbor Improvements," *NYT*, Mar. 2, 1854. For more on the

low wharf rate, see New York State Comm. on Commerce, *Report of the Comm. on Commerce on the Bill to Amend the Law of March 31, 1801*, S. 77–99 (1854).

16. N.Y. City Landmarks Preservation Commission, *Greenpoint Historic District Designation Report* (New York, 1982), 3; William L. Felter, *Historic Green Point: A Brief Account of the Beginning and Development of the Northerly Section of the Borough of Brooklyn, City of New York, locally known as Green Point* ([Brooklyn, N.Y.?], 1918), 13–15; Act of Apr. 10, 1849, ch. 302, 1849 N.Y. Laws 434 (authorizing Neziah Bliss and others to erect and maintain docks in Bushwick); and *Assem. Report on Encroachments, supra* note 1, at 61.

17. Notice of Henry Ruggles, *BE*, June 1, 1852; "Opinion of Charles O'Connor, US District Attorney for the Southern District of New-York, to the Attorney General of the State, in Regard to the Ruggles Grant," in New York State Senate Comm. on Commerce and Navigation, *Report of the Majority and Minority of the Comm. on Commerce and Navigation on the Encroachments upon the Harbor of New-York*, S. 77-49, at 29–39 (1854) [hereinafter *S. Comm. on Commerce and Navigation Report on Encroachments*]; and "United States Circuit Court: Injunction as to the Docks in Brooklyn," *NYT*, Sept. 13, 1853. The resolution annulling the letters patent received by Ruggles is found in Resolution of Jan. 11, 1855, 1855 N.Y. Laws 1115 (letters patent of Henry Ruggles). For brief biographical information on Ruggles, see "Death List of the Day: Henry Joseph Ruggles," *NYT*, Mar. 7, 1906.

18. Act of May 26, 1853, ch. 270, 1853 N.Y. Laws 573 (fixing a permanent line of piers in Brooklyn); and "Harbor Encroachments," *NYT*, Feb. 7, 1854.

19. "For the Journal of Commerce," *JoC*, June 29, 1853, called the May 26, 1853, act pertaining to the permanent line in Brooklyn a development of an "alarming character." Act of July 18, 1853, ch. 577, 1853 N.Y. Laws 1057 (concerning the consolidation of Brooklyn, Williamsburgh, and Bushwick); and Rosenwaike, 31, table 4.

20. "New York Harbor," *JoC*, July 16, 1853 (quotation); and "A Visit to the Harbor," *EP*, July 19, 1853.

21. Albion, 19–21; "Query—'Hell Gate?'" *Journal of the American Geographical and Statistical Society* 1, no. 2 (1859): 63; "Hell Gate vs. Hurl Gate," *EP*, July 30, 1816; "Description of Hell-Gate," *NYG*, Nov. 7, 1789; Gerard R. Wolf, "Hell Gate and Hell Gate Bridge," in Jackson, 588–89; and *Assem. Report on Encroachments, supra* note 1, at 82–84.

22. *Hurl Gate and the Proposed Canal* (New York, 1832); Act of Apr. 11, 1832, ch. 111, 1832 N.Y. Laws 172 (amending Act of Apr. 15, 1828, incorporating Hallet's Cove Rail-Way); and "Hurl Gate Rocks," *JoC*, June 17, 1851. On the papier-mâché model, see "A Very Curious and Valuable Plan of the Bottom of the East River . . ." *DNI*, June 6, 1850 ("very curious" and "two or three" quotations).

23. B. Maillefert to E. Meriam, Nov. 30, 1849, EML; Klawonn, 74–76; Extract, Washington A. Bartlett to A. D. Bache, Dec. 19, 1851, EML ("erase the rock" quotation); "Terrible Disaster at Hurlgate," *WH*, Apr. 3, 1852; Washington A. Bartlett to E. Meriam, Mar. 27, 1852, EML ("Twenty one and a half" quotation); and letter of B. Maillefert and W. Raasloff to Freeman Hunt in "The Blasting of Rocks Under Water Without Drilling," *Hunts Merchants' Magazine and Commercial Review* 27, no. 3 (Sept. 1852): 321 ("terror" quotation).

24. "Ruinous" and "permanent line" quotations are from "Encroachments on the Harbor of New York," *JoC*, July 20, 1853. This piece is signed E.M., for Ebenezer Meriam. All other quotations are from "Movements of the Chief Magistrate," *WH*, July 16, 1853.

25. The governor, according to one member of the legislature familiar with his opinions, "believes no further docking out on the east River side ought to be allowed, as it injured navigation by making the tide very rapid." A survey of the harbor, the governor felt, was in order, a move that would have revealed just how much the city had overstepped its legal authority to build out around its shores. But with the Erie Canal nearing completion and New York not, as yet, threatened by other commercial rivals, the survey was shelved. Indeed, just two years later, the state granted the city control of more underwater land. See Thomas Hyatt to Mayor of the City of New York, Feb. 18, 1824, CCP, box 94, folder 1913, Wharves, Piers, and Slips; and Act of Feb. 25, 1826, ch. 58, 1826 N.Y. Laws 43 (regarding New York City improvements). *S. Report on Encroachments, supra* note 13, at 32–33; and *S. Comm. on Commerce and Navigation Report on Encroachments, supra* note 17, at 13.

26. Frederick Clifford, *A History of Private Bill Legislation*, 2 vols. (London, 1885), 1:478. As intoned by Governor Horatio Seymour, whom the merchants had recruited to their cause: "The history of the world admonishes us that the seats of commercial prosperity have frequently been changed, and sometimes from causes similar to those which are now supposed to threaten your own great City." See "Harbor Encroachments," *WH*, Dec. 24, 1853.

27. M. R. Werner, *Tammany Hall* (Garden City, N.Y.: Doubleday, Doran, 1928), 85 (Tweed quotation); "State Affairs," *NYT*, Feb. 9, 1855; and Xavier Donald MacLeod, *Biography of Hon. Fernando Wood, Mayor of the City of New-York* (New York, 1856), 322 ("boundaries" quotation).

28. "New-York City," *NYT*, Dec. 17, 1853; and Act of Mar. 30, 1855, ch. 121, 1855 N.Y. Laws 191–92 (appointing a commission for the preservation of New York Harbor).

29. On King, see "Latest News," *Trenton (N.J.) State Gazette*, May 15, 1866; and Ernest P. Muller, "Preston King: A Political Biography" (PhD diss., Columbia Univ., 1957), 555, 740–41.

30. Hugh Richard Slotten, *Patronage, Practice, and the Culture of American Science: Alexander Dallas Bache and the U.S. Coast Survey* (Cambridge, UK: Cambridge Univ. Press, 1994), 6–9, 12, 27 ("rationalize" quotation), 80.

31. Slotten, *Patronage, Practice, and the Culture of American Science*, 90, 104–5 ("sandbars" quotation); and "Harbor Encroachments," *NYT*, Dec. 22, 1853 ("prosperity" quotation).

32. "Obituary" [Edmund Blunt], *American Journal of Science and Arts*, 2nd ser., 42, no. 126 (Nov. 1866): 433; and *Assem. Report on Encroachments, supra* note 1, at 22 (Bache quotation).

33. *Assem. Report on Encroachments, supra* note 1, at 110, 111–12, 68–69 ("depot" quotation), 71, 73 ("invasions" and "regret" quotations).

34. "Steam-Ships Sirius and Great Western: Splendid Sight from the Battery," *Jamestown (N.Y.) Journal*, May 2, 1838 ("abridge" quotation); Burrows & Wallace, 649–50; "The Great Eastern," *Tait's Edinburgh Magazine* 25 (Nov. 1858), 680 ("furlong" quotation); and *Assem. Report on Encroachments, supra* note 1, at 77 ("cannot enter"

quotation). Christened *Leviathan*, the ship's name was changed to *Great Eastern*. In 1860 the ship made it across the bar at Sandy Hook. See "Reception of the Great Eastern at New York," *NYH*, June 29, 1860; and William A. Wallace, *The Great Eastern's Log* (London, 1860), 19.

35. *Assem. Report on Encroachments*, *supra* note 1, at 77 ("second class" quotation); and "New-York Harbor: Extracts from the Report of the Superintendent of the United States Coast Survey for the Year 1857," in *ARCCNY, for the Year 1858* (New York, 1859), 191, which discusses the need for a "systematic plan" for the harbor.

36. *Assem. Report on Encroachments*, *supra* note 1, at 4, 7, 31.

37. "Harbor Encroachments," *BE*, Feb. 1, 1854; "Brooklyn Water Rights," *BE*, Feb. 15, 1854; "The Harbor Encroachment—Minority Report of Senator Hutchins," *BE*, Feb. 23, 1854 (quotation); *S. Report on Encroachments*, *supra* note 13, at 157–60; and "Exterior Line of the City," *JoC*, Nov. 15, 1856.

38. Burrows & Wallace, 835–36; and Hartog, 237–39.

39. *Assem. Report on Encroachments*, *supra* note 1, at 64; and *S. Report on Encroachments*, *supra* note 13, at 25–26, 28, 32–36 ("neglected passage" quotation, 36), 58, 97–99 ("control" quotation).

40. "Harbor Encroachments," *EP*, Mar. 31, 1857; and Act of Apr. 17, 1857, ch. 763, 1857, vol. 2, N.Y. Laws 638 (establishing bulkhead and pier lines).

41. Edward L. Glaeser, "Urban Colossus: Why Is New York America's Largest City?" *NYFedEPR* 11, no. 2 (Dec. 2005): 10.

6. The Open Loop

1. Dominique Laporte, *History of Shit*, trans. Nadia Benabid and Rodolphe el-Khoury (1978; repr., Cambridge, Mass.: MIT Press, 2000), 131 ("worker" and "every last one" quotations); and Ceri Crossley, "Pierre Leroux and the *Circulus*: Soil, Socialism and Salvation in Nineteenth-Century France," in *Histoires de la terre: earth sciences and French culture 1740–1940*, ed. Louise Lyle and David McCallam (Amsterdam: Rodopi, 2008), 107.

2. GWD, 6:66. On Washington's views on agricultural improvement, see Steven Stoll, *Larding the Lean Earth: Soil and Society in Nineteenth-Century America* (New York: Hill and Wang, 2002), 33–34.

3. Johann Heinrich von Thünen, *Von Thünen's Isolated State: An English Edition of Der Isolierte Staat*, trans. Carla M. Wartenberg, ed. Peter Hall (Oxford, UK: Pergamon, 1966), xiii, 10. Von Thünen's insight into the spatial dimension of economic life became the basis for what is called central place theory. See William Cronon, *Nature's Metropolis: Chicago and the Great West* (New York: W. W. Norton, 1991), 48–52; and Marc Linder and Lawrence S. Zacharias, *Of Cabbages and Kings County: Agriculture and the Formation of Modern Brooklyn* (Iowa City: Univ. of Iowa Press, 1999), 24–26.

4. Ezra L'Hommedieu, "Observations on Manures," *Transactions of the Society for the Promotion of Agriculture, Arts and Manufactures Instituted in the State of New-York* 1, 2nd ed. (1801), 238; and Timothy Dwight, *Travels in New England and New York*, ed. Barbara Miller Solomon, with the assistance of Patricia M. King, 4 vols. (Cambridge, Mass.: Belknap Press of Harvard Univ. Press, 1969), 3:227.

5. *MCC, 1784–1831*, 2:532–33 (1799); and Duffy, 185.

6. Duffy, 186–188; and "Hints for the Corporation or Its Officers of Police," *EP,* May 11, 1811.

7. Edward K. Spann, *The New Metropolis: New York City, 1840–1857* (New York: Columbia Univ. Press, 1981), 129 (quotation); Clay McShane and Joel A. Tarr, *The Horse in the City: Living Machines in the Nineteenth Century* (Baltimore: Johns Hopkins Univ. Press, 2007), 58–63, 26. Complicating the horse-population issue is the fact that many horses commuted into the city from New Jersey and Brooklyn, certainly by the period after 1850, meaning that the daytime and nighttime population would differ significantly. Clay McShane, email message to author, Jan. 19, 2009.

8. Brian Donahue, *The Great Meadow: Farmers and the Land in Colonial Concord* (New Haven, Conn.: Yale Univ. Press, 2004), 57; Samuel Akerly, "Agriculture of Richmond County," *Transactions of the New-York State Agricultural Society, Together with an Abstract of the Proceedings of the County Agricultural Societies, for the Year 1842* 2 (1843): 207; and "Queens," *Transactions of the New-York State Agricultural Society, with an Abstract of the Proceedings of the County Agricultural Societies* 8 (1848): 528–29.

9. Richard Wines, *Fertilizer in America: From Waste Recycling to Resource Exploitation* (Philadelphia: Temple Univ. Press, 1985), 10; and "Manure Used on Long Island," *American Agriculturalist* 20 (1861): 285 ("almost incredible" quotation).

10. Rosenwaike, 16, table 2; 63, table 19; Linder and Zacharias, *Of Cabbages and Kings County,* 47; Street Committee, "Report Relative to the Depositing of Street Manure South of Twenty-Eighth Street," Dec. 7, 1835, *DBA,* 2:234 (1835); Duffy, 360; Spann, *The New Metropolis,* 131; and Joint Special Committee, "Report . . . Relative to the New York and Albany Rail Road," July 24, 1840, *DBA,* 7:113–14 (1841).

11. *MCC, 1675–1776*, 2:103 (1700). The modern understanding of how rivers clean themselves is based on three main processes: aeration, wetland ecology, and deposition. The last is rooted in the ability of the saltwater interface to cause small particles to flocculate and settle out.

12. The petition is reproduced in Paul A. Gilje and Howard B. Rock, eds., *Keepers of the Revolution: New Yorkers at Work in the Early Republic* (Ithaca, N.Y.: Cornell Univ. Press, 1992), 219–21 (quotations from 220). See also Burrows & Wallace, 588.

13. "Night soil, n.," *OED Online,* www.oed.com; Wines, *Fertilizer in America,* 26–28; and "Manures.—No. 11," *WF* 1 (1849): 168. Entering the phrase *night soil* into Google Books, Ngram Viewer, http://books.google.com/ngrams/ shows a steep upsurge in use beginning roughly in 1790.

14. *In Common Council, February 28th, 1831: Mr. Townsend presented the following Communication from the Committee of the Lyceum of Natural History of the City of New-York, in Answer to an Enquiry from Mr. Townsend on the Source, Quality and Purity of the Water on This Island . . .* (New York, 1831), 9 ("100 tons" and "excrementitious" quotations). All other quotations are from John H. Griscom, "Communication of the City Inspector, with an Ordinance Regulating the Emptying of Sinks, Privies, and Cispools," Sept. 12, 1842, *DBA,* 9:164, 166, 167 (1843). To convert cubic feet to tons and make the 1831 and 1843 figures comparable, I converted cubic feet to cubic yards and then used the factor of 0.608 to arrive at a figure of 16,889 tons, or 19,611 tons less than the total annual excrement in 1831.

15. *In Common Council, February 28th, 1831*, 10 (emphasis in original).
16. Henry B. Livingston to Henry Remsen, Apr. 11, 1810, AHMC—Manhattan Company, New-York Historical Society, New York; Gerard T. Koeppel, *Water for Gotham: A History* (Princeton, N.J.: Princeton Univ. Press, 2000), 187, 197; and Burrows & Wallace, 625–28.
17. Peter H. Gleick, "Basic Water Requirements for Human Activities: Meeting Basic Needs," *Water International* 21, no. 2 (1996): 88; and Weidner, 58, table 3. Gleick recommended 50 liters, or 13.2 gallons. Weidner recorded a consumption figure of 40 million gallons a day in 1850, at a time when New York's population was 515,547. That works out to 77.6 gallons per person per day.
18. Koeppel, *Water for Gotham*, 120; and Joanne Abel Goldman, *Building New York's Sewers: Developing Mechanisms of Urban Management* (West Lafayette, Ind.: Purdue Univ. Press, 1997), 72.
19. Duffy, 406, 409–11, 414; Goldman, *Building New York's Sewers*, 24, 72, 92; and Metropolitan Sewerage Commission of New York, *Sewerage and Sewage Disposal in the Metropolitan District of New York and New Jersey* (New York, 1910), 228, table II.
20. Communication from the city inspector in "New-York City," *NYT*, Aug. 9, 1853.
21. "Town Sewerage," *WF* 5 (May 1, 1853), 51.
22. William H. Brock, *Justus von Liebig: The Chemical Keeper* (1997; repr., Cambridge, UK: Cambridge Univ. Press, 2002), 250–51. On Chadwick, see also Joel A. Tarr, *The Search for the Ultimate Sink: Urban Pollution in Historical Perspective* (Akron, Ohio: Univ. of Akron Press, 1996), 300. Marguerite Holloway, *The Measure of Manhattan: The Tumultuous Career and Surprising Legacy of John Randel Jr., Cartographer, Surveyor, Inventor* (New York: W. W. Norton, 2013), 287–88; and [James Jay Mapes], "Manures.—No. 20," *WF* 1 (Nov. 1, 1850), 205 (on Randel), 206 (quotation). For a biographical sketch of Mapes, see William H. Shaw, comp., *History of Essex and Hudson Counties, New Jersey,* 2 vols. (Philadelphia, 1884), 1:657–60.
23. George E. Waring Jr., *Draining for Profit, and Draining for Health* (New York, 1867), 227; and Tarr, *The Search for the Ultimate Sink,* 298, 300. See also Nicholas Goddard, "19th-Century Recycling: The Victorians and the Agricultural Utilisation of Sewage," *History Today* 31, no. 6 (June 1981): 32–36. Given the fact that the New York metropolitan area has plenty of precipitation, the sewage would have likely flooded farmland. According to one estimate, it would require an acre of land to deal with the waste of "every five hundred to one thousand people contributing sewage." See Daniel Schneider, *Hybrid Nature: Sewage Treatment and the Contradictions of the Industrial Ecosystem* (Cambridge, Mass.: MIT Press, 2011), xxv, 15. The word *sewage* dates from the 1830s. See "sewage, n.," *OED Online*, www.oed.com. One historian has argued that before the 1830s, the word "was defined as any surface runoff involving liquids. It was perceived as a source of nuisances but not particularly dangerous. . . . Although common sense led most people to suspect filthy water, 'sewage' was not defined as pollution until 1834, when a parliamentary select committee on metropolitan improvements used it to refer specifically to household cesspool discharges and street runoff." See Dale H. Porter, *The Thames Embankment: Environment, Technology, and Society in Victorian London* (Akron, Ohio: Univ. of Akron Press, 1998), 54.

24. James T. Carlton, email message to author, Mar. 22, 2009; James T. Carlton, "Molluscan Invasions in Marine and Estuarine Communities," *Malacologia* 41, no. 2 (1999): 439–454; "To the Street Commissioner, to whom had been referred the annexed Resolution . . . ," Apr. 15, 1833, *DBA&A*, 2:460 (1833); and New York State Commissioners on Encroachments, *Report of Commissioners Relative to Encroachments in the Harbor of New-York*, S. 80–40, at 255, 188, 198 (1857) [hereinafter *S. Report on Encroachments*]. There is a brief mention of the sea worm in "Report of the Committee on Wharves, Relative to the Erection of a Great Pier in the North River," Dec. 7, 1836, *DBA*, 3:423 (1837).

25. In addition to declining oxygen saturation, it is possible that the area around sewage outfalls may have undergone a decrease in salinity (from all the freshwater released) and that trend also would have compromised the shipworm. James T. Carlton, email message to author, Mar. 29, 2009.

26. Robert W. Howarth et al., "Wastewater and Watershed Influences on Primary Productivity and Oxygen Dynamics in the Lower Hudson River Estuary," in Levinton & Waldman, 122, table 10.1, 131–33; and Dennis J. Suszkowski and Christopher F. D'Elia, "The History and Science of Managing the Hudson River," in Levinton & Waldman, 315, 317. On the long-term forest history of New England, see David R. Foster, Glenn Motzkin, and Benjamin Slater, "Land-Use History as Long-Term Broad-Scale Disturbance: Regional Forest Dynamics in Central New England," *Ecosystems* 1, no. 1 (Jan.–Feb. 1998): 96–119, doi:10.1007/s100219900008.

27. David M. Scobey, *Empire City: The Making and Meaning of the New York City Landscape* (Philadelphia: Temple Univ. Press, 2002), 5. In the 1850s, New York emerged as the most advanced capital market—underwriting railroad securities—that the world had ever seen. The demand for new buildings and office space proceeded apace and so did a new, more optimistic vision of New York's future. See Burrows & Wallace, 657–59; and Iver Bernstein, *The New York City Draft Riots: Their Significance for American Society and Politics in the Age of the Civil War* (New York: Oxford Univ. Press, 1990), 199.

28. [William Martin], *The Growth of New York* (New York, 1865), 5, 45. On the larger issue of economic growth as a limitless proposition, see Steven Stoll, *The Great Delusion: A Mad Inventor, Death in the Tropics, and the Utopian Origins of Economic Growth* (New York: Hill and Wang, 2008). For biographical information on Martin, see Scobey, *Empire City*, 35.

29. [Martin], *The Growth of New York*, 19–21.

30. Richard A. Winsche, "When Nassau Supplied Brooklyn's Water," in *Nassau County: From Rural Hinterland to Suburban Metropolis*, ed. Joann P. Krieg and Natalie A. Naylor (Interlaken, N.Y.: Empire State Books, 2000), 150; and Walt Whitman, "A Plea for Water," in *The Uncollected Poetry and Prose of Walt Whitman*, ed. Emory Holloway, 2 vols. (Garden City, N.Y.: Doubleday, Page, 1921), 1:254.

31. I. M. de Varona, *History and Description of the Water Supply of the City of Brooklyn* (Brooklyn, N.Y., 1896), 145; Winsche, "When Nassau Supplied Brooklyn's Water," 150–51, 166–67, 174–75, 169–71; and Act of Feb. 11, 1857, ch. 22, 1857, vol. 1, N.Y. Laws 35 (providing Brooklyn with a water supply). See also Richardson Dilworth, *The Urban Origins of Suburban Autonomy* (Cambridge, Mass.: Harvard Univ. Press, 2005), 82–83.

32. Varona, *History and Description of the Water Supply*, 186–87, 203, 209 (quotation); Act of Feb. 18, 1871, ch. 47, 1871, vol. 1, N.Y. Laws 56 (providing for the further supply of Brooklyn with water); and Rosenwaike, 63, table 19. See also David Soll, "Watershed Moments: An Environmental History of the New York City Water Supply" (PhD diss., Brandeis Univ., 2009), 135–36. The information on per capita consumption is from Varona, *History and Description of the Water Supply*, n.p., table 9.

33. Dilworth, *The Urban Origins of Suburban Autonomy*, 82; "Reports upon the Ports and Cities of the North Atlantic Coast," app. O, in Nat'l Bd. of Health, Dep't of Treasury, *Annual Report of the Nat'l Bd. of Health*, H. Exec. Doc. No. 46–10, at 318 (2nd Sess. 1879); and "The Utilization of Sewage," *BE*, May 2, 1871.

   Joel A. Tarr, "Sewerage and the Development of the Networked City in the United States, 1850–1930," in *Technology and the Rise of the Networked City in Europe and America*, ed. Tarr and Gabriel Dupuy (Philadelphia: Temple Univ. Press, 1988), 164, argues that New York's sewers, before 1860, at least, did not constitute a "sewerage system" because they were a hodgepodge of private and public pipes. Brooklyn, Chicago, and Jersey City, however, drawing on the sanitary experiences of the English, built the first systematic sewer networks. For more on Brooklyn sewers, see Goldman, *Building New York's Sewers*, 5, 109.

34. *S. Report on Encroachments*, *supra* note 24, at 22 (quotation); Act of Apr. 16, 1857, ch. 671, 1857, vol. 2, N.Y. Laws 487 (establishing regulations for the port of New York); "Reports of Special Committees," in *Seventeenth ARCCNY, for the Year 1874–'75* (New York, 1875), 55; "Reports upon the Ports and Cities of the North Atlantic Coast," 310, table; 310 (on pier at West Thirteenth Street); and Goldman, *Building New York's Sewers*, 163.

35. Miller, 40, 41, 44.

36. "The Floating Carcasses," *BE*, Sept. 8, 1870; Act of Apr. 26, 1871, ch. 756, 1871, vol. 2, N.Y. Laws 1741 (preventing carrion, offal, and dead animals in North and East Rivers, New York or Raritan Bays); "New York's Danger," *NYH*, Aug. 21, 1879; Steven Hunt Corey, "King Garbage: A History of Solid Waste Management in New York City, 1881–1970" (PhD diss., New York Univ., 1994), 81–82; and "Garbage War," *BE*, July 23, 1880 ("not pleasant" quotation). On Barren Island in the 1870s, see Miller, 54–55.

37. *Daily Constitution* (Middletown, Conn.), June 18, 1875. In 1837 the Harlem Marsh yielded before the grid, having initially escaped the rectilinear logic of the 1811 plan. See Hilary Ballon, ed., *The Greatest Grid: The Master Plan of Manhattan, 1811–2011* (New York: Museum of the City of New York/Columbia Univ. Press, 2012), 107. On the tidelands just south of Harlem marsh and creek and their use as dumping areas, see Corey, "King Garbage," 80.

38. William R. Martin, "The Growth of New York," *RERBG*, Apr. 3, 1875 (supplement); Suellen Hoy, *Chasing Dirt: The American Pursuit of Cleanliness* (New York: Oxford Univ. Press, 1995), 61, 63–64; and Charles E. Rosenberg, *The Cholera Years: The United States in 1832, 1849 and 1866* (Chicago: Univ. of Chicago Press, 1962), 203–11.

   The emerging open-loop system did, however, offend the calculating sensibilities of New York's business class. "Is it not time some action was taken to utilize the sewage of New York City?" asked the *Real Estate Record*, the newly formed trade journal of what would come to be one of the city's signature enterprises. "The waste of valuable manure is unmistakably enormous, and this waste is more obvious in view of the fact that, within forty or fifty miles of New York, lands are to be found which, if this sewage was applied, would be of enormous value." In 1870 the Chamber of Commerce entertained the idea that sewage could be discharged and disinfected in such a way that it would become "a very valuable manure" instead of "an expense, a source of great discomfort." See Untitled editorial, *RERBG*, July 17, 1869; "A Question of Garbage," *RERBG*, Apr. 18, 1885; and "Report of Committee Number Five" in *Thirteenth ARCCNY, for the Year 1870–'71* (New York, 1871), 18.

39. Edward Hagaman Hall, *The Catskill Aqueduct and Earlier Water Supplies of the City of New York* (New York, 1917), 66n (Tiemann quotations); and Weidner, 61.

40. Scobey, *Empire City*, 207; Burrows & Wallace, 929–31; Rosenwaike, 77, table 29; and Weidner, 58, table 3. Samuel Ruggles seemed to argue that with a proper rapid transit system, there would be no limit to New York's future growth. See Samuel B. Ruggles, *The Rise and Growth of the Metropolis* (New York, 1875), 9–11. In 1875 Fernando Wood projected that all of Manhattan Island was destined for development as a metropolis. See "Fernando Wood's Remarks," *RERBG*, Apr. 3, 1875 (supplement). The *Times*, which was strongly opposed to Tammany, ran an editorial in 1870 casting doubt on the idea of endless growth and seemed to have Martin in mind when it wrote that "the general tendency after rapid growth is to a certain equilibrium." The paper concluded: "Our population *may* within the space we have named exceed the most extravagant estimates; but it is much more likely to fall considerably short of them." See "The Growth of New-York," *NYT*, Nov. 30, 1870.

7. The Exploding Metropolis

1. Serrell argued that the excavated earth could even be used to reclaim the marshlands of Queens and bring them up to grade. This "New New York" then could be divvied up according to the same rectangular logic that prevailed "north of Houston Street." See James E. Serrell, *Memorial of James Serrell, City Surveyor and Civil Engineer, of the City of New York, Asking the Action of Congress on the Proposed Change of the Eastern Boundary of the City of New York . . .* (New York, 1867), 6, 7, 9, 14. For a brief sketch of Serrell's life, see "An Older Surveyor's Funeral: James E. Serrell's Work in Manhattan Island Improvements," *NYT*, June 14, 1892. See also James E. Serrell, *Compilation of Facts Representing the Present Condition of the Sewers and Their Deposits in the City of New York* (New York, 1866).

2. "What Shall Be Done with the East River?" *EP*, Mar. 28, 1857; Alan Trachtenberg, *Brooklyn Bridge: Fact and Symbol*, 2nd ed. (Chicago: Univ. of Chicago Press, 1979), 67; David Everett Wheeler, *The New York Harbor and the Improvements Necessary for Its Accommodation of Commerce, and the Removal of the Dangers at Hell Gate* (New York, 1856), 16–19; and "Suggestions from Correspondents," *NYH*, Apr. 26, 1857.

3. "Remodelling New York City," *NYH*, Mar. 21, 1867.

4. [William Martin], *The Growth of New York* (New York, 1865), 11; and "The Building Season," *RERBG*, Mar. 21, 1865. Martin included not just Brooklyn and Wil-

liamsburg in his reckoning of population growth in the metropolis but even Jersey City. Even a reformer such as Frederick Law Olmsted agreed on the inevitability of growth, arguing in 1879 that New York must not be "confined by arbitrary political boundaries." See Frederick Law Olmsted, "The Future of New York (1879)," in *Frederick Law Olmsted: Essential Texts*, ed. Robert Twombly (New York: W. W. Norton, 2010), 118.

5.   "Necessity of Marsh Drainage," *RERBG*, Sept. 5, 1868. The paper continued: "The subject [of marsh drainage] is one of sufficient importance to demand State legislation, and liberal appropriations ought to be made for the purpose, the same as the Papal Government has done for the drainage of the Pontine marshes." The paper urged the people of Williamsburg and Hoboken, in particular, to call on their representatives to compel state action and relieve them of living "in the midst of oozing, slimy swamps, the veriest stronghold of miasmatic fevers."

6.   New Jersey, *Report of the Commissioners on the Extent and Value of Lands Under Water in the County of Hudson*, at 6 (1849) [hereinafter New Jersey, *Report of the Commissioners*]. In 1837 the New Jersey legislature empowered a company to lay claim to a thousand acres of land under water at Harsimus Cove, north of the City of Jersey (as Paulus Hook came to be called), though the project stalled because of conflicting claims to the property. See Bonnie J. McCay, *Oyster Wars and the Public Trust: Property, Law, and Ecology in New Jersey History* (Tucson: Univ. of Arizona Press, 1998), 97.

7.   On the geometry of New York Harbor and the Jersey Flats, see *Report to the Commissioners on the Preservation of New-York Harbor from Encroachment, by the Advisory Council on the Comparative Map of New-York Bay and Harbor and the Approaches*, prepared by the US Coast Survey, 1857, in *ARCCNY, for the Year 1858* (New York, 1859), 186–87.

8.   George H. Farrier, *Memorial of the Centennial Celebration of the Battle of Paulus Hook, August 19th 1879* (Jersey City, N.J., 1879), 157; Harriet Phillips Eaton, *Jersey City and Its Historic Sites* (Jersey City, N.J., 1899), 18; and Frederik Muller, *Catalogue of Books, Maps, Plates on America, and of a Remarkable Collection of Early Voyages . . .*, pt. 3 (Amsterdam, 1872), 42.

9.   Farrier, *Memorial of the Centennial Celebration of the Battle of Paulus Hook*, 32–33, 153.

10.   Farrier, *Memorial of the Centennial Celebration of the Battle of Paulus Hook*, 32, 154; and New Jersey, *Report of the Commissioners, supra* note 6, at 37, 38. In 1850 the population of Jersey City was 6,856. See US Census Office, *The Seventh Census of the United States: 1850* (Washington, D.C., 1853), 139.

11.   Peter Linebaugh, *The Magna Carta Manifesto: Liberties and Commons for All* (Berkeley: Univ. of California Press, 2008), 6; *Arnold v. Mundy*, 6 N.J.L. 1, 77, 39 (Sup. Ct. 1821); and *Gough v. Bell*, 21 N.J.L. 156, 163 (Sup. Ct. 1847).

12.   Act of Mar. 9, 1848, 1848 N.J. Laws 217 (protecting the rights of dock and pier owners); New Jersey, *Report of the Commissioners, supra* note 6, at 22; and, for all quotations, *Gough v. Bell*, 22 N.J.L. 441, 464, 493 (Sup. Ct. 1850).

13.   Act of Mar. 18, 1851, 1851 N.J. Laws 335 (authorizing landowners to build wharves).

14. *Obituary Address and Proceedings of the Bar on the Occasion of the Death of Abraham O. Zabriskie*... (Jersey City, N.J., 1874), 33, 41–42; and William Edgar Sackett, *Modern Battles of Trenton, Being a History of New Jersey's Politics and Legislation from the Year 1868 to the Year 1894* (Trenton, N.J., 1895), 68. Zabriskie was certainly no friend of the Magna Carta. In a leading case on underwater land rights, Zabriskie argued that in New Jersey, riparian rights extended to the low-water mark. The people of New Jersey had been ignoring the high-water mark for years, he said. He argued that the Jersey Associates had been at work since 1804 reclaiming mudflats and that almost half of all Jersey City was built "below the old high water mark." "I contend," he wrote, "that the common law of England on this subject, in its strictness, never has been applied in this state." See *Bell v. Gough*, 23 N.J.L. 624, 1852 N.J. Lexis 41, 50, 47 (E. & A. 1852).

15. *Bell*, 23 N.J.L. at 696. See also, Norene Napper, "Water Law—States' Rights and Riparian Rights—Riparian Jurisdiction: Ordinary and Usual v. Extraordinary," *Tennessee Law Review* 76, no. 1 (Fall 2008): 191.

16. Vincent J. Cannato, *American Passage: The History of Ellis Island* (New York: Harper-Collins, 2009), 20, 26; Act of Apr. 16, 1857, ch. 671, 1857, vol. 2, N.Y. Laws 487 (establishing regulations for the Port of New York); "New Jersey Boundary Dispute," *NYH*, Oct. 12, 1859 ("Ellis Gibbet island" quotation); and "Commercial Topics," *NYT*, Oct. 7, 1859 ("destruction" quotation). See also, "The Oyster Island Boundary Dispute," *NYH*, Oct. 26, 1859.

17. Lorett Treese, *Railroads of New Jersey: Fragments of the Past in the Garden State Landscape* (Mechanicsburg, Pa.: Stackpole Books, 2006), 50, 70–71; and *Charters of the Central R. R. Company of N.J., the American Dock and Improvement Co., and the Central Land Improvement Co.* (Newark, N.J., 1880), 13–14, 17–20, 21–22, quotation from p. 21.

18. The Jersey Central reportedly paid the state handsomely for the right to the underwater land. Earlier, Johnston and various New York colleagues formed the American Dock and Improvement Company, designed to secure underwater land from Communipaw Cove to Cavan Point. But the state saw through its efforts and appointed a commission to determine the extent of the state's rights to underwater land. See Sackett, *Modern Battles of Trenton*, 69–72; and Act of Apr. 11, 1864, ch. 391, 1864 N.J. Laws 681 (to ascertain rights to land under water in New York Bay). In New York, the Chamber of Commerce worried, as it had since the 1850s, that expansion onto underwater land would destroy the harbor by causing changes in stream flow and shoaling. See "The New York Chamber of Commerce and the American Dock and Improvement Co.," *DSG*, Mar. 21, 1864. On the Jersey Central's encroachment on New York Harbor, see *People v. Central R. Co.*, 42 N.Y. 283, 1870 N.Y. Lexis 51, 4 (1870). See also Raymond J. Baxter and Arthur G. Adams, *Railroad Ferries of the Hudson and Stories of a Deckhand* (New York: Fordham Univ. Press, 1999), 46.

19. William H. Richardson, *Jersey City: A Study of Its Beginning, Its Growth and Its Destiny* (Jersey City, N.J.: Jersey Journal, 1927), 19 ("once famed" quotation); Act of Mar. 30, 1868, ch. 248, 1868 N.J. Laws 551 (to enable the United Railroad and Canal Companies to build a Jersey City terminal); and New Jersey, *Report of the Com-*

missioners Appointed to Ascertain the Rights of the State and of Riparian Owners to the Lands Lying Under Water, at 28 ("deep" and "great measure" quotations), 14 (1865).

20. "List of Patents Issued," *Plough, the Loom, and the Anvil* 8, no. 8 (Feb. 1856): 510; "Spencer Bartholomew Driggs (1821–1883)," http://records.ancestry.com; US Census Office, 1860 manuscript schedule, New Brunswick, Middlesex County, N.J., p. 254, www .ancestry.com; Kevin W. Wright, *The Hackensack Meadowlands: Prehistory and History* (report no. 1988-039, MERI, 1988), 61–62; and Hunter Research, Grossman and Associates, and Dorothy Peteet, *Cultural Resource Investigation of Ten Sites in the Hackensack Meadowlands* (prepared for the US Army Corps of Engineers, 2006), V-47–48.

21. *Proceedings of the Second Annual Meeting of the New Jersey Mosquito Extermination Association of the State of New Jersey* (Trenton, N.J., 1915), 16; "Reclamation of New Jersey Meadows," *RERBG*, Aug. 29, 1868; "Improving the Marsh Lands," *DSG*, Aug. 26, 1867 ("docks" quotation); "Reclaiming the Meadows," *Bergen County (N.J.) Democrat*, June 12, 1868 ("reaching down" quotation); Hunter Research, Grossman and Associates, and Peteet, *Cultural Resource Investigation*, V-48; Wright, *The Hackensack Meadowlands*, 65; and "The New System of Reclaiming Lands," *Frank Leslie's Illustrated Newspaper*, Nov. 16, 1867, 136–38.

22. National Board of Health, *Annual Report* (Washington, D.C., 1879), 320. Jersey City's population in 1870 is from Campbell Gibson and Kay Jung, "Historical Census Statistics on the Foreign-Born Population of the United States: 1850 to 2000" (Population Division, Working Paper No. 81), table 23, www.census.gov/popula tion/www/documentation/twps0081/twps0081.html.

23. "Opinion of Cortlandt Parker, Esq.," in New Jersey, *Report of the Commissioners on the Extent and Value of Lands Under Water in the County of Hudson*, at 56 (1864).

24. "New Jersey Her Present and Future: An Address delivered by Hon. Cortlandt Parker before the Trenton Board of Trade, on Wednesday evening, February 9th, 1870," *Trenton (N.J.) State Gazette*, Feb. 15, 1870.

25. "Charter of the City of New York Granted in the Year 1731 by Governor John Montgomerie," in Seymann, 280; Act of Jan. 1, 1828, ch. 9, tit. 5, art. 4, § 67, 1827 N.Y. Laws 69, 81 (commissioners of land have power over the waters adjacent to New Jersey); and Act of June 28, 1834, ch. 126, 4 Stat. 708, 710, 709 (giving consent for a compact between the states of New York and New Jersey).

26. The Central Railroad Company of New Jersey and the New York and Erie Railroad went beyond the established lines. See New Jersey Riparian Commissioners, *Report*, at 1018 (1870); and *Central R. Co.*, 42 N.Y. at 283, 303. See also, McCay, *Oyster Wars and the Public Trust*, 101. George Blunt, secretary of the Board of Commissioners of Pilots, was particularly incensed by the actions of the New Jersey railroad, writing, "The great encroachment into the harbor by the New Jersey Central Railroad, amounting to over 5,000,000 square feet of surface, is an accomplished fact. It shows the spirit of the age. Money is power." See George W. Blunt, letter to the editor, *BE*, May 1, 1871.

27. Klawonn, 95–96, 76.

28. John Newton, "The Improvement of East River and Hell Gate," *PS*, Feb. 1886, 434; Klawonn, 78; and "Real Estate Market," *RERBG*, May 16, 1868. In 1872 the *RERBG* noted that "free passage of steamers of the largest draught through Hell

Gate . . . will double and treble the value of all real estate in the vicinity of the East River from Corlears Hook to Harlem Bridge." See "Real Estate and City Improvements," *RERBG*, Sept. 21, 1872.

29. David C. Hammack, *Power and Society: Greater New York at the Turn of the Century* (1982; repr., New York: Columbia Univ. Press, 1987), 189; and Andrew H. Green, "A Prophetic Glance into the Future," in John Foord, *The Life and Public Services of Andrew Haswell Green* (Garden City, N.Y.: Doubleday, Page, 1913), 284, 290. See also Burrows & Wallace, 1220–22; and Richardson Dilworth, *The Urban Origins of Suburban Autonomy* (Cambridge, Mass.: Harvard Univ. Press, 2005), 36, 56, 61.

30. "Progress of the Work at Hell Gate," *Manufacturer and Builder* 7, no. 7 (July 1875): 148.

31. William Wallace Tooker, *Indian Names of Places in the Borough of Brooklyn* (New York, 1901), 40 (quotation); Jeffrey A. Kroessler and Vincent Seyfried, "Hunter's Point," in Jackson, 631; and Letters Patent granted to Jonathan Crane and Charles Ely for land under water in Newtown Creek and East River, Newtown, Queens County, Mar. 28, 1855, bk. 31, p. 288, NYSA. For reports that mention the earlier history of Newtown Creek back in the days when there were oyster beds, see "Newtown Creek," *BE*, June 28, 1884; and "A Trip by Water," *BE*, May 20, 1893. On fish that formerly existed in the creek, see "Newtown Creek," *BE*, July 18, 1880; "Unsavory," *BE*, Aug. 24, 1881; and "The Creek," *BE*, Apr. 30, 1885.

32. Jeffrey A. Kroessler, "Building Queens: The Urbanization of New York's Largest Borough" (PhD diss., City Univ. of New York, 1991), 26, 80; Burrows & Wallace, 937; Act of May 6, 1870, ch. 719, 1870, vol. 2, N.Y. Laws 1729 (incorporating Long Island City); and Vincent F. Seyfried, *300 Years of Long Island City, 1630–1930* ([Hicksville, N.Y.?]: Edgian, 1984), 105 (quotation).

33. Seyfried, *300 Years of Long Island City*, 105–7; and Dilworth, *The Urban Origins of Suburban Autonomy*, 75. Sunswick Creek flowed through the tidal wetlands that once defined the area. Seyfried briefly charts the decline of these landforms.

Long Island City also shared with New York a history involving underwater land and the drainage problems that grew out of that practice. The idea behind Thomson's entire earth-moving scheme was to raise up the city out of the marsh and create a sufficient grade for the water to drain off through sewers, leaving the land dry enough for building purposes. See, for example, "Towns on Stilts," *NYT*, Oct. 23, 1875.

Drainage was an issue for Long Island City right from the start. Indeed, one of the very first things the new city in Queens did was to dedicate several thousand dollars to ditch digging in an effort to combat the dampness of the marshes. A new development effort that began in 1874, however, wound up defeating these earlier measures. Embankments thrown across meadows in the process of street building somehow managed to choke off the culverts built earlier in the decade. See Seyfried, *300 Years of Long Island City*, 107–8.

As the *Times* reported in 1877, "earth being thrown up across the original water courses" interfered with the land's predevelopment drainage pattern. "The costly mistake of damming up the water courses," the paper continued, "is now discovered with some mortification." Malarial conditions ensued. See "Malarial Sickness," *NYT*, Oct. 1, 1877.

34. Andrew Hurley, "Creating Ecological Wastelands: Oil Pollution in New York City, 1870–1900," *Journal of Urban History* 20, no. 3 (May 1994): 341, 343, 346; and Burrows & Wallace, 1045 (on Pratt). On the underwater land granted in Newtown Creek, see Letters Patent granted to J. Augustus Herriman, Gertrude Schoonmaker, John Barnett, Daniel T. White, Samuel S. Schieffelin, and William Cooper, June 10, 1871, bk. 42, pp. 110–15; and William H. Furman and Euglantine E. Furman, Dec. 8, 1871, bk. 42, pp. 164–65, NYSA.

35. *Nineteenth ARCCNY, for the Year 1876–'77* (New York, 1877), ix; Klawonn, 87; Seyfried, *300 Years of Long Island City*, 117; and Act of June 13, 1881, ch. 493, 1881, vol. 1, N.Y. Laws 667 (regarding pilots at Hell Gate).

36. Klawonn, 82, describes Hallett's Point Reef as being three acres in extent. Flood Rock was reckoned at roughly nine acres. See NOAA, "Hell Gate and Its Approaches," http://celebrating200years.noaa.gov/new_york_charts/ny_harbor.html. According to the Army Corps of Engineers, 21,110 feet of galleries were driven and 81,851 cubic yards of rock excavated at Flood Rock between 1878 and 1885. I compiled these figures from "East River, N.Y.," in *Analytical and Topical Index to the Reports of the Chief of Engineers . . . 1866–1879*, comp. Henry M. Robert et al. (Washington, D.C., 1881), 194; and "East River, N.Y.," in *Analytical and Topical Index: River and Harbor Improvement*, comp. Henry M. Robert, Louis Y. Schermerhorn, and Holden B. Schermerhorn, 3 vols. (Washington, D.C., 1889), 2:189. The football field figure was arrived at by converting the figure for cubic yards excavated (81,851) into cubic feet and then dividing by the area of a football field, which is 57,600 square feet, including the end zones. On Sheridan and Beecher, see "Blown Up," *Cincinnati Commercial Tribune*, Oct. 11, 1885. On the scale of the explosion relative to those in the nuclear age, see, for example, Sanderson, 85.

37. On the theory that removing rocks at Hell Gate would cause shoaling at Sandy Hook, see "The Hell Gate Improvement," *Boston Journal*, Feb. 8, 1883. A man named Sandy Gibson lived on Big Mill Rock and fished the waters. After he died in 1871, the land was sold to the federal government, which used the rock to store dynamite for its demolition project. For a brief discussion of Gibson, see Abner J. Weisman, *"Hell Gate Hill Section" of New York: A Brief Sketch of an Interesting Part of the Island of Manhattan . . .* (New York, 1965), 6.

38. "Eighteen Miles Around New York," *Harper's Weekly*, May 6, 1871, 421. On George Washington's exercise routine, see GWD, 5:506. There were earlier maps that were even more expansive in their reach. See, for example, John H. Eddy et al., *Map of the Country Thirty Miles Round the City of New York* (New York, 1828).

39. Friedrich Ratzel, *Sketches of Urban and Cultural Life in North America*, trans. Stewart A. Stehlin (1876; repr., New Brunswick, N.J.: Rutgers Univ. Press, 1988), xiii–xiv, 20n, 14–15. On his use of the word *Hudsonmündung*, see Ratzel, *Städte- und Culturbilder aus Nordamerika* (Leipzig, 1876), 18.

40. *The Harbor of New York: Its Condition, May 1873: Letter of Prof. Benjamin Pierce, Superintendent of the United States Coast Survey, to the Chamber of Commerce of New-York, with the Report of Prof. Henry Mitchell, on the Physical Survey of the Harbor* (New York, 1873), 8; *Twenty-First ARCCNY, for the Year 1878–'79* (New York, 1879), xxiii; and Letter of Committee on the Harbor and Shipping, Apr. 3, 1879,

in *Twenty-First ARCCNY*, 139 (quotation). In 1896 George Waring instituted primary separation in New York. See Steven Hunt Corey, "King Garbage: A History of Solid Waste Management in New York City, 1881–1970" (PhD diss., New York Univ., 1994), 100.

41. Burrow & Wallace, 1046, 1047, 1049–50, 1051; "sky-scraper, n," *OED Online*, www.oed.com; and "Street Cleaning Abuses," *NYH*, Mar. 7, 1881.

42. Letter of A. Foster Higgins, chairman of the Committee on the Harbor and Shipping, Chamber of Commerce, June 4, 1884, in *Twenty-Seventh ARCCNY, for the Year 1884–'85* (New York, 1885), 13 (quotation), as well as Higgins's letter of Oct. 2, 1884, on 20–22; "Reports of Standing Committees" in *Twenty-Sixth ARCCNY, for the Year 1883–'84* (New York, 1884), 146; Corey, "King Garbage," 87–88; and Letter of Oelrichs and Company et al. to Chamber of Commerce in *Twenty-Eighth ARCCNY, for the Year 1885–'86* (New York, 1886), 66–67, as well as p. xx of the Annual Review of the Chamber of Commerce. Steam-powered suction dredges were used to deepen Gedney's Channel to thirty feet between Apr. 1887 and Feb. 1891. Some 4.3 million cubic yards of material was removed. See M. Grant Gross, "Man's Effects on Estuarine Shorelines—New York Harbor, A Case Study," in *San Francisco Bay, Use and Protection: An Investigation into Man's Activities and Impacts on San Francisco Bay, Government and Private Sector Responses to Those Impacts, and Prospects for its Future Use and Protection* (sixty-first annual meeting of the Pacific Division/American Association for the Advancement of Science, held at Univ. of California, Davis, Calif., June 22–27, 1980), 10–11. On standard time and the railroads, see Michael O'Malley, *Keeping Watch: A History of American Time* (1990; repr. New York: Penguin, 1991), 67, 99–144. For more on the steamship lines and their desire for a deeper channel into New York Harbor, see Klawonn, 166–67.

43. "Reports of Standing Committees" in *Thirty-Sixth ARCCNY, for the Year 1893–'94* (New York, 1894), 66 ("crying evil" quotation). The supervisor's report for 1893 is discussed in 26 Cong. Rec. 4376 (1894). The 1888 law required dumpers to apply for permits, but did not allow for prosecution of those who dumped without a permit. In 1889 the supervisor of the harbor reported that he had overseen the disposal within the harbor of nearly three-quarters of a million cubic yards of material in just a seven-week period. That was material "equal to one of the larger buildings in this city." See *Estimate of Appropriations to Prevent Deposits in New York Harbor*, H. Exec. Doc. No. 50–69, at 2, 4, 6 (2nd Sess. 1889). See also the discussion in Congress about amending the 1888 law to allow the supervisor the resources to carry out his duty to prevent obstruction or injury to New York Harbor in 20 Cong. Rec. 1301–1302 (1889); and the resolution by the Chamber of Commerce complaining about the "lack of necessary steamers to keep a rigid espionage over the harbor and detect violations" in "Resolutions," *Thirty-Second ARCCNY, for the Year 1889–'90* (New York, 1890), 101.

Congress passed legislation amending the 1888 act in 1894. See Act of Aug. 18, 1894, ch. 299, §§ 2–3, 28 Stat. 338, 360–61 (prohibiting obstruction and deposits in New York Harbor). See also *Dumping in New York Harbor*, H. Exec. Doc. No. 53–57 (2nd Sess. 1894). "The amount of refuse matter from a great city like New York is almost inconceivable," lamented one congressman. See 26 Cong. Rec. 4376 (1894).

44. Susan Strasser, *Waste and Want: A Social History of Trash* (New York: Metropoli-

tan Books, 1999), 127; Corey, "King Garbage," 89–93; Joseph P. Viteritti, "Rikers Island," in Jackson, 1105; and Act of May 8, 1881, ch. 262, 1884 N.Y. Laws 328 (providing for the purchase of Rikers Island).

45. Andrew H. Green, *Communication from Andrew H. Green, on the Subject of a Consolidation of Areas about the City of New York Under One Government*, N.Y. State Assem. 113–71, at 15 (1890).

46. Green, *Communication from Andrew H. Green*, 14, 11, 50.

47. Population density figure is derived from Roger S. Tracy, "The Growth of Great Cities," *Century Magazine*, Nov. 1897, 79–81.

48. J. E. Rosenthal et al., "One Hundred Years of New York City's 'Urban Heat Island': Temperature Trends and Public Health Impacts" (abstract, American Geophysical Union, 2003), http://adsabs.harvard.edu/abs/2003AGUFM.U32A0030R; and Monica Peña Sastre, "The History of the Urban Heat Island Effect in New York City" (master's thesis, Columbia Univ., 2003), 76–78.

49. Tracy, "The Growth of Great Cities," 79 ("bodies of water" quotation); and "The Topography of Greater New York," *RERBG*, Nov. 20, 1897.

8. Two-Dimensional Gotham

1. James Reuel Smith, *Springs and Wells of Manhattan and the Bronx New York City at the End of the Nineteenth Century* (New York: New-York Historical Society, 1938).

2. Smith, *Springs and Wells of Manhattan*, viii–ix; and Smith, *Springs and Wells in Greek and Roman Literature* (New York: G. P. Putnam's Sons, 1922).

3. Smith, *Springs and Wells of Manhattan*, 48–50. On Riverside Park and Olmsted, see Jonathan Kuhn, "Riverside Park," in Jackson, 1109.

4. Smith, *Springs and Wells of Manhattan*, 97–98, 108.

5. Smith, *Springs and Wells of Manhattan*, xiii.

6. Thomas A. Janvier, *In Old New York* (New York: Harper & Brothers, 1894), 58; Stokes, 1:ix. Volume one of Stokes encompasses the years from 1498 to 1811. Even those who benefited directly from the grid's packaging of space evinced a concern with topography. On the eve of consolidation, the *Real Estate Record* defended Greater New York's topographic virtues relative to other cities. See "The Topography of Greater New York," *RERBG*, Nov. 20, 1897.

7. "[I]t was a common occurrence," wrote Smith, "to meet city people who had lived for years within a few blocks of a spring, who either never knew of it or had forgotten its location." See Smith, *Springs and Wells of Manhattan*, xiv. Manhattan's population in 1910 was 2,331,542. See US Census Bureau, *Population of the 100 Largest Cities and Other Urban Places in the United States: 1790 to 1990* (prepared by Campbell Gibson, 1998), www.census.gov/population/www/documentation/twps0027/twps0027.html.

8. Roughly 35 billion gallons of storage capacity were added in the 1890s to the New York water system. See Edward Hagaman Hall, *The Catskill Aqueduct and Earlier Water Supplies of the City of New York . . .* (New York, 1917), 68. Thirty-five billion gallons is equal to 107,411 acre-feet; dividing by the 2010 land area of Manhattan Island (13,636 acres) equals 7.88 feet.

9. "The Water Supply," *NYH*, Oct. 19, 1876 ("Croton River" quotation); and "The Water Famine," *NYH*, Nov. 1, 1876 (remaining quotations). I derived the figures on daily per capita water consumption from Weidner, 58, table 3 (which provides figures on total daily water consumption) and divided by population figures provided by Rosenwaike, 16, table 2, and 77, table 29. On the frontage system, see Weidner, 165; and Revell, 123.

10. "The Water Supply"; and Weidner, 63–65.

11. "Ending a Troubled Life," *NYT*, Sept. 26, 1884; "The City's Water Supply," *NYT*, Apr. 29, 1881 (quotation); and Weidner, 69, 77. For more on the New Croton Aqueduct, see David Soll, "Watershed Moments: An Environmental History of the New York City Water Supply" (PhD diss., Brandeis Univ., 2009), 25–28.

12. "Message from His Honor the Mayor," *City Record*, Feb. 1, 1888.

13. Weidner, 75, 80–82, 86–87, 89, 91, 92–93; and Rosenwaike, 63, table 19, which gives the 1870 population of New York City as 942,292 and the 1890 population as 2,515,301. For a convenient table that shows the storage capacity and years that the reservoirs went into service, see Hall, *The Catskill Aqueduct*, 68. The figures for the rise in water consumption with the start of the New Croton Aqueduct are from Merchants' Association of New York, *An Inquiry into the Conditions Relating to the Water-Supply of the City of New York* (New York, 1900), 130.

14. Weidner, 114, 129; Diane Galusha, *Liquid Assets: A History of New York City's Water System* (1999; repr., Fleischmanns, N.Y.: Purple Mountain Press, 2002), 78, 266; and "World's Biggest Reservoir New York's New Year Gift," *NYT*, Dec. 24, 1905 (Wegmann quotations). The New Croton storage capacity was nearly thirty-four billion gallons. See Hall, *The Catskill Aqueduct*, 67.

15. I. M. de Varona, *History and Description of the Water Supply of the City of Brooklyn* (Brooklyn, N.Y., 1896), table 9, 231; Act of May 27, 1898, ch. 942, 1896, vol. 1, N.Y. Laws 1025 (concerning the provision of pure water); and Burrows & Wallace, 1229.

16. Merchants' Association of New York, *An Inquiry into the Conditions Relating to the Water-Supply*, 11, indicates a daily average of 371 million gallons was consumed in 1899. The Empire State Building has a volume of 37 million cubic feet. Converting gallons into cubic feet and dividing by the volume of the Empire State Building yields the figure 1.34.

17. John R. Freeman, *Report upon New York's Water Supply with Particular Reference to the Need of Procuring Additional Sources* . . . (New York, 1900), 6. Merchants' Association of New York, *An Inquiry into the Conditions Relating to the Water-Supply*, 191, 193, indicates that the daily average total consumption per person was 117 gallons and that 23.85 gallons per capita were used for trade purposes. On skyscrapers and the American Tract Society Building, see Revell, 115; and Freeman, *Report upon New York's Water Supply*, 55. On Berlin, see "Waste Reduction in American and German Cities," app. D, in *Waste and Water in New York and Its Reduction by Meters and Inspection: A Report by James H. Fuertes* . . . (New York, 1906), 220, 58 (quotation). For toilets and cleanliness, see Suellen Hoy, *Chasing Dirt: The American Pursuit of Cleanliness* (New York: Oxford Univ. Press, 1995), 68, 92.

18. Revell, 125; Merchants' Association of New York, *An Inquiry into the Conditions Relating to the Water-Supply*, 123; "Views on the New Real Estate Association,"

RERBG, Mar. 28, 1903; "Taxpayers Want Plenty of Water," *RERBG,* Oct. 9, 1909; and "Water Metering," *RERBG,* June 17, 1911 (quotation). See also, Soll, "Watershed Moments," 180–82.

19. *Report to the Aqueduct Commissioners . . . of the Chief Engineer, Alphonse Fteley . . .* (New York, 1895), 82–83.

20. Weidner, 140–49, 157; Revell, 117–18; "Ramapo Company's Big Land Options," *NYT,* Aug. 23, 1899; Act of Mar. 10, 1901, ch. 122, 1901, vol. 1, N.Y. Laws 302 (repealing ch. 985 of the laws of 1895 on the powers of the Ramapo Water Company); Freeman, *Report upon New York's Water Supply,* 8; Hall, *The Catskill Aqueduct,* 78; Act of June 3, 1905, ch. 723, 1905, vol. 2, N.Y. Laws 2022 (establishing a state water commission); and Act of June 3, 1905, ch. 724, 1905, vol. 2, N.Y. Laws 2027 (providing for an additional pure water supply for New York City).

21. Weidner, 193. See also "Mayor Turns Sod For Big Aqueduct," *NYT,* June 21, 1907.

22. "Coming from Washington," *NYT,* Apr. 29, 1889; "Honored by the Nation," *NYT,* Apr. 30, 1889; "Old Skippers at the Oar," *Philadelphia Inquirer,* Apr. 8, 1889; and "Water Carnival," *Boston Evening Journal,* Apr. 30, 1889. The weather at Harrison's inauguration is from Inauguration of President Benjamin Harrison, 1889, http:// inaugural.senate.gov/history/chronology/bharrison1889.cfm.

23. On the effects of low dissolved-oxygen levels on fish and invertebrates, see D. W. Crawford et al., "Historical Changes in the Ecological Health of Newark Bay Estuary, New Jersey," *Ecotoxicology and Environmental Safety* 29, no. 3 (Dec. 1994): 287–88, doi:10.1016/0147-6513(94)90004-3; and L. A. Levin et al., "Effects of Natural and Human-Induced Hypoxia on Coastal Benthos," *Biogeosciences Discussions* 6, no. 10 (2009): 2063–98, doi:10.5194/bg-6-2063-2009. I surmise that the waters around Manhattan were experiencing declining oxygen levels because of the disappearance of the sea worm. See chapter 6.

24. Norman F. Brydon, *The Passaic River: Past, Present, Future* (New Brunswick, N.J.: Rutgers Univ. Press, 1974), 109, 111; Crawford et al., "Historical Changes in the Ecological Health of Newark Bay Estuary," 280; and Stuart Galishoff, "The Passaic Valley Trunk Sewer," *New Jersey History,* 88, no. 4 (Winter 1970): 197.

25. Timothy J. Iannuzzi et al., *A Common Tragedy: History of an Urban River* (Amherst, Mass.: Amherst Scientific, 2002), 71; Brydon, *The Passaic River,* 111; Albert R. Leeds, "Water Supply of the State of New Jersey," *Journal of the Franklin Institute,* 3rd ser., 105 (Apr. 1878): 241–43, on the conditions that caused fish kills; Galishoff, "The Passaic Valley Trunk Sewer," 200–1; and Albert R. Leeds, "The Monstrous Pollution of the Water Supply of Jersey City and Newark," *Journal of the American Chemical Society* 9, no. 5 (May 1887): 87, 95. In 1890 Newark had the highest death rate in a class of twenty-eight cities of over one hundred thousand. See Galishoff, "The Passaic Valley Trunk Sewer," 202–3. On the abandonment of the Passaic by Newark and Jersey City as of 1892, see George W. Rafter and M. N. Baker, *Sewage Disposal in the United States* (New York, 1894), 58. On the fact that only those fish robust enough to tolerate the degraded conditions lived in the Passaic, see Iannuzzi et al., *A Common Tragedy,* 99.

26. Galishoff, "The Passaic Valley Trunk Sewer," 204, 206. The formation of the state commission to investigate the pollution of the Passaic is discussed in MSC, *Sew-*

erage and Sewage Disposal in the Metropolitan District of New York and New Jersey (New York, 1910), 326.

27. Transcript of Record, *New York v. New Jersey*, US Supreme Court, Oct. term, 1916, 4:2968 (available at the Jersey City Free Public Library, Jersey City, N.J.).

28. *New York v. New Jersey*, 256 U.S. 296, 309–10 (1921); and Refuse Act, ch. 425, § 13, 30 Stat. 1152 (1899). Nothing in the historical record explains the exemption for liquid material. See Jamie Benidickson, *The Culture of Flushing: A Social and Legal History of Sewage* (Vancouver: UBC Press, 2007), 50–51. Completed in 1924, the Passaic district's sewer brought about a brief renaissance along the Passaic River, even enticing a yacht club to open. See Brydon, *The Passaic River*, 172.

29. Transcript of Record, *New York v. New Jersey*, 4:2964 ("remember" quotation); and Clive G. Jones, John H. Lawton, and Moshe Shachak, "Organisms as Ecosystem Engineers," *Oikos* 69 (Apr. 1994): 373–86. The sewage discharge in 1910 was 741 million gallons per day. See Dennis J. Suszkowski, "Sewage Pollution in New York Harbor: A Historical Perspective" (master's thesis, State Univ. of New York at Stony Brook, 1973), 7–9. Suszkowski also has a good brief history of the various commissions appointed beginning in 1903 to look into the pollution of New York Harbor on 54–55.

30. On the declining oxygen saturation beginning in 1909, see Suszkowski, "Sewage Pollution in New York Harbor," 19.

31. Transcript of Record, *New York v. New Jersey*, 1:207–8 (quotation); and Charles F. Breitzke, "An Investigation of the Sanitary Condition of the Gowanus Canal, Brooklyn, New York," *Technology Quarterly and Proceedings of the Society of Arts* 21 (Sept. 1908): 250. One report observed: "Fish have not been caught in the canal for many years." See "Investigations Made by Charles F. Breitzke in 1906 of the Sanitary Condition of Gowanus Canal," in MSC, *Digest of Data Collected Before the Year 1908, Relating to the Sanitary Condition of New York Harbor* (New York, 1909), 62. On the 0 percent dissolved-oxygen reading in part of the Gowanus Canal, see Breitzke, "An Investigation of the Sanitary Condition of the Gowanus Canal," 258, table. See also, *Report of the New York Bay Pollution Commission to Hon. Frank Wayland Higgins* . . . (Albany, N.Y., 1906), 31.

32. MSC, *Sewerage and Sewage Disposal*, 413, table III, 220, 54.

33. Transcript of Record, *New York v. New Jersey*, 1:249, 250 (Townsend quotation); and William T. Hornaday, "The Wild Animals of Hudson's Day," *Zoological Society Bulletin* 35 (Sept. 1909): 519–20. On the sea horse, see "*Hippocampus hudsonius*, Dekay, 1842," World Register of Marine Species, last modified Feb. 28, 2008, www.marinespecies.org/aphia.php?p=taxdetails&id=306796. By 1917, the New York Aquarium had gone so far as to put oysters—at one point one of the most prolific species in the region—on display. See *Guide to the Nature Treasures of New York City* . . . , prepared by George N. Pindar with the assistance of Mabel H. Pearson and G. Clyde Fisher (New York, 1917), 138. A 1901 report on the aquarium concluded that "the fishes of the neighboring waters are well represented." See Charles L. Bristol, "The New York Aquarium," *PS*, Feb. 1901, 412.

34. Kathleen Eagen Johnson, *The Hudson-Fulton Celebration: New York's River Festival of 1909 and the Making of a Metropolis* (New York: Fordham Univ. Press, 2009); and

"Address by George Frederick Kunz, Ph.D., Sc.D.," *Fifteenth Annual Report, 1910, of the American Scenic and Historic Preservation Society* (Albany, N.Y., 1910), 439.

35. Sigmund Freud, *The Standard Edition of the Complete Psychological Works of Sigmund Freud*, trans. and ed. James Strachey et al., 24 vols. (London: Hogarth Press/Institute of Psycho-Analysis, 1953–74), 9:174. "It is probable that there is no other city in the world within whose crowded districts so much sewage is discharged," read a report by (among others) George Soper, famous for discovering Typhoid Mary. See MSC, *Main Drainage and Sewage Disposal Works Proposed for New York City . . .* (New York, 1914), 643.

36. Not until 1931 did New York City come up with a plan for financing the reform of the sewerage system based on some of the recommendations made by the MSC in 1914. See Dennis J. Suszkowski and Christopher F. D'Elia, "The History and Science of Managing the Hudson River," in Levinton & Waldman, 320. Six sewage treatment plants were in operation by 1898. See R. Lawrence Swanson et al., "Science, Policy and the Management of Sewage Materials: The New York City Experience," *MPB* 49, nos. 9–10 (Nov. 2004): 680, doi:10.1016/j.marpolbul.2004.06.025. The Gowanus flushing tunnel, built between 1905 and 1911, was 6,280 feet long and included a four-hundred-horsepower pump. See "Gowanus Canal, Narrative History for Historic American Engineering Record Documentation," app. B, in James Lee, Patrick Harshbarger, and Richard Hunter, *Archaeological Sensitivity Study, Gowanus Canal, Brooklyn Borough, City of New York, Kings County, New York* (draft report prepared for the US Environmental Protection Agency, 2011), R-38.

37. The scientific names for the oyster and menhaden at issue here are, respectively, *Crassostrea virginica* and *Brevoortia tyrannus*. "When actively feeding, an average three-inch oyster will consume 10 to 20 thousand cells of phytoplankton daily. In order to fulfill its food requirement, oysters will siphon 10 to 100 gallons of seawater daily. In fact, some oysters will siphon 10 gallons an hour for short periods." See Timothy Visel, "Life History of the American or Eastern Oyster, *Crassostrea Virginica*," *Aquaculture Center News* (published by Sound School Regional Vocational Aquaculture Center, New Haven, Conn., n.d.), 2. Sara Gottlieb notes that menhaden can filter 15.2 liters (four gallons) of water a minute. See Sara Jean Gottlieb, "Ecological Role of Atlantic Menhaden (*Brevoortia tyrannus*) in Chesapeake Bay and Implications for Management of the Fishery" (master's thesis, Univ. of Maryland, College Park, 1998), 3. The "ocean's kidneys" quotation is from W. Jeffrey Bolster, *The Mortal Sea: Fishing the Atlantic in the Age of Sail* (Cambridge, Mass.: Belknap Press of Harvard Univ. Press, 2012), 127. Bolster was referring to menhaden when he made the kidney analogy, though he notes that oysters and menhaden "serve the same function," with oysters working on the bottom of the harbor and menhaden in the water column. For a study that argues that overharvesting of oyster populations may have contributed to anoxia, see Roger I. E. Newell, "Ecological Changes in Chesapeake Bay: Are They the Result of Overharvesting the American Oyster, *Crassostrea virginica*?" in *Understanding the Estuary: Advances in Chesapeake Bay Research; Proceedings of a Conference* (1988): 536–46. It is estimated that oysters could have filtered the waters of Chesapeake Bay every three days. See Jeremy B. Jackson et al., "Historical Overfishing and the Recent Collapse of Coastal Ecosystems," *Science* 293, no. 5530 (July 27, 2001): 634, doi:10.1126/science.1059199.

38. William Livingston et al., *The Independent Reflector Or Weekly Essays on Sundry Important Subjects More Particularly Adapted to the Province of New-York*, ed. Milton M. Klein (Cambridge, Mass.: Belknap Press of Harvard Univ. Press, 1963), 436; and Pehr Kalm, *The America of 1750: Peter Kalm's Travels in North America . . .*, ed. Adolph B. Benson, 2 vols. (1937; repr., New York: Dover Publications, 1966), 1:126.

39. "Ordinance of the Director General and Council of New Netherland Against cutting Sods or Dredging Oyster Shells on Manhattan Island . . . ," Apr. 11, 1658, in *Laws and Ordinances of New Netherland, 1638–1674*, comp. and trans. E. B. O'Callaghan (Albany, N.Y., 1868), 347; "An Act for Preserving of Oysters," 16th assembly, 1st sess. (1715), ch. 290, in *The Colonial Laws of New York from the Year 1664 to the Revolution . . .* 5 vols. (Albany, N.Y., 1894), 1:845; and "An Act for the Better Preservation of Oysters," 20th assembly, 3rd sess. (1730), ch. 552, in *The Colonial Laws of New York*, 2:655–56 (emphasis added). On the decline of the natural oyster beds by the early nineteenth century and the rise of oyster planting, see Ernest Ingersoll, *The Oyster-Industry* (Washington, D.C., 1881), 112; and William V. Askins, "Sandy Ground: Historical Archaeology of Class and Ethnicity in a Nineteenth Century Community on Staten Island" (PhD diss., City Univ. of New York, 1988), 93–95. For more on oyster planting, see Bonnie J. McCay, *Oyster Wars and the Public Trust: Property, Law, and Ecology in New Jersey History* (Tucson: Univ. of Arizona Press, 1998), 10–11.

40. Askins, "Sandy Ground," 95, 58–59, 52, 98–99, 111; Mark Kurlansky, *The Big Oyster: History on the Half Shell* (2006; repr., New York: Random House, 2007), 125, 214; and "Our New York Letter: All About Oysters . . ." *Troy (N.Y.) Weekly Times*, Feb. 27, 1869.

41. Askins, "Sandy Ground," 101–3; Clyde L. MacKenzie Jr. et al., eds., *The History, Present Condition, and Future of the Molluscan Fisheries of North and Central America and Europe*, NOAA Technical Reports National Marine Fisheries Service 127, 3 vols. (1997), 1:3, 114; McCay, *Oyster Wars*, 156; and Kurlansky, *The Big Oyster*, 256.

42. "Join to Resist Oyster Trust," *Pawtucket (R.I.) Times*, Aug. 9, 1905 ("oyster trust" and "under the law" quotations); Act of June 16, 1887, ch. 584, 1887 N.Y. Laws 797 (protecting shellfish cultivation in the state of New York); and Act of Apr. 7, 1893, ch. 321, 1893, vol. 1, N.Y. Laws 617 (amending the game law regarding shellfish cultivation). In the late nineteenth century, the Chamber of Commerce succeeded in lobbying Congress to pass legislation making it unlawful "to engage in fishing or dredging for shell fish in any of the channels leading to and from the harbor of New York." See Act of Aug. 18, 1894, ch. 299, § 2, 28 Stat. 360 (prohibiting fishing and dredging for shellfish in channels of New York Harbor). See also, "Resolutions," in *Thirty-Seventh ARCCNY, for the Year 1894–'95* (New York, 1895), 17.

43. On bans relating to steam-powered dredging, see, for example, Act of May 21, 1878, ch. 302, § 2, 1878 N.Y. Laws 391 (prohibiting the use of steam power for shellfish dredging); Act of May 5, 1892, ch. 488, § 191, 1892, vol. 1, N.Y. Laws 999 (also prohibiting dredging for shellfish with steam power); and Act of Feb. 19, 1900, ch. 20, § 125, 1900, vol. 1, N.Y. Laws 47 (prohibiting steam-powered dredging on natural-growth beds).

44. Askins, "Sandy Ground," 117; Joel A. Tarr, *The Search for the Ultimate Sink: Urban Pollution in Historical Perspective* (Akron, Ohio: Univ. of Akron Press, 1996), 55; and

Andrew Hurley, "Creating Ecological Wastelands: Oil Pollution in New York City, 1870–1900," *Journal of Urban History* 20 (May 1994): 355–56.

45. Clyde L. MacKenzie Jr., "A History of Oystering in Raritan Bay, with Environmental Observations," in *Raritan Bay: Its Multiple Uses and Abuses: Proceedings of the Walford Memorial Convocation*, Sandy Hook Laboratory Technical Series, report no. 30, 1984, 58, 61, fig. 15; Klawonn, 166, 170; "Report of the Committee on the Harbor and Shipping," Jan. 31, 1898, in *Fortieth ARCCNY, for the Year 1897–'98* (New York, 1898), 87; and Elliott B. Nixon, "John W(olfe) Ambrose," in Jackson, 25. The extensive dredging may have increased the tidal range in New York Harbor. See M. Grant Gross, "Man's Effects on Estuarine Shorelines—New York Harbor, A Case Study," in *San Francisco Bay, Use and Protection: An Investigation into Man's Activities and Impacts on San Francisco Bay, Government and Private Sector Responses to Those Impacts, and Prospects for its Future Use and Protection* (sixty-first annual meeting of the Pacific Division/American Association for the Advancement of Science held at University of California, Davis, Calif., June 22–27, 1980), 11.

46. "Ate 228 Oysters in Half An Hour," *New York American*, Mar. 10, 1898; and N.Y. State Conservation Commission, "In the Matter of the Decline of the Oyster Industry," in *Department Reports of the State of New York . . .* , 78 vols. (1920), 22:176.

47. For a clear discussion of eutrophication, see Callum Roberts, *The Unnatural History of the Sea* (Washington, D.C.: Island Press/Shearwater Books, 2007), 221–22. A more technical treatment of the effects of hypoxia can be found in Raquel Vaquer-Sunyer and Carlos M. Duarte, "Thresholds of Hypoxia for Marine Biodiversity," *PNAS* 105, no. 40 (2008): 15452–57, doi:10.1073/pnas.0803833105.

48. H. Bruce Franklin, *The Most Important Fish in the Sea: Menhaden and America* (Washington, D.C.: Island Press/Shearwater Books, 2007), 6, 58; Frederick R. Black, *Jamaica Bay: A History; Gateway National Recreation Area New York-New Jersey* (Historic Resource Study prepared for the National Park Service, Cultural Resource Management Study No. 3, 1981), 17, 28; and Miller, 85 (quotation).

49. Black, *Jamaica Bay*, 30–31; Franklin, *The Most Important Fish in the Sea*, 6, 105; and "Reviving the Glories of Jamaica Bay," *BE*, Apr. 17, 1890.

50. Ezra L'Hommedieu, "Observations on Manures," *Transactions of the Society for the Promotion of Agriculture, Arts and Manufactures Instituted in the State of New-York* 1, 2nd ed. (1801), 231; Ralph H. Gabriel, "Geographic Influences in the Development of the Menhaden Fishery on the Eastern Coast of the United States," *Geographical Review* 10, no. 2 (Aug. 1920): 92, www.jstor.org/stable/207707; Bolster, *The Mortal Sea*, 118, 172–73, 148, 175, 146–47; Act of Feb. 24, 1865, ch. 313, 1865 Me. Laws 283 (protecting menhaden on the Maine coast); and G. Brown Goode, *A History of the Menhaden . . .* (New York, 1880), 110 ("unutilized" quotation).

51. Bolster, *The Mortal Sea*, 179; Franklin, *The Most Important Fish in the Sea*, 104; "Menhaden Fisheries," *New Haven (Conn.) Register*, Sept. 11, 1882; and *Protecting fisheries on the Atlantic coast*, S. Rep. No. 48–706, at 258, 116 ("one hundred acres" quotation), 227 ("Government only" quotation) (1st Sess. 1884). On the depletion of menhaden from inshore waters, see also Gabriel, "Geographic Influences in the Development of the Menhaden Fishery," 95.

52. *Protecting fisheries on the Atlantic coast*, 80, 81 (Brown quotations); "The Menhaden

Fisheries," *Trenton (N.J.) State Gazette*, Sept. 7, 1882; and Franklin, *The Most Important Fish in the Sea*, 100. The only exception to the lack of regulation was in the waters to the north of Cape Cod. See also, Bolster, *The Mortal Sea*, 178–82.

53. Act of June 9, 1888, ch. 547, 1888 N.Y. Laws 901 (protecting fish in Richmond County waters); Act of May 5, 1892, ch. 488, § 138, 1892, vol. 1, N.Y. Laws 995 (regulating fishing nets); Franklin, *The Most Important Fish in the Sea*, 110; "To Lay Off Menhaden Steamers," *NYT*, July 29, 1899; Bolster, *The Mortal Sea*, 219–20; Gabriel, "Geographic Influences in the Development of the Menhaden Fishery," 99; and Black, *Jamaica Bay*, 32. By early in the twentieth century, a report on the Atlantic Coast menhaden fishery noted that factories "should be within a few hours' run of the fishing grounds," underscoring how the fish had fled inshore waters. See Rob Leon Greer, *The Menhaden Industry of the Atlantic Coast*, Bureau of Fisheries, Doc. No. 811 (Washington, D.C., 1915), 6.

54. MSC, *Main Drainage and Sewage Disposal*, 182.

55. MSC, *Main Drainage and Sewage Disposal*, 643 (quotation). It is important to note that there was eutrophication of the coastal waters of the Mississippi River Bight and Chesapeake Bay in the nineteenth century. See, for example, James E. Cloern, "Our Evolving Conceptual Model of the Coastal Eutrophication Problem," *Marine Ecology Progress Series* 210 (Jan. 2001): 233, fig. 14, and 235, fig. 16, doi:10.3354/meps210223. For the timing of eutrophication during the twentieth century in different places around the world, see Donald F. Boesch, "Challenges and Opportunities for Science in Reducing Nutrient Over-Enrichment of Coastal Ecosystems," *Estuaries and Coasts* 25, no. 4 (2002): 889, table 1, and 890, fig. 2, doi:10.1007/BF02804914.

56. MSC, *Main Drainage and Sewage Disposal*, 378, 375, table LXI, 376 ("Berlin farms" quotation), 366. On sewage farms in the United States, see Tarr, *The Search for the Ultimate Sink*, 293–308.

57. "In the important field of sanitary engineering," the engineer Alfred Flinn declared in 1913, "New York must confess to being laggard, at least in so far as the disposal of its sewage is concerned." See Alfred D. Flinn, "Engineering Achievements and Activities of New York City," *TASCE* 76 (1913): 1775; and MSC, *Main Drainage and Sewage Disposal*, 384 ("primary question" quotation). By the early twentieth century, US and British engineers "were in agreement that sewage was a nuisance that should be disposed of by any means, regardless of the potential to profit from its fertilizing power." The development of the activated sludge process for the biological treatment of sewage in 1914 allowed cities to grow much bigger without the worry of having to dispose of tons of waste material on the land or completely and utterly fouling the local waters. See Daniel Schneider, *Hybrid Nature: Sewage Treatment and the Contradictions of the Industrial Ecosystem* (Cambridge, Mass.: MIT Press, 2011), 140, xxvii, 15–16.

58. Wilbur N. Torpey, "Response to Pollution of New York Harbor and Thames Estuary," *Journal* (Water Pollution Control Federation) 39, no. 11 (Nov. 1967): 1799–1800, www.jstor.org/stable/25035857.

59. Gerard T. Koeppel, *Water for Gotham: A History* (Princeton, N.J.: Princeton Univ. Press, 2000), 289; Weidner, 256–57; and Galusha, *Liquid Assets*, 270, on the number

of people and communities displaced in building the Ashokan Reservoir. A report from a local paper captured the full impact of the dislocation. "People who knew every foot of the section find themselves compelled to ask which way out, when they get toward Brown Station and the Olive City side, owing to the clearing and houses gone, which makes a complete change of scenery." See "Many Ashokan Changes," *Kingston (N.Y.) Daily Freeman*, May 20, 1913.

Meeting, Jan. 20, 1913, *Bulletin of the American Institute of Mining Engineers*, no. 74 (1913): xvii, notes that since the start of construction on the Catskill Aqueduct in 1906, the number of fatalities amounted to 237. It was another four years (1917) before the aqueduct went into service. Galusha, *Liquid Assets*, 272, indicates that 283 lives were lost building the aqueduct. Although the official number of deaths at Hoover Dam was 96, the Bureau of Reclamation has calculated, despite the lack of completely clear evidence, a total of 213 fatalities over the course of the project. See US Department of the Interior, Bureau of Reclamation, "Fatalities at Hoover Dam," www.usbr.gov/lc/hooverdam/History/essays/fatal.html.

60. Hall, *The Catskill Aqueduct*, 5, 6 (McClellan quotation); Tarr, *The Search for the Ultimate Sink*, 59; Joel A. Tarr and Robert U. Ayres, "The Hudson-Raritan Basin," in *The Earth as Transformed by Human Action: Global and Regional Changes in the Biosphere over the Past 300 Years*, ed. B. L. Turner (Cambridge, UK: Cambridge Univ. Press, 1990), 631, table 38-1b; and Weidner, 284. In the period from 1891 to 1895 water consumption increased by 73 million gallons, an increase of 14.6 million gallons per year. See Weidner, 84.

61. Revell, 137; and Crawford et al., "Historical Changes in the Ecological Health of Newark Bay Estuary," 295.

62. Torpey, "Response to Pollution of New York Harbor," 1800; David R. Franz, "An Historical Perspective on Molluscs in Lower New York Harbor, with Emphasis on Oysters," in *Ecological Stress and the New York Bight: Science and Management*, ed. Garry F. Mayer (Columbia, S.C.: Estuarine Research Federation, 1982), 187, 188, table 3; Tarr, *The Search for the Ultimate Sink*, 59 ("enough oxygen" quotation, which is originally from an Army Corps of Engineers report at the National Archives and Records Administration that I was unable to find and verify); and Ann S. Loop, *History and Development of Sewage Treatment in New York City* (New York: City of New York Department of Health, 1964), 45. In 1910 there were only seven sewage treatment plants operating in New York City; they were rudimentary facilities that treated just nineteen million gallons per day. See Suszkowski, "Sewage Pollution in New York Harbor," 11. For more on declining oxygen saturations during the 1920s, see Harold M. Lewis, *Physical Conditions and Public Services* (New York: Regional Plan of New York and Its Environs, 1929), 55, which documents the dramatic decline of the Harlem River and the lower part of the East River.

63. Torpey, "Response to Pollution of New York Harbor," 1806–7. For more on the Hudson River shad fishery, see Stephen C. Esser, "Long-Term Changes in Some Finfishes of the Hudson-Raritan Estuary," in *Ecological Stress and the New York Bight*, ed. Mayer, 302–6; and Karin E. Limburg et al., "Fisheries of the Hudson River Estuary," in Levinton & Waldman, 195–96.

64. Franz, "An Historical Perspective on Molluscs," 183, table 1, 183–84; Gottlieb,

"Ecological Role of Atlantic Menhaden," 1; and Clyde L. Mackenzie Jr., *The Fisheries of Raritan Bay* (New Brunswick, N.J.: Rutgers Univ. Press, 1992), 32.

65. Jeremy B. C. Jackson and Enric Sala, "Unnatural Oceans," *Scientia Marina* 65, no. S2 (2001): 277, 279, doi:10.3989/scimar.2001.65s2273.

66. Edward K. Spann, "The Greatest Grid: The New York Plan of 1811," in *Two Centuries of American Planning*, ed. Daniel Schaffer (Baltimore: Johns Hopkins Univ. Press, 1988), 34.

9. The Road to Hermitville

1. Ecologists began using the word *wetland* instead of the "value-laden" term *swamp* in the 1950s. See Ann Vileisis, *Discovering the Unknown Landscape: A History of America's Wetlands* (Washington, D.C.: Island Press, 1997), 7. The 300-square-mile figure is from E. Porter Felt, "New York State's Part in Mosquito Extermination," in *Proceedings of the First General Convention to Consider the Questions Involved in Mosquito Extermination* (Brooklyn, N.Y., 1904), 52. A geologist reported that even as late as 1924, "the enormous tidal wetland systems in the eastern Bronx, Staten Island and Jamaica Bay were largely intact." See Daniel C. Walsh, "Reconnaissance Mapping of Landfills in New York City" (paper available from the National Ground Water Association, n.d.), 394, info.ngwa.org/gwol/pdf/910155209.pdf.

   The historical GIS analysis conducted for this book analyzed the marshlands in Staten Island, Jamaica Bay, Flushing Meadows, and the New Jersey Meadows, and determined that in 1900 they alone extended over an area of 79.22 square miles. The 300-square-mile figure for marshland noted here was for an area (within a 25-mile radius of city hall) that extended beyond the bounds of my study. The figure was also put forth by a man preoccupied with the elimination of marshland for mosquito control and who could have been exaggerating to convince public officials to provide more funding. But the figure is plausible.

2. C. C. Vermeule, "Drainage of the Hackensack and Newark Tide-Marshes," in *Annual Report of the State Geologist for the Year 1897*, Geological Survey of New Jersey (Trenton, N.J., 1898), 301; and New York City Department of Street Cleaning, *Report of the Department of Street Cleaning for the Four Years Ending December 31, 1905* (New York, 1906), 73, 74 ("possibilities" quotation).

3. See Donald F. Squires, "Quantifying Anthropogenic Shoreline Modification of the Hudson River and Estuary from European Contact to Modern Time," *Coastal Management* 20, no. 4 (1992): 347, table 1, 345, doi:10.1080/08920759209362183. The historical GIS conducted for *Gotham Unbound* indicate that the combined area of marshlands at Flushing, Staten Island, New Jersey, and Jamaica Bay in 1900 was 79.22 square miles. In 2010 the area amounted to just 11.12 square miles, for a decline of 86 percent and comparable to the drop Squires observed. See appendix E.

4. "Development of Water Front Facilities," in *Fifty-Fourth ARCCNY, for the Year 1911–'12* (New York, 1912), 156. "Our city location on three islands separated from the mainland," Calvin Tomkins, the city's dock commissioner, pointed out, "while originally an advantage is now a disadvantage." See "Remarks of Calvin Tomkins," in *Fifty-Eighth ARCCNY, for the Year 1915–'16* (New York, 1916), 191.

5. Revell, 60–61; Jameson W. Doig, *Empire on the Hudson: Entrepreneurial Vision and Political Power at the Port of New York Authority* (New York: Columbia Univ. Press, 2001), xvi, 28; and "Freight Congestion Loosens," *Wall Street Journal*, Jan. 7, 1918.

6. T. Kennard Thomson, *A Really Greater New York: Address Before the Republican Club of New York* . . . (New York, 1914), 8 (Barnes quotation); and "President Marks' Interesting Address," *GNY*, Mar. 30, 1914, 2.

7. "Big Steamship Lines Want Chelsea Piers," *NYT*, Dec. 22, 1903; and Harry Chase Brearley, *The Problem of Greater New York and Its Solution* (New York: Search-Light Books, 1914), 11–12 (quotation).

8. Doig, *Empire on the Hudson*, 8, 28–30; New York, New Jersey Port and Harbor Development Commission, *Joint Report with Comprehensive Plan and Recommendations* (Albany, N.Y., 1920), 5 (quotation), 12–13, 29–30; "Reclamation Has Progressed Well," *Newark (N.J.) Evening News*, May 19, 1914; "Big Project on Marsh Now Taking Form—Landmarks for Generations to Disappear—At Least One Pier to Be Built This Year," *Call* (Newark, N.J.), June 24, 1914; James M. Reilly, *Port Newark Terminal* (Newark, N.J., 1915), 7; and Eric Darton, *Divided We Stand: A Biography of New York's World Trade Center* (New York: Basic Books, 1999), 48.

9. Doig, *Empire on the Hudson*, 79–80, 89–90, 114–15.

10. "Adding Six Square Miles to Manhattan Island," *Illustrated World*, Dec. 1921, 517, 519.

11. Robert Murray Haig, "Toward an Understanding of the Metropolis," *Quarterly Journal of Economics* 40, no. 3 (1926): 188 ("explaining why" quotation); and Thomas Adams, "Discussion," *Proceedings of the Seventh National Conference on City Planning, Detroit, June 7–9, 1915* (Boston, 1915), 160.

12. "Decentralization a Necessity," *NYHTr*, May 7, 1928 ("bring the place" quotation); Regional Plan Association, *The Graphic Regional Plan: Atlas and Description* (New York: Regional Plan of New York and Its Environs, 1929), 1:147–48, 327 ("vast schemes" quotation), 395 ("new city development" quotation); and Michael Simpson, "Meliorist *Versus* Insurgent Planners and the Problems of New York, 1921–1941," *Journal of American Studies* 16, no. 2 (Aug. 1982): 211, 216, doi:10.1017/S0021875800010513. For an interesting discussion of the Regional Plan Association's approach to development, see Tom Angotti, *New York for Sale: Community Planning Confronts Global Real Estate* (Cambridge, Mass.: MIT Press, 2008), 67–69.

13. The name of the group was the Regional Planning Association of America. Lewis Mumford, "The Plan of New York," in *Planning the Fourth Migration: The Neglected Vision of the Regional Planning Association of America*, ed. Carl Sussman (Cambridge, Mass.: MIT Press, 1976), 232 ("extension" quotation), 255 ("prejudices" and "Manifest Destiny" quotations); and Geddes Smith [Lewis Mumford], "'Friction of Space' among 20,000,000," *Survey*, Mar. 15, 1927, 799 ("nothing bolder" quotation).

14. For a good historical discussion of the emergence of the regional city and its role in the history of planning, see Andrew A. Meyers, "Invisible Cities: Lewis Mumford, Thomas Adams, and the Invention of the Regional City, 1923–1929," *Business and Economic History* 27, no. 2 (Winter 1998): 292–306.

15. Robert Caro, *The Power Broker: Robert Moses and the Fall of New York* (1974; repr., New York: Vintage, 1975), 25, 28, 33–34, 270.

16. Simpson, "Meliorist *Versus* Insurgent Planners," 222, on Smith and his initial inclination toward Mumford's Regional Planning Association of America plan.

17. Kenneth T. Jackson, "Robert Moses and the Rise of New York: The Power Broker in Perspective," in *Robert Moses and the Modern City: The Transformation of New York*, ed. Hilary Ballon and Jackson (New York: W. W. Norton, 2007), 70; and Robert Fitch, *The Assassination of New York* (London: Verso, 1993), 59.

18. On Moses as a "force of nature," see Caro, *The Power Broker*, 830.

19. Marc Bloch, *French Rural History: An Essay on Its Basic Characteristics*, trans. Janet Sondheimer (Berkeley: Univ. of California Press, 1966), 6.

20. Charles Denson, *Coney Island: Lost and Found* (Berkeley: Ten Speed Press, 2002), 3–6, 18–19; Benjamin F. Thompson, *History of Long Island . . .* (New York, 1839), 20, 39; and Act of Apr. 26, 1905, ch. 339, 1905, vol. 1, N.Y. Laws 614 (concerning nets in Coney Island Creek).

21. Michael Immerso, *Coney Island: The People's Playground* (New Brunswick, N.J.: Rutgers Univ. Press, 2002), 13; Stephen F. Weinstein, "The Nickel Empire: Coney Island and the Creation of Urban Seaside Resorts in the United States" (PhD diss., Columbia Univ., 1984), 37–38; J. Disturnell, comp., *A Gazetteer of the State of New-York . . .* (Albany, N.Y., 1842), 187 (quotation); and Elizabeth Bradley, "Coney Island," in Jackson, 299.

22. "The Private Ownership of Land," *RERBG*, Jan. 3, 1885. One commoner insisted on knowing whether "[n]o one except a favored few are allowed to set foot on the soil. . . . We want to know whether we have a right to walk on this part of the beach or not." See "Sheepshead Bay," letter to the editor, *Kings County (Brooklyn, N.Y.) Rural Gazette*, Feb. 10, 1877. The Coney Island common lands are discussed in Denson, *Coney Island*, 4–6.

23. Benjamin Miller, "Fat of the Land: New York's Waste," *Social Research* 65, no. 1 (Spring 1998): 88–90; "M'Carren Accused in Woodbury Inquiry," *NYT*, May 10, 1906; "Marrone Knows Nothing and Keeps No Books," *NYT*, May 1, 1906; "Brooklyn's Added Acres," *NYT*, Apr. 8, 1906 (quotation); and "M'Carren Stays Away from Woodbury Hearing," *NYT*, May 17, 1906, on the valuation of the made land. On the state of Coney Island Creek and vicinity in the early twentieth century, see the map titled "Coney Island Creek and Its Inlets and Marshes," in *Proceedings of the First General Convention to Consider the Questions Involved in Mosquito Extermination . . .* (Brooklyn, N.Y., 1904), following p. 62.

24. At one point, there were plans to turn Coney Island Creek into a ship canal, but the plan was abandoned. See Act of May 9, 1918, ch. 588, 1918, vol. 3, N.Y. Laws 1910 (appropriation for a ship canal between Gravesend Bay and Sheepshead Bay). The Belt Parkway was finished in 1941. See Hilary Ballon and Kenneth T. Jackson, eds., *Robert Moses and the Modern City: The Transformation of New York* (New York: W. W. Norton, 2007), 225–27. The same year the Belt Parkway opened, the state passed Act of Apr. 14, 1941, ch. 360, 1941 N.Y. Laws 1045 (amending New York City code regarding disposition of lands once under water at Coney Island Creek). On the filling of the creek for the Belt Parkway, see Charles Denson, "Coney Events: Charles Denson Shares the Secrets of Coney's Creek," *Kinetic Carnival* (blog), Oct. 2, 2007, http://kineticcarnival.blogspot.com/2007/10/coney-events-charles-denson-shares.html.

25. "Warfare on Mosquitos," *NYT*, May 23, 1903; and Gordon Patterson, *The Mosquito Crusades: A History of the American Anti-Mosquito Movement from the Reed Commission to the First Earth Day* (New Brunswick, N.J.: Rutgers Univ. Press, 2009), 40–42. "New Jersey swamps" quotation is Weeks speaking, as reported in "No Quarter to Be Given in Mosquito Warfare," *NYT*, Oct. 16, 1904. On the relative values of Manhattan and New Jersey marshland real estate, see the quotation from Weeks in *Proceedings of the First General Convention to Consider the Questions Involved in Mosquito Extermination . . .* , 4. Weeks advocated gates at both ends of Coney Island Creek to rid the area of mosquitos. See "Report on Mosquito War," *NYT*, July 16, 1903; and Weeks's letter, Sept. 20, 1903, in *Proceedings of the First General Convention to Consider the Questions Involved in Mosquito Extermination . . .* , 63–64.

26. C. C. Adams, "Mosquito Control Work in Nassau County, L.I., N.Y.," in *Proceedings of the Fourth Annual Meeting of the New Jersey Mosquito Extermination Association . . .* (Trenton, N.J., 1917), 173. The Weeks disciple was Cromwell Childe, writing in "Mosquito Engineering," *NYT*, May 18, 1902.

27. Patterson, *The Mosquito Crusades*, 44; K. Bromberg Gedan, B. R. Silliman, and M. D. Bertness, "Centuries of Human-Driven Change in Salt Marsh Ecosystems," *Annual Review of Marine Science* 1, no. 1 (2009): 126, doi:10.1146/annurev.marine.010908.163930; and "Interstate Mosquito War Begins Tomorrow," *NYT*, Apr. 30, 1916 (Bolduan quotation). One study determined that in 1907 Jamaica Bay consisted of 9,979 hectares of water and wetlands, which would be 38.5 square miles. See Ellen Kracauer Hartig et al., "Anthropogenic and Climate-Change Impacts on Salt Marshes of Jamaica Bay, New York City," *Wetlands* 22, no. 1 (Mar. 2002): 74. Fishermen harvested from the bay some 450,000 tons of oysters a year. See *Report of the Jamaica Bay Improvement Commission* (New York, 1907), 24.

28. Gayne T. K. Norton, "Mosquito Extermination in New York," *Nature-Study Review* 12, no. 9 (Dec. 1916): 384 ("western front" quotation); "Killing the Mosquito," *NYT*, Oct. 28, 1917; and Eugene Winship, "Mosquito Extermination in Greater New York, 1900–1916," in *Proceedings of the Fourth Annual Meeting of the New Jersey Mosquito Extermination Association*, 166–67, 168–69. For a report on the bird life that once inhabited Dyker Beach (and the rise of a man-made set of lakes in the Flushing Meadows that would, it was hoped, offer a substitute habitat), see "Lakes at World Fair Site to Be Haven for Wild Fowl," *LIP*, July 8, 1937.

29. Gedan, Silliman, and Bertness, "Centuries of Human-Driven Change in Salt Marsh Ecosystems," 127; and Winship, "Mosquito Extermination in Greater New York, 1900–1916," 171.

30. Gedan, Silliman, and Bertness, "Centuries of Human-Driven Change in Salt Marsh Ecosystems," 127. The changed landscape also likely created a habitat that was hostile to some kinds of bird life, such as seaside sparrow. See Glenn D. Dreyer and William A. Niering, eds., *Tidal Marshes of Long Island Sound: Ecology, History and Restoration* (New London: Connecticut College Arboretum, 1995), 45, and also available at www.conncoll.edu/green/arbo/tidal-marshes-of-long-island-sound.htm.

31. Adams, "Mosquito Control Work in Nassau County," 174, 177; and Act of May 3, 1916, ch. 408, 1916, vol. 2, N.Y. Laws 1053 (amending the public health law to establish mosquito extermination commissions).

32. Adams, "Mosquito Control Work in Nassau County," 175, 181; R. Marc Fasanella, "The Environmental Design of Jones Beach State Park: Aesthetic and Ecological Aspects of the Park's Architecture and Landscape" (PhD diss., New York Univ., 1991), 34–35; and Kenneth E. Nagle, "High Hill Beach, II," *LIF* 37, no. 12 (Dec. 1974): 224, on the profusion of steamers (*Mya arenaria*).

33. Patterson, *The Mosquito Crusades*, 81, 7–8, 14–15; Adams, "Mosquito Control Work in Nassau County," 181; and C. A. Holmquist, director, Division of Sanitation, New York State, "Mosquito Extermination (Nassau County)," in *Forty-Second Annual Report of the State Department of Health . . .*, part 2, (Albany, N.Y., 1922), 1:317.

34. Remarks of Royal S. Copeland at a special meeting of the Medical Society of the County of Kings, *Long Island Medical Journal* 16 (Dec. 1922): 516.

35. Caro, *The Power Broker*, 160–61; and Thomas Floyd-Jones, *Thomas Jones, Fort Neck, Queens County, Long Island, 1695 and His Descendants . . .* (New York, 1906), 17, 20 (quotations).

36. "Waste, n.," *OED Online*, www.oed.com; "Report of Engineers of Town Meadows Surveys," Oct. 22, 1908, TLS, box 2, folder 5; "Lessees of Town Lands," n.d., and "Lessee's of Marsh Lands," n.d., TLS, box 2, folder 34; and Town Board Resolution "for cutting the grass on the Common Marshes," Mar. 12, 1907, TLS, box 2, folder 39.

37. Daniel M. Tredwell, *Personal Reminiscences of Men and Things on Long Island*, pt. 1, (New York: Charles Andrew Ditmas, 1912), 136, 140, 141. For the agroecology of mixed husbandry, see Brian Donahue, *The Great Meadow: Farmers and the Land in Colonial Concord* (New Haven, Conn.: Yale Univ. Press, 2004), 55–60. For a sense of avian life, see John Treadwell Nichols and Francis Harper, "Field Notes on Some Long Island Shore Birds," the *Auk* 33, no. 3 (July 1916): 237–55; and William Vogt, "Notes from Jones Beach, N.Y.," the *Auk* 50, no. 4 (Oct. 1933): 445–47.

38. Robert Moses to Officers of the Town Board, Aug. 3, 1925, PS, box 3, folder 9.

39. Robert Moses, "A 'Ditchdigger' Replies," *Newsday* (N.Y.), n.d., in "Robert Moses" vertical file, LISI. Moses's reply was made after the publication of a thirteen-part series on him in *Newsday*.

40. *First Annual Report of the Long Island State Park Commission . . .* (Albany, N.Y., 1925), 17, table; and "Joint Hearing Before State and Assembly Committees on Conservation," Mar. 14, 1923, 174, 195 (quotation), RMP, box 2, legislation 1923 folder.

41. Edwin G. Burrows, "Gotham Without Long Island: Thinking the Unthinkable," *NCHSJ* 55 (2000): 39, 41. On the decline of the forests of Long Island, see *First Annual Report of the Long Island State Park Commission*, 9.

42. *First Annual Report of the Long Island State Park Commission*, 9–10, 21. Moses, along with Townsend Scudder and Clifford L. Jackson, wrote this first report.

43. "Don't Surrender Babylon's Oceanfront," *Babylon (N.Y.) Leader*, Aug. 1, 1924; and "'Time to Crab,'" *Long Island Sun* (Amityville, N.Y.), repr. in *Babylon Leader*, Aug. 1, 1924.

44. Fasanella, "The Environmental Design of Jones Beach State Park," 51–53, 57–59. The vote on what was known as Town Proposition No. 1 was 12,695 against, 5,331 for the proposition, and 8,578 ballots left blank. See Town Board of Canvassers' Return and Statement of Canvass, Nov. 7, 1925, PS, box 3, folder 9. McWhinney and

Townsend Scudder were members of the Hempstead Planning Commission. The Planning Commission's report recommending that the town convey the beach to the state is in *Second Annual Report of the Long Island State Park Commission* ... (Albany, N.Y., 1926), 81, and 42 for a report on the 1926 election results indicating that voters approved the Jones Beach plan by a margin of nearly four to one. A fuller rendering of the story of Moses and Jones Beach is in Caro, *The Power Broker,* 204–5, 208, 209, 210, 231–37.

45. Julian Denton Smith, "High Hill Beach," *NCHSJ* 32 (1971): 7; Chester R. Blakelock, "History of Jones Beach State Park," *LIF* 16, no. 2 (Feb. 1953): 23; and County of Nassau, Town of Hempstead, and Long Island State Park Commission, *Improvement of Jones Inlet* (n.p., 1940), 6.

46. Kenneth E. Nagle, "High Hill Beach, 1905–1939," *LIF,* 37, no. 8 (Aug. 1974): 176; "High Hill Beach Lures Imaginative Explorers," *NDR,* July 3, 1928 ("sand dunes" quotation); Nagle, "High Hill Beach, II," 224 ("so prolific" quotation); and "Guide to the Will Cuppy Papers Circa 1884–1949," Special Collections Research Center, Univ. of Chicago Library, www.lib.uchicago.edu/e/scrc/findingaids/view.php ?eadid=icu.spcl.cuppyw#idp46846576 ("Tottering" quotation).

47. "Robert Moses from the Bridge," *Newsday,* May 28, 1966; and Will Cuppy, *How to Be a Hermit or A Bachelor Keeps House* (1929; repr., New York: Liveright Publishing, 1987), 319. Though Cuppy was no longer allowed to live permanently at Jones Beach, the shack he lived in was not destroyed, and he was able to periodically return to it. See "Guide to the Will Cuppy Papers Circa 1884–1949."

48. Sidney Shapiro, "Diary of the Jones Beach Causeway," (1927–1928), 26, available from the New York State Office of Parks, Recreation and Historic Preservation, Long Island Region, Babylon, N.Y.

49. Sidney Shapiro, "Diary of the Jones Beach Causeway," 8, 41, 44, 45, 12; Kenneth E. Nagle, "High Hill Beach, IV," *LIF* 38, no. 6 (June 1975): 105; and Marshall Berman, *All That Is Solid Melts into Air: The Experience of Modernity* (1982; repr., New York: Penguin, 1988), 296.

50. Jackson, "Robert Moses and the Rise of New York," 68 ("greatest builder" quotation); Julian Denton Smith, "Unnative Plants on Jones Beach," *LIF* 13, no. 10 (Oct. 1950): 191–92; and Clarence C. Combs, "Jones Beach State Park," *Parks and Recreation* 18 (Oct. 1934): 37. On Combs's use of native plants, see Fasanella, "The Environmental Design of Jones Beach State Park," 119.

51. Fasanella, "The Environmental Design of Jones Beach State Park," 134–35; and "Carey Says Moses Is a Propagandist," *NYT,* Oct. 11, 1939 (Moses quotation).

52. Donald Worster, *Dust Bowl: The Southern Plains in the 1930s* (1979; repr., New York: Oxford Univ. Press, 1982), 13; Raymond P. McNulty, "Obstacles Encountered on the Way to a Great Public Improvement," *World Ports* 21 (Nov. 1932): 32; Fasanella, "The Environmental Design of Jones Beach State Park," 79; and William Oliver Stevens, *Discovering Long Island* (1939; repr., Port Washington, N.Y.: Ira J. Freidman, 1969), 240–41.

53. "Roosevelt Renews Challenge on Parks," *NYT,* Aug. 5, 1929 ("socialistic" quotation).

54. Both letters to the editor are in "More Taxpayers Resent Parking Fees Which Bar Short Stop at Jones Beach," *NDR,* June 26, 1931. In an effort to compel towns-

people to support the conveyance of land to the state for Jones Beach, Moses swore there would be no tolls. See Caro, *The Power Broker*, 236.

55. Robert Moses, "Park Commission Answers Editorial Referring to Prices at Jones Beach," *NDR*, June 29, 1931 ("no apologies" and "stupid" quotations); Robert Moses, "Hordes from the City," *Saturday Evening Post*, Oct. 1931, 15 ("shrubbery" and "contraband" quotations); and *People v. Brennan*, 142 Misc. 225, 229 (N.Y. County Ct. 1931).

56. Robert Moses, "The Building of Jones Beach" in *Robert Moses: Single-Minded Genius*, ed. Joann P. Krieg (Interlaken, N.Y.: Hearts of the Lakes Publishing, 1989), 137; and see the map following p. 8 in *First Annual Report of the Long Island State Park Commission*, which labels the barrier island "Jones Beach." On the New England colonists and their "ideology of conquest" regarding Indian land, see William Cronon, *Changes in the Land: Indians, Colonists, and the Ecology of New England* (New York: Hill and Wang, 1983), 56–57.

10. The Landscapers of Queens

1. Hilary Ballon and Kenneth T. Jackson, eds., *Robert Moses and the Modern City: The Transformation of New York* (New York: W. W. Norton, 2007), 67; and Robert Caro, *The Power Broker: Robert Moses and the Fall of New York* (1974; repr., New York: Vintage, 1975), 458 ("Nature" quotation).

2. George A. Soper to George McAneny, May 24, 1929, GMP, box 69, Department of Sanitation, Misc. folder; and Robert Moses, "Backyard Conservation," *Forum and Century* 99, no. 1 (Jan. 1938): 58. Moses also shared the Regional Plan Association's sense that in planning one must think about "the totality rather than the parts." See Regional Plan Association, *The Graphic Regional Plan: Atlas and Description* (New York: Regional Plan of New York and Its Environs, 1929), 1:125.

3. Robert Moses, "New York City's Parkways," 8 ("islandic" quotation), NYCDPGF, mn. 22839, roll 39, box 102421, Flushing Meadows Park, Articles-Newspaper folder, 1939; and Moses, "New York City: An All Year Vacation Playground," 2 ("sprawling" quotation), NYCDPGF, mn. 22842, roll 42, box 102423, Flushing Meadows Park, Literature, folder 3, 1939.

4. "Jones Beach State Park," *American City*, May 1931, 126–27; Victor Bernstein, "West Side Highway to Open," *NYT*, Oct. 10, 1937; Ballon and Jackson, eds., *Robert Moses and the Modern City*, 206–9, 161–62, 200–1; Caro, *The Power Broker*, 556–57, 534–35, 540–49, 365–67; and Robert Moses, *Public Works: A Dangerous Trade* (New York: McGraw-Hill, 1970), 238 ("slopover" quotation).

5. Max Horkheimer, *Eclipse of Reason* (1947; repr., London: Continuum, 2004), 25–26; and Donald Worster, "Hoover Dam: A Study in Domination," in *Under Western Skies: Nature and History in the American West* (New York: Oxford Univ. Press, 1992), 64–78.

6. "Site Virgin Land," *World's Fair Bulletin* 1 (Aug. 1936), 11.

7. Benjamin Miller, "Fat of the Land: New York's Waste," *Social Research* 65, no. 1 (Spring 1998): 92; John H. Barry, "Flushing from a Sanitary Standpoint," in *Illustrated Flushing and Vicinity* . . . , comp. and ed. Darby Richardson (Flushing, N.Y.,

1917), 24; and "The Origin of Community Names in Queens Borough" (compiled by the Queens Borough Historian as a supplement to his First Annual Report, 1944, and available at the LISI), 8.

8.   Vincent F. Seyfried, *Corona: From Farmland to City Suburb, 1650–1935* (s.l., 1986), 67 ("conveyor belt" quotation); Miller, "Fat of the Land," 88; and Richard J. Harrison, *Long Island Rail Road Memories: The Making of a Steam Locomotive Engineer* (New York: Quadrant Press, 1981), 8 ("Talcum" quotation).

9.   *Examination and Survey of Flushing Bay and Creek, New York*, H.R. Doc. No. 68–124, at 6–7 (1923); Daniel C. Walsh, "Incineration: What Led to the Rise and Fall of Incineration in New York City?" *Environmental Science & Technology* 36 (Aug. 2002): 319A; and Miller, "Fat of the Land," 92. In 1913 the Tammany-supported governor of New York, William Sulzer, signed legislation granting New York City land under water in Flushing. The grant was made to support the "straightening [of] Flushing Creek," in order to aid navigation. See Act of Mar. 6, 1913, ch. 62, 1913, vol. 1, N.Y. Laws 103 (granting New York City land under water in Flushing Bay and Flushing Creek).

10. F. Scott Fitzgerald, *The Great Gatsby* (1925; repr., New York: Scribner, 2004), 23; Miller, "Fat of the Land," 92; and "Mountains of Garbage Which Dotted Flushing Meadow Are Gone but Not Forgotten by North Shore Residents," *LIP*, Apr. 29, 1939.

11. "Asks a City Prison on Rikers Island," *NYT*, Mar. 27, 1925; Ellen Fletcher, "Roosevelt Island," in Jackson, 1122; "Remarks of Dr. Woodbury," in *Forty-Fifth ARCCNY*, for the Year 1902–1903 (New York, 1903), 106; "Fight Plan to Add to Riker's Island," *NYT*, Sept. 11, 1925; and "City to Forbid Rat Shoot," *NYT*, May 26, 1931 ("poison gas" quotation).

12. "Walker Lays Cornerstone for Riker's Building," *NSJ*, July 29, 1931 ("garbage heap" quotation); John J. Dorman to Joseph F. Higgens, Oct. 30, 1928, GMP, box 69, Department of Sanitation, Misc. folder; and Guy Hickok, "City's Ashes Have Expanded Rikers Island from 67 Acres in 1654 to 700 Acres in 1934," *BE*, Apr. 20, 1934 ("Christmas trees" quotation). The 130-foot figure is from Joseph K. Blum, "Preliminary Report on New York City Refuse Disposal Situation," Dec. 15, 1935, p. 1, GMP, box 69, Department of Sanitation, Misc. folder. For more on rats and Rikers, see Robert Sullivan, *Rats: Observations on the History and Habitat of the City's Most Unwanted Inhabitants* (New York: Bloomsbury, 2004), 38–39, 226.

13. "Preparing the Fair Site," *NYHTr*, Apr. 10, 1937. Steven Gregory, *Black Corona: Race and the Politics of Place in an Urban Community* (Princeton, N.J.: Princeton Univ. Press, 1998), 182, notes that together La Guardia Airport and the Grand Central Parkway wound up "displacing the shoreline one hundred yards into the bay."

14. Boyden Sparkes, "Fortune's Built on Gold from Garbage," *PS*, Jan. 1932, 20 ("English park" quotation); "Rosoff's Proposed Dump Would Hurt State's Parkway Plans, Says Official," *LIP*, Apr. 6, 1933; "Harvey Joins Fight on New Refuse Dumps," *LIP*, Apr. 7, 1933; and "History of 'Mt. Corona,'" *FMI* 2 (Mar. 1937): 22.

15. Helen Harrison, ed., *Dawn of a New Day: The New York World's Fair, 1939/40* (Flushing, N.Y.: Queens Museum/New York Univ. Press, 1980), 3; and "Percy S. Straus, 67, Dies in Home Here," *NYT*, Apr. 8, 1944.

16. Whalen's salesmanship is described in "In Mr. Whalen's Image," *Time*, May 1, 1939,

72–74. See also Grover A. Whalen, *Mr. New York: The Autobiography of Grover A. Whalen* (New York: G. P. Putnam's Sons, 1955); and Peter J. Kuznick, "Losing the World of Tomorrow: The Battle over the Presentation of Science at the 1939 New York World's Fair," *American Quarterly* 46, no. 3 (Sept. 1994): 351–52, http://www .jstor.org/stable/2713269.

17. Howard Elkinton, "Tribute to George McAneny," *NYT*, Aug. 15, 1953; Eric Darton, *Divided We Stand: A Biography of New York's World Trade Center* (New York: Basic Books, 1999), 24–25; and Henry Farrand Griffin, "George McAneny: What He Has Done and Hopes to Do for New York," *Independent*, July 31, 1913, 247 (McAneny quotation).

18. George McAneny to John P. O'Brien, statement made on McAneny's last day as commissioner of sanitation, Sept. 18, 1933, GMP, box 69, Department of Sanitation, Speeches, Releases, Data folder. The following letters are from NYWFR, Central Files, box 1, folder 4: George H. Macbeth to Board of Estimate, Nov. 2, 1935 ("ocean breezes" quotation); Frank Joyce to George McAneny, Jan. 20, 1936 ("beautiful shores" quotation); Arthur H. Hill to Grover Whalen, June 16, 1936; George H. MacBeth to N.Y. State Legislature, Mar. 30, 1936 ("bog lands" and "bottomless" quotations); and John H. Ward to Fiorello H. La Guardia, Oct. 15, 1935 ("anomalous" quotation).

19. Norman Thomas and Paul Blanshard, *What's the Matter with New York: A National Problem* (New York: Macmillan, 1932), 201; and John J. Halleran, "The World's Fair and Development of Flushing Meadows Park," *World's Fair News* 1 (Aug. 1936): 15. The Flushing Meadows site was also sold as the geographic center of New York City. See, for example, *New York World's Fair 1939: Hearings Before the Comm. on Foreign Affairs . . . on H. J. Res. 234 and H. J. Res. 304*, 75th Cong. 19 (1937) (statement of Grover A. Whalen).

20. Robert Moses to Mr. Andrews, Oct. 3, 1935, NYCDPGF, mn. 22838, roll 38, box 102392, Flushing Meadows–World's Fair Project, folder 3; "The New Plan for Riker's Island," *FMI* 3 (Sept. 1937): 18 ("Eternal Lights" quotation); "Moses Gives Plan for Rikers Island," *NYT*, Aug. 8, 1936 (Moses quotation); "Plans Perfected for Rikers Island," *NYT*, Oct. 18, 1936; "Work to Start at Once Beautifying Riker's Island," *LIP*, Oct. 19, 1936; and "Moses Has Plan for Beautifying Rikers Island," *LIS*, Oct. 19, 1936.

21. "Ash Fill on Muck Base Makes Airport," *Engineering News-Record* 120 (June 2, 1938): 779; "North Beach, Dedicated Today, Monument to a Dogged Mayor," *NYHTr*, Oct. 15, 1939; "Plans Perfected for Rikers Island"; "End of Vesuvius," *FMI* 1 (Oct. 1936): 4; and Moses, *Public Works*, 329.

22. Grover A. Whalen, "A Survey Submitted," n.d., NYWFR, Central Files, box 10, folder 22; "Army of Men Shape Swamp into Fair Site," *LIP*, Aug. 23, 1936; "Site Virgin Land," 11; "Metropolitan Pelts," *NYT*, Oct. 25, 1936; John G. Grimley to John L. Rice, May 24, 1938, 3–4, NYWFR, Central Files, box 224, folder 2; and "Swamps, Ash Dumps, Saga of Fair Grounds," *NSN*, Nov. 16, 1936.

23. "Corona Exodus, Called by Moses, Enlists Help of Old Gray Mares When Families Vacate for Fair," *LIS*, July 1, 1936 ("ancient nags" quotation); "City Ousting Families," *NYWT*, n.d. ("heartache" quotation); and "Needy Family of Eight 'Holds

the Fort,'" *LIS*, n.d., copies in NYWFR, Promotion and Development Division, box 1971, folder 1; and "'Tiki Tik,' Monarch of Ballino, Mourns as World's Fair Dooms Corona Courts," *LIS*, Aug. 5, 1936.

24. J. C. Balcomb to Col. John P. Hogan, July 29, 1936, NYWFR, Operating Division, box 1566, folder 8; "Fair Area Experiences Its Worst Dust Storm Since Work Was Begun," *LIS*, Sept. 18, 1935; "Work of Filling Site Done in Record Time," *NYHTr*, Apr. 11, 1937; "Fair Corporation Reports Progress of Work," *GNY*, Dec. 18, 1936, 9 ("white way" quotation); "Five Miles Progress in Preparation for Greatest World Fair," *NSN*, Nov. 9, 1936 ("completely changed" quotation); and "Site Virgin Land," 12 ("pave" quotation).

25. "Versailles for Millions," *LIS*, Dec. 8, 1936 ("Versailles" quotation). McAneny was quoted as saying that because of the Flushing River and the marshland, "you can make lagoons out there with a spoon." See "Vast Trade Opportunities Seen in 1939 Fair," *GNY*, Mar. 17, 1936, 12.

26. "Queens Community Councils Knew World's Fair Site When—," *LIS*, Mar. 29, 1937, which describes the transformation of the ash heap into the fair as "fairy-like"; and "Army of Workers Making Dirt Fly at Fair Grounds," *LIS*, Dec. 15, 1936 ("geography" quotation). See also, Untitled, *NSJ*, [Aug. 1936?], copy in NYWFR, Promotion and Development Division, box 1971, folder 8.

27. Caro, *The Power Broker*, 830.

28. "Mammoth Sewers Drain Park Area," *FMI*, 1 (Nov. 1936): 4; Benjamin Eisner, "Sanitation at the New York World's Fair," Mar. 15, 1939, NYWFR, Central Files, box 237, folder 12; "Sewer Improvements at Fair Site," *Jackson Heights Herald* (Whitestone, N.Y.), May 27, 1937 (quotation); Revell, 134–35; and Edward T. O'Donnell, "Maurice E. Connolly," in Jackson, 305.

29. "Flushing, n.1," *OED Online*, www.oed.com; "Tide Gate and Dam—Flushing River," *FMI* 1 (Dec. 1936): 8; "Tide Gate, Dam and Bridge," *FMI* 2 (Apr. 1937): 2; and "The Part of Planting in the Future Park," *FMI* 3 (May 1939): 40. The idea of tide gates at Flushing Meadows was suggested to Robert Moses as early as 1935. See Robert Moses to John O'Connor, Oct. 12, 1935, NYCDPGF, mn. 22838, roll 38, box 102392, Flushing Meadows–World's Fair Project, folder 3.

30. Herman L. Fellton, "Control of Aquatic Midges with Notes on the Biology of Certain Species," *Journal of Economic Entomology* 33 (Apr. 1940): 252–54 ("decidedly green" quotation), 260–63 (on measures taken to control midges); and John G. Grimley, "The Midge," Mar. 16, 1940, 3 ("stop about" quotation), NYWFR, Central Files, box 223, folder 21. As the algae blooms collapsed, the remains sunk to the bottom and served as a food supply for insects, increasing their survival and growth rates.

31. "'Inaugural' Party Travels in a Bus," *NYT*, Apr. 20, 1939; "Washington's Party, Blushing, Hopes Bus Ride Was Its Last," *NYWT*, Apr. 20, 1939 ("where's the horses" quotation); Gilbert D. Phillips to Boatswain Holmes, May 15, 1939, NYWFR, Promotion and Development Division, box 2138, folder 4; "'Washington' Here, a Bit Coach-Weary," *NYT*, Apr. 25, 1939; and "Inaugural Scene of 1789 Is Enacted," *NYT*, May 1, 1939.

32. GWD, 5:458; and William F. Fox, *Tree Planting on Streets and Highways* (Albany, N.Y., 1903), 14. The Parks Department eventually banned ailanthus because it

tended to split. See Max Page, *The Creative Destruction of Manhattan, 1900–1940* (Chicago: Univ. of Chicago Press, 1999), 205.

33. "Man-Made Forest for a World's Fair," *PS*, Sept. 1937, 44; "10,000 Live Trees Sought for Fair," *NYT*, Feb. 25, 1937; "3 Rare Sycamores Set at Site of Fair," *NYT*, Apr. 3, 1937; "Tree Planting on Fair Site," *FMI* 2 (May 1937): 6; and "Landscape Features of the New York World's Fair of 1939," n.d., p. 2, NYCDPGF, mn. 22839, roll 39, box 102421, Flushing Meadows Park–Articles and Magazines folder, 1939.

34. "New York Opens the Gates to the World of Tomorrow," *Life*, May 15, 1939, 19; Regional Plan Association, "Planning the Fair Site," *Information Bulletin*, no. 45, June 26, 1939, 4; and *Your World of Tomorrow* (New York: Rogers-Kellogg-Stillson, 1939), www.1939nyworldsfair.com/worlds_fair/wf_tour/theme-7.htm#.

35. Horkheimer, *Eclipse of Reason*, 26; "Landscape Features of the New York World's Fair of 1939," 1, 2 ("bumper" quotation); and Arthur Pound, *The Golden Earth: The Story of Manhattan's Landed Wealth* (New York: Macmillan, 1935), 12. In the late 1920s, *landscape* was being used for the first time as a verb meaning to "lay out a landscape." Prior to this time, the word meant "to depict." See "landscape, v.," *OED Online*, www.oed.com. Entering the word *landscaping* in Google's Ngram Viewer shows a graph with a steep upsurge after 1925. See Google Books, Ngram Viewer, http://books.google.com/ngrams/.

36. Bruce Bliven Jr., "Fair Tomorrow," *New Republic*, Dec. 7, 1938, 116 ("chromatically" quotation); "Jones Beach State Park," *American City*, May 1931, 126–27 ("color planning" quotation); Ed Tyng, *Making a World's Fair: Organization, Promotion, Financing, and Problems, with Particular Reference to the New York World's Fair of 1939–1940* (New York: Vantage, 1958), 30 ("function" quotation); and William Oliver Stevens, *Discovering Long Island* (1939; repr., Port Washington, N.Y.: Ira J. Freidman, 1969), 342 ("shimmering" quotation).

37. "Largest Willow Grove," *FMI* 1 (Oct. 1936): 8 ("ecological system," "special consideration," and "landscape effects" quotations). By the time of the fair, an economic paradigm founded on the control of nature had come to rule the science of ecology, replete with a lexicon packed with words such as *productivity* and *efficiency*. See Donald Worster, *Nature's Economy: A History of Ecological Ideas* (1977; repr., Cambridge, UK: Cambridge Univ. Press, 1985), 311–14. At Willow Lake, this new technocratic vision found expression on the ground.

38. "When You See Those Trees at the New York World's Fair," *American City*, May 1940, 66. For more on landscape losing its roots in place, see "Meadow and Willow Lakes Wild Life Sanctuaries," *FMI* 2 (July 1937): 17. "Sanctuaries for migratory waterfowl," the article explains, "have been successfully established in all parts of the country and it has been found that geographical location is not of paramount importance."

39. "New York Fair's Wonder Exhibit to Rest on Fir Piles," *American Lumberman*, June 5, 1937, 48. The quotation is from promotional literature reprinted in Larry Zim, Mel Lerner, and Herbert Rolfes, *The World of Tomorrow: The 1939 New York World's Fair* (New York: Harper & Row, 1988), 34. The fair corporation claimed 758 miles of piling were driven.

40. Moses used the word *landscape* as a verb, as in "I never liked the idea of attempt-

ing to landscape these two mountains." He also used the word *landscaping* when discussing the need for "further landscaping in 1940." See Robert Moses, "From Dump to Glory," *Saturday Evening Post*, Jan. 15, 1938, 13 ("unspoiled," "route," "logical," and "general reclamation" quotations), 72 ("geographical and population" and "never liked" quotations), 74. The geographic center of New York City is not in Flushing at all. In fact, it is not even in Queens. It is found in the Bushwick section of Brooklyn. On the geographic center of New York, see Michael Pollak, "The Middles of the City," *NYT*, Feb. 27, 2005. It is, however, true that by 1930 Nassau and Queens were in terms of population the first and second fastest-growing counties in the nation. See Thomas Parran Jr. et al., *Report of the Governor's Special Long Island Sanitary Commission* (Albany, N.Y., 1931), 8.

11. The Wilds of Staten Island

1.   William T. Davis, *Days Afield on Staten Island* (1892; repr., Lancaster, Pa.: Science Press, 1937), 5; Charles W. Leng and William T. Davis, *Staten Island and Its People: A History, 1609–1929*, 5 vols. (New York: Lewis Historical Publishing, 1930), 1:3; Ralph W. Tiner, *Wetlands of Staten Island, New York: Valuable Vanishing Urban Wildlands* (Hadley, Mass.: US Fish and Wildlife Service, 2000), 14, maps; and Richard Buegler and Steven Parisio, *A Comparative Flora of Staten Island, Including the 1879 and 1930 Floras by Arthur Hollick and Nathaniel Lord Britton* (Staten Island, N.Y.: Staten Island Institute of Arts & Sciences, 1982), 29.

2.   For details on Davis's family history, see Mabel Abbott, *The Life of William T. Davis* (Ithaca, N.Y.: Cornell Univ. Press, 1949), 7–9, 13, xi ("200 feet" quotation). "The whole island is like a garden," Thoreau wrote, "and affords very fine scenery." See Henry David Thoreau, *Familiar Letters of Henry David Thoreau*, ed. F. B. Sanborn (Boston, 1895), 84.

3.   Leng and Davis, *Staten Island and Its People*, 2:620, 625; Patricia M. Salmon, "The Original Cause and Beyond: Clay Pit Ponds State Park Preserve and the Formation of Protectors of Pine Oak Woods," *PSILAS* 36, no. 1 (2004): 69, 71; and William T. Davis, "Staten Island Names: Ye Olde Names and Nicknames," *PNSASI* 5, no. 5 (1896): 50.

4.   E. R. Carhart, "The New York Produce Exchange," *Annals of the American Academy of Political and Social Science* 38, no. 2 (Sept. 1911): 206–21; Abbott, *The Life of William T. Davis*, 52 (diary quotation); and William T. Davis, *Days Afield on Staten Island* (New York, 1892), 129, 72.

5.   Davis, *Days Afield on Staten Island* (1892), 85; and Davis, "Staten Island Names," 20.

6.   Abbott, *The Life of William T. Davis*, 153 ("ramble" quotation from a journal entry); Davis, "Staten Island Names," 49; "The Mosquito War," *Public Opinion*, Aug. 22, 1901, 239 ("Hunter's Point" quotation), 240 ("Dead sea" quotation); and Joseph M. Lonergan, "Fly and Mosquito Elimination Work in New York City," *Engineering and Contracting* 54, no. 10 (1920): 243. In 1908 one veteran of the mosquito war wrote about the ditching of the island's salt marshes: "The land already drained has entirely changed its character; instead of being soft and dangerous to walk upon, as before drainage it was unable to support the weight of the body, it is now firm and

hard, and may be driven over by trucks." See Alvah H. Doty, "The Mosquito: Its Relation to Disease and Its Extermination," *New York State Journal of Medicine* 8 (May 1908): 229.

7. Davis, *Days Afield on Staten Island* (1937), 5; Gerald Sullivan, "Brush Fires Cost Million in One Year," *SI*, Apr. 25, 1931; "$200,000 Toll Taken by Flames," *SI*, Apr. 22, 1931; Lonergan, "Fly and Mosquito Elimination," 243; Rosenwaike, 133, table 64; and Abbott, *The Life of William T. Davis*, 84 ("devilopments" quotation).

8. Davis, *Days Afield on Staten Island* (1937), 5; and Leng and Davis, *Staten Island and Its People*, 1:28. On the diversity of Staten Island's flora as late as 1930, see George R. Robinson, Mary E. Yurlina, and Steven N. Handel, "A Century of Change in the Staten Island Flora: Ecological Correlates of Species Losses and Invasion," *BTBC* 121, no. 2 (Apr.–June 1994): 125, www.jstor.org/stable/2997163.

9. As his biographer once observed, Davis "wanted no tree cut down, no underbrush removed, no wild flower exterminated, and no bird or beast killed or frightened away." See Abbott, *The Life of William T. Davis*, 242.

10. "Heard About Town," *NYT*, May 20, 1901; Jonathan Franzen, "Emptying the Skies," *New Yorker*, July 26, 2010, 53; and William T. Hornaday, *Our Vanishing Wild Life: Its Extermination and Preservation* (New York: Charles Scribner's Sons, 1913), 101. For more on the criminalization of customary activity in the Progressive Era, see Karl Jacoby, *Crimes Against Nature: Squatters, Poachers, Thieves, and the Hidden History of American Conservation* (Berkeley: Univ. of California Press, 2001).

11. "To Save Our Birds," *SI*, Apr. 12, 1916 ("tends to further" quotation); New York (City) Board of Aldermen, *Code of Ordinances of the City of New York . . .* Compiled by Arthur F. Cosby, c. X, § 430 (1912); New York (City) Board of Aldermen, *The Code of Ordinances of the City of New York . . .* Compiled by the Committee on Codification of Ordinances, c. 11, art. 1, § 2 (1917); "No Shooting on Island," *SI*, Nov. 15, 1916; and "Mayor Asks Power . . . Vetoes Ordinance Allowing Hunting on Staten Island, as Residents and Police Oppose It," *NYT*, Nov. 13, 1916 ("my opinion" quotation).

12. Stefan Bechtel, *Mr. Hornaday's War: How a Peculiar Victorian Zookeeper Waged a Lonely Crusade for Wildlife That Changed the World* (Boston: Beacon Press, 2012), 153 ("virgin forest" quotation); "Bird Club and Our Wood Areas," *SI*, June 9, 1923 ("natural a condition" quotation); "Spoiling the Parks," *NYTr*, June 4, 1923; and "Staten Island Bird Club: Devoted to the Conservation of Bird Life on Staten Island," 1926, WTDC, Staten Island Bird Club, 1917–28 ("mistaken idea" quotation). For more on the cultural construction of nature, see William Cronon, ed., *Uncommon Ground: Rethinking the Human Place in Nature* (New York: W. W. Norton, 1996); and Jennifer Price, *Flight Maps: Adventures with Nature in Modern America* (New York: Basic Books, 1999).

13. "Staten Island Bird Club: Devoted to the Conservation of Bird Life on Staten Island" ("natural state" quotation); Loring McMillen, *Staten Island: The Cosmopolitan Era from 1898* (Staten Island, N.Y., 1952), 5; Committee on Parks of the Staten Island Chamber of Commerce, *Report on a Proposed Park System for the Borough of Richmond, New York City* (1902), 6; Community Councils of the City of New York, press release including "Report by Chairman of Committee on Parks," Great Kills

Marine Park, 1930, 3, PC, box 4, folder 73; "The Garden Spot of New York City—Staten Island," radio talk by W. Lynn McCracken, July 24, 1929, PC, Committee on Parks, 1924–1940, box 1, folder 8; "Swamp at Willowbrook Park Becomes Artificial Lake," *SIA*, June 14, 1932; and "Marsh Becomes a Lake," *SIA*, June 15, 1932. On parks and real estate values, see John J. Halleran, "The World's Fair and Development of Flushing Meadows Park," *World's Fair News* 1 (Aug. 1936): 10.

14. J. Otis Swift, letter to the editor, "News Outside the Door," *New York World*, June 2, 1926; "The Garden Spot of New York City—Staten Island" ("Attorney" quotation); W. Lynn McCracken, letter to the editor, "McCracken Again Makes Plea for Island's Natural Parks," *SIA*, Sept. 24, 1932; and W. Lynn McCracken, letter to the editor, "Nature Lover Deplores 'Landscraping' in Clove Lakes Park," *SIA*, May 12, 1932 ("overtaming" quotation).

15. New York (City), Dept. of Parks, *Ordinances, Rules and Regulations of the Department of Parks of the City of New York*, c. 17, art. I, §§ 6, 7, 17 (1931); Untitled report on meeting of the Natural Science Association, *PNSASI* 8, no. 12 (1902): 29 ("thoughtless plucking" quotation); New York (City), Dept. of Parks, *Rules and Regulations of the Department of Parks of the City of New York*, c. 17, art. II, §§ 4, 5, 6, 10 and art. III, § 24 (1938); and W. Lynn McCracken, letter to the editor, "The Parks Need Care," *NYT*, Apr. 29, 1932. We can infer that the earlier prohibition against hunting and trapping must have been ineffective because the language of the rule required that people be caught in the act of engaging in these activities. The 1938 rules fixed the problem by criminalizing mere "possession [of] any feral animal, reptile, bird, bird's nest or squirrel's nest."

16. Gretchen Ernst, "When East Siders Come to Our Parks: Common Property—Trees and Birds," *SIA*, June 21, 1932.

17. Clara J. Hemphill and Raymond A. Mohl, "Poverty," and Kathleen Hulser, "Unemployment Movements," in Jackson, 1030, 1344; "6,525 Fatalities in City Last Year," *NYT*, Mar. 19, 1931; William V. Askins, "Sandy Ground: Historical Archaeology of Class and Ethnicity in a Nineteenth Century Community on Staten Island" (PhD diss., City Univ. of New York, 1988), 105; and Interstate Sanitation Commission, *Annual Report* (1940), 41. On oysters and Indians, see Jerome Jackson, *Burial Ridge, Tottenville, Staten Island, N.Y.: Archaeology at New York City's Largest Prehistoric Cemetery* (Staten Island: Staten Island Institute of Arts and Sciences, 1980), 5, 18.

18. Samuel L. Mitchill, "The Fishes of New-York," *Transactions of the Literary and Philosophical Society of New York* 1 (1815): 422–23; "All Staten Island on Fishing Spree," *NYT*, Aug. 6, 1932 ("hungry schools" quotation); "Bay Alive with Big Schools of Tiny Mackerel Driven to Inland Shelter by Bluefish," *SIA*, Aug. 2, 1932 ("Men" quotation); and "Consideration for the Needy," *SIA*, Aug. 2, 1932 ("are driven" quotation).

19. "O'Rourke Seeks 500 Men to Cut Firewood for Needy," *SI*, Nov. 18, 1932. "Some men seem to have an insane passion for cutting trees, 'clearing out' shrubbery, and exposing the face of Nature to the scarifying hands of man," wrote William Hornaday. "We see it everywhere." See William Hornaday, letter to the editor, "Some More Protectors of Nature Are Wanted," *SI*, Nov. 29, 1932.

20. "A Treeless Staten Island," invitation to a meeting of the Conservation Association

of Staten Island, Oct. 23, 1933, WTDC, Conservation Committee/Borough President's Planning Commission, DN 159, box 26; "Conservationists Suggest Special Police in Park Areas," *SIA*, Jan. 21, 1933; "Seven Men Are Arrested in Conservation Group's Drive to Preserve Trees," *SIA*, Feb. 21, 1933; "6 Who Cut Trees Are Convicted," *SIA*, Mar. 16, 1933; "Protection Requested for Trees," *SIA*, Oct. 7, 1933; and "Punishing Tree Theft," *SIA*, Mar. 20, 1933 ("householder" quotation). Angelo Pietroangelo, one of the men charged with cutting down the oak trees in question, was a carpenter, and Nicholas Valente was in trucking. See US Census Office, 1930 manuscript schedule, Tompkinsville, Richmond County, N.Y., p. 12-B, and Concord, Richmond County, p. 1-A, www.ancestry.com.

21. "Police Can't Stop It," *SIA*, Nov. 18, 1939 ("true sportsmen," "belong to the tribe," and "invade" quotations); Davis, "Staten Island Names," 26; Robert Moses, "Hunting Banned in City, Moses Insists," letter to the editor, *SIA,* Dec. 5, 1939; and "Vigilant Cop Won't Allow Any Hunting in Borough," *SIA,* Dec. 6, 1939 ("carrying a gun" quotation).

22. "Petition from Citizens of Richmond County, N.Y.," n.d., WTDC, Staten Island Bird Club, 1917–28, DN 163A; "Mr. Woodward's Pledge," *SIA*, Mar. 29, 1940; "Game Protector's Duties Unchanged by Hunting Bill," *SIA*, Apr. 3, 1940; "Richmond G.O.P. Hits Hunting Ban on Island," *SIA*, Mar. 28, 1940; "pot-hunter, n.," *OED Online*, www.oed.com; and "The Bormann Bill," *SIA*, Jan. 26, 1940 ("common sense" quotation). Those interested in the rational behavior of the commoners should see E. P. Thompson, *Customs in Common* (New York: New Press, 1991), 107. Ironically, the biblical Nimrod is depicted as a good hunter.

23. Robert Moses to Robert S. Woodward, Mar. 8, 1940, NYCDPOC, mn. 22706, roll 6, box 107863, *Staten Island Advance*, folder 34, 1940; Act of Apr. 22, 1940, ch. 623, 1940 N.Y. Laws 1770 (amending the penal law to ban hunting "in any county wholly embraced within the territorial limits of a city"); William T. Davis to Charles Bormann, Feb. 3, 1940, Staten Island Conservation, WTDC, DN 71, 1919–40; and "Hunting Once Flourished as Staten Island Sport," *SIA*, Nov. 21, 1931.

12. The Massifs of Fresh Kills

1. Bruce Kershner, *Secret Places of Staten Island: A Visitor's Guide to Scenic and Historic Treasures of Staten Island* (Dubuque, Iowa: Kendall/Hunt Publishing, 1998), 42; and William T. Davis, "Staten Island Names: Ye Olde Names and Nicknames," *PNSASI* 5, no. 5 (1896): 41. *Dood* is the Dutch word for death, so it is entirely possible it evolved into the word *todt* (which is closer to the German form) over time.

2. Victor Garnice, "Local Place Names of Staten Island," *Staten Island Historian* 31 (July–Sept. 1974): 172. E. B. O'Callaghan, comp., *Calendar of N.Y. Colonial Manuscripts: Indorsed Land Papers in the Office of the Secretary of State of New York, 1643–1803* (1864; repr., Harrison, N.Y.: Harbor Hill Books, 1987), 11, mentions land patents from 1676 and their relationship, spatially, with "Fresh kill." The scientific name for common reed is *Phragmites australis*.

3. The legal status of the land at Fresh Kills was complicated by Queen Anne of

England, who issued letters patent to a loyal British officer turned astute businessman named Major Lancaster Symes. The document purportedly gave Symes title to all ungranted land on Staten Island. On the effect of the resource recovery plant at Barren Island on neighboring property, see "Craig Says Odors Bothered Reynolds," *NYT*, Oct. 22, 1917. See also, "Fatal Explosion on Barren Island," *NYT*, May 1, 1910. Presumably in deference to the interests of real estate, the city took Manhattan Island and Jamaica Bay off the table as potential sites for a new facility. See "Fight Against Garbage Destructor," *SI*, Mar. 25, 1916 ("Fresh Kills meadows" quotation); and "Garbage Disposal Goes to Richmond," *NYT*, Apr. 11, 1916.

4.   Miller, 130; "Asleep at the Switch," *SI*, May 20, 1916; "Further Action in Garbage War," *SI*, July 8, 1916; "Doyle's Navy Gets Garbage Site Fort," *NYT*, June 9, 1916; "Garbage Men Beaten," *SI*, Apr. 28, 1917; "Anti-Garbage Defeated," *SI*, May 12, 1917; and "Hylan Makes Issue of Richmond Garbage," *NYT*, Oct. 28, 1917 (Hylan quotation). On Thoreau and Lakes (Lake's) Island, see Mabel Abbott, *The Life of William T. Davis* (Ithaca, N.Y.: Cornell Univ. Press, 1949), 77.

5.   Susan Strasser, *Waste and Want: A Social History of Trash* (New York: Metropolitan Books, 1999), 128; Steven Hunt Corey, "King Garbage: A History of Solid Waste Management in New York City, 1881–1970" (PhD diss., New York Univ., 1994), 42, 101–2; "Garbage Plant Products," *NYT*, Dec. 2, 1917; "What Can Be Done with Garbage," *American Journal of Public Health* 8, no. 2 (Feb. 1918): 176; Charles W. Leng and William T. Davis, *Staten Island and Its People: A History, 1609–1929*, 5 vols. (New York: Lewis Historical Publishing, 1930), 1:371; "Ask Government to Take Garbage Plant," *NYT*, July 20, 1918; "Garbage Dumped at Sea," *NYT*, June 29, 1918; and "Order Stops Garbage Plant," *SI*, Oct. 9, 1918.

6.   Strasser, *Waste and Want*, 170, 171–73, 191, 199–201. Two periods (1920 to 1930 and 1963 to 1973) stand out in New York City's waste history for the "sustained increase in rates of per capita mass discard of residential refuse." See Daniel C. Walsh, "Urban Residential Refuse Composition and Generation Rates for the 20th Century," *Environmental Science & Technology* 36, no. 22 (2002): 4938, doi:10.1021/es011074t.

7.   Richard Fenton, "Current Trends in Municipal Solid Waste Disposal in New York City," *Resource Recovery and Conservation* 1, no. 2 (Oct. 1975): 170; "The Polluted Beaches," *NYT*, July 24, 1923; *New Jersey v. New York*, 283 U.S. 473 (1931); and *New Jersey v. New York City*, 290 U.S. 237 (1933). In response to New Jersey's legal campaign to end the dumping, New York City made two main arguments: that the city had long discharged garbage into New York Harbor under the supervision of the harbor master, and, moreover, that the US Supreme Court had no jurisdiction over the three disposal areas—described as eight, twelve, and twenty miles to the southeast of Scotland Lightship, a floating beacon—because they existed outside US waters. Certainly, the court argued, it had jurisdiction over the injured property in New Jersey. Nor did complying with the harbor supervisor's decisions with respect to the location of discharge give the city the right to create a nuisance.

8.   City of New York, Department of Sanitation, *Annual Report* (1934), 7, and app. no. 1, p. 7.

9.   Robert Moses, *Public Works: A Dangerous Trade* (New York: McGraw-Hill, 1970),

329; "W. F. Carey Is Elected Chairman of International Utilities Corp.," *NYT*, Aug. 7, 1941; and "W. F. Carey Elected by Curtiss-Wright," *NYT*, July 12, 1938.

10. "Fight on Dumping Is Taken to Court," *NYT*, July 23, 1938; Edward T. Russell, "Refuse Dumping Opposed," letter to the editor, June 8, 1938 ("Dark Ages" quotation); Robert Moses, *The Future of Jamaica Bay* (New York, 1938), 3, 4; "Carey Bows to Protest on Jamaica Bay Dump," *NYT*, Sept. 23, 1938; and "Carey Says Moses Is a Propagandist," *NYT*, Oct. 11, 1938.

11. "Carey Is Indicted in Dumping Dispute," *NYT*, Jan. 11, 1939 ("land-fill method" quotation); Martin V. Melosi, *The Sanitary City: Urban Infrastructure in America from Colonial Times to the Present* (Baltimore: Johns Hopkins Univ. Press, 2000), 271; "New York's Landfills," *NYT*, Apr. 15, 1940; New York, N.Y., Sanitary Code art. 13, § 252 (1948); and Daniel C. Walsh, "The History of Waste Landfilling in New York City," *Ground Water* 29 (July–Aug. 1991): 592 ("most prolific" quotation).

12. Richard Fenton, *An Analysis of the Problems of Sanitary Landfills in New York City* (a report for the Bureau of Sanitary Engineering, New York City Health Department, 1947), 64–65; Walsh, "Urban Residential Refuse Composition," 4936, 4938; and Walsh, "The History of Waste Landfilling," 592, fig. 1. A salt marsh survey of New York City conducted in 1946 and 1947 revealed that total acreage in four boroughs (not including Manhattan, which presumably had no extensive marsh reserves) was just 14,310 acres, roughly half the amount that was estimated to exist in 1935. See the table in Fenton, *An Analysis of the Problems of Sanitary Landfills*, unnumbered page following p. 63. A later study revealed that roughly 23,400 acres of land was filled in in New York City in the period from 1924 to 1954–57. The boroughs of Queens (11,040 acres) and Brooklyn (5,640 acres) accounted for the bulk of the new land. See Daniel C. Walsh, "Reconnaissance Mapping of Landfills in New York City" (paper available from the National Ground Water Association, n.d.), 394, info.ngwa.org/gwol/pdf/910155209.pdf.

13. "Sanctuary for Water Fowl Urged by Planning Group," *SIA*, June 6, 1940; Robert Moses, *Improvement: Richmond Marine Park* ([New York?], 1940), 2–3; John Milner Associates, Report, n.d., 69, 78, ch. 5, Staten Island Unit, c. 1978, PC, box 8, folder 140; and "Staten Island Bog Gives Way to Park," *NYT*, Feb. 18, 1949. On the earlier history of what French settlers called La Grand Kil, see Col. H. C. Newcomer, *Report on Great Kills Harbor, Staten Island, New York* (prepared for the Committee on Commerce of the Great Kills Community Council, 1923), 1–3, PC, Great Kills Harbor, box 4, folder 71.

14. Fenton, *An Analysis of the Problems of Sanitary Landfills*, unnumbered page following p. 63. The land Moses had in mind at Fresh Kills was part of the notorious Symes grant. But by this point, the courts had ruled the grant void on the grounds of its imprecision, and, with that obstacle out of the way, the state conveyed the city title to the property. See Memorandum in Support of Senate Introductory No. 569, Mar. 2, 1945 ("unimproved" quotation), and Nathaniel L. Goldstein, Memorandum for the Governor, Mar. 6, 1945, NYCDPOC, mn. 22725, roll 25, box 107874, Legislation, folder 16, 1945. See also Act of Mar. 17, 1945, ch. 171, 1945 N.Y. Laws 553 (granting New York City lands under water and meadow lands at Fresh Kills).

15. "'46 Capital Budget Voted by Board," *NYT*, Dec. 1, 1945; "Fresh Kills Dump Fund

Again Put in Budget," *SIA*, June 7, 1946; Robert Moses to William F. Carey, Nov. 17, 1945, NYCDPOC, mn. 22720, roll 20, box 107872, folder 1 ("disgraceful" quotation); "Big Capital Budget Sharply Attacked," *NYT*, Nov. 16, 1945 ("Don't" quotation); and "Staten Islanders War on 'Landfill,'" *NYT*, July 10, 1946.

16. "Hall Backs Fresh Kills Dump" *SIA*, June 8, 1946 (Hall quotations); and "'No Other Way of Meeting Problem,' Says Moses, Defending Kills Dump," *SIA*, June 25, 1946 (Moses quotation).

17. Robert Moses to *SIA*, June 22, 1946, p. 2, NYCDPOC, mn. 22740, roll 40, box 107883, folder 41 ("no other way" quotation); and "Waste Disposal in New York City," July 18, 1946, pp. 7, 6, NYCDPOC, mn. 22742, roll 42, box 107884, folder 22.

18. "Staten Island Problem," *NYT*, July 23, 1946.

19. "Waste Disposal in New York City," 1–2, which notes that roughly 55 percent of the waste was ashes, cans, and bottles and could not be burned in incinerators, and thus had to be shipped to landfills like Fresh Kills; Daniel C. Walsh, "Incineration: What Led to the Rise and Fall of Incineration in New York City?" *Environmental Science & Technology* 36 (Aug. 1, 2002): 320A; and New York City Department of Sanitation, *Annual Report* (1946), 30, 31. I derived the ten-plant figure from the table on p. 30 of the 1946 Department of Sanitation annual report. As for capacity, the same table indicates that roughly one million tons were burned. In 1937 Walsh says two million (metric) tons were burned. See Walsh, "Incineration," 320A.

20. "Buck Asks U.S. Aid to Preserve Fresh Kills," *SIA*, June 22, 1946, which reprints Buck's letter to the Fish and Wildlife Service; "Waterfowl to Suffer, Buck Told," *SIA*, July 9, 1946; "Other Boroughs Need Site Here, Keegan Claims," *SIA*, July 12, 1946; and "City Council Votes $208,853,423 Budget," *NYT*, July 12, 1946.

21. "Will Back Secession from City If Islanders Want It, Says Radigan," *SIA*, Jan. 3, 1947; "New Appeal Sent to Governor on Anti-Dump Bills," *SIA*, Apr. 5 1947; "Johnson, Berge Pledge Dumping Fight Renewal," *SIA*, Apr. 14, 1947; "City Studies Dump Site in Another Borough," *SIA*, Jan. 31, 1947; and "Alternate Dumping Site Is Branded Unsuitable," *SIA*, Feb. 20, 1947.

22. "Manhattan Firm Given 'Go' Sign on Dump Plant," *SIA*, Feb. 21, 1947; "City Calls for Speed on Fresh Kills Work," *SIA*, Mar. 14, 1947; "Dump Getting 1st Scowload of Garbage," *SIA*, Apr. 17, 1948; "More Land to Be Taken for Dump at Fresh Kills," *SIA*, Mar. 4, 1948; and Daniel C. Walsh, "Solid Wastes in New York City: A History," *Waste Age*, Apr. 1989, 122 ("world's largest" quotation).

23. US Census Office, 1910 manuscript schedule, Northfield Township, Richmond County, N.Y., p. 5-B, and 1920 manuscript schedule, Borough of Richmond, Richmond County, N.Y., p. 11-A, www.ancestry.com; Joseph Mitchell, *The Bottom of the Harbor* (1959; repr., New York: Vintage, 2001), 69, 70–71; and Interstate Sanitation Commission, *Annual Report* (1940), 41.

24. Mitchell, *The Bottom of the Harbor*, 72–73, 74.

25. "'Ugly Ducklings' Ply Backwaters," *NYT*, Nov. 6, 1952; Interstate Sanitation Commission, *Annual Report* (1951), 15; and New York City Department of Sanitation, *Annual Report 1959–1960* (1960), 33.

26. Robert Moses to William O'Dwyer and attached memorandum, Aug. 12, 1948, NYCDPOC, mn. 22752, roll 52, box 107890, folder 29; Cornelius A. Hall, Robert

Moses, and Andrew W. Mulrain, *Fresh Kills Land Fill=100 Acres of Parks Arterials Public Works=100 Acres for Private Development* ([New York?], 1951), quotations from 13; and "Big Opportunity for City Planning Is Seen in Landfill on Staten Island," *NYT*, Nov. 26, 1951.

27. Hall, Moses, and Mulrain, *Fresh Kills Land Fill*, 2. The Empire State Building contains 37 million cubic feet, or 1.37 million cubic yards, of space. The Flushing reclamation involved roughly 7 million cubic yards of fill.

28. "The Claypit Ponds Battle: 'Wildlife' Vs. 'Progress'" and "Don't Ruin Beauty, Rare Bird Refuge, Naturalists Plead," *SIA*, Nov. 28, 1951; Samuel R. Mozes, "Staten Island: Today and Tomorrow; A Comprehensive Planning Study for Future Development of the Borough of Richmond, New York City" (master's thesis, Columbia Univ., 1954), 170–71; and "Park Proposed in Claypit Pond Area," *SIA*, Mar. 21, 1951, which notes that Moses advocated turning some of the Claypit Pond area into a park, a development that came to fruition.

29. "Great Kills Landfill Rats Attract Rare Snowy Owl," *SIA*, Jan. 5, 1946; "Bird Counts on Staten Island 1950–1974," EC, box 2, folder 28 (quotations). A later study showed that ring-billed gulls were more dependent on landfills for food than herring gulls (*Larus argentatus*). See Jerrold L. Belant, Sheri K. Ickes, and Thomas W. Seamans, "Importance of Landfills to Urban-Nesting Herring and Ring-Billed Gulls," *Landscape and Urban Planning* 43, no. 1 (1998): 11–19, doi:10.1016/S0169 -2046(98)00100-5.

30. The fossil record indicates that *Phragmites australis* was present in North America as long as forty thousand years ago. But recent research has revealed evidence of a nonnative variety that likely was introduced early in the nineteenth century, possibly when ship ballast was used to fill in marsh at a coastal port somewhere. Regardless of its provenance, there is no questioning the explosion of the plant in the New York metropolitan area's littoral over the last century. Moreover, the boom in common reed seems to be linked to anthropogenic change, specifically the man-made hydrology and accompanying eutrophication that characterize an area crammed with so many human beings. See Kristin Saltonstall, "Cryptic Invasion by a Non-Native Genotype of the Common Reed, *Phragmites australis*, into North America," *PNAS* 99, no. 4 (Feb. 19, 2002): 2445, 2448, doi:10.1073/pnas.032477999; Carlo Popolizio, "An Invasive Foe or a Resilient Friend?: *Phragmites australis* in the Hackensack Meadowlands," *Field Notes* (US Fish & Wildlife Service, N.J. Field Office), Dec. 2002, 20; and Marianne Marks, Beth Lapin, and John Randall, "*Phragmites australis (p. communis)*: Threats, Management, and Monitoring," *Natural Areas Journal* 14 (Oct. 1994): 285–86.

31. Alfred G. Haggerty, "Progress Seen Killing Off Island Wildlife," Mar. 18, 1960, PC, Parks on Staten Island, box 7, folder 122; and "Staten Island's Wildlife Periled by Reclamation and New Homes," *NYT*, May 9, 1960 (quotations). Polevoy claimed that but fifteen years before, forty trappers bagged eighteen thousand skins, whereas he now counted only fifteen trappers, of whom just five worked at it for a living. By 1960, rabbits were the only significant population of small game on the island. See Haggerty, "Progress Seen Killing Off Island Wildlife."

32. In 1960 Staten Island's population density was 3,803 people per square mile.

33. "City Set to Fill In 20,000 Acres in Vast Shoreline Reclamation," *NYT*, Jan. 21, 1957; and "James Felt, Former Chairman of City Planning Agency, Dies," *NYT*, Mar. 5, 1971 ("conscience" quotation).

34. Eric Darton, *Divided We Stand: A Biography of New York's World Trade Center* (New York: Basic Books, 1999), 34; and Robert Fitch, *The Assassination of New York* (London: Verso, 1993), xii–xix, 135, 91–96. Robert Moses continued to believe in the viability of waterfront reclamation. See Robert Moses, *The Expanding New York Waterfront* ([New York?], 1964); and Moses's introduction to *A Tour of Staten Island Improvements and the Next Steps* (published by the Triborough Bridge and Tunnel Authority, 1965).

35. Regional Plan Association, *Waste Management: Generation and Disposal of Solid, Liquid and Gaseous Wastes in the New York Region* (New York, 1968), 5, 65. On the virtues of the city's many landfill projects, see 52, 59–61. Maps contrasting wetland with man-made land appear on 62–63.

36. New York City Planning Commission, *Plan for New York City, 1969: A Proposal*, 6 vols. (Cambridge, Mass.: MIT Press, 1969), 1:159. On the master plan, see Tom Angotti, *New York for Sale: Community Planning Confronts Global Real Estate* (Cambridge, Mass.: MIT Press, 2008), 73–74.

37. Nancy Moran, "Garbage Piles Up, and Suburbs Seek Places to Put It," *NYT*, Aug. 22, 1969; Peter Kihss, "Kearing Warns Landfills for Refuse Disposal Will Be Filled in Eight Years," *NYT*, Feb. 20, 1967; and Paul Wilkes, "The Garbage Apocalypse," *New York*, Mar. 10, 1969, 24 (Kearing quotation). The nine sanitation commissioners are named in Martin Tolchin, "Mayor Swears in Sanitation Chief," *NYT*, Apr. 27, 1971.

38. Department of Sanitation, *Annual Report 1959–1960*, 33; Walsh, "The History of Waste Landfilling," 592; Walsh, "Reconnaissance Mapping of Landfills," 397; David Bird, "City Incinerator Is Closed," *NYT*, May 21, 1969 ("contouring" quotation); and Edward C. Burks, "Hill of Landfill Backed for S.I.," *NYT*, Dec. 1, 1970 ("endanger" quotation). City Council President Sanford Garelik proposed to end the landfill shortage by piling the city's daily twenty thousand tons of refuse into a mountain projected to rise twenty-five hundred feet above Pelham Bay in the Bronx. See "Trash Mountain Urged for City Grand Slalom," *NYT*, Aug. 16, 1970.

39. Walsh, "Incineration," 321A (quotation), 320A; and Charles Grutzner, "City's Dirty Air Called a Factor in Rising Deaths," *NYT*, June 23, 1965.

40. Corey, "King Garbage," 306–7, 267–68; and David Bird, "City to Shut Dirty 73d St. Incinerator," *NYT*, Dec. 30, 1972 ("merely trading" quotation).

41. Samuel J. Kearing Jr., "The Politics of Garbage," *New York*, Apr. 1970, 32.

42. "Littering, n.1," *OED Online*, www.oed.com; "City to Intensify War on Littering," *NYT*, Mar. 9, 1955; "Did *You* Make New York Dirty Today?" newspaper advertisement, Citizens Committee to Keep New York Clean, HHP, box 56, folder 3 ("Cleaner New York" quotation); Corey, "King Garbage," 282; *Annual Report of the Citizens Committee to Keep New York City Clean, Inc. 1960–1961*, pp. 28, 29, Citizens Committee to Keep New York Clean, HHP, box 56, folder 4; Ted Steinberg, "Can Capitalism Save the Planet? On the Origins of Green Liberalism," *Radical History Review* 2010, no. 107: 14; and Walsh, "Urban Residential Refuse Composition," 4938.

43. Julia Martin, "Staten Islanders See Wildlife Refuge Threat," *Newark (N.J.) News*, Nov. 2, 1969; and Herbert Elish, "The Crisis in Solid Waste Disposal," *New York*

Affairs 1, no. 2 (1973): 95. Since 1980, the annual per capita rate of residential refuse declined to 430 kilograms and remained steady from that point until 2002. See Walsh, "Urban Residential Refuse Composition," 4938.

44. Wehran-New York, *Draft Environmental Impact Statement for the Fresh Kills Ash/ Residue Landfill, Staten Island, New York* (report for the City of New York Department of Sanitation, Middletown, N.Y., 1991), III-35; and K. A. Boriskin, "Civilization's Colossal Creation," letter to the editor, *Science News* 139, no. 3 (Jan. 19, 1991), 43. An archeological study of Fresh Kills, written in 1992, projected that the Fresh Kills Landfill, when closed down in 2005, would reach 505 feet in height. See William Rathje and Cullen Murphy, *Rubbish!: The Archaeology of Garbage* (1992; repr., New York: HarperPerennial, 1993), 3–4.

45. Kearing, "The Politics of Garbage," 30.

13. The Great Hackensack Disappearing Act

1. Charles Stafford, "A Reclamation Challenge," newspaper clipping, no source, ca. 1958, box 1 (Mar. 1888–Oct. 1963), MERI ("My father" quotation); and John Brooks, "A Reporter at Large: The Meadows—II," *New Yorker*, Mar. 16, 1957, 113, 110 ("Mayor" quotation).

2. Ralph W. Tiner, John Q. Swords, and Bobbi Jo McClain, *Wetland Status and Trends for the Hackensack Meadowlands: An Assessment Report from the U.S. Fish and Wildlife Service's National Wetlands Inventory Program* (Hadley, Mass.: US Fish and Wildlife Service, 2002), 20, table 11. On the bird life present in the wetlands circa 1990, see Richard P. Kane, "Hackensack Meadowlands Special Area Management Plan," *New Jersey Audubon*, Winter 1990–1991, 26.

3. Brooks, "A Reporter at Large: The Meadows—II," 113, 118; and US Census Office, 1900 manuscript schedule, East Rutherford, Bergen County, N.J., 14, and 1910 manuscript schedule, East Rutherford, Bergen County, 22-B, www.ancestry.com.

4. Thomas J. Headlee, "Report on Mosquito Work for 1915," *Thirty-Sixth Annual Report of the New Jersey State Agricultural Experiment Station* . . . (Paterson, N.J., 1916), 349 ("destroyed" quotation); Gordon Patterson, *The Mosquito Crusades: A History of the American Anti-Mosquito Movement from the Reed Commission to the First Earth Day* (New Brunswick, N.J.: Rutgers Univ. Press, 2009), 72–73; Act of Mar. 21, 1912, ch. 104, § 3, 1912 N.J. Laws 149 (empowering county mosquito extermination commissions to eliminate breeding areas); and John W. Harshberger and Vincent G. Burns, "The Vegetation of the Hackensack Marsh: A Typical American Fen," *Transactions of the Wagner Free Institute of Science of Philadelphia* 9, pt. 1 (May 1919): 13. On the mosquito and property values, see William E. Sackett, *Modern Battles of Trenton, Volume II, from Werts to Wilson* (New York, 1914), 93–94. No one played a more important role in initiating mosquito eradication than the Rutgers University entomologist John B. Smith. Around 1900, Smith recommended ditching to cause water on the marsh to rise and fall and to allow killifish, a predator of the mosquito, to enter the area. See Thomas J. Headlee, *The Mosquitoes of New Jersey and Their Control* (New Brunswick, N.J.: Rutgers Univ. Press, 1945), 273. For the figures on the amount of drainage ditches by county, see appendix D.

5. Harshberger and Burns, "The Vegetation of the Hackensack Marsh," 35 ("Hackensack marsh" quotation). On the unintended effects of ditching, see Headlee, "Report on Mosquito Work for 1915," 361, and on the new diking method, see 352–53. On the loss of tidal and freshwater wetlands between 1905 and 1932, see Michael Reis, "Wartime Mobilization and the Newark Bay Home Front Environment: A Case Study Revealing Opportunity for Federal Leadership in Resolving Mega Site Problems," *Environmental Claims Journal* 18, no. 4 (Fall 2006): 297, doi:10.1080 /10406020600996315.

6. Kevin W. Wright, *The Hackensack Meadowlands: Prehistory and History* (report no. 1988-039, MERI, 1988), 6; John Brooks, "A Reporter at Large: The Meadows—I," *New Yorker*, Mar. 9, 1957, 105; and Adrian C. Leiby, *The Hackensack Water Company, 1869–1969* (River Edge, N.J.: Bergen County Historical Society, 1969), 61, 163, 181.

7. William S. Sipple, "The Past and Present Flora and Vegetation of the Hackensack Meadows," *Bartonia: Journal of the Philadelphia Botanical Club*, no. 41 (1971–72): 23–24; US Fish and Wildlife Service, *The Hackensack Meadowlands Initiative: Preliminary Conservation Planning for the Hackensack Meadowlands, Hudson and Bergen Counties, New Jersey* (2007), 112; and William Stanton Sipple, "The Past and Present Flora and Vegetation of the Hackensack Meadows New Jersey and Suggestions for Management" (master's thesis, Univ. of Pennsylvania, 1971), 118.

8. Environmental Defense Fund, *The New Jersey Hackensack Meadowlands: The Need to Establish the Scope of Federal Clean Water Act Jurisdiction and to Prepare a Programmatic EIS to Consider Alternative Management Strategies* (New York, 1985), 4–5; and John P. Peterson, "The Development and Use of Machinery for Crushing Grasses, Reeds, and Sedges on the Salt Marshes," *Proceedings of the Nineteenth Annual Meeting of the NJMEA* (New Brunswick, N.J., 1932), 71 (quotation).

9. Brooks, "A Reporter at Large: The Meadows—II," 114 ("Mostly muskrat" quotation); Sipple, "The Past and Present Flora and Vegetation of the Hackensack Meadows New Jersey and Suggestions for Management," 144; Charles A. Urner, "Relation of Mosquito Control in New Jersey to Bird Life of the Salt Marshes," in *Proceedings of the Twenty-Second Annual Meeting of the NJMEA* (New Brunswick, N.J., 1935), 132–33; and Lisa Goodnight, "In the Dumps No More," *Record*, Apr. 10, 2001, on the new license plate design.

10. Steven Hart, *The Last Three Miles: Politics, Murder, and the Construction of America's First Superhighway* (New York: New Press, 2007), 10–11. The Venetian plan mentioned was put forward by the Regional Plan Association. The canals were a virtual necessity, for there would be no other way of securing the monumental 172 million cubic yards of fill anticipated for the project. Lewis Mumford called the idea "[p]erhaps the most drastic transformation of land use" in the entire Regional Plan Association plan for the region. See George McAneny, "Waterways and Port Development," July 3, 1931, GMP, box 56 (New York City Files, Planning and Regional Plan Association); "A Magic City from a Swamp," *PS*, Oct. 1928, 49; "A Model Industrial City Rising on Hackensack Meadows," *Regional Plan News* 2 (Dec. 1930): 1–2; and Lewis Mumford, "The Plan of New York," in *Planning the Fourth Migration: The Neglected Vision of the Regional Planning Association of America,*

ed. Carl Sussman (Cambridge, Mass.: MIT Press, 1976), 237. For other bold plans, see New Jersey Waterways and Highways Improvement Association, *The Hackensack and Passaic Valleys as Part of the Port of New York* (Jersey City, N.J., 1926), 4–5, 6, 7, 9, 17; and *Report of Meadow Reclamation Commission: Appointed Under Joint Resolution No. 8 of the Legislature of the State of New Jersey, Session of 1930* ([Trenton, N.J.?], 1930), 19, 22, 31, 35.

11. Hart, *The Last Three Miles*, 4; and "Jersey Meadows Viaduct," *NYT*, Nov. 25, 1932.

12. Tiner, Swords, and McClain, *Wetland Status and Trends for the Hackensack Meadowlands*, 20, table 11. Development took a different, more expedited course to the south, on the more manageable and accessible Newark Meadows. As late as the first decade of the twentieth century, the meadows outside of the city of Newark covered forty-five hundred acres. Construction at Newark Airport and even more extensive improvements carried out by the US Army Air Forces (which leased the field) during the early 1940s led to significant filling in of the Newark area marshlands. By 1944, more than half the original salt marsh had been turned into railroad yards, highways, runways, and docks. See Reis, "Wartime Mobilization," 313–14; and Frederick W. Becker, "The Story of Mosquito Control in Essex County," *Proceedings of the Thirty-First Annual Meeting of the NJMEA* (New Brunswick, N.J., 1944), 154.

13. Clarence D. Smith Jr., "The Destructive Storm of November 25–27, 1950," *Monthly Weather Review* 78, no. 11 (Nov. 1950): 208–9; Samuel Gofseyeff and Frank L. Panuzio, "Hurricane Studies of New York Harbor," *TASCE* 128, no. 4 (Apr. 1963): 397, table 1; "21 Die in Suburbs; Loss Is in Millions," *NYT*, Nov. 26, 1950; and "Flood Waters Add to Devastation as Coast Staggers Under Chill Blast," *Washington Post*, Nov. 26, 1950.

14. Vernon Conant, "The Conversion of the North Arlington Meadow Salt Marsh from a Dike-Enclosed Meadow to an Open Meadow," *Proceedings: Fifty-Third Annual Meeting, NJMEA* (Atlantic City, N.J., 1966), 116. For a nice explanation of the counterproductive effects of the dikes, see the comments of Don Smith in "Meadowlands Haven," *SL*, July 31, 1983. On the change in avian life, see Irving H. Black, "Past and Present Status of the Birds of the Lower Hackensack River Marshes," *New Jersey Nature News* 25, no. 2 (1970): 59.

15. Tiner, Swords, and McClain, *Wetland Status and Trends for the Hackensack Meadowlands*, 20, table 12.

16. John T. George and Thomas W. Ryley, "The New Jersey Turnpike," *Land Economics* 33, no. 2 (May 1957): 154, 161, www.jstor.org/stable/3144904; Tom Lewis, *Divided Highways: Building the Interstate Highways, Transforming American Life* (1997; repr., New York: Penguin, 1999), 48, 69; and "Construction Men Rush Turnpike over Jersey Marshes for '51 Use," *NYT*, Aug. 9, 1950. On Laurel Hill, see Wright, *The Hackensack Meadowlands*, 108.

17. On the ecological impact of the turnpike, see John R. Quinn, *Fields of Sun and Grass: An Artist's Journal of the New Jersey Meadowlands* (New Brunswick, N.J.: Rutgers Univ. Press, 1997), 167.

18. Marc Levinson, *The Box: How the Shipping Container Made the World Smaller and the World Economy Bigger* (Princeton, N.J.: Princeton Univ. Press, 2006), 39, 43–44, 70.

19. Levinson, *The Box*, 85–86, 92; and Moray Epstein, "Reclamation Challenge," *NSDN*, Aug. 22, 1965. One of those hay farmers was Bill Ballenski, whose father, a German immigrant, had been cutting hay since the 1890s. See "Haymakers Kayoed in Meadows," *NSDN*, Feb. 22, 1959.

20. Hawthorne Hill, "Special Reports on Waste Disposal: The Private Collection of Garbage," *Municipal Affairs*, suppl. 2 (June 1898): 128–30; New Jersey Department of Community Affairs, Division of State and Regional Planning, *Introduction to the Meadows: The Developmental History*, technical report no. AA ([Trenton, N.J.?], 1968), 22; Thomas D. Mulhern, "Mosquito Control in New Jersey in 1940 and Its Contributions to National Defense," *Proceedings of the Twenty-Eighth Annual Meeting of the NJMEA* (New Brunswick, N.J., 1941), 82; Joan Cook, "Pigless Secaucus, 75, Points with Pride," *NYT*, Apr. 29, 1975; "Henry Krajewski, Pig Farmer Who Ran for President, Dies," *NYT*, Nov. 9, 1966 (quotation); Fred Ferretti, "About New Jersey," *NYT*, Apr. 11, 1976; Norman R. Stoll, "This Wormy World," *Journal of Parasitology* 33, no. 1 (Feb. 1947): 2–4, www.jstor.org/stable/3273613; and Department of Health of the State of New Jersey, *Eighty-Fourth Annual Report* (Trenton, N.J., 1961), 103.

21. Department of Health of the State of New Jersey, *Eighty-Fourth Annual Report*, 101; Department of Health of the State of New Jersey, *Seventy-Seventh Annual Report* (Trenton, N.J., 1955), 125; and "New Jersey Mosquito Control Activities During 1956," *Proceedings: Forty-Fourth Annual Meeting NJMEA* (New Brunswick, N.J., 1957), 178.

22. Howard Fast, "The Meadows," *Esquire*, Dec. 1958, 68, 70; George Cable Wright, "Meyner to Press Plan on Meadows," *NYT*, Mar. 12, 1959 (Meyner quotation); and "Requiem for the Meadows," *NYT*, Mar. 25, 1959.

23. Charles C. Morrison Jr., "The Hackensack Meadows—A Metropolitan Frontier" (master's thesis, Columbia Univ., 1961), 1, 88, 61, 87, 89, 145, 62. The term "garbage dumps" was chosen carefully, since New Jersey did not enact a law requiring an earth cover for refuse until 1958, a full generation after New York City had done so. Even after the 1958 reform, the state remained notorious for the open dumping of garbage. See Department of Health of the State of New Jersey, *Eighty-Second Annual Report* (Trenton, N.J., 1959), 8.

24. Brooks, "A Reporter at Large: The Meadows—II," 116, 123; and John T. Cunningham, "Natural Wonderland," *NSDN*, Mar. 1, 1959.

25. Zurn Environmental Engineers, *Analysis of Alternative Solid Wastes Management Systems for the Hackensack Meadowlands District* (Trenton, N.J., 1970), II-2, II-4, V-5, V-10; "The Hackensack Meadowlands—1968," *Jersey Plans* 17 (Summer 1968), 13; and "N.Y. Landmarks' Rubble Bears Jersey Industry," *NYT*, Oct. 13, 1968.

26. "Birds Aid Jersey War on Marijuana," *NYT*, Aug. 21, 1968.

27. Tiner, Swords, and McClain, *Wetland Status and Trends for the Hackensack Meadowlands*, 20, table 11. Bruce Davidson's 1965 photograph of Royka can be seen at the website of Magnum Photos, accessed May 30, 2013, www.magnumphotos.com/image/NYC102615.html. Biographical information on Royka can be found in Quinn, *Fields of Sun and Grass*, 143–49.

28. "Ecologist Tangles with McDowell," *North Arlington (N.J.) Leader*, May 13, 1971; "The Tidelands of Megalopolis," *Record*, July 11, 1964; *Sisselman v. State Hwy. Dep't*, No. A769-59 (N.J. Super. Ct., App. Div., 1961), available from the Office of the Clerk, Superior Court of New Jersey, Trenton, N.J.; Alfred A. Porro Jr., and Lorraine S. Teleky, "Marshland Title Dilemma: A Tidal Phenomenon," *Seton Hall Law Review* 3, no. 2 (Spring 1972): 325; Moya Keys, "The Hackensack Meadowlands—State or Private Interest?: An Analysis of the Tidelands Doctrine," *Rutgers Law Review* 38, no. 2 (Winter 1986): 387; and Wayne H. Dawson, "Tideland Ownership—Time for Reform," *University of Cincinnati Law Review* 36, no. 1 (Winter 1967): 121. The Meadowlands Owners' Association was formed to fight the legal ruling. More than a thousand parcels of land were thrown into dispute.

29. Peter Hellman, "In the Big Dump: A Sweet Smell of Success," *NYT*, Jan. 26, 1975; Bruce Lambert, "Paul Ylvisaker, 70, Educator and Urban Planner," *NYT*, Mar. 20, 1992; David Stout, "Fairleigh S. Dickinson Jr., 76, Who Helped Save the Meadowlands," *NYT*, Oct. 17, 1996; Act of July 1, 1968, ch. 404, 1968, vol. 1, N.J. Laws 1313 (creating the HMDC); and art. 1, § 1, 1968, vol. 1, N.J. Laws at 1314.

30. HMDC, *Hackensack Meadowlands Comprehensive Land Use Plan* ([Lyndhurst, N.J.?], 1970), 28, 29; Chester P. Mattson, *The Hackensack Meadows: An Ecological Perspective* (Philadelphia, 1970), 14, 8; and Sipple, "The Past and Present Flora and Vegetation of the Hackensack Meadows New Jersey and Suggestions for Management," 26, 63. The ditching, for example, opened channels for killifish to enter, removed water from the land so that Phragmites could flourish, and, in the process, created a food supply that muskrats above all other animals thrived on.

31. HMDC, *Hackensack Meadowlands*, 42, 40, 39, 57.

32. "Meadowlands Plan to Help Ecology," *NYT*, Nov. 24, 1970; and Mattson, *The Hackensack Meadows*, 20 (quotation).

33. "Dream City," *Daily Journal* (Elizabeth, N.J.), Nov. 27, 1970 ("no instance" quotation); "Meadowland Dream Stirs Ecologists' Fears," *Record*, Nov. 27, 1970 ("do not need" quotation); and Ania Savage, "Dangers Descried in Meadows Plan," *Record*, Nov. 29, 1970.

34. "Case Comments: Environmental Law—New Jersey Sports and Exposition Authority Act . . . ," *Rutgers Law Review* 26, no. 4 (Summer 1973): 868, 873 (quotation); Tiner, Swords, and McClain, *Wetland Status and Trends for the Hackensack Meadowlands*, 10; and Act of May 10, 1971, ch. 137, 1971 N.J. Laws 314 (providing for stadiums and other facilities in the Hackensack Meadowlands). On the western spur of the turnpike as well as the hope that it would speed development, see Act of Feb. 16, 1966, ch. 6, 1966, vol. 1, N.J. Laws 17 (authorizing an addition to the N.J. Turnpike); Joseph C. Ingraham, "Regional Plan Urges New Link for Jersey Pike," *NYT*, Feb. 1, 1965; Joseph C. Ingraham, "Turnpike Is Being Widened in Jersey," *NYT*, Jan. 11, 1968; New Jersey Department of Conservation and Economic Development, Division of State and Regional Planning, *Land Use and Development Trends in the Hackensack Meadows*, Technical Report No. 2B ([Trenton, N.J.?], 1966), 2B-1; and James F. Lynch, "Development of Meadows Crawls On amid Conflict," *NYT*, May 4, 1969.

35. "Broker Looks at Meadowlands' Future," *Record*, July 16, 1971 (Klatskin quo-

tation); Glenn Fowler, "Jersey Meadowlands 'Making It,'" *NYT*, Nov. 7, 1971 ("helter-skelter" quotation); and Edward J. Flynn, "Industry Giving Meadows New Image," *Record*, Oct. 20, 1971 (Goldman quotation).

36. "N.J. Meadowlands Becoming Prime Property for Building," *Daily Journal*, Apr. 26, 1974; and "What's Doing in the Meadowlands? Just Ask Klatskin," *New Jersey Business*, Dec. 1976, 45 (Klatskin quotation). It turned out that the most intense period of annual wetland loss overlapped with the commission's formation and early years. The period 1966 to 1976 saw 304 acres a year of wetland loss. See Tiner, Swords, and McClain, *Wetland Status and Trends for the Hackensack Meadowlands*, 20, table 12. However, a 1988 news report noted that since 1972, the HMDC had only allowed 824 acres to be developed out of a total of 8,624 acres of both wetlands and water. See Adriana Reyneri, "A Balancing Act with Nature," *Jersey Journal* (Jersey City, N.J.), Feb. 19, 1988.

37. Robert Hanley, "Hackensack Meadowlands Still Paradise for Trappers," *NYT*, Dec. 1, 1978 (Royka quotation); and Tom Tiede, "Trapping Is Willie's Way of Survival," *Park City (Bowling Green, Ky.) Daily News*, Dec. 27, 1972. See also, Martin Gottlieb, "Braving the Wilds for $2 a Pelt," *Record*, Nov. 14, 1973. Royka said that, in one reporter's words, "urbanization has pushed muskrats closer together." See "Fur Trappers Flourish in Wilds of New Jersey," *Daytona (Fla.) Beach Morning Journal*, Nov. 21, 1978.

38. Martin Gansberg, "Federal Agency Praises Cleanup of Once 'Stinking' Meadowlands," *NYT*, May 8, 1978 ("water-quality" quotation); Mattson, *The Hackensack Meadows*, 12; Richard Kane, "Birds of the Kearny Marsh," *New Jersey Audubon Supplement* 4 (Winter 1978): 22–27 ("phenomenal" quotation); Environmental Defense Fund, *The New Jersey Hackensack Meadowlands*, 19; and Tiner, Swords, and McClain, *Wetland Status and Trends for the Hackensack Meadowlands*, 20, table 11. For favorable interpretations of ecological change in the Meadowlands, see Chester P. Mattson and Nicholas C. Vallario, *Water Quality in a Recovering Ecosystem: A Report on Water Quality Research and Monitoring in the Hackensack Meadowlands, 1971–1975* ([Secaucus, N.J.?], 1976); and Reyneri, "A Balancing Act with Nature," which quotes HMDC naturalist Don Smith, who argued that the meadows, though smaller, were still rich in wildlife.

39. Judy Temes, "EPA Irks Builders," *Hudson Dispatch* (Union City, N.J.), July 25, 1988, on the small projects the EPA put on ice; Robert Hanley, "Environmentalists' Tough Balancing Act in Meadowlands," *NYT*, Aug. 15, 1987 (EPA quotation); Scott Friedman, "HMDC and Feds Clash on Meadowland," *Hudson Dispatch*, Sept. 6, 1989; and Tiner, Swords, and McClain, *Wetland Status and Trends for the Hackensack Meadowlands*, 20, table 12. For more on the poor business environment created by regulations, see Jeffrey Hoff, "The Wetlands Nightmare," *Business Journal of New Jersey*, May 1988, 117–19.

40. Ronald Sullivan, "Huge Incinerator Planned in Jersey," *NYT*, Aug. 19, 1971; "Progress on Garbage Disposal," *Herald-News* (Passaic, N.J.), July 23, 1971, on the 116 municipalities dumping refuse in the Meadowlands in 1971; Robert Podesfinski, "Meadowlands Title Battle Continues," *Herald-News*, Dec. 7, 1970, on the virtues of open marshland; Eileen McGurty, "Solid Waste Management in 'The Garden

State': New Jersey's Transformation from Landfilling to Incineration," in *New Jersey's Environments: Past, Present, and Future*, ed. Neil M. Maher (New Brunswick, N.J.: Rutgers Univ. Press, 2006), 36–37, on the development angle with respect to incinerators; Clifford A. Goldman, "The Hackensack Meadowlands: The Politics of Regional Planning and Development in the Metropolis" (PhD diss., Princeton Univ., 1975), 347–49; and Edward J. Flynn, "Trash: Is Any Hope Left?" *Record*, Nov. 17, 1971.

41. Robert Hanley, "Meadowlands Balancing Environment and Development," *NYT*, Aug. 15, 1987; Thomas J. Lueck, "Not Just Football Booming in Jersey Meadows," *NYT*, Jan. 11, 1987; and David Blomquist, "Where Will the Trash Go?" *Record*, Dec. 29, 1985.

42. Donald F. Squires, "Quantifying Anthropogenic Shoreline Modification of the Hudson River and Estuary from European Contact to Modern Time," *Coastal Management* 20, no. 4 (1992): 343, 347, table 1. Table 1 shows that the original marsh declined from 71,500 acres to 15,500 acres in 1980, a loss of 56,000 acres (78 percent), equal to 4.1 times the size of Manhattan Island in 2010 (13,636 acres). See also appendix E. For wetland loss around the world, see World Water Assessment Programme (United Nations), *Water for People, Water for Life: A Joint Report by the Twenty-Three UN Agencies Concerned with Freshwater* (New York: UNESCO and Berghahn Books, 2003), 143; and M. Sufia Sultana, G. M. Tarekul Islam, and Zahidul Islam, "Pre- and Post–Urban Wetland Area in Dhaka City, Bangladesh: A Remote Sensing and GIS Analysis," *Journal of Water Resource and Protection*, 1 (Dec. 2009): 414, doi:10.4236/jwarp.2009.16050. For more on the drainage of wetlands in the twentieth century, see J. R. McNeill, *Something New Under the Sun: An Environmental History of the Twentieth-Century World* (New York: W. W. Norton, 2000), 186–89. On the simplification of habitat and adaptable generalists such as gulls and pigeons, see D. F. Squires and J. S. Barclay, *Nearshore Wildlife Habitats and Populations in the New York/New Jersey Harbor Estuary* (report prepared for the New York/New Jersey Harbor Estuary Program, 1990), 87.

14. The Age of Limits

1. Owen Moritz, "Plan a $1.2B Wonderful Town on East River Landfill," *DN*, Apr. 13, 1972 (Lindsay quotation).

2. Regional Plan Association, *The Region's Growth: A Report of the Second Regional Plan* ([New York?], 1967), 11, 36, 19.

3. Albin Krebs, "Big Apple Polishers Brighten City's Image," *NYT*, Mar. 27, 1975; and "Notes and Comments," *New Yorker*, Aug. 6, 1984, 21.

4. Second Report, Nov. 1963, DLMAP, box 189, folder 1733; and David Rockefeller with Dick Reeves, radio interview, WCBS, Nov. 20, 1963, DLMAP, box 189, folder 1733. On the 1962 plan by the Department of Marine and Aviation, see "The Lower Manhattan Plan," in *The Lower Manhattan Plan: The 1966 Vision for Downtown New York*, ed. Carol Willis (1966; repr., New York: Princeton Architectural Press, 2002), 30.

5. Marc Levinson, *The Box: How the Shipping Container Made the World Smaller and*

the World Economy Bigger (Princeton, N.J.: Princeton Univ. Press, 2006), 94; David Rockefeller, "Progress Report," Oct. 8, 1959, DLMAP, box 189, folder 1733; Robert Fitch, *The Assassination of New York* (London: Verso, 1993), 134–35; and Eric Darton, *Divided We Stand: A Biography of New York's World Trade Center* (New York: Basic Books, 1999), 93–95.

6.   Steven V. Roberts, "Governor Urges 'City' at Battery," *NYT*, May 13, 1966.

7.   "Jackhammers Bite Pavement to Start Trade Center Job," *NYT*, Aug. 6, 1966; "Work on the World Trade Center Is Moving into a Higher Gear," *NYT*, July 6, 1967; Darton, *Divided We Stand*, 83; Paul Willen and James Rossant, "In Retrospect," in *The Lower Manhattan Plan*, ed. Willis, 32; Steven V. Roberts, "Conflicts Stall Landfill Plans," *NYT*, Jan. 17, 1967; Charles Grutzner, "Hudson Landfill Project to Start," *NYT*, Dec. 24, 1966 ("fatten" quotation); and Terrence Smith, "Moses Urges Hudson Fill as a Stock Exchange Site," *NYT*, Dec. 7, 1966.

8.   Ann Buttenwieser, "'Fore and Aft: The Waterfront and Downtowns' Future," in *The Lower Manhattan Plan*, ed. Willis, 22–24; Ada Louise Huxtable, "City Gets a Sweeping Plan for Rejuvenating Lower Manhattan," *NYT*, June 22, 1966; "The Lower Manhattan Plan," vi; and Willen and Rossant, "In Retrospect," 30 (quotation). McHarg would go on to write the classic *Design with Nature* (1969), a manifesto that called for applying an ecological sensibility to regional planning.

9.   Eugene J. Morris, "Legal Bars to Overwater Developments," letter to the editor, *NYT*, Jan. 3, 1967; Charles W. Merritt to John B. Goodman, Jan. 11, 1967, DLMAP, box 77, folder 963; BPCCA Act, ch. 343, § 1971, 1968, vol. 1, N.Y. Laws 1301 ("blighted" quotation); Act of May 26, 1969, ch. 1144, 1969, vol. 2, N.Y. Laws 3048 (authorizing the Board of Estimate to lease land under water in the Hudson River to the BPCCA); and River and Harbor Act of 1968, Pub. L. No. 90–483, § 113, 82 Stat. 736 (1968) (declaring parts of the East and Hudson Rivers nonnavigable). The Battery Park City Corporation Authority responded to my Freedom of Information Law request on the decision to landfill the site by indicating that there were no such records in their possession. Carl Jaffee (FOIL officer) to author, email, June 8, 2011. Nelson Rockefeller and Mayor John Lindsay entered into an agreement to plan and develop Battery Park City. Lindsay said that the project "adds to the greatness of the city, one that creates new land and a new urban environment." See Nelson A. Rockefeller, *Public Papers of Nelson A. Rockefeller Fifty-Third Governor of the State of New York 1968* ([Albany, N.Y.?], 1968), 1068.

10.   Ada Louise Huxtable, "Architecture: How Not to Build a City," *NYT*, Nov. 22, 1970; "Battery Park Plan Is Target of a Suit," *NYT*, Apr. 16, 1969 ("destroy" quotation); David K. Shipler, "Battery Park Plan Is Shown," *NYT*, Apr. 17, 1969 ("Riviera" quotation); and City Planning Commission, "Dissenting Opinion—Commissioner Walter McQuade," Aug. 20, 1969, DLMAP, box 77, folder 967 ("speculation" quotation).

11.   Citizens Budget Commission, *New York City's Waterfront: Opportunities and Options* (New York, 1969), 16, 17; Ada Louise Huxtable, "Plan's 'Total' Concept Is Hailed," *NYT*, Apr. 17, 1969; and Park Association of New York City, *The Waterfront* (New York 19[67?]), 4.

12.   David Bird, "Environment Superagency Asks City for Half Billion for Projects," *NYT*, Oct. 30, 1968 (Eisenbud quotations). The Second Regional Plan endorsed

"[t]opographic modification [that] reflects a more positive approach to landfilling than has been traditional in the past." See Regional Plan Association, *Waste Management: Generation and Disposal of Solid, Liquid and Gaseous Wastes in the New York Region* (New York, 1968), 76. Construction of a colossal 66.7 million square feet of office space took place in Manhattan between 1967 and 1973. See Kim Moody, *From Welfare State to Real Estate: Regime Change in New York City, 1974 to the Present* (New York: New Press, 2007), 13.

13. Act of Apr. 10, 1913, ch. 247, § 20, 1913, vol. 1, N.Y. Laws 438 ("navigation" quotation); *American Dock Co. v. New York*, 174 Misc. 813, 825 (N.Y. Sup. Ct. 1940), which seemed to affirm the 1913 law, and containing the "private business" quotation; John V. Lindsay to Nelson A. Rockefeller, Apr. 28, 1970, NYSL, bill jacket for Act of May 20, 1970, ch. 994, 1970, vol. 2, N.Y. Laws 3113 (authorizing cities to utilize waterfront for public, commercial, and business purposes); and David K. Shipler, "Manhattan Is Expanding Out as Well as Up," *NYT*, Aug. 25, 1971. Residential development on inland lots could cost upward of one hundred dollars per square foot, whereas landfill could produce buildable lots for a third to half that amount. See New York City Planning Commission, *The Waterfront: Supplement to Plan for New York City* ([New York?], 1971), 30.

14. Judith Pratt, "Charles J. Urstadt '53," Cornell Law School Spotlights, www.law school.cornell.edu/spotlights/Charles-Urstadt-53.cfm ("Trump" quotation).

15. Charles J. Urstadt, "Building a New City Within a City," speech before the New York Academy of Sciences, Oct. 12, 1977, p. 4, DLMAP, box 78, folder 975, series 3.2; and Charles J. Urstadt, "The Development of Downtown Manhattan," *Record of the Association of the Bar of the City of New York* 26, no. 8 (Nov. 1971): 672 ("merely following" quotation), 673 ("gold" quotation). The island of Manhattan (not the borough, which also includes Roosevelt, Ellis, Liberty, Governors, Randall's, and Ward's Islands) was 11,351 acres in 1609 and expanded to 13,636 in 2010. See appendix F.

16. Charles J. Urstadt, "Man-Made Land for Commercial and Residential Use—A Case Study," speech before Annual and National Environmental Engineering Meeting, Oct. 20, 1970, pp. 3–4, 8 ("Battery Park City" quotation), DLMAP, box 77, folder 968. See also Adam Rome, *The Genius of Earth Day: How a 1970 Teach-In Unexpectedly Made the First Green Generation* (New York: Hill and Wang, 2013). Urstadt's strategy with respect to the ecological benchmark is an example of what ecologist Daniel Pauly dubbed "shifting baseline syndrome." See Daniel Pauly, "Anecdotes and the Shifting Baseline Syndrome of Fisheries," *Trends in Ecology and Evolution* 10, no. 10 (Oct. 1995): 430, which is arguably one of the most influential single-page articles ever written.

17. Pub. L. No. 90–483, *supra* note 9, § 113, 736; and US Army Corps of Engineers, New York District, *Final Environmental Statement: Battery Park City Authority Project; Hudson River, New York* (prepared Nov. 15, 1971, and secured through a Freedom of Information Act request), 19, 13, 15. The Corps dismissed the idea of letting the site remain a node for marine shipping, noting that regional and city authorities had committed themselves to "high-density, multiple-use development in the lower Manhattan area."

18. Jack Moffly, "Renaissance Realtor: The Twin Careers of Charles Urstadt," *Greenwich Magazine*, June 2010, www.greenwichmag.com/g/June-2010/Renaissance-Realtor/; and Eric Lipton, "Battery Park City Is Success, Except for Pledge to the Poor," *NYT*, Jan. 2, 2001. Badillo quotations are from Nat Hentoff, "Herman Badillo: The Making of a Rationalist-Revolutionary," reprinted in 123 Cong. Rec. 24213 (1977). While some of the fill came from the building of the Twin Towers, the bulk of the remaining fill for the Battery Park City project came from Lower New York Bay. LeFrak eventually bailed out of the project and built housing across the river in New Jersey. See Darton, *Divided We Stand*, 174.

19. Peter Blake, "Walking on New York's Water," *NYT*, Apr. 2, 1974.

20. Initially, the project was called Wateredge. Proposed in 1971, it called for a seven-hundred-acre expansion of Manhattan along the Hudson and involved an eight- to ten-lane road that would stretch from the Battery Tunnel to Seventy-Second Street. A shelf built atop the road was to create space for housing and parkland. Wateredge was the brainchild of the Urban Development Corporation. The idea proved too ambitious and was scaled down, in part to speed the project along after an accident involving an asphalt truck that plummeted through the run-down West Side Highway. Instead, a joint city and state task force called the West Side Highway Project, headed by Lowell Bridwell, a former administrator at the Federal Highway Administration, proposed Westway, which received its name from Deputy Mayor John Zuccotti. See New York State Urban Development Corporation, *Wateredge Development Study: Hudson River Edge Development Proposal* ([New York?], 1971), 3–6; Owen Moritz, "West Side Hwy. Plan Is Unveiled," *DN*, July 20, 1971; Owen D. Gutfreund, "Urban Development Corporation," in Jackson, 1354; Fitch, *The Assassination of New York*, ix; Michael B. Gerrard, "The Saga of Westway," *Amicus Journal* 2, no. 2 (Fall 1980): 11; and Ann L. Buttenwieser, *Manhattan Water-Bound: Manhattan's Waterfront from the Seventeenth Century to the Present*, 2nd ed. (Syracuse, N.Y.: Syracuse Univ. Press, 1999), 212.

21. Tom Morganthau et al., "The Death of a 'Boondoggle'?" *Newsweek*, Aug. 19, 1985, 28. I derived the figure on the amount of fill from the US Army Corps of Engineers, *Report on Application for Department of Army Permit by the New York State Department of Transportation to Dredge and Fill in the Hudson River . . .*, Sept. 14, 1979, in *Westway Project: A Study of Abuses in Federal/State Relations; Hearings Before the Subcomm. of the Comm. on Gov't Operations House of Representatives*, 98th Cong. 1226, (1983), which indicated that the project would require 9,742,000 cubic yards of sand fill and 1,583,000 cubic yards of stone. The filling in of the Hudson varied over the four-mile proposed course from 150 to 970 feet from the shore.

22. US Department of Transportation, Federal Highway Administration, and New York State Department of Transportation, *West Side Highway Project, Environmental Impact Statement* (draft report, 1974); Federal Highway Administration, *West Side Highway Project: Final Environmental Impact Statement* (1977); and Alpine Geophysical Associates, *West Side Highway Project: Technical Report on Water Quality*, pt. 2 (1974), all available in *Westway Project*, 98th Cong., 1171, 1197, 1205.

23. Robert H. Boyle, *The Hudson River: A Natural and Unnatural History* (New York: W. W. Norton, 1969), 22, 252, 253.

24. The three agencies initially opposed were the EPA, the Fish and Wildlife Service, and the National Marine Fisheries Service. In 1978 the EPA prevailed on the New York State Department of Transportation overseeing Westway to study more closely the biology of the "interpier" area to be filled in. The history of Westway is from *Sierra Club v. U.S. Army Corps of Engineers*, 701 F. 2d 1011, 1021–1024 (2d Cir. N.Y. 1983). On the impact of the Army Corps of Engineers on the eastern United States, see Marc Reisner, *Cadillac Desert: The American West and Its Disappearing Water* (1986; repr., New York: Penguin Books, 1987), 504.

25. Phillip Lopate, *Waterfront: A Walk Around Manhattan* (New York: Anchor Books, 2004), 93; "Downtown-Lower Manhattan Association Backs Westway," press release, July 10, 1978, DLMAP, box 190, folder 1740; and "The Real Dimensions of Westway," *NYT*, Feb. 16, 1981. The environmental groups involved included the Sierra Club, the Clean Air Campaign, Action for Rational Transit, and the Hudson River Fishermen's Association (which Boyle himself had played a role in founding).

26. Guidelines for Specification of Disposal Sites for Dredged or Fill Material, 45 Fed. Reg. 85345 (Dec. 24, 1980) (to be codified at 40 C.F.R. pt. 230) (quotation); Tom O'Keeffe, "The Lower Hudson: Environmental Resource in Megacity," *EPA Journal*, Nov. 1987, 45; and Lopate, *Waterfront*, 99.

27. Roger Starr, "Making New York Smaller," *NYT*, Nov. 14, 1976; and Marshall Berman, *All That Is Solid Melts into Air: The Experience of Modernity* (1982; repr., New York: Penguin Books, 1988), 330 (quotation). An article about Starr singles out Westway as one of his life's great disappointments. See Jack Rosenthal, "Roger Starr, B. 1918: The Contrarian," *NYT*, Dec. 30, 2001.

28. *Action for Rational Transit v. West Side Highway Project*, 536 F. Supp. 1225, 1237–1238 (S.D.N.Y. 1982), on the Chesapeake and Hudson striped bass fisheries; Shannon Petersen, "Congress and Charismatic Megafauna: A Legislative History of the Endangered Species Act," *Environmental Law* 29, no. 2 (Summer 1999): 479–80; and Lopate, *Waterfront*, 96. Westway's opponents tried to present the striper as right at home in New York because supporters of the project viewed the fish as intruders. As late as 1983, James Larocca of the State Department of Transportation, operating on the assumption that nature had ended on lower Manhattan's inshore, characterized the area as "a man-created, utterly blighted habitat" that striped bass ventured into by "accident." See Testimony of James L. Larocca in *Westway Project*, 98th Cong., 1002. Apart from the effect of the project on the striped bass, some also argued that Westway would increase flooding in some parts of the harbor, including in northern New Jersey. The Corps felt reasonably certain that the project would not increase flood heights.

29. William W. Buzbee, "The Regulatory Fragmentation Continuum, Westway and the Challenges of Regional Growth," *Journal of Law and Politics* 21, nos. 2–3 (Spring–Summer 2005): 333; *Sierra Club v. U.S. Army Corps of Engineers*, 614 F. Supp. 1475, 1494 ("Battery Park landfill" quotation), 1495 ("adverse impact" quotation) (S.D.N.Y. 1985); and *Sierra Club v. U.S. Army Corps of Engineers*, 772 F.2d 1043 1053 ("Orwellian-like" quotation) (2d Cir. N.Y. 1985).

30. 614 F. Supp. at 1513 ("basic transportation" quotation).

31. 614 F. Supp. at 1514 ("redevelopment" quotation), 1515 ("defined" quotation).

Technically, what I am calling the environmental impact statement was actually the final supplemental environmental impact statement, or FSEIS.

32. Michael Oreskes, "House Votes by Big Margin to Bar Funds for Westway," *NYT*, Sept. 12, 1985; and Oreskes, "Moynihan Sees No Way to Win a Westway Vote," *NYT*, Sept. 19, 1985. The quotations are from 131 Cong. Rec. 23373, 23377, 23384 (1985). Congress could have rescued the venture by pushing through legislation (as it did for both Battery Park City and Manhattan Landing) declaring the inshore waters nonnavigable. See Buzbee, "The Regulatory Fragmentation Continuum," 333n26.

33. In 1985, with the Westway corpse still warm, Meyer Frucher, the new president of the Battery Park City Corporation Authority, introduced a pier-and-platform plan that extended more than two hundred acres into the Hudson River. Eventually Frucher plunged ahead with a less ambitious plan and, without the necessary federal permit, began excavating in the Hudson River to build a platform for an esplanade. Who knows what would have happened had a division chief with the Army Corps of Engineers not glanced out the window of one of the World Trade Center towers and noticed the backhoe at work. Frucher claimed the infraction was "a mistake." See Michael Moss, "River Structure Gives Its Foes Their Platform," *Newsday* (N.Y.), June 26, 1988. This news report refers to a three-page memo that Frucher sent to Governor Mario Cuomo, but it seems that only the first page of the memo survives. See Meyer S. Frucher to Mario Cuomo, Oct. 9, 16, 1985, NYSA, ser. 13682-96D, New York State Governor Central Subject and Correspondence Files, reel 9.

34. New York City Council, Legislative Panel on Waterfront Development, *The Future of New York City's Waterfront: Proud Legacy? Lost Opportunity?* ([New York?], 1989), 47–48; Alan S. Oser, "City Efforts Trapped in Multiple Reviews," *NYT*, Nov. 29, 1987 ("aquatic" quotation); and Robert O. Boorstin, "U.S. Official Urges a Riverfront Development Plan," *NYT*, Jan. 18, 1987. The last two overwater projects referred to were called, respectively, Hudson River Center and River Walk.

To help spur development, the Koch administration went so far as to invite the city's most prominent real estate minds—Larry Silverstein, John Tishman, Samuel LeFrak, Larry Fisher, Donald Trump—to suggest a way forward on the waterfront. "Give them a section of the waterfront to look at in Brooklyn, Queens and the other boroughs," Koch wrote a deputy, "and ask them to give you their ideas as to what the city should be doing by way of development." See Edward I. Koch to Steven Spinola, Sept. 21, 1984, and Steven Spinola to Edward I. Koch, Waterfront Development Task Force, Dec. 13, 1984, EKP, mn. 41030, box 75A, folder 24.

35. Boorstin, "U.S. Official Urges a Riverfront Development Plan"; and New York City Council, Legislative Panel on Waterfront Development, *The Future of New York City's Waterfront*, v, vi, ix. On Congress declaring areas surrounding Manhattan nonnavigable, see Water Resources Development Act of 1974, Pub. L. No. 93–251, § 51, 88 Stat. 26.

Stuckey offered evidence from a PDC study that he said showed "piers may better the aquatic habitat." An official with the National Marine Fisheries Service, however, criticized the study for merely demonstrating "the presence of fish in the different habitats" without explaining "what value the different habitats offer the fish." See New York City Council, Legislative Panel on Waterfront Development, *The Future of New York City's Waterfront*, 36; and Roy R. Stoecker, Janet Collura, and Phillip J. Fallon Jr., "Aquatic Studies at the Hudson River Center Site," in *Estuarine Research in the 1980s: The Hudson River Environmental Society Seventh Symposium on Hudson River Ecology*, ed. C. Lavett Smith (Albany, N.Y.: State Univ. of New York Press, 1992), 407–27.

36. David W. Dunlap, "West Side Planning Panel Rules Out Landfill for Hudson Riverfront," *NYT*, July 20, 1989 (Del Giudice quotation). The time seemed ripe for the state bill halting development in the Hudson in that the EPA in 1988 had designated New York Harbor as an "estuary of national significance" (providing money to create a management plan). One of the bill's sponsors deplored the rampant development that "would fill in land and construct high-rise luxury housing for the yuppie crowd while destroying the Hudson River." See Water Quality Act of 1987, Pub. L. No. 100–104, § 320, 101 Stat. 61 ("national significance" quotation), 62; and Marianne Arneberg, Alexis Jetter, and Rex Smith, "Steps Taken on Proposal to Break Budget Impasse," *Newsday*, June 27, 1988 ("yuppie" quotation). On Stuckey's and Frucher's opposition (the latter's opposition, I infer) to the bill, see Michael Moss, "Battle over Bill to Ban Building on Hudson," *Newsday*, Mar. 22, 1989. On the Koch administration's views on the legislation, see Stanley E. Grayson to Jack Rosenthal, Mar. 14, 1989, and Stanley E. Grayson to Edward I. Koch, Mar. 30, 1989, EKP, mn. 41023, box 56, folder 11.

37. West Side Waterfront Panel, *A Vision for the Hudson River Waterfront Park* (New York, 1990), 5, 13 ("lifeless" quotation), 1 ("band of green" quotation), 7 ("restricting" quotation).

38. Michael Moss, "Gold Coast Rush Feared on West Side," *Newsday*, Sept. 1, 1988; West Side Waterfront Panel, *A Vision for the Hudson River Waterfront Park*, 8 (quotations); and New York City Planning Commission, *New York City Waterfront Revitalization Program* (New York, 1982), 72, on the rationale for a water-dependent standard.

39. Statements of Marcy Benstock, Clean Air Campaign; John Mylod, Hudson River Sloop Clearwater; Kirkpatrick Sale, Wetlands Restoration Project; and Stephen Short, Oct. 15, 1990, in West Side Waterfront Panel, *A Vision for the Hudson River Waterfront Park* (New York, 1990), app., 2:15, 142, 167–68, 172.

40. New York City Department of City Planning, *Plan for the Manhattan Waterfront: New York City Comprehensive Waterfront Plan* (New York, 1993), 16 ("nothing remains" quotation), 68 ("original" quotation); and Hudson River Park Trust, *Hudson River Park Estuarine Sanctuary Management Plan* ([New York?], 2002), 1–3.

41. New York City Department of City Planning, *New York City Comprehensive Waterfront Plan: Reclaiming the City's Edge* (New York, 1992), 148–51. A detailed analysis of the plan was carried out by the office of Manhattan borough president Ruth Messinger. See "The Department of City Planning's Proposed Waterfront Zoning: What Does It Mean for Manhattan Communities," Apr. 14, 1993, DLMAP, box 189, folder 1735. Trump's expansive plan for the Upper West Side is explained in David W. Dunlap, "Trump Offers Unusual Plan to Use 'Underwater Zoning,'" *NYT*, June 28, 1989. Trump eventually scaled down his plans and agreed to have

parkland, and subsequently apartment buildings went in along the abandoned Penn Central rail yards at Riverside Park South.

42. Sam Roberts, "Consensus Means Waterfront Project for West Side May Actually Get Built," *NYT*, May 21, 1992; *Hudson River Sloop Clearwater v. Cuomo*, 222 A.D. 2d 386 (N.Y. App. Div. 1st Dep't 1995); and Hudson River Park Conservancy, *Hudson River Park: Concept and Financial Plan* (New York, 1995), 46 ("high-tech" quotation).

43. Hudson River Park Act, ch. 592, § 8.3(b), 1998, vol. 3, N.Y. Laws 3516. On the entrepreneurial impulse at the core of the new approach to parks, see David Harvey, "From Managerialism to Entrepreneurialism: The Transformation of Urban Governance in Late Capitalism," *Geografiska Annaler*, ser. B, 71, no. 1 (1989): 3–17, www.jstor.org/stable/490503.

44. William Bridges, *Map of the City of New-York* (New York, 1811), 26; Michael J. Del Giudice and Fran Reiter, "Open Letter to Future Park Users," May 1995, in Hudson River Park Conservancy, *Hudson River Park: Concept and Financial Plan*; and Elizabeth Hawes, "The Waterfront 2004," *NYT*, Nov. 20, 1994.

45. Quotations are from Hudson River Park Act, *supra* note 43, § 3(l), § 8.3(c), 3509, 3516. On shade and fish habitat, see Kenneth W. Able, John P. Manderson, and Anne L. Studholme, "The Distribution of Shallow Water Juvenile Fishes in an Urban Estuary: The Effects of Manmade Structures in the Lower Hudson River," *Estuaries* 21, no. 4 (Dec. 1998): 731–44, www.jstor.org/stable/1353277; J. T. Duffy-Anderson and K. W. Able, "Effects of Municipal Piers on the Growth of Juvenile Fishes in the Hudson River Estuary: A Study Across a Pier Edge," *Marine Biology* 133, no. 3 (Apr. 1999): 409–18, doi:10.1007/s002270050479; and Kenneth W. Able and Janet T. Duffy-Anderson, "Impacts of Piers on Juvenile Fishes in the Lower Hudson River," in Levinton & Waldman, 428–40.

Supporters of the park dismissed these ecological concerns. "The only thing that would be acceptable to these people would be if the West Side waterfront reverted to how it was when Henry Hudson came up the river in 1609, which might be great if there were only fish there," said Tom Fox, the former president of the Hudson River Park Conservancy and a proponent of allowing private development to subsidize public open space. While it is true that critics called for leaving the Hudson's waters "in their natural state," by this they simply meant to object to further intrusion on the river. See Josh Benson, "A Fierce Coalition Prepares Last Stand Against Hudson Park," *New York Observer*, Jan. 10, 2000, http://observer.com/2000/01/a-fierce-coalition-prepares-last-stand-against-hudson-park/ (Fox quotation); and Marcy Benstock et al. to John Ferguson, June 12, 1998, p. 3, RGP, mn. 60318, box 02/03/008, folder 347 ("natural state" quotation). These issues might have been sorted out had the Army Corps of Engineers undertaken a full review of the park, but the agency deferred to an earlier environmental impact statement conducted by the state that found that "adverse impacts to aquatic resources would not be likely to occur." See Empire State Development Corporation and Hudson River Park Conservancy, *Hudson River Park Project: Final Environmental Impact Statement* (New York, 1998), S-13.

46. Vincent McGowan to Board of Directors, Hudson River Park Conservancy, Sept.

5, 1996, RGP, mn. 60388, box 02/09/006, folder 219 ("relocation" quotation). For more on the life of Poppa Neutrino, see Alec Wilkinson, *The Happiest Man in the World* (New York: Random House, 2007). Neutrino once wrote, "Without being attached to my garden, and continuing to receive instruction on how to cultivate it, my garden at this point covers the entire earth." See David Pearlman, "Poppa Neutrino Speaks," last modified Mar. 21, 2011, www.floatingneutrinos.com/Message /Poppa%20Neutrino%20Speaks.html. On the docking of the *Town Hall* in 1991, see P. J. Partridge, "The Floating Neutrinos," accessed June 7, 2013, http://most fascinating.blogspot.com/.

47. Working Waterfront Association, "Hudson River Park Trust Misconduct: Fact Sheet," faxed on Nov. 1, 2000 ("communal" quotation); and Adam Brown to Janis Schulmeisters, Oct. 6, 2000, RGP, mn. 61092, box 02/02/1/004, folder 98; John J. Donohue, "A New Voice for the Sailors," *NYT*, Feb. 22, 1998 ("wasteland" quotation); and *supra* note 43, § 2(a), 1998, vol. 3, N.Y. Laws 3506 ("blighted" quotation). On the seizure of the vessel, see Partridge, "The Floating Neutrinos."

48. Matthew Schuerman, "A Ribbon of Green That Hasn't Got Any," *New York Observer*, Feb. 27, 2006, http://observer.com/2006/02/a-ribbon-of-green-that-hasnt -got-any-2/.

49. Moody, *From Welfare State to Real Estate*, 227, 231; Marcha Johnson, "Guiding the Design of Post-Industrial Waterfronts in Relation to Their Ecological Context" (PhD diss., Univ. of Pennsylvania, 1991), 2; and Mark B. Bain, Marcia S. Meixler, and Geof E. Eckerlin, *Biological Status of Sanctuary Waters of the Hudson River Park in New York: Final Project Report for the Hudson River Park Trust* (Ithaca, N.Y., 2006), 18 ("malformed" quotation), 15, table 3.

15. The Big Apple Biome

1. Rohit Aggarwala left McKinsey to develop PlaNYC. See Annie Karni, "The Planner Behind Bloomberg's PlaNYC," *New York Sun*, May 29, 2007, www.nysun.com /new-york/planner-behind-bloombergs-planyc/55342. The various initiatives are spelled out in Michael Bloomberg, *PlaNYC: A Greener, Greater New York* (New York, 2007), 146–55.

2. Michael Bloomberg, "Mayor Bloomberg Delivers PlaNYC: A Greener, Greater New York," press release, Apr. 22, 2007, www.nyc.gov (Bloomberg quotations); and Bloomberg, *PlaNYC*, 130 ("growing" quotation).

3. Bloomberg, "Mayor Bloomberg Delivers PlaNYC."

4. David Owen, *Green Metropolis: Why Living Smaller, Living Closer, and Driving Less Are the Keys to Sustainability* (New York: Riverhead Books, 2009), 3–6. Current population figures suggest that there are 69,464 people per square mile in Manhattan, somewhat denser than the figure that Owen uses (67,000). Much of New York City's positive ecological reputation rested on its smaller per capita carbon footprint. In this sense, there was a very good argument to be made for the sustainability of high-density living. But the ecological case for New York becomes more complicated when other major factors responsible for global environmental change—alterations, for example, in the nitrogen cycle or in land cover—are raised.

See Peter M. Vitousek, "Beyond Global Warming: Ecology and Global Change," *Ecology* 75, no. 7 (Oct. 1994): 1861–76, doi:10.2307/1941591.

5. Owen, *Green Metropolis*, 32, 34. On the population density of the New Jersey cities, see my discussion above, p. 394, note 2.

6. Owen, *Green Metropolis*, 10. The historian Kenneth Jackson, in resuscitating the image of Robert Moses (who had received unflattering treatment by his biographer), noted that for all of Moses's alleged highway-building sins, the city had the virtue of low per capita gasoline consumption. See Kenneth T. Jackson, "Robert Moses and the Planned Environment: A Re-Evaluation," in *Robert Moses: Single-Minded Genius*, ed. Joann P. Krieg (Interlaken, N.Y.: Heart of the Lakes Publishing, 1989), 24.

7. Regional Plan Association, *The Region's Growth: A Report of the Second Regional Plan* ([New York?], 1967), 19.

8. Robert D. Yaro and Tony Hiss, *A Region at Risk: The Third Regional Plan for the New York–New Jersey–Connecticut Metropolitan Area* (Washington, D.C.: Island Press, 1996), 1–3, 110, 120, 88. There is no question that the Third Regional Plan represented a significant break with past plans in its adoption of an ecological paradigm. The emphasis on safeguarding both terrestrial and marine reserves, revitalizing green spaces in highly urbanized settings, and addressing the fragmentation of regional ecology by linking these various conservation lands is evidence enough. Though the plan was criticized for conceiving of areas not designated as green space as somehow "devoid of living systems," there is no escaping the reality that the third plan, in contrast to the others, aspired to an ecologically advanced vision of urban life. See Alejandro Flores et al., "Adopting a Modern Ecological View of the Metropolitan Landscape: The Case of a Greenspace System for the New York City Region," *Landscape and Urban Planning* 39, no. 4 (Jan. 1998): 306, doi:10.1016/S0169-2046(97)00084-4.

9. The year 1997 witnessed the launching of the journal *Urban Ecosystems*. "In the urban environment," the journal's editor wrote, "man so dominates the landscape that it is the natural component of the urban ecosystem that is often obscured." One author in the journal's inaugural issue called cities "the most significant human ecological event of the past 100 years" but lamented the failure of scholars to pay attention to the role of ecological forces in urbanization. A Rutgers biologist would later go so far as to claim that if Charles Darwin were alive at the dawn of the twenty-first century, "he might be studying Staten Island instead of the Galapagos." See Mark R. Walbridge, "Urban Ecosystems," *Urban Ecosystems* 1, no. 1 (1997): 1 ("dominates" quotation), doi:10.1023/A:1014307007437; William E. Rees, "Urban Ecosystems: The Human Dimension," *Urban Ecosystems* 1, no. 1 (1997): 63 ("most significant" quotation), doi:10.1023/A:1014380105620; Mark J. McDonnell et al., "Ecosystem Processes Along an Urban-to-Rural Gradient," *Urban Ecosystems* 1, no. 1 (1997): 21–36, doi:10.1023/A:1014359024275; and Alexander Stille, "Wild Cities: It's a Jungle Out There," *NYT*, Nov. 23, 2002 ("Galapagos" quotation).

10. Robert Sullivan, *The Meadowlands: Wilderness Adventures at the Edge of a City* (New York: Scribner, 1998), 87. Although the Meadowlands was often dismissed as little more than a "toxic wasteland," in 1997 a naturalist wrote of it, "the timeless heartbeat of nature pulses here." See John R. Quinn, *Fields of Sun and Grass: An Artist's*

Journal of the New Jersey Meadowlands (New Brunswick, N.J.: Rutgers Univ. Press, 1997), 2, 3.

11. Anne Matthews, *Wild Nights: The Nature of New York City* (London: Flamingo, 2001), 11 (quotation), 13; and Allison Sloan, "Migratory Bird Mortality at the World Trade Center and World Financial Center, 1997–2001: A Deadly Mix of Lights and Glass," *Transactions of the Linnaean Society of New York* 10 (Sept. 2007): 197.

12. Alan Weisman, *The World Without Us* (New York: Thomas Dunne Books, 2007), 28. The body of water near the Empire State Building was called Sunfish Pond.

13. D. F. Squires and J. S. Barclay, *Nearshore Wildlife Habitats and Populations in the New York/New Jersey Harbor Estuary* (report prepared for the New York/New Jersey Harbor Estuary Program, 1990), 4.

14. M. Llewellyn Thatcher and Cesar Mendoza, *Hydrologic Modifications* (report prepared for the New York/New Jersey Harbor Estuary Program, 1991), 5. The report notes that 1,444 hectares of land were added to Upper Bay Harbor (Upper New York Bay), which converts to 3,568 acres.

15. US Coast and Geodetic Survey, *United States Coast Pilot: Atlantic Coast, Part IV; From Point Judith to New York* (Washington, D.C., 1904), 139. The amount of marshland in 1907 is from Jamaica Bay Environmental Study Group, *Jamaica Bay and Kennedy Airport: A Multidisciplinary Environmental Study*, 2 vols. (Washington, D.C., 1971), 2:59. On dredging in the 1930s, see Frederick R. Black, *Jamaica Bay: A History; Gateway National Recreation Area New York–New Jersey* (Historic Resource Study prepared for the National Park Service, Cultural Resource Management Study No. 3, 1981), 78, and 79, which mentions that fourteen million cubic feet of fill was used to build Floyd Bennett Field. Between 1941 and 1945, La Guardia's administration supervised the amassing of 4,527 acres around Jamaica Bay. See George Scullin, *International Airport: The Story of Kennedy Airport and U.S. Commercial Aviation* (Boston: Little, Brown, 1968), 30, 37.

16. Scullin, *International Airport*, 40, 41 ("Holland" quotation); Jamaica Bay Environmental Study Group, *Jamaica Bay and Kennedy Airport*, 2:44, 78, 59; and John Waldman, *Research Opportunities in the Natural and Social Sciences at the Jamaica Bay Unit of Gateway National Recreation Area* (prepared for the National Park Service, 2008), 5 ("alterations" quotation). The amount of material dredged out of Jamaica Bay prior to 1971 was conservatively estimated at 125 million cubic yards, or enough sand and muck to bury Manhattan to a depth of over five feet. There were four sewage treatment plants in operation sending effluent into Jamaica Bay by the 1950s. An area known as Grassy Bay, originally made up of salt marsh islands and accompanying channels, was rendered into one very deep hole. The pit was eventually obstructed by a runway that acted like a dike and penned up the partially treated effluent coursing into the water from a nearby pollution-control plant.

17. Squires and Barclay, *Nearshore Wildlife Habitats*, 16; and table in appendix E.

18. David Soll, "Watershed Moments: An Environmental History of the New York City Water Supply" (PhD diss., Brandeis Univ., 2009), 160, 194.

19. Soll, "Watershed Moments," 198–99, 208–9; and "Ripples of Doubt Cast on City's Water Ideas," *NYWTS*, Apr. 30, 1952, for Moses's thoughts on the water supply. Figures on water consumption for the years 1979 to 2009 are available at "His-

tory of Drought and Water Consumption," www.nyc.gov/html/dep/html/drinking _water/droughthist.shtml. On the Hudson River's discharge per day, see New Jersey Marine Sciences Consortium, *The Hudson-Raritan: State of the Estuary* (Fort Hancock, N.J., 1987), 5.

20. Debra Tillinger et al., "Hydrologic Functions of Green Roofs in New York City," and William D. Solecki et al., "Potential Impact of Green Roofs on the Urban Heat Island Effect," in *Green Roofs in the New York Metropolitan Region: Research Report*, ed. Cynthia Rosenzweig, Stuart Gaffin, and Lily Parshall (New York, 2006), 27, 19, table 2; Thatcher and Mendoza, *Hydrologic Modifications*, 30; and Alex Prud'Homme, *The Ripple Effect: The Fate of Freshwater in the Twenty-First Century* (New York: Scribner, 2011), 54. Combined sewer overflows (CSOs) contribute less in the way of nutrients than they do bacteria and floating debris. See Leo J. Hetling et al., "Effect of Water Quality Management Efforts on Wastewater Loadings During the Past Century," *Water Environment Research* 75, no. 1 (Jan.–Feb. 2003): 37, www.jstor.org/stable/25045659.

21. New Jersey Marine Sciences Consortium, *The Hudson-Raritan*, 5; and Soll, "Watershed Moments," 311–18, 315 ("porcelain" quotation).

22. Hetling et al., "Effect of Water Quality Management Efforts," 37. This report notes that in 1996, the National Academy of Sciences singled out eutrophication as "one of the two biggest threats to biodiversity in marine ecosystems." To return the estuary to a state that would bear some resemblance to the one that Henry Hudson found would require removing the bulk of the nutrients present in the effluent, a complicated and very costly proposition. See Bostwick H. Ketchum, "Population, Resources, and Pollution, and Their Impact on the Hudson Estuary," *ANYAS* 250 (May 1974): 155–56, doi:10.1111/j.1749-6632.1974.tb43900.x.

23. Linda M. Puth and Catherine E. Burns, "New York's Nature: A Review of the Status and Trends in Species Richness Across the Metropolitan Area," *Diversity and Distributions* 15, no. 1 (Jan. 2009): 12, 16, doi:10.1111/j.1472-4642.2008.00499.x.

24. Squires and Barclay, *Nearshore Wildlife Habitats*, 15, 19, table 4, 84, 87. This study estimated the original tidal marsh in the New York/New Jersey Harbor estuary at 70,000 acres in 1609 and 15,000 acres in 1990, when the study was written. The historical GIS conducted for this book suggests that an estimated 37,800 acres of underwater land were filled. Staten Island is 37,437 acres. See also appendix E.

25. The presence by the 1960s of three landfills around the perimeter of Jamaica Bay went a long way toward explaining why Kennedy Airport had more bird-aircraft collisions than any other airfield in the United States. In 1975 a flock of herring gulls struck a DC-10 on takeoff as it headed for Saudi Arabia, causing the engine to burst into flames and drop off the wing. Though no one was killed, the event led to calls for the closing of the landfills. See Jamaica Bay Environmental Study Group, *Jamaica Bay and Kennedy Airport*, 1:22; Richard Witkin, "139 Escape DC-10 Afire at Kennedy," *NYT*, Nov. 13, 1975; and Witkin, "Proposals Made to End Kennedy Airport Bird Peril," *NYT*, Mar. 9, 1976. On the sludge and worm issue, see R. Lawrence Swanson et al., "Science, Policy and the Management of Sewage Material: The New York City Experience," *MPB* 49, nos. 9–10 (Nov. 2004): 680, 682, 683, doi:10.1016/j.marpolbul.2004.06.025.

26. Peter M. J. Woodhead, *Inventory and Characterization of Habitat and Fish Resources, and Assessment of Information on Toxic Effects in the New York–New Jersey Harbor Estuary* (report prepared for New York–New Jersey Harbor Estuary Program, 1991), sec. 3, pp. 35–37; and Thomas M. Brosnan, Andrew Stoddard, and Leo J. Hetling, "Hudson River Sewage Inputs and Impacts: Past and Present," in Levinton & Waldman, 344.

27. Ian Frazier, "Back to the Harbor," *New Yorker*, Mar. 21, 2011, 36–37, 39. Upgrades made to sewage treatment plants and other environmental reforms have improved the habitat of the New York Bight. See, for example, Jack B. Pearce, "The New York Bight," *MPB* 41, nos. 1–6 (2000): 44–55, doi:10.1016/S0025-326X(00)00101-6. However, increasing evidence suggests that former marine species abundances in the Northwest Atlantic Ocean were much higher than commonly supposed. See, for example, W. Jeffrey Bolster, Karen E. Alexander, and William B. Leavenworth, "The Historical Abundance of Cod on the Nova Scotian Shelf," in *Shifting Baselines: The Past and the Future of Ocean Fisheries*, ed. Jeremy B. C. Jackson, Karen E. Alexander, and Enric Sala (Washington, D.C.: Island Press, 2011), 109–10; and Andrew A. Rosenberg et al., "The History of Ocean Resources: Modeling Cod Biomass Using Historical Records," *Frontiers in Ecology and the Environment* 3, no. 2 (Mar. 2004): 88, fig. 4. For the importance of complexity for ecological health, see Stephen R. Palumbi, Karen L. McLeod, and Daniel Grünbaum, "Ecosystems in Action: Lessons from Marine Ecology About Recovery, Resistance, and Reversibility," *Bioscience* 58, no. 1 (Jan. 2008): 38, fig. 6.

28. Squires and Barclay, *Nearshore Wildlife Habitats*, 47; Flores et al., "Adopting a Modern Ecological View of the Metropolitan Landscape," 299; and Robert DeCandido, Adrianna A. Muir, and Margaret B. Gargiullo, "A First Approximation of the Historical and Extant Vascular Flora of New York City: Implications for Native Plant Species Conservation," *Journal of the Torrey Botanical Society* 131, no. 3 (July–Sept. 2004): 244, www.jstor.org/stable/4126954.

29. DeCandido, Muir, and Gargiullo, "A First Approximation of the Historical and Extant Vascular Flora," 245, table 1.

30. Jamaica Bay Environmental Study Group, *Jamaica Bay and Kennedy Airport*, 1:1, 3, and 2:87, 89 (quotation), 89–90; and Gateway National Recreation Area Act, Pub. L. No. 92–592, 86 Stat. 1308 (1972). The Gateway recreation area included four units: Jamaica Bay, Breezy Point, Sandy Hook, and Staten Island, as well as Hoffman and Swinburne Islands, two small man-made islands in Lower New York Bay.

31. *Gateway National Recreation Area: Hearings Before the Subcomm. on Parks and Recreation of the Comm. on Interior and Insular Affairs . . . on S. 1193 and S. 1852*, 92nd Cong. 160 (1971) ("Fort Knox" quotation). The four plants were Coney Island, Twenty-Sixth Ward, Jamaica, and Rockaway. See Interstate Sanitation Commission, *Annual Report* (1985), A-1. In 2005 the city of New York passed a law to establish a watershed protection plan for Jamaica Bay. See New York, N.Y., Local Law to Develop a Watershed Protection Plan for Jamaica Bay, no. 71 (July 20, 2005). The figures on marshland loss are from Patti Rafferty and Charles Roman, "Wetland Loss—A Closer Look at Wetland Loss Research Activities in Jamaica Bay" (slide presentation prepared for the "State of the Bay" symposium, 2006), 4.

32. D. R. Franz and W. H. Harris, "Seasonal and Spatial Variability in Macrobenthos Communities in Jamaica Bay, New York—An Urban Estuary," *Estuaries* 11, no. 1 (Mar. 1988): 15–16, www.jstor.org/stable/1351714; Joanna Burger, "Jamaica Bay Studies VIII: An Overview of Abiotic Factors Affecting Several Avian Groups," *Journal of Coastal Research* 4, no. 2 (Spring 1988): 195, www.jstor.org/stable /4297393; and Kevin M. Brown et al., "Changes in the Nesting Populations of Colonial Waterbirds in Jamaica Bay Wildlife Refuge, New York, 1974–1998," *Northeastern Naturalist* 8, no. 3 (2001): 275, www.jstor.org/stable/3858484.

    In some ways, the preservation of open space in Jamaica Bay succeeded too well. Laughing gulls, for example, first began to nest at Jo Co Marsh in 1979. Not seen on Long Island for a century, laughing gulls—named for their distinctive call—established a colony in the refuge that happened to be located near a Kennedy Airport runway. The colony grew explosively from just a few nesting pairs to well over seven thousand pairs over the next decade or so. It is conceivable that the development of salt marshes in New Jersey forced the gulls to flee to Queens, where they found a congenial salt marsh environment largely free from predators. The habitat likely improved with the closing of the Pennsylvania Avenue and Fountain Avenue Landfills in 1980 and 1985, respectively. The closures caused the population of herring gulls—a considerably larger species that competed with the laughing gulls—to decline. By the latter part of the 1980s, laughing gulls accounted for over half of all the bird-aircraft collisions at Kennedy. The bird strikes proved so problematic that the federal government stationed marksmen at the airport who killed an astonishing fourteen thousand gulls in 1991 alone. See Richard A. Dolbeer, Jerrold L. Belant, and Janet L. Sillings, "Shooting Gulls Reduces Strikes with Aircraft at John F. Kennedy International Airport," *Wildlife Society Bulletin* 21, no. 4 (Winter 1993): 442, 448, www.jstor.org/stable/3783417; Anne C. Fullam, "East End Cheering Return of Gulls," *NYT*, Aug. 23, 1992; Joanna Burger, "Feeding Competition Between Laughing Gulls and Herring Gulls at a Sanitary Landfill," *Condor* 83, no. 4 (Nov. 1981): 328–35, www.jstor.org/stable/1367501; and Brown et al., "Changes in the Nesting Populations of Colonial Waterbirds," 280.

33. John G. Mitchell, *High Rock and Green Belt: The Making of New York City's Largest Park*, ed. Charles E. Little (Chicago: Center for American Places, 2011), 33–39. A tenacious group of conservationists acting on behalf of the Staten Island Greenbelt Natural Areas League (SIGNAL), founded by the journalist John G. Mitchell, defeated Moses's parkway plan. In 1970 SIGNAL published a position paper titled "Wetlands Aren't Wastelands," in which it decried the loss of the city's tidal marshes and worried that further urbanization would so upset the habitat as to leave people "observing how well concrete relates to cement." See Staten Island Greenbelt Natural Areas League, "Wetlands Aren't Wastelands," p. 4 (position paper, n.d.), EC, Greenbelt, box 3, folder 63.

34. Wehran-New York, *Draft Environmental Impact Statement for the Fresh Kills Ash/ Residue Landfill, Staten Island, New York* (report for the City of New York Department of Sanitation, Middletown, N.Y., 1991), III-66, III-35, III-37, III-38; New York Department of Sanitation, *Draft 6 NYCRR Part 360 Permit Application for the Fresh Kills Landfill* (submitted to the N.Y. State Department of Environmental

Conservation, 1994), III-139, III-146; and Bruce Kershner, *Secret Places of Staten Island: A Visitor's Guide to Scenic and Historic Treasures of Staten Island* (Dubuque, Iowa: Kendall/Hunt Publishing, 1998), 62 (quotation).

There is no denying the significant changes in plant life that have taken place on Staten Island. One study showed that increasing suburban development since the 1930s had transformed the landscape from forests and fields to housing tracts and set the stage for a radical decline in flora. More than 40 percent of the native plant species had gone missing by the 1990s. In this context, the Greenbelt—because of its potential to counteract this trend—assumed increased significance. See George R. Robinson, Mary E. Yurlina, and Steven N. Handel, "A Century of Change in the Staten Island Flora: Ecological Correlates of Species Losses and Invasion," *BTBC* 121, no. 2 (Apr.–June 1994): 119, 126, 127.

35. Dana Gumb et al., "The Staten Island Bluebelt: A Case Study in Urban Storm-water Management" (paper prepared for NOVATECH 2007, Sixth International Conference on Sustainable Techniques and Strategies in Urban Water Management, Lyon, France, 2007), 20–21, http://hdl.handle.net/2042/25201; James Garin et al., "Bluebelt Beginnings—Green Preserves Blue on Staten Island," *Clear Waters*, Winter 2009, 10–11; Dana F. Gumb Jr., "Staten Island History and Bluebelt Acquisitions," *Clear Waters*, Winter 2009, 23–24; Ian L. McHarg, *Design with Nature* (Garden City, N.Y.: Natural History Press, 1969), 103–15; and Abeles Schwartz Associates, *Open Space and the Future of New York: Programs and Policies* ([New York?], 1987), 58. On the state's tidal and freshwater wetland laws, see Norman Marcus, "New York City Zoning—1961–1991: Turning Back the Clock—But with an Up-to-the-Minute Social Agenda," *Fordham Urban Law Journal* 19, no. 3 (1992): 712.

36. Garin et al., "Bluebelt Beginnings," 10–11; and "Bluebelt Generates Grateful Community Response," *Clean Waters*, Winter 2009, 20.

37. Norman Steisel to Edward I. Koch, Congressman Molinari's Waste Disposal Proposals, Aug. 15, 1983, mn. 41022, box 55, folder 14 ("500-foot-high" quotation); Norman Steisel to Fellow New Yorkers, Dec. 17, 1985, mn. 41121, box 255, folder 3; Norman Steisel to Edward I. Koch, Nathan Leventhal, and James R. Brigham, Mar. 3, 1980, mn. 41026, box 64, folder 11; and Norman Steisel to Edward I. Koch, Sept. 26, 1980, and Susan J. Raila to Norman Steisel, Sept. 24, 1980, mn. 41095, box 207, folder 3. All these documents are in EKP. On the struggle over the Brooklyn Navy Yard incinerator, see Matthew Gandy, *Concrete and Clay: Reworking Nature in New York City* (2002; repr., Cambridge, Mass.: MIT Press, 2003), 203–10; and Julie Sze, *Noxious New York: The Racial Politics of Urban Health and Environmental Justice* (Cambridge, Mass.: MIT Press, 2007), 77–80. Molinari hailed the closing of the landfill as "the highlight of my twenty-seven-year career, and perhaps the greatest victory in our borough's history." See "Opening the Door to the New Staten Island," *The New Staten Island* (prepared by Borough President Guy V. Molinari, n.d.), EC, box 3, file 105.

38. Gandy, *Concrete and Clay*, 210–11; William D. Solecki and Cynthia Rosenzweig, "Biodiversity, Biosphere Reserves, and the Big Apple," *ANYAS* 1023 (June 2004): 112, table 2, doi:10.1196/annals.1319.004; Kirsten Engel, "Reconsidering the Na-

tional Market in Solid Waste: Trade-Offs in Equity, Efficiency, Environmental Protection, and State Autonomy," *North Carolina Law Review* 73, no. 4 (Apr. 1995):
1493–94; and *Philadelphia v. New Jersey*, 437 U.S. 617 (1978). The formation of an
activist community group called the Organization of Waterfront Neighborhoods
took place in 1996 when Fresh Kills was slated to close. Some of the group's leaders
were members of a task force formed by Mayor Giuliani and Governor George
Pataki to contemplate a solid-waste plan in the wake of the closing of Fresh Kills
Landfill. The task force was wary about the prospect of exporting garbage. See Sze,
Noxious New York, 115, 125.

39. For an archeology of Fresh Kills Landfill, see William Rathje and Cullen Murphy, *Rubbish!: The Archaeology of Garbage* (1992; repr., New York: HarperPerennial,
1993). Robert Sullivan, "Wall-E Park," *New York*, Nov. 23, 2008, http://nymag
.com/news/features/52452/; George R. Robinson and Steven H. Handel, "Forest
Restoration on a Closed Landfill: Rapid Addition of New Species by Bird Dispersal," *Conservation Biology* 7, no. 2 (June 1993): 271–78, www.jstor.org/stable
/2386424; New York City Parks and Recreation, Freshkills Park Frequently Asked
Questions, Natural Systems, www.nycgovparks.org/park-features/freshkills-park
/more-information#naturalSystems; Lisa W. Foderaro, "From Dump to Paragon of
Ecology," *NYT*, Sept. 29, 2011 ("atonement" quotation); and Mitchell, *High Rock
and Green Belt*, 77. A student of Ian McHarg's named James Corner, known for
his efforts at restoring open spaces (he dreamed up Manhattan's High Line, a park
built atop an abandoned railroad spur), landed the Fresh Kills design job in 2003.

40. Andrew R. Davis, "Meadowlands Commission Revises Master Plan, Rewrites
Zoning Regulations—Finally," *New Jersey Law Journal*, Feb. 2, 2004, www.lexis
nexis.com; and Maria Newman, "Plan to Revive the Meadowlands Is Approved,"
NYT, Jan. 9, 2004. The New Jersey Meadowlands Commission Master Plan of
2004 is available at www.njmeadowlands.gov/doc_archive/economicgrowth_mp
_maps_doc_archive.html. According to one study, the total wetland acreage of the
Meadowlands (Hackensack Meadows) in 1889 was 20,045. By 1970, the plan was
to develop the area so that there would be 1,500 acres remaining. Also, it is worth
noting that the 8,400-acre figure for the preservation of the Meadowlands put forward in the 2004 master plan included open water in addition to wetlands. In 1889
there were 2,943 acres of deepwater habitat in addition to the 20,045 acres of wetland. See Ralph W. Tiner, John Q. Swords, and Bobbi Jo McClain, *Wetland Status
and Trends for the Hackensack Meadowlands: An Assessment Report from the U.S. Fish
and Wildlife Service's National Wetlands Inventory Program* (Hadley, Mass.: US Fish
and Wildlife Service, 2002), 20, table 11.

41. Tiner, Swords, and McClain, *Wetland Status and Trends for the Hackensack Meadow-
lands*, 20, table 12; David M. Herszenhorn, "Fighting over the Ugliest Wilderness,"
NYT, Mar. 16, 1998; Lauren Otis, "The Malling of the Meadowlands," *New Jersey
Monthly*, Mar. 2000, 95 ("undermalled" quotation); and Matthew Futterman, "A
Watershed Clash Roils the Meadowlands," *SL*, June 21, 1998.

42. Tom Topousis, "Meadowlands Revival," *Record*, Oct. 15, 1995 ("lawns" quotation).
In 1995 the Hackensack Meadowlands Development Commission hatched a plan
to allow developers to plow under more than eight hundred acres of wetlands if they

contributed $875 million toward restoring the ecosystem. The ecology behind the idea was that when the Phragmites die, their biomass causes the land to rise and eventually to dry out and become upland.

On the other side of the debate were those environmentalists who were inclined to eschew development and restoration and leave the Phragmites be and who were basing their decision on some research suggesting that the plant actually favored more invertebrates than native grass would. Their idea was to replicate the effects of the 1950 nor'easter, which washed out dikes and tide gates and led to the decline of Phragmites, spurring the rise of an ecological reserve of mudflats and low salt marsh with more native vegetation. As Bill Sheehan, an environmentalist with the Hackensack Estuary and River Tenders, put it: "It may take thirty or fifty years, but let's let the river decide where the restoration is going to happen." Ecologist Joan Ehrenfeld at Rutgers said, "Building another megamall in one of the last remaining areas of open space in that area is just about the stupidest thing we can do." These two quotations are from Futterman, "A Watershed Clash." See also Mark McGarrity, "Keeper of the Gate," *SL*, July 12, 1998; and Philip Silva, "Phragmites: Friend or Foe?" *Wallington (N.J.) Leader*, Mar. 1, 2001.

43.   Ana M. Alaya, "Letters Explore Proposal for Mall," *SL*, Feb. 20, 2001; Act of Aug. 27, 2001, ch. 232, 2001, vol. 2, N.J. Laws 1492 (changing the HMDC to the New Jersey Meadowlands Commission); US Army Corps of Engineers, New York District, *Meadowlands Environmental Site Investigation Compilation* ([New York?], 2004), ES-1; and John Brennan, "Xanadu Proposal Making Progress," *Record*, Aug. 30, 2003. The environmental movement split over the master plan, with more moderate groups supporting the preservation of thousands of acres of open space. More radical factions, such as the Sierra Club, called the decision to allow the mall in return for the space "welfare to the developers." The new mall, named Xanadu (inspired by a Mills mall in Spain with a ski track), required the filling in of more than seven acres of wetlands, but some environmentalists, perhaps worn down by years of battle and triangulated into a corner where they were beginning to look extreme, saw the sacrifice as necessary to preserve the vast expanse of open land. See Carolyn Feibel, "State to Buy Empire Tract for $26.8M," *Record*, Oct. 5, 2004 ("welfare" quotation). The Sierra Club filed a lawsuit against the New Jersey Meadowlands Commission, a move that some environmentalists vehemently opposed. See Rick Grossman, "Wetlands Dispute," *Secaucus (N.J.) Reporter*, Sept. 24, 2004. The mall stalled, but as of this writing, a Canadian conglomerate has revived the project (calling it American Dream Meadowlands) in an even more ambitious form, with a water park to be built on wetland nearby. See Charles V. Bagli, "Work to Begin Soon to Revive Mall in Meadowlands, New Owner Says," *NYT*, June 10, 2013.

44.   On the Sawmill area, see US Army Corps of Engineers, New York District, *Meadowlands Environmental Site Investigation Compilation*, VII-1. Of course, cynics might argue that if the metropolitan area supports a robust open-space system, it is also home, in New York City alone, to at least three major Superfund sites at the Gowanus Canal, Newtown Creek, and the Hudson River, the last one involving the cleanup of PCBs (polychlorinated biphenyls) released by General Electric. The Newtown Creek site hosts an underground oil spill believed to contain millions of

gallons of petroleum—estimated to outstrip the 1989 *Exxon Valdez* disaster, when an oil tanker rammed into a reef in Prince William Sound, Alaska, and released at least eleven million gallons of oil. In 1988 the New York State Department of Environmental Conservation negotiated a consent decree with Mobil, one of the responsible parties, that required no damage payment and hardly spurred the company and the other culprits to address the problem. See Mireya Navarro, "Between Queens and Brooklyn, an Oil Spill's Legacy," *NYT*, Aug. 3, 2010; and Frank Koughan, "Breathless in Brooklyn," *Mother Jones*, Sept.–Oct. 2007, 33. A complete listing of all the cleanup sites in New York and New Jersey is available at the EPA's Region 2 website, www.epa.gov/region2/cleanup/sites/index.html.

45. US General Services Administration, *Draft Environmental Impact Statement for the Disposition of Governors Island, New York* ([New York?], 1998), III D-33, III A-1; and Ann L. Buttenwieser, *Governors Island: The Jewel of New York Harbor* (Syracuse, N.Y.: Syracuse Univ. Press, 2009), 90–91, 94–95, 100, 111, 116, 122–23.

46. Governors Island Alliance, "About the Alliance," www.governorsislandalliance.org /about/; and Quitclaim Deed, United States of America, by and through the General Services Administration to National Trust for Historic Preservation, Jan. 31, 2003, Trust for Governors Island, New York, 6–8 (copy at Governors Island National Monument). For more on the design competition, see John Gendall, "Five Variations on the Theme of Governors Island," *Architectural Record*, July 2007, 58 ("Babylonic" quotation); and Alexandra Lange, "Five Teams Compete to Make Governors Island an Urban Paradise," *New York*, June 4, 2007, www.lexisnexis.com.

47. US General Services Administration, *Draft Environmental Impact Statement for the Disposition of Governors Island*, III B-5; Brian Davis, "The New Public Landscapes of Governors Island: An Interview with Adriaan Geuze," *Places: Forum of Design for the Public Realm*, Feb. 2, 2011, http://places.designobserver.com/feature/the-new -public-landscapes-of-governors-island-an-interview-with-adriaan-geuze/24228; and Lange, "Five Teams Compete" ("national park" quotation). Governors Island contains 103 acres of landfill, which is 60 percent of its 172 acres. The "man-altered" quotation is from US General Services Administration, *Draft Environmental Impact Statement for the Disposition of Governors Island*, vi.

48. The idea to allow the island to "revert back to nature" was, however, raised by a *Times* reader who responded to a call by the paper to send in ideas about how to handle Governors Island. See James Barron, "On the Blank Slate of Governors Island, Imaginations Run Wild," *NYT*, Apr. 16, 2010.

16. The Future of New York

1. Max Page, *The City's End: Two Centuries of Fantasies, Fears, and Premonitions of New York's Destruction* (New Haven, Conn.: Yale Univ. Press, 2008), 4.

2. Charles Scawthorn and Stephen K. Harris, "Estimation of Earthquake Losses for a Large Eastern Urban Center: Scenario Events for New York City," *ANYAS* 558 (June 1989): 447, 436, doi:10.1111/j.1749-6632.1989.tb22590.x. The first edition of the National Earthquake Hazards Reduction Program's *Recommended Seismic Provisions* was released in 1985.

3. William K. Stevens, "Eastern Quakes," *NYT*, Oct. 24, 1989; and Jim Dwyer, "Trump's Folly Shakes City," *DN*, Nov. 11, 1997.

4. Michael W. Tantala et al., "Earthquake Loss Estimation for the New York City Metropolitan Region," *Soil Dynamics and Earthquake Engineering* 28, nos. 10–11 (Oct.–Nov. 2008): 821, table 1, 824, 816–17, 813, doi:10.1016/j.soildyn.2007.10.012.

5. F. P. Ellis, F. Nelson, and L. Pincus, "Mortality During Heat Waves in New York City: July, 1972 and August and September, 1973," *Environmental Research* 10, no. 1 (Aug. 1975): 11; Edward P. Kohn, *Hot Time in the Old Town: The Great Heat Wave of 1896 and the Making of Theodore Roosevelt* (New York: Basic Books, 2010), x, 235; Steven Whitman et al., "Mortality in Chicago Attributed to the July 1995 Heat Wave," *American Journal of Public Health* 87, no. 9 (Sept. 1997): 1515; and Laurence S. Kalkstein and J. Scott Greene, "An Evaluation of Climate/Mortality Relationships in Large U.S. Cities and the Possible Impacts of a Climate Change," *Environmental Health Perspectives* 105, no. 1 (Jan. 1997): 91, table 4, www.jstor.org/stable/3433067.

6. William D. Solecki et al., "Potential Impact of Green Roofs on the Urban Heat Island Effect," in *Green Roofs in the New York Metropolitan Region: Research Report*, ed. Cynthia Rosenzweig, Stuart Gaffin, and Lily Parshall (New York, 2006), 15; J. E. Rosenthal et al., "One Hundred Years of New York City's 'Urban Heat Island': Temperature Trends and Public Health Impacts" (abstract, American Geophysical Union, 2003), http://adsabs.harvard.edu/abs/2003AGUFM.U32A0030R; and S. R. Gaffin et al., "Variations in New York City's Urban Heat Island Strength over Time and Space," *Theoretical and Applied Climatology* 94, nos. 1–2 (2008): 3, doi:10.1007/s00704-007-0368-3.

7. Laurence S. Kalkstein et al., "Analog European Heat Waves for U.S. Cities to Analyze Impacts on Heat-Related Mortality," *BAMS* 89, no. 1 (Jan. 2008): 1, 7, 8, table 3, 9, doi:10.1175/BAMS-89-1-75.

8. Kalkstein et al., "Analog European Heat Waves," 9; US Environmental Protection Agency, *Excessive Heat Events Guidebook* (Washington, D.C., 2006), 12, 27; Richard Pérez-Peña, "New York's Tally of Heat Deaths Draws Scrutiny," *NYT*, Aug. 18, 2006 (quotation); and Pérez-Peña, "Heat Wave Was a Factor in 100 Deaths, New York Says," *NYT*, Nov. 16, 2006. Ironically, the *Times* itself underreported the number of excess deaths. See "Corrections: For the Record," *NYT*, Nov. 18, 2006.

9. Kim Knowlton et al., "Projecting Heat-Related Mortality Impacts Under a Changing Climate in the New York City Region," *American Journal of Public Health* 97, no. 1 (Nov. 2007): 2028, 2030 (quotation), doi:10.2105/AJPH.2006.102947; and Brodie Ramin and Tomislav Svoboda, "Health of the Homeless and Climate Change," *Journal of Urban Health: Bulletin of the New York Academy of Medicine* 86, no. 4 (July 2009): 655–56, doi:10.1007/s11524-009-9354-7.

10. Office of the New York City Comptroller, "NYC: A Fragile Recovery After Seven Quarters of Recession," *Economic Notes*, Apr. 2010, 1; Vivien Gornitz et al., "Impacts of Sea Level Rise in the New York City Metropolitan Area," *Global and Planetary Changes* 32, no. 1 (Dec. 2001): 61, 65, doi:10.1016/S0921-8181(01)00150-3; Rae Zimmer, "Global Warming, Infrastructure, and Land Use in the Metropolitan New York Area," *ANYAS* 790 (June 1996): 75, doi:10.1111/j.1749-6632.1996 .tb32470.x; and US Army Corps of Engineers et al., *Metro New York Hurricane*

Transportation Study: Interim Technical Data Report ([New York?], 1995), 3. Before the US National Weather Service's Sea, Lake, and Overland Surges from Hurricanes (SLOSH) computer model, older studies of storm-surge risk were based solely on historical data.

11. Brian A. Colle et al., "New York City's Vulnerability to Coastal Flooding: Storm Surge Modeling of Past Cyclones," *BAMS* 89, no. 6 (June 2008): 829, 840, doi:10.1175/2007BAMS2401.1; and US Army Corps of Engineers et al., *Metro New York Hurricane Transportation Study*, 4, 37, 39.

12. US Army Corps of Engineers et al., *Metro New York Hurricane Transportation Study*, 28, 29, table 10, 1, 42 (quotations).

13. Elyse Scileppi and Jeffrey P. Donnelly, "Sedimentary Evidence of Hurricane Strikes in Western Long Island, New York," *Geochemistry, Geophysics, Geosystems* 8 (June 2007): 1–25, doi:10.1029/2006GC001463; Nicholas K. Coch, "Hurricane Hazards Along the Northeastern Atlantic Coast of the United States," *Journal of Coastal Research*, special issue no. 12 (1994): 136, fig. 23, www.jstor.org/stable/25735594; Cynthia Rosenzweig et al., "Climate Component: MTA 8.8.07 Task Force Report," in *August 8, 2007 Storm Report*, ed. Metropolitan Transportation Authority ([New York?], 2007), 9; Colle et al., "New York City's Vulnerability to Coastal Flooding," 829; and US Army Corps of Engineers et al., *Metro New York Hurricane Transportation Study*, 20.

14. US Weather Bureau, *Hurricane Donna, September 2–13, 1960: Preliminary Report with the Advisories and Bulletins Issued* (Washington, D.C., 1960), 40; Samuel Gofseyeff and Frank L. Panuzio, "Hurricane Studies of New York Harbor," *TASCE* 128, no. 4 (Apr. 1963): 396–97, table 1, 398, 414, fig. 13, 418; *Atlantic Coast of New York City from East Rockaway Inlet to Rockaway Inlet and Jamaica Bay, New York*, H.R. Doc. No. 89–215 (1965), at 1–2; and Louis J. Lefkowitz, "Jamaica Bay: An Urban Marshland in Transition," *Fordham Urban Law Journal* 1, no. 1 (Summer 1972): 16–17. The figure for total water level at the Battery in Donna derives from data provided by the Battery station (no. 8518750) using the station datum and available at http://tidesandcurrents.noaa.gov/data_menu.shtml?stn=8518750%20The%20Battery,%20NY&type=Extremes. The data coverage at this station spans from 1856 through the present. I accessed the data on Nov. 5, 2012.

15. Coch, "Hurricane Hazards," 131; and Colle et al., "New York City's Vulnerability to Coastal Flooding," 837. The key paper on the AMO is Michael E. Schlesinger and Navin Ramankutty, "An Oscillation in the Global Climate System of Period 65–70 Years," *Nature* 367, no. 6465 (Feb. 24, 1994): 723–26, doi:10.1038/367723a0.

16. Malcolm J. Bowman et al., *Hydrological Feasibility of Storm Surge Barriers to Protect the Metropolitan New York–New Jersey Region* (s.l., 2004), 26 (quotation), 3, 20; and Patrick Barry, "Sooner or Later, the Water Will Arrive," *New Scientist*, June 3, 2006, www.lexisnexis.com. The potential ecological impacts of the barriers are discussed in R. L. Swanson and R. E. Wilson, "Storm Surge Barriers: Several Ecological and Social Concerns" (paper presented at "Against the Deluge: Storm Surge Barriers to Protect New York City," American Society of Civil Engineers, Metropolitan Section, Infrastructure Group Seminar, New York, 2009). The storm barrier in England is called the Thames Barrier. The massive barrier in the Netherlands is known as the Delta Works.

17. Diane Cardwell, "New City Plan Outlines Evacuations in Hurricane," *NYT*, June 29, 2006; and *2006 Hurricane Forecast and At-Risk Cities: Hearing Before the Subcomm. on Disaster Prevention and Prediction of the Comm. on Commerce, Sci., and Transp., U.S. Senate*, 109th Cong. 12 (2006), emphasis in original.

18. R. J. Nicholls et al., "Ranking Port Cities with High Exposure and Vulnerability to Climate Extremes: Exposure Estimates," *OECD Environment Working Papers*, no. 1 (2008): 3, 8.

19. Nicholls et al., "Ranking Port Cities," 9, 33, table 6, 39–40; N. Lin et al., "Risk Assessment of Hurricane Storm Surge for New York City," *Journal of Geophysical Research* 115, no. D18 (Sept. 2010): 1 ("catastrophic" quotation), doi:10.1029 /2009JD013630; and Scileppi and Donnelly, "Sedimentary Evidence of Hurricane Strikes," especially sec. 6.1.

20. New York City Office of Emergency Management, *Natural Hazard Mitigation Plan* ([New York?], 2009), sec. III, 116 ("substantially lower" quotation), 129 ("dense population" quotation), sec. IV, 137–40; Metropolitan Transportation Authority, *August 8, 2007 Storm Report* ([New York?], 2007), 9; and Klaus Jacob, "Multi-Hazard Mitigation Needs and Opportunities for the Greater New York City Metropolitan Area with Examples for Earthquake and Coastal Storm Surge Hazards" (paper prepared for Urban Hazards Forum, John Jay College, N.Y., 2002), 19.

21. Gornitz et al., "Impacts of Sea Level Rise," 85, 78 (quotation); and Juliana Maantay and Andrew Maroko, "Mapping Urban Risk: Flood Hazards, Race, and Environmental Justice in New York," *Applied Geography* 29, no. 1 (2009): 111, 123, doi:10.1016/j.apgeog.2008.08.002. To call attention to the flooding problem, an artist from Texas named Eve Mosher pushed a line-painting machine around New York to help show where the floodwater would come in the event of a one-in-a-hundred-year flood. She called her piece of art *The High Water Line*. See Eve S. Mosher, "Highwaterline," accessed Nov. 9, 2012, www.highwaterline.org.

22. Benjamin Strauss, "NYC's One-Inch Escape from Irene," *Huffington Post*, Aug. 30, 2011, www.huffingtonpost.com/benjamin-strauss/nyc-hurricane-irene_b_942503 .html; and Jean Casella and James Ridgeway, "Rikers Island Prisoners Left Behind to Face Irene," *Mother Jones*, Aug. 27, 2011, www.motherjones.com/mojo/2011/08 /rikers-island-prisoners-irene. Kerry Emanuel, a climate scientist at MIT, thought the "one-inch" characterization might be an exaggeration but concurred that some slight changes could have resulted in a disastrous outcome. See Andrew C. Revkin, "Warnings and the Cost of Storms and Climate Change," *Dot Earth* (blog), *NYT*, Aug. 31, 2011, http://dotearth.blogs.nytimes.com/2011/08/31/warnings-and-the -cost-of-storms-and-climate-change/.

23. As late as 1965, an urban historian called the grid "a disaster whose consequences have barely been mitigated by more modern city planners." See John W. Reps, *The Making of Urban America: A History of City Planning in the United States* (Princeton, N.J.: Princeton Univ. Press, 1965), 299. On the fiscal crisis, see David Harvey, *A Brief History of Neoliberalism* (Oxford, UK: Oxford Univ. Press, 2005), 45–47.

24. Rem Koolhaas, *Delirious New York: A Retroactive Manifesto for Manhattan* (1978; repr., New York: Monacelli, 1994), 18, 20.

25. Hartog, 163–64; Edward K. Spann, "The Greatest Grid: The New York Plan of

1811," in *Two Centuries of American Planning*, ed. Daniel Schaffer (Baltimore: Johns Hopkins Univ. Press, 1988), 35 (quotation); Alan Ehrenhalt, "The Return of the Grid," *Governing Magazine*, Nov. 2005, www.governing.com/topics/transportation-infrastructure/The-Return-The-Grid.html; Herbert Muschamp, "Of Mondrian, Street Grids and Cities Transcendent," *NYT*, Dec. 7, 1995; and Paul H. B. Shin, "Manhattan Phenom 'Henges' on Sun," *DN*, May 27, 2006.

26. Sam Roberts, "200th Birthday for the Map That Made New York," *NYT*, Mar. 21, 2011; Michael Kimmelman, "The Grid at 200: Lines That Shaped Manhattan," *NYT*, Jan. 3, 2012; Alec Appelbaum, "New York's Green Grid," *NYT*, Apr. 17, 2011; and Henry James, "New York Revisited," *Harper's Monthly Magazine*, May 1906, 900.

27. Roberts, "200th Birthday" (Hiss quotation); and ch. 8, *The Cruise*, DVD, directed by Bennett Miller (Santa Monica, Calif.: Lionsgate, 1998).

28. Edward Glaeser, *Triumph of the City: How Our Greatest Invention Makes Us Richer, Smarter, Greener, Healthier, and Happier* (New York: Penguin, 2011), 14, 222.

29. The quotation is that of Thaddeus Pawlowski. See Amy O'Leary, "Everybody Inhale," *NYT*, Mar. 4, 2012.

30. As early as 1968, the Federal Aviation Administration (FAA) implemented what it called a High Density Rule to control the number of takeoffs and landings at Kennedy and La Guardia. In the intervening period, the congestion problem was further aggravated by the tendency of airlines to build hubs in the region. Early in the twenty-first century, Newark and Kennedy emerged as particularly gridlocked, spurring the FAA to issue a congestion-management rule. A report revealed that the New York area's three main airports accounted for one-third of all the nation's flight delays. A remarkable three-quarters of all the delays experienced across the nation could be traced to problems that began in the airspace over the city. The Partnership for New York City (a group dedicated to maintaining New York's "position as a global center of commerce, finance, and innovation") noted that the congestion problem "is largely a product of space limitations." See US Government Accountability Office, *FAA Airspace Redesign: An Analysis of the New York/New Jersey/Philadelphia Project*, GAO-08-786, 2008, 9n12; Congestion Management Rule for John F. Kennedy International Airport and Newark Liberty International Airport, 73 Fed. Reg. 60544–571 (Oct. 10, 2008); Port Authority of New York and New Jersey, *Flight Delay Task Force Report* (s.l., 2007), 1; and Partnership for New York City, *Grounded: The High Cost of Air Traffic Congestion* (New York, 2009), 7.

31. Regional Plan Association, *Upgrading to World Class: The Future of the New York Region's Airports* (New York, 2011), 13, 123, table 10.2A.

32. Gateway National Recreational Area (National Park Service) and Jamaica Bay Watershed Protection Plan Advisory Committee, *An Update on the Disappearing Salt Marshes of Jamaica Bay, New York* (s.l., 2007), 2 ("ecological" quotation); and John Waldman, *Research Opportunities in the Natural and Social Sciences at the Jamaica Bay Unit of Gateway National Recreation Area* (prepared for the National Park Service, 2008), 13.

33. Gateway National Recreational Area (National Park Service) and Jamaica Bay Watershed Protection Plan Advisory Committee, *Update on the Disappearing Salt Marshes*, 6–7; Waldman, *Research Opportunities*, 8; Ellen Kracauer Hartig et al., "Anthropogenic and Climate-Change Impacts on Salt Marshes of Jamaica Bay, New

York City," *Wetlands* 22, no. 1 (Mar. 2002): 85–86; Regional Plan Association, *Upgrading to World Class*, 120; and Lisa L. Colangelo, "Local Residents Fighting Plan to Extend JFK Runways into Jamaica Bay," *DN*, Apr. 7, 2011 (Riepe quotation).

34. Director of the Department of City Planning Amanda Burden noted that if the 1992 plan precipitated the redevelopment—some would say gentrification—of the waterfront, the new vision ventured a step further, "into the water itself." She went so far as to call the surrounding waters the "Sixth Borough." Burden, it bears noting, worked in the 1980s for the Battery Park City Corporation Authority. See New York Department of City Planning, *Vision 2020: New York City Comprehensive Waterfront Plan* (New York, 2011), 3, 7.

35. Julie Satow, "19 Months Left to Finish Remaking New York," *NYT*, May 20, 2012; and New York Department of City Planning, *Vision 2020*, 13, 12, fig. 4, 36.

36. New York Department of City Planning, *Vision 2020*, 9, 68, 74–76.

37. New York Department of City Planning, *Vision 2020*, 75–76. However, a human encampment on Shooter's Island may have in part chased the birds away beginning in 1998. See Tony Hiss and Christopher Meier, *H2O, Highlands to Ocean: A First Close Look at the Outstanding Landscapes and Waterscapes of the New York/New Jersey Metropolitan Region* (Morristown, N.J.: Geraldine R. Dodge Foundation, 2004), 70.

38. Michael Bloomberg, *PlaNYC: A Greener, Greater New York* (New York, 2007), 58; and Christopher Rizzo, "Protecting the Environment at the Local Level: New York City's Special District Approach," *Fordham Environmental Law Journal* 13, no. 2 (Spring 2002): 255.

39. New York Department of City Planning, *Vision 2020*, 106, 107.

40. New York City Panel on Climate Change, "Climate Change Adaptation in New York City: Building a Risk Management Response," *ANYAS* 1196 (May 2010): 8 (quotation), doi:10.1111/j.1749-6632.2009.05415.x. New York is actually subsiding by three to four inches every century because the areas north and west of the city are rebounding from the effects of the melting of the extremely heavy ice sheets. See New York City Panel on Climate Change, "Climate Change Adaptation," 45, 54. After Hurricane Sandy, Mayor Bloomberg called a second meeting of the New York City Panel on Climate Change to assess the latest models and the potential impact on the city. See New York City Panel on Climate Change (NPCC2), *Climate Risk Information 2013: Observations, Climate Change Projections, and Maps* (prepared for the City of New York Special Initiative on Rebuilding and Resiliency, 2013), 18, 20.

41. New York City Panel on Climate Change, "Climate Change Adaptation," 9, 10, 95. Nor did the *Vision 2020* plan, which relied on the task force's findings, offer much in the way of substantive reforms with respect to climate change. Granted, the plan briefly mentioned the prospect of retreating in the face of a rise in sea level, itself remarkable given the city's longstanding aggressive stance toward the sea. But otherwise the plan embraced the idea that extreme natural conditions—not extremism in development—were the root cause of the natural disaster problem. "As a coastal city exposed to the ocean," the plan pointed out, "New York has always faced risks from severe storms and coastal flooding." But such an ahistorical statement masked the role that waterfront development and the quest to expand into the sea

with landfill played in increasing the vulnerability to disaster. In other words, floods and storms were viewed in the plan as resulting from timeless natural hazards, as opposed to what could be called an extreme set of development policies that had placed increasing amounts of land at risk. "There is inherent unpredictability in storm events and the risks they present," the authors of the *Vision* plan declared. But in reality, the uncertainty regarding New York's natural disaster future could just as easily be ascribed to the volatility of high-density development as it could to the mercurial workings of nature. In contrast, a British team assessing flood risk drew attention to the "critical uncertainty that socio-economic development presents to the future of flood risk." Nor should we overlook that by seeking to expand the allowable commercial use of the waterfront—replacing the state's stricter "water-dependent" standard with the wishy-washy "water-enhancing" one—the *Vision* plan, while indeed improving public access to the coast, was also helping to place more people and property in harm's way. See New York Department of City Planning, *Vision 2020*, 109, 17, 111, and 27, 40, on "water-enhancing" uses; and Environment Agency, *Thames Estuary 2100: Managing Flood Risk Through London and the Thames Estuary*, TE2100 plan (London, 2009), 20.

42. "Washout at Jones Beach," *NYT*, Dec. 30, 2012, www.nytimes.com/2012/12/31 /opinion/washout-at-jones-beach-for-trump-project.html?_r=0.

43. "Devastation in Long Beach, N.Y. After Hurricane Sandy," YouTube video, Nov. 2, 2012, www.youtube.com/watch?v=sgkVdnxyGDk ("nineteenth century" quotation).

44. Eric S. Blake et al., "Tropical Cyclone Report: Hurricane Sandy," National Hurricane Center, AL182012, Feb. 12, 2013, 9, www.nhc.noaa.gov/data/tcr/AL182012 _Sandy.pdf; Archie Tse, "A Survey of Destruction by Hurricane Sandy in New York City," *NYT*, Nov. 21, 2012; Peter Donohue, "Dozens of MTA Workers, Stranded in Coney Avenue Terminal, Faced Death as Hurricane Sandy Waters Rushed In," *DN*, Nov. 13, 2012, www.nydailynews.com/new-york/mta-workers-trapped-flood -sandy-article-1.1200933; and "Gowanus Canal Hurricane Sandy Flooding Map," accessed May 6, 2013, http://bit.ly/SandyGowanusMap.

45. Blake et al., "Tropical Cyclone Report," 18, 120, table 9, 9; Kirk Semple, "At Home Again, but Only to Mourn," *NYT*, Dec. 5, 2012; James Barron, Joseph Goldstein, and Kirk Semple, "Staten Island Was Tragic Epicenter of Storm's Casualties," *NYT*, Nov. 2, 2012; Tse, "A Survey of Destruction by Hurricane Sandy"; Jennifer Peltz, "Plan for NYC Ferris Wheel Rolls On, Despite Sandy," Associated Press, Jan. 1, 2013, http://bigstory.ap.org/article/plan-nyc-ferris-wheel-rolls-despite -sandy; and Ian Frazier, "The Toll: Sandy and the Future," *New Yorker*, Feb. 11 and 18, 2013, 38. A report by the Special Initiative for Rebuilding and Resiliency, formed by the Bloomberg administration in December 2012, concluded that in the future "the risks faced by the North Shore [of Staten Island] from extreme weather events are likely to increase due to climate change." See Michael Bloomberg, *A Stronger, More Resilient New York* (New York, 2013), 281.

46. David Ariosto, "First Irene, Then Sandy: Jersey City Recovers, Again," *CNN Wire*, Nov. 14, 2012, www.lexisnexis.com; David M. Halbfinger, "New Jersey Reels from Storm's Thrashing," *NYT*, Nov. 1, 2012; and Blake et al., "Tropical Cyclone Report," 17.

47. "Manhattan Subway Floods . . . Cars Float Down Wall Street," *Washington's Blog*, Oct. 30, 2012, www.washingtonsblog.com/2012/10/manhattan-floods-cars-float -down-wall-street.html; Tse, "A Survey of Destruction by Hurricane Sandy"; Blake et al., "Tropical Cyclone Report," 18; Bloomberg, *A Stronger, More Resilient New York*, 373; Lisa W. Foderaro, "Hudson River Park Still Without Power Weeks After Storm Damaged Equipment," *NYT*, Dec. 14, 2012, www.nytimes .com/2012/12/15/nyregion/hudson-river-park-still-without-power-because-of -hurricane-sandy.html; Glenn Collins, "A Wall Once Unseen, Now Revered," *NYT*, June 23, 2003, www.nytimes.com/2003/06/23/nyregion/wall-once-unseen-now -revered-ground-zero-symbol-survival-mended-for-posterity.html?pagewanted =all&src=pm ("indomitable" quotation); and Steven Rosenbaum, "The Bathtub: Lower Manhattan's Wall Against Water," *Forbes*, Nov. 5, 2012, www.forbes.com /sites/stevenrosenbaum/2012/11/05/the-bathtub-lower-manhattans-wall-against -water/.

The storm also made a mockery of the region's wastewater infrastructure. More than ten billion gallons of raw or partially treated sewage were released in New York and New Jersey. The largest sewage overflow anywhere was the responsibility of the Passaic Valley Sewerage Commission. That was the agency established in 1902 to deal with the pollution of the Passaic River by channeling the waste to Upper New York Bay. Sandy's storm surge submerged the commission's vast Newark plant and led to the release of 840 million gallons of untreated sewage directly into Newark Bay—more than four times the oil spilled in the 2010 Deepwater Horizon disaster off the coast of Louisiana—though the ecological impact is difficult to gauge. The New York City Department of Environmental Protection found, based on water samples, that the sewage it tested did not have a significant impact on water quality. Nevertheless, the hard reality is that sewage treatment plants must be located close to water and that means that they are always going to be at risk from storm surge and rising sea level. See Alyson Kenward, Daniel Yawitz, and Urooj Raja, *Sewage Overflows from Hurricane Sandy* (Princeton, N.J.: Climate Central, 2013), 1, 9, 10, www.climatecentral.org/pdfs/Sewage.pdf; Jarrett Renshaw, "Hurricane Sandy Delivered a Body Blow to N.J. Sewage Plants," *nj.com*, Dec. 25, 2012, www.nj.com /politics/index.ssf/2012/12/hurricane_sandy_delivered_a_bo.html; and Bloomberg, *A Stronger, More Resilient New York*, 210–11.

48. Susanne Craig, "Goldman Sachs's New Palace Creates Princes, Serfs," *Wall Street Journal*, Apr. 16, 2010, http://online.wsj.com/article/SB1000142405270230382830 4575180581255747658.html; and Goldman Sachs, *Environmental Progress Report 2009*, 16–17, www.goldmansachs.com/citizenship/esg-reporting/env-report-2009 .pdf. The building has a gold LEED (Leadership in Energy and Environmental Design) rating.

49. Adam Volland, "Comparing the Winds of Sandy and Katrina," NASA Hurricanes/ Tropical Cyclones, Nov. 9, 2012, www.nasa.gov/mission_pages/hurricanes/archives /2012/h2012_Sandy.html; and Tom Schlatter, "Weather Queries," *Weatherwise*, Mar.–Apr. 2013, www.weatherwise.org/Archives/Back%20Issues/2013/March -April%202013/weather-queries-full.html. The 1938 storm had a somewhat lower central pressure of 941 millibars. Sandy's central pressure at landfall in New Jersey

was estimated at 945 millibars. See Blake et al., "Tropical Cyclone Report," 6, and 4 on the storm's status as a posttropical cyclone.

50. James Barron, "After the Devastation, a Daunting Recovery," *NYT*, Oct. 31, 2012 (Obama quotation); Winnie Hu, "Cuomo Waives a Tax to Allow Docking Tankers to Unload Their Fuel More Quickly," *NYT*, Nov. 2, 2012, www.nytimes.com/2012 /11/03/nyregion/cuomo-says-gas-tankers-are-on-the-way-to-new-york.html (Cuomo quotation); James Barron, "Region Faces Rescues, Looting, and a Rising Death Toll," *NYT*, Nov. 1, 2012 (Bloomberg quotation); and Matt Chaban, "On the Waterfront, There's No Place Like Home: Mayor Bloomberg's Tidal Wave of Development Washes Out," *New York Observer*, Oct. 31, 2012 (Spinola quotation), www.lexisnexis.com.

51. Blake et al., "Tropical Cyclone Report," 8; and Bloomberg, *A Stronger, More Resilient New York*, 13. The storm tide is defined as the storm surge plus the astronomical tide.

52. Mireya Navarro, "New York Is Lagging as Seas and Risks Rise, Critics Warn," *NYT*, Sept. 11, 2012, www.lexisnexis.com (Jacob quotation).

53. National Public Radio, "As Storm Recovery Continues, Looking to the Future," *Talk of the Nation: Science Friday*, Nov. 2, 2012, www.lexisnexis.com ("managed retreat" quotation); Matt Chaban, "New New Amsterdam: Should New York Do Like the Dutch and Build Some Skyscraper-Sized Sea Gates?" *New York Observer*, Oct. 31, 2012, http://observer.com/2012/10/new-new-amsterdam-should -new-york-do-like-the-dutch-and-building-some-skyscraper-sized-sea-gates (Chakrabarti quotation); and Jim Dwyer, "Still Building at the Edges of the City as Tides Rise," *NYT*, Dec. 5, 2012. On the Center for Urban Real Estate's plan for LoLo, or Lower Lower Manhattan, a proposal to fill in so much of the land under water around Manhattan as to connect it with Governors Island and, in the process, summon forth eighty-eight-million square feet of development, see Julie Satow, "Visions of a Development Rising from the Sea," *NYT*, Nov. 23, 2011; and Matt Chaban, "Why Build a Bridge to Governors Island? Competition of Course," *New York Observer*, Nov. 23, 2011, http://observer.com/2011/11/why -build-a-land-bridge-to-governors-island-competition-of-course/.

54. Data extraction, Nov. 5, 2012, NOAA data on tides at the Battery station, http:// tidesandcurrents.noaa.gov/data_menu.shtml?stn=8518750%20The%20Bat tery,%20NY&type=Extremes; NOAA, "Mean Sea Level Trend: 8518750 The Battery New York," accessed Nov. 9, 2012, http://tidesandcurrents.noaa.gov/; National Weather Service Twitter page, "Storm Surge Was 9.23 FT," Oct. 31, 2012, https:// twitter.com/NWSNewYorkNY/status/263727333112942592; Blake et al., "Tropical Cyclone Report," 8; and Coch, "Hurricane Hazards," 130, 136, fig. 23. The New York City Panel on Climate Change estimates the sea level rise by the 2020s as four to eight inches in the middle range, and eleven inches on the high end. These new estimates are up significantly since the study made in 2009. See New York City Panel on Climate Change (NPCC2), *Climate Risk Information 2013*, 4.

55. Bloomberg, *A Stronger, More Resilient New York*, 25, 41.

56. Mike Davis, *Planet of Slums* (London: Verso, 2006), 134.

INDEX

Entries in italics refer to illustrations.

Adams, Thomas, 188, 189
Adirondack Mountains, 95
aerial photography, 208, 216, 339–40
African-Americans, 43, 69, 113–14, 133, 167–68, 407n14. *See also* slaves
Ahasimus (Harsimus) Cove, 130, 134
Ailanthus altissima, 221, 452–453n32
air pollution, 212, 255
airports, 265, 309, 339, 340, 490n30. *See also* Kennedy Airport; La Guardia Airport; Newark Liberty Airport
Albany, N.Y., 30, 45, 108
    grid plan in, 56, 59
    as seat of state government, 107–8, 236–37, 298, 301
Albion, Robert, 77
Ambrose, John W., 170
Ambrose Channel, 170
American Can Company, 256
American Fisheries Company, 173
American Littoral Society, 340
American Philosophical Society, 78
American Revolution, 36, 49, 55, 56, 233, 264
    as a dividing line, 30, 33–34, 48, 52, 95
American Scenic and Historic Preservation Society, 165, 176
Andros, Edmund, 20–21, 25
Angotti, Tom, xviii

Argall, Samuel, 9
Army Corps of Engineers. *See* US Army Corps of Engineers
Arthur Kill, xxi, 169, 226, 238, 250, 332
    industry on, 227, 249
Ashokan Reservoir, 176
Astor, John Jacob, 74–76
Astral Oil Company, 142
Atlantic Dock Company, 83, *84*
Atlantic Flyway, xvii, 246, 318, 323
Atlantic Multidecadal Oscillation (AMO), 332
automobiles, 197, 199, 200, 203, 264, 306

Babylon, L.I., 201
Bache, Alexander D., 102–5, *106*, 122
bacteria, 119, 163, 170, 177
Badillo, Herman, 292
Baisley Pond Park, 245
barges, 184. *See also* garbage scows
Barnes, Thurlow Weed, 184–85
Barren Island, 4, 123, 171–72, *173*, 309
    joining of, to mainland, 5, 309
    resource recovery plant on, 123, 172, 239, 240
Bartlett, Washington, 100
Battery, the, 90–93, *94*, 102, 164, 216, 221
    water level at, 331, 348, 350

Battery Park City, 283, 286–92, 299, 346
ecological impact of, 291–92, 296, 316
as last major expansion of Manhattan, 284
Battery Tunnel, 330, 335, 345, 349
Bayard's Mount (Bunker Hill), 43, 49, 87
Bayonne Peninsula. *See* Bergen Neck
beavers, 15, 70
Bedloe's Island, 133, 187
Beecher, Henry Ward, 143
Beekman, William, 42
Beekman's Swamp, 25, 42, 43, *75*
Beeren Eylandt. *See* Barren Island
Belt Parkway, 193, 445n24
Bergen Neck, 6, 128–31, 133–34, 135–39, 188, 345
Berlin, 149, 158, 174
Berman, Marshall, 295
Bestevars Killitie (Mannette), 27, 56, 58
"Big Apple" (term), 284
biodiversity, xv, 6, 15–16, 70, 226–27, 303, 316
decline of, 177–79, 251, 256–58, 273, 314–15 (*see also* fish: declining varieties of)
in marshes, 6, 8, 183, 191, 226, 238, 271, 277
partial rebounding of, 318, 323–24
Blackstone, William, 93
Blackwell's Island, 127
Blake, Peter, 292
Bliss, Neziah, 96
Bloomberg, Michael, 304–5, 308, 348
mayoral administration of, 333, 337, 341–43
Blunt, Edmund M., 77, 103, *104,* 122
Blunt, George, *104,* 122, 430n26
Bog Brook, 156
Bolduan, Charles F., 194
borrow pits, 316
Boston, 25, 26, 31
Boudreau, Clarence, 206
Bowery Bay, 141
Boyle, Robert H., 293–94
Bradford, William, 28

Brady, Anthony N., 192, 193, 211. *See also* Brooklyn Ash Removal Company
Breezy Point, Queens, 317, 331
bridges, 191–92, 209, 226, 232, 264, 265. *See also* Brooklyn Bridge; George Washington Bridge; Triborough Bridge; Verrazano-Narrows Bridge
Britain. *See* Great Britain
Bronx, the, 156, 200, 210, 246
marshes in, 183, 243–44, 245, 247
see also Bronx Zoo
Bronx River, 48–49, 155
Bronx-Whitestone Bridge, 209
Bronx Zoo, 231, 232
Brooklyn, 4, 27, 52, 67–68, 80–85, 192
expansion of, 97, 309
parks in, 245
population of, 52, 66, 81, 97, 121
and waste disposal, 212, 213, 246, 250, 255, 320 (*see also* Brooklyn Ash Removal Company)
waterfront development in, 77, 81–85, 90, 96–97, 101, 106, 349
water supply of, 120–21, 157–58, 200
Brooklyn, marshes in, 13, *344*
decline of, 83–85, 140–41, 163–64, 194–95
Brooklyn Ash Removal Company, 192, 211–12, 213–14, 215–16, 217
Brooklyn Bridge, 25
Brooklyn Bridge Park, 303
Brooklyn Daily Eagle, 106, 121
Brown, William, 173
Browne, Joseph, 48–49
Brunel, Isambard Kingdom, 105–6
Buck, Ellsworth B., 246
bulkheads, 17, 85, 134, 170, 192
in Jamaica Bay, 318, 340
and Manhattan shoreline, 97, 284, 300, 303
Bunker Hill (Bayard's Mount), 43, 49, 87
Burgis, William, 26
Burling Slip, 53
Burnet, William, 26
Burr, Aaron, 69

Bushwick, Brooklyn, 96, 97
Bushwick Creek, 141
Buttermilk Channel, 81–82, 92–93, 102,
    105, 108, 344
  and Brooklyn's development as port,
    82–83, 90, 93
Butzel, Albert, 295–96, 301
Byram River, 155

canals, 19, 350
  for drainage, 14, 49, 74 (*see also*
    Gowanus Canal; Heere Gracht)
  for navigation, 73, 98, 133 (*see also* Erie
    Canal)
  in the Netherlands, 14, 15
Canal Street, *35,* 43, 68, *75,* 331, 346
Canarsie, Brooklyn, 216, 245
Canarsie Indians, 5
Carey, Hugh, 294
Carey, William, 217, 242–43, 247
Carlstadt, N.J., 323
Carson, Rachel, 273
Carteret, Sir George, 70
Castle Clinton, 91
Castle Point, 135
Catskill Mountains, 159–60, 175–76
cedar trees, 191, 259, 260, 262, 263. *See
    also* white cedar swamps
Center for Urban Real Estate, 349
Central Park, 48, 125, 126, 308
  impact of, 216, 301
  relative size of, 293, 319, 322
  shaping of, 86–87, 240
Central Railroad Company of New Jersey,
    128, 133–34, 138–39, 143, 430n26
cesspools, 175
Chadwick, Edwin, 117
Chakrabarti, Vishaan, 349–50
Chamber of Commerce. *See* New York
    Chamber of Commerce; Staten
    Island Chamber of Commerce
Charles II (king of England), 19
Chelsea, 80. *See also* Chelsea Piers
Chelsea Piers, 186
Cherry Pond, 228

Chesapeake Bay, 51, 168, 295
Chicago, 214, 328, 329, 426n33
cholera, 82, 116–17, 123, 134
Christiaensen Basin, 315
Churuti, Jack, 270
Cicindela beetles, 76
cisterns, 44
Citizens Budget Commission, 289,
    310
Citizens Committee to Keep New York
    Clean, 256
Civil War, 123, 125, 127, 139, 141
clams, 16, 204
  harvesting of, 164, 196, 201, 203, 207
Clark, Myron, 101–2
clay mining, 227–28, 233
Clay Pit Ponds, 227, 250
Clean Water Act (1972), 277–78, 294,
    314, 316
climate change, xxiii, 50, 329, 332,
    334, 340, 342–43. *See also* global
    warming
Clinton, De Witt, 69, 71, 85, 91
Clinton, James, 58
closed loop, 109–13, 123, *124,* 174–75,
    240–41
  in Europe, 174
  pig farms and, 268–69
  see also resource recovery
coal, 133, 142, 211
coastal flooding, 67–68, 326, 330–35, 342,
    348, 350
Coast Survey. *See* US Coast Survey
Colden, Cadwallader, 27
Collect Pond (Fresh Water Pond, "the
    Collect"), 43–44, *45,* 46–50, *75*
  elaborate plans for, 56–57, 73
  filling of, 49–50, 68, 87, 148
  health concerns about, 47–48, 49
  as water resource, 44, 48, 125
Colman, John, 6–7
Combs, Clarence, 204
common law, English, 131, 132, 272
common rights, 32–33, 168, 200, 236.
    See also commons tradition

commons tradition, 291, 302–3
  disruption of, 131–33, 205–7, 218, 222,
    227, 230–32, 234–37
  on Long Island, 191, 195, 198–99,
    205–7, 217–18, 222
  in New Jersey, 131–33, 270
  on Staten Island, 168, 227, 230–32,
    234–37
communal rights, 11. *See also* commons
    tradition
Communipaw Cove, 130, 134
Concord, Staten Island, 227, 228
Coney Island, xx, 77, 191–93, 206,
    243
  commons tradition on, 192, 195
  and Hudson's voyage, 6, 7
  joining of, to mainland, 192–93
  marshland on, 183, 191
  resort located on, 123
  storm damage on, *347*
Coney Island Creek, 191–93, 211, 344,
    347
congestion pricing, 304
Congress. *See* US Congress
Connecticut, 170
Connolly, Maurice, 219–20
conservation movement, 227, 230–34,
    235–37, 244, 253
  and commons tradition, 230–32,
    233–37
consolidation of five boroughs (1898),
    148, 149, 158, 161, 196, 200
containerports, 267–68, 309. *See also* Port
    Elizabeth
Continental Can Company, 256
cordgrass. *See* salt marsh cordgrass
Corlear's (Corlaers) Hook, 27, 48, 95, 105
Corona, Queens, 211, 212, 214, 218, 224
corporations, 146–47, 170, 222, 256. *See
    also specific companies*
corruption, 140, 147, 159, 211–12, 214
Cosby, William, 92
Cozzens, Issachar, Jr., 49
crabs, 171, 191, 271, 273, 303. *See also*
    fiddler crabs

Cross Island Parkway, 209
Croton Aqueduct, 115–16, 155. *See also*
    New Croton Aqueduct
Croton River, 115, 155, 159
  diversion of, for New York City,
    115–16, 121, 125, 155–57, 159
crows, 248, 315
Cruger, John, 27
Cuomo, Andrew, 348
Cuomo, Mario, 298, 302
Cuppy, Will, 202, 203, 448n47
Cushing, Caleb, 100

dams, 115, 155, 157, 161, 220. *See also*
    Hoover Dam; Oradell Dam
Danckaerts, Jasper, 84
Davis, Charles Henry, 102
Davis, William Thompson, 227–30, 238,
    259, 345
  and conservation movement, 230, 231,
    232, 233, 236
deforestation, 36–37, 95, 119, 130, 146,
    419n13
  in Manhattan, 36, 406n28
Degnon, Michael, 211–12
De Lancey, James, 33
Delaware River watershed, 310
Del Giudice, Michael J., 298–99, 301
De Witt, Simeon, 57–60
Dey, Anthony, 130, 135
Dickinson, Fairleigh, Jr., 272
dikes, 8, 24, 135, 309
  in New Jersey, 71, 72, 135, 262, 266
Dinkins, David, 300
disease, 123, 162, 170, 197, 255. *See also*
    cholera; malaria; yellow fever
Doctor's Creek, 275
Dongan, Thomas, 23, 36, 77, 90, 101, 106,
    131. *See also* Dongan Charter
Dongan Charter, 23, 24, 26, 92
Douglass, David B., 83–84
Downtown-Lower Manhattan
    Association (DLMA), 286, 287
dragonflies, 195
dredge-and-fill permits, 294, 296, 297

dredging, 95, 247
  of harbor slips, 95, 133
  for landfill, 203–4 (*see also*
    dredge-and-fill permits)
  for navigation, 170, 247, 309
  and oyster beds, 168, 169
Driggs, Spencer Bartholomew, 135
drinking water, 44, 48–49, 115, 116, 162,
    313
droughts, 125, 155, 162, 230, 262
dumping (into the water), 24, 123,
    147–48, 241
  of dead animals, 48, 53, 74, 122–23
  of human waste, 114–15, 117
  legal restrictions on, 122–23, 241,
    245
  from ships, 94–95
Dunham, David, 82
Dutch colonists, 9–18, 20, 84, 167, 171,
    398n15
  continuing legacy of, 19, 21
  limited reshaping of landscape by,
    17–18, 348, 350
  in New Jersey, 128, 130
  place names given by, 4, 14, 19, 43, 51,
    56, 64, 98, 238
Dutch Farms section. *See* Concord,
    Staten Island
Dwight, Timothy, 111
Dyker Beach, 194–95
Dyker Beach Park, 194, 245
Dyker Meadows, 223

Earth Day, 291, 304
earthquakes, 326, 327–28, 334
East River, 96, 126–27, 141, 345–46
  controversies over, 100–101, 106–8
  early description of, 15
  islands in, 210 (*see also* Rikers Island)
  and Manhattan wetlands, 43, 74, 88
  navigation on, 80, 98, 105 (*see also*
    Hell Gate)
  waste disposal in, 24, 47, 117, 122
  water quality in, 163, 164, 177,
    249

East River, waterfront development on,
    37, 51, 52–53, *75,* 81–85, 89, 90,
    96–97
  in colonial era, 23–24, 25, 26, 27, 32, 34
  since Second World War, 283, 288,
    298, 349
East Rutherford Meadows, 269
Edgemere Landfill, 246, 320
egrets, 196, 226, 318, 341
Eisenbud, Merril, 289–90
Elish, Herbert, 255
Elizabeth, N.J., 37, 70, 133, 134, 221, 262
  containerport at (Port Elizabeth), 268,
    286, 309
Elizabeth Meadows, *229, 259n, 261, 279*
  disappearance of, 268, *279*
Elliott, Donald H., 253
Ellis Island, 133
Ellsworth company, 168, 169
Empire State Building, 158, 226, 250, 308
Endangered Species Act, 295
Engels, Friedrich, 94
English common law, 131, 132, 272
environmentalists, 274–75, 294, 299, 304,
    323
  and Hackensack Meadows,
    485nn42,43
Environmental Protection Agency (EPA).
    See US Environmental Protection
    Agency
Erie Canal, 59, 60, 71, 80, 112, 115
  and New York's growth, 66, 73, 76, 79,
    331
Ernst, Gretchen, 234
Esopus Creek, 159–60
estuaries, xvi, xvii, xxii, 113. *See also* New
    York Harbor
eutrophication, 118–19, 162, 220, 318,
    441n55
  impervious ground cover and, 149
  natural defenses against, 123, 173
  see also oxygen levels
evacuations, 266
  planning for, 330, 333, 334, 335
excrement. *See* human waste; manure

factory fishing. *See* industrial fishing
False Channel Meadow, 198
Fast, Howard, 269
Federal Emergency Management Agency
   (FEMA), 277, 324, *347*
Federal Highway Administration
   (FHWA), 296–97
Federalists, 62–63
Felt, James, 252
ferry service, 81, 82, 130, 141, 202, 268
fiddler crabs, 195, 197, 211, 324
Fifth Avenue, 115
firewood, 36, 217, 235
First World War, 166, 184, 194, 241
fish, 4, 6, 46, 141, 143, 172, 235
   declining varieties of, 161–62, 164–65,
      171, 285, 302, 303
   in Hudson River, 15, 94, 177, 293–96,
      302, 303
   partial comeback of, 316, 318
   see also fishing; flounder; killifish;
      menhaden; shad; striped bass
fishing, 164, 192, 202
   in colonial era, 46, 171
   industrial, 171, 172–73
Fitzgerald, F. Scott, 193, 212, 224
Five Points, 69
flash floods, 334
Flatbush, Brooklyn, 13
Flat Creek, 203
Floating Neutrinos, 302–3
Flood Rock, 98, 142–43
flooding, 95, 164, 319
   due to poor drainage, 36–37, 69, 116
   of wetlands, 220, 277
   see also coastal flooding; flash floods
flood-insurance maps, *347, 348*
flounder, 171, 191, 198, 202, 302
Floyd Bennett Field, 309
Flushing Bay, 211, 213, 224, 265, *312*
Flushing Creek, 211, 212, 219, 220
Flushing Meadows, 13
   airport in: *see* La Guardia Airport
   ash heap in ("Mount Corona"),
      211–12, 213–14, 215–16, 218

commons tradition in, 217–18, 222
landscape change in, 217, 218–24, 245,
   249, 349
as marshland, 183, 210–11, 213, 217,
   222, 224, 310, 339
origin of, 4
World's Fair in, 214–24, 242, 243
   see also Flushing Meadows Park
Flushing Meadows Park, 249, 253
Flushing Railroad, 141
flush toilets, 158, 314
forests, 36, 86, 200, 235
   old-growth, 12, 36, 153
   see also deforestation
Fort George, 90
Forty-Second Street, 65, 298
Fountain Avenue Landfill, 320
France, 26, 114, 328
Franklin, Benjamin, 103
Freeman, John Ripley, 158, 159
Fresh Kills, xxi, 183, *229,* 258
   native flora and fauna of, 238–39,
      246–47, 248
   resource recovery efforts in, 239–40,
      247
   see also Fresh Kills Landfill; Freshkills
      Park
Fresh Kills Landfill, 238–39, 248, 249–50,
   252–53, 289–90, 325
   closing of, 320–21
   and ecological change, 238–39, 250–51,
      256–58
   growth of, 238, 254–58, 463n44
   origins of, 244–47, 249
Freshkills Park, 321–22
Fresh Water Pond. *See* Collect Pond
freshwater wetlands, 15, 123, 194, 243,
   319–20
   in New Jersey, 263, 273, 277
Freud, Sigmund, 152, 166
Fteley, Alphonse, 159

garbage collection, 111, 122, 241
garbage scows, 241, 247
Gardiners Bay, 171

Gateway National Recreation Area, 317–18, 481n30
Gaynor, William, 159
Gedney, Thomas, 77, 78, 79
Gedney's Channel, 77, 79, 105, 433n42
George II (king of Great Britain), 44–45
George Washington Bridge, 263, 267
Geuze, Adriaan, 324
Gibbet, Ellis, 133
Giuliani, Rudolph, 301, 302, 321
glaciers, 3–4, 50–51, 190, 191, 219
Glaeser, Edward, xvii, 337
global warming, 305, 328, 329, 337, 341n
glossy ibis, 341
Goerck, Casimir, 56–57
Goethals Bridge, 232
Goldman, Clifford A., 276
Goldman Sachs, 346
golf courses, 194, 213, 237, 271, 309
Governors Island, 9, 102, 187, 324–25, 349
  and Buttermilk Channel, 81
  landfill on, *178*, 324, 486n47
Gowanus Canal, 85, 164, 166, *338*, 344
Gowanus Creek, 83–85, 163–64
Gramercy Park, 96, 125
Grand Central Parkway, xix, 209, 213–14, 249, 450n13
Grassy Bay, 340, 479n16
Gravesend Bay, 192, 223
Great Britain, 70, 81, 97, 105–6, 174
  in colonial era, 18–19, 20, 26, 30, 44–45, 130
  waste disposal in, 174, 243
  see also London
Great Depression, 205, 217, 227, 234–35
  Staten Island in, 227, 230, 234–36
  World's Fair and, 214, 222
Great Dock, 20, 26–27
Great Falls (Paterson, N.J.), 161
Great Gatsby, The (Fitzgerald), 193, 212
Great Kill (Manhattan stream), 48
Great Kills, 13, 183, *229*, 244, *257*, 345
  landfill in, 244, 251
  see also Great Kills Park

Great Kills Park, 233, 244, 253, 317
Great South Bay, 195
Green, Andrew Haswell, 139–40, 148–49
Greene, Thomas G., 170–71
Green Island, 161
Green Metropolis (Owen), 305–6
Green Point (Greenpoint), Brooklyn, 96
Greenville, N.J., 184
Greenwich Street, 23, 34
Greenwich Village, 27, 48, 55–56, 80
grid plan, 41–42, 65, 66, 80
  anniversaries of, 179, 335–37
  as basis for population density, xix, 65, 304–6, 335, 337
  contents of, 61, 63
  creation of, 56–63
  criticisms of, 41, 87–88, 154, 188, 335, 337, 411n51
  and drainage, 87–88
  goals of, 61–63, 65
  and open space, 62, 82
  precedents for, 53, 56, 78
  relation of, to waterfront development, xix, 55, 63, 201
  and wetlands, 63–65, 73
Grinnell, Henry, 83, 99, 100, 108
Grinnell, Moses H., 108
Griscom, John, 114–15
Griswold, Nathaniel L., 83
ground cover. *See* impervious ground cover
growth imperative, xviii, 119–20, 140, 190, 293, 351
  adaptation of, to new conditions, 291, 297, 305, 314
  attacks on, 273, 284, 349
  in New Jersey, 136
  Regional Planning Association and, 187–88
  and waste disposal, 258, 325
  and water supply, 120, 158
  and World's Fair, 222
gulls, 239, 280, 315, 318, 482n32. *See also* herring gulls
Guttenberg, N.J., 306

Hackensack Meadowlands Development
    Commission (HMDC), 272–78,
    484–85n42
Hackensack Meadows, 114, 120, 134–35,
    183–84, *225*, 259–60, 270, 271–80
    decline of, as marshland, 183–84,
        260–71, 273–80
    ecological changes in, 260, 263–64,
        266, 271, 273, 276–77, 280
    extent of, 183–84, 260, *261*, 265,
        484n40
    and Hackensack River, 260, 263
    highways in, 264–65, 266–67, 268, 270,
        277
    as "The Meadowlands," 269, 275–78
    mosquito control in, 260–62
    origin of, 4
    and port development, 267–68
    proximity of, to Manhattan, 184, 253,
        259
    Swartwout brothers and, 70, 71–73,
        120, 128, 134, 274
    waste disposal in, 268–69, 270–71,
        278
Hackensack River, 71, 114, 135, 162,
    274
    and Clean Water Act, 277
    damming of (Oradell Dam), 262–63
    and Hackensack Meadows, 260, 263
Hackensack Water Company, 262–63
Haerlem Creek (Pension's Creek),
    48, 64
Haerlem (Harlem) Marsh, 63, 426n37
Hall, Cornelius, 244–45, 249
Hall, Edward Hagaman, 176
Halleran, John J., 216
Hallett, William, 139
Hallett's Point Reef, 139, 140, 142
Hamilton, Alexander, 69
Harlem, 12, 13, 48, 61, 98, 123, 140. *See
    also* Haerlem Marsh
Harlem Flats, 123
Harlem Property Owners' Association,
    159
Harlem River, 107, 140, 149, 164, 177

Harper's Weekly, 143–44, *145*
Harrison, Benjamin, 160–61
Harsimus (Ahasimus) Cove, 130, 134
Hartz Mountain Industries, 275, 278
Hassler, Ferdinand Rudolph, 78–79, 102,
    103
Hawkins, J. W. "Mossbunker," 172, 173
Headlee, Thomas, 196
heat waves, 326, 328–29, 334, 342
Heere Gracht, 18, 19, 73, 350, 400–
    401n36
Hell Gate (Hurl Gate), 97–100, 126
    demolition projects for, 98–100, 107,
        139, 140, 142–43
    as obstacle to navigation, 98, 106
Hempstead, L.I., 198, 199, 201–2, 203
Hempstead Creek, 121
Hempstead storage reservoir, 121
herring gulls, 250–51, 256, 315, 482n32
Hewitt, Abram, 156
High Hill Beach, Long Island, 202–3,
    204
High Rock Park, 318–19
Hiss, Tony, 337
Hoboken, N.J., 7, 69–70, 136, *137*, 144,
    306
    storm damage in, 67, 266, 332, 345
    water supply for, 162, 263
hogs, 24, 112, 122. *See also* pig farms
Holland. *See* Netherlands, the
Holland Tunnel, 219, 264
homelessness, 234, 302, 329, 334
Hoover Dam, 176, 210, 332
Hornaday, William, 165, 231, 232,
    456n19
horses, 111–13, 423n7
    carcasses of, 24
Housatonic River, 159
Howard, Leland, 196
Hudde, Andries, 12
Hudson, Henry, 1609 voyage commanded
    by, 3–8, 147
    anniversaries of, 52, 165, 304
    ecological changes since, xviii, 3, 291,
        309, 315, 316, 324, 341n

Hudson River, 4, 63, 122, 138, 177
in colonial era, 9, 14, 15, 36, 42–43,
46, 58
fish in, 15, 94, 177, 293–96, 302, 303
New York Harbor as estuary of, 3, 119,
144
sediment carried by, 119, 133, 136
shipping on, xvii, 76, 80
watershed of, 119, 157 (*see also* Croton
River)
Hudson River, waterfront development
on, 23, 27, 50, 52, 53, 73, *75,* 89, 101,
209–10
since Second World War, 294–95,
297–98, 300, 302–3, 310–13, 345–46
(*see also* Battery Park City; Hudson
River Park; Westway project)
Hudson River Landfill Project. *See*
Battery Park City
Hudson River Park, 300–303, 307, 346,
476n45
controversy over, 301–3
Hudson River Park Conservancy,
300–301, 307
Hudson River Waterfront Park. *See*
Hudson River Park
Hudson Yards, 350
Hughes, Richard, 272
human waste, 95, 109, 113–15, 117, 118,
122, 163
Hunter, Douglas, 4
Hunter, George, 141
Hunter, Robert, 197
Hunter Island, 210
Hunter's (Hunters) Point, Queens, 141,
142, 228
hunting, 191, 231, 456n15
and commons tradition, 191, 236
decline of, 190, 231–32, 236–37,
456n15
Huntington Bay, 194
Hurl Gate. *See* Hell Gate
Hurricane Carol (1954), 265n
Hurricane Donna (1960), 331, 332,
412n5

Hurricane Irene (2011), 34–35
hurricane of 1821, 66, 67, 72, 331, 350
hurricanes, 66–67, 265n, 330–31, 332,
342, 346, 350, 412–13n5
in early twenty-first century, 34–35 (*see
also* Hurricane Sandy)
see also Hurricane Donna; hurricane of
1821
Hurricane Sandy (2012), xxiii, 326, 328,
343–48, 349–51, 493n47
Hutchinson River, 247
Huxtable, Ada Louise, 289
hygiene, 123, 158
Hylan, John F., 215, 240
hypoxia, 161

Idlewild Airport. *See* John F. Kennedy
Airport
immigrants, 69
Impellitteri, Vincent, 313
impervious ground cover, 149, 164, 313,
320, 326
efforts to reduce, 304, 320
incinerators, 214, 254–55
and air pollution, 255
ashes from, 192, 211–12, 213–14,
215–16, 218
and Fresh Kills Landfill decisions,
246–47, 249, 254–55, 256, 321
limitations of, 245, 246, 249, 255, 278,
460n19
Independent Reflector, 29–30, 31, 167
India, 109, 313n
Indians, 10–12, 22–23, 43, 84, 130, 171,
197
conflicts involving, 7, 19, 22, 43, 45,
238
and Hudson's voyage, 5, 7
and oyster beds, 7, 234
place names given by, 6, 12–13, 27, 56,
125, 141
relationship of, with land, 10–12,
207
see also Lenape Indians
industrial fishing, 171, 172–73

industrial revolution, 28, 30
  second, 142
Interborough Parkway, 209
International Longshoremen's
  Association, 288–89
interstate waste trade, 321, 322
Inwood Hill Park, 210
Irish, 69, 70
Iron Dike and Land Reclamation
  Company, 135
Isle of Meadows, 238, 239, 341
Italians, 218, 231, 236, 248

Jackson, John B., 336
Jacob, Klaus, 349
Jacobs, Jane, 305
Jamaica Bay, 216, 242–43, 317–18, 332,
  341
  dredging in, 309, 479n16
  and Hudson's voyage, 4–5,
  size of, 309, 446n27
  waste management in, 239, 310,
    479n16, 480n25
  see also Barren Island; Kennedy Airport
Jamaica Bay, marshes in, 13, 172, 183,
  186, 194, 258, 309, 396n3
  decline of, 194, 195–96, 309–10, 318,
    339–40, 349
Jamaica Bay Wildlife Refuge, 318
Jamaica Creek, 121
James, Duke of York, 18–19, 70
James, Henry, 41, 337
James, Zachariah, 202
Janvier, Thomas, 154
Jay, John, 47
Jefferson, Thomas, 59, 78
Jersey Central. See Central Railroad
  Company of New Jersey
Jersey City, N.J., 9, 133, 134, 137, 219, 262
  rise of, 130–31, 135, 136
  sewer system in, 426n33
  storm damage in, 67, 266, 332, 345
Jersey Flats, 107, 146, 169
  expansion of, 136–39, 143
  origins of, 7, 130

Johnson, Lyndon, 272
Johnston, John Taylor, 133–34
Jones, Thomas, 197–98
Jones, Walter R., 97, 100
Jones Beach Causeway, 203
Jones Beach State Park, 205–7
  creation of, 199–205
  storm damage to, 343
Jones's Island, 183, 199, 201, 202–4,
Juet, Robert, 3–5, 8
Juniper Valley Park, 245

Kalm, Pehr (Peter), 167
Kane, Richard, 277
Kearing, Samuel, 254, 255, 258
Kennedy, Milton, 192
Kennedy Airport, 309, 480n25,
  490n30
  construction of, on marshland, 5, 243,
    309, 339, 340
  proposed enlargement of, 317,
    339
  vulnerability of, to storms, 330,
    344
Kew Gardens, 218
Kieft, Willem, 12
killifish, 194, 273
  and mosquito control, 194, 197, 262,
    264, 266, 273, 463n4
Kill Jordan, 220
Kill Van Kull, 6, 16, 37, 128, 135, 160,
  221, 226, 249
Kimmelman, Michael, 336
King, James G., 100
King, John Alsop, 107
King, Martin Luther, Jr., 301
King, Preston, 102
King George's War, 30
Kings County, 19, 66, 112, 140, 197. See
  also Brooklyn
Kingsland Creek, 277
Klatskin, Charles, 275, 276
Koch, Edward, 294, 297, 298
Koolhaas, Rem, 335, 336
Kopp, Mary, 218

Kraft, Jacob, 259–60, 262, 263–64, 267, 270
family background of, 260, 264, 269
uses made by, of meadows, 259, 264, 270
Krajewski, Henry, 268
Kreischer, Balthasar, 227
Kreischerville, Staten Island, 227
Kunz, George Frederick, 165

La Guardia, Fiorello, 214, 215, 217, 221, 242, 309
La Guardia Airport, 242, 265, 331
construction of, on filled land, 243, 339, 450n13
Lakes Island, 239
landfills, 243, 246, 250, 254, 309, 320–21, 482n32
herring gulls and, 251, 315, 339
mass consumption and, 255–56
in New Jersey, 269, 271, 278
see also Fresh Kills Landfill; "Mount Corona"
land patents, 12
landscaping (term), 210, 222, 231, 232, 453n35, 453–54n40
landscraping (term), 231, 233
Lanza, Charles, 270
LeFrak, Samuel J., 292
Lenape Indians, 5, 6, 11–12, 22–23, 27, 130
displacement of, 22
resource use by, 16, 23, 43
Leroux, Pierre, 109, 117, 123, 125
Levitch, Timothy "Speed," 337
L'Hommedieu, Ezra, 110–11
Liberty State Park, 134
Lima, Peru, 56
Lindsay, John, 254, 283, 284, 290
liquefaction, 327
Lispenard, Leonard, 44
Lispenard Meadows, 44–46, 49–50, 73, 75
disappearance of, 88, 89, 123
drainage in, 46, 56, 68

littering (term), 256
Little Ice Age, 6n, 36, 46
littoral drift, 4, 93, 140, 191, 202
Locke, John, 12
Lodi Manufacturing Company, 114
LoLo (Lower Lower Manhattan) plan, 494n53
London, 61, 69, 97, 109, 333
grid plan in, 56
as port, 51, 62, 95, 105
relative economic importance of, 67, 100, 166, 333
relative size of, 61, 108, 149, 394n2
Long Beach, N.Y., 265, 343–44
Long Island:
airports on, 309 (see also Kennedy Airport; La Guardia Airport)
and Brooklyn water supply, 121, 157
in colonial era, 19, 36
farming on, 110, 111, 112, 113, 117, 174–75
and Hudson's voyage, 4, 6
marshes on, 183, 191–207, 247 (see also under Flushing Meadows and Jamaica Bay)
menhaden factories on, 171, 172
and New York City consolidation, 195–96
north shore of, 193–94
south shore of, 183, 191–93, 194–207 (see also Jamaica Bay)
storm damage on, 265, 331, 342
see also Brooklyn; Nassau County; Queens; Suffolk County
Long Island City, 128, 141, 142, 431n33
Long Island Railroad, 141, 193
Long Island Sound, 122, 194, 296
and disaster planning, 331, 332
and navigation, 51, 140
Long Island State Park Commission, 189, 199, 207
longshoremen, 288–89
Lorillard, Peter, 108

lower Manhattan, xx, 7, 46, 88, 226
    coastal-flooding vulnerability of, 331,
        332, 345–46, 349, 350
    real estate development in, 252,
        286–92, 349, 471n7 (*see also* Battery
        Park City; Westway project)
Lower Manhattan Plan, 287–88
Lower New York Bay, 3, 51, 293, 331
Lyceum of Natural History of New York,
    49, 114, 115

mackerel, 235
Madison, James, 70
Magna Carta, 131
Maillefert, Benjamin, 99–100, 139
Main Creek, 238
malaria, 193, 196, 197
malls, 323, 345
Mangin, Joseph, 56–57
Manhasset Bay, 194
Manhattan Island
    choice of, as center of Dutch colony,
        9–10
    deindustrializing of, 215, 252, 286,
        288–289
    expanding area of settlement in, 34,
        47–48 (*see also* grid plan)
    grand dreams to expand, 126–128, *185*,
        283, 349, 472n20, 494n53 (*see also*
        Westway project)
    lower: *see* lower Manhattan
    oysters and, 7, 16–17, 167
    parks on, 60, 76 96, 125, 153 (*see also*
        Central Park; Hudson River Park)
    ponds and springs on, 48, 152–154,
        226, 479n12 (*see also* Collect Pond)
    prior to European impact, xv, 15–16,
        55–56
    purchase of, 10–11
    relative size of, 243, 269, 272, 280,
        310
    vulnerability of, to natural hazards, 331,
        332, 345–46, 349, 350
    zoning on, 215, 252, 286, 300, 340,
        341

Manhattan Island, changing landscape of,
    8, 14, 34–37, 68–69, 73–76, 86–88,
    89, 123, 153–54
    and deforestation, 36, 406n28
    see also Battery, the; Hudson River
        Park
Manhattan Island, changing shoreline of,
    33–34, 52–53, *75*, 89, 284, 300
    and bulkheads, 97, 284, 300, 303
    in colonial era, 23–24, 26–27, 30,
        33–34, 36–37
Manhattan Island, marshlands on,
    12–13, 14, 34, 42–43, 47, 63–64
    (*see also* Haerlem Marsh; Lispenard
        Meadows; Stuyvesant Meadows)
    disappearance of, 14, 34, 68, 73–76, 80,
        89, 123, 125
Manhattan Island, population of, 31, 50,
    61, 65, 108, 113, 157, 331
    density of, xvi, 34, 37–38, 305,
        471n15
Manhattan Island, real estate on:
    in colonial era, 12, 28, 33 (*see also*
        water-lot grants)
    growing importance of, 76, 119, 186,
        222, 287, 291, 294, 297, 332, 350
    in reclaimed marshland, 68, 73,
        74, 80
    see also real estate speculation
Manhattan Island, water supply on, 43,
    44, 48–49, 115, 116
    off-island, 115–16, 123, 125, 154,
        155–60, 175–76, 177
"Manhattanhenge," 336, 337
Manhattan Landing project, 283
Mannette (Bestevars Killitie), 27, 56, 58
manufacturing, 98, 148, 215, 270, 274
    limits placed on, 215, 252, 286
manure, 109–13, 117, 123, 149, 198
Mapes, James Jay, 117
marijuana, 271
Marine Mammal Protection Act (1972),
    316
Marine Society of New York, 161
Marks, Marcus M., 185

marshes:
  biodiversity in, 6, 8, 183, 191, 226, 238, 271, 277
  Dutch colonists and, 12–13, 14
  extent of, in New York area, 184–85, 243
  filtering functions of, 123, 308, 313
  Indians and, 5, 6, 23
  locations of: *see under* Coney Island; Bronx, the; Brooklyn; Jamaica Bay; Long Island; Manhattan; New Jersey; Queens; Staten Island
  old customs of: *see* commons tradition
  origins of, 4, 5
  plants in, 8 (*see also* salt marsh cordgrass; salt meadow hay; phragmites)
  as storm buffers, 319–20, 228–30, 233, 244–45
marshes, decline of, 5, 184, 190, 243, 254, *279*, 280, 310, 349
  and metropolitan planning, 184–89, 208–10
  and resulting ecological change, 190, 195, 197, 250–51, 263–64, 266, 273, 277, 303, 315
  see also mosquito control
Martin, William, 119–20, 123, 125, 127
Marx, Karl, 34, 94
Maspeth, Queens, 217
Massachusetts colony, 23
Massapequa Indians, 197
mass consumption, 241, 255–56
Matthews, Ann, 307
Mayfield, Max, 333
McAneny, George, 214, 215–16, 452n25
McCarthy, John A. "Fishhooks," 211–12
McClellan, George B., Jr., 160, 176
McCracken, W. Lynn, 233, 236
McHarg, Ian, 288, 319
McKinsey & Company, 304
McLean, Malcolm, 267–68
McNulty, Raymond, 205
McWhinney, Thomas A., 196, 202

Meadow Lake, xix, 218–19, 220–21, *312*, 341
Meadowlands, xx, 70, 269, 275–78. *See also* Hackensack Meadows
Meadowlands Sports Complex, 275, 276, 323
menhaden, 166–67, 171–73, 175, 177, 438n37
merchant elite, 23, 27, 33, 52, 95, 108
  in Dutch period, 14
  opposition of, to harbor encroachment, 92–93, 94, 97
  water lots gained by, 24–25, 26, 27, 30–31, 33, 52
  see also New York Chamber of Commerce
Meriam, Ebenezer, 99, 100
Metropolitan By-Products Company, 239–40, 247
Metropolitan Transit Authority, 254
Meyner, Robert, 269
Middle Crow Island, 198
midges, 220
Midland Beach, Staten Island, *257*, 345
migratory birds, 307
  habitats for, 195, 246, 260, 266, 294
  see also Atlantic Flyway
Mills Corporation, 322–23
Millstein, Gilbert, xxiii
Minetta Water, 48, 88
Minuit, Peter, 10, 12
Mitchel, John Purroy, 232, 240
Mitchell, Joseph, 248
Mohawk Indians, 12–13
Molinari, Guy, 321
mollusks, 178. *See also* clams; oysters; shipworms
Montgomerie, John, 27, 63, 73, 77, 81, 131, 138, 345. *See also* Montgomerie Charter
Montgomerie Charter, 27, 52, 58, 73, 92
  extensive underwater land granted by, 27, 138, 287
  later questioning of, 93

Montgomerie Charter (*cont.*)
　legacy of, and Hurricane Sandy,
　　345–46
　as a turning point, 28, 33, 42, 44, 53, 63
Moore, Clement Clark, 41
Morningside Heights, 48
Morris, Gouverneur, 57–58, 59, 63, 65,
　73, 201
Morris Canal, 133
Morrison, Charles, 269–70
Moses, Robert, 189–90, 208–9, 225, 232,
　287, 289, 290, 291, 313
　background of, 189
　building accomplished by, 189–90, 193,
　　209, 210–11, 213–14, 293 (*see also*
　　Jones Beach State Park)
　and commons tradition, 233–34, 236
　eventual loss of power by, 190, 253–54,
　　288
　and Flushing Meadows, 213–14,
　　216–17, 218–19, 220, 224, 242, 341
　and Long Island waterfront, 197,
　　199–207, 242–43, 318, 343
　and Regional Planning Association,
　　189, 190, 201, 209, 216, 253
　and Staten Island, 231, 236, 244,
　　245–46, 249, 256, 318
mosquito control, 463n4
　on Long Island, 193–97, 199,
　　454–55n6
　in New Jersey, 196, 260–62, 263, 266
　on Staten Island, 228, 230, 250, 251
　success of, against malaria, 197
mosquitoes, 47, 193, 217, 262. *See also*
　mosquito control
Moulton, Gretta, 318
"Mount Corona," 212, 217, 218
Moynihan, Daniel Patrick, 294
Mud Hole Hassock, 198
Muller's (Miller's) Pond, 228–30
Mulrain, Andrew, 249
Mumford, Lewis, 188, 189, 251, 252,
　464n10
Murray Hill, 115
Muscoot River, 157

Museum of the City of New York, 336
muskrats, 70, 226
　and drainage projects, 72, 135, 264,
　　273, 276, 467n30
　trapping of, 217, 250, 259, 270, 271,
　　276

Nassau County, 195–96, 197, 199, 454n40
National Earthquake Hazards Reduction
　Program, 327
National Marine Fisheries Service, 277
National Park Service, 318
natural hazards, 326–27, 334, 337, 349.
　See also earthquakes; coastal flooding;
　heat waves; storms
Navesink River, 16
Netherlands, the, 12, 16, 17, 19, 332
　land reclamation in, 8–9, 24, 309,
　　349–50
Neutrinos. *See* Floating Neutrinos;
　Pearlman, David
New Amsterdam. *See* Dutch colonists
Newark, N.J., 162, 176, 262, 274
　storm damage in, 264, 265, 331
　See also Port Newark
Newark Bay, 6, 37, 128, *261,* 263, 493n47
　changing dimensions of, 309
　oysters in, 167, 169
　pollution in, 162, 176, 263
Newark Liberty Airport, 262, 339,
　490n30
Newark Meadows, 6, 143, 194, *229, 259n,*
　279, 465n12
　drainage in, 194, 262, 264
New Croton Aqueduct, 155–57
New Croton Dam, 157
New Deal, 205
New Jersey, 70, 306
　commons tradition in, 131–33, 270
　ecological change in, 262, 263–64, 266,
　　273, 276–77, 280, 323
　highways in, 264–65, 266–67, 268, 270,
　　277
　mosquito control in, 196, 260–62, 263,
　　266

pig farms in, 268–69
rivers in: *see* Hackensack River; Passaic
    River
railroads in, 133–34, 146, 161, 184, 186,
    262, 266 (*see also* Central Railroad
    Company of New Jersey)
waste disposal in, 162–63, 170, 248,
    263, 269, 270–71, 274, 278, 321
New Jersey, marshes in, 70–73, *229,*
    259n, 261, 279 (*see also* Elizabeth
    Meadows; Hackensack Meadows;
    Newark Meadows)
decline of, 128, 135–36, 183–84,
    260–71, 272–80
salt hay in, 71, 259, 260, 262, 268
New Jersey, waterfront development in,
    128–32, 133–34, 136–38
ports in, 186–87, 262, 267–68, 286,
    309
underwater land in, 86, 131, 132, 134,
    138
wharves and piers in, 67, 132, 133, 134,
    138
New Jersey Audubon Society, 277
New Jersey Meadowlands Commission,
    323. *See also* Hackensack
    Meadowlands Development
    Commission
New Jersey Meadows. *See* New Jersey:
    marshes in
New Jersey Railroad and Transportation
    Company, 134
New Jersey Turnpike, 266–67, 271, 275,
    277, 307
Newton, Isaac, 156
Newton, John, 139, 140, 142–43
Newtown Creek, 128, 140–42, 184
declining water quality in, 164, 228,
    249
industry on, 128, 142, 228
as Superfund site, *338,* 485–86n44
New York Academy of Sciences, 49. *See*
    also Lyceum of Natural History of
    New York
New York Aquarium, 164–65, 437n33

New York Bay, 16, 98, 122, 134, 143–44,
    162, 164–65. *See also* Lower New
    York Bay; Upper New York Bay
New York Bight, xx, 315, 330, 345
New York Chamber of Commerce, 103,
    160, 170, 186, 439n42
formation of, 33
and Hell Gate clearance, 97–98, 100,
    142
opposition of, to harbor encroachment,
    92–93, 97, 108, 429n18
on waste management, 146, 147, 162,
    427n38
New York City Board of Health, 241, 268
New York City Department of City
    Planning, 300, 319
New York City Department of
    Environmental Protection, 319, 339
New York City Department of Health
    and Mental Hygiene, 329
New York City Department of Marine
    and Aviation, 286
New York City Department of Parks,
    245, 248
New York City Planning Commission,
    244, 247, 252, 253, 254, *285*
and waterfront projects, 287, 289, 300
New York City Sanitation Department,
    242, 247
New York Conservation Department,
    236, 248
New York Convention and Visitors
    Bureau, 284
New York Dry Dock Company, 76
New York Evening Post, 127
New-York Gazette, 32
New York Harbor, xx, 95, 101–6
entrances to, 51, 77, 79, 98, 105–6 (*see*
    also Sandy Hook)
as estuary of Hudson River, 3, 119, 144
geological history of, 3–4, 50–51
Hudson's exploration of, 3–8
maps of, *13, 28, 29,* 86, *104, 145*
marine life in, 115, 154, 164–65 (*see*
    also fish; oysters)

New York Harbor (*cont.*)
  navigational advantages of, 16, 30,
    50–51
  tides in, 51, 95, 409n25
  transformed waters of, 110, 118–19,
    121–23, 154, 161, 173–79, 314 (*see
    also* eutrophication)
New York Herald, 127, 155
New-York Historical Society, 52
New York Public Library, 115
New York Times, 159, 215, 231, 336, 340
  on waste disposal, 241, 243, 246
  on waterfront development, 95–96,
    287, 290, 294, 301, 340
  on wetlands projects, 193, 209, 265,
    267, 269
New York World's Fair (1939), 214–17,
    243
  choice of Flushing Meadows as
    location for, 216
  communal customs uprooted by,
    217–18
  and Great Depression, 214, 222
  landscape changes brought by, 217–24,
    242
Nicolls, Richard, 19
night men, 113–14, 115
night soil. *See* human waste
nitrogen, 117–18, 163, 166, 176, 241, 314
Nooten Eylandt, 9, 10. *See also* Governors
    Island
nor'easters, 26–27, 265–66, 319, 330, 347
North Beach Airport. *See* La Guardia
    Airport
North River. *See* Hudson River
North Shore Improvement Association,
    194

O'Brien, John, 214
Ocean Parkway, 204
O'Dwyer, William, 247
Oesters Eylandt. *See* Bergen Neck
offal, 24, 122–23, 134, 147, 172
office buildings, 250, 252, 288
Ogden, James De Peyster, 83

oil companies, 142, 170. *See also* Standard
    Oil Company
Old Croton Dam, 115. *See also* New
    Croton Dam
old-growth forests, 12, 36, 153
Old Hackensack Neck. *See* Bergen Neck
Old Place Creek marsh, 228, *229, 257*
Old Slip, 53
Old Wreck Brook, 42, 47, 88
Olmsted, Frederick Law, 41, 87, 153, 210,
    322, 335, 428n4
One Chase Manhattan Plaza, 252
open-loop system, 117–18, 146, 165–66.
    See also waste disposal
open space, 91–92, 337, 351
  and grid plan, 62, 82
  preservation of, 316–25
  and regional park system, 188
  shortage of, 62, 86, 199–200, 201, 301
Oradell Dam, 262–63
Orchard Beach, 210, 243–44, 245
Organization for Economic Co-operation
    and Development (OECD), 333–34
O'Rourke, John, 233, 235
osprey, 165, 183, 320, 324
otters, 64
Outerbridge Crossing, 232
overfertilization, 119, 314
Owen, David, 305–6
oxygen levels, 149, 161, 163, 175–77
  crustaceans and 161
  fish and, 161, 162, 176, 177
  impact of sewage on, 118–19, 164,
    175
  importance of, 161
  oysters and menhaden and, 167, 171,
    175, 177
  rebounding of, 277, 316
  see also eutrophication
oyster beds, 7, 141, 248
  in New Jersey, 128, *129,* 131, 132, 133,
    134, 135, 248
  threats to, 16–17, 128, 132, 133, 134,
    135, 157–58, 167, 179
oyster reefs. *See* oyster beds

oysters, 94–95, 166–71
  in colonial era, 16–17, 84, 128, 167
  ecological importance of, 166–67, 171,
    173, 175, 177, 179
  former abundance of, 7, 16, 133, 134,
    136, 141, 167, 170–71
  as important food source, 167, 168,
    234–35
  Indians and, 7, 43, 234
  see also oyster beds; oyster shells
oyster shells, 19, 94–95

Palisades Interstate Park, 200
Paris, 62, 108, 109, 126, 149, 174
Park Association of New York City, 233,
  289
Parker, Cortlandt, 136–38
parkways, 193, 204, 209, 224, 445n24. See
  also Grand Central Parkway
Passaic River, 71, 161–63, 262, 266
  bridges over, 264, 267
  sewage in, 162–63, 164
Passaic River Sewerage District, 162
passenger pigeons, 16
Pataki, George, 321
PATH (Port Authority Trans-Hudson)
  transit system, 286–87, 330
Patterson, George Washington, 102, 106
Paulus Hoeck (Powles Hoeck), 67,
  130–31, 136
Pauw, Michael, 130
Peace of Utrecht (1713), 26
Pearlman, David ("Poppa Neutrino"), 302
Pelham Bay, 210
Pell, Robert L., 117
Pennsylvania Avenue Landfill, 482n32
Pennsylvania Railroad, 211
Pension's Creek (Haerlem Creek), 48, 64
Perit, Pelatiah, 97, 108
Perkins, George W., 200
Petit Marsh, 198
Philadelphia, 51, 78, 266, 329
  grid plan in, 56
  relative size of, 31, 37, 50, 108
Philipse family, 27

phosphorus, 119, 166, 220, 314
Phragmites (common reed), 251, 263,
  264, 285, 461n30, 467n30
  in Fresh Kills, 239, 250, 251, 256
  in New Jersey, 262, 263–64, 266, 273,
    277, 280, 323
phytoplankton, 167, 178, 239
  and oxygen levels, 119, 177
  oysters and menhaden and, 167, 172,
    177
Pierce, Franklin, 97, 98, 100
piers, 51, 118, 249
  in Brooklyn, 83, 97
  in colonial era, 17, 18, 20
  controversies over, 93, 97, 106–7
  as fish and bird habitat, 294–95
  in New Jersey, 133, 134
  and shoreline transformation, 86, 97,
    185, 186, 242, 300
  and waste disposal, 114–15, 116,
    122
pigeons, 280. See also passenger
  pigeons
pig farms, 268–69
Pike, Samuel N., 135
Pintard, John, 73
plankton. See phytoplankton
PlaNYC, 304–5, 341, 343
platforms, 297–302
Pleistocene epoch, 50
Polevoy, Sergius, 251
ponds, 260
  human-made, 227–28, 250, 277, 318
    (see also Meadow Lake; Willow
    Lake)
  in Manhattan, 48, 479n12 (see also
    Collect Pond)
  and mosquito control, 194, 195,
    228–29
population:
  of Brooklyn, 52, 66, 81, 97, 121
  of Jersey City, 136
  of Manhattan borough, 154, 305
  of metropolitan area, 140, 177, 251,
    294n5

population, of New York City, 201, 304, 341
  in colonial era, 31
  in nineteenth century before consolidation, 50, 61, 65, 108, 113, 157, 331
population density, xv
  of Manhattan, xvi, 34, 37–38, 305, 471n15
  of metropolitan area, 140, 177, 251
  of New York city after consolidation, 149, *285*, 306
  of Staten Island, 251, 461n32
porpoises, 37
Port Elizabeth, 268, 286, 309
Port Newark, 186, 262, 267–68, 309
Port Newark-Elizabeth Marine Terminal, 268
Port of New York Authority, 186–87, 267–68, 286–87, 317
Pot Rock, 98–100
Pound, Arthur, 222
Powell, William, 247
Powles Hoeck. *See* Paulus Hoeck
Prall's Island, 239, 341
Pratt, Charles, 142
Prince, William, 221
Prince's Bay, 168, 170, 248
privies, 175
Progressive Era, 187, 188, 231–32, 240, 248, 267
Provost, David, 96
Public Development Corporation (PDC), 297–98
Pulaski Skyway, 264–65
Putnam County, 125

Queen Anne's War, 26
Queens, 211, 292, 349
  airports in: *see* Kennedy Airport; La Guardia Airport
  before 1898 consolidation, 19, 98, 111, 112–13, 140, 196–97
  farming in, 111, 112–13

Long Island City in, 128, 141, 142, 431n33
  parks in, 245, 249, 253 (*see also* Flushing Meadows Park)
  proposed canal through, 98, 126
  waste disposal in, 219–20, 246, 320 (*see also* Brooklyn Ash Removal Company)
Queens, marshes in, 128, 141 (*see also* Flushing Meadows)
  decline of, 128, 141, 211–24

raccoons, 183, 259, 303, 215, 216
Radcliff's Pond, 228
railroads, 141, 168, 187, 192, 200, 211, 212
  in New Jersey, 133–34, 146, 161, 184, 186, 262, 266 (*see also* Central Railroad Company of New Jersey)
Randall's Island, 140, 210
Randel, John, Jr., 55–56, 58, 60–61, 103, 117, 126
Randel, John, Sr., 55
Raritan Bay, 122–23, 173
Raritan River, 4, 16, 131, 167, 176
rats, 213, 217, 237, 244
Ratzel, Friedrich, 144
Reagan, Ronald, 294, 295
Real Estate Record and Builders' Guide, 127–28, 135, 151, 192, 426–27n38
real estate speculation, 73, 155, 201, 252, 290, 291, 324
  and choice of World's Fair location, 216
  in water lots, 53, 74, 90, 101
Red Hook, Brooklyn, 82, 344
Refuse Act of 1899, 163
Regional Plan Association (RPA), 187–89, 214, 215, 269, 317, 339
  boundless growth advocated by, 187–88, 189, 209, 216, 222, 253, 283–84
  critics of, 188, 251, 464n10
  Robert Moses and, 189, 190, 201, 209, 216, 253
  Second Regional Plan of, 253, 471n12
  Third Regional Plan of, 306–7, 478n8

rent control, 290
Republican Party, 87, 102, 107
reservoirs, 115, 121, 125, 156–57, 176,
    310, 313. *See also* dams
resource recovery plants, 123, 171–72, 241
    on Staten Island, 239–40, 247
Revolution. *See* American Revolution
Reynolds, William H.
Richards, Daniel, 82–83, 84–85
Richmond County. *See* Staten Island
Richmond Creek, 238
Riepe, Don, 340
Riker, Richard, 69–70
Rikers Island, 141, 148, 217, *312,* 335
    prison on, 148, 212–13
    waste dump on, 148, 212–13, 216–17,
        241–42, 244
Ring, Welding, 162
Riverside Drive, 153, 210
Riverside Park, 153
Riverside South towers, 327
Rockaway, Queens, xxi, 51, 196, 210, 327
Rockaway Inlet, 4, 147, 243, *311*
    and disaster planning, 317, 331–32
    and Hudson's voyage, 4, 7, 147
Rockaway Peninsula Mosquito
    Extermination Association, 196
Rockefeller, David, 252, 286–87
Rockefeller, John D. (*see also* Standard Oil
    Company), 142
Rockefeller, Nelson, 253–54, 287, 290
Rodman's Neck, 210
Roebling, John, 127
Roettinger, Josephine, 206
Roosevelt, Franklin, 205, 267
Roosevelt, John, 27
Roosevelt Island, 213
Rosoff, Samuel, 213–14
Ross, Ronald, 196
Rotten Row, 32–33
Royka, Willie, 271–72, 276
Ruggles, Henry, 96–97
Ruggles, Samuel, 96, 125
Russell, John Scott, 105–6
Russell Sage Foundation, 187

Rustin, Bayard, 289
Rutgers, Anthony, 44–46, 47, 68
Rutherfurd, John, 57–58, 59, 272
Rycken, Abraham, 148

Sale, Kirkpatrick, 299
salt hay, 8, 84, 248
    on Long Island, 13, 191, 195, 198, 204,
        224
    in New Jersey, 71, 259, 260, 262, 268
salt marsh cordgrass, 7–8
    and ecological change, 266, 273, 277,
        340
    on Long Island, xix, 191, 211, 217
salt marshes. *See* marshes
Sandy Ground, 167, 168
Sandy Hook, 51, 143, 164, 187, 317, 331
    channels through, 51, 77–78, 79, 101,
        106
    growth of, 93, 140, 147
sanitary code, 243, 250
Saw Kill, 48
Sawmill Creek, 277, 324
Sawmill Wildlife Management Area,
    323–24
Schagen, Pieter, 10
Scully, Vincent, 41
seabirds. *See* gulls; herring gulls
Seaford Creek, 197
Sea Gate, *347*
sea grass, 163, 178–79
seahorses, 164–65
sea level, 4, 5, 44, 50–51, 191, 330, 494n54
    recent rise in, 334, 342, 350
seals, 16, 316
sea worms (shipworms), 118, 316, 425n25
Secaucus, N.J., 70, 265, 267, 268–69, 275
Second World War, 246
sediment, 51, 95, 130, 133, 340. *See also*
    littoral drift; siltation
seines, 172–73
September 11 attacks, 307, 346
Serrell, James E., 126–28, 134, 143
Seven Years' War, 30
sewage. *See* waste disposal

sewage (term), 118, 441n57

sewage treatment plants, 166, 308, 310, 318

   limitations of, 166, 313–14

   in New Jersey, 248, 263, 274

sewers, 116–17, 219–20, 426n33

   in Brooklyn, 121, 426n33

   delivery of waste by, to surrounding
      waters, 116, 118, 121–22, 130, 164,
      169, 175, 176, 313–14

   and storm-water runoff, 313–14

shad, 15, 82, 161–62, 177, 179

Shapiro, Sidney, 203

Sheepshead Bay, 192, 193

Sheridan, Philip, 143

shipworms (sea worms), 118, 316, 425n25

shipyards, 82, 96

Shooter's Island, 341, 491n37

shorebirds, 196, 213, 260, 318

   migrating, 191, 266, 318

   see also egrets

Short Beach, 202

Silent Spring (Carson), 273

siltation, 53, 93, 101, 122

   and Jersey Flats, 130, 134, 136

skyscrapers (term), 146–47

slaughterhouses, 43, 47–48

slaves, 24, 43, 44, 79, 167

slave trade, 17, 19

slips, 24, 28, 286

   dredging of, 111, 133

   filling of, 24, 51, 53, 94–95, 114–15,
      116, 122

   public access to, 32, 33, 53

Smith, Adam, 90

Smith, Al, 189, 205

Smith, James Reuel, 152–54, 155, 228

Smith, John B., 463n4

Smitt, Hendrik Jansen, 43

snakes, 70, 153, 183, 217, 248, 319

Soundview Park, 245

South Brother Island, 122

South Street, 37, 53

Spain, 8, 9, 26

Special Natural Waterfront Areas, 341

speculation. *See* real estate speculation

Spinola, Steven, 348

Springfield Brook, 121

springs, xv, 43, 44, 116, 120, 152–54, 226

squatters, 86, 217–18

squirrels, 237, 315

Standard Oil Company, 128, 142, 146,
   170, 173, 228

Starr, Roger, 295

Staten Island, 226–237, 341, 345, 349,
   483n34

   in colonial period, 13

   commons tradition on, 168, 227,
      230–32, 234–37

   conservation movement on, 227,
      230–37, 244, 253

   geographical setting of, 3, 6, 50, 51, 128

   open space preservation on, 317,
      318–22, 341

   and oyster beds, 167–68, 170

   population density of, 200, 226, 461n32

Staten Island, marshes on, xvi, 226–27,
   228, *229,* 244, *257,* 310 (*see also*
   Fresh Kills; Great Kills)

   decline of, 228–30, 233, 244–45,
      250–51, 310 (*see also* Fresh Kills
      Landfill)

Staten Island Association of Arts and
   Sciences, 232

Staten Island Bluebelt, 319–20, 341

Staten Island Chamber of Commerce,
   233

Staten Island Greenbelt, 318–19, 320,
   483n34

Staten Island Museum, 231

Staten Island Sound. *See* Arthur Kill

Statue of Liberty, 187, 323

steamships, 94, 105–6, 147, 170, 186

Stokes, Isaac Newton Phelps, xvii, 41, 42,
   154

Stony Brook University, 332

storms, 67, 202, 205, 265, 317, 412n5

   in nineteenth century, 67 (*see also*
     hurricane of 1812)

   see also hurricanes; nor'easters

storm-surge barriers, 331–33
storm-water runoff, 36, 116, 313
Straus, Isidor, 214
Straus, Nathan, Jr., 233
Straus, Percy, 214
Stringer, Scott, 336
striped bass, 171, 172, 259, 294, 295, 303
    and Westway project, 294, 295–96,
        473n28
Stuckey, James P., 297, 298
Stuyvesant, Petrus (Peter), 17–18, 44, 350
Stuyvesant Meadows, 60
Stuyvesant Square, 76
subway system, 330
Suffolk County, 157–58
Sullivan, Robert, 307
Sulzberger, Iphigene Ochs, 208
Sunken Meadow, 210
Superfund sites, 338, 485–86n44
Sutton, Percy, 289
Swartwout, brothers (John, Robert, and
    Samuel), 69–70, 135
    wetlands project of, 70, 71–73, 120,
        128, 134, 274
Swinburne Island, 316

tanneries, 46, 47–48
Terhune, John, 191–92
Terrell, Betsy, 302
Thirteenth Avenue, 80
Thirty-Fourth Street, 62, 65, 86, 300
Thomson, James, 141
Thoreau, Henry David, 203, 227, 228,
    239, 240, 307
tidal range, 51, 95, 409n25
"tidelands doctrine," 272
Tiede, Tom, 276
Tiemann, Daniel, 125
Tiffany & Company, 160
Tilden, Samuel J., 140
Times Square, 48, 216
Titicus River, 156–57
Todt Hill, 238
Tompkins, Daniel D., 76
Tompkins Square Park, 60, 76

Totten, Joseph, 102
Townsend, Charles, 164–65
trapping, 270, 456n15
    and commons tradition, 217, 222, 227,
        236
    on Long Island, 217, 222
    of muskrats, 217, 250, 259, 270, 271,
        276
    on Staten Island, 227, 230, 231, 232,
        233, 236, 250, 461n31
Tredwell, Daniel M., 198
trenches, 194–95, 228–30, 262. See also
    mosquito control
Triborough Bridge, 209, 224
Triborough Bridge and Tunnel Authority,
    253–54
Trump, Donald, 239, 290, 300, 327, 343,
    475–76n41
tunnels, 117–18, 166, 187, 211
    flooding danger in, 300, 331, 335, 345,
        349
    see also Battery Tunnel; Holland Tunnel
Tweed, William M. "Boss," 101, 125, 155
Twelfth Avenue, 50, 63
typhoid fever, 170

underwater land, 22, 53, 63, 81, 88
    in colonial era, 22, 24–25, 26, 27–28,
        31, 32
    encroaching of waste disposal on, 244,
        254
    extent of filling of, xviii, 315, 480n24
    grant of, by New York State, 58, 73, 74,
        80, 92, 106, 142
    New Jersey and, 131, 132, 134, 138
    sale of, 24–25 (see also water-lot grants)
Union City, N.J., 306
Upper New York Bay, xviii, 7, 36, 128,
    130, 162, 166
    Hudson's voyage and, 6, 7
    and shipping, 51, 93, 144, 160
Urban Development Corporation
    (UDC), 300–301, 472n20. See also
    Hudson River Park Conservancy
urban heat-island effect, 149, 328, 329

Urstadt, Charles, 290–91, 292
US Army Corps of Engineers, 102, 177,
    249, 291–92, 298
    and disaster planning, 317, 330–32
    and Hell Gate projects, 139 (*see also*
       Newton, John)
    and New Jersey wetlands, 277, 323
    and Westway project, 291–92, 294,
       296–97, 323
US Coast Survey, 78–79, 99, 102, 103
US Congress, 78, 170, 173, 288, 318
    and disaster planning, 327, 351
    and East River projects, 100, 139
    and Westway, 297
US Environmental Protection Agency
    (EPA), 277–78, *338*, 475n36
US Fish and Wildlife Service, 246–47,
    277
US Supreme Court, 47, 321, 458n7

Van Cortlandt family, 25
Van Cortlandt Park, 245
Vanderbilt, Cornelius, 187
Van der Donck, Adriaen, 11, 13–16, 17, 18
Vaux, Calvert, 87
Verhulst, Willem, 9–10, 12
Verrazano, Giovanni da, 4
Verrazano Narrows, 4, 6, 7, 51, 235, 332.
    See also Verrazano-Narrows Bridge
Verrazano-Narrows Bridge, 251, 318, 319
Viele, Egbert Ludovicus, 85–88
Vierlingh, Andries, 9, 68
Vision 2020 plan, 340–42, 491–92n41
Von Liebig, Justus, 117
Von Thünen, Johann Heinrich, 110, 111,
    112

wading birds, 341
Walden Swamp, 275, 307
Walker, Jimmy, 213, 214
Wallabout Bay, 81, 82, 84, 141
Wall Street, 37, 89, 108, 161, 307
    in colonial era, 25, 43
    as financial center, 100, 252
Walton, William, 31–33

Walton, William, Jr., 33
Wantagh, L.I., 203
Waring, George, 117–18, 240–41,
    242–43, 247, 433n40
warming. *See* global warming
War of 1812, 78, 82, 102
Washington, George, 58, 211, 221
    arrival of, as president-elect, 37–38,
       160–61, 221, 283, 299, 345
    extent of change in New York area
       since lifetime of, xviii, 89, 108,
       143–44, 161, 165–66, 211, 324
    observations of New York by, 34, 36,
       109–10
Washington, D.C., 56
Washington Heights, 153
Washington Square, 27, 56
waste disposal, 109–18, 146, 239–42, 243,
    252–56, 315, 320–21
    and closed-loop recycling, 109–13, 123,
       124, 174–75, 240–41, 247
    interstate trade in, 321, 322
    in New Jersey, 162–63, 170, 248, 263,
       269, 270–71, 274, 278, 321
    see also dumping; human waste;
       incinerators; landfills; sewage
       treatment plants; sewers; wastewater
wastewater, 118, 121, 123, 174, 313–14.
    See also sewage treatment plants
water consumption, 156–59, 174, 310–13,
    314
waterfowl, 16, 195, 196, 201, 223, 264, 294
    impact of drainage projects on, 195,
       196, 204, 251, 264, 273, 277
water-lot grants, 24–25, 27–34, 51–55, 74,
    94, 96–97
    in Brooklyn, 82
water meters, 155, 158–59, 314
Water Street, xx, 32, 68, 69
water supply, 43, 44, 48–49, 115, 116
    off-island, 115–16, 123, 125, 154,
       155–60, 175–76, 177, 310–13
    for Brooklyn, 120–21, 157–58, 200
    see also springs; wells
Watson, John D., 174

Watts, John, 36
weasels, 259, 315, 319
Weed, Thurlow, 184–85
Weehawken, N.J., 184
Weeks, Henry Clay, 193, 194
Wegmann, Edward, 157
Weisman, Alan, 308
Welfare (now Roosevelt) Island, 213
wells, 48, 115, 116, 120, 153
Werpos village, 84
Westchester County, 115, 140, 148, 149,
    159, 176, 187
West India Company, 9, 12, 17, 18
West Indies, 19, 20, 21, 26, 28
West New York, N.J., 306
West Side Waterfront Panel, 298–99,
    302
West Street, 53, 80, 346
Westway project, 284, 292–93, 472n20
    Army Corps of Engineers and,
        291–92, 294, 296–97, 323
    battle over, 284, 292–93, 295–97, 301,
        473n28
    and changing ecology, 293–95
    Congress and, 297
    death of, 295, 296–97
wetlands. See marshes
wetlands mitigation, 322–23
Whalen, Grover, 214, 215, 217
whales, 15, 398n13
"wharfing out," 24, 32, 138
wharves, 67, 93, 95–96, 118
    in Brooklyn, 82, 84–85
    in colonial era, 20, 24, 25, 26–27, 28,
        32
    congestion of, 52–53
    fees for dockage at, 32, 95
    in New Jersey, 67, 132, 138
    public access to, 32–33
    and transformation of shoreline, 86,
        89, 185

Whig Party, 102
white cedar swamps, 6, 70, 183, 191
    decline of, 263, 273, 275, 276
Whitestone Parkway, 209
Whitman, Walt, 7, 41, 83, 85, 120
Whitney, William C., 193
Whyte, William H., 336
Williams, Jonathan, 81, 82
Williamsburg(h), Brooklyn, 82, 97
Willowbrook marsh, 233
Willow Lake, 218–19, 223, *312*, 341,
    453n37
Wilson, Woodrow, 262
Winship, Eugene, 194–95, 197
Wolfe's Pond marsh, 233
wolves, 6, 22, 237, 295
Wood, Fernando, 101, 107, 125
Woodhull, Maxwell, 92–93
Working Waterfront Association, 302
World's Fair. See New York World's Fair
World Trade Center, 256, 286–87, 289,
    307, 328
    construction of, 141, 203, 241–42,
        307
    2001 attack on, 307, 328, 346
Wright, Henry, 188

Yates, Joseph, 101
yellow fever, 46, 47, 48, 49, 57
Ylvisaker, Paul, 272
Yonkers, N.Y., 148
York Island. See Manhattan

Zabriskie, Abraham Oothout, 132, 136,
    429n14
Zach's Bay, 202, 203–4, 343
Zach's Inlet, 202
Zeckendorf, William, 290
Zenger, John Peter, 28
Zimmer, Andrew, 248, 250
zoning, 215, 252, 286, 300, 340, 341